CALIFORNIA RISING

THE LIFE AND TIMES OF PAT BROWN
CALIFORNIA RISING

ETHAN RARICK

UNIVERSITY OF CALIFORNIA PRESS

BERKELEY   LOS ANGELES   LONDON

University of California Press
Berkeley and Los Angeles, California

University of California Press, Ltd.
London, England

Library of Congress Cataloging-in-Publication Data

Rarick, Ethan
    California rising : the life and times of Pat Brown /
Ethan Rarick.
        p. cm.
    Includes bibliographical references and index.
    ISBN 0-520-23627-0 (cloth : alk. paper)
    1. Brown, Edmund G. (Edmund Gerald), 1905–
    2. Brown, Edmund G. (Edmund Gerald), 1905—Family.
    3. Brown family. 4. Governors—California—Biography.
    5. California—Politics and government—1951–
    6. California—Social conditions—20th century.
    I. Title.
    F866.4.B75R37 2004
    979.4'053'092—dc22

                                        2004009697

Manufactured in Canada

14   13   12   11   10   09   08   07   06   05
10   9   8   7   6   5   4   3   2   1

The paper used in this publication meets the minimum
requirements of ANSI/NISO Z39.48-1992 (R 1997)
(Permanence of Paper).

FOR MY PARENTS

CONTENTS

Photographs follow page 184

Prologue / 1

PART I: RISING

1. Go-getters / 7
2. A New Religion / 21
3. The Chairs of Politics / 39
4. Waiting / 66
5. Victory / 87

PART II: BUILDING

6. The Big Wallop / 113
7. All These Students / 135
8. Anguish / 154
9. Cigar Smoke / 180
10. Building a River / 205
11. "By God, I Can Beat That Son of a Bitch" / 229

PART III: FALLING

12. Race and Politics / 255

13. Rejection / 271

14. Berkeley / 292

15. Watts / 314

16. Tired Old Governor / 341

17. Dynasty / 367

Epilogue / 381

Acknowledgments / 385

Notes / 389

Selected Bibliography / 459

Index / 485

PROLOGUE

THREE DAYS AFTER CHRISTMAS, twenty men on horseback, dressed in the coonskin caps and buckskin clothing of mountain men, rode up to the Capitol in Sacramento. They presented the governor with a leather scroll commemorating the day, a milestone for their state. Dignitaries said a few words, and the bells of nearby churches chimed out "Clementine." To consecrate the moment, the riders fired a volley from their black-powder muzzle loaders that thundered through the winter air.[1]

But the guns were loaded with blanks, and the bystanders shocked by the sudden fusillade were not nineteenth-century pioneers but twentieth-century office workers emerging for lunch. It was 1962. California was celebrating not the Gold Rush, or statehood, or the completion of the transcontinental railroad, but a more modern brand of triumph, one revealed first in the formulas of demographers. California was proclaiming itself the most populous state in the nation, the ultimate beneficiary of Americans' restless westward push.

The governor who greeted the riders and received the scroll—Edmund G. Brown, a man universally known by his nickname, "Pat"—was the father of the day's ceremonies. Almost a year before, reviewing the projections of his state's experts, Brown had seen the coming breakthrough, the final surge past New York, and decreed that an observance was in order. "On that day," Brown told reporters, "the balance of the most powerful nation in the world will shift from the Atlantic to the Pacific."[2]

There was hyperbole in the governor's words, but there was also an element of truth. Through the quiet 1950s and the turbulent 1960s, California seized a place of prominence in American life such as it had never held before, and not merely because of its newfound numerical supremacy. In those years, in rapid and related succession, the state provided the blueprint for three great impulses of the day, leading the nation to postwar optimism, and then to sixties activism, and then to conservative backlash.

First came the siren song. The sunny good life lured millions of newcomers who saw the state as an American promised land. Then came the doubts, a new and querulous mood that started in California and moved east to engulf the country. Student protests at Berkeley sparked an era of student rebellion; the anger and frustration of poor blacks in the Watts section of Los Angeles touched off the first massive urban riot of the period. And finally the reaction: California produced a politician, Ronald Reagan, who launched a conservative counterattack that reshaped American politics for years to come.

As a result, California not only changed the country, but the country changed the way it thought about California, a shift that reverberates to the present day. By the end of the twentieth century, it was a commonplace to portray California as the proving ground of America's future. The state, it was said, offered a preview today of what the rest of America would experience tomorrow. The writers of the 1990s hailed California as the place "where the new American society is first coming into full view," where the future "continues to take shape," where the nation first embraced everything from computer culture to "sexual experiment."[3]

Yet in recognizing California as pacesetter for the nation, it's easy to forget how recently the perception emerged. For much of its history, California was seen as an American rebel that resisted rather than established the nation's norms. The most common reference to California in the journals and books of the century that followed the Gold Rush is as a strange and inexplicable wonderland. California did not reveal what America would become; it simply stood apart from much of what America was. There was always a sense that California was a place of great promise, an almost mythical land where gold lay underfoot. The dream was that in California life would begin anew, would be better and fundamentally different from the way it had been. In the 1940s John Gunther toured the United States to write about the country and declared California "a whole great world of its own" and "the outside fringe."[4] As late as 1949 Carey McWilliams, history's most astute observer of things Californian, surveyed past and present and decided that the state was, as he titled his book, "The Great Exception."

By the late 1960s, less than two decades later, McWilliams was arguing not that California stood apart but that it pointed the way. "California," he wrote, "is the future."[5] The intervening years—the time just before and after Brown's celebration with the mountain men—had been a pivot point of American history. California's postwar migration, sixties ferment, and conservative reply set the tone for America, and Americans started thinking of California as example rather than anomaly. During that time, the historian Kevin Starr once said, the state "assembled itself as the cutting edge" of the nation's story.[6] American history bounced off the Pacific Ocean and started running west to east. The balance of the nation, as Pat Brown put it, had shifted.

———

Brown did more than merely articulate that change. He was central at every turn. When Californians brimmed with confidence, he was their activist governor. A landslide victory in 1958 launched him into a first term of vigor and accomplishment. Brown funded the expansion of public colleges and universities in a burst of growth unequaled in the history of the United States. The legislature and voters approved his plan to build a vast system of dams and canals to move water from the wet north to the arid south, at that time the largest single public works project ever undertaken by a state and an achievement that had eluded previous governors. Brown signed a major civil rights bill, increased funding for social programs, even proposed and enacted a major tax increase to pay for it all. As reward, the voters gave him reelection over Richard Nixon, an upset victory that Brown cherished. Only weeks later came the numerical triumph over New York, in the midst of the holiday season of 1962. As the governor stood outside the Capitol to greet the ceremonial riders, he was at a high point of his life and career.

Yet there were already hints of a changing mood. The ceremonies to note the great day were sparsely attended, sometimes mocked. There were those who grumbled that the state was marking a curse rather than an achievement, the newcomers bringing more problems than possibilities. In the years of Brown's second term, the doubts only deepened, and again the governor was at the center of affairs. When rebelliousness struck, he was the authority figure to be spited. It fell to him to order the arrest of protesting college students, and it was his National Guard that occupied Watts. At the end, when regular Californians grew angry at the turmoil around them, Brown was the victim. It was Brown they pitched from office in favor of Reagan, marking the first great victory of the modern conservative movement.

In time, Brown became more than a character in the California drama of those years. He became the emblem. The kindness of nostalgia burnished memory, and Californians began to associate their aging former captain with the successes of his early years as governor, not the turmoil and defeat of his later ones. They remembered the great challenges that were conquered and came to believe, with much justification, that Brown was the last California governor to ready the state for the future, the last provident leader. Eventually, he became the new icon of California politics, hailed by both Democrats and Republicans, liberals and conservatives. When he died, three decades after he was thrown from office, one writer remembered Brown as "the grand man of the California boom."[7]

For good or ill, California still leads the way to the nation's future. The digital revolution launched in Silicon Valley is transforming culture and commerce alike. The ethnic diversity of the state, where whites are already a minority, will spread to the country as a whole in the years to come. The recall of Gov. Gray Davis in fall 2003 may prove a political watershed, although it will take years to sort through the full effects. Even the state's sheer size remains of note. One of every eight Americans lives in California, the largest proportion for any state since the Civil War. The growth shows no signs of abating. McWilliams was right: California is the future, in part because in the future an extraordinary percentage of Americans will be Californians.

But if California still creates tomorrow, it's important to understand fully the moment when that role first emerged—the extraordinary years when Brown was governor. It is a joyful and turbulent tale, filled with great dreams and vast accomplishments, unrestrained optimism and angry protest, dynastic visions and private disappointments. Legendary leaders connive in back rooms. A new generation seizes the streets. Politics changes forever. And through it all, California rises, not just in demographic bulk, but to a new and unique standing in the American experience.

PART I
RISING

GO-GETTERS

PAT BROWN STOPPED AS HE walked down the aisle of his official gubernatorial plane, the *Grizzly,* and peered out the window. Calling out to make himself heard over the drone of the propellers, he exclaimed with wonder, "Gee, will you look at that!" People sitting nearby, seeing nothing spectacular, asked Brown what he was referring to. "California," he replied, unabashed. "Did you ever see anything like it?"[1]

Like many Americans, Brown was a man of joyful geographic bias. He lived his entire life in California and never doubted he was lucky for the privilege. As his career brought him prestige and opportunities, he traveled the world and enjoyed its wonders, but he always loved Yosemite most of all.

Perhaps family history was at work. Perhaps Brown cherished California so deeply because his ancestors, like so many others, had endured hardships to make a life there. California was no accidental homeland, but a hard-earned goal, an accomplishment to savor. In that, Brown was tied to an essential story of his nation's experience. For among his forefathers were people who had possessed the courage or desire or desperation to abandon their old lives and strike out for something new, hunting for the future in the West.

Both of Brown's grandfathers sought new lives twice, first by leaving the old country for America and then by heading west to California. The first to arrive in the state was Brown's maternal grandfather, a tough German immigrant named Augustus Schuckman. Schuckman came to America in about 1850, worked for a time in the Midwest, then beat the winter snows over the Sierra Nevada in a wagon train in 1852. For Americans, California was then a new and enticing place. Less than a decade before, it had been a Mexican province—and not one of particular lore or fame. The preferred destination for western pioneers had been Oregon. The Gold Rush had changed that, and by the time Schuckman and his comrades arrived California had burst into the consciousness of both the United States and the world.

Coming down the western slope of the mountains, Schuckman stopped in the mining boomtown of Placerville, where, he later claimed, he struck up a drinking friendship with John Marshall, the discoverer of the first nugget. Schuckman had once worked as a boatman on rivers around the Great Lakes, and as a way to see the countryside he soon took up the same work in California. On a trip up the Sacramento River, he found Colusa County, a stretch of rolling hills and grasslands, and decided to make it his home.

He bought a small ranch and ran cattle, but his real goal had always been life as a country innkeeper. As he prospered, he bought first one stagecoach stop, then another, transforming himself into a hotelier. As would his grandson, he liked the company of people: Even after a bout of self-reform made him a teetotaler, he tended the bar at his inn.[2]

Schuckman married while on a trip back to Germany, and although his wife disliked her rustic new home in America, the couple eventually produced nine children. The last was a girl, named Ida, born in 1878. Mrs. Schuckman died when Ida was still young, and perhaps because of the loss, or simply because of her nature, the girl did not much like country life. She found a little relief from the boredom when, still in her teens and the postmistress in a nearby town, she steamed open all the letters and read them, but she soon resolved to leave. When she was a young woman, friends moved to San Francisco, and she seized her chance to follow them, determined to make her way in the great city.[3]

———

Brown's other grandfather, Joseph Brown, came to America at almost the same time as Schuckman, fleeing his native Ireland amid the miseries of the potato famine. A few weeks after his twenty-first birthday, in 1850, he sailed into Boston harbor in the cold of a New England November. He headed straight for the little town of Framingham, Massachusetts, where a large and established Irish community allowed him to hear the comforting accents of home. Brown made a life for himself in his new country, finding work as a laborer, then becoming a citizen, and finally marrying and starting a family. By the Civil War, his attention, like Schuckman's before, was turning westward. The specific reasons are lost to history, but Brown decided that he and his family would strike out for California. They made it—no sure thing in those days—and by summer 1866 they were living in San Francisco.[4]

Brown drove a team for a while and later worked in foundries, but he was never the most reliable of men. He pitched into drinking binges, then obeyed his wife's admonition to stay off the bottle for a few months, then headed back to the bars as soon as the promise expired. In time, though, he landed a gardening job with the city, a steady civil service post that became his sinecure. The fourth of his five children—and the second born in California—was a son, born in 1871, named Edmund Joseph Brown.[5]

From an early age, the younger Brown was determined to make something of himself, at least financially. Drawn more to the risky world of business than to the safety of the municipal job his father enjoyed, Edmund found work as a porter lugging crates for wholesale grocers, then began driving a laundry route. By his mid-twenties he had already struck out on his own and was operating a small laundry business, the first in a long series of entrepreneurial ventures. Then and for the rest of his life, he was a man on the make, always with some new scheme that might bring riches. A talker and a charmer—a "young blade" as one of his sons would later say—he was the kind of man who must have seemed endlessly exciting to a girl from the sticks.[6]

———

Precisely how Ida Schuckman and Edmund Brown met remains a mystery, but a romance blossomed, the big-city boy wooing the country girl new to the metropolis. Youthful attraction apparently overcame what should have been obvious differences, and the couple courted, then married. Their first child was born on April 21, 1905, and they named him Edmund Gerald, the first name for the father, the second for the family doctor. The tot was doted on. The elder Edmund Brown liked to dress the boy in the finery of tiny infant clothes, then take him downtown and proudly show him off to business associates.[7]

Three days before the boy's first birthday, at a little after 5:00 A.M. on April 18, 1906, a massive earthquake roiled the streets as if they were water. Standing on a corner, one police sergeant saw waves of solid ground roll toward him. At least one apartment building sank until the second story was even with the street. Thrown off level, church bells rang madly, as if to herald the Judgment Day. Fires broke out, then merged into a conflagration against which there was no hope, since the water mains had been shredded by the quake. The fire would rage unchecked for three days, killing hundreds and razing 521 city blocks. Chicago's Great Fire thirty-five years earlier had leveled an area only two-thirds as large.[8]

Miraculously, the Browns were unharmed, but the reactions of husband and wife suggested their dissimilarities. Terrified, Ida bundled up her only child and temporarily fled back to her girlhood home in the comforting—and unmoving—hills of Colusa County. She feared earthquakes the rest of her life. Edmund was characteristically blithe. He owned a cigar store downtown, where the destruction was near total, but he knew there was nothing he could do to stop the flames. So he climbed to the top of one of the city's steep hills, lay down on the spring grass, and, as he said later, "watched the city burn."[9]

His nature precluded discouragement. He found a new partner and started over, eventually operating a series of small-time dreams: an arcade, another cigar store, a movie theater, photography shops, curio stores. Hungry for profit, Brown had no objection if some of his ventures skirted the edge of legality. As a young man he made book on the horses, then switched to running small-time poker rooms.[10]

His family grew along with his business ventures. The first boy was followed by three more children, boys named Harold and Frank and a girl named Constance, known as Connie. At times the patriarch provided amply for his brood. At times they scraped by. "Anything but a steady provider," as Harold remembered, the elder Brown was invariably either rich or poor. When he had money, his free-spending spirit emerged. There were diamonds for Ida and a maid to help with the housework.[11] A few years after the earthquake, Brown was able to commission an architect to build three flats, one atop the other, on an empty lot by the panhandle of Golden Gate Park, toward what was then the western edge of the city. The top and bottom units were rented out; the Browns lived on the middle floor, the first time the family owned a home. By the standards of the day, it was a comfortable life: a big living room, a dining room, three bedrooms. There was even the small luxury of a second toilet, tucked away in a tiny room separate from the regular bathroom. The only possible drawback was the lack of a garage. The architect said the automobile was a passing fad.[12]

———

Growing up in that neighborhood, young Edmund Gerald Brown had no worries about serious crime, but there was a need to be tough. Wander too far from your own block, and there was a good chance of fisticuffs with the kids whose turf you had invaded. The Brown boys were part of the Grove Street Gang, enemies of the nearby Fulton Street Gang. Burnishing the powers of persuasion that would later serve him so well, Brown once convinced a Fulton member to switch sides. The poor boy's former comrades captured him, tied a rope around his body, and hanged him from a pulley, though fortunately not by the neck. "You had to be able to handle your dukes," Brown said later.[13] His father encouraged a pugnacious streak. Once the boy came home and said another youngster had hit him. On learning his son had not fought back, the elder Brown suggested that he "do something." Young Edmund found the other boy, challenged him to a fight, and, at least according to his later retelling, whipped him.[14]

In his younger brother Harold, Edmund found the companion of his early years. They played Cowboys and Indians, sneaked into a nearby reservoir to swim, pounded on a punching bag in the basement, and went to San Francisco Seals baseball games with their father.[15] Both readers, the brothers gathered their books and opened a neighborhood lending library downstairs next to the boxing equipment, although they soon closed up shop, realizing that often the books failed to return. In 1915, when Edmund was ten, the city hosted a world's fair, the Panama Pacific International Exposition. The boys took the streetcar down to the waterfront and wandered amid the exhibits and crowds, surviving on fifty cents apiece from their father and gawking at the amazing sights: the sparkling Tower of Jewels, 435 feet high and encrusted with more than 100,000 glass "gems"; the Machinery Palace, the biggest wooden and steel building in the world; the glittering Horticultural Palace, with its magnificent 185-foot-tall glass dome; an eatery whose name reflected the popular new snack that was its fare, the Frankfurter Inn. In the car race the winner averaged an astonishing fifty-six miles per hour.[16]

At Easter vacation Ida would take the children back to Colusa County, an annual adventure. They crossed the bay on a ferry to Oakland, then boarded a train north. The train itself was put aboard a ferry to cross the Carquinez Straits at the mouth of the Sacramento River, the choppy neck of water framed on either side by big hills rising out of the river. After that the train headed into California's flat and hot Central Valley and then finally into the brown rolling hills of Colusa. They stayed with Ida's elder sister, Emma Allen, on a farm that Brown would later describe as "a pretty poor piece of habitation." It must have been a shock for the city kids. There were outhouses, hand-pumped water, and rattlesnakes. When the Brown kids went to school with their cousins, they rode horses. Edmund sometimes stayed inside to read rather than join Harold in farm chores, but there were times when the brothers enjoyed the fun of the countryside. They hiked, a country cousin taught them how to spear fish in a nearby creek, and at night dances attended by local farm families offered music and entertainment. Another cousin "taught" young Edmund how to catch snipes, taking him half a mile into the woods at night with a sack and then leaving him there to wait for the fictitious creatures to appear.[17]

But if it was a childhood with a lot of fun, there was also a lot of work. Ever the hustling businessman, the elder Edmund Brown had determined that his boys would learn the ways of commerce. He gave them one thing after another to sell, mimicking in miniature his own fickle career. There were Christmas cards they boxed themselves and a mysterious elixir called Fire of Life, bottled and labeled by the Brown boys at home. On the streetcar after work, their father lugged two big bundles of newspapers, one for each of his older sons to sell. On Saturday nights he would buy the early editions of the Sunday paper, and the following morning the boys would be up by 6:30, walking through the dank streets of San Francisco calling out "Chronicle, Examiner."[18] Young Edmund took to it, displaying the energy that would mark his life. He ushered at a theater on Powell Street, hawked sodas at the fights, and worked in one of the shops his father owned on Market Street, awash in bric-a-brac and cheap jewelry and polished seashells with "San Francisco" painted across one side. The shops had a camera too, and people came in to have their portraits taken, three for twenty-five cents. World War I proved a boon: Soldiers wanted a keepsake of themselves in uniform. From his father, the boy picked up the hustler's ceaseless thirst for a little more profit. At Christmas he told passersby that a prize awaited if only he sold a few more cards, although it wasn't true. At the fights he always asked for an extra glass, then took a little from each of the sodas so he had one more to sell. His father, he said later, would have approved.[19] Surely that was correct. Brown Sr. never doubted the value of the long hours, never thought there were better ways to spend a childhood than peddling newspapers and snapping cheap pictures. "I wanted them to be businessmen, and learn how," he once said of his sons.[20] "He made them," their younger sister said years later, "into go-getters."[21]

———

By the time young Edmund reached the seventh grade, America was hurling itself into World War I, and the youngsters were assigned to give four-minute speeches in school urging people to buy liberty bonds. Brown gave his a big finish—"Give me liberty or give me death"—and his classmates dubbed him Patrick Henry Brown. By high school the nickname had been shortened to Pat, and it stuck, then and for the rest of his life. The senior Edmund hated that his son was now known by another name. If friends came to the door of the family house and asked for Pat, his father would insist that no such person was living there, then add, "You're not referring to Edmund, are you?" But the newly minted Pat Brown didn't mind, neither then, when he took it as a sign of other children's friendship, nor later, when he realized that the name gave the half-German Brown a thoroughly Irish air in a city where the Irish dominated politics.[22]

Like his siblings, Brown went to Lowell, by far the best of San Francisco's public high schools. Physically, he was small, limited to the 100-pound basketball team as a sophomore and junior, then to the 120-pounders as a senior. As part of the school's ROTC program, he had to take a physical exam with other boys, and when they stripped down to wait for the doctor, he was embarrassed that he was the only one without pubic hair. At dancing school all the girls were taller.[23]

But he was everywhere, not merely a joiner, but the leader of the groups he joined. He was president of the camera club and the debating society. He organized the rowing club, then became the president of that too. Organizing groups was a skill he displayed often: When the school's fraternities wouldn't admit one of Brown's friends because he was Jewish, Brown created a new fraternity, the Nocturnes, open to all. He ran for "yell leader," a position of great status among the students, and won. At football games he was out in front of the crowd, natty in white flannel trousers and red jersey, hurling confetti as the team charged onto the field. He was a Big Man On Campus, and he took advantage of it, squiring the girls to parties thrown by his fellow Nocturnes.[24]

When not in charge, Brown was unhappy. Fearful of losing to the captain of the football team, he refrained from running for student body president, opting for the safer race for secretary. He won, but taking the minutes as other people made the decisions bored him, and he vowed that in the future he would be willing to risk defeat.[25]

————

If Pat Brown inherited an entrepreneur's energy from his father, he took other traits from his mother. Neither of Brown's parents attended high school, but Ida was always the more intellectual of the two. Her husband's long hours often left her alone in the early years of their marriage, before they had children, and she filled the void by attending lectures. When she became a mother, she took the children along. Brown remembered going to see Hiram Johnson, California's famous governor, at the Dreamland Auditorium. At night, when his father was out tending to business, Brown and his siblings would crawl into bed with their mother and listen to her read children's versions of biblical stories. "When I was in school I knew even more than the Jewish kids about the Old Testament," Brown said. "My mother was left alone, so we became very close, my mother and my brother Harold."[26]

But if religious stories brought mother and children closer together, theological differences drove the parents even further apart. Edmund Sr. was an Irish Catholic who wanted his children taken to mass, even though he never went. Ida was a Protestant raised in the countryside at a time when many rural Americans saw "papists" as a threat to the nation's independence. She felt only enmity for the Catholic church, mild at first, later bitter. She found its dogma silly, objected to Catholic schooling, and ridiculed the idea of a celibate clergy. She refused to attend her daughter's first communion.[27]

The old, stereotypical differences that had marked husband and wife from the beginning—he the gay Irishman, she the stern German—now became almost unbearable. When Pat was a teenager one of his father's periodic business setbacks ruined the family finances, increasing the strain even more. By the time Pat's younger sister, Connie, reached high school a few years later, the marriage was purely a facade. The couple maintained separate rooms at home—Edmund in the front, Ida in the back—and they kept to their corners. Eventually Edmund headed for a hotel downtown, and although the couple never legally divorced, they never lived together again. Ida kept the flats, the rent from the tenants above and below giving her an income; Edmund scraped by on his businesses. The separation was no great surprise to the children. "You could tell they actively disliked one another," Connie recalled. "And then finally my father just moved out."[28]

———

Brown graduated from high school in June 1923 and took off for a vacation, the first of many breaks that would fill the summers of his early adulthood and acquaint him more than ever before with the natural wonders of his state. He spent time on the Russian River and at Lake Tahoe, but it was Yosemite that always grabbed him. The great national park offered, he said once, "the greatest splendor this earth affords." Through his late teens and early twenties he went every summer, usually with friends, hiking in the backcountry and swimming in the bracing lakes and streams. On one trip Brown and his friends scaled Half Dome, the massive granite escarpment that looms over Yosemite Valley. At the end, like everyone else, they pulled themselves along on chains strung down the steep face, the toughest climb Brown had ever done.[29]

They were young men, and the trips featured less sublime diversions too. At night they sat on the lodge porch and waited for the bus that brought young women to the evening dance. "We used to call it 'look at the stock,'" Brown remembered years later. "Then we'd pick them out. We'd say, 'This one is for you, this one is for me.' Of course, we weren't always successful in getting the ones we wanted."[30]

———

After high school Brown went to work for his father. Ostensibly he was the cashier in a cigar store, but his real task was to guard the door to the poker game in a back room, admitting only those who could be trusted. On the side, the gambler's son ran his own craps game, and between his paycheck and his dice winnings Brown was flush with cash. His father had fallen on hard times, so Brown would float him loans, the winnings of the son papering over the losses of the father, a situation that cannot have been easy for either man.[31]

Looking ahead in life, Brown possessed enough drive and ambition to want something more, but he was uncertain what to do. His grades had slipped toward the end of high school, and it was not at all clear that he would be admitted the following fall to the University of California, across the bay in Berkeley. A neighbor suggested that he consider San Francisco Law School, where an undergraduate degree was not required. Brown liked the idea. He was a young man of hurried ambition, and a college education meant four years of delay. A bachelor's degree was still a rarity in American life, and if there was no need of it, better to move ahead.[32]

The law was an old ambition anyway. At Lowell he had occasionally gone down to the courthouse to watch trials, and enjoyed it.[33] The public speaking surely appealed to the outgoing youngster who would be yell leader and debating club president. And the prestige and financial rewards of a legal career must have attracted the ambitious boy whose father had endured stretches of hardship.

Less than two months after high school graduation, Brown filled out an application to law school, then started classes that fall. Harvard it was not. Founded only fourteen years earlier from the remnants of a YMCA program that offered night legal classes, Brown's new school relied on rented office space, shaky finances (a bankruptcy would be narrowly averted in 1941), and a few dozen students. But it suited a streetwise kid with a work ethic, and Brown settled in, his academic performance improving year by year.[34]

After two years he had made a sufficiently strong impression that he was offered a job by a blind lawyer named Milton Schmitt. The pay was less than Brown earned working for his father and running his own craps game, but the opportunity was too good to ignore. Brown wanted some practical experience with the law, and although Schmitt's career was in the midst of a long, downward slide, he was still a man with connections. Years earlier, before losing his sight, Schmitt had served four terms in the state assembly, the lower house of the California legislature, and was once a serious candidate for the speakership.[35]

Schmitt needed a personal assistant as much as a legal one, so Brown's new job required long hours. He rose early and took three streetcars before reaching Schmitt's house by 8:30. Reboarding the trolley, Brown guided Schmitt to work, where his main task was to read material aloud. At the end of the day, he led Schmitt home, and then most nights attended classes. Brown studied whenever possible, however brief the opportunity. As they clattered along on the streetcar, he perfected the habit of reading while Schmitt was talking, since the lawyer obviously could not see that his assistant was devoting much of his attention to something other than the conversation.[36]

Somehow he also managed to make time for student politics. In his final year, forsaking the timidity he had regretted in high school, he ran for student body president and won a three-way race in a landslide, 60 to 22 to 5. The yearbook attributed Brown's victory to his "likeable traits and ability." The student president, the yearbook writers said, "has stamina and an energy born of quenchless zeal."[37]

Brown graduated in spring 1927, took the bar exam, and found out in the fall that he had passed it. Feeling his oats on the day he learned the result, he bet the extraordinary sum of $100 (almost an entire year's tuition at his former law school) on a football game between Stanford and St. Mary's, a small Catholic school across the bay. Night school man that he was, he took St. Mary's because he considered Stanford snooty. St. Mary's won in an upset, 16–0, and the bookmaker's son walked away with $400.[38]

———

Through his years in law school and those just after, Brown kept his habit of a summer idyll, but increasingly he stayed in at night when his friends went hunting for girls. Brown was less interested in chasing the girls at Yosemite than in writing to one back home.

In high school history class he had met Bernice Layne, although it was hardly love at first sight. Initially Brown regarded her as merely "a little kid with long braids." She was indeed three years younger than he, but already had shown great promise. Most of her early schooling had been in an experimental program that allowed students to work at their own pace, and hers was fast. She completed eight grades in three and a half years while reading her way through every Horatio Alger book she could find. By the time she met Lowell's worldly-wise yell leader, she was a high school junior even though she was only thirteen. Brown walked her home a few times and discovered that the braided kid was in fact "a bright, sparkling girl." Bernice's mother at first refused to let her daughter go out with a boy, declaring her too young, but Brown proved a persistent suitor, and in time he and Bernice began to date.[39]

In some respects the differences in their personalities mirrored those of Brown's parents. Pat was always ebullient, Bernice more bookish. Once at a basketball game when he was yell leader, he called her down from the stands to lead a cheer, which delighted him and embarrassed her.[40] But if he thought about the potential for an echo of his parents' troubled relationship, he gave no sign of it. His surviving letters to her chronicle a romance that grows from boyish playfulness to ardent love affair.

"Well, how are things with you, kid?" he wrote in one of the first, which described his summer vacation just after high school graduation. "Bernice, Rio Nido is the only place on the river and there are pretty girls and handsome men galore."[41] By the following year he was complaining that her family's busy phone line sometimes kept him from talking to her, and begging that she send him a picture of herself.[42] The summer after that, Brown pined for her during his Yosemite jaunt. "I feel," he wrote to her, "like shouting our love from the highest mountains hereabouts."[43]

Not that things always went smoothly. They often quarreled, occasionally broke it off, invariably reconciled. His letters to her are filled with hints of little jealousies, and sometimes they seem to have been justified. Once, while Bernice was living in Berkeley and attending the University of California, she canceled one of their dates. Sensing an implausible excuse, he went to her apartment and found another man. Brown stormed off, and, not surprisingly, the romance fell apart for a few months. But they reunited as always, and by the year of his law school graduation, Brown was madly in love, chattering away in his letters about their future together. He wanted to set a wedding date and occasionally referred to himself and Bernice as husband and wife, as though the ceremony were a mere formality.[44]

———

Fresh from his bar exams, Brown kept working for Schmitt, but the older man began acting strangely, in minor ways at first and then more pronounced. He rented an office beyond his means, gave peculiar instructions to Brown, and declared that he planned to make a million dollars for both of them. At times Schmitt grew so angry and talked so incessantly about death that Brown actually feared Schmitt might attack him. Finally, Schmitt's legal skills deserted him, and Brown felt compelled to tell a judge there was "something wrong" with his employer. Schmitt was losing his mind; Brown thought later that perhaps the poor man's collapse was the result of syphilis that had stolen his eyesight. Whatever the cause, he was taken to a psychiatric hospital, and he died the following spring.[45]

Brown inherited Schmitt's clients, and, although he was only a few months into his legal career, found himself unexpectedly independent. The source of his good fortune troubled him a little, but he shook off the nettlesome worries with plainspoken acceptance. "I have been somewhat fortunate at the misfortune of another," he confessed in a letter to Bernice. "I do not believe it is anything to lament over, nor do I believe it calls for huzzah and self-congratulations. It just is."[46]

Troubled at their new lawyer's obvious youthfulness—Brown needed to shave but once a week—a few of Schmitt's clients went elsewhere, but many stayed. Eager and ambitious, Brown formed a loose association with another lawyer in the building and logged the long hours of a young man trying to make good. When he won a case against a local cab company, earning a small fee, he wrote to Bernice that if the judgment had been for $1 million, it would not have brought him more confidence. "Bern," he wrote to her, "I am going to be a success."[47]

And yet at times, perhaps suffering from the crises of confidence that would mark his career, it sounded as if he were trying to reassure himself. "Business continues bad but find myself quite busy," he wrote in yet another letter to his girlfriend. "All professional men advise me not to be discouraged for at least two years, for it takes that long to get anywhere. Rather difficult to reconcile my mind to two years on bread and water, especially when this is the age of good health and youthful exuberance. Well, as long as I have any money left there will be a smile on my face."[48]

———

By summer 1928 Brown had been out of law school barely a year. He was twenty-three, single, and living at home. And yet he decided to run for the state legislature. That he would even consider such an idea is extraordinary, evidence of his determination to climb the ladder even if he had to take a running leap merely to grab the first rung. "I just had that political bug from the very, very beginning," he said later. "It was part of me." When an interviewer suggested to Brown that he was dreaming of the presidency of the United States as soon as he left law school, he didn't deny it.[49]

He filed to run for the local seat in the state assembly, though there was nothing to suggest the incumbent was vulnerable. Ray Williamson, who held the seat, was an established figure and a loyalist of Tom Finn, a former sheriff and the boss of the Republican machine that ran the city.

Brown was challenging a member of his own party, for he too was a Republican, a fact as predictable at the time as it was surprising in retrospect. In the 1920s the Democratic Party remained largely a creature of the South. The United States was a Republican country, California a Republican state, San Francisco a Republican city. In the six decades since the Civil War, only two Democrats had been elected president. Through the 1920s only a handful of Democrats were elected to the California legislature. In one session the eighty-member state assembly consisted of seventy-eight Republicans and two Democrats. Republican dominance was just as pronounced in San Francisco. Of the city's twenty seats in the state legislature, Republicans held nineteen.[50] Brown's ideological convictions remained amorphous, but for an ambitious young man who wanted to get into politics in San Francisco, the Republican Party was the only realistic alternative, so he joined.

He adopted the best slogan he could think of—"23 Years in the District," reflecting nothing but his age—and convinced his old fraternity brothers at Lowell to put up signs. Bernice agreed to ring doorbells, though she was so embarrassed at having to identify the candidate as her boyfriend that she claimed he was her brother.[51]

With no real platform and no campaign help save his high school buddies and his girlfriend, Brown plugged away as best he could. He plodded up and down the steep hills of San Francisco to knock on doors and make his pitch, but these were disheartening days. So meaningless was his campaign that his name barely made the papers. On the day of the August primary, he finished third in a field of three Republicans, the victim of a thorough whipping. He tallied just 653 votes, barely 15 percent of those cast. Williamson won easily.[52]

Like many ambitious young men before him, Brown had tried to go too far too soon. In his first try at winning the thing he wanted most—public office—he had fallen flat on his face. But he had no plans to give up. Giving up was not what had brought his grandparents across oceans and continents, not what had caused his father to start over again after watching his business burn, not what Brown himself had learned by peddling newspapers and hawking sodas. Even as a schoolboy he had always been the leader, and in the aftermath of his humiliating defeat, he knew he still wanted the honor and glory of politics. First he would change much about himself: his party, his skills as a politician, his profile around town. Then, when he was ready, he would try again.

2   A NEW RELIGION

ON A CLEAR FALL DAY in late October 1930, Capt. Arthur D. Layne of the San Fran-
cisco Police Department received a brief, unexpected telegram from Reno:
"Married this morning at Trinity Cathedral. Now staying at Riverside
Hotel." It was signed by his daughter, the former Bernice Layne, now Mrs.
Edmund G. Brown.[1]

Pat and Bernice had been a couple for the better part of a decade and had
been thinking about marriage and children for years. Yet the elopement was
a surprise. They had discussed wedding dates and started planning the big
event for Grace Cathedral, high atop the city's famed Nob Hill. The father
of the bride insisted that the couple eloped simply because they decided
against a big wedding. Bernice, who had graduated from college the previous spring and was a beginning schoolteacher, said later they wanted to
keep the marriage a secret because new teachers were not allowed to wed.

Whatever the reason, their elopement was no secret. A police captain was
a prominent man, and his daughter's wedding was big news. All the San
Francisco papers ran stories the next day, some including a picture of the
bride. But the groom received little mention. The complete insignificance
of Brown's bid for public office just two years earlier was obvious; none of
the papers even mentioned it. The kindest words came from his new father-
in-law, who referred to him as "a promising young attorney."[2]

In the short run, times were tough. Back from Reno, the Browns moved into a downtown hotel—she hated it, he didn't mind—and set about their new life. Young lawyers can rarely afford to be selective about their clients, and Brown was no exception. His caseload was a hodgepodge: bankruptcies, estate work, personal injury suits. He handled a lot of divorces, although he had a tendency to tell prospective clients that perhaps they should reconcile. He started representing the union of streetcar workers—unions would eventually represent a cornerstone of his political support—and he did some blindingly tedious paper shuffling for the Excavators and Dump Truck Owners' Association of Northern California. Once he used his mother as a nominal client and sued a private streetcar company for failing to do required maintenance work. The case was sufficiently strange that it made the papers, but he and Ida lost. At least in private, he had a sense of humor about the need to find business. "Would like to meet more people," he wrote to Bernice before their marriage. "Old rich ones preferred. Probate, you know."[3]

As he had in school, Brown made time for a whirl of ceaseless activities. At one time or another he seemed to be a member of everything: the Elks, the Marina Boosters, the Haight-Ashbury Neighbors, the Knights of Pythias, the Junior Chamber of Commerce, the Olympic Club, the Community Chest. He launched a morning Bible-reading class that met weekly over breakfast, and he cobbled together the Contact Club so that local professionals could network. Not surprisingly, he maintained connections with the people he met. Though still a young man, Brown's Christmas card list soon numbered in the hundreds.[4]

By the time Brown turned thirty, in spring 1935, he was an established lawyer with numerous contacts around town, but he was still one among many in San Francisco's legal community, no more obviously a rising public star than any other young man of promise. Politics remained his goal, but he had learned the hard way that a premature bid for office was often useless. So instead of running again, he reverted to type and built from scratch. The teenager who had created his own fraternity was now a young man intent on organizing a new force in San Francisco politics, one that would simultaneously advocate reforms he thought proper and put his name before the public.

Brown borrowed his model from Seattle, where young reformers had organized themselves as the New Order of Cincinnatus, named for a Roman general famous for selfless patriotism. Brown took the same name for the new San Francisco organization and adopted a slightly vague but sweet platform—an end to partisan bickering and deadlock in city politics. To emphasize the dedication to change, the members would be young. Those over forty were to be admitted only as "associate" members. The practical goal was to field a slate of candidates for the city's Board of Supervisors, the election for which would be held that fall. To generate interest and raise money, Brown organized a public meeting at a San Francisco hotel on July 11, a debut that might hint at the group's viability.

Chairing the meeting as the group's founding president, Brown looked out over a pleasingly big crowd, hundreds of people jamming into the auditorium and others spilling out into the summer night. There was some heckling early on, but Brown was surprisingly firm. The dissenters were, as the *San Francisco Chronicle* put it colorfully, "cut off at the pockets" by the chairman. When the real recruiting got going, the results were good: More than five hundred in the crowd took the Cincinnatus pledge to work toward a "clean, honest and efficient" City Hall, and at least twenty promised to raise $100 each toward campaign expenses for the organization's slate.[5]

The big crowd was a good beginning, and soon the new organization had a permanent headquarters on Market Street, then eventually eleven neighborhood offices scattered around the city. They produced a four-page newspaper, the president pictured on page 2, firm-jawed and staring straight ahead, as if he were trying to look older than his thirty years. "For 25 years the citizens of San Francisco have been fooled and befuddled by the old-line politicians," he wrote in a statement beneath the photograph. "With the approach of a world-class exposition and the completion of two of the greatest bridges in the world, it is realized that new blood and new methods will be necessary to push San Francisco to its place in the sun."[6]

On election day Cincinnatus met with mixed success. Of the four candidates for the Board of Supervisors, one won. It was not a spectacular showing, but for a new group fighting the established parties, one victory was respectable. It laid the groundwork for stronger results in later years. In the meantime, the campaign had transformed Brown into a prominent man. From beginning to end, he was in the spotlight, issuing statements to reporters, chairing the big public meetings, posing for newspaper photographers. Unlike his failed and obscure campaign for the assembly, Cincinnatus had made Brown a man with a reputation. Three months after the election, the city held a ceremony to mark Abraham Lincoln's birthday, a big occasion that drew thousands. For the principal speech, the organizers settled on the founder of the New Order of Cincinnatus.[7]

Brown relished his new prominence. When he was asked to serve as an appeal agent for the local draft board, his pleasure sprang less from the work than from the mere opportunity. "Don't know what I have to do," he wrote a friend, "but appreciate getting my name in the paper."[8]

———

In later years, Brown proved himself the most inveterate of glad-handers. Even by the standards of an extroverted profession, Brown was astonishing. If he found himself waiting briefly in an airport or a hotel lobby, he would greet the nearest stranger. If the car in which he was riding stopped to fill up with gasoline, he would jump out and chat up the attendant. The habit persisted even to retirement. As an old man, the need for votes nothing but a fading memory, Brown would look around for someone to greet if the car in which he was riding stopped at a stoplight. His window would roll down, and any available bystander would suddenly find himself accosted with happy affability: "Hi, I'm Pat Brown. What's your name?"[9]

Endless repetition made the tendency seem entirely natural, and in one sense it was. Brown was always a man inherently interested in people. But he also perfected his native skill, an accomplishment that began during his years as a young lawyer. About town as always, Brown was introduced to Joe Murphy and Jim Brennan, old-style Irish pols in whom he found able teachers. Brown learned how to take his natural ebullience and hone it to a vote-winning spiel. The lessons were simple—use a little charm, tell a joke or two, don't argue with people, keep your spirits up—but the results were plain. "I would laugh and everybody would laugh with me," Brown remembered later. "I could see that I was getting over with people." He took the tutoring to heart and settled on the tools that would serve him through a lifetime of campaigning.[10]

———

An able young lawyer like Brown could avoid the worst miseries of the depression, but the soup lines and jobless queues had one profound effect: They destroyed the old party allegiance that had governed both Brown and his city.

For Brown, it was a cautious transformation. As late as 1932 he was supporting Herbert Hoover's bid for another term in the White House. Two years after that, when California witnessed a bitter and divisive campaign for governor—the Democrats nominating the Socialist muckraker Upton Sinclair, the Republicans a hardcore conservative—Brown opted for the middle ground. He supported a former Republican making a third-party bid as a centrist, though the man lost badly.[11]

As the depression dragged on, Brown began to wonder if he should complete his move across the ideological spectrum and join his old opponents. Faced with war veterans selling apples on the street, he had grown tired of the Republicans' devotion to the free market and frustrated by the argument that help from the government would erode the self-reliance of men near ruin. Republicans, he said later, thought government "should be merely a policeman." Democrats, he remembered approvingly, "wanted to do things for people and felt that the government had a part in it[,] . . . felt that the government should aid and assist." Much of the country had been won over, and so had many of Brown's neighbors. San Franciscans switched from Republican to Democrat in such a flood tide that the city's political life was forever reordered.[12] Brown's friend and fellow lawyer Matt Tobriner made the switch and often urged Brown to do the same. Finally, the appeal was too great to resist, and Brown decided he would join the party of the activist president attacking the nation's woes. As Franklin Roosevelt prepared to run for a second term, Brown stopped at the San Francisco elections office and changed his party affiliation. For the first time in his life, he was a Democrat, the political label that would define his career. In the long years that followed, he never thought of going back. Changing parties, he sometimes said, was akin to finding a new religion.[13]

———

Brown embraced his new faith with a convert's zeal. In the summer of 1938, he attended the Democratic state convention in Sacramento, rooming with Tobriner. A future justice of the California Supreme Court, the brainy Tobriner remained in the room working on the party platform. Brown wandered the hotel, making as many friends as possible among his new colleagues. "Before the convention was over," Tobriner said later, "everybody knew Pat Brown."[14]

In the fall Brown added new duties to his already hectic schedule by taking on campaign chores for the Democrats' candidate for governor, a tall, silver-haired lawyer from Los Angeles named Culbert Olson. A member of the party for only two years, Brown was nonetheless named to head the Olson fund-raising committee for San Francisco and the speakers' bureau for all of Northern California, both significant jobs. Money was critical for obvious reasons, and in the days before television and videotape, equally important was a campaign's ability to organize surrogate speech makers to stand in for the candidate. At the behest of party leaders, Brown also checked out rumors of corruption at the State Compensation Insurance Fund, hoping to dig up dirt on the incumbent Republican administration.[15] In November Olson won, becoming the first Democrat elected governor of California in the twentieth century.

Having labored for the winner, Brown expected some reward. He wrote to the governor-elect immediately after the election, ostensibly offering legal advice but also putting his name before the great man's eyes. "I have been trying to ingratiate myself with the new administration and believe that I am going to be successful," he wrote to a friend on New Year's Eve, 1938, still before Olson's inauguration.[16] But after so many years out of power, the Democratic lines were long. Olson received twelve thousand job applications in the days right after his election; nearly two months later he was still getting five hundred a day.[17]

Brown kept trying. He pitched himself for job after job: manager of the compensation insurance fund, chief counsel to the state Highway Department, membership on the Board of Prison Directors. He even tried for a judicial appointment, drawing a letter of recommendation from another young San Francisco lawyer, Melvin Belli, who was destined for a famous career studded with high-profile cases.[18] But none of Brown's appeals worked, and before long he was reduced to churlish complaints. Olson was having "an awful time," Brown wrote to a friend. The new governor had left most people unhappy, "particularly the patronage seekers," a group that obviously included Brown.[19] A few weeks later he complained to other friends. "I have been using all of the pressure that I can think of to bring my abilities to the attention of the governor," he wrote, "but whether it will suffice or not, I do not know."[20] And in yet another letter a few months later: "I found in the past that I waste a lot of effort" trying to land state jobs. "I do not believe that anyone, including Governor Olson, knows what motivates his appointments."[21] Finally he wrote to Franck Havenner, a former San Francisco newspaper reporter now in Congress, and let his frustration pour out in rage: "[Olson] is doing the Democratic Party in California terrific harm by absolute bull-headedness. He has shown absolutely no statesmanship. I am in complete sympathy with everything that he is trying to do, but his manner of attempting to do it is beyond the pale."[22]

———

Frustrated by his failure to land a job through the governor, Brown decided that instead he would once again try to build his own political career, and so he turned his attention back to hometown politics.

San Francisco's incumbent district attorney, Matthew Brady, had held the job for nearly twenty years, but his longevity flew in the face of his record. When he originally announced his candidacy in 1919, Brady inexplicably told reporters that he "never was considered a 'good convicter,'" and in the years since he had often proved himself right. Brady's critics—a group that ranged from the San Francisco Bar Association to the Women's Vigilant Committee—had for years accused the district attorney of being lazy, ineffective, and even dishonest. The bar association once concluded he had misappropriated more than $53,000 in taxpayer money, some of it because he faked payroll records. In September 1939, two months before Brady would be on the ballot to seek yet another term, word leaked out that his office was again under investigation, this time by the local grand jury.[23]

Brown was not an obvious choice as a replacement, for he had virtually no experience in criminal matters. For most of the preceeding decade, he had handled civil work almost exclusively, and his few forays into criminal law had not been promising. Once as a young defense attorney he became so flummoxed that he had to ask the prosecutor for advice on making a dismissal motion. In another case he represented a young prison inmate who was already serving time for statutory rape of a teenage girl. The man was charged with sending her an obscene, threatening letter, and Brown, lacking much of a defense, had the man plead guilty and hope for leniency. Instead the client was sentenced to five more years in prison, a penalty so stiff that the crestfallen Brown asked to be removed from the list for court-appointed criminal defense work.[24]

Still, he was eager to run. It had been a decade since his race for the assembly, and in many ways his life and politics had acquired a weightiness that previously had been lacking. He was a married man, and he and Bernice had three children, girls named Barbara and Cynthia and a son, Edmund Gerald Jr. More important politically, Brown was a well-known man in the community, the benefit of his constant networking and affability. He had learned the details of campaigning and had adopted a new philosophy and party that both matched his true beliefs and kept him squarely in the majority. He was a Democrat in what was now a Democratic town.

So he entered the race, a field of five candidates that shrank almost immediately when two men withdrew. That left Brady, Brown, and a man named John Reisner. Reisner immediately charged that Brown had double-crossed him by reneging on a handshake deal under which Brown had agreed to withdraw if Reisner convinced the other two challengers to quit. The idea, Reisner said, was to consolidate the anti-Brady vote behind a single challenger. Reisner had succeeded in convincing the other two men to quit, so the fight should be his alone. "[Brown] broke his word to me," Reisner told one reporter, although it's impossible to know now if the claim was true or false.[25] Regardless, Brown responded with a lawsuit alleging that Reisner lived in Marin County, across the new Golden Gate Bridge that had opened just two years before. That meant he would be ineligible to run in San Francisco, although he was registered to vote there. The case went all the way to the state supreme court, but the justices threw out Brown's suit, and Reisner stayed on the ballot.[26]

Brown pitched himself into the campaign with a frenzy, shaking hands and making speeches at his usual nonstop clip. Yet for all his troubles, Brady remained the heavy favorite, a familiar figure for voters in a city where politics was often turbulent. He had the support of all four of the city's major newspapers, and the challengers could barely get their names into print. With two days left in the campaign, the *Examiner* reported that the incumbent was so far ahead that voting itself was a "mere formality."[27]

On election night the returns were, from Brown's perspective, both disappointing and heartening. Brady won easily, but Brown finished a strong second, with more than a third of the vote. Eleven years before, the first time he had sought office, he had finished third in a three-way field, so far back as to be inconsequential. This time he had shown himself a viable candidate, an up-and-comer with a political future. He said later that the race was "an opening wedge."[28]

———

By 1940 Brown was consumed with Democratic politics. The party's national convention was to be in Chicago that summer, but unfortunately Brown had not been appointed a delegate. Determined to see the great show anyway, he simply decided to attend, intending to watch from the galleries and soak up the excitement. He was, he joked, "an alternate to an alternate."[29]

The trip took two and a half days by train. It took nine hours just to cross the Utah salt flats—"one tremendous white blanket," Brown said. But the long journey didn't bother Brown a bit; it was a chance to drink and chat with California's true politicos, an opportunity he took full advantage of. He made sure to talk with the governor and with the famous movie actress Helen Gahagan Douglas, an activist who was about to be elected to the Democratic National Committee.[30]

They arrived a day early, so Brown saw the sights of Chicago, a metropolis so big and busy that it impressed even a young man from the most cosmopolitan city of the West. He walked along the shore of Lake Michigan, struck by the size of the apartment buildings and hotels, some of which, he felt certain, were the largest in the world. Boarding the "El," he headed to Wrigley Field for a treat that no westerner could enjoy at home, a major league baseball game. He saw a doozy, the hometown Cubs beating the New York Giants on a home run in the bottom of the thirteenth inning.[31]

Roosevelt had played coy all year, refusing to say if he would seek to be nominated for a third term. There were plenty of Democrats who thought he should not, including members of the president's inner circle. James Farley, the chairman of the Democratic National Committee and the manager of FDR's first two presidential campaigns, was so determined that Roosevelt not run again that he insisted his own name would be placed in nomination, a protest against the concept of a three-term presidency.

In later years, presumably out of deference to FDR's iconic status, Brown would claim that he had always wanted Roosevelt to run again. But in fact, as the convention began on Monday, July 15, Brown was opposed to a third term for the president. The Democrats should pick someone else, he wrote home to Bernice the next morning, perhaps his fellow westerner, Montana Sen. Burton Wheeler. The idea of another term for Roosevelt, Brown insisted, was so troubling that unless the president refused to run, Brown intended to boycott the convention he had traveled so far to see.[32]

A political animal to his soul, it was a vow he couldn't keep. That night Brown was back in the galleries, watching as the delegates staged a wild demonstration for Roosevelt, chanting the president's name with such fervor that the two-term tradition was shouted down in favor of another nomination.[33]

The critical issue was settled, and with no actual role at the convention, Brown grew bored. He decided to leave and the next morning headed for

New York, a city he had never seen, on a mode of transportation most Americans had yet to experience, an airplane. The prospect worried Brown—he could get no sleep the night before—and as the plane approached New York the passengers had some anxious minutes. Flying into thick fog, the pilot could not find La Guardia airport and finally had to land at another field. Brown was still captivated. "I was a little scared," he confessed in his daily letter home, "but have now definitely concluded that it is the only way to travel."[34]

Brown took a room at the Astor Hotel, but the tourist bug had worn off. Tired and far from home, he experienced the ironic, age-old malady of the traveler: loneliness amid a great city. He wrote to Bernice to ask that she meet him at the train station when he returned, and headed back to California.[35]

———

In theory, Brown had been raised a Catholic. His father, although not a churchgoer, insisted the children be brought up in the faith of their Irish ancestors. Pat and Harold took first communion, were dispatched to mass, attended catechism. But with their business-obsessed father so often absent, Ida's anti-Catholicism had more impact, at least on her eldest son. When a scuffle in confirmation class brought Pat a smack on the hand from a nun's ruler, he walked out and never returned. On Confirmation Sunday he played hooky from church, and as neither of his parents attended the ceremony, they were never the wiser. As an adult, eager for something spiritual in his life, Brown occasionally went to mass, or even to the Unitarian church that offered his mother solace, but religion was hardly central to his character.[36]

Then when Brown was in his mid-thirties a friend from Democratic politics invited him on a weekend retreat at El Retiro, a Catholic center in Los Gatos, south of San Francisco. From Thursday night until Monday morning, Brown endured a strict regimen of order and discipline: early morning prayers, mass, breakfast, then spiritual exercises and lectures throughout the day, the last one starting at 8:00 P.M. For most of the day silence was required; participants could talk for only half an hour every night before lights out. It might seem a routine of agony for a talkative, gregarious pol, but Brown loved it, perhaps precisely because it was so different from the frenetic, ladder-scaling existence he had created for himself.[37] The weekend at El Retiro left Brown in a contemplative mood—he started reading a lot of philosophy—that soon brought him back to the church. He even asked his Protestant wife if she would renew their vows in a Catholic ceremony, and she agreed.

Catholicism would remain a touchstone for the rest of Brown's life. There were times when he did not attend mass regularly, but he always considered himself a member of the church. Years later, when he had an audience with the pope, his daughter Kathleen would remember seeing in her father more deference than she had ever witnessed before. Always, he remembered a prayer he had been taught at that first weekend at El Retiro. Brown had been taught to pray for his family, for the sick, for the priests, and, at one point, for the most forgotten soul in purgatory. "When I became governor and I'd go to church," he once said, "I would pray that my works as governor would reach the most forgotten person in the state of California."[38]

———

Three days after the bloody shock of Pearl Harbor, Brown contacted the San Francisco office of the FBI and asked for a job application. At thirty-six, with a wife and three children to support, he would not be drafted, but he wanted to contribute in some way to the war effort that had just begun.[39] He was not particular. Less than two weeks later he tried a different tack, writing to a former client now working in Washington, D.C., and asking him to investigate whether Brown might obtain "a legal position in some governmental capacity connected with the prosecution of the war." The firm of Brown and Brown, which now included his brother Harold, was doing well, but patriotism was calling:

> I feel somewhat derelict in my duty to my country if I continue in the private practice of the law, although I have just completed my most successful year in twelve years of practice. There must be someplace where I could fit in which would permit me to support my wife and three children and permit me to be of service to my country.[40]

Neither effort led to a job, but it's not surprising that Brown tried. California was taut with war tension. Many people were convinced their state could be attacked at any moment, and blackouts and deserted streets became the norm. Earlier that year, Pat and Bernice had bought a comfortable home in a hilly, foggy neighborhood on the west side of San Francisco, and now at night they sometimes gathered the children in a little pantry off the kitchen, where the windows had been covered so that no light could escape during blackouts.[41] Brown even considered buying a home in Marin County, a safer place if the city were attacked. "It is mighty serious business here on the Pacific Coast," Brown wrote to a friend.[42]

In many respects, it was more serious on the Pacific Coast than elsewhere, and during the next few months, Brown dealt directly with one of the most tragic events in American history. In June 1942 he wrote to Yoneo Bepp, a businessman and former client who was now literally a prisoner of his own country. Along with thousands of other Japanese Americans, Bepp had been forced into an internment camp. Stirred by groundless fears of disloyalty, Roosevelt had signed Executive Order 9066, giving the military the authority to forcibly evacuate Japanese Americans from the West Coast.

Brown's initial letter to Bepp is lost, but Bepp's heartrending reply survives:

> Life in the center is all according to how one views it. As for myself, this place is virtually a "concentration" camp. We have no civil rights here and are subject to many restrictions, and our individual status is nothing more than that of a common laborer, all of which contributes to make this existence very miserable. Although conditions are bearable in spite of many inconveniences, I expect to see real cases of hardships particularly with respect to the sick, who even now are not getting sufficient medical attention. There are only 6 doctors to care for more than 18,000 persons and the hospital facilities are most inadequate. There is a small epidemic of measles, so we try to keep our little one away from other children as much as possible. Life as we have lived it and enjoyed in the past was beautiful compared to the circumstances and unnatural surroundings in which we now find ourselves. We try to be philosophic about the whole thing, for after all this is war, and this is the sacrifice we have been called upon to make.

He asked Brown to tidy up a final legal matter for his company, then closed by adding matter-of-factly that he was working for the very government that had imprisoned him, helping to make camouflage netting for the army.[43]

Months later, having been transferred to the Heart Mountain camp in Wyoming, Bepp wrote to Brown again and tried valiantly to put the best face on things:

The weather is getting colder and colder week by week and the surrounding hills are covered with snow, but the cold is not as bad as we imagined it would be. The thermometer has registered as low as 12 degrees . . . but if one is clothed warmly it is not bad at all. The climate is healthy due to the dry air and many people formerly affected by nose trouble do not complain as before.

Still, the inherent outrage of the situation shone through. Once a successful businessman, Bepp was now working for the camp administration as a statistician, earning just $19 a month.[44]

Brown knew that ethnic background could be used against people unjustly. Only a few months earlier, his brother Harold had been told that his application for service in the Intelligence Department of the navy was being rejected because his grandparents came from Germany. Enraged, Pat wrote to the secretary of the navy on his brother's behalf, complaining about the "rigid rule" that destroyed Harold's chances. "We are proud of our ancestry, but to have this thrown in our faces is like telling us to move out with the Japanese aliens into a concentration camp," Brown wrote. "If there is any disunity in this country, such silly rules as this are the cause of it."[45]

So it is all the more remarkable that Brown answered Bepp's letters by suggesting that in the end the internment of Japanese Americans might prove best. Before the war Brown had apparently told Bepp that such a thing would never happen, an error he now acknowledged, but then he went on:

I must, however, say that whether the reason for the movement is for reasons of National Defense, or protection of the Japanese people, it will, in the long run, turn out to be better for everybody. As a matter of fact, I am quite a fatalist and believe that things always turn out for the best. When the war is over, and I hope it will be soon, your health and that of the family will probably be much better than that of us who still remain in the cities. With food rationing and tire and gasoline rationing, we will be pretty near as restricted in movement as you are.

When I think of you up in the country and the beautiful mountains of Wyoming, I am, frankly, somewhat envious. I hope that you will have time to do some of the things that you probably wanted to do all your life and that this enforced restriction of movement will give you that opportunity.[46]

Months later, in January 1943, Brown wrote again and astonishingly managed to get in a little campaigning. Later that year he was likely to run again for district attorney, he noted. "If I do and if there are any people from San Francisco in Heart Mountain, Wyoming, I would appreciate your marking their ballots for them."[47]

To be fair, it should be noted that, at Bepp's request, Brown wrote twice to the War Relocation Authority to urge that Bepp be released. He was a man of the highest character, Brown wrote, "as much of an American as I am."[48] But Brown's direct correspondence with Bepp shows a man normally devoted to civil liberties losing his way in a time of crisis. The pursuit of votes is obviously shameless. Far worse is the ugly fact that Brown told a man imprisoned solely for his ethnicity that he was the object of envy and that his captivity might ultimately be for the best. Perhaps he was just trying to cheer up a friend, but it is still horrific nonsense.

———

Over time, Brown's father lost his touch, both as a gambler and as a businessman. The loans from his son grew more frequent, and his health deteriorated. Exhausted, suffering the curses of a hard life, the elder Brown eventually ended up in a hospital, obviously on his deathbed. Called to administer last rites, a priest arrived and found Frank, Brown's youngest son. Frank tried to wave off the clergyman. His father had not been to mass in years, Frank said, and there wasn't much religion in him. But the priest persisted, talking his way into the room. He bent close to the dying man and said he was there to take a last confession. "Oh father," the old huckster answered, "it would take too long."[49]

———

In summer 1943 Pat Brown went to see Frank Clarvoe, the editor of the *San Francisco News*. Although he didn't know it, Clarvoe and the paper were crucial to Brown's next career move—another run for district attorney. Brown wanted to capitalize on the work of the past ten years: the publicity from Cincinnatus, the connections from constant networking, the popularity of the Democrats, the experience from a second-place finish in 1939. All meant that Brown was ready to chase Matthew Brady from his sinecure.[50]

But Brown also knew that four years before, he had lacked a critical component of a winning campaign in those pretelevision days—support from at least one newspaper. The first half of the twentieth century was an era of journalistic bias such as can hardly be imagined by later generations. Newspapers picked a candidate, then supported him not merely with editorial endorsements but also with news coverage so lopsided as to be risible. The chosen candidate was celebrated with long features, sometimes accompanied by flattering photographs, while the names of other candidates often were omitted from the paper entirely. If Brown were to mount a winning campaign, he needed the benefit of such treatment.

As he went to see Clarvoe, Brown had good reason to think the meeting might produce an endorsement. Like all aspiring politicians, Brown kept a careful eye on the papers. He watched for scoops, for leaks, for evidence of how the city's four major papers competed. Brady had a well-earned reputation for leaking almost exclusively to the *Examiner,* the bigger of the two Hearst papers and perhaps the most powerful in town. Brown knew that the *News,* owned by Scripps Howard, resented Brady's favoritism to the *Examiner* and thus was a good prospect for supporting a challenger. If the *News* promised an endorsement, Brown believed, he could probably convince the *Chronicle* to go along too, equalizing the newspaper score at two to two: the *News* and the *Chronicle* for Brown, the two Hearst papers for Brady.

Watching Brady's methods paid off. Although all the papers had backed the incumbent in 1939, Clarvoe readily agreed to endorse Brown this time, and the *Chronicle* soon followed suit. When Brown announced his candidacy in early September, the *News* played it up, matching a sweetheart story with a stern-faced picture of the candidate, his hair neatly parted, his tie perfectly knotted, the very image of respect and authority. The *Examiner* didn't publish a word about it.

Brady presented an even fatter target the second time around. A few months before Brown joined the race, the incumbent had been stung yet again with criticism. The city's grand jury had issued a public report denouncing Brady as so mediocre that the mayor should step in to run the office, or perhaps even call in the state's attorney general. Brady, the grand jury foreman said, "did exactly nothing" to fight juvenile delinquency, then a hot topic among San Franciscans.[51]

The day before Brown officially filed papers to join the race, he caught an ironic break. Giving a radio speech in which he attacked Brady's job performance, Brown twice wandered from his script, which had been approved by the station's lawyers. Engineers abruptly switched to organ music, cutting off Brown partway through his talk. He thought it helped, inciting curiosity and interest in what he had planned to say.[52]

The basic message varied little throughout the campaign: Brady was ineffective, a has-been, too old. The office needed fresh blood, and Brown was the man to drag it into the present day. Brady should be challenged to "name one single case he has ever tried in his public or private career." By contrast, Brown vowed to spend at least two hours a day in court, a questionable use of the district attorney's time but an appealing campaign stunt.[53]

Four years earlier the first Brown-Brady race had hardly registered in the press. This time the campaign was in the newspapers almost every day. By October 21 the *News* was reporting that in political betting circles much of the new money was riding on Brown. It was a critical sign of a campaign on the move. With sophisticated modern polling not yet a part of local races—it was only beginning to be used in national campaigns—betting odds were the accepted way of judging a candidate's viability. Technically illegal, political betting was so widely practiced that two well-known oddsmakers in San Francisco were regularly quoted in the papers as the city's "betting commissioners." Expressed as odds, their predictions were judged as important as those of pollsters and consultants in later decades. When the campaign started, the *News* reported, bettors had been putting money on Brady to win by at least thirty thousand votes. Now he was no better than even money to win at all.

If their pockets were deep enough, campaigns were known to bet heavily on their own man in the early going, in the hope of creating a sense of momentum. Brown knew it too, and as his challenge to Brady gained steam, he used the same tactic. When a cousin ponied up $500 for the campaign, Brown took it to Tom Kyne—one of the "betting commissioners"—and put it all on himself at 5–1. The result of course was to drive down the odds on himself, adding heft to the campaign's aura. But Brown added an ingenious personal twist. He demanded his chit in the form of fifty $10 tickets, then handed them around to campaign volunteers and told each worker that a $60 payoff awaited if he won. The result was, as he once said, "fifty of the greatest campaign workers you'd ever seen."[54]

Sensing a possible victory, Brown redoubled his pace, keeping up a frenetic style that exhausted the thirty-eight-year-old challenger, let alone the sixty-eight-year-old incumbent. In the morning Brown shook hands everywhere he could find an early shift: slaughterhouses, produce stalls, flower shops. During the day he worked the neighborhoods. At night he hit the familiar speechmaking circuit.[55]

Brady responded by increasing the vehemence of his attacks. From the beginning of the campaign, he had intimated that there was something vaguely dishonest about his challenger's campaign. But with Brown on the rise and only four days to go before the election, Brady replaced his rhetorical scalpel with a cleaver.

In what the *Examiner* called a "fighting speech"—dutifully reported on the front pages of the pro-Brady Hearst papers and ignored by the pro-Brown *News* and *Chronicle*—Brady charged point-blank that Brown was the tool of criminals. During a famous corruption investigation seven years before, Brady said, Brown had represented gamblers when they were called before the city's grand jury and advised them to cite their Fifth Amendment right against self-incrimination. "And this is the opponent who boasts his civic mindedness," Brady mocked. Two days later the *Examiner* reported that when he was a young lawyer, Brown had filed the incorporation papers for two "social clubs" that were actually poker parlors hiding behind a law that allowed private clubs to offer limited gambling.[56]

Brown responded in a radio broadcast on the night of Monday, November 1, just hours before the polls opened. The incumbent, he said, was grousing about old legal cases, "routine activities" that were "entirely legal" and accepted by the California secretary of state, who had received the incorporation papers. More to the point, it was Brady who had been responsible for prosecuting criminals in San Francisco for the past twenty-four years. "San Francisco's gamblers know exactly where they stand with Mr. Brady," said Brown, the son of one of the gamblers who had benefited from the district attorney's laxity. "They know how conveniently blind he is to their activities."[57]

Privately, Brown was convinced that Brady's charges had backfired. San Francisco had always been a city tolerant of vice, and Brown thought the district attorney sounded puritanical, perhaps silly. Brown talked to his friends at the *Chronicle,* and, whether due to his lobbying or not, the paper mocked Brady with an election-eve editorial. "So we have gambling in San Francisco," the piece began. "Isn't that interesting?" There were hundreds of "social clubs" in the city, the paper said, and everybody knew that from time to time money changed hands. If Brady wished, he should go out that day and cite them all. "Then we'll have everything wrapped up neat and tidy for election day, and the public can go to the polls and decide whether it wants to re-elect a district attorney whose crowd has the effrontery after twenty-four years to have a quiet stroke of apoplexy about gambling in San Francisco."[58]

On election morning the outcome was still uncertain. Brown voted as early as possible, giving the afternoon papers the chance for a picture that might appear in print before the polls closed that night. There was nothing else to do the rest of the day—it was too late for meaningful campaigning—so Bernice suggested killing time with golf. With the press still in tow, they headed to the city's Lincoln Golf Course. The photographers waited at the first tee to get a shot of Pat's drive. Nervous and unsettled, he swung mightily—and rolled the ball three inches. It set two patterns for Brown: He always played golf on election day, and he remained a duffer for the rest of his life.[59]

Almost as soon as Brown arrived at his Market Street headquarters that evening, there were signs that it might be a good night for challengers. A local shipping executive had routed a three-term incumbent in the mayor's race, and a twenty-year veteran had been booted from the Board of Supervisors. The district attorney's race, however, remained agonizingly tight. First returns put Brady up by 900 votes. The war had robbed many precincts of their traditional workers, and updated tallies barely crept in as first-time clerks struggled with the system. But slowly Brown began to whittle the margin, first to a few hundred votes, then thinner and thinner, then eventually pulling ahead. At last, well after midnight, the final totals came in. Brown: 97,229. Brady: 90,127. It was a slim victory—7,102 votes out of nearly 200,000 cast—but it was Brown's.

He was elated. Years later, long after he had retired, he said that he was more excited the night of that first victory than on any of those that followed. For fifteen years he had tried but failed to get the one thing he most wanted, a rung on the ladder of politics. Now he had his grasp. Beaten twice at the polls, Pat Brown, age thirty-eight, was finally in office. He dropped off a victory statement at the newspapers, and then everybody headed to Vanessi's, a joint on Broadway. They took a side room so the party could be private, and then, into the wee hours, the newly elected district attorney of San Francisco and his friends drank and talked and laughed and celebrated.[60]

3 THE CHAIRS OF POLITICS

ON A BLEAK SATURDAY in early January 1944, San Francisco's new district attorney took the oath of office. For Brown, it was a grand day. At thirty-eight he had achieved in every way the respectability that had graced his father only fleetingly if at all. He lived in a nice house in a good neighborhood. He had a good marriage and three children. His law degree gave him public stature as well as marketable skills. Most of all, he was newly elected to one of the most important jobs in his hometown. Popular and dynamic, he was a man on the rise. Standing in the cavernous rotunda of City Hall for the swearing-in ceremony, he even looked natty, a gaily patterned necktie and a perfect triangle of white handkerchief setting off a double-breasted suit.[1]

In the speech that followed his swearing in, he promised a renewed sense of vigor among the city's prosecutors. The district attorney could, he said, enjoy a tenure of "pleasant leisure" overseeing an agency "complacent or conveniently blind in the execution of its sworn duty." These were obvious references to the defeated Brady, and Brown promised there would be no such sloth among his men. The new district attorney's office would "move vigorously" to "seek the full penalty of the law against deliberate, malicious and unrepentant offenders."

The new era started with a change in personnel. Brown decided he would replace almost the entire staff of the district attorney's office, retaining only four people from Brady's operation. Already a good politician who knew how to gain the most profitable attention, he dribbled out the news of his appointments, earning several stories in the papers for what might otherwise have been a single day's news.

His first appointment was a Republican, Bert Levit, who was named chief deputy. Levit's appointment set a pattern that would continue throughout Brown's career. Both in this job and in those that followed, Levit functioned as a catalyst, stepping into government briefly whenever Brown assumed a new office, reshuffling personnel and procedures, then returning a few months later to private law practice. Energetic and bright—although more conservative politically than many of Brown's followers—Levit added a dose of hustle to any new staff Brown was organizing. He was, Brown once said, a "real goer."[2]

A week later Brown set another pattern, including among five new deputies a local San Francisco lawyer named William Jack Chow, whom Brown touted as the first deputy district attorney of Chinese descent anywhere in the country. It was the first of many such groundbreaking appointments for Brown, although in talking to the papers he insisted he was not catering to interest-group politics. "My selection of Chow is in no sense a recognition of the Chinese of San Francisco, because my office represents no particular class or group," he told reporters. "It is our duty to function on behalf of all the people, but I am sure that a deputy with an Oriental background will prove of great value because of his specialized experience."[3]

But in the long run the most significant of Brown's early appointments was Thomas Connor Lynch, a tall, lanky federal prosecutor with a no-nonsense bearing. The son of an immigrant Irishman, Lynch had been orphaned as a child, gone to sea, then, like Brown, worked his way through law school without an undergraduate degree. They had known each other for years. Lynch was among the young lawyers who had gone along on the hiking and girl-hunting trips to Yosemite back when Brown was attending law school. For a decade, Lynch had been a deputy U.S. attorney in San Francisco, but now Brown prevailed on his old friend to move to the district attorney's office. Six months later, when Levit jumped back to private practice, Lynch was made the chief deputy. His personality complemented Brown's—he was less affable, more intellectual—and in time he would become one of Brown's closest and most important confidants, handling delicate political matters or helping out when crisis struck the governor's office.

Other hiring decisions were less noble. Given money to hire three investigators, Brown used two of the slots for unqualified cronies. One was a chauffer with good political connections, the other a publicity man whose principal duty was to promote his boss's ambition for statewide office.[4]

———

Brown inherited a shambles. The district attorney's office had two typewriters, few files, and a record-keeping system that relied mostly on handwritten entries. Astonishingly, the deputy district attorneys were not full-time employees, although San Francisco's population already numbered more than six hundred thousand. Brown found that often his staff failed to show up, preferring to work in their private offices.

Worse still, the prosecutors rarely decided which cases would be prosecuted. The office was "a mere arm of the Police Department," in Brown's words. Unless the arresting officer was bribed—which happened with disturbing regularity—charges were filed automatically after an arrest, without a lawyer's review. The result was a lot of weak cases that were dismissed by a judge after costly preliminary hearings.[5] Brown empowered his staff; he ordered his deputies to review police reports after arrests and decide if charges should be filed. It was a simple but effective reform that focused resources on the cases with the best legal footing, and the result was fewer charges but more convictions.[6]

Other changes were impossible, at least right away. The budget would not support full-time deputies, although Brown said publicly he hoped to create a full-time staff soon, perhaps after the war ended and things got back to normal.[7] In the meantime, the district attorney himself did a little private legal work on the side. In later years moonlighting by a public official would have been scandalous, ruining his reputation at the ballot box or sparking allegations of serious ethical violations. At the time nobody seems to have given it a second thought. While district attorney, Brown appeared regularly as a private lawyer in divorce and estate cases, even basing the work out of his city office at 550 Montgomery Street in downtown San Francisco. At various times he drove across the relatively new Bay Bridge to handle a case in Alameda County or down the peninsula to appear in San Mateo courts. Once he represented a client before the state Railroad Commission. On another occasion he handled an estate in San Francisco and was awarded a court-ordered fee, although obviously the judge—along with everyone else involved—knew he was a local elected official. He even had the chutzpah to complain that his real job, the one for which he had campaigned and to which he had promised unlimited commitment, was interfering with his private business. "Please pardon the delay in answering your recent letter," he wrote to one former client whose divorce he had handled and who now needed a copy of a document, "but what with daily rapes and murders, as well as husbands beating their wives and children—my private practice is entirely neglected."[8] It is no surprise that he wanted to maintain a private practice, for it was lucrative work: In his first year as district attorney, outside cases nearly doubled his salary.[9]

––––––––

From the beginning, Brown blended a streak of liberalism—or at least pragmatism—into his law enforcement. He intended to be more vigilant than Brady, but hardly draconian. His inauguration speech promised an office that would seek "the full penalty of the law" against criminals, but Brown also vowed that it would not become "an agency of grim, blind and implacable justice." A prosecutor given to inflexibility or vindictiveness—"a dark revival of medievalism," as he put it—was not the American tradition, let alone that of famously bohemian San Francisco.[10]

The realities of wartime soon allowed Brown to implement his modulated justice. When the army and the navy pushed to close all the whorehouses in town in an effort to prevent servicemen on leave from contracting venereal diseases, Brown intentionally took it slow. "Of course, you can close those places up but you can't make screwing unpopular," he said later, "so you've probably got more venereal disease from streetwalkers when you closed up the whorehouses."[11] Faced too with the need to do something about the city's most notorious brothel, Brown waited to file charges until the madam was found to be employing a minor.[12]

On gambling, Brown restrained a growing personal vehemence. Perhaps scarred by his father's troubled life, Brown was becoming adamant about the dangers of a bettor's life. He once wrote in a letter to a friend that gambling was "the greatest of evils."[13] As district attorney, he intended to prosecute gambling cases as felonies under state law, rather than follow the traditional San Francisco practice of pursuing them merely as misdemeanors under a city ordinance. But the former craps game operator offered a shot across the bow for his onetime colleagues. Even before he took office, he let it be bruited around town that the new district attorney—along with the new mayor—intended to be more aggressive in hunting bookies, a rumor that dried up the trade. "San Franciscans who place their bucks on the bangtails," the *Call-Bulletin* reported between Brown's election and his inauguration, "today found themselves with virtually no bookmaking establishments where they could place bets on eastern horse races."[14] After taking office, Brown filed an early case as a felony, then asked the court to impose probation rather than jail time. "I thought the gambling fraternity was entitled to notice," he said later.[15]

Even the city's most notorious culprits got a grace period. Soon after his election, Brown's friend and political fund-raiser William Newsom arranged a meeting between Brown and the McDonough brothers, crooked bail bondsmen who had once been dubbed the "fountainheads of corruption" in the city. Brown knew them. His father had been a friend of one of the brothers and had borrowed money from them when times got tough.[16] Brady had tolerated the McDonoughs' activities, and now they wanted to know if the city's new prosecutor would be as beneficently neglectful. Brown said no, but also gave them sixty days of unmolested operation to close up shop in an orderly fashion. The brothers tried to reciprocate the generosity. When Brown got home, he found $1,000 in cash in the pocket of his coat. He called Newsom and told him to return the largesse. Newsom stopped by Brown's house to pick up the money, then went back to the bar and found the McDonoughs still in the back room. "Edmund picked up the wrong coat," Newsom told them.[17]

———

There was more than a little do-gooder in District Attorney Brown. Soon after he took office he created the new Department of Crime Prevention in his office and then ordered an investigation into why juvenile crime was said to be on the rise. The result was a dowdy twenty-two-page booklet bearing all the hokey earnestness of both its era and its author. "Youth, Don't Be a Chump" started off with a promise from Brown that if only San Francisco youngsters would stop by the district attorney's office and ask to see him, he would help them with their troubles. On the premise that youngsters needed to "know the rules" of the "game of life," the pamphlet then ticked off laws applying to juveniles: no entering pool halls, no loitering after 10:00 P.M., no upbraiding teachers. It's hard to know how much effect the booklet had—it's difficult to imagine a troubled kid opting for a talk with the well-meaning D.A. rather than snatching something from the corner store—but it enjoyed a wide distribution. During Brown's first term, his office produced at least three editions with a total print run of 275,000.[18]

Keeping kids on the straight and narrow was obviously the kind of issue politicians love, but it also reflected a genuine concern, which surfaced again and again in Brown's career, about stressing prevention over punishment. Two months after he became district attorney, his office produced a report on crime prevention, the sort of document that many new prosecutors might use as a call for strict law enforcement typified by more arrests and longer sentences. Brown urged that something be done to reduce the divorce rate, in part by greater use of the city's Court of Reconciliation, which tried to hammer out marital difficulties. "The relationship between broken homes and juvenile delinquency is definite and startling," his report said. Faced with complaints that a department of crime prevention was not truly in the district attorney's purview, Brown insisted that to the contrary it was "mandatory."[19] When two academics published a significant new book on criminology that had a bent toward rehabilitation and other well-intentioned measures, Brown took the time to write to them, praising the book and suggesting a meeting if the two men ever came to San Francisco.[20]

In a long tenure as district attorney, Brown played to the grandstand only rarely. The most egregious case came almost at the end. After an acquittal in a murder case, Brown announced that judges "lean over backwards to give the defendants every possible break. They pay more attention to the civil rights of defendants than to the civil rights of the people who were killed." This was irresponsible nonsense, not to mention entirely out of character. In an editorial the *Chronicle* rightly praised the judge for pointing out that the American system of justice is based on a concern for the rights of the accused. "We would add that if district attorneys occasionally find it inconvenient," the paper said, "that is just too bad."[21]

Brown's most famous prosecution involved what a local newspaper termed "one of San Francisco's oldest and best-known institutions," although it was as illegal as it was prominent. Inez Burns ran a clinic on Fillmore Street where hundreds of abortions were performed every year. It was clean, professional, and discreet. Madams sent their girls there, but much of the clientele was far more respectable. The wives and girlfriends and daughters of the San Francisco establishment patronized Burns's business. Movie stars came up from Hollywood when in need of her services. Authorities had made a few efforts to crack down on Burns—performing an abortion was then a felony, and the issue was not yet one of ideological division in American politics—but they never got very far. After one raid they could find no one willing to testify against Burns, since her customers were generally grateful. Lynch, Brown's new assistant, had indicted her for tax evasion when he was in the U.S. attorney's office, but Burns, a millionaire with a chauffeur-driven car and a horse ranch at Half Moon Bay, simply paid a fine and kept right on going.

Fired up with the energy of a newcomer, Brown vowed to wage a crusade. Twice he raided Burns's clinic, but each time his investigators came up empty. Thinking that crooked cops had tipped off Burns, who was famous for her extensive bribery, investigators finally followed up one raid on the clinic by going to Burns's house. There they found nurses and orderlies waiting in hospital uniforms, ready to return to work as soon as their boss gave the all-clear.

The prosecution wasn't easy. The grand jury refused to hand down an indictment, so Brown filed the case himself, a district attorney's prerogative. When the case went to trial, juries hung twice; who knows whether any of the jurors had had need of Burns's services? At one point Brown had to petition the city's Board of Supervisors for extra cash to launch another investigation. For Burns's third trial, Brown's deputies brought into the courtroom the tools of her trade: operating tables, anesthetic machines, the long, narrow instruments she used to perform the actual procedure. After deliberating more than six hours, the jury finally convicted, and Burns was sentenced to prison. [22]

———

In summer 1944, about a year and a half after he took office, Brown turned his attention back to his real love—politics. Four years earlier, he had attended the Democratic National Convention as nothing more than an observer. Now, befitting his status as an elected Democrat in California's most important city, he traveled to Chicago as a delegate. [23]

There was no question that Franklin Roosevelt would be nominated for his fourth term, so the only real issue at the convention was the identity of the vice presidential nominee. The second spot on the ticket was hotly disputed, in part because Roosevelt's health was faltering badly. It was increasingly obvious that the president might not survive a full term and thus that the convention was probably choosing his successor as much as his running mate. Henry Wallace, the incumbent vice president, was the liberal's liberal. An intellectual, an author, a fervent New Dealer, he was a hero to most of the party activists who served as delegates. But to the party's hardheaded, backroom leaders, Wallace seemed like a dilettante, a man who liked to study languages and play with a boomerang and who had no grasp of practical politics. An eloquent believer in civil rights, he was hated in the South, the Democrats' electoral hole card. The pols' solution was to dump Wallace in favor of a little-known but noncontroversial Missouri senator named Harry Truman. The president, who did not attend the convention and gave his acceptance speech from a West Coast location kept secret for reasons of wartime security (it was San Diego), left everybody hanging, suggesting at various times that he wanted Wallace, would accept Truman, or preferred any number of other contenders.

As the convention opened on July 19 in Chicago Stadium, delegate Brown was uncertain. He was no Wallace man. Although a liberal, Brown was already positioning himself as a practical politician, and he had been disgusted by a Wallace speech earlier that year at the Palace Hotel in San Francisco. The vice president had given vent to his idealistic, scholarly side. "He got up and wandered all over hell's half acre and didn't say anything," Brown said. "He appeared to me to be a dreamer."[24] But on the convention's second night, Wallace gave one of the seconding speeches for the president's nomination—and electrified the delegates:

> The future belongs to those who go down the line unswervingly for the liberal principles of both political democracy and economic democracy regardless of race, color or religion. In a political, educational and economic sense, there must be no inferior races. The poll tax must go. Educational opportunities must come. The future must bring equal wages for equal work, regardless of sex or race.

The delegates rose and roared again and again. The organist began to bang out the Wallace theme song, and a chant surged out of the crowd, "We Want Wallace." Looking up at the podium, Brown was one of those who swooned. He decided that the next day, when the balloting for vice president was to be held, he would vote for Wallace.

The party insiders were still determined to ditch the vice president. They had settled on Truman, and as a nine-hour session dragged on the following day, they began to haul delegates to a small room beneath the rostrum for a browbeating session designed to turn votes to the Missourian. Brown got the treatment from Bill Malone, the Democratic Party boss in San Francisco, and Ed Pauley, a rich Southern California oilman. Pauley, destined to become one of Brown's most important financial and political backers, was already a national player in Democratic politics; he had been involved in White House meetings where he and others worked to convince FDR that Wallace was deadweight. "Gee Pat, really this Wallace is a nut," Pauley told Brown in the makeshift woodshed beneath the convention's dais.[25] Although forty-eight hours earlier he would have agreed, now Brown tried to defend the vice president. The labor people all liked him, Brown told Pauley, and so did Helen Gahagan Douglas, the glamorous actress and Democratic National Committeewoman from California.

But Brown knew he was in the presence of men who understood the intricacies of national politics far better than he did, so, characteristically, he struck a middle course. He told Pauley and Malone that he would vote for Wallace on the first ballot, but if the vice president did not capture the nomination immediately, he would switch to Truman on the second ballot. That was fine with the Truman forces. Their strategy was to push the matter to two ballots, letting idealistic delegates blow off steam with an initial vote for Wallace. They had encouraged sixteen favorite-son candidacies, forcing those delegations to support the local figures and drawing off enough Wallace supporters to ensure a second ballot.

The strategy worked. Wallace led on the first ballot, though not with a majority, and the second vote produced a stampede to Truman. Sticking by his commitment, Brown joined in. "Thank God I changed because Wallace later turned out to be a traitor to Roosevelt," Brown said later. "He ran on a third-party ticket in '48 against Harry Truman and he got way off in left field and was really kind of a pie-in-the-sky fellow." In Brown's view, Wallace's idealism was so exaggerated that it disqualified him from the nation's highest office. Wallace was "sincere, but not the kind of man that you'd want to be president of the United States."[26]

———

Brown turned forty in spring 1945, barely a week after Franklin Roosevelt died. Looking ahead to the next year's election, the ever-ambitious Brown could ponder many options. Culbert Olson, the governor who had rejected Brown's job entreaties, had lost a reelection bid in 1942. Worse, he took most of his fellow Democrats to defeat with him. In Sacramento the party held only one statewide job—Attorney General Robert Kenny was a hero of the left—and thus ambitious Democrats like Brown had an opportunity to advance. Kenny planned to run for governor in 1946, challenging the one-term Republican incumbent, Earl Warren, so the attorney generalship would be an open seat. It was the logical job for a local prosecutor to seek, and Brown was a logical Democratic candidate—a popular and vigorous figure in the state's second-largest city. Hoping to hammer out a consensus ticket, Kenny called a meeting of key Democrats in his San Francisco office, and Brown emerged with the nod for attorney general.[27]

Ironically, the threat in the primary was not from Democrats but from Republicans. California elections were held under an unusual law known as "cross-filing," a relic of Progressive reforms that allowed candidates to run in the primaries of multiple parties. The candidate's party affiliation did not appear on the ballot, which made it impossible for a voter to know, simply by looking at the ballot, if he or she was voting for a Democrat or a Republican. Warren had led the Republicans to a majority in the legislature, and because they were now well-known incumbents Republicans were often winning the primaries of both parties, effectively rendering the fall election meaningless. In the statewide races for 1946, all the Republicans cross-filed to run in the Democratic primary, and Brown and his colleagues on the ticket were worried they might not win their own party's nomination.

As the gubernatorial nominee, Kenny was their leader, but he wasn't much help. In one of the strangest political decisions in California history, he left the state the day after he announced his candidacy, declaring that he planned to attend the Nuremberg trials and would not return for weeks. Leaderless, low-level Democratic officials began announcing their support for Warren, who was immensely popular, and by the time Kenny returned from Germany it was clear he might lose in the primary. Brown and others huddled with Kenny in Los Angeles and told him of the disastrous condition of his own neglected campaign. He fell apart, got drunk, and—then and there—faded into meek defeatism.[28]

Brown, however, kept plugging away. In contrast to his later campaigns, he ran wholeheartedly as part of the Democratic ticket, perhaps because in partisan affairs he had the fervor of a convert. At one point a group of his fellow district attorneys—almost all Republicans—approached him and suggested he could have their support if only he would split from the Democratic ticket and run independently. Brown said no; he had already promised to run as part of the team.[29]

Not a man innately given to strategic concerns, Brown was nonetheless directing the campaign himself, handling details normally beneath a candidate's altitude. Dictating memo after memo, he directed aides toward specific potential donors, ordered that certain reporters be contacted on this story or that, and devised strategy and tactics.[30] In May—the primary was

June 4—he spent so much time on the hustings that he announced he would reimburse the city for that month's salary as district attorney. "I, of course, keep my office notified of my whereabouts and am available for contact," he told reporters, "but I am not spending my entire time in my office and it's only right that I should return my salary."[31]

Brown supporters had once been confident to the point of cockiness, but by election night there was speculation that Brown might suffer the same ignoble fate as Kenny—losing to a Republican in the Democratic primary. Frederick Howser, the district attorney in Los Angeles County, was a Republican who was running for attorney general in both party primaries, and it appeared he might beat Brown on the Democratic side. Brown claimed later that he was almost wishing for it. He knew that a general election race without a Democratic candidate at the top of the ticket would be difficult, and if he lost now it could all be blamed on Kenny's lackluster effort. But surprisingly, Brown took a lead over Howser and held it, narrowly, throughout the night. As the vote continued to come in the following day, Brown's lead shrank, eventually leaving him only six thousand votes ahead out of nearly a million cast. Then, three days after the election, as returns still trickled in and the outcome hung in the balance, officials in Alameda County, across the bay from San Francisco, discovered their tally system was hopelessly bungled. Thousands of votes had been incorrectly added to Howser's total through a series of goofs. One precinct worker, for example, had been subtracting when she should have been adding. Once cleared up, the new totals padded Brown's margin—and assured him of the Democratic nomination. Narrowly, by a little more than 2 percent of the vote, Brown had survived his first statewide campaign. In November he and Howser, who had won the Republican primary, would battle in the general election.[32]

———

By 1946, Brown's father had been dead for four years, and Brown had won public office and established himself as a substantial figure in his city. So perhaps he had forgotten his own past. Little else explains the bizarre attack he launched against Howser.

In October, as the fall campaign heated up, Brown used the opportunity of a statewide radio address to charge that his opponent had ties to gamblers. Brown alleged that one of Howser's aides in the Los Angeles district attorney's office had once been the lawyer for a gambling ship that prowled the waters off Southern California and that Howser's campaign treasurer had once been a shareholder and director of a company owned by the gambling ship operators. Howser, Brown suggested, had allowed the ship to operate because of the close connections.[33]

It was a reckless and stupid thing to say—and not just because some of Brown's information proved wrong.[34] Brown was the son of a gambler, had once been the lawyer for gamblers, and had been a professional gambler himself, running the craps game that helped to fund his education and his father's losses. In his campaign for district attorney, he had thought Brady's antigambling attacks foolishly prudish, and yet now he was trying to use similar material against Howser. Brown even knew that gambling still thrived in his own jurisdiction. As district attorney he had strengthened the prosecution of such cases, but he had hardly eliminated betting altogether. Privately at least, Brown acknowledged that San Francisco remained a gambler's haven. "I have my greatest difficulty with the gambling situation," he wrote to a friend in 1945, barely a year before he launched his attack on Howser. "As you know, San Francisco is a city that has gambled before I was born and will probably gamble long after I die. It is inbred in people of high moral principles and to eradicate it is like trying to cure a cancer."[35]

Even friends recognized the unfairness of Brown's attack. Less than a week later two prominent Southern California supporters—former assemblyman Maurice Atkinson and former state supreme court justice Louis Meyers—abandoned the Brown campaign. Meyers said nothing, and Atkinson referred only to a dispute "over policy," but the timing left little doubt as to the reason. Two weeks later Atkinson decided he disliked no-man's land and went clear over to the opposite trench, endorsing Howser in a statewide radio address and specifically praising the Republican's handling of the gambling ship case.[36]

Recalculating, Brown abandoned personal attack in the campaign's final days and focused more of his speeches on policy matters. He promised to keep order impartially during labor disputes, inoculating himself against charges that a liberal Democrat would let union thugs run riot. He also vowed aggressive action against the underworld and sex criminals and promised to fight for the state's right to control revenues from offshore oil drilling.[37]

But most voters heard nothing about these ideas, since often Brown couldn't get his name in the paper. The journalistic bias that Brown had skillfully manipulated in his district attorney campaign was now working against him. In California nearly all the big newspapers were Republican.

Despite its crucial endorsement of Brown for district attorney just three years earlier, the *San Francisco Chronicle* backed Howser for attorney general and virtually ignored the Democrat, even though he was a local figure. When Brown was mentioned, it was usually as the target of Howser attacks. The same was true for the staunchly conservative *Los Angeles Times*. The Hearst papers were even more obvious in their rightward leanings. Bannered across the front page in the days leading up to the election was the slogan "Vote Against New Deal Communism—Vote Republican—Vote American." Virtually the only major Democratic paper in the state was the *Sacramento Bee,* which was as favorable to Brown as the *Chronicle* and the *Times* were dismissive. The *Bee* covered almost everything Brown said and often ignored the Republican nominee. The weekend before the election, the paper ran a puffy profile of the Democrat, complete with a picture of the candidate and his family. Howser's name did not appear in the paper that day.[38]

Doubtless the cheerleading helped Brown carry Sacramento County, but statewide he was a doomed man. It was a Republican year. Nationally, voters were tired of the Democrats who had ruled the country for so long, and Harry Truman seemed to many people a weak and prosaic imitation of the great man he had succeeded. Democratic fortunes were especially weak in California, where Kenny's ignominious defeat in the primaries meant the party had a headless ticket. Brown lost by 344,000 votes, a thorough defeat but, given the circumstances, not a rout.

In his first try for statewide office, Brown had come up a loser, just as he had the first time he ran for district attorney. Yet he had made a respectable showing, and as he reviewed the returns a lesson emerged. Howser had run up much of his margin in Southern California, especially his home county of Los Angeles. Outside the south, the race was roughly even. Once, Northern California, the home of the Gold Country and San Francisco, had lorded over the state. But through the final decades of the nineteenth century and the first ones of the twentieth, Southern California had surpassed its northern rival. If he was to have a political career in California, Brown, though a born northerner, would have to strengthen his ties to the south.

The prospect did not daunt him. A resilient man by nature, he had lost before and survived to fight another day. Now he resolved to do the same. "I am not a bit discouraged, but feel that it was just one of the cyclical sweeps that are going to happen in this country as sure as the night follows the day," he wrote to Glenn Anderson, a Democratic assemblyman who would eventually go on to be Brown's lieutenant governor. "In the meantime, we will all prepare for two, four and six years hence when we again fight for those things we think are right."[39]

——————

With the end of World War II California's growth had become, in at least one sense, more a festering problem than an opportunity. With GIs returning home and starting families—for the first time demographers were noticing the record-setting birthrate that would swell into the baby boom—America's cities were soon filled to bursting. There simply was not enough housing, and the homes and apartments that existed were rapidly being priced out of middle-class incomes. In San Francisco, a metropolis constricted into a finger of land, the problem was acute.

It was not a topic obviously under the district attorney's purview, but Brown decided that he could call for better housing on the basis that slums bred crime. To find out how bad things really were, Brown dispatched a staff member—a former navy WAVE named Janet Aitken—to study the issue. In spring 1947, as Brown was nearing the end of his first term as district attorney, Aitken wandered through San Francisco's seedier neighborhoods and recorded her impressions.

She found squalor. South of Market, rats scurried around rooming house floors at night. In Chinatown whole families lived in "dark cubicles." In the Western Addition seat-of-the-pants remodeling had transformed old homes into dangerous mazes of apartments. In North Beach Aitken walked down a dank, garbage-strewn alley to enter a flat where a family of seven lived, the rooms so dark that it was necessary to keep the lights on throughout the day. It was damp inside and the slipshod wiring was a fire hazard. "The whole family was sickly," Aitken reported. "After seeing such depressing and inadequate living conditions, it is easy to understand why, as statistics prove, these areas have the highest disease, delinquency and crime rates."[40]

The evidence of such misery transformed Brown into an aggressive advocate for public housing programs. The construction industry, he noted when releasing Aitken's report to the newspapers, was building barely a third of the housing the city needed. What was worse, private industry was getting rich in the meantime. "Slums are and always have been very profitable and a source of large revenue to the owners," he said. "They produce little tax, however, and cost much in policing, public health and fire protection."[41] The solution was to use public muscle where private efforts had failed.

Brown headed for Sacramento and testified on behalf of a housing subsidy bill then pending in the legislature, one of his first formal encounters with the state government that would dominate the rest of his career. It was a bruising, infuriating debut. He and other supporters of the bill were quickly brushed aside by a senate committee that questioned the need for a solution funded by taxpayers. Brown believed he had been victimized by the influence rich slumlords wielded with rural senators, who did not face the housing shortage in their own districts. Back in his San Francisco office the next day, he wrote to the committee chairman and gave vent to his rage:

> In my long experience in public life, I have never seen anyone treated so badly as you treated me and the other citizens who tried to present a case to their elected representatives in the state of California. It was disgraceful. Those senators outside of the metropolitan areas can use the great powers that they have to stifle free expression, but, in the long run, they will do this great democracy of ours much harm.

Then an acid postscript: "In all fairness to you, I will say that you were equally unfair to each side."[42]

Frustration with the legislature did nothing to diminish his commitment. During the next year, he produced two more reports on slums in San Francisco, encountering at every turn the same resistance—the argument that housing was a problem best solved by private industry. It was a contention that held no sway with Brown. When the *San Francisco Call-Bulletin,* Hearst's evening paper, editorialized that government subsidies for housing should be avoided, Brown wrote a letter to the editor, ostensibly agreeing but in fact calling precisely for public programs. "Government . . . has found that it is necessary to eliminate conditions that are harmful to the health of the community. We do not permit bad and defective meat to be sold because we know that it is dangerous to the community. The same is true of housing. Slums are injurious to the health of the community and must be eliminated. The only possible way that this can be done is with government aid and assistance." California voters, he urged, should approve a $100 million housing bond slated for a statewide ballot. (It failed.) And he supported an expansive federal housing program—recently rejected by the Republican Congress in favor of a more modest bill—that would have provided subsidies for public housing projects.[43]

———

There was never a doubt that Brown would run for a second term as district attorney. In the fall of 1947, as his first term drew to a close and the deadline for filing candidacy papers approached, it appeared he might face an uncontested campaign. Late in the afternoon on the last day for filing, with only fifteen minutes to go before the clerk's office closed, someone on Brown's staff produced a cake and a bottle of champagne so that they might celebrate the boss's certain victory. Then the clerk's office phoned: a former policeman and assistant U.S. attorney named George Curtis had jumped into the race. "We drank the champagne and we ate the cake," Brown remembered later, "but it was the bluest party I've ever seen in my life."[44]

When the first crush of disappointment wore off Brown recognized Curtis as an impotent enemy. "This was our first general staff meeting since some nonentity filed against our boy on the closing day of the filing," read a memo describing a Brown staff meeting the next day. At the meeting—which was utterly typical then but would today be considered a scandalous blend of governmental and campaign business—Brown laid out for his deputies the strategy of the fight ahead: Curtis should never be attacked, his name never mentioned. Whenever possible the Brown forces would simply ignore their opponent. Deputies were expected to be available for campaign work five nights a week. They were to hand out Brown cards whenever the opportunity presented itself and convince their friends to slather bumper stickers on their cars. If they were members of a lodge, they were to attend every meeting until election day. When giving a talk, staff members were to stress the increase in prosecutorial vigor since Brady's day. "Mention the major cases and take credit for everything the police have done," they were told. For fear of angering real estate interests, they were to avoid any mention of the slum housing Brown had so consistently condemned.[45]

The last point is the most interesting, for it reflected a pattern—and a tension—coursing through Brown's career. Often during his long run of politics, he indulged his liberal heart between elections, only to heed his pragmatic head during campaigns. Sometimes a little disingenuous, it was a strategy that allowed him to construct successful, centrist campaigns out of a liberal, activist record.

In this case, caution proved unnecessary. Brown's strong first term had made him popular to a wide array of San Franciscans. He was endorsed for reelection by organizations as ideologically distant as the *San Francisco Examiner*—incessantly conservative, Republican, even nativist—and the local chapter of the resolutely liberal National Lawyers Guild. On election day Brown more than tripled Curtis's vote total to win a second term.[46]

———

Soon after Brown took the oath of office for a second time in January 1948, he began to hear troubling scuttlebutt from political reporters. California Democrats were gripped with lethargy, the writers said. Democrats lacked the "vigor and vitality" of their Republican counterparts.[47]

The rumors ushered in Brown's second flirtation with national politics. Again he would be a delegate to the Democratic National Convention. The difference was that this time he would be far more involved in the key decisions of the California delegation. No longer merely a political hopeful, he had blossomed into a figure of moderate importance in his state. His navigation through the complicated shoals of the 1948 campaign would show some of the traits that had already brought him success: pragmatism, a good political nose, flexibility (albeit a brand of flexibility that sometimes teetered close to pliancy). But 1948 would also foreshadow future troubles for Brown. Years before a debacle at a future Democratic National Convention would seriously damage his career, there were hints that his gabby, folksy style might sometimes be overwhelmed by the high-pressure maelstrom of a national arena.

There was no surprise in the reporters' assessments that Democrats seemed a little blue. For the first time since the beginning of the Great Depression, they were facing a presidential election without the reassuring presence of Franklin Roosevelt. Democrats still held the White House, but Truman was immensely unpopular, even within his party. In the South the president's support for various civil rights measures stamped him as a traitor. Nationally, he seemed certain to lead the party to defeat, just as he had in the midterm elections two years earlier.

Despite these problems, or perhaps because of them, Brown was typically eager for a campaign. He wrote to Jimmy Roosevelt, son of the late president and now the chairman of the California Democratic Party, and urged a little hustle. "Things are moving along but a little bit too slowly to suit me," Brown wrote in mid-January. "I am very anxious to have a meeting and start a radio campaign throughout the state of California, attacking the

Republican Party and all of its pomps and pretensions." A month later he was still frustrated. He sent Roosevelt essentially the same letter again: "I trust that you will pardon my constant reiteration of this point, but I would invite your attention to the fact that there is absolutely no publicity moving out of Democratic headquarters in this state."[48]

Roosevelt was less concerned with jump-starting a campaign than with merely holding one together. When the delegates, including Brown, were picked weeks earlier, they swore allegiance to Truman. But as winter turned to spring, many party activists became increasingly disenchanted with the president. Hard-core liberals cozied up to a third-party bid by Henry Wallace, the former vice president and hero of the left. Moderates hoped to dragoon Gen. Dwight Eisenhower into accepting the party's nomination, though his politics remained an enigma. As the party's chairman in California, Roosevelt was trying to hold the delegation for Truman, a chore made only more difficult when two of his brothers announced in late March that they were joining the Ike bandwagon. Three days later Brown wrote to Roosevelt and bluntly made the case for abandoning the president:

> I wanted to say that we should face the fact that Truman cannot be re-elected and even if he could we really should not want him. He is not strong enough in these perilous times to achieve even the smallest goal. At the convention four years ago I refused to permit the same voices that spoke so loudly in favor of Truman to influence me. I felt then, as I feel now, that the nomination of Truman was one of the most serious mistakes ever made. I feel that it could well influence the entire course of history. I feel, also, that the delegation from California could be a potent force in encouraging a man like Eisenhower to become a candidate.[49]

Publicly, however, Brown was sticking with his Truman pledge. In less than two weeks he was scheduled to be the chairman of a big Democratic fund-raising dinner in San Francisco, and Sen. J. Howard McGrath, chairman of the Democratic National Committee, was to attend and give a speech. McGrath was there to rouse the troops for Truman, and under such circumstances Brown could hardly say publicly what he believed privately, that the president should not be renominated.

Roosevelt was similarly ambivalent. He harbored serious doubts about Truman's chances for victory, but as state party chairman, he had to be diplomatic. He decided that he would use another fund-raising dinner, this one held in Los Angeles and also attended by McGrath, to test the waters.

In his remarks Roosevelt omitted the president's name entirely and praised Eisenhower as "a lieutenant colonel of 1938 [who] became the supreme Allied commander in 1943." The Eisenhower line drew cheers from the crowd, some of whom later heckled McGrath's pro-Truman speech.

Brown attended the dinner too, and afterward, as a man of increasing influence in the party, he was cornered by reporters curious about his reaction to Roosevelt's comments. Undoubtedly, Roosevelt expected Brown to say something noncommittal. Privately, Brown had been an active proponent of dumping Truman, and now Roosevelt had made a public feint in the same direction. There was every reason to think Brown would leave the door open to an Eisenhower draft, just as Roosevelt had intimated.

Instead, Brown essentially attacked Roosevelt, saying that the affair had been "in bad taste." The heckling of McGrath had put the party chairman "on the spot." As for the possibility of an Eisenhower draft, Brown insisted that he intended to stand by Truman, although he was far from enthusiastic. The delegates should stick with the president as a "moral obligation," he said.[50]

Roosevelt was understandably enraged. Just two weeks earlier Brown had written to him stating flatly that Truman could not be reelected, did not deserve a second term even if he could win one, and was a great mistake of history. Now, when Roosevelt offered a far milder version of the same sentiments by omitting the president's name from a speech, he found himself attacked in the papers by Brown for orchestrating a meeting in "poor taste." Furious, he leaked Brown's earlier letter to the *San Francisco News*, embarrassing Brown in his hometown paper. "Pat Brown Center of State Demo Row," the *News* headlined, then quoted Brown as drawing a thin distinction between his private views (anti-Truman) and his public commitment (pro-Truman).[51]

Knowing that he had double-crossed Roosevelt, Brown immediately wrote a letter and tried to patch things over.

I am sorry that I commented upon the dinner last Monday night, particularly in view of your extremely gracious invitation and kindness in placing me at the speaker's table. I was a guest and should most certainly not have commented upon my host. Those are things that people simply do not do. . . . I am also sorry that you saw fit to release my personal and confidential letter. I think that if we are not careful neither of us will achieve our joint objectives. I would like to suggest that we start all over, beginning now, to accomplish together those things we are each trying to do.[52]

The damage was done. Neither man came off well. Roosevelt's decision to leak the letter was spiteful, but Brown looked wishy-washy at best, duplicitous at worst. He had been quoted as saying it was in "bad taste" to express doubts about Truman's renomination, then been revealed as the author of a letter that only days before had flatly stated that the president should be dumped. Party leaders, including the old San Francisco Democratic boss Bill Malone, were said to be so annoyed that they decreed a punishment for Brown: He would no longer be considered a possible state party chairman the following year.[53]

———

By the time Democrats gathered in Philadelphia for their national convention, in mid-July, the delegates were filled with gloom. Eisenhower had adamantly refused to run, and it was obvious that Truman would be nominated. Yet even among party regulars, few people held out hope for Truman's reelection. Brown had grudgingly come to accept a Truman candidacy, yet he too was beset by pessimism. Arriving in town, Brown thought the atmosphere seemed more like a funeral than a political convention. Discouraged even before the opening gavel, he almost left Philadelphia immediately. He decided to stay, but on Monday, the first night, he could not bring himself even to go to the hall. Instead, he sat in his hotel room and listened to the proceedings on the radio, much as he had done eight years earlier when he was hoping someone other than FDR would be nominated.[54]

To his surprise, Brown heard the convention come alive. Alben Barkley, an old-line senator from Kentucky, inspired the delegates with a fiery defense of the New Deal that immediately made him the front-runner for the vice presidential nomination. Brown thought Barkley, at seventy-one, was too old for the job, but he agreed that the senator had made a dead convention breathe.[55]

By Wednesday, when Truman was to be formally nominated and give his acceptance speech, Brown was not only in attendance, he had finagled his way backstage. He managed a few words with the president and found a man so determined and confident that he abandoned the anti-Truman beliefs he had been harboring for months. "I am compelled to retreat from the statements made in the letters that I wrote to Jim Roosevelt this year," Brown confessed in a letter to a friend. "I still do not believe that Truman is a great man, but then who is?" Thomas Dewey, the Republican nominee, was too cold, Brown said. He thought Truman had given a great acceptance speech, boosting the delegates' morale and launching his campaign with zest. "He will make a fight," Brown wrote admiringly, "and I think he has a chance."[56]

The convention over, Brown and two friends bolted for the urban wonders of New York. One of these was Yankee Stadium, where they saw Joe DiMaggio go hitless. "He is a good player," Brown wrote to his thirteen-year-old son, Jerry, with striking understatement, "but is a little bit off stride."

Brown flew home on what he described as a "huge plane"—a TWA Constellation that seated fewer than fifty people—and was greeted at the San Francisco airport not only by Bernice, but also by the newest member of the Brown family, three-year-old Kathleen. The whole family was soon off to a summer vacation at Yosemite, where the patriarch for once refused to think about politics, preferring instead to while away the long evenings on the porch playing bridge with Bernice.[57]

————

As Brown looked ahead to the elections of 1950, he was certain to run for something. He never intended to remain a local prosecutor his entire career, and he now had a good base from which to build: the twin booster shots of his respectable bid for attorney general and his overwhelming reelection as San Francisco's district attorney. The question was whether he should take one step at a time and run again for attorney general or leap immediately to the big leagues and challenge Earl Warren for the governor's chair.

Warren was not yet an icon. Later, as his years on the Supreme Court made him a national figure and a hero to many liberals, the memories of California Democrats would soften, and many would look back on him with fondness, even awe. But at the time many Democratic activists and politicians saw Warren as a frustrating and difficult opponent. The governor was a wizard at projecting nonpartisan purity when appealing to the electorate as a whole yet remaining a vigorous and committed Republican when the need arose. He was the keynote speaker at the 1944 Republican National Convention and the party's vice presidential nominee in 1948, yet between those two elections managed to win both parties' gubernatorial primaries in 1946. Democrats grew so annoyed at Warren's deft maneuvering that they began handing out little cards—labeled "Earl Can't Fool Me"—outlining the governor's GOP activism.[58]

Brown was among those who were sometimes skeptical of Warren. He knew that years before Warren had run a much-respected district attorney's office in Alameda County, but in some regards Brown was not particularly impressed. Warren struck him as "grim and ambitious" and "not always fair." Warren regularly attended prosecutors' conventions when Brown was district attorney, warming their relationship a little, but they were hardly confidants. As Brown scanned the political horizon, Warren was not an untouchable idol; he was simply a potential Republican opponent.[59]

Yet the governor was a man of undeniable political popularity. Brown had seen firsthand how Warren crushed Kenny's gubernatorial campaign in 1946, winning both parties' nominations and ending the contest in the primary. As the vice presidential nominee, Warren had escaped blame for Dewey's disastrous collapse in 1948, and he was thought a serious contender for the Republican presidential nomination in 1952. He was a weighty, national figure, a politician far grander than San Francisco's district attorney.

By contrast, running again for attorney general seemed an easy battle. Howser had suffered through a ruinous first term. At best, he seemed a bumbler. Once he gave local officials a list of one hundred fifty "known gangsters" said to be threatening the peace, only to learn later that several of the men were dead, including one who had been executed in the electric chair. At worst, rumors circulated that Howser was a crook, precisely the intimation that Brown had made, however foolishly, during their campaign four years before. There were accusations that people close to Howser's office were demanding bribes and kickbacks. A Howser crony was convicted in Mendocino County of trying to extort money from slot-machine operators. Most suspicious of all, a shady political operative from Los Angeles was found dead in a San Francisco hotel room under circumstances that suggested odd ties to the attorney general's office. His hotel reservation had been made by Howser's staff, for example. Howser's troubles led to a nasty feud with Warren, who had formed a Commission on Organized Crime that was a rival of the attorney general's office. Weakened and demoralized, Howser checked himself into a hospital, citing "nervous tension and high blood pressure."[60] Brown believed that Howser would not be renominated by the Republicans, thus ensuring a wide open race for the attorney general's office in the general election. If a Democrat "has anything on the ball at all," Brown thought, he would win.[61]

As a high school student a quarter century before, Brown had allowed the threat of a strong opponent to intimidate him into seeking an office he did not want and as a result had vowed that he would always give full play to his ambitions, that he would never let the fear of losing deter him from running for a post he craved. He had tried that tactic a few years later, running for the state legislature when he was barely out of school, and endured a stinging defeat. As he matured, he had settled on a middle ground. He spent a decade building his career and connections, then set his aim on a reasonable target, the district attorney's office. When he lost he did not allow discouragement to set in, tried again, and won. Now, well into middle age—he was about to turn forty-five—he returned to the prudent strategy that had brought him victory. Aware of Warren's strengths and Howser's weaknesses, Brown decided to delay his gubernatorial ambitions and pass up a possible race against Warren. Instead, he would run again for attorney general. He would continue, as he put it later, "going through the chairs of politics."[62]

In the days after New Year's, 1950, Brown was in the midst of his typical election-year milieu: out on the road, giving speeches and shaking hands. "Frankly, I am sounding out the state to see what support I may have if I decided to be a candidate," he told a business group in San Bernardino. "I am interested only in the attorney general's office. I think there is a job to be done in that office and I would like to do it."[63]

In mid-February he made his candidacy official, positioning himself as the cleaner alternative to Howser's grimy record. "Today the office of attorney general has sunk in public esteem to a level unparalleled in the history of California," Brown said in his announcement. "Its function has been diverted from one of public service to the point where its actions meet with public ridicule and even contempt." With such a broad target at hand, Brown kept himself free of any controversy, offering a platform of Pablum so bland as to be laughable: "nonpartisan administration of justice," "legal opinions based on the facts," "conduct of a friendly office." As one newspaper reported demurely, "He did not particularize."[64]

The June primary proved no obstacle. No other major Democrats entered the race, and Brown easily won the nomination. His instincts about the Republicans proved right. Howser lost to Edward Shattuck, a lawyer and former state GOP chairman.

The outlook for November was uncertain. Brown polled more total votes than Shattuck, but Howser had taken almost seven hundred thousand. No one knew where those voters would go in the general election—to Brown or to Shattuck—and they were clearly enough to swing the outcome. Brown had beaten Shattuck in thirty-eight of the fifty-eight counties, but he ran second in Los Angeles County, which had more than 40 percent of the state's voters.

Democrats nominated two famous names for the top of the ticket: Jimmy Roosevelt to challenge Warren for governor and Helen Gahagan Douglas to run for an open U.S. Senate seat against an ambitious fellow House member, Richard Nixon. It was a stark contrast to the race four years earlier, when Warren's sweep of both primaries left the Democrats with no candidate for governor. Yet Brown was wary of his party's new leaders. Both Roosevelt and Douglas had reputations as liberals, and Brown wanted to avoid too close a tie to his party's left wing.

He told Roosevelt point-blank that he would campaign with the ticket in places where it would help and stay clear of the Democratic label in places where it would hurt. "Wherever [Roosevelt and Douglas] were strong I went with them, but wherever I thought they were weak I dumped them or ducked them," Brown said later, unselfconsciously. "It was really a very practical political situation."[65]

Tailoring the campaign geographically was possible because campaigning remained largely a localized practice. Statewide television was yet to become a real force, and newspaper ads could be aimed at specific areas. In at least one Northern California district where he sensed little support for Roosevelt, Brown even took out ads touting himself for attorney general, the local Democratic candidate for Congress, and Warren for governor.[66]

Still, for all his careful cultivation of a moderate image, Brown was soon accused of dangerous left-wing sympathies. Nixon was running a horrific smear campaign against Douglas, intimating communist sympathies by calling her "the pink lady." To a lesser degree, Shattuck began to adopt the same tactics against Brown. Shattuck noted that Brown had once been a member of the liberal National Lawyers Guild and that he had opposed the deportation of Harry Bridges, the Australian-born leader of the International Longshoremen's Association who had repeatedly been accused of being a communist. Even Brown's incessant politicking came back to haunt him. He had known so many people and lent his name to so many events that Shattuck was able to dig up obscure items that supposedly revealed Brown's subversive tendencies. He had supported something called the Salute to Young America Committee, for example, which was said to have suspicious ties, although the group's purpose is now lost to history. In another case, Brown and Bridges had jointly sponsored a dinner for Henry Wallace in 1946, as Wallace was drifting to the left of the mainstream Democratic Party.[67]

It was the first time, although by no means the last, that Brown would be accused of dubious sympathies. For years thereafter, internal memos of the FBI would reference Brown's opposition to Bridges's deportation. Shattuck's intimations were ridiculous. If anything, Brown's flaw was that he stayed too carefully in the political middle, not that he was a sympathizer with the far left. In a bit of overheated campaign rhetoric, he once even said that he harbored an "inborn hatred of communism."[68] In truth, he found Red-baiting foolish and wrong. Years later when he was governor, the FBI called Brown and told him that the wife of a governor's office staff member had once been a member of the Communist Party. In fact, she had been only a supporter of such causes, but it was still enough, in that era, to cause panic in many politicians. The staff member fretted about repercussions, but a few days later at a cocktail party hosted by the governor during a statewide political convention, Brown made a point to greet the woman graciously, then take her by the hand and lead her inside. It was a show of public support and reassurance that touched her husband, who still grew misty eyed at the memory decades later. "If he had done nothing else," the man said, "he would have been my hero."[69]

As late as mid-October 1950, Brown was still dubious about his chances against Shattuck. The betting was at even money, and a survey by Mervin Field, a pioneer in political polling in California, showed the race tight, with a huge undecided vote. "This election will be a very close fight and probably will be decided during the next two weeks," Brown wrote to a friend. "I only hope I will be successful, but unless there is a swing back to the Democrats I may go down with Roosevelt and Douglas."[70]

Then he got a break. The Los Angeles County chairman of the Republican Party, angry at Shattuck over some forgotten matter, leaked to Brown a series of letters Shattuck wrote during World War II. At the time Shattuck had been assigned to the Selective Service office in Washington, D.C. He was already politically ambitious, and the letters revealed that he had retained a publicity agent in a ceaseless effort to get his name in the papers. More valuable for Brown, Shattuck had voiced a little frustration at Warren's decision to pass him over for appointment as state draft director. It wasn't much, but Warren cherished his aura of rectitude, and the slightest wisp of criticism rankled him. Brown knew that if he could make the Shattuck letters public, he would drive a sizable wedge between Warren and Shattuck. It would guarantee that Warren would stay out of the attorney general's race completely.

Warren might have stayed mute anyway. He rarely endorsed anyone, including other Republicans. But there was always the chance he might offer veiled support of Shattuck or criticism of Brown. Given the closeness of the race, a nod from the popular governor might turn the day. Hoping to curry favor with the Great Man, Brown had already proposed that the governor's crime commission be made permanent, exactly the issue over which Warren and Howser had disagreed so fervently.

The problem was getting the letters out. Sensing a Democratic plant, no California reporter would write the story. Then Harry Lerner, a shrewd San Francisco public relations man who was one of Brown's friends and supporters, got the letters to Drew Pearson, whose muckraking column was often a friendly forum for Democrats. In the first of many favors he would do for Brown, Pearson wrote about the letters. He quoted Shattuck's most ill-advised passages—his vexation with Warren; his unguarded remark, "I feel I can go a long way on the 'veteran-of-two-wars idea'"—and suggested that Shattuck was an opportunist trading on his military service.[71]

For Brown, it was risky and perhaps even unseemly politicking. In some ways it hearkened back to 1946, when the former gamblers' attorney attacked Howser for his ties to gamblers. Now Brown, through a surrogate, was trying to shame Shattuck for publicity hunting, even though for years Brown had worked as hard as anyone to keep his name in the papers. Even worse, Shattuck quickly pointed out that at least he had been in the service twice, in both world wars, whereas Brown had never donned his nation's uniform.

But the ploy worked because the real target was not public opinion; it was Warren. Only two days before the election, the governor offered a semi-concealed endorsement of Nixon in the Senate campaign—a valuable boost for the young congressman. About the attorney general's race, however, Warren was silent, almost surely annoyed by Shattuck's impertinence. In his memoirs he described his attitude toward Brown's campaign as "benevolent neutrality." Brown believed he would have lost the race if Warren had backed Shattuck.[72]

Even with Warren on the sidelines, Brown was by no means guaranteed a victory. The final Field Poll, released two days before the voting, showed that what had once been a close race was now a dead heat: 45 percent for Brown, 45 percent for Shattuck, 10 percent undecided.[73]

As always, Brown voted early on election day. He indulged himself with a little revenge. Brown had not forgotten that Roosevelt embarrassed him two years earlier by releasing his anti-Truman letter. Now, in a tiny way, Brown struck back. Cloistered in the privacy of the voting booth, the Democratic nominee for attorney general marked his ballot for the Republican nominee for governor.[74]

For different reasons, a lot of Americans voted for Republicans that day. With Truman's sagging popularity as a handicap, Democrats lost seats in both houses of Congress. The California results were no better. Nixon beat Douglas for the Senate seat. Republicans expanded their control of the legislature, and Warren routed Roosevelt for the governorship. Down the ticket, Republicans won every statewide race but one.

But that one race was the contest for attorney general. Brown ran up a huge margin in his hometown, San Francisco. He was almost as strong in the three counties—Sacramento, Fresno, and Stanislaus—served by the McClatchy-owned *Bee* newspapers. The result was a narrow win—225,000 votes—the slimmest margin Brown would ever enjoy in a statewide victory. In January 1951 he would become the only Democrat in California holding a statewide office.

The victory was a lofty moment for Brown, not just because he had achieved statewide office, but also because throughout the 1940s he had laid the foundation of his politics. In 1944 he had listened to the wise men of his party and abandoned the liberal Henry Wallace for the moderate Harry Truman. In 1948 he had toyed with the Eisenhower draft, then switched back to Truman just in time. In 1950 he had avoided too close an embrace with Roosevelt and Douglas, proving that he could win when so many other Democrats lost. By the time he was elected attorney general, Brown had cast his lot: He would be the liberal Democrat always careful to avoid too much liberalism or too Democratic a tinge. Brown's would be the politics of cautious commitment, holding in constant and careful tension a desire to do the right thing and to get reelected.

On election night, he focused on more prosaic matters. As attorney general, he announced, he would give no quarter to crooks, would shirk no fight with the state's legal opponents, would work hand-in-glove with the governor. But Brown's career would head almost unavoidably for larger arenas. For, at forty-five, he was now the most important Democrat in the nation's second-biggest state, a place fast becoming the embodiment of the American future.

4 WAITING

WHEN PAT BROWN TOOK statewide office for the first time, California was experiencing one of its periodic population explosions. The bustling shipyards of World War II had started the most recent boom, luring thousands of workers westward with the promise of better jobs. In the years after the war, the flood of migrants persisted. The 1950 census figures, released just days before Brown's election as attorney general, showed that during the previous decade, more than 3.5 million people had moved to the state, a rate of about 1,000 a day. In ten years California had added more new residents than in its first seventy years of statehood, 1850 to 1920. California had surged past Pennsylvania to become the second most populous state in the nation, and metropolitan Los Angeles was now the country's third biggest urban center. In a phrase that Brown would use often in later years, Earl Warren called it "the greatest mass migration this country has ever known."[1]

The westward torrent showed no signs of abating, and it was catching the nation's attention. California was more than just big; it was gleaming. Sunshine and beaches and a healthy outdoorsy brio made the state seem, more than at any time since the Gold Rush a century before, like a magical place. In one poll Americans cited it as their favorite vacation spot.[2] John Gunther's *Inside U.S.A.*, a popular book of the time that sought to capture the mood of various parts of the country, described California as "the most spectacular and most diversified American state[,] . . . ripe, golden, yeasty."[3] Gunther devoted four chapters to California. Ohio, which at the time had almost as many people, got just one. Even the old Gray Lady of American journalism, the *New York Times,* announced that the very core of the country had been pulled toward the Pacific. "After a hundred hurrying years," the *Times* said, California was "something to marvel at."[4]

Yet for those who ran the state—a group that now included Brown more than ever—the excitement was mixed with challenge. The newcomers were so numerous they threatened to destroy the good life they sought. Old roads were overwhelmed by the modern rush hour, which in many places was bloating well past sixty minutes. Schools were packed: new elementary schools were needed immediately, new high schools soon enough, new college campuses in the years to come. Experts predicted that for the next two decades, merely to keep pace with its expanding population, metropolitan Los Angeles would have to open a new hospital every five months.[5] Without a burst of public energy and investment, California risked being overwhelmed by its own good fortune, a business where the rush of customers tramples the merchandise.

––––––

In the district attorney's office, Brown had only a few dozen employees, all centrally located and almost all exempt from civil service protections. He could hire and fire at will, and when he first took office he had done so, bringing in an almost entirely new staff. The state Department of Justice, by contrast, had six hundred employees spread among offices in San Francisco, Los Angeles, and Sacramento.[6] Nearly all were civil servants, and their new boss wondered to himself if they would be entirely on his side.[7] It proved a needless worry: Within six months he declared in a letter to a friend that his new staff was "very cooperative."[8]

The civil service structure made the office less valuable to Democrats as a political tool. Just as twelve years before Brown had hounded the Olson administration for a job, hundreds of people now looked to the only statewide Democratic officeholder as a potential sugar daddy. There was little candy to give away. "There are so few exempt employments in the office of the attorney general," Brown wrote to Assemblyman Glenn Anderson, who would eventually become his lieutenant governor, "that the Democratic Party will have a difficult time building on the basis thereof."[9]

Aware of Howser's squabbles with Warren, Brown wasted no time trying to mend fences with the governor, though they faced one potentially major disagreement. Although during the campaign, in what was surely an early attempt to curry favor with Warren, Brown had endorsed the idea of making the governor's commission on organized crime a permanent fixture of state government, in the wake of victory he wasn't so sure. The commission had been a rival to Howser, and Brown wanted no similar competitors.

Hoping to impress the governor, Brown hired two old Warren hands for top positions in the Department of Justice, then took them along for a meeting with Warren. He urged Warren to forget about the crime commission. If Warren were the attorney general, Brown argued, he would want no rivals. Neither did Brown. Crime was in the attorney general's bailiwick, not the governor's.

Warren listened, then delivered a lesson in practical politics. Reporters had staked out the session, he noted, and either Brown could accede to the governor's wishes or he could start his new job with headlines recounting a split between the attorney general and the state's revered three-term chief executive. The younger man knew when to concede. "Governor," Brown responded, "we shall have a crime commission."[10]

The relationship between the two men improved with time. Brown kept his headquarters in San Francisco, but every few months on one of his trips to Sacramento he and Warren had lunch together amid the quiet comforts of the Del Paso Country Club. They talked politics, with Warren, the older and more experienced man, offering counsel. Once the governor held his hands up to his chest, as if holding cards in a poker game, and—taciturn Swede to the core—told Brown that in politics one should always "play them very close to the vest." It was advice that Brown, as sociable and gabby as a man could be, was monumentally unsuited to follow.[11]

———

Fighting crime made headlines, but in fact it was only a piece of Brown's job. Although attorneys general always like to portray themselves as something approaching high-powered police officers, most of the office's duties had nothing to do with breaches of the peace. Department of Justice lawyers spent most of their time representing state agencies, and Brown was now essentially the managing partner of a very large law firm.

The formal opinions issued by Brown's office—perhaps the most revealing product of his tenure—show his liberal heart. The state law prohibiting the sale of liquor to Indians—such things were still on the books—was "anachronistic" and of "doubtful validity." A state employment commission had the right to investigate racial and religious discrimination in hiring. Japanese Americans who owned bars or restaurants or package stores could reacquire the liquor licenses they lost when they were interned. Every county in the state had to provide Indians with welfare checks on the same basis as other citizens. Cities had the right to move forward on their own with local ordinances prohibiting racial discrimination.[12] In yet another case, Brown tempered justice with reason and insisted in a memo to a staff member that a family should not have to forfeit their Packard sedan solely because their teenage son had been caught with a little marijuana while driving it.[13]

A trio of opinions entwined Brown in the perilous thicket of religion and the schools. The decisions prohibited officially sanctioned classroom prayers, the schoolhouse distribution of Gideon Bibles, and the reading of scripture for purposes of religious instruction. The latter opinion actually lessened slightly the restrictions on the use of scripture, but letters still poured in complaining that Brown had banned the word of God.

All three decisions took some courage, given the zeitgeist. Just the year before, President Eisenhower had ordered that the words "under God" be added to the Pledge of Allegiance, and though the U.S. Supreme Court had already outlawed religious instruction in public schools, it would be years before the justices expanded their restrictions to include prayer and Bible reading. Brown appealed to America's civil scripture to justify his stance. The Constitution, he said, must protect everyone, "even atheists and agnostics." Then, straying a little from the strictures of the law, he painted his defense of dissent in global terms: "In the great ideological struggle in which the world is now engaged, enforced conformity of thought is one of the evils against which we fight."[14]

———

By early 1952 Brown was back on one of his periodic anti-Truman jags. "I am hoping that the president will withdraw and that [Illinois] Governor [Adlai] Stevenson will announce his candidacy," he wrote to Drew Pearson, the columnist. "If he does, I think the Democrats will be in for another four years."[15]

A month later Brown got his wish. After losing the New Hampshire primary to Tennessee Sen. Estes Kefauver, Truman announced he would not accept renomination. Brown was in Hawaii, but he quickly got a phone call from William Malone, the old San Francisco Democratic kingpin who had helped convince Brown to abandon Henry Wallace in favor of Truman for the vice presidential slot in 1944. Aware of the role Malone played, Truman had made him the administration's man to see in California. Now Malone wanted to protect his turf by ensuring that the next president would also be beholden.

Kefauver already had a slate of delegates submitted for the California primary, but that was of no use to Malone. Kefauver was a man much disliked by party regulars, especially by Truman devotees like Malone. (The president referred privately to Kefauver as "cowfever.")[16] If Kefauver controlled California's delegation at the national convention, Malone effectively would be shut out from any meaningful influence.

Malone needed a stand-in candidate, someone who could win the California primary and deny the delegation to Kefauver. With the substitute as the nominal candidate, the delegation could be held together until the convention, where Malone could work his backroom magic. There was only one possible choice as the favorite son: the Democrats' only statewide elected official, Attorney General Pat Brown. Given Truman's weakness, Brown had seen it coming. Weeks earlier in Washington, D.C., he had talked with Pearson and said that he did not want to run against Kefauver if Truman withdrew.[17] But over the phone Malone proved convincing. He sweet-talked Brown into allowing his name to be placed at the head of what would have been Truman's delegation. Just two years into his first term as attorney general, Brown was technically a candidate for the presidency of the United States.

Not that anybody expected him to win the California primary. He didn't expect it himself. When he met Kefauver in debates, the atmosphere was almost jocular. Both men knew that Kefauver was a serious candidate for the White House and that Brown was nothing more than a placeholder. There wasn't much money for Brown's campaign, which soon ran up a deficit, and he made a frankly halfhearted effort. Even publicly, Brown made no bones about his stand-in status. "We entered this race with our slate to give the Democrats of California a true democratic choice," he said a few days before the primary. "If they think that any of the fine candidates other than Senator Kefauver should be nominated at Chicago, then they should vote for my delegation."[18]

The result was a shellacking at the primary: more than a million votes for Kefauver, fewer than half that for Brown. Of the state's thirty congressional districts, the Brown slate carried not a one. Still, he did not regret the game little effort. "My theory in politics in those days," he said later, "was always get your name before the public as much as possible and try to maintain a good image and be a good human being."[19]

In the long run, the more important item to go before California voters in the spring of 1952 was an initiative to alter the state's unusual cross-filing system. In the decade since Warren had captured the Governor's Mansion, Democrats had been frustrated that their numerical superiority in voter registration failed to translate into power in Sacramento. Warren had retained the state's top office, and Republicans held control of both houses of the legislature and nearly every lesser statewide post. Compared with their rivals, Democrats had far more voters and far fewer officeholders.

There were plenty of reasons—the writer Irving Stone once said that California's peculiar politics "were very nearly inexplicable to anyone who has not drunk them in with his mother's milk"—but one factor was surely cross-filing.[20] Republicans regularly filed to run in Democratic primaries. The Republicans were most often the incumbents, with better name recognition, and because the ballot did not specify the party affiliation of the candidate, incumbents usually did well. Also, incumbents were always listed first on the ballot, a huge advantage for the party in power.[21]

To Brown, the biggest problem with cross-filing was financial. Because candidates had to protect against their opponent winning both nominations at the primary, everybody had to run hard from the first day. Even if you were the only candidate from your party, you had to mount a major effort in the primary as well as the general election. That cost money, and Republicans were typically better funded than Democrats. If the system were changed, a Democrat who had no intraparty opposition in the primary could simply hoard his money until the fall campaign.[22]

Controlled by Republicans, the legislature was never going to change the system. But for Democrats, an odd savior was at hand, a rich oilman who had made politics his hobby for decades. John B. Elliott attended his first Democratic National Convention in 1900, when the party nominated William Jennings Bryan for the second time. By 1916 Elliott was a sufficiently important figure to run Woodrow Wilson's campaign in California. For years after, Elliott claimed credit for crucial decisions that gave Wilson a narrow edge in California and thus a slim electoral college majority. By the 1950s Elliott was an old man and decided he would add one final achievement on behalf of California Democrats—the abolition of cross-filing.[23]

Personally fronting the necessary cash, Elliott had an initiative petition drawn up to abolish cross-filing, and he circulated it during the 1950 campaign. At the time California law required that initiatives go first to the legislature, which could enact them verbatim. If the legislature refused, the measure went automatically to the voters. So once Elliott's supporters gathered the required number of signatures, the Republican leadership of the legislature knew it could not simply kill the measure. As an alternative, legislators decided to approve a second ballot measure dealing with cross-filing that would appear on the ballot at the same time as Elliott's. The legislative measure altered cross-filing without eliminating it. Candidates would still be able to file in both primaries, but their party affiliation would at least be reflected on the ballot. The strategy of putting both measures on the ballot was simple: Republicans hoped that voters would become confused and reject both, or at least opt for the more cautious of the two. The Republicans used every tool they had. The numbering of ballot measures was done at the discretion of the secretary of state, and Republican Frank Jordan assigned to the Elliot measure the number 13, hoping that superstitious voters would reflexively mark down a "no." He gave the legislative measure the lucky number 7.[24]

In the immediate sense, Republicans got their wish. Voters narrowly rejected Proposition 13—who knows if the numbering had any effect—while approving Proposition 7 in a landslide. But the legislature had outsmarted itself. Although it did not eliminate cross-filing, Proposition 7 was still a milestone reform. For the first time in decades, voters would now be able to see the party affiliation of candidates. Democratic voters in Democratic primaries, in other words, could finally avoid inadvertently supporting Republicans.

California Democrats were on the rise in many ways. A few months after the change in the cross-filing system, state senator George Miller called a meeting of party leaders and activists at Asilomar, a conference center on the Central Coast. Miller was a gruff but brilliant political strategist, and a man who would play a huge role in California politics for years to come. Already the Democratic Party's hapless condition had struck him a blow. In 1950 he ran for lieutenant governor, only to lose in both the Democratic and Republican primaries to the GOP nominee, Goodwin Knight. Knight was assured of a victory in the general election; Miller was infuriated.

In the wake of Adlai Stevenson's losing 1952 presidential campaign, Miller saw a way to fortify the party's influence. Stevenson's clean, brainy style had lured thousands of volunteers to Democratic activism. Stevenson

Clubs sprouted throughout the state. Miller sensed that the newcomers had to be kept involved, lest they drift away when faced with less inspiring candidates. At Asilomar—the conference was titled "What's Wrong with the Democratic Party in California"—Miller urged the creation of a new Democratic organization, one that would build on the enthusiasm of the Stevenson Clubs. The group would endorse candidates *before* the primary rather than wait for voters to have their say. By picking true Democrats, as opposed to Republicans who had cross-filed into the Democratic primary, the new organization would educate the voters, and, combined with the new party affiliation on the ballot, the endorsements might finally allow Democrats to take advantage of their numerical superiority among voters.[25]

Given the weakness of the formal party structures, Brown and others had known for years that a new Democratic organization was needed. As early as 1948 Brown wrote to the secretary of state and reserved the legal rights to the names Associated Democrats of San Francisco and Associated Democrats of California. Later, he and Matt Tobriner, the lawyer friend who had urged him to switch parties way back in the 1920s, tried to create a group that would issue endorsements before the primaries. They drafted bylaws and picked a name—the Democratic Council—but nothing ever came of it. For one thing, neither Brown nor Tobriner was half the political tactician Miller was. For another, they tried to launch the idea before the 1952 Stevenson campaign produced so many eager volunteer clubs. In the wake of that campaign, Tobriner surrendered the rights to the name Democratic Council to Miller's infant organization.[26]

The Asilomar conference, which led to the formal creation of this new California Democratic Council (CDC) a few months later, was a huge success. Activists vowed a reinvigorated Democratic effort. There was talk of raising $200,000 for the next campaign. Organizers had to book extra hotel rooms in other towns because of the overflow crowd. It was an auspicious beginning, and it was yet another sign that California Democrats were finally finding their stride.

Brown gave a speech urging Democrats to take on Governor Warren when necessary and not shy away from criticizing him simply because of his popularity, but Brown's presence on the podium was more significant than what he had to say.[27] As the party's only elected official, Brown had become the Democrats' public face. It was a workhorse role he loved. For years he toured the state again and again, appearing in small towns and large, hustling to a dinner speech, or stopping at the local newspaper for an interview. Aware of their momentum, Democrats were focusing on the special elections called when a legislative seat became vacant. In those cases Brown was the party's designated campaigner. Occasionally the appearance of a statewide official brought charges of carpetbagging, but nobody really cared. "We knew it was good," said Don Bradley, a former union activist brought in by Miller as executive director of the party. "Pat was popular, and people were willing to accept the Democratic leadership role from him, and he was willing to take it."[28]

————

Never wild about public life, Bernice had to accustom herself to even longer absences from her husband. As district attorney, he had spent evenings darting around San Francisco. Now he was gone for days or even weeks, trooping the length and width of the state. Even when no campaign was under way, Brown kept going. Once, when the next election was more than a year off, he gave fourteen speeches in a month, roughly one every other day. Normally indefatigable about such things, Brown confessed to a friend that "no man can do a good job and still make that many talks."[29] Bernice remembered it later as feeling like a campaign that lasted years. On one trip, Pat was gone so long that she flew to Santa Barbara, where he was making a stop, just to see him for a day.[30]

Like all ambitious politicians, Brown was missing a lot at home. The couple's four children were growing up, far more often under the eye of their mother than their itinerant father. Barbara and Cynthia, their eldest daughters, were by now young women, creating their own lives. The youngest, Kathleen, was still in school. But it was the couple's only son, Edmund Gerald Jr., already known as Jerry, who stood out. Perhaps this was because he was his father's namesake, the male child in an age of sexist assumptions. Or perhaps it was because the boy was already proving to be, in every sense, an unusual person. Strikingly bright and inquisitive, he sometimes drove his teachers nuts with his incessant but insightful questions. Around the neighborhood he was always an energetic, rambunctious handful, occasionally a hellion. One way or another, he was often in trouble. When he scratched his name into the wet cement of a neighbor's newly poured driveway, the Browns had to replace it. Years later, when the boy had grown into early manhood, his father wrote to ask for his views on the prevention of juvenile delinquency, then added, "I can think of no one whose experience would fit in better to tell us how to prevent it."[31]

To all of the children, Brown was a caring, concerned father, although often an absent one. His remaining letters to them show both his hectic schedule and his simple, charming affection. To Jerry when he was ten and away at summer camp:

> There are many, many interesting things that occurred [at the Democratic convention, from which Brown had just returned], and I will tell you about them on the way up to Yosemite on Monday. . . . I hope you are having a good time. I am sure that you brush your teeth, wash your hands and face and say your prayers at least three times a day. . . . I hope you have not gotten into any fights, but if you have, I hope you haven't lost them.[32]

Later to Kathleen, twelve and also at camp:

> I sure missed not seeing you on Sunday, but I had to make the television show and speech in San Diego. It always seems that politics interfere with my family life. . . . I do hope that you have improved your leg kick because it has always been a disappointment in my life that I was not a great swimmer, but I think you will be much better than your father or your mother.[33]

And to twenty-year-old Barbara, who was attending school in Berkeley and had just written home pleading for more money—at least $32.20—and signed her missive "Your most extravagant daughter":

> Dear Miss Extravagance:
> A close audit of your bills and expenditures indicates to me that you have charged yourself with a failing that is not too evident from the exhibits attached to your letter. I must confess, however, that the $4.00 gift for a sponsee (whatever that might be) could probably have been cut in half, and I think the "miscellaneous spending money" covers a multitude of sins or virtues. As for the $25.00 item for clothes, although I have four women in my family I am not prepared to pass judgment upon it. My experience indicates that although it might be extravagant it is certainly not profligate.

He noted that he had already sent along $100—enough to take his daughter "out of bankruptcy"—then signed his letter, "Your most liberal father."[34]

As California Democrats began looking around for someone to challenge Warren if he decided to seek a fourth term, they naturally turned to Brown. The attorney general wanted no piece of it. The governor was immensely popular, and if Brown were to challenge him in 1954, he would have to give up his current post as attorney general. When he had made a bold leap before—for example, running for attorney general in 1946—he was in the middle of a term, which allowed him to make a safe bid for a promotion while holding his current job as a fallback. If he challenged Warren and lost, he would be out of politics completely. So in May 1953, eighteen months before the election, Brown publicly declared he would not seek the governorship.[35]

A few months later, in the fall, the political landscape changed radically. After more than a decade as governor, Warren announced he would not seek a fourth term. He was sixty-two, and it seemed time to go. Eisenhower, who was likely to run for reelection in 1956, blocked his presidential ambitions. The Republican nomination probably would not be open until 1960, when Warren would be approaching his seventieth birthday. Furthermore, Eisenhower had promised him the next vacancy on the U.S. Supreme Court, a guarantee made good only weeks later when Chief Justice Fred Vinson died and was replaced by the California governor.

For California politics, Warren's decision not to run again was an earthquake. He had first moved into the Governor's Mansion in the gloomy early days of the war, when Brown was still a lawyer in private practice. Opinions differed about his achievements as governor, but he was undeniably popular, a stumbling block for other ambitious politicians, many of whom, like Brown, were afraid to challenge him.

Goodwin Knight, Warren's lieutenant governor and now, thanks to Warren's appointment to the Court, the state's chief executive, was a far less certain commodity. The son of a Utah lawyer, Knight moved to Los Angeles as a boy and later worked his way through Stanford as an undergraduate and Cornell as a law student. He practiced law for a few years and then bought a gold mine in the Mojave desert. The miners struck a vein, and Knight was rich.

Knight's real interest was politics. Almost as affable as Brown, he loved to shake hands, tell jokes, even occasionally dance or sing or juggle. He was reputed to have once said, "With my luck, who needs brains?" He was appointed a judge in 1935, but gave up the bench to run for lieutenant governor in 1946. In the years since, he had spent most of his time angling for Earl Warren's job. Now that he had it, now that Warren was gone, nobody knew how Knight would do running for a term of his own.[36]

Democrats sensed that for the first time in years they had an opening to take the governorship, and they began urging Brown—their lone first-string candidate—to make a move. Ed and Ellie Heller, a wealthy couple who were perhaps the Democrats' most important donors at the time, invited Brown over to their house, where he found many of the party's big financial backers. They promised critical financial support if he would seek the governor's chair.[37] Pressure came from within his own office too. At one event, Bill O'Connor, Brown's chief deputy at the Department of Justice, put up a "Pat for Governor" banner, although Brown ordered it yanked down immediately.[38]

Any election was tempting. Like all instinctive people with a particular talent, Brown longed to exercise it. "I wanted to run—period," he once said of his political career, describing a trait more than a mood. This time, though, he held his fire. His earlier losses had come in smaller races, the campaigns serving simply to widen his reputation. But if he tried too quickly for the state's most important office, he might be tagged a loser. He would also have to give up the attorney general's post, a job he liked. It was too soon, Brown told Graves and the others. He wanted to wait.[39]

Brown was the only Democrat likely to win, so a delegation of party activists—including Don Bradley, a strategist who had run the Brown for president primary campaign in 1952, and Alan Cranston, the president of the CDC and a man with a big future himself—went to Brown and asked him to reconsider. He wouldn't budge. Shortly before Christmas 1953, almost a year before the election, Brown announced his decision publicly. The *New York Times* called it a "heavy blow" for Democrats, who now "must be prepared virtually to give the governorship to the Republicans by default."[40]

———

Reelection as attorney general appeared easy, although it did not come without political intrigue. Before the primary Brown got a call from Kyle Palmer, the political editor of the *Los Angeles Times* and a kingmaker of Republican politics in California. Even in a time of openly partisan journalism, Palmer was unusual. Forgoing any appearance of objectivity, Palmer worked more like a political operative, cutting deals and giving advice almost constantly.

Palmer proposed a simple pact: The *Times* would support Brown's bid for reelection if he would refrain from endorsing the Democratic candidates for governor and the U.S. Senate. Brown slept on it a night, then called Palmer and turned him down. Despite the *Times*'s great influence, it was a relatively easy decision. Although he typically shied away from lashing himself too tightly to the Democratic ticket, Brown was always careful to offer a pro forma endorsement when necessary. He had no intention of becoming a man without a party. He knew that somewhere along the campaign trail he would be asked point-blank if he was supporting his fellow Democrats at the top of the ticket. To say absolutely nothing—as Palmer was demanding—would look disloyal and selfish. Brown also knew he was headed for an easy reelection, with or without the *Times*. His first term had gone well, and he was facing marginal opposition. Palmer was offering an insurance policy Brown did not need to buy.[41]

The primary results made that obvious. On the Democratic side it was a rout; Brown took more than 90 percent of the vote. But he also cross-filed into the Republican primary. His main opponent was the disgraced Howser, hoping somehow to resuscitate himself. Even on the Republican side, Brown won by almost three hundred thousand votes, a remarkable display of strength given that the new election law required that he be plainly identified on the ballot as a Democrat.[42] Like Warren in 1946, Brown had captured the nomination of both major parties, essentially ensuring himself of victory in November.

He had no intention of sharing his popularity with his fellow Democrats. At the top of the ticket, nobody really thought they had a chance anyway. After his failed attempt at getting Brown to run, Graves had allowed himself to be talked into accepting the Democratic nomination for governor. He was running against Knight, now seeking a full term in his own right. Brown regarded Graves as a likable man who was politically doomed. Brown had even less fondness for his party's Senate nominee, Congressman Sam Yorty. Yorty had begun his career as a left-winger and would end it as a race-baiting reactionary. Brown disliked Yorty from the start and would eventually come to despise him.

So Brown offered only the faintest of endorsements—and then fled the country. His own victory had been sealed at the primary, and a week before the general election he headed to South America. Ostensibly he was attending something called the Inter-American Congress of Public Law Administrators in São Paulo, Brazil, but that meeting was still nearly a month off, and in his candid moments Brown recognized that he was actually sidestepping too public a connection with Democratic colleagues he considered surefire losers. "I really 'took a walk' to stay out of the last week of the campaign so I wouldn't be embarrassed," he said later.[43]

Accompanied by Bernice and an assistant from the Department of Justice, Brown went first to Mexico City, then down through Central America to Peru. On election night a confident and relaxed Brown went to the Lima Country Club for dinner. Halfway through a steak, he paused to boast. "At this moment," he told a local reporter at 10:00 P.M., "I am being re-elected."[44]

He had not been worried. A letter to a staff member back in San Francisco offers both a travelogue of a busy Grand Tour and a glimpse at views about Latin America that were, for the day, typical and perhaps even generous.

> The trip has been terrific. The letter from Richfield, the Standard Oil man, and Otis McCallister has opened the doors in every country that we have visited. In Mexico we saw the great university, talked with the attorney general, attended a state dinner and found out how to stop wetbacks and narcotics from moving into California. Then to Guatemala where we met Jim Collins, the W. R. Grace man, and Monsignor Collins' brother (please call the good monsignor and tell him he has a good brother). We settled the crime situation not only in Guatemala City but also at Antigua. It is a beautiful country but economically very bad. Thence to Panama. This community is teeming with people and poverty but they seem very happy. We saw the canal and ships going and coming but business very bad here. On to Lima, a beautiful, clean progressive city. The folks were very friendly to the U.S. but they all want aid and dollars. We then went 350 miles inland over the Andes to Cuzco. . . . Back to Lima and our newfound friends, who gave a farewell party. The next morning to Santiago and now here in Valparaiso in a beautiful hotel.[45]

Brown was having a ball. As he returned from South America to start his second term as attorney general—his fiftieth birthday only a few months off—he knew there would be plenty of openings for higher office down the road. In the meantime, he had a great job, prominent, enjoyable, substantial. Unlike almost any other political post, he was able to stay in San Francisco, the hometown of his boyhood, a city his wife liked, the place where he had raised—and was raising—his children. He had a nice house in a good part of town and every morning could be driven to his office in the grand state building downtown. Even the fringe benefits were nice. Every year at Christmas, for example, his larder filled to bursting. A gift list from one of those years is as copious as it is reflective of the time: nearly four cases of whiskey, a case of wine, subscriptions to *Reader's Digest* and *American Heritage,* an ashtray, a wooden meat platter, handkerchiefs, a case of canned pineapple, two boxes of cigars, cigarettes, a necktie, a tie pin, five cases of tomato juice, a clock, a case of canned peaches, champagne, five books, enrollment in the Jesuit Seminary Association to share in Masses, Prayers and Apostolic Labors of Jesuits of California Province of the Society of Jesus, a membership in the Fruit of the Month Club, and—unavoidably—a fruitcake.[46]

———

Early in fall 1955, Brown made a pilgrimage to the prairies of northern Illinois. He stopped at a small town with the almost ludicrously quaint name of Libertyville, the home of Adlai Stevenson. In the latest of a string of career decisions, Brown was trying to decide if he should run for the U.S. Senate in 1956, and he wanted to talk things over with the presidential nominee.

For Brown, as for so many liberals of the day, Stevenson was very nearly an idol. Devoted to liberal causes, as Truman had been, Stevenson was also many things that Truman was not (or at least did not seem to be): intellectual, sophisticated, witty in a dry way. He was strikingly pedigreed: His paternal grandfather had been vice president of the United States under Grover Cleveland; his schooling had been at Choate and Princeton. And though he was actually the product of the Chicago machine, somehow Stevenson seemed almost the opposite of a machine politician, clean and scrupulously honest and well intentioned. His loss in 1952 had done nothing to cool the ardor of his fans. Brown thought him "the greatest man that I have ever met."[47]

At Libertyville the discussion centered on Brown's immediate future. Should he challenge Tommy Kuchel, a moderate Republican appointed to the U.S. Senate to replace Richard Nixon when Nixon became vice president. In 1954 Kuchel had won the right to serve out the final two years of Nixon's term by defeating Yorty, but in 1956 he would have to run for a full term in his own right.

Musing about the Senate race was keeping Brown up at night. Winning the seat for the Democrats might give the party control of the Senate, a huge prize that would make Brown all the more important. The timing was right: The 1956 election would come halfway through his second term as attorney general, so he could run for the Senate and still hold his current job as a fallback. But then Warren's absence would creep into his mind. "I know," he wrote, "that if I wait three years and run against Knight that the entire course of history in the state of California could be changed, provided, of course, that I win."[48]

Although we have no record of their meeting, Stevenson must have urged caution. He wanted Brown campaigning full-time for the 1956 Democratic presidential nominee, whom Stevenson hoped to be, and in the wake of the Libertyville meeting rumors flew that if Brown stayed out of the Senate race and Stevenson were elected, he might be in line to become U.S. attorney general. Even the vice presidential nomination was talked up for Brown, although that seems improbable. Whatever their exact conversation, Brown returned to California with little enthusiasm for a challenge of Kuchel.

He announced his decision through a powerful new tool of political life: television. Appearing on a weekly San Francisco public affairs program called "Column 1"—the name was not the only thing that symbolized the new medium's reliance on the old; all the questioners were newspaper reporters—Brown was asked about his future. He said he would bypass the Senate race, the first time he made such an announcement over the airwaves. The duties of the attorney general's office pressed upon his time, as did his work organizing an Adlai Stevenson delegation to the next summer's Democratic National Convention.[49]

In one sense it was an unusual time for Brown. Throughout the mid-1950s he repeatedly passed up chances to run for bigger offices. Earlier in his career he had jumped at everything, running for district attorney twice, for attorney general twice, even (under highly unusual circumstances) for president in 1952. But now Brown could see an advantage to waiting.

For California Democrats, the mid-1950s were a time of gathering strength, a time of success even though they remained a minority in Sacramento. Voters might now get a slate card from the CDC endorsing a set of candidates before the primary. If not, they could see plainly on the ballot which candidates were real Democrats and which were simply Republican interlopers cross-filed into a primary in which they did not belong. The changes were making a difference. After fifteen years of frustration and glum wondering about the value of their majority on the voting rolls, they were finally realizing substantial gains. In the 1952 election, the last one under the old system, Democrats won 27 of the 80 seats in the state assembly. Two years later they won 32, two years after that 38. Progress was quick in the senate too, from 11 seats to 16 to 20. If Brown kept waiting, he might actually have an army to lead.

———

By the time Edmund Gerald Jr. turned seventeen, in 1955, he was a deeply religious young man. Friends threw him a surprise party, but because his birthday that year happened to fall on Maundy Thursday, he was out at church all night and missed the festivities. At his insistence, he had attended St. Ignatius, a Jesuit high school in San Francisco, and now, having graduated, he asked his parents for permission to enter the Sacred Heart Novitiate in Los Gatos, south of San Francisco, to begin studying to become a Jesuit priest. They thought him too young to make so important a decision and refused, so Jerry enrolled instead at Santa Clara University, a few miles from the seminary. Even at Santa Clara religion was central to his life. He joined the student Sanctuary Society, donning a cassock and surplice to officiate at mass. The following year, his eighteenth birthday freed him from the need for parental permission to begin studies for the priesthood, and on August 15, 1956, the Feast of the Assumption, he and some friends drove down to the novitiate, where young Jerry Brown began his new life.[50]

It was a choice that left his father ambivalent. A devout Catholic, Pat was proud that Jerry was choosing to serve the church, especially as a Jesuit, the elite of the clergy. But having his son choose a life so different from his own—almost, it seemed, pointedly rejecting everything the father loved—was hard to understand. For Pat, there was nothing better than the gabbiness and gossip of politics, the constant stream of people to meet and connect with. He was impulsive, undisciplined, ebullient, endlessly human. He loved to get the papers, keep up with things, chatter away with everyone he met. Now his son was entering a world of almost medieval regimentation. At the novitiate, there were no newspapers, no radios, no television. Unnecessary talking was discouraged. At 5:00 A.M. the novices rose from their straw mattresses, dressed, and spent an hour meditating on the lesson of the day, the time strictly divided into three periods, one when they knelt, another when they stood, the last when they sat. They were to accept the rules of St. Ignatius unquestioningly, even to bind or flog themselves to mortify the flesh. Despite his ambivalence, Pat was proud that his son would someday be a priest and decided that the training was "some kind of necessary evil."[51]

As parents, Pat and Bernice could visit for two hours one Sunday a month, almost the only contact Jerry had with the outside world. They walked through the grounds, chatting, and sometimes their visits grew a little tense. "It is silly to waste our time discussing things that you will probably reach in theology six or seven years from now," Pat wrote in one letter to his son after an obvious argument, then added awkwardly, "It would be like your discussing intricate problems of legal bond financing during the first six months of law school." Bernice was mystified by her son's choice. She was an immensely practical person, a Protestant to boot. Pat, ever the conciliator, tried to smooth things over. Perhaps Jerry, who always loved abstract philosophical questions, could write a little more about the daily routine of life at the novitiate. It might, Pat suggested gently, help his mother to understand his experience.[52] Occasionally, the father put aside his worries. Once he wrote to Jerry urging him to eat well, the better to gain a little weight. "It is my observation," he said, "that fat friars are always happier."[53]

————

Brown was not there when his son disappeared into near-isolation. It was another presidential year, and he was boarding a train for Chicago and the 1956 Democratic National Convention. It bothered him to miss his son's departure. "It was like getting married," he said later, "getting married to the church."[54] But national conventions, coming only once in four years, could not be lightly cast aside. And this one would be a milestone. For the first time, Brown would head the California delegation.

Stevenson would again be the nominee. That was obvious. The question as the delegates arrived in Chicago was the vice presidential nomination. In some friendly quarters Brown himself had even been mentioned for the second spot. He offered the obligatory remarks that he did not want the job but would take it if drafted. Surely he was actually yearning to be picked, but the talk never got beyond California, and by the time of the convention his moment of would-be glory had passed. On a more serious level, Hubert Humphrey was interested, as was Estes Kefauver, Brown's old opponent from the California primary four years before. And there was an insurgent bid by a young senator from Massachusetts, John F. Kennedy.

As the head of a huge delegation, Brown was invited to Stevenson's hotel room to discuss the convention. Stevenson said he had no intention of picking his own running mate. He planned to throw the matter to the convention, the better to generate excitement and interest. Stevenson announced his decision on August 16. It happened to be the birthday of Clary

Heller, the son of the big Democratic donor Ellie Heller, so after that day's floor session she invited people to her suite for birthday cake. Brown hitched a ride and sat in the front seat of the car, next to Heller. At a stoplight another car pulled alongside and the window rolled down. An accented voice—Heller later figured out that it was JFK—called out, "Hey Pat, where are you going now? I want to talk to you."

Heller passed along her suite number, and within minutes Kennedy was working the room at her son's birthday party, hunting for spare delegates. Along with his younger brother Bobby, Kennedy cornered the chairman of the California delegation and made his pitch for the vice presidency. Brown was impressed, as he so often was by well-educated, eloquent men of national stature, and he decided on the spot to back Kennedy for the nomination.

When the balloting for vice president got under way the next day, no one controlled a majority. Humphrey soon dropped out, leaving the second-ballot contest to Kennedy and Kefauver. It was a complicated situation. From the dais, they began calling the roll, and doing it quickly. Delegations had to be re-counted for the new ballot, and a lot of delegates were switching. Kennedy was gaining steam. Nowhere was the situation more chaotic than in the California parcel of the floor. The delegates had been assigned to sit in rows, with a row captain counting each row. The numbers were to be passed to Brown or one of his lieutenants, who would tally the total. But the system had collapsed. Sociable and friendly as always, Brown had let people wander from their assigned seats, chatting here and there, pumping a few hands, enjoying a grand time. He was surrounded by his friends, but the order and discipline of the seating chart was nowhere to be seen. With the roll call of the states rushing along and the bedlam of a convention floor all around them, Brown found it impossible to count his own delegates quickly enough.

Memories differ as to what happened next. In some versions, Brown simply got caught up in the Kennedy mania and tried to announce all of California's votes for him. In that telling, Kefauver supporters literally seized the microphone and demanded a true tally. One writer claimed that Jimmy Roosevelt grabbed Brown by the lapels and threatened to break his leg if he handed the delegation to Kennedy. Brown remembered his role as that of a Kennedy defender. According to his version, he decided that since the ticket was likely to lose in November, he did not want the first Catholic vice presidential nominee to serve as a convenient scapegoat. So he sandbagged the man he was ostensibly supporting, pulling numbers out of the blue and giving a big margin to Kefauver.

Either way, it was a messy affair. For the first time Brown had led his state's delegation to the national convention—the World Series of hardball political maneuvering—and it had not gone well. It was a bad omen, one that would come to haunt him horribly four years later, when the convention would be held in California, when it would be filling the top slot on the ticket rather than the second, and when Brown would be even more unquestionably the man in charge.[55]

———

Back in California after the convention, Brown found himself busy with the kind of political exertions that normally go unnoticed. He was actively recruiting Democratic candidates, stocking the legislature with future allies in anticipation of his own rise. On the last day a candidate could file his papers for the 1956 election, Brown phoned Bill Beard, a lawyer from Imperial County who had worked on Brown's campaigns. The attorney general told Beard that there were already supporters waiting at the county clerk's office, a petition in hand that would make Beard a candidate for the state senate. After years in the local district attorney's office, Beard had only recently started private practice, and he was not eager to abandon his lucrative new enterprise for a paltry legislative salary. But Brown persisted. Someday soon he hoped to be in the governor's office, and he would need a Democratic majority in the legislature. Imperial County's senate seat was held by a Republican, but Beard could wrest it away. Sweet-talked into submission, Beard agreed to run. In November he won the election.[56]

———

The attorney general's staff was also laying the groundwork for a future battle. For three months Department of Justice investigators burrowed their way into the state's mental hospital in Modesto. They found horror stories. Patients, it was said, had their arms twisted until the bones broke. They were beaten with rubber plungers or forced to drink from toilet bowls. The hair was ripped from their scalps. And if there was little humanity, there was less treatment: few patients received adequate psychiatric care, record keeping was slipshod, doctors shirked their duties.

The accusations, compiled into a thirty-seven-page report, were released publicly by Brown in early September. Anticipating the document's release, the director of the hospital had resigned suddenly due to "ill health," and soon the legislature was quizzing administrators about their treatment of the state's most helpless residents. The report sparked a call for improvements to the archaic system—staff members were still called "bug housers"—that lasted for years.

There is little doubt that Brown would have been concerned about conditions in the hospital; it fits with much else in his life and career. But he also admitted years later that, influenced by his own ambitions, he worked to his own advantage. In the old days, when Warren was governor and Brown was content to bide his time, he would have told the chief executive about his findings, even made it a joint investigation of the attorney general and governor. With Knight in power, Brown kept the report to himself until he could blindside the Republican with its public release. "If I really explore my own inner feelings," he once said, "I was trying to build myself up."[57]

Now in his fifties, a decade of patience behind him, Brown wanted no more to tarry. He had his eye on the prize.

5 VICTORY

BROWN'S TRUE AMBITION WAS no secret to those who knew him. He wanted to be governor, had *always* wanted to be governor. The San Francisco district attorney's office had an east-facing window that offered a glimpse of the Ferry Building down by the water, then the Bay Bridge and the Berkeley hills beyond. Tom Lynch remembered Brown standing at that window, back in the winter of 1944 when he first took office, and peering into both the distance and the future. "You know, Tom," Brown told him, "I can almost see Sacramento from here."[1]

But he had waited, sometimes forced to by defeat, sometimes choosing to out of prudence. There was the loss in 1946, then the long decade of the 1950s with its constantly bypassed options, a potential race against Earl Warren that was too tough, one against Goodwin Knight that was too early, and again and again the Senate seats that just did not seem right. Now, as 1958 loomed, Brown sensed his chance.

———

California's senior U.S. senator, William Fife Knowland, was born into a dynasty of power and politics like the one Pat Brown was destined to create. Lured west by dreams of gold, William Knowland's grandfather, Joseph Knowland, arrived in California on a steamer in 1857. He failed as a miner, hawked oranges on the streets of San Francisco, then finally moved across the bay and found success in the lumber business. By the time he died in 1912, his empire had spread to mining and shipping and banking, and he was one of the richest and most powerful men in Oakland. Joseph Knowland's son, J. R. Knowland, parlayed the family connections into a political career, winning election to the state assembly at twenty-five and Congress at thirty. A staunch conservative, he was defeated for the U.S. Senate in 1914 when he split the Republican vote with a Progressive candidate, handing victory to a Democrat. The following year he bought a controlling interest in the *Oakland Tribune* and set about reclaiming as a publisher the power and prestige he had once enjoyed as a politician. He succeeded, transforming the *Tribune* into a successful business and a relentless advocate for conservative politics and the Republican Party. The newspaper life apparently suited him: He died more than half a century later, at the age of ninety-two, still holding the publisher's title.[2]

William Fife Knowland was born in 1908, when his father was in his third term in Congress. For Billy Knowland, life and politics were inseparable. He followed his father through the halls of the Capitol as a young boy, campaigned for Warren Harding at twelve, and served as a Republican precinct worker when he was in high school. In 1928, while he was a student at the University of California, Knowland attended the Republican National Convention in Kansas City, where he watched his father nominate Herbert Hoover for president. He managed to win election to the assembly at twenty-four—one year younger than his father had been—and then moved up to the state senate two years later. Drafted into the army during World War II, he was serving in Paris when he received word of a decision that elevated him instantly to a figure of national politics: He had been appointed to the U.S. Senate.[3]

Hiram Johnson, the old Progressive warhorse of California Republican politics, had died after almost thirty years in the Senate. Speculation that Knowland would be his replacement started immediately, and for good reason. Years before, the *Oakland Tribune* had supported the political aspirations of a young Alameda County district attorney named Earl Warren. Now governor, Warren was ready to repay the favor by appointing the son of the *Tribune*'s publisher to the Senate.

In Washington, Knowland built a record so solidly conservative that he was typically seen as the heir to Robert Taft's status as Mr. Republican. Obsessed with the fate of the Nationalist Chinese, he was sometimes referred to as the "senator from Formosa," but this was not apparently a problem for his GOP colleagues. After Taft's death, they elected him their leader, and for two years when Republicans held control of the chamber, Knowland was the Senate majority leader, one of the most powerful jobs in Washington. Honest and forthright, his popularity back home was such that in 1952 he won both the Republican and Democratic primaries, thus avoiding a November race altogether. It was widely assumed that he would be reelected in 1958, and then mount a serious bid for the presidency in 1960.

Yet for all that, Knowland was often the object of ridicule. Big and plodding and stolid—a block of wood with a crew cut—Knowland bulled his way through life. Though he loved politics, he was notoriously uncomfortable around people. When constituents came to visit him in Washington, his wife, Helen, often took them to lunch, pleasant chitchat being outside the ken of the senator. Richard Russell, the old Senate lion from Georgia, once said of Knowland that "he walks like he thinks," which, for those who had seen the Californian trudge along heavy-footed, could not have been an intimation of mental alacrity. In his diary Dwight Eisenhower wrote of Knowland, "In his case, there seems to be no final answer to the question, 'How stupid can you get?'"[4]

What few people knew was that Knowland's personal life was a mess. Long a philanderer, in recent years his amorous adventures had become shocking, even weird. Helen Knowland had been carrying on an affair with Blair Moody, a dashing and energetic former newspaper reporter who had been appointed to the Senate from his home state of Michigan, and who was one of Bill Knowland's best friends. In turn, Knowland began an affair with Moody's wife, Ruth, eventually becoming so taken with her that, in his forties, he had himself circumcised at her request. It is unclear whether Knowland knew that his wife was sleeping with the husband of his mistress, but in effect the couples were engaged in a spouse swap, even while remaining friends and taking vacations together.

In summer 1954 Blair Moody died suddenly of a heart attack. Eight weeks later a distraught Helen Knowland tried to kill herself with sleeping pills and alcohol, but she survived and soon recovered. With Moody gone, she became increasingly bitter about her husband's affair with Ruth Moody, and wanted to get him out of the capital, which she sometimes called a "candy shop" of sexual temptation. Drew Pearson wrote in his diary that Helen Knowland was the captive of a "desperate anxiety to take her husband away from Washington," so much so that it was "pathetic." "When there's another woman in the case," Pearson wrote, "the wife will do anything." It was even said that Helen Knowland issued a blunt ultimatum:

Her husband must return to California or she would leave him, ruining his chances at the White House.[5]

If he had to head west, one option would be the California governorship, although of course the incumbent Republican, Goodwin Knight, was planning to run again in 1958. Knowland's aides wanted him to stay in the Senate. The governorship, even if he could win it, would offer no better platform for a presidential campaign, they argued. Knowland's father—the aging publisher of the *Oakland Tribune* and the patriarch of the family—felt the same way. But pressed by his wife, Knowland apparently felt he had no choice. On January 7, 1957, two years before his term was up, he announced during a CBS radio interview that he would not seek reelection to the Senate, although he insisted he did not know his other plans.

In style the announcement was almost nonchalant. Knowland mentioned it only in the closing seconds of the interview, and only then in response to a direct question. But in substance it shook the California political world as had no news since Warren's appointment to the Supreme Court.

Sent over the wires, the news reached Sacramento in the middle of Knight's annual State of the State address in the assembly chambers. Even before he was finished, reporters were scrambling out of the hall to pursue the news of Knowland's decision. State Controller Robert Kirkwood announced that he was a candidate for the Senate while Knight was still talking. Reporters blockaded the governor at the rostrum as he tried to leave after his speech and pelted him with the obvious question: Did he believe Knowland was leaving the Senate to challenge Knight for the governor's chair? Knight pleaded ignorance.[6]

Knowland's announcement was as much a surprise to Brown as to anyone else. Quizzed by reporters about how the decision might alter his career—he was obviously the Democrats' best hope to capture the governorship—he refused to be drawn in. "I haven't any plans for 1958 so they couldn't be changed," he insisted.[7]

In the narrowest sense, that was true, but Knowland's decision still left Brown with a whole new script to ponder. Along with everybody else in California politics, Brown assumed that Knowland was in fact running for governor, and he was not the opponent Brown had expected to face. Knowland's decision to give up his seat seemed to open another option for Brown: run for the Senate.

Brown started talking to everybody, asking what he should do "almost to the point of monotony," as he put it. The governorship held an undeniable allure: better to be one of one in Sacramento than one of many in the Senate. But it would be a tougher race, and he was worried, both about the newspapers—most were Republican and would oppose him—and about money. If he ran for governor and if Knight stayed in the race, a good many moderate donors might fade away. In a Senate bid, he believed, cash would be plentiful.[8]

In spring 1957, just a few months after Knowland's announcement, Brown met with California's Democratic congressional delegation in Washington, D.C., and told them he would run for governor if one of them would run for Knowland's Senate seat, thus ensuring a full Democratic slate. Clair Engle, a tough little man from Red Bluff, up in the northernmost reaches of the state, agreed to run, and he and Brown shook hands on the deal. But Brown spent the night tossing around in his hotel room, unable to sleep at the thought that he had made a foolish bargain. The Senate seat, after all, would be vacant and thus an easier target. Why should he, the only Democrat in statewide office, give away the safer race to a mere congressman? He went down to Engle's congressional office the next day and tried to renege. Brown would run for the Senate, Engle for governor. But Engle stood his ground. The men had a deal, he insisted, and now they should both live up to it. Chagrined, Brown agreed to honor his earlier commitment, although it was understood the matter would be kept secret.[9]

Once Brown got back to California, he began again to waiver. He put his concerns on paper in a letter to his son, Jerry, now nineteen and deep into his studies for the priesthood:

> I love being attorney general and cannot even think of anybody else sitting in this chair. . . . The United States Senate would open a completely new vista and permit me to have a box office seat on world affairs. The governorship, of course, would be like your first two years at the Novitiate— tough but very enjoyable!
>
> I am being criticized by some of my Democratic friends for not making a decision, but I can't help it. I just don't know what I am going to do. I may injure my chances by delaying, but would also injure them by too quick a decision.[10]

Financially, the best path was the most timid one: run for reelection as attorney general. He would almost surely succeed, and Bernice in particular saw it as the best option. They were not rich people after all. Kathy was still headed for college, maybe even Jerry too if he decided to abandon priestly training. Pat was worried. If he ran for higher office and lost, returning to private practice in his mid-fifties, after fifteen years in government, would be tough. So he essentially took out some insurance. He went around to his rich friends, people like Ben Swig, who owned the swanky Fairmont Hotel atop Nob Hill in San Francisco, and laid it on the line. He did not want to run and lose and then have to scratch around for clients, like a youngster fresh out of law school. Instead, he wanted a promise that if he ended up out of government and had to sign on with a firm, they would direct some business his way, maybe $5,000 or $10,000 a year in retainers for five years. His friends came through, and by the end of his rounds, Brown was confident that if he needed it, there would be a cushioned landing.[11]

By summer Democrats were getting worried that their best horse might not leave the starting gate. They knew Brown could be cautious, had seen him sit out race after race in the past few years, waiting for just the right move. Now he was holding everybody up. He was so clearly the party's best statewide candidate that nobody else in the political world could make any decisions until his choice was set. So Democrats in the legislature called an informal party huddle to discuss the ticket for 1958. Meeting in the merciless August heat of Bakersfield, a farming town in the Central Valley, they demanded of Brown that he make a decision by the middle of September, although it was utterly unclear how they intended to enforce their order. Brown stalled. He would decide what office to seek, he said, only after a sounding-board trip around the state and a long vacation to Hawaii.

He was already doing a lot of relaxing that summer, enjoying life a little before the frenzy of an election year. He perfected his skills at the barbecue, acquiring particular expertise, at least in his eyes, in the proper grilling of a steak. In July he and Bernice flew back to Missouri for the dedication of the Truman Library, basking in the reflected glow of titans: Herbert Hoover, Lyndon Johnson, Sam Rayburn. For once, even Bernice savored the limelight. "I think it was the very first time Mother really enjoyed politics," Pat wrote to Jerry after their return. "She admitted it, which, I think, was quite an admission for her." Then a few weeks later they had a frolic at the Lake Tahoe estate of Henry Kaiser, the Bay Area industrialist whose wartime shipyards had produced both a personal fortune and a new kind of workplace medical insurance, the Health Maintenance Organization. At Kaiser's fabulous lakeside compound, they played volleyball, swam, and motorboated across what Mark Twain called the most beautiful spot on earth.

Even the trip back was fun: They flew home on a small airline that used float planes and took off right from the water.[12]

But the summer's last trip was the best, both because it was the longest—a week in Hawaii—and because it was the most important, for the Browns' host would be one of the richest and most powerful Democrats in California.

———

Ed Pauley had made a fortune out of oil and a hobby out of politics. Long a man of influence, Pauley was the one who had convinced young delegate Pat Brown to suppress his sudden infatuation with Henry Wallace at the 1944 Democratic National Convention and support instead the vice presidential nomination of Harry Truman. In time Pauley would give so much money to his hometown university, the University of California, Los Angeles, that the school would put his name on its basketball arena—Pauley Pavilion—making him famous to a later generation.

In August 1957, as the attorney general was surveying the Republican maneuverings and trying to figure out his next move, Pauley invited him to vacation at Coconut Island, Pauley's private estate in Hawaii. Pauley owned the entire island, and it was spectacular. Slides led from the bedrooms straight down to the water, so that you could rise from bed, pull on your trunks, and, seconds later, splash into the warmth of a Pacific lagoon. Bernice came along, as did Kathy and one of her school friends. Bernice insisted that Pat leave his omnipresent briefcases behind, so instead he took some novels. At night there were dinners and cocktails, by day swimming and sunbathing and boating. At least once Brown and Pauley took one of the outdoor slides together, one behind the other, two paunchy middle-aged men in swimsuits roaring down the ramp, then flying off the end, arms and legs splayed wildly as they plopped into the water, like little boys at play.[13]

Aside from all the fun, there was serious political brinksmanship. Pauley was a Democrat, but a conservative one with many Republican friends. He counted Goodwin Knight among them, and it was still possible, perhaps even likely, that Knight would meet Knowland's primary challenge and seek another term as governor. Like all powerful people with a rooting interest in politics, Pauley did not want his two good friends—Goodwin Knight and Pat Brown—competing in the same race, thus guaranteeing that one would be eliminated. Better for Pauley if they both remained in office. So Pauley was hoping to convince Brown to stay clear of the governor's race entirely and run either for reelection as attorney general or for the Senate seat vacated by Knowland. Drew Pearson claimed in his column that Pauley had promised Brown $500,000 for his campaign if he ran for the Senate—an extraordinary amount in those days. Brown denied it, and it seems likely it was at the very least exaggerated, but everybody knew Pauley was pushing hard.

More than two thousand miles away in California, Democrats were worried that Brown might succumb. Nowhere was the fretting more pronounced than in Brown's own office, where a young aide named Fred Dutton desperately wanted his boss to run for governor. Dutton was a World War II veteran who had spent time in a German POW camp. He became a lawyer and had caught Brown's eye a few years earlier by writing occasional op-ed pieces for the *Los Angeles Times*. Always on the lookout for astute talent, Brown called him up, and the two men soon struck up a correspondence. For Dutton, barely into his thirties, it was heady stuff, a chance to whisper in the ear of a big-time politician rather than plod his way up the career ladder of a law firm. As it turned out, he was a natural political strategist, with the kind of quick yet practical mind that is invaluable in politics. Volatile and demanding, Dutton sometimes annoyed people—he and his assistant Meredith Burch once got into such a heated argument that they chucked dinner rolls at one another—but everybody recognized him as a comer.

Brown hired him. Ostensibly Dutton oversaw the criminal division in the Department of Justice, a position for which he had no relevant experience, but his real role was to tend Brown's political ambitions. In 1956 he ran the Stevenson campaign in Southern California, and when the state proved one of the few in which Stevenson improved on his 1952 performance, Dutton's reputation as a wunderkind—he was thirty-three—was secure.[14]

By the time Brown flew off to Hawaii to contemplate his future, Dutton knew him well enough to worry. Pauley's goal was no secret, and Dutton knew that Brown liked to agree with people, liked to please them, often sounded like the last person he talked to. Saying no, telling someone what he did not want to hear—these were not Pat Brown's most finely honed skills.[15]

So Dutton mounted a long-distance counteroffensive to Pauley's lobbying. Planning ahead, even before Brown left, Dutton wrote a form letter asking prominent California Democrats if Brown should run for governor. He knew in advance what the answer would be: Brown was the party's only hope to seize the state's top job. Soon the responses—every one encouraging—starting pouring in. Each day Dutton and his staff would collect the most laudatory and cable them to Coconut Island.[16]

It worked. Often a man who needed a pat on the back, Brown loved the praise. He answered one of the letter writers with a cable—"Tell all who signed not to have the slightest worry about next year"—that left little doubt what decision he would announce when he returned to the mainland.[17]

Having sworn off a reelection bid to the Senate, Knowland tried to play it coy about the governor's race. He was not very good at it. At a Republican fund-raiser in Hollywood, he declared he would be traveling around the state later in the year. Asked if it would be a vacation, he said, "You can't take a vacation when you're campaigning." A few months later he went to Washington and had breakfast with the state's GOP congressional delegation. Within a day, word leaked that Knowland had told the congressmen he would run for governor.[18]

All of which left Goodie Knight in a bind. He deeply wanted to fight it out with Knowland for the Republican gubernatorial nomination, but he knew it was an uphill fight. He had been governor for a little more than four years, since Warren had gone to the Supreme Court, and had won a term of his own only against a political nonentity, the California League of Cities lobbyist Richard Graves. It was a résumé that did not suggest victory against a former majority leader of the U.S. Senate. And as time went on, the messages Knight was getting from the rest of the political world were worse and worse.

Since Warren's departure, Knowland, Knight, and Nixon had coalesced in the public mind into "the Big Three," the Republican masters of the state. Their names even sounded good together, like a particularly euphonious law firm. In fact, they were not a happy clan. All three thought of themselves as potential presidents and correctly saw the others as rivals. Nixon especially was disliked by the other two. But now the vice president sensed an opportunity to eliminate his rivals, or perhaps to have them eliminate themselves. If Knight dropped out of the governor's race and ran for Knowland's seat in the Senate, it would appear to voters to be a smarmy deal, an attempt at trading important public offices as if they were positions on a softball field. Both men might lose, and thus no longer pose a threat to the rise of Richard Nixon.

Through intermediaries, including Kyle Palmer, the influential political editor of the *Los Angeles Times,* and Clint Mosher, who held the same job with William Randolph Hearst's *San Francisco Examiner,* Nixon began suggesting that Knight stood no chance against Knowland and should switch to the Senate race. Mosher even went to the Governor's Mansion to pass along word that Knight should get out of the race. If he did not, the big Republican donors would reject him and the money for his campaign would dry up, a threat, as Knight knew, that Nixon and the *Times* were perfectly capable of enforcing.[19]

Faced with such heavy pressure, Knight left the state for a supposedly secret vacation, although it soon leaked out that he was in Phoenix with his wife and two top campaign advisers. Even there, he took calls from Palmer telling him to abandon the governor's race. Knight was happy and joyful by nature, perhaps even a bit silly; he was not especially tough. Beset from all sides by the worst threat that a politician can receive—stingy contributors—he finally caved. The jolly man who wanted nothing more than to be governor of California headed for Washington, D.C., there to tell the president that he would not seek a second term.[20] "I had no other choice," a woebegone Knight said later. "I was like a man in the middle of the ocean, standing on the deck of a burning ship."[21]

It was a bitter experience, and the bitterness would not fade. In the months to come, as Brown campaigned, he would sometimes run into Virginia Knight, who still resented the role that Knowland had played in her husband's trouble. Republican or not, she always said she planned to vote for Brown.[22]

———

Home from Hawaii, Brown called a news conference and made plain his plans. There would be enough Democratic money for a major statewide race, he said, and he ruled out a bid for the Senate seat Knowland was vacating. The sole reason for delaying an official announcement, Brown suggested, was decorum: "I don't feel it's fair to spend 15 or 16 months running for public office." Then, as the meeting broke up, he posed for pictures and, beaming, asked rhetorically, "Do I look like a governor?"[23]

Privately, preparations were at full bore. Dutton was dispatched to the

East, charged with throwing himself into a crash course in American governors. He asked for meetings with the Democratic chiefs of four big states: New York, New Jersey, Michigan, and Massachusetts. The goal was to learn as much as possible, quickly, about all matters gubernatorial: the mechanics of campaigning, what issues played well, dealing with the press.[24]

Another sharp young lawyer from Los Angeles, Warren Christopher, was asked to cobble together a brain trust. In recognition of the talents that would later make him U.S. secretary of state, he was told he could have any position in the campaign he might desire.[25] Brown's old law partner and friend Frank Mackin plotted the actual announcement, urging that the Republicans' troubles be exploited. "I think that 'Time for a Change' and apathetic, confused non-leadership of the Republicans in this state should be stressed," he wrote in a memo to Brown.[26]

By the end of October everything was ready. The formal announcement came on October 30, 1957, the Browns' twenty-seventh wedding anniversary. For Pat, it was surely a magnificent way to celebrate, although less so for Bernice, who admitted openly that she would have preferred a reelection bid for the attorney general's office, then added simply, "This is what he wants to do." In a tacit acknowledgment that Brown's native San Francisco had now been surpassed by its southern rival, the event was held in Los Angeles.

Decked out in a new blue suit bought just for the occasion, Brown told reporters that he expected Knight to withdraw, leaving Knowland as the only opponent. He left little doubt about his hopes for the state: He wanted it to get bigger, and he wanted to be the governor who would help it to do so.

> I deeply believe we still have a great state to build. We have millions of children to school—and school well. We have water to transport, and tidelands to tap [for oil]. We have highways to build and highway safety to achieve. We have discrimination to dispel, genuine underprivileged to provide for, and perhaps most important of all, hundreds of thousands of new jobs to be created for an expanding population.

Then, aware that a busy year of campaigning lay ahead, the Browns headed off for a round of golf.[27]

Knight finally capitulated formally a few days later, officially acknowledging what everybody already knew. He would drop out of the gubernatorial race and instead seek Knowland's seat in the Senate. In effect, the two men would try to trade jobs.

The next day, knowing he would face Knowland, Brown had dinner with Drew Pearson, who recorded the event in his diary in his usual chatty, self-absorbed, observant style:

> Pat Brown came for dinner. He is bubbling over with enthusiasm for his chances to become governor. He didn't say so, but if he becomes governor of California, he has a good chance to be president of the United States. He would be the first Catholic in American history. He still claims that I was responsible for electing him attorney general of California. He is a wonderful guy personally, but I wish he had a little more backbone. Last week for the first time I met his wife, who is the lady who doesn't want him to step forward and run for anything. She is a beautiful, charming gal, but I can see that she doesn't like the limelight. Maybe however, her timing has been best for Pat because he now may be in for really big things.[28]

It soon became apparent that Pearson was right to be optimistic about Brown's chances. The Knowland-Knight switch proved an incomprehensible blunder, an affront to the voters' sensibilities. Earlier polls testing potential match-ups in the gubernatorial race showed Brown losing to either Knowland or Knight, sometimes by double-digit margins. In the wake of the switch, Mervin Field, the California equivalent of George Gallup, dispatched his interviewers to ask about what was now definitely a Brown-Knowland race. The result was breathtaking. In the previous two months—the time during which Knowland formally announced his gubernatorial candidacy and Knight dithered, then finally abandoned the campaign—Brown had picked up 20 points. Where he had previously trailed Knowland badly, now he led easily. And the shift came from voters of both parties: Brown had shored up his already strong support among Democrats, doubled his showing among Republicans. Voters simply disliked the idea that Knowland and Knight would try to trade jobs. Before the switch, Brown never led in a poll of the governor's race. After it, he never trailed.[29]

The economy was slowing down, and almost from the start Brown used it as a weapon. Republicans, after all, had ruled the state for fifteen years, the country for seven. Anyone willing to travel around the state a bit, he told newspaper publishers meeting in Oakland, would find "serious economic dislocations" in everything from poultry farming to home building. Yet Knowland offered only "a bigger dose of trickle-down economics."[30]

Brown's economic prescription was a little hazy, but in general he kept offering the same dose of government activism he had suggested when he entered the race. He promised to appoint a "consumer counsel" to represent the public interest in legislative hearings, regulatory procedures, and court cases. An economic development department would be created to lure new businesses to the state. Discrimination based on age should be outlawed, a Fair Employment Practices Commission created to stamp out racial bias in hiring. If a Brown administration had its way, there would be more and better schools, more roads, limits on interest charges on credit purchases, stiffer traffic-law enforcement to cut down on fatalities, even more boat launches so that Californians could enjoy their striking terrain.

Always, at every stop, there was mention of water. Brown knew it was the defining issue of the West, and he hammered at it mercilessly. Never mind that the attorney general and his fellow Democrats in the legislature had connived to stall water legislation so long as a Republican was in the governor's office, now he promised that he would move forward if given the chance.[31] California's problem was not lack of water, he told the crowds, but the location of it. The water was in the north, the people in the south. The solution was obvious: move the water. Existing federal projects fell short, so it was time for California to create its own solution. He promised to find the money to build a huge state waterworks that would move massive amounts of water to the parched farmers and cities of the Central Valley and the South Coast.

Knowland was horribly adrift. Much of the time the most noticeable thing about his campaign was the lack of a candidate. He stayed in Washington, D.C., to attend to Senate business, so his wife, two daughters, and a daughter-in-law filled in on the hustings. They did their best, but were essentially left to beg the indulgence of crowds that were disappointed that the man who would be governor was nowhere to be seen.

When Knowland did talk, he was simply off kilter. He ranted about the Chinese Communists until Brown finally responded with a statement ridiculing the strange fixation of a man who was seeking a state, rather than a federal, office: "The senator has become almost silly with his obsession that I state my stand on Red China. I frankly think it has little to do with a campaign for the governorship." His own effort, Brown said, would be based on state issues. He recommended that "the senator do his homework so that he does not have to try to divert public attention elsewhere." For the record, Brown added, he agreed with the platforms of both major parties opposing recognition of "Red China" or its admission to the United Nations.[32]

Then there was labor. Knowland talked constantly of his support for Proposition 18, a so-called right-to-work ballot measure that would have outlawed the union shop. Early polling suggested the measure might pass, and Knowland had always been hostile to organized labor, so he talked about it often. It was, he insisted, a matter of civil rights: People should not have to join a union to get a job.

Publicly, Brown denounced Knowland's position as "class warfare." Collective bargaining was a basic right. If that led to a closed shop, so be it. Anything else would amount to "a return to the ugly and destructive law of the economic jungle."[33] Privately, he was gleeful. "The money just poured in from the labor leaders," he said years later with a chuckle. "It was like manna from heaven. We didn't have to worry about fundraising drives or anything. They just put it in—it was really something—in buckets!"[34]

———

On the trail, the two men were as different personally as politically. Knowland was a clunker. Born to wealth and power, he looked right past people, fumbling over their names, forgetting who they were. June Stephens, one of his campaign volunteers, once spent an entire day driving him around the Bay Area. The next day, at another event, she was introduced to Knowland by a staff member unaware of their previous time together. The candidate was equally oblivious. "So nice to meet you," he said to the woman who had spent hours with him the day before.[35]

Brown, on the other hand, was in his element. He loved it, rushing up and down the state, finding crowds to work and hands to pump. In Eureka he drew the biggest crowd for a political dinner in the county's history; more than 600 people jammed into a room where only 490 place settings had been arranged. In Santa Barbara he made a bid for the opposition's support: "I always ask Democrats to vote the ticket straight and ask Republicans to vote for the best man." In Modesto, before another overflow crowd, he blamed the Republicans for a recession that was hamstringing his state.

Had the economy continued to grow at the old Truman-era rate, he maintained, California would have had millions more in tax revenue to handle its ever-growing school enrollment.[36]

Even when familiar faces were lacking and people had other concerns, he managed to forge ahead. Once when he was being trailed by a *Time* magazine reporter, he and his entourage stopped for the night at Cal-Neva, a Lake Tahoe resort literally astride the California-Nevada state line, where guests could stand in the great lodge and hop back and forth between states. Brown marched into the casino, then stopped short. The big, gaudy room was packed, but mostly with out-of-state tourists, people he did not recognize and who in any event seemed more interested in a blackjack or a lucky seven than in prospective chief executives. Flummoxed, he paced around a bit at the edge of the room, for once a little shy. Then an aide brought over the manager and introduced the candidate as "the next governor of California."

The old juices flowed, and instantly Brown was shaking hands and slapping backs. In a place where he had not known a soul only minutes before, he was suddenly everyone's pal. He wagered a dollar on the blackjack table, lost it, and didn't mind a bit. "Pat Brown was happy," the *Time* man wrote. "He was among friends. He was being liked."[37]

———

For Bernice Brown, campaigning was less instinctive. For the first time since going door-to-door for her Republican boyfriend thirty years before, she was on the trail. During Pat's earlier races, the children had been younger (Kathy, the youngest, was now thirteen), and in any event a campaign for attorney general was a smaller, lower-profile affair. Now campaign aides began drawing up a separate schedule for her, with interviews or charity events or luncheons. She said she liked it, but the claim rang more of duty than truth. Pictures invariably show a proper, self-possessed woman smiling tightly, almost grimacing, as if working through her chores because it was expected.[38]

Nor can so intelligent and thoughtful a person have appreciated the limited role to which she was confined. Those who knew Brown knew that his wife was a significant and trusted adviser—often adding a little steel to his shaky resolve—but publicly that was not a woman's place. Bernice Brown's interviewers were almost always from the women's pages, her events and publicity of a very restricted kind. Early in the campaign, after she met with reporters at the Biltmore Hotel, aides issued a press release highlighting details about her that they thought would be publicly appealing: She liked to freeze leftovers so they could be heated up later, she packed a light suitcase when she and Pat traveled so they could avoid overweight charges on airplanes, and she liked to play golf. In retrospect, most striking of all was the first sentence: "There's nothing like a press conference to make a woman wish she were back in her kitchen."[39]

Knowland's goof in focusing on the antilabor proposition was killing him. Voters didn't care, and the labor money that was pouring into the Brown campaign was giving the Democrats their most vigorous effort in years.

On February 1, 1958, still nine months from election day, Dutton finally left the state payroll, where he had never really belonged, and officially went on the campaign payroll. He handled everything, from tiny detail to grand concept, laying out strategy, editing speeches, scheduling events, handing out commands almost as if he were the candidate himself. Brown trusted him so much that he would later think back to that campaign and refer to Dutton, with only slight exaggeration, as "my alter ego," "my brains," "my Svengali," "my prime minister."[40]

Foreshadowing in miniature the Kennedy administration's reliance on Ivy League academics and other intellectuals, Dutton used California's burgeoning collection of bright lights for volunteer speechwriting and policy research. Dean McHenry, a UCLA political scientist who had once run for mayor of Los Angeles and Congress and in the latter case had been smeared as a Red by, as he put it, "the young Nixonites," wrote up something on reorganizing the executive branch of state government.[41] Eugene "Bud" Burdick, a UC Berkeley political scientist whose best-selling novel, *The Ugly American,* would cause a sensation later that year by exposing the boorish behavior of many Americans overseas, worked on international affairs. Even Wallace Stegner, the Stanford writing professor whose picaresque novel, *The Big Rock Candy Mountain,* had already made him famous, and who would eventually become a legend, helped smooth out some speech drafts.[42]

There was plenty of money for broadcast ads, mostly on radio, since television was still something of a riddle to the political world. The Brown campaign recorded spots on everything: inflation, law enforcement, agriculture, labor unions, governmental efficiency, utility rates, economic development, the state's revenue from offshore oil drilling. In one ad Brown charged that Knowland wanted to be governor only so that he could run for president two years later. The Republican, Brown told listeners, represents "only himself and his own national political ambitions" and, if given the chance, might "wreck California's future."[43]

As usual, Brown wanted to avoid too strong a connection with other Democrats, although, because he was now at the head of the ticket, he could not abandon his troops completely. The result was that the campaign walked a tightrope between party fealty and independent success. Slate mailers listing all the Democratic candidates were fine, but lawn signs connecting his name with the rest of the ticket were too much. Down-ticket Democrats could put their literature inside Brown campaign offices, but he was careful to point out that those offices would be manned by his own troops, not the Democratic Party.[44]

Yet he expected loyalty directed upward toward himself. He sent Dutton to see Richard Graves, the 1954 gubernatorial nominee whom Brown had largely snubbed. Dutton told Graves that they hoped he would actively support Brown's campaign. Remembering Brown's distance from the ticket four years earlier, when he spent the final weeks of the campaign gallivanting around South America, Graves said he would do for Brown exactly what Brown had done for him.

"He'll scream," Dutton replied.

"Then let him scream," Graves said.[45]

———

In a certain sense the June primary was meaningless. Both major candidates faced only token opposition and thus were assured of their party's nomination. But both men had cross-filed into the other party's primary, so the vote totals represented the best of all possible polls, a dry run for November.

Amazingly, Knowland had campaigned in the state only fourteen days, whereas Brown had spent the entire seven months since his Halloween eve announcement trudging up and down the state. It was a recipe for a big Democratic edge, which is exactly what happened: Brown topped Knowland by more than 660,000 votes. Even in the Republican primary, Brown took 22 percent of the vote.

Dutton knew he had a rare commodity among California Democrats— a two-term incumbent who had been popular enough in his reelection bid to get both the endorsement of the *Los Angeles Times* and the nomination of the Republican Party, which some people might have regarded as the same thing. But Dutton also knew there was the potential for trouble. The party's liberal activists did not entirely trust Brown—he had been a law-and-order prosecutor, after all—but if the campaign veered too far left it might suffer the same fate as Upton Sinclair's famous bid nearly twenty-five years before. Brown had to stay in the middle and somehow drag his party's left wing, however reluctantly, with him. To avoid a splintering, Dutton decided to keep the focus on the Republican Big Switch and the GOP's anti-labor stand, in effect unifying the Democrats with a common enemy.[46]

So from the start, Brown hit hard and kept punching. Two days after he announced his candidacy, he appeared at a Democratic fund-raising dinner with former president Truman and hammered away at Knowland mercilessly. The senator, Brown said, had publicly proclaimed himself in favor of a vigorous Republican primary, then sat back quietly while his backroom supporters shoved Knight aside. It was an act of "deceit," of "no integrity." Knowland was a man not interested in California but consumed by "selfish personal ambitions elsewhere," an obvious reference to his presidential hopes. He was a force for "class warfare [and] trickle-down economic theories [that would leave] the American Negro and most other Americans only the crumbs on our economic table."[47]

Now, in the wake of the primary, Brown stayed on the offensive. The senator's support centered in a group that was "arrogant, ingrown and out of touch with twentieth century realities," and the senator himself was increasingly "silly and desperate." The Big Switch had shown Knowland capable of "political strong-arm methods [that] threaten the essence of free and rational public processes." He was guilty of "bully-boy intemperance and irresponsible invective."[48]

At the same time, Brown touted his own activist program, playing on the likelihood that in a booming state with nearly incalculable public needs voters would turn to the party of the New Deal rather than to that of Herbert Hoover. Invariably, he appealed to California pride, to the self-confidence of a place where old people could still remember the days of the pioneers and children would grow up in the nation's biggest state. Knowland, he warned, could wreck that glittering future. California needed to be "a major spring of national vigor and vision[,] . . . a symbol of the future, of opportunity ahead." In the next four years the state needed to add 600,000 new jobs, more than 70,000 schoolteachers, and nearly as many hospital beds. To keep up, twenty-three new schoolrooms would have to be opened every day. But those were possibilities, not problems. All that was needed was "leadership which is concerned with people, with individuals and their needs, leadership which is understanding and personal, not cold and grim and aloof."[49]

When a campaign clicks, it's a heady thing, and Brown and his men were doing everything right. In secret focus groups, voters were telling the Democrats exactly what they wanted to hear. Republicans had been in power too long. It was "time for a change." The state needed energy, somebody who would go out and attract new businesses to create new jobs. Knowland's right-to-work nonsense "bored" people. When asked, virtually nobody cited it as a key issue. Even worse, the senator was perceived as a career climber, somebody who had engineered the Big Switch so that he could win the governorship, then use that office as nothing more than a launching pad to the White House. Brown's lead grew over the summer, then kept widening.[50]

With the primary done and the Republicans collapsing, Brown dipped his toe into television, recording a series of commercials for the fall campaign. By later standards they were achingly primitive. First there was a weird, incongruous shot of Brown's smiling face, disembodied, no neck or shoulders attached at all, then an announcer with a slightly florid style offering a catchphrase—"First with all the people because people are first with Pat Brown" or "Pat Brown: first choice for governor, vote for Brown"—and finally the candidate himself. He was the avatar of respectability: horn-rimmed glasses, gray suit, dark tie, a tasteful collar pin attached to his white shirt. His hair was slicked back, his round face suggesting a middle-aged—he was fifty-three—man of substance. He stared straight ahead, stern and grim and serious, all of his typical warmth and approachability sucked away by the strange mechanical audience he was addressing.

Once he started talking, the message varied, for the campaign recorded more than a dozen spots. There was an occasional touch of liberalism: In one ad he promised "equal job opportunities for all Californians," a clear reference to outlawing racial discrimination in hiring and a continuation, he said, of the state's "great progressive tradition." There was also some of the Republican-bashing he often used on the stump: Knowland was the "grand architect of Republican wreckage in this state," a man who might "wreck our state's future" and who represented "only himself and his own national political ambitions."

But most of the ads showed a man staying away from the rough edges of the campaign, playing it safe with a lead, sticking to the middle. He boasted about California's growth, insisting that the state's "abundance is here for all to share" and scoffing at the idea that the newcomers might overwhelm things. "Problems?" he said. "I'd rather say challenges." He bragged that he had been a tough attorney general and promised more of the same as governor. He vowed to be frugal with tax dollars and ensure government efficiency. He insisted that attracting new businesses and protecting agriculture would be priorities.[51]

For some, it was too timid, too moderate. Phil Burton, a liberal Democratic activist who was running for the assembly—and who in time would have a long, glorious, and controversial career in Congress—kept bickering with Dutton, saying that Brown was hiding his true colors, was muffling himself and his beliefs and his causes. Dutton thought that was ridiculous. Brown was being honest but not foolish. The point was to win, not just in lefty places like San Francisco or West Los Angeles, but across the whole state. And to do that you had to soft-pedal the liberalism, avoid beating your chest or ranting or crusading. Dutton, very much a liberal himself, believed that ultimately a touch of moderation at the top of the ticket would help the Burtons of the world. The bigger Brown's margin, the more Democrats he would drag into office with him. "California was not and would not be a liberal state unless Pat got elected," Dutton said later.[52]

———

In mid-September, with less than two months to go before election day, Knowland's already staggering effort received a death blow. Ironically, or perhaps appropriately, it came from the wife who had so often borne the pain of his neglect. Whatever her personal problems, Helen Knowland was a true believer, an archconservative, a Republican to the core, a woman dedicated to the blunt politics of her husband. When he and Brown both spoke at the same event, their wives in tow, Helen Knowland became so agitated when Brown spoke that he sometimes wondered if she would pick up something and hurl it at him.[53]

Among the causes of her frequent distress was organized labor, about which she seethed. And so in the midst of the campaign, when she came across a pamphlet titled "Meet the Man Who Plans to Rule America," about United Auto Workers chief Walter Reuther, she seized on it. She sent hundreds of copies to leading California Republicans and was about to distribute thousands more when the *New York Times* called.

The *Times* knew that the author of the anti-Reuther diatribe was Joseph Kamp, a right-wing extremist who had been jailed for contempt of Congress, had been denounced as a fascist by mainstream conservatives, and had written a book titled *We Must Abolish the United States.* The paper published a story about the connection between Kamp and the Knowland campaign.

Brown pounced on it. His opponent, he said, had been "caught red-handed doing business with elements that would not stop at imposing a fascist dictatorship over the American people." When Knowland was slow to denounce the material, Brown started noting his continued silence in press releases issued with almost comic regularity. On September 15: "Nearly 48 hours have elapsed since the New York Times revelation . . ." On September 16: "Over 60 hours have now elapsed . . ." Then again later on the same day: "Over 70 hours after public disclosures . . ." Eventually Knowland ordered his wife to stop distributing the pamphlet, but the damage was done.[54]

The Knowland campaign literally started to fall apart, shedding pieces of itself like a cheap boat in a storm. Within days the chairman of the veterans' committee, frustrated by the feeling that he was being ignored, resigned. A week after that, one of the fund-raisers quit, complaining that the campaign was lifeless. Finally, with a month to go, a scorned and embittered Goodwin Knight took his revenge, announcing that he would not support his fellow Republican for governor. At the very end Knowland was a desperate sideshow. On the campaign's last weekend, he staged a ludicrous twenty-hour telethon, sitting beneath the baking lights of a television studio, haggard and in shirtsleeves, answering question after question phoned in by voters.

It was a final push that reflected the new political world. Both candidates were northerners—they had been born in the Bay Area, raised there, built their careers there—but they spent the end of the campaign in Los Angeles, where the votes were now. On Sunday they appeared together on *Meet the Press,* the national broadcast reflecting the ever-growing importance of California.

By Sunday night there was nothing left to do. Everybody knew Brown was going to win. Liberated from the pell-mell schedule of campaigning, Pat and Bernice decided to take in a movie. They went to see *The Last Hurrah,* a John Ford picture starring Spencer Tracy as an old-time Irish pol—a big-city mayor—running for one last term against a young, handsome, vapid rival who relied more on television than handshaking. For a politician in a political season, it was a natural choice, and the Browns weren't the only ones with the idea. At intermission they wandered out into the lobby—and ran into William Knowland and his family.[55]

———

Brown flew home the next night, election eve, grinning irrepressibly as he marched off the plane, thirteen-year-old Kathy sauntering along beside him, even Bernice looking happy for the photographers. There was one last pitch to the waiting reporters—California was "too big, too complex [and] too important" to be left to the likes of Knowland—and then it was over.[56]

Election day was clear and warm, picnic weather even in San Francisco after a morning fog burned off. The pleasant day sparked predictions of a big turnout, always a good sign for Democrats. Up early, Brown voted, went to church, then returned home for breakfast. He and Bernice managed their traditional election day round of golf at the Olympic Club, where photographers caught them teeing off as usual. Home from the links, Brown read part of a new novel someone had sent him, then changed into a suit, making sure that for luck he put on the same tie he had worn when announcing his candidacy. When it was time, he went downstairs to join the growing party of family and close friends.

It was a gleeful bunch. The first returns were coming in from the eastern time zones, and Democrats were on a roll. They were picking up congressional seats, knocking off governors, and seizing control of state legislatures. Right-to-work measures were failing in state after state. Even the flinty Yankee Republicans of Vermont were swooning: They elected a Democrat to a major office for the first time in 102 years.

Finally, the polls closed and the California returns began. From the start they confirmed what everybody expected: Brown was a sure thing, and he seemed to be pulling the rest of the ticket along with him. The Browns got a police escort to campaign headquarters downtown, sirens blaring all the way, and when they got there it was pandemonium. The place was packed. For the first time in twenty years, since before World War II, a Democrat had been elected governor, and the Democrats were ready to celebrate. It took Brown fifteen minutes just to work his way from the door to the dais, shaking hands, laughing, smiling, waving, basking in the adulation and victory. He kissed his wife for the photographers, introduced his kids, threw his arm around his eighty-year-old mother, and announced that she had thought he would lose. The crowd, loyalists all and by now feeling pretty good, loved it. Dutton remembered the whole thing as "just a ball," the candidate as "euphoric." Somebody put a corsage on Kathy, which, to her, made it all seem quite grand.

Brown waited a little—decorum seemed to require that—and then at 10:30, just two and a half hours after the last polling places had closed, he claimed victory. As he sometimes did for a speech, he turned solemn, reading a short statement quickly and seriously, almost sounding a little tired. The election, he said, was a "historic Democratic triumph[,] . . . a mandate for progressiveness in our public life." It was time to make California "a still better and more prosperous state."[57]

When the final numbers came in, they showed a landslide. Brown topped Knowland by more than a million votes, carrying all but four of the state's fifty-eight counties. Engle beat poor old Goodie Knight for the Senate. Democrats won a majority of seats in the congressional delegation. In the legislature they seized control of both the senate and the assembly for the first time in the twentieth century. Even the bottom of the ticket went Democratic. Whereas Brown had been the lone Democrat in statewide office for the past eight years, the situation was now reversed. Only one Republican, Secretary of State Frank Jordan, survived the onslaught.

The victory was a blend of luck and skill. In one sense, Brown was graced again with a weak opponent. He had been elected district attorney by beating a tired old man. As attorney general he followed a predecessor widely thought to be a crook. Now, in his biggest election, Brown had faced an opponent who foolishly transformed himself from giant to dwarf. Knowland ran for the wrong office, emphasized issues of little concern to the voters, and even failed to show up for long stretches of the campaign. But it was also true that Brown ran a great campaign. He saw his opponent's weakness and exploited it mercilessly, stayed away from his party's fringe, and spoke most often to the reality that voters saw around them every day: the new housing subdivisions, the crowded schools, the clogged freeways. Back in August, at the Democratic State Convention, Brown had denounced Knowland as a "right-wing extremist." "We must help turn back the last great charge of American reaction now being mounted in our state," he told the delegates.[58] As the governor-elect rose and dressed the morning after the election, it seemed they had done exactly that.

Not that everyone was as excited as the partyers the night before. Trying to make a television interview, Brown hurried out of the house, then discovered that the show was later than he thought. Finding himself with a little extra time, he spotted a six-stool corner tavern that also served breakfast and popped in for a quick bite. Perhaps the waitress failed to recognize him, or perhaps she was just understandably exhausted from the morning rush, but she seemed to show a little less than the expected deference. She mumbled when she asked for his order and, when he requested ham and eggs, demanded, "On a raft, scrambled or what? How?" Brown asked for the eggs over, then whispered to a reporter trailing him around for the morning, "As you can see, greatness is very thin."[59]

PART II
BUILDING

6   THE BIG WALLOP

IN THE DAYS AFTER his victory, the new governor-elect and his closest aides fled to
Palm Springs. They wanted time to contemplate the chores that lay ahead,
and they did it in California style, planning the new administration at pool-
side, clad in swimsuits and slathered in suntan lotion. The only drawback
was olfactory: The resort's lawns were under repair, subjecting Brown and
his team to the omnipresent stench of fertilizer.[1]

Brown offered the preeminent job of chief of staff to Fred Dutton, ring-
leader of the campaign and one of those along on the trip. For other posts,
Brown plundered his old San Francisco crowd. Adrienne Sausset was
named his personal secretary, the job she had held when he was both district attorney and attorney general. Cecil Poole, whom Brown had made
the first black prosecutor in the city, would be the clemency secretary, sorting through death penalty cases and making recommendations about
clemency. Bert Levit, the Republican friend who always served as the fix-it
man in any new Brown administration, was named director of the Department of Finance, a critical position because the agency drew up the
state budget. Brown thought the job should go to a loyal Democrat, but he
relented when Levit said he wanted it.[2]

For one important job they picked an outsider, *San Francisco Chronicle*
reporter Hale Champion. Champion was a bright and blunt midwesterner
whose Democratic roots ran deep. His grandfather had been elected district

attorney of Branch County, Michigan, in 1896, the last Democrat to win an election in the area until FDR. Champion had been in the army during the war and then worked as a reporter and a political staff member before going to Stanford, where he studied writing under Wallace Stegner. After a Niemann Fellowship at Harvard he took over political coverage at the *Chronicle* while one of the regular reporters was out ill. Champion was resourceful. Once as a young man he headed west to see the country but was forced to hitchhike when his car broke down. He finally arrived in Sacramento with $8 in his pocket, so he walked into the *Bee* and talked his way into a job. He was also, like his boss-to-be, practical. Champion thought of himself as a liberal, but he liked the idea of getting things done, of accomplishing things rather than just making a point. He had been a Truman man when his friends supported Henry Wallace. From his work as a political reporter, he and Dutton had struck up an acquaintance, and now Dutton asked him to become the press secretary. Champion was eager to get back into government, to see once again how things worked from the inside, so he said yes.[3]

Down the ladder, Brown wanted all new people. By comparison to the sparse patronage opportunities offered by the attorney general's office, the governor's chair was fertile ground from which to reward supporters. He told all of Knight's political appointees—those not protected by civil service—to submit their resignations. The voters wanted change, Brown announced, and now they were going to get it.[4]

By Inauguration Day, the first Monday of 1959, the new administration was ready. Key jobs were filled. The proposed state budget stood ready for release. The new governor's agenda had been made real, reduced to the bland, unreadable language of legislative bills. In both chambers of the Capitol, new and friendly majorities from Brown's own party held sway. "The new year," wrote one local political columnist, "rides in on a Democratic donkey."[5]

The day itself was a mess. After nine months of drought, a storm blew into Sacramento from the Pacific. Wind gusts reached fifty-five miles an hour. Trees blew over and knocked down power lines, leaving much of the city without electricity. At the Cathedral of the Blessed Sacrament downtown, two blocks from the Capitol, metal sheathing on the great dome ripped loose and began flapping about, threatening to tear away completely and become giant, deadly missiles.

Mercifully, the ceremony was indoors, in the big assembly chamber on the north side of the Capitol. Brown took the oath, then began his inaugural speech. At first he was at pains to establish his authenticity as a man of the left: He used the word *liberal* or *liberalism* seven times in the first eight paragraphs. "Offered reaction by the radical right, the voters emphatically declined," he said in his most partisan passage. "Offered government by retreat, the people preferred progress." In only nine weeks between the election and the inauguration, Brown noted, the state's population had increased by seventy-five thousand. The state government could no longer be on "dead center, unresponsive and inert." Yet he swore off profligacy and pipe dreams, and insisted to the point of repetition that his would be a sober reign. Brownish activism was to be "reasonable, rational, realistic." Offering personal credo as much as programmatic motto, he coined the catchphrase of his administration, "responsible liberalism."[6]

Moving to specifics, he unleashed a whirlwind of ideas. California should ban racial discrimination in hiring, limit consumer credit charges, expand publicly funded medical care for the poor, establish a minimum wage, improve campaign finance reporting, speed up the tabulation of votes on election night, streamline the state bureaucracy, offer treatment to drug addicts convicted of crimes, implement new training programs for prison inmates, improve the public schools, research the dangers of smog, and even fund an ongoing plan to discourage alcoholism and promote temperance. Still, that was not enough. But for the limits of time, he would say more, and he promised that in the weeks ahead he would propose a plan on traffic safety and a commission to study urban problems. He even suggested that government should go looking for extra responsibilities. The state should mimic private industry and establish a research and development program, the nation's first in the public sector. Bright young men would be gathered up and put to work on nettlesome problems of the future: health insurance, crowded airways, and the need for workers to have portable pensions. Taken as a whole, it was a program of striking ambition, one that would be matched by no other newly elected California governor for the rest of the century.

It was all a little heady, and it put Brown to babbling. At a big family dinner hours after the inauguration, he posed for newspaper photographers, his wife on one side and his mother on the other, Jerry in his liturgical collar, fine china and grandchildren and smiles all around. Taken with the moment, Brown joked out loud, or maybe half-joked, "These are the kind of pictures that will get me into the White House."[7]

Brown took charge of a state brimming with energy. In the 1950s, as he waited for the right chance to run, America's postwar boom charged along—and California led the way. The state attracted roughly 500,000 new residents a year, almost one a minute. During the eight years that Brown was attorney general, the state added more than 3.6 million new residents, as if the entire city of Chicago had moved to California.[8] In many parts of the country, central cities shrank as people moved to the suburbs. In California new residents flocked to big city and suburb alike. Of the country's largest cities, Los Angeles was one of the few to add population during the 1950s; sleepy Orange County was transformed from orchards to sprawling suburbs, its population suddenly tripling.[9]

Blessed with the economic godsend of the Cold War, Southern California's aerospace industry was harvesting so many contracts from the Pentagon that the state received one out of every five research dollars spent by the federal government. Jealous New York officials launched a counterattack to draw away some of the money, but theirs was a hopeless cause.[10] California was still the nation's most productive agricultural state, but by the time Brown was elected governor, more Californians were employed making aircraft than producing food.[11]

Cultural lures mingled with economic ones. Move to California and get a good job, the story went, and you'll have a pool in your backyard, sunny barbecues year-round, and a set of friends who are, compared to the staid folks back home, "more outgoing, fun-loving [and] happy-go-lucky." James Michener, then the nation's most famous chronicler of place, described Western Man almost as if he were a new species, a fresh branch on the evolutionary tree. Compared to hidebound easterners, Michener insisted, the westerner "had a rough and ready acceptance of new ideas," enjoyed a special vitality, even was taller and "ate more salads." Looking back, it sounds almost comical. At the time, it was as real as any dream can be. People kept packing the station wagon and heading for California because it was a chance at the good life, not by getting lucky or rich or famous, just by moving. In California, one transplanted Chicago man said, he and his family "just get more sheer pleasure out of being alive."[12]

Nothing, however, seemed so fundamentally American a sign of the state's growth and power as the arrival, finally, of major league baseball. In the world of sports, maybe even in the world of American popular culture, baseball was king. For years, even as California became bigger and richer than its older eastern counterparts, even as San Francisco and Los Angeles cemented their status as two of the country's most important cities, big league baseball remained a distant show, a thing to read about in the papers rather than to watch and feel and smell.

The bizarre fact was that the National Pastime was a regional enterprise. For most of their history, the major leagues had no team west or south of St. Louis. In 1955 the Philadelphia A's moved to Kansas City, but that was hardly the real West. Then, in 1957, in search of newer stadiums and bigger profits, the owners of the Brooklyn Dodgers and the New York Giants declared the unthinkable: they were moving their teams to California.

No symbol could have been more perfect. Americans had been going to California for decades. Now their most beloved sports heroes would too. New York was the self-appointed capital of the world, the biggest state in the country, an imperium utterly certain of its own greatness. Yet it was losing two of its most cherished institutions to a place that, when Americans first played baseball, still belonged to another country. The scientist Stephen Jay Gould later said that it "ripped out the soul of New York City." The writer Pete Hamill and a friend, both Brooklyn fans, once independently wrote down the names of the three worst human beings in history. Along with Hitler and Stalin, both men included Walter O'Malley, the owner of the Dodgers.[13] On the other side of the country, Angelenos gave O'Malley a California Bear flag and hailed him as a hero.[14]

Californians loved their triumph. Two San Franciscans who happened to be in New York on Opening Day 1958 stopped by the city's information booth in Times Square and, rubbing salt in the wound, asked when the Giants would be playing their next game at the Polo Grounds, the team's hallowed Manhattan home, now abandoned.[15]

It was more than Schadenfreude. Californians knew, New Yorkers knew, everyone knew, that something big had happened. When the two teams met in San Francisco and played the first major league game west of the Rockies, the story made the front pages even on the East Coast. The *New York Times* said the National League was finally a national fact. The *Christian Science Monitor* wrote that "big league baseball's manifest destiny" had finally come true "at the ocean's glorious edge."[16]

In California both the people and the papers showed even less restraint. The first game was covered by the *San Francisco Chronicle* in a "Baseball Extra," with an eight-column picture of the packed stands dominating the front page. "This is how it was at Seals Stadium yesterday," the caption read, "big league in every way." When the Dodgers played their first game in Los Angeles three days later, they drew 78,672 people to the city's vast Memorial Coliseum. Americans had been attending major league baseball for eighty-three years and had never produced so large a crowd for a regular-season game. In less than a week in the big leagues California had overwhelmed the record books.[17]

––––––

Brown had been a San Franciscan all his life, but his election to the governorship meant a new home in a new city. The prospect was not greeted with universal enthusiasm in the household. Kathleen, the only Brown child who remained at home, told her aunt during the campaign that she hoped her father would lose so they could all stay put.[18]

In Sacramento home would now be an eighty-two-year-old mansion a few blocks from the Capitol, originally built by a rich merchant named Albert Gallatin and later sold to the state to serve as the official gubernatorial residence. It was a wondrous old place, big and rambling and creaky and pleasantly dilapidated, with winding staircases and dark wood banisters and heavy, burgundy drapes. Guards were stationed outside, although security was hardly restrictive. Touring the house just after the election, Bernice was told by Goodie Knight's wife, a little melodramatically, that a table by the front door contained a hidden "panic button" to summon the police. The Browns never had need of rescue, but one of the grandchildren eventually found the button and pushed it: A bell rang in the Carriage House, but nobody came.[19]

During the first few weeks, Brown occasionally lived the bachelor life: Bernice spent part of the time in San Francisco with Kathleen until the teenager could change schools.[20] But in time both Bernice and Kathleen settled in at the mansion, and Barbara and Cynthia began to bring their kids often, giving a crowded air to what might have been a lonely house. For the grandchildren, the mansion was a giant playland. Three stories tall and with a full basement, it was filled with nooks and crannies and quirky niches. The third floor, uninhabited and essentially unused, was a place of ghosts, a challenge to brave and then scurry from in fear. Best of all, there was a cupola—built so Gallatin could watch for freighters coming up the Sacramento River—that soared high above the rest of the house, two stories up a winding staircase, ending in a tiny room with floor-to-ceiling windows. The cupola was a great little spot. As a teenager, Kathleen Brown and a friend used it as a bombing platform from which to rain down water balloons on unsuspecting trick-or-treaters.

The location was undistinguished. Once, the neighborhood had been a tony part of town, but now the house was surrounded by a commercial district, and traffic clanged along incessantly just outside the windows. The sound of trucks was so bad that Bernice eventually took to running her bedroom air-conditioner all night long, even in the dead of winter, so as to smother the bedlam with white noise.

Worse still was the weather. Accustomed to the cool seaside fog of their native city, the Browns had to acclimate to summers in Sacramento, where triple-digit highs are common and it sometimes tops 110 degrees. As the heat started to bake the city during Brown's first summer as governor, he took relief where he could find it. Directly across the street was the Mansion Inn, a hotel with a pleasant little swimming pool. Brown tucked his trunks under his arm and walked over and explained himself to the desk clerk. Management gave him a key to a room so that he could change, and soon enough he was splashing around. He began doing it all the time, which was fine until Bernice happened to ask him one day where he changed. By chance, that day there had been no empty rooms, so instead he had used the men's room. Brown was not bothered at all. The first lady was appalled: No governor of California should be stripping naked in a public restroom. She demanded a swimming pool on the mansion grounds, and supporters ponied up the money. The governor's staff griped that a swimming pool was a rich man's toy, hardly the right symbol for a new Democrat fresh into office. But Bernice insisted, and eventually she got lucky. The public announcement that a pool would be added to the mansion grounds came on a day so painfully, aggressively hot that only the most miserly would begrudge the governor of California a chance for a cool, private dip.[21]

———

Perhaps aware of the amplified historical weight granted by his new office, Brown began keeping a diary, apparently the only time in his long life he did so with regularity. His dedication to the idea lasted only two years, but so long as he continued, he recorded his thoughts and moods in a fitful, honest, occasionally revealing fashion. His first entry was the simple reflection of a new beginning. "This begins second week of my administration," he wrote. "Slept well."[22]

Brown knew there was a tiny window of opportunity if he were to accomplish the goals laid out so ambitiously in his inaugural speech. At the time California's legislature held a full-blown session—six months of dicker and drink—only once every two years, in the odd-numbered, nonelection years. In the even-numbered years there were short sessions limited only to the state budget, so in a governor's four-year term, he had only two chances to work his will on a full and unrestricted meeting of the legislators. Brown knew that his best hope for real accomplishment lay in that first legislature, the one that began with his swearing in and would continue for the first six months of 1959. His million-vote landslide hung in the air, and the new Democratic majorities still remembered who headed the ticket that brought them to power. "I packed a big wallop," Brown said later.[23]

The problem was that the new governor had no money to spend. Seemingly the flushest of states, home to the good-time dreams of 1950s America, California was in fact going broke. For years the state had been running in the red, a practice underwritten by huge surpluses from the war, when military production gave a boost to the West Coast economy and generated extraordinary revenues. In the three years before Brown took office, the state spent $323 million more than it received, and the problem was worsening. As the economy slowed in 1958—the minor slump used by Brown as an anti-Republican weapon during the campaign—revenues dropped even further, while costs mounted for government social programs. The shortfall for the previous year alone was almost $150 million, all of it papered over with the old surpluses. Now the savings accounts were almost empty. Amiable Goodie Knight had used up the household savings, then dashed out the door and left his successor to face the inevitable reckoning day. As Brown was planning his administration, financial experts announced that by the end of the current fiscal year the state would be almost $88 million in the hole. For the year that would start July 1, 1959—the year for which Brown had to draw up a budget—the gap would be more than twice that. The total shortfall was almost a fifth of the expected state budget, a staggering amount.[24]

California had not had a major tax increase in more than twenty years. First the state had been too poor (during the depression) and then it had been too rich (during the war and the surplus years right after). Now, faced with a bare financial cupboard and massive growth he had neither the desire nor the ability to check, Brown decided he would restock the public larder. The biggest piece of the resulting proposal was a progressive increase in the personal income tax. Brackets would be narrowed so as to create a steeper climb into the higher rates, and the top rate would be increased from 6 to 7 percent. Personal and dependent exemptions would be shifted so that taxes went up for the rich, down for the poor. The capital gains tax would be increased slightly. There was also a big increase proposed for the income tax paid by banks and corporations, and, for the first time in California, a tax on tobacco products, three cents a pack on cigarettes and 15 percent of the wholesale price for cigars. Smaller proposals included a severance tax on oil and natural gas—this would prove particularly contentious—an increase in the beer tax, a bigger cut for the state from horse-track betting, and a jump in inheritance taxes. All in all, once they were fully implemented, the changes would bring in an additional $256 million a year, a huge amount of money for the time.[25]

It was a critical decision, and one largely forgotten in later years. Political considerations played a role. Brown had won by a million votes, giving him enormous political capital. He thought he could push for a big tax increase immediately, at the beginning of his term, thus avoiding the need for anything similar when a reelection campaign would be closer at hand.[26] But Brown also deserves credit for recognizing the necessity of an unpopular policy and then for following it through. He saw that in a state growing as rapidly as California, cutting programs would be foolish in the long run, so he insisted in his budget proposal that every penny of the new money was needed. In his diary he was more candid. "I have nothing but contempt for those who say that no new taxes are necessary," he wrote.[27]

————

The new governor often found himself lying awake amid the mansion's nighttime creaks, for his added responsibilities brought him new stresses, personal as well as professional. He thought he was spending insufficient time with his aging mother, and he missed his cloistered son, who was "out of this world," as Brown wrote in his diary.[28]

Typically, he started the day early, often with a working breakfast in a little dining room above the mansion's porte cochere. Once at the office, there were often tasks that an attorney general did not face. Brown now had far more interaction with the press, for example. He held news conferences twice a week and initially followed tradition and held separate sessions for the newspaper and broadcast reporters. Soon Brown's staff combined the two, causing a furor in the press corps. The result was a bizarre effort by the print reporters to effectively block the broadcasters from using their questions as an on-air preface to the governor's remarks. Unwilling to provide material for their hated new competitors, the newspapermen would lard their questions with obscenity: "Governor, what about this fucking bill you've got?"[29]

By night Sacramento was a fraternity party writ large. Watering holes were plentiful. There was Bidell's, just across the street from the Capitol, or the bars at the Senator and El Mirador hotels, or Frank Fat's, a Chinese restaurant just down the street that doubled as a second office for many lawmakers. After drinks and dinner, women were the typical prey. Away from their wives and families, ensconced in a world of adolescent masculinity, legislators made philandering a sport. Secretaries, almost the only women in the world of Sacramento officialdom, were fair game. A short drive produced alternatives. The town of Jackson, fifty miles away in the Sierra Nevada foothills, had so many whorehouses it was sometimes known as "the legislators' bedroom."[30]

Brown ducked the scene. Conventional in his personal life, he was never a heavy carouser, nor was he a devotee of insider legislative machination—the stuff that so fascinated the Sacramento bar crowd. Usually Brown went home at night. Often he worked. There was an office on the third floor of the mansion, in a converted section of what had once been a grand ballroom. The office had a sturdy walnut desk that had been made for Earl Warren by inmates at San Quentin, but the room was cold and far from the home's heart, and Brown didn't use it much. Most evenings, he settled into his favorite chair in the main living room downstairs, the overstuffed briefcase at his side offering a steady diet of paperwork and reading. On nights dedicated to relaxation, Brown preferred entertainments far quieter than those pursued by legislators. He and Bernice had friends to the mansion for private screenings of new movies: musicals, westerns, and, in later years, the popular spy series featuring the president's favorite protagonist, James Bond.[31]

Brown's new role often took him away from Sacramento altogether. More than ever before, he was a highly public figure, expected to be everywhere at once in his large state, cutting a ribbon or giving a speech or opening a factory. Los Angeles, its bulk always looming over the state's political landscape, required constant attention. Weekend trips were frequent even during the legislative session. Brown loved the whirl, but it could be a bit much even for him. Less than a month into his term he was already writing to his son to say that he wanted nothing more than a day of solitude and books.[32]

————

At the end of January Brown signed his first bill, a minor measure extending a deadline for auto registrations. Reporters gathered around to watch, but ironically Brown's pen failed at the critical moment. His signature was rendered a feeble scrawl, but he wanted everyone to know the weakness was not his. "It looks as though it was signed by an old man," he said. "I'm not that timorous."[33]

The first major bill to begin moving through the long legislative maze was also the one that Brown had identified as his top priority: the creation of a Fair Employment Practices Commission. During World War II, thousands of blacks migrated west for jobs in the shipyards, yet more than a decade later big pieces of the working world remained off-limits. The Los Angeles Urban League surveyed job opportunities for blacks and found doors firmly closed. Almost all businesses hired blacks as custodians, but often that was about it. Two of the state's biggest banks segregated their black employees in four branches serving predominantly black areas. Of the seven major oil companies in the state, only one employed blacks for office jobs. The four big California brewers employed no blacks. Especially restricted were jobs that might cause the public to see a black face. Top Los Angeles hotels hired no blacks as waiters or waitresses, and the big department stores had all-white sales forces.[34]

The obvious solution was a Fair Employment Practices Commission, universally known as an FEPC, a panel that already existed in fourteen states.[35] Technically, a commission by the same name had already been created in California, but it had no teeth and received almost no public attention. Black leaders, who had chafed under what they saw as the opposition or indifference of Earl Warren and Goodwin Knight, had supported Brown passionately precisely because he was committed to creating a meaningful FEPC.[36]

As governor, Brown quickly encountered a chance to display his devotion to the idea. After the bill passed the assembly, the lower house of the legislature, opponents began threatening to put the measure on the ballot, letting the voters decide its fate. Fearing racism in the electorate, some supporters suggested appeasement. If the bill were weakened in the legislature, opponents might be mollified and the threat of a statewide vote eliminated. Brown was no stranger to compromise, but in this case he stood firm. Privately, in conversations with aides and others, the governor decreed that the administration would stand by the original bill.[37]

Rebuffed, opponents turned to the state senate, which was far less comfortable ground for the liberal governor. As in many states, California's legislature was modeled after Congress, the two houses divided in structure and thus in outlook. Like the House of Representatives, the assembly was apportioned by population and therefore dominated by legislators from the huge metropolitan areas surrounding Los Angeles and San Francisco. The senate mimicked its national counterpart too, for it reflected geography rather than population. No county could have more than one senator, with the troubling result that the millions of people living in Los Angeles County had no more representation than the few thousand living in sparsely populated counties in the far north. For years the different compositions of the two chambers had produced different results—liberal legislation passing in the assembly, only to die in the senate—and it was closer to realism than to pessimism to anticipate the same result for the proposed ban on employment discrimination.

The effort to wreck the bill was launched almost as soon as it reached the senate—and ironically was engineered by members of the governor's party. As drafted, the bill allowed the commission to investigate discrimination allegations on its own, prior to a complaint, and to try persuasion as a way to resolve cases, in effect negotiating with employers. If that failed a formal case would precede fines or other penalties. The amendments, supported by an employers' group and adopted in a senate committee, required a formal complaint first, before any action at all. Stifled until a complainant came calling, the panel would be effectively robbed of initiative. Byron Rumford, one of only two African Americans in the assembly and the author of the bill, thought the change so damaging to the measure's intent that he compared it to emasculation.[38]

The morning after the amendment was adopted in committee, Brown opened his news conference by declaring his opposition to the changes and, along with legislative allies, began working to undo the damage on the senate floor.[39] Less than a week later, they succeeded. Almost along party lines—Democrats favoring the stronger version, Republicans the weaker one—the full senate stripped out the amendments and restored the bill's original language, a victory hailed by the *Bee* as "a striking show of political muscles by the new Democratic regime."[40] Signed by Brown, the new law proved its worth through the accretion of small victories. In its first three years, the commission created by the bill reviewed almost two thousand discrimination complaints and ushered black Californians into jobs that had once been inaccessible: the first black teachers in many school districts, the first supervisors in two bus companies, the promotion to foreman of shipyard and aircraft workers, the promotion by a bakery of three janitors who became bakers, even the first golf teacher at a municipal course.[41]

———

Shepherding bills through the legislature required constant applications of power, often in small measurement. It was not work to which Brown was naturally suited, for he was not a tactician. "I am a horse, not a jockey," he once wrote of himself.[42] He was also an unusually forgiving man and thus disinclined to hold in balance the necessary political tools of reward and punishment, tending to favor too much reward and too little punishment. At times, though, he showed flashes of toughness. In late March, not quite three months into the legislature's session, a rebellious assemblyman from Santa Barbara voted against an administration proposal to shift money around in the state budget to pay for a series of local projects. Hours later, he found that a local canal vital to his area had been deleted from the list of items to be funded. Asked about the retribution at a news conference, Brown claimed complete ignorance, although he didn't seem unhappy. The governor's aides said it was all the work of Bill Munnell, the Democratic leader in the assembly. Munnell pointed to Jesse Unruh, the young assemblyman who had managed Brown's Southern California campaign and was now chairman of the assembly Ways and Means Committee. Unruh said it was all done by Ralph Brody, a lawyer working for the governor. In reality, it was a circle of people passing off credit rather than blame. Privately, in the pages of his diary, Brown admitted his role in punishing the renegade, who had been taught the need for reciprocal loyalty. "Took on one poor legislator," Brown wrote, "to let them all know that this was a two-way street."[43]

Occasionally the dressing-down was done in public. When a Republican assemblyman named Harold Levering attacked the governor's income tax bill as too easy on the rich and too hard on the middle class, Brown responded that Levering was irrelevant, an incessant naysayer heeded by no one in the Capitol. If the assemblyman truly thought the administration's proposal was too favorable to the affluent, Brown said during a news conference, perhaps he should prepare an amendment to raise rates in the upper brackets. The governor would gladly take a look.[44]

Complaints about the onerous burden of taxation rarely received a favorable hearing from Brown. In a speech at the Commonwealth Club in San Francisco, he let loose a populist blast against such feelings. Critics of the governor's proposed tax increase were selfish men, he said, "unwilling to pay their fair share." He insisted that many were magnates who hid behind tax shelters while collecting huge profits, a practice of which he plainly disapproved.[45]

Less than four months into his term, on April 21, Brown celebrated his fifty-fourth birthday, his first as governor. He noted the milestone in his diary. The requirements of office still pressed on him, and he acknowledged that his journal entries were distressingly rare. Yet he was content. "God has been good to me and I am thankful that my mother is still with me, my family are all well and happy." He counted no major losses in the legislature so far and vowed a steady effort in the months ahead. In straightforward language, he described the goal of his tenure: "life a little more comfortable for the average human being."[46]

———

By May the legislature was deep in its labors, hoping to finish work within a few weeks and escape Sacramento before the worst of the summer heat. The governor was increasingly unhappy with the senate, and for cause. On a number of key administration proposals, the earlier dynamic of the FEPC bill was now being repeated: relatively easy passage in the assembly, trouble in the senate. Brown thought the senate's leadership unimpressive, and he was right.[47]

The senate president pro tem—the leader of the body—was a Fresno Democrat named Hugh Burns, a man so conservative that it occasionally seemed his party affiliation had ended with his registration. Burns had authored the amendments weakening the FEPC bill, for example, an effort in which he was allied mostly with Republicans. He owed the governor nothing. Unlike the Democratic leaders in the assembly, Burns had acquired his power before the 1958 Brown landslide. He had been elected senate leader two years earlier, after the 1956 election, when he convinced two renegade Republicans to bolt their party and support him. He was also not the most impressive of men. He viewed the California Democratic Council, home to so many true liberals, as "a wart on the body politic." He acknowledged, "I got on in the Legislature because I never tried for too much." He said he would have enjoyed being secretary of state partly because "you're never facing issues."[48] Occasionally Burns could be strange or perhaps even stupid. Once during a hearing of the state's Un-American Activities Committee—a "baby HUAC" modeled after the Red-baiting congressional panel—Burns questioned a witness, seriously and at length, about the dangers posed by a race of little aliens with metal heads.[49]

Of nearly equal concern for Brown were the chairmen of senate committees, for many did not share the governor's basic views. By tradition, the senate awarded chairmanships based on seniority, regardless of party. Some of the old bulls still survived, with the result that most of the senate committees were run by Republicans, although Democrats outnumbered them two to one in the chamber as a whole.

Fortunately for the governor, the single most powerful member of the senate was a brilliant ally, the chairman of the Finance Committee, George Miller Jr. A labor lawyer from Contra Costa County—a safe Democratic district filled with blue-collar workers from the local shipyards and oil refineries—Miller was at once one of the ablest members of the legislature and one of the most liberal. He had been a key figure in creating the CDC, the grassroots group built from the volunteer "clubs" that had sprung up to support Adlai Stevenson's 1952 campaign for the presidency. Close to Brown, Miller bridged to some degree the gap between the activists of the party's left wing and the pragmatic, moderate governor. Brown's confidence in Miller was such that the senator was used as a watchdog for Brown campaigns, with the candidate asking Miller to let him know if things were askew.[50] A far keener political strategist than Brown, Miller was smart, intense, driven. He held a focus on legislative business despite a horrible case of psoriasis that worsened with stress, almost becoming unbearable. At times he would bleed through his shirts or leave in his wake little gatherings of pale flakes where he had scratched away the scaly skin.[51]

The governor consulted Miller often. They would share a drink in the late afternoon in Brown's office, and once a week with other key legislators retreat to a private room for dinner at the Sutter Club, home to Sacramento's establishment. Once, a meeting with Miller left the governor's head so busy with strategic calculation that he could not get to sleep until 4:30 A.M.[52]

Buttressed by Miller's help, the administration's bills started to clear the senate one after another: first the cap on loan rates, then the car pollution guidelines, then the health care expansion and the end of cross-filing, the old California system that had allowed candidates to run in the primary of more than one party.

The increases in the income tax and the cigarette tax—the most important of the tax bills in the governor's program—were the last to pass. On the senate floor Miller laid out the case for both bills with uncluttered argument: "There's no money in the till." Both bills passed, almost strictly along party lines, and went to Brown, who signed them into law. Together they represented more than half of all the new revenue to be generated by the governor's tax package. They were also politically significant. In an administration that touted itself as liberal, the income tax increase represented the program's most progressive component. The Brown-era reforms shifted California's tax burden away from other sources and toward income taxes, imposing a bigger burden on the rich.[53]

On one issue Brown could accomplish much by doing almost nothing. And by chance, it was a topic as crucial to California as any other: roads. As it became more populous, people sometimes forgot that California was equally vast. Laid along America's eastern seaboard, the state would stretch from Boston to South Carolina, from the Atlantic almost to Ohio. The largest county, San Bernardino, is twice the size of Massachusetts.

Not surprisingly, California became synonymous with car culture, especially in the years just before Brown took office. One national magazine sent a writer out to take the measure of the place, then headlined his impressionistic piece "Cars, Cars, Cars, Roads, Roads, Roads."[54] The state had 7 percent of the nation's people and 12 percent of its cars.[55] Overseeing it all, the state Department of Motor Vehicles outgrew its new headquarters in half the expected time and then needed an additional wing four times the size of the original building. Turning a nice phrase, a young reporter for the *Sacramento Bee* stared at the massive new structure and declared perceptively that it showed California was growing "like a weedpatch after a spring rain."[56]

For years the scale of road-building projects had been grand. In 1939, to cite the most striking example, Lloyd Aldrich, the city engineer of Los Angeles, proposed a six-hundred-mile concrete web crisscrossing the city, complete with freeways, tree-lined parkways, a downtown bypass, connections to the suburbs, special bus lanes, extra right-of-way for future mass-transit lines, and parks and recreational facilities in the outlying areas. Aldrich proposed, quite literally, urban surgery. His giant parkways would run smack through the middle of the city. Chunks of Los Angeles would be ripped apart, the roads laid down, the city built back up around them. It was a plan so ambitious that it dwarfed anything built to that point by New York's public works czar, Robert Moses, so ambitious that it would have required Los Angeles to increase its road-building budget by fifteenfold, so ambitious that its cost was one and a half times greater than the road-building budget of the entire state. And yet, given its outsized dreams, the most extraordinary thing about the Aldrich plan is that it was, more or less, implemented. It became, in the words of one historian, "the blueprint that guided freeway development in Los Angeles during the postwar years."[57] Anyplace else, a scheme so grand would have been laughed at. In California, it was built.[58]

The state had even bigger plans as Brown took office. California's highway engineers were proposing a state system of freeways stretching for more than twelve thousand miles. Most of the work involved improvements; existing roads would be transformed from country lanes or regular highways into limited-access freeways, the straight wide slabs that were then celebrated as the safest and most efficient way to move traffic. It was a massive project. Once completed, the plan would lay asphalt the length and breadth of the state. It was said that a freeway would link every city in the state that had a population of at least five thousand. Freeways would cross the Sierra Nevada and edge Big Sur, the stunning coast south of San Francisco. Three parallel giants would run down the spine of the Central Valley. Built in a straight line, the system would have run halfway around the earth.[59]

The true size of the behemoth can best be judged by the fact that only a fraction of it exists. In the early 1970s the OPEC oil embargo swelled gas prices, which caused people to drive less and thus reduced gas-tax revenues. At the same time, inflation raised construction costs, and growing environmental concerns produced stiff opposition to more freeways. As a result legislators trimmed the plans. By century's end, though California often seemed a land of endless freeways, it actually had less than half the system that had once been envisioned.[60]

But in 1959 the need to truncate the plans was years off, and largely unforeseeable. At that time the freeway plan seemed like pure progress. Certainly so to the governor, who even chastised his old hometown when San Franciscans, proud of their gorgeous topography and wary of ruining the views, rejected a proposal for freeways through the city. "There isn't any way in the world to avoid it," Brown told a news conference. He insisted that more freeways were needed to lessen the "stupendous" problem of traffic jams, blissfully ignoring the possibility that more roads might simply attract more cars.[61]

Most amazing, however, was the ease with which the state could pay for all those roads. Projected costs over the next twenty years totaled $10.5 billion, this at a time when the entire state budget was only about $2 billion a year. Federal money, mostly from the Interstate Highway Program approved by Congress three years before, would provide some help but not the lion's share.[62] Yet the state's fiscal experts insisted that no tax increase was needed. The existing gas tax—six cents a gallon paid by drivers every time they filled up—would provide most of the money.[63] All that was required of Brown and the legislature was, really, to do nothing, to hold the tax at its current rate, an easy task politically. Californians were now so numerous, driving around their immense domain so far and so often, that the natural course of economics would do the rest. Quite reasonably, in other words, Californians believed that they could, virtually by themselves and with no special effort, pay for a modern concrete colossus such as the world had rarely seen.

———

Legislative losses were rare, but they happened. In a sign of the times, lawmakers balked at an administration-backed bill to declare drivers drunk if their blood-alcohol level was 0.15 percent. That was seen as too aggressive, although in later years the standard was lowered to barely more than half that. Also killed was a bill increasing the regulation of labor unions. In the Capitol's normal give-and-take, the tax program was shaved. The beer tax was increased less than Brown requested, and cigars were deleted from the tobacco tax bill, much to the annoyance of some liberals who regarded fat stogies as the emblem of the rich.

Big agriculture proved a tougher foe even than drinkers or cigar lovers. Brown's initial proposal for a state minimum wage of $1.25 included farmworkers, a remarkable provision given the influence wielded by both corporate and small farmers. (The federal minimum wage, which did not cover farmworkers, was $1.00 an hour.) By the time the bill came up for a hearing in an assembly committee, the administration had agreed to lower the mark for farmworkers to $0.90 an hour, but even that was controversial. Hundreds crowded into the hearing. Some were farmworkers or their advocates, including a young community service worker named César

Chávez, who three years later would found the country's first farmworkers' union. But many in the crowd were farmers claiming impending economic disaster if they had to pay laborers $0.90 an hour. One San Joaquin County grower got so carried away he claimed the proposal for a minimum wage had been "conceived in hate." The testimony raged on for more than three hours, and then finally two rural Democrats joined with Republicans to kill the measure. The next day reporters asked Brown if he would continue the fight, but he declared a strategic surrender. Other issues remained before the legislature, he said, and he was done battling over this one. Agriculture, an industry unaccustomed to losing in California, had won again.[64]

By late May one key fight remained. The oil and gas tax, the final piece of the tax-increase package, was stalled in the assembly. Oil industry lobbyists, always powerful figures around the Capitol, were fighting hard, and they were on friendly turf. The bill had been sent to the Revenue and Taxation Committee, a conservative bulwark hostile to the administration. On May 28 the panel rejected the bill, 10–6.

The governor dug in his heels, showing precisely the kind of fighting resolve he had lacked on the minimum wage measure. The bill should be pulled from committee, he told reporters, a rare maneuver that, in the world of the legislature, signals vehemence. The $23 million that would be raised by the tax, Brown insisted, meant nothing to so rich and powerful an industry, but would pay for much in the hands of the state. If the tax were to die, the budget would have to be sliced up painfully: aid to the aged and infirm would be cut, so would school funding, even help for veterans. "I don't see how anybody can call himself a liberal," Brown said, using a term that had yet to be transformed from accolade to insult, "and vote against this . . . tax."[65]

Word went out that the governor would veto the increased school aid—a perennially popular item with legislators—unless the oil tax were approved. When that didn't work, Brown and Unruh, who was leading the fight for the bill, announced that revenue raised through the tax would be dedicated to old-age pensions and faculty salary increases at the state colleges, two other popular items. It was something of a fiction, since money is fungible, but it sounded good and gave wavering Democrats a reason to support the bill. Then, in a sleepy moment when few members were actually on the floor, Unruh quickly pushed through a motion to move the bill from the hostile revenue committee to his own Ways and Means Committee, a far friendlier venue for the administration.

Briefly it looked as if the bill might survive, but by the following week, a coalition of Republicans and conservative Democrats had regrouped. Remembering Unruh's shrewd gambit and aware that to win they needed every member present, they demanded a call of the house, a parliamentary procedure requiring that the members be penned up in the chamber, the doors blocked off by the sergeants at arms. As often happens when the legislature has been in session for a few months, members were weary and drained, and they had scattered. One man was riding in a hometown parade, another attending his son's graduation. Near the little town of Quincy, way up in the Sierra Nevada north of Sacramento, Highway Patrol officers found two of the wayward lawmakers as they pulled into Bucks Lake for a fishing trip.

Six hours later, the wanderers retrieved, the full assembly voted to undo Unruh's handiwork and return the bill to its burial ground in the revenue committee. Twelve Democrats joined nearly every Republican and, in effect, killed the bill. Brown conceded defeat, the biggest loss he suffered that year. Rightly, he called it a victory for industry over individuals, noting that personal income tax rates were going up. "When the taxpayers put their money on the line to pay for the needs of California," he told reporters, "what will they think about the oil industry?"[66]

It was a noble defeat, but it was also an early reminder of political reality. Even at the peak of Brown's legislative influence, even when helped by tactical geniuses like Unruh and Miller, even when friendly and accommodating Democratic majorities filled both chambers, the governor and his men could still lose a few.

———

By the time the final gavel fell and the session ended, at six minutes to midnight on June 19, scattering the legislators back to hometowns and constituents and wives and sobriety, the administration's few nettlesome defeats were forgotten. Exhausted senators set off a string of firecrackers and launched a shower of paperwork into the air. Across the Rotunda in the assembly, Unruh tacitly acknowledged the pugnacious tactics he used to push the governor's bills. A quarter hour before the scheduled adjournment, he rose and asked the speaker to excuse him from the floor early. "I think," he half-joked, "you should give me at least 15 minutes head start to get out of town."[67]

The governor walked over from his suite of offices and took to the podium in each chamber, first in the assembly and then the senate, greeted both places by clamorous standing ovations. After the noise died away, Brown said that his first legislative session as the state's chief executive had been "the most exhilarating six months" he had ever experienced. He pointed especially to the antidiscrimination bill that created the Fair Employment Practices Commission. It was, he said, a "great symbol of human progress—an achievement of enlightenment and understanding."[68]

There was much to be proud of. He had already signed into law 1,109 bills and had at least 1,000 more waiting on his desk. The increased aid to schools was only the second such boost since World War II.[69] More than nine thousand poor, disabled people were provided with state-funded health care. For the first time, standards were set for air quality and for pollution from cars. Safety regulations for farm labor trucks were increased. Consumer protections were stiffened. Disability benefits were raised. Unemployment insurance payments were increased and the time limit for benefits lengthened, at least during periods of high unemployment.[70] State workers got a pay raise.[71]

All of it was funded by the biggest California tax increase in a quarter century, which was perhaps the most important accomplishment of all, since it provided money desperately needed by an ever-growing state with ever-growing public demands. This was not necessarily an obvious outcome. Republicans and business groups complained that the proposed tax increases were too steep. Brown said no. Cautious legislators suggested that the tax increases be phased out after two years. Brown said no. The legislative analyst urged steeper budget cuts and an increase in college tuition. Brown said no. The governor's own budget director recommended that the state's oil-drilling revenues be raided rather than preserved for dam building. Brown said no. Again and again, in other words, the governor and his allies fought to keep intact an ambitious fiscal program that raised taxes—mostly on rich people, corporations, and cigarette smokers—in order to pay for important and expanding public programs. "Responsible liberalism," it turned out, was an activist's creed.

To be sure, there were compromises. Politics is a realm of practical accomplishment—the perfect is the enemy of the good, as the old saw goes—and Brown was a practical man. The smog standards fell short of more vigorous proposals to require pollution-controlling equipment on new cars. The pay raise was less than the State Personnel Board had recommended as a fair boost for state employees. The increase in school aid, although substantial, was less than that sought by the state Department of Education. The interest rate limit, proposed by Brown and crafted by Unruh, was a piece of devilish genius: The cap was low enough to hamper loan sharks, who had neither popularity nor lobbyists, but high enough to win the support of big department stores, which had both.[72] There was even some shameless flimflam passed off as achievement: Brown fulfilled his promise to create an economic development department, even though privately he knew it was a house of bureaucracy. "It was really just a publicity item," he said later. "All they could do was jawbone."[73]

Still, on many topics, Brown was in front of the public, taking stands that were as much to his personal credit as his political detriment. One in three Californians still believed that employers should be able to reject a job applicant because of race, precisely the kind of thing the FEPC was designed to eliminate.[74] On that issue and others, Brown had used his popularity, getting things done even if it meant losing some of the luster from his huge victory. Californians could afford the tax increase—the postwar boom was making them richer every year—but they grumbled nonetheless. Toward the end of the session, even as successes piled up, pollsters found that the governor's approval rating had slid to just 51 percent. Among those who judged him inadequate, the most commonly cited objection was "too much taxation."[75]

But looking back, it is the accomplishments that shine, and even then, plenty of people saw it that way. The *Sacramento Bee* called the 1959 session "a striking personal triumph" for the new governor, but then the *Bee* was always friendly.[76] More significant was the hard-earned homage of enemies. Norman Chandler, the publisher of the *Los Angeles Times* and thus the keeper of California's Republican flame, wrote that Brown was to be commended. The governor, Chandler said, had shown "firm leadership" and pursued a program that was "well thought-out." Even the tax increases, so unpopular with so many Republicans, were "necessary." A bit stilted perhaps, not exactly laudatory, but for a Chandler to offer anything approaching praise to a Democrat was a rare thing indeed.[77] Around the Capitol, the hallway chatter was more effusive. The legislature had not enjoyed so productive a session, it was said, since 1911, when Hiram Johnson and the Progressives reordered the state's political world.

In his diary Brown satisfied himself with plainspoken understatement: "Legislature has gone home. It was a great session. Many fine things were accomplished."[78] But, as always in California, there was still more to do.

7　ALL THESE STUDENTS

SHORTLY AFTER HE BECAME GOVERNOR, Pat Brown received the first two issues of a newsletter produced by the bustling Los Angeles campus of the University of California. UCLA was, according to one of the newsletters, "the campus where the hammers never cease to ring." Fourteen construction projects were under way simultaneously: a botany building, an addition to the geophysics hall, a neuropsychiatric wing, a student union, dormitories, a nursery and kindergarten for the children of students. Nor would the expansion soon stop. The university boasted that it was planning more than a dozen other projects, from an institute for nuclear medicine and radiation biology to a theater arts building.[1]

UCLA was not alone. When Brown took office, California's public colleges and universities were growing pell-mell. Westward migration and California's low tuition had combined to lure more and more students to the state's campuses. In the previous seven years, enrollment had doubled, stuffing to the bursting point what was already the biggest such system in the United States.[2]

Yet a glance at the bulging elementary schools across the country revealed a still larger impending onslaught. The oldest baby boomers were at the edge of puberty, already launched on their generation's bull-in-a-china-shop rush through the nation's demography. Experts projected that by 1975 the UCLA and Berkeley campuses—both already large—would more than double, and Los Angeles State College would grow by a remarkable 756 percent.[3] Californians took pride that the state's public colleges and universities were affordable and accessible, but the enrollment projections for the baby boomers led educators to begin referring to a "tidal wave" of future freshmen. "The question was," University of California president Clark Kerr remembered later, "who was going to handle all of these students?"[4]

———

Looking ahead, the state's educational bureaucrats were doing more than hammering nails at UCLA. The university had already started transforming two dusty agricultural research outposts—in the citrus groves of Riverside, east of Los Angeles, and in the flat farmlands of Davis, near Sacramento—into full-fledged campuses. The campus in Santa Barbara, restricted to undergraduate work since the university had been forced to acquire it in 1944, was adding graduate programs. And the year before Brown was elected, the university's governing body, the Board of Regents, had approved three new campuses, one near San Diego, another in Los Angeles or Orange County, the third somewhere south of the Bay Area. (In the end they were built in La Jolla, Irvine, and Santa Cruz.)

Enrollments were shooting up even faster at the university's poorer, less distinguished cousins, the state's public colleges. By 1958 there were twelve of them, and enrollment had doubled in eleven years, far outpacing even the university's expansion. The legislature had just authorized the creation of four more college campuses, and there was every reason to believe the system would soon expand again. (Eventually it would comprise more than twenty campuses, and is known today as the California State University.)

It was a situation that might have gladdened the hearts of educators: millions of dollars would have to be spent to build campuses, repair aging facilities at existing schools, and hire professors. But hidden in the boom times were two problems that threatened to tear apart the country's best system of public higher education. The first threat was Turkey Tech. The second was the war over the Golden Fleece.

"Turkey Tech" was the nickname that would soon be applied to a new college campus near Turlock, in Stanislaus County, that had been approved by the legislature the year before Brown was elected governor. The problem was that nobody outside Stanislaus County thought there should be a college campus there. A flat patch of California's stifling San Joaquin Valley, it was an area filled with poultry farms, better known for producing future

Thanksgiving dinners than students looking for a college education. Although the state college system aimed to spread itself around California's vastness, providing opportunities for kids throughout the state, there had to be at least some logic in the decision to place new campuses. A joint panel representing both the university and the colleges had drawn up a list of needed new campuses, and Stanislaus County had come in fifth, behind growing suburban areas where large numbers of potential students would soon be living. But the legislature ignored the recommendations, approving the Stanislaus campus in part because its chief backer was a Republican. Lawmakers skipped higher-priority sites pushed by Democrats, who were then—before Brown's landslide—still in the minority.[5]

Unwanted by all but the locals, Turkey Tech thus reflected a kind of helter-skelter, politically driven growth that worried educators. Legislators believed, often correctly, that a college campus brought an area not only prestige but also jobs, innovation, and a better-trained workforce. Everybody wanted one, and as statisticians began to foresee the coming surge of students, everybody had an excuse. In the 1955 session, legislative campus-hunting got so out of control that state senator George Miller, the powerful chairman of the Senate Finance Committee, spoofed the trend by proposing a new campus called Frog U., to be located in Angels Camp, the site of Mark Twain's famous story "The Celebrated Jumping Frog of Calaveras County." He then invited other senators to toss their own districts into the bill, with the ridiculous result that the measure eventually proposed establishing nineteen new campuses, something the state clearly could not afford. Larded up to the point of absurdity, the bill died. But the thirst for more campuses did not. The next general legislative session, in 1957, saw proposals for seventeen new campus sites, and four of them, including Turkey Tech, were approved.[6] To many in the state's educational community, it seemed almost that Miller's 1955 joke had become a 1957 reality, Turkey Tech being not much better than Frog U. If things kept going as they were, the state could end up with campuses in places they did not belong. "If Turlock could get a state college," one educator remembered years later, "who couldn't?"[7]

The second problem, related to the first, was a gnawing competition—unavoidable, relentless, at times almost childish—between the university and the colleges. And the fulcrum of that competition was what would come to be termed the "Golden Fleece" of higher education, the Ph.D. The doctorate was the sole possession of the University of California. Since their founding as "normal schools" designed to train schoolteachers, the colleges had steadily expanded into other fields and had begun to offer the master's degree. But they had never acquired the right to award the Ph.D. and—just as important—everything else that went with it: prestige, bigger faculty salaries, and funding for laboratories and other research facilities. The prohibition on research at the colleges was so absolute, in fact, that if a prospective faculty hire indicated a desire to expand the boundaries of his or her field, the candidate was not considered for the job.[8] The coming tidal wave made the competition both more vicious and, for the university, more dangerous. There would soon be more to fight over, and as the colleges grew the university's traditional dominance was seeping away. Many people at the colleges believed that the time had come for the schools to be acknowledged as full-fledged universities—the oldest and largest of the colleges, in San Jose, was the twenty-fifth largest institution of higher learning in the United States[9]—and they saw the Ph.D., not unreasonably, as the symbol of that recognition. The university was just as determined to maintain its place at the top of California's educational heap.

By the time Brown and his fellow Democrats swept into power in Sacramento, it was clear that some sort of truce was needed, both to end the biting competition between the colleges and universities and to plan for the inevitable rush of students. The tidal wave had to be channeled, preferably in a logical, careful way. The haphazard free-for-all of the past, whether driven by political pork barreling or educational infighting, had to be controlled.

The eventual result was the grandly named Master Plan for Higher Education, both a closely negotiated peace treaty among rival educational factions and a noble design for the state's future. It also came to be perceived as a big piece of Brown's legacy. When he died his obituary in the *New York Times* hailed the document as "the high point of [his] first term."[10] Textbooks occasionally attributed the plan directly to Brown, and Brown sometimes fostered the idea himself. He often asked young people, "Which one of my colleges are you going to?" Worse, he liked to tell a charming but untrue story that appeared to give him complete credit for the added campuses. In 1958, the tale went, he failed to carry only Santa Cruz, Orange, and San Diego Counties, so he mentioned to his wife that the people there simply had to be educated, and then he built a university campus in each county.[11]

The problem with this canonical version of the Master Plan is that it is misleading at best, false at worst. The story about the three new campuses is just plain wrong. Those were not the only counties Brown lost, the campuses had already been authorized before he took office, and as a regent he favored putting a campus in Santa Clara rather than Santa Cruz County. But more important, the idea that Brown created the Master Plan out of whole cloth obscures a far more complex and engaging story. The Master Plan is a tale not merely of one man's commitment to higher education but also of the nuances and vagaries of public policy, especially of executive leadership. Brown did not conceive the overall plan, or negotiate it, or write it. Rather, he midwifed it. He prodded and pushed and urged. He helped the idea when it was in trouble, left it alone when it was flourishing. And then he made sure the state would spend the money to complete the vision.

———

The Master Plan was in the works even before Brown took office, thanks largely to a change in leadership as dramatic for the University of California as Brown's landslide victory would be for the entire state. Since 1930 the university's presidency had been occupied by Robert Gordon Sproul, a legendary figure on the Berkeley campus who had landed the job when he was only thirty-eight. As a student he had been a drum major and a track star, and as president his rich voice and dazzling oratorical talents allowed him to retain something of a dramatic mien. With the university facing depression-induced budget cuts in 1933, he took to the radio to warn of what the legislature's parsimony might do to California's students. His speech caused a whirlwind. Students wrote home to their parents, asking that they contact local legislators on the university's behalf. Business groups announced their support for the school. Farmers wired the Capitol, alarmed that they might lose agricultural programs. One assemblyman was said to have received two hundred telegrams in two days. The legislature relented, adding back at least some of the money sliced from the budget earlier. A few years later when Sproul was offered the princely sum of $50,000 a year to become the president of a bank—more than three times his current salary—thousands of students gathered in front of the President's House at Berkeley and urged him to stay. He did, winning praise from newspapers for his devotion and sacrifice. From time to time Sproul was even chatted up as gubernatorial material. But by the late 1950s, Sproul was an old man. Weakened by a devastating controversy surrounding a 1949 "loyalty oath" that sundered the university, he had lost some of his magic. So in summer 1958, as Brown was stumping the state in his bid to become governor, the Board of Regents settled on a replacement for the aging

Sproul. They chose Clark Kerr, a specialist in labor negotiations who had spent six years as chancellor of the Berkeley campus.[12]

Kerr was as much the urbane man of learning as Sproul was the grand showman and Brown the glad-handing pol. The son of a farmer-schoolteacher who valued hard work and education, Kerr went to Swarthmore, then arrived at Berkeley in 1933 as a graduate student. He completed his Ph.D. in economics, taught briefly at the University of Washington, and returned to Berkeley to settle in. He was utterly at home in the academy. Balding and bespectacled, he was precise, knowledgeable, and able to speak at length on almost any subject touching on the university, citing details and statistics without the use of a single note. He always remained calm, never raised his voice, and enunciated every syllable of every word. The institution he led was invariably the "u-ni-ver-si-ty," each letter present, never the final *i* slurred over as most people do: *universty*. He could be witty but always in a dry, intellectual vein. Once he said that his main job as chancellor was to provide enough parking for the faculty, athletes for the alumni, and sex for the students. On another occasion he livened up a speech at Harvard with the clever use of a limerick. Then, when the speech was published in a book, he footnoted the poem. It would be hard to say which—the use of the limerick or the use of the footnote—was more Kerr-like.[13]

The institution Kerr inherited from Sproul was unusual in that it was public, vast, and excellent. It was inextricably woven into California's history and society. Founded by an easterner who went west specifically to establish a college, the school had overcome a rocky beginning through the most California of schemes—a risky land development and profitable water deal.[14] The university grew in tandem with its state. Even before the turn of the century it was among the ten biggest universities in the country; by the 1920s it was the biggest. And it was excellent. Well regarded even early in the century, by the postwar years it was clearly one of the best universities in the country. In 1957, just a year before Brown's election as governor and Kerr's appointment as president, a survey of American educators ranked Berkeley third among American universities, behind only Harvard and Yale. Twenty-four of Berkeley's twenty-eight departments were rated "outstanding."[15] Two years later Kerr was able to write to the new governor that of the thirty-five living American Nobel Prize winners who had been educated in the United States, 20 percent held UC degrees. Of the Nobel Prize winners teaching in America, the same proportion—one out of five—was on the UC faculty.[16]

Within the state the university's reach was extraordinary, having grown far beyond the original campus in Berkeley. Medical and law schools churned out California's doctors and lawyers. Scientists designed weapons for the Pentagon, helping to cement the state's status as the home of a burgeoning aerospace industry. Agricultural researchers kept advancing the state's biggest industry, inventing tomato pickers, cotton harvesters, even a mechanical thumb that pressed down on a head of lettuce to determine if it should be cut.[17] The university owned ranches, apartment buildings, forests, hospitals, vineyards, and movie studios. Its campuses—six already, with more in the offing—stretched almost the length of the state. It enrolled almost 47,000 students, offered 7,900 courses, and employed 3,000 professors. *Time* magazine once put Kerr on its cover and noted of his domain: "On its 25,877 acres, a man can freeze or fry without leaving the premises."[18] When Kerr took over the reins in 1958, he was inaugurated in a seventeen-day series of ceremonies that seemed more like a coronation: thirteen receptions, four full-scale academic processions, five inaugural convocations, seven luncheons, four formal banquets, a review of the university's oceangoing research fleet, production of a Greek trilogy and an opera, and a concert of chamber music. To get to it all, the new president traveled more than thirty-five hundred miles.[19]

Once he was done listening to operas and inspecting ships, Kerr settled into his new post and quickly realized he had a rare chance to do something about the unbridled competition between the university and the colleges. From the university's perspective, it was time to seek peace. Combined, the colleges already had twice as many students as the university, and the colleges were growing faster. From the standpoint of pure self-interest, they might have been well advised to do nothing, biding their time until they grew naturally into a competing research institution. "The thing," Kerr would remember years later, "was moving in their direction."[20] Dean McHenry, an old friend of Kerr's from their graduate school days and now a university administrator and Kerr confidant, noted that the university still had more alumni than the colleges. That was an advantage in gaining public support, but given the growth of the colleges, it was an edge that would soon be lost. "If we are ever going to remold the higher education picture nearer our heart's desire," McHenry wrote to Kerr, "we ought to strike soon."[21]

Kerr briefly considered adopting the problem children. If the university absorbed the best of the college campuses, the pressure to share the doctorate would be reduced. The remaining colleges would live on in such a weakened state that they could not threaten the university's preeminence.

Kerr devised a plan to take over the best of the college campuses—San Francisco, San Jose, Fresno, and San Diego—and make them branches of the university. He broached the idea with the college presidents, but they rejected it, justifiably concerned that if they were absorbed they would forever be the poor stepchildren of the university system.[22]

That left Kerr with no choice but a negotiated deal, a prospect certain to involve complicated maneuvers through a network of competing and sometimes hostile interests. The university's Board of Regents would have to approve. So too would the state Board of Education, which operated the state colleges, a remnant from the days when the colleges almost exclusively trained teachers. The legislature would eventually be involved as well. But those players were familiar, each possessing identifiable interests easy to predict from past behavior. By contrast, one potentially important player remained a mystery. The state's new governor had no substantial record on higher-education issues, or any obvious preference among the competing parties, or a pronounced desire to delve into the campus wars. For that matter, he did not even have an undergraduate degree.

———

When Brown took the oath of office in January 1959, he instantly became a critical player in California's system of public colleges and universities. As governor, he was automatically president of the Board of Regents. His predecessors had often skipped the meetings—the press of other business pulling them away—but if a governor of California wished, he could at any time take the gavel and preside over the university's governing body. What was more, Brown would now appoint members to both the Board of Regents and the Board of Education, the two groups crucial to forging a deal. Perhaps most important, Brown would now have enormous influence over state spending and thus over the fiscal health of the campuses.

Brown's inauguration was not greeted with glee at the university. The college presidents were whispering that during a campaign speech months before in Chico, Brown had promised to let the state colleges create Ph.D. programs. Brown later denied saying such a thing, but as he settled in as governor, the rumor coursed through faculty clubs and academic halls, as worrisome to administrators at the university as it was comforting to those at the colleges.[23]

Brown's first budget proposal soothed no nerves. Strapped for cash, the new governor eliminated $24 million in capital requests from the university, arguing that before launching major new building efforts, the University of California should wait until an agreement on new campuses was worked out with the state colleges.[24] It was a reasonable position, but alarm bells still clanged in Berkeley. Accustomed to getting virtually everything they wanted, university administrators were shocked by even the most minor cuts. Brown proposed that general state support for the university be held about even, but administrators had requested an increase, and for many the proposal only reconfirmed doubts about the new governor.[25]

When he discussed the ongoing academic competition—in his diary he called it "a real war"—Brown hardly made it clear which side he was on. "I want to be sure that we don't have a new state college and a new university in the same area and at the same time," he said. "Apparently there hasn't been the coordination."[26]

Kerr was trying to work toward a deal, but he wasn't having much luck. In mid-March, the Board of Regents and the Board of Education met jointly in hopes of reaching an accord. The session went poorly. Roy Simpson, the state superintendent of public instruction and thus overseer of the colleges, pushed ahead with a list of possible new campuses. That infuriated Kerr, who thought there should be a moratorium on new sites until both sides agreed to a long-range plan. In the governor's office, Fred Dutton heard of the meeting's contentious outcome and grew worried that the whole effort to fashion some sort of plan might collapse. From an aide, Dutton ordered up specific recommendations as to what the governor should do "if an indefinite stalemate develops."[27]

Then Malcolm Love, the president of San Diego State College, launched a frontal assault on the university, increasing tension even more. Love suggested not only that the colleges should offer the doctorate, but that they should take most of the enrollment growth expected in the years to come. The university should abolish many of its programs offering master's degrees, Love said, and limit itself to students headed for a professional career or the academic life. In a memo to Kerr, McHenry noted that the university had no proposal ready as an answer. "Tactically, it appears that we were outmaneuvered at the outset," he wrote. "They had a definite proposal in writing; we had some ideas that were fuzzy by comparison." Yet both Kerr and McHenry were sure Love's ideas had to be fought off, for they would limit the university to a small percentage of California's students. The university was proud of its strict academic standards, but it was not about to become so highbrow as to be irrelevant. Kerr worried that Love's proposal would render the university so elitist that it might not survive.[28]

Worse still, the university was failing to present a unified front. The chancellors at Berkeley and UCLA—Glenn Seaborg, a Nobel Prize–winning chemist, and Vern Knudsen, a physicist—had mused about letting the colleges hand out Ph.D.'s. This may have been academically reasonable, but politically it was a foolhardy sacrifice of the university's hard-won standing. "Read the photocopies of their drafts . . . and weep with me," McHenry wrote to Kerr. "Having failed to do their homework, these boys have practically given on a silver platter what we have kept from [the colleges] by force of logic and by power in the Legislature. Deliver us from naïve scientists!"[29]

With progress toward a deal thus stymied, Brown decided to weigh in. In April, to celebrate the triumphs of the new governor's first legislative session, the state Democratic Party rented a plane and sent their new star on a bragging tour of the state, north to south. The two-day trip ended on April 14, the day before the Board of Regents and the Board of Education were to meet for a second time, hoping for a friendlier session than their first try a month before. At his last stop, in San Diego, Brown spoke to a school administrators' convention and turned his attention to the tug-of-war under way between the university and the colleges. After some internal debate among his staff, it had been decided that the governor would attend the next day's meeting and wield the gavel. Brown said bluntly that he intended to warn the boards about the potential consequences of the "vague and increasingly conflicting relationship" between the university and the colleges. "I am determined that practical steps shall be taken to relate their respective responsibilities," Brown said. "If such is not undertaken voluntarily by them—if a psuedo-cooperation should lead to mutual log-rolling by which each approves the projects of the other in order to have license for its own—then we may be compelled to consider other structural possibilities." Duly reported in the next morning's papers just as the two boards prepared to meet for the second time, the threat was obvious. The academicians must come to an agreement, or the politicians would do it for them.[30]

The next day Brown kept the pressure on. Chairing the joint meeting, he urged the two boards to work toward some kind of deal and to do it quickly. When people started talking about a report that might be sent to the legislature by 1961, the governor insisted on 1960, less than a year away. Key legislators had flown in from Sacramento to magnify the message even more, and in league with Brown they gave "a sizzling hotfoot" to the educators, as one reporter put it. Successfully pushed, both panels voted to create a joint committee that would develop a long-range plan before the end of the year. Brown told reporters after the meeting that it had been "a fine first step." He was referring to the overall meeting, but the phrase just as aptly described his own role. The governor had embraced a posture that would prove greatly useful during the negotiations to follow: He would stand to the side, using his power and that of the legislature as a looming threat to the academicians, impelling them toward an agreement.[31]

———

Privately, the relationship between Brown and Kerr was strained. In later years they would become friendly, sometimes attending UC Berkeley football games together, but in the early going there was tension. They were starkly different—Brown the gregarious backslapping pol, Kerr the studious intellectual—and by summer their relationship was so touchy that surrogates were bemoaning the bad blood.

"I am sad at the way the university-gubernatorial relations have worked out, but still think that Clark and Pat are natural allies," UC Berkeley political scientist Eugene Burdick wrote to Dutton. Dutton answered that he hoped to have lunch with Kerr and some of his lieutenants "to try to mend some difficult personal relations at the moment." Dutton knew things were getting worse: "At the last meeting of Kerr and the governor, I was in Los Angeles and hoped perhaps there might be an improvement in the situation. Unfortunately, I gathered from both sides that the reverse was true."[32]

Fortunately, trouble between the governor and the university president was not an impediment to developing the long-range plan, a task that had been delegated to a panel of educators. To head the team, Kerr and Simpson agreed on Arthur Coons, the president of Occidental College in Los Angeles and a grand old man in California higher education. There had been some talk that the job might go to A. Alan Post, the legislature's chief policy analyst, but he was rejected in part because the job would give him a chance to rummage through the university's books. "I mention to you also," McHenry wrote to Kerr in a memo advising against Post's selection, "the danger that such a role might provide the opportunity for Alan to dig into delicate matters of teaching load, expense accounts and other matters which the university has tended to obscure."[33]

Glenn Dumke, the president of San Francisco State College, was the main representative of the state colleges. McHenry served the same role for the university. But it was often a process controlled from the top. McHenry talked to Kerr almost daily, and Dumke was under just as tight a rein. Forced to request frequent breaks so he could consult higher-ups by telephone, Dumke began to ask for recesses by saying, "Sorry, on this one I have to go call Moscow," a line McHenry soon adopted.[34] Though not directly involved, the governor's office at least kept tabs, detailing a staff member to spend two or three days a week tracking the issue.[35]

Less contentious matters were resolved quickly, but the toughest point—the prideful battle over the right to confer the Ph.D.—dragged on without resolution through the summer and into the fall. By November the governor was turning up the pressure, as he had the previous spring. Higher education needed some sort of coherent plan, he said, and he wanted the educators to develop something soon.[36] At the end of the month, the newspapers were quoting a more blatant threat. "If they don't come up with something," Brown said, echoing his own comments from months before, "we will do it ourselves."[37]

The regents and the Board of Education were to meet jointly again in mid-December to hear recommendations from the negotiating team, but as the meeting date approached it was by no means clear there would be agreement on what to present. Desperate, Kerr cobbled together an informal meeting of the key figures one night in his Berkeley office. Stealing an idea from a joint Ph.D. program he had read about—memories vary as to whether it was in Indiana or Michigan—Kerr proposed a similar agreement for California. Speaking for the colleges, Dumke insisted that the schools needed the prestige of the Ph.D., that they could never agree to a role of endless deference to the university. The colleges, Kerr replied, were holding open the idea of growing into a second full-fledged research institution, exactly what the state could not afford and the university feared. More to the point, what the colleges really wanted was a new governing board, separate from the Board of Education. Ideally, the new entity would be placed in the state constitution, a mark of independence already possessed, and cherished, by the university's regents. But it was the university that had the power in the legislature to make that happen, Kerr said. Without the university's backing, the colleges could not win the freedom they craved even more than the Ph.D. So the two sides struck a deal, to be sent first to the university's Board of Regents and the state Board of Education and then to the legislature.[38]

The proposal boiled down to a simple trade. The colleges agreed to abandon their quest to award the doctorate, satisfying themselves with the half-measure Kerr had proposed: joint Ph.D. programs involving both the colleges and the university. In return the university would use its lobbying power in Sacramento to help the colleges win their constitutional independence, thus freeing them from the most invasive meddling by the legislature. (That offered a side benefit to the university; if the deal were locked into the constitution, the colleges would have a harder time changing it later.)

The other critical component of the deal was that the university and the colleges agreed to raise their admissions standards. The university, which had admitted students from the top 15 percent of high school classes, trimmed that to 12.5 percent. The colleges moved their bar from the top 40 to 50 percent (calculations varied) to the top one-third. The changes, it was projected at the time, would divert about fifty thousand prospective students from the university and the four-year colleges into junior colleges. Accordingly, the junior college system would be greatly expanded. The university and the college system would go ahead with new campuses already on the drawing boards and with two new college campuses specifically mentioned in the proposed deal, but no more. No other new campuses would be built until there were sufficient junior colleges in the area. This was critical, for it produced the most statesmanlike aspect of the Master Plan. Because it was cheaper to build and operate junior colleges than four-year schools, the state could promise a larger expansion, so large that it could ensure a place for every high school graduate who wanted a college education. That guarantee of "universal access" received less attention at the time, while the plan was being negotiated, but eventually became the bragging point of the Master Plan, cited proudly by California's educators and politicians alike.[39]

———

Exactly one week before Christmas, the Board of Regents and the Board of Education met in Berkeley to consider the deal, now formally dubbed the Master Plan. It was approved unanimously. Talking to reporters, Brown said it was "the high step forward in higher education in the state of California." He took the opportunity to portray the higher-education deal as a template for California. Given the state's hurly-burly population growth, long-range plans were needed for everything from mental hospitals to penitentiaries to recreation facilities, he said.[40]

But for all the excitement, Brown avoided an endorsement of the new plan's details. And he signaled that as the plan moved from the academic world to the political one, the greatest focus of controversy was shifting too. To the educators, the critical point of contention had been control of the Ph.D. To the politicians, the great issue was the proposed constitutional independence for the colleges. In the Capitol, minds naturally focused less on who would confer advanced degrees and more on who would control the purse strings. On that issue the governor remained uncertain. "I'm interested to find out how much of a limitation on the fiscal control of the governor and the legislature creation of the new board would involve," he told reporters. "But that doesn't mean I disapprove of the suggestion. I intend to keep an open mind and review the matter carefully."[41]

The regular 1960 legislative session was limited to the state budget, so in January, one year to the day after taking office, Brown called a special session of the legislature to consider the new higher-education plan. A little grandly, he phrased the issue in Cold War terms. "If—as we all pray—the epic contest in which the world is involved is not settled on the battlefield, it will be settled in the classrooms and laboratories," Brown insisted. "It is here that we can best serve the cause of freedom."[42]

But he still indicated nothing about his position on the fundamental practical dispute, whether the plan should be locked into the state constitution. When legislators arrived in Sacramento for the special session three weeks later, the governor remained on the fence. He insisted that as a regent he had voted for the Master Plan "with some reservation." Some changes might be needed. "I have not as yet made up my mind," he said. Asked specifically if it was wise to reduce the legislature's control over higher education by giving the colleges fiscal independence, Brown said simply that he wanted to "leave the door slightly ajar in that connection."[43]

———

Before deciding the constitutional issue, Brown had to deal with one criticism of the plan that was coming from his own office. Don Leiffer, the lead staffer on higher-education issues, believed the whole thing was basically elitist. Top students, Leiffer noted, would enjoy the university's advantages: bigger and better campuses, with better buildings, more extensive facilities, better-paid faculty members. Lesser students would be shunted to lesser schools, either state colleges or junior colleges. "The greatest block of students will be entitled to go to institutions with the lowest student per-capita expenditures," he noted. This had always been true, but now it would be worse, since the university would raise its admission standards. Worse still, the schools serving the bulk of students—the colleges—would be forever hog-tied. The university, Leiffer noted, was trying to "promote itself and protect its well-deserved prestige by arbitrarily and artificially placing limits on the growth of other, and presumably competing, institutions. It is difficult to subscribe to the argument that greatness in an educational institution can be furthered by placing a ceiling on education development elsewhere."[44]

There were plenty of faculty members at the colleges echoing Leiffer's argument, but in early February Brown effectively rejected it, characteristically opting for the possible over the ideal. "None of these things are perfect," he told reporters, "but I think they're far better than the haphazard fighting for state college sites and things that we have been running through here in this state for the last 20 years. There has been no planning whatsoever, and it's destructive of higher education and is costing and has cost the people millions of dollars."[45]

On the more controversial issue of whether large chunks of the deal should be put in the state constitution—and thus protected from legislative tampering—Brown was being urged by many in the Capitol to say no. The university's vaunted status—so sacred a touchstone to the faculty— was a nuisance to the legislature. Lawmakers had long resented their limited control over the vast sums spent at Berkeley and, in more recent years, Los Angeles. They also liked their ability not only to influence, but if necessary to command, the state colleges. The power to order the creation of a campus back home was as valuable politically as it was imprudent academically. No matter its provisions, a plan enacted only in statute could be changed by the legislature at any time. The law might say that no new campuses would be built, for example, but any legislator able to corral the votes could simply rewrite the law. Putting the plan into the constitution would require a vote of the people and then would require another vote to change any of the provisions. Now the Master Plan threatened to give to the colleges precisely the kind of maddening freedom the university already possessed. George Miller, the governor's ally in the state senate, bluntly told Glenn Dumke that the constitutional provisions were a dead letter. "If you think that we are going to give you constitutional status and remove you from our control in the way the university is removed from our control, you've got another think coming. We're never going to do it."[46]

The university had foreseen that. Weeks before the special session opened, James Corley, the university's lobbyist in Sacramento, passed word to Kerr that such autonomy "will not be accepted at this time by the Department of Finance, legislative analyst and many legislators."[47] By the end of the month, Corley had become blunter about Capitol reaction. In a terse memo, he said he had been told there was "too much 'garbage' proposed to be placed in the constitution."[48]

Still, nobody from higher education wanted to give up. For the colleges, the importance of a constitutional amendment was obvious: They would finally be free of legislative shackles. But, ironically, Kerr and the UC contingent also wanted to write the deal into political stone. For the university, a key piece of the whole idea was to effectively lock the colleges into permanent educational second place by denying them the Ph.D. In the constitution, such a prohibition would be more or less permanent, safe at least from legislative tinkering. But if it were merely a provision of law, the legislature could at any time allow the colleges to begin offering the doctorate. "The stability we sought cannot be attained if each biennium we must fight off revisionists who wish to alter the pattern of assigned functions," McHenry wrote to Kerr.[49]

McHenry was already trying to drum up public support for the original deal. Like a politician on the hustings, he was traveling almost constantly, speaking two and three times a week at Rotary Clubs or YWCAs.[50] He wasn't the only one. The university was running the rough equivalent of a speaker's bureau on behalf of the plan.[51] Corley and his fellow lobbyists were working too, playing on long-standing relationships in the Capitol. It was the kind of thing the university was good at, mostly because the school used every tool it had to make and keep friends. Each year every legislator got two free season tickets for football games, for example: UCLA for lawmakers from the south, Berkeley for those from the north. They were good seats, and the university even assigned a staff member to ensure that political enemies were not placed next to one another.[52]

Yet for all its connections, the university made little headway in the legislature. Donald Grunsky, a rural Republican who chaired the senate's Education Committee, introduced a bill implementing the Master Plan more or less as drafted by the academicians, complete with constitutional independence for the new state college board. Miller quickly rallied the votes to kill that proposal, favoring instead his own bill, which didn't include most of the constitutional provisions.[53]

Desperate, the academics turned to new strategies, including some that in retrospect seem a little odd. In a memo to Kerr, McHenry mused that perhaps the Master Plan should be given "an aloof name" such as "The Organic Act of California Higher Education," which might discourage future legislative tampering. But in the end he acknowledged that no legislature can bind a future version of itself—the law can always be changed—so they might do no better than a compromise. Their only real hope in the short run was to convince the governor that his own party's legislators were wrong. "In the meantime," McHenry said in the memo, "try to enlist the active support of the governor. His own silence has induced much of the wrangling."[54]

Brown had not really been silent—he had hinted from the beginning that he might oppose a plan that included constitutional provisions—but neither had he weighed in with certainty. In late March, he finally did so, although even then he used a surrogate. Kerr and the key academic players were called up to the governor's office to be given the bad news. Miller played the heavy, telling the educators that the constitutional provisions were a dead issue. There was a silence, and then the governor, always the friendly consensus builder, jumped in to suggest that everybody simply agree on a statutory plan. Brown didn't need to speak. Kerr would recall years later, "As soon as George committed himself, I knew that was the end of it."[55] Brown issued a brief statement backing the legislation as it stood, which did not include most of the constitutional provisions.[56]

Two days later, the educators publicly surrendered, with Kerr, Simpson, and the heads of both the regents and the Board of Education issuing a written statement accepting the statutory language. Thus stripped down, the bill passed the senate easily, 36–1.[57]

Kerr sent a note to Miller, both to celebrate the plan's passage and to gently needle the lawmaker about the one key topic on which the politicians had rejected the educators' plan. "Great appreciation for your interest and understanding and hard work on the Master Plan," Kerr wrote. "Some real progress has been made." Still, he added, the "best solution" would have been a permanent one in which the changes were written into the constitution. "Perhaps some other time."[58]

———

Dorothy Donahoe was never an enormously influential figure in the legislature generally or in the Master Plan specifically. Although she chaired the assembly Education Committee, such issues were not her primary interest. Treatment of the disabled was her passion, perhaps because of a childhood bout with polio that left her with a pronounced limp and a long and difficult battle with asthma that required her to carry an inhaler. She authored the resolution calling for creation of the Master Plan primarily because it was brought to her by the lobbyist for the university, an institution of which, like many legislators, she was in awe. As the plan progressed, she was not always involved in the crucial meetings. Years later her aide, Keith Sexton, remembered once sitting in George Miller's office as he and his allies plotted strategy on the Master Plan. They would puff on big cigars and hatch their plans, then turn to Sexton and mockingly ask, "Think that will be all right with Dorothy?" as if her opposition might have killed any of their schemes.

But Donahoe was well liked, her toughness evidenced by her mere presence in what was then still very much a man's world. She was one of only two women in the legislature and had shown spunk to get there. When the Bakersfield school district, where she worked when she first ran for the assembly, denied her a leave of absence she simply quit her job and started campaigning.

So it was unfortunate that she could not preside over her committee when the Master Plan, having passed the senate, finally came up for a hearing on a Monday in early April. Despite a bad cold, Donahoe had gone to Bakersfield over the weekend for a political dinner she felt she could not miss, and by the time she returned to Sacramento she was too sick to chair the meeting. She stayed home, and the panel's vice chairman, Carlos Bee, saw the measure through. There was some tension at the hearing. Two powerful groups, California's biggest teachers' union and the state employees retirement system, had objected to minor provisions, so there was some relief when an agreement was hammered out and the bill passed. Sexton and his wife headed for a celebratory drink at the hotel suite maintained by Jim Corley, the university's lobbyist. While they were there, there was a call for Sexton from Sen. Walt Stiern, who also represented Bakersfield and was a friend of Donahoe's. Stiern had gone to check on her and found her unconscious. A Christian Scientist, Donahoe had refused to see a doctor, and the cold had apparently turned into pneumonia. She was taken to a hospital, where she died that night. The following day the bill was renamed the Donahoe Higher Education Act and then passed unanimously by the assembly. Three weeks later the governor signed it into law.[59]

———

In the years that followed, the Master Plan came to be celebrated as one of the great accomplishments of its day, although it was never without critics.

The joint doctoral program that had been so crucial to negotiating the deal never truly flourished, perhaps because it was caught tenuously between the university and the colleges, loved by neither. One college president joked that the idea of a Ph.D. issued by two schools had "all the ambiguities of a mermaid, only with far less allure." More significant, there were faculty members at the colleges who complained vehemently that the Master Plan was really a "Master Sham," nothing but a ruse that protected the university from competition and kept it atop the pecking order.[60]

There was some truth to the complaints, but in the most important respects, the Master Plan worked. The political warfare for campuses was lessened—although never eliminated—and the plan codified a system of public higher education that remained, in many respects, the envy of the nation. California's public colleges and universities grew at an extraordinary pace. Including the junior colleges, enrollment roughly doubled while Brown was in office, a burst of growth that kept California's college attendance rates well above the national average. It was true that many of those students had no choice but to attend a junior college, but given the size of the coming generation, that had been the only affordable alternative. One historian of the topic, John Aubrey Douglass, concluded that the Master Plan "fulfilled its basic promise, fostering ordered growth at a manageable cost to the people of California."[61]

Not that the cost was negligible, and Brown met it with more enthusiasm than any of his predecessors. In the years after the Master Plan was adopted, the governor and the legislature poured unprecedented millions into higher education. From Brown's first budget to his last, state spending on the university more than doubled, on the colleges more than tripled.[62] The results were literally concrete. During Brown's administration, four new state colleges were opened, a total unmatched by the next four governors combined. Three new university campuses were built during Brown's time; during the next thirty years, the state added none.

It was a record that made Brown justly proud, but even before the construction began he was convinced that the Master Plan was yet another reason to boast about California. When he signed it, in spring 1960, he insisted that his state had seized "the lead among the nation's states in giving direction and purpose to higher education."[63] He could not have known that in a few short years, the glittering flagship of California's academic fleet would become a place of such trouble and turbulence that it would help swamp his career.

8   ANGUISH

IF BROWN'S FIRST YEAR brought astonishing successes—the glory of the 1959 legislative session, the development of the higher education Master Plan—
there was one issue that hung over him. Before long, everyone knew, he
would have to deal with the death penalty, the public policy issue that bothered him more than all others. And he would have to do it flush in the glare
of international publicity.

On the state's death row at San Quentin Prison, just across the Golden Gate
Bridge from San Francisco, California held the world's most famous prison inmate, Caryl Whittier Chessman. When he arrived on death row, Chessman
was just another convicted felon and Brown was still the district attorney of
San Francisco, but before their shared drama would be completed, the story
would mark indelibly all its participants, even the state where it occurred.

For Chessman, it was the fight to save his life, although the struggle eventually attracted the attention of Marlon Brando, Albert Schweitzer, and the
queen of Belgium.[1] For Brown, it was an example of how his best instincts—those that had led him to the height of power and popularity—
could take him just as easily down the path of self-ruin. For California, it
was a story that added yet again to the fame of the place, revealing along
the way both the present and the future. The Chessman case occurred at
the apex of liberal conscience and compassion, yet it hinted at a nascent
conservative urge that eventually would dominate the politics of the state

and then the nation. As nothing had before, the Chessman case roiled Californians' emotions and ushered in a troubled decade. Before it was done, the story of Caryl Chessman and Pat Brown became, in the words of the governor's closest aide, "law and sex and bloodlust incarnate. . . . It was deep in the psyche of the state."[2]

––––––––

Caryl Whittier Chessman claimed that his middle name was the bequest of a distant ancestor, the poet John Greenleaf Whittier. If true, the genes had weakened, for Chessman's early life offered no hint of inherited greatness.

He was born in Michigan, but when he was still a tot the family moved to Southern California for the most typical of reasons: sunshine and opportunity. His father hoped to make a fortune in the movie business, but it did not come to pass. The elder Chessman bounced from job to job, until eventually the Great Depression forced the family onto the dole, humiliating their only son. When Caryl was nine his mother was paralyzed in a car accident, and eventually his father, worn down by their woes, tried twice to commit suicide.

By the time he was a teenager, Caryl's troubled home led to a troubled life. Smart, argumentative, often friendless, he began stealing groceries, then cars for joy rides. First arrested at sixteen for auto theft, he escaped from the local juvenile hall but was picked up hours later while burglarizing a drugstore. His rage at the world was obvious: Rather than take anything, he simply piled up the store's cigars and smashed whiskey bottles over them.

After his release, Chessman proved he was recidivism defined, stealing cars, robbing people, at least once shooting it out with the police. He spent time in a variety of juvenile institutions, including the state-run Preston Industrial School in Ione, near Sacramento, hundreds of miles from home. After his eighteenth birthday, he began a grand tour of California's adult prisons: San Quentin, Folsom, and a model minimum-security facility at Chino from which he quickly and easily escaped. Freedom was an oddity; inevitably he was back in custody almost instantly. When he was paroled in December 1947, he had been incarcerated for nearly the entire decade since he turned sixteen.[3]

The month after Chessman's parole, Los Angeles experienced a spate of crimes that might have been overlooked in later years but was big news at the time. A man with a gun, sometimes wearing a handkerchief across his face, robbed several drivers and their passengers. Often he preyed on couples parked on lovers' lanes; usually he began the crime by shining a red spotlight on their cars, perhaps to make them believe he was a police officer. Two of the cases went far beyond robbery. Twice the robber took women back to his car, where he forced them to perform oral sex, and in one case he attempted to rape his victim as well.

The day after the second sexual attack, the victim of which was only seventeen years old, Chessman and another man were arrested after a robbery at a men's clothing store in Redondo Beach. The clothing store robbery was an easy case to make: The car the men were driving contained many of the pilfered items. The police maintained that during subsequent questioning, Chessman admitted to the crimes of the "Red Light Bandit," as the papers had dubbed the case, and some of the victims picked Chessman from a lineup. Chessman insisted that police fists beat the confession from him and that problems tainted the identifications. One of his accusers, for example, saw him being questioned by detectives before the lineup, an obvious tip-off that he was the suspect.[4]

Fairly or not—the arguments about his guilt or innocence would rage for years—Chessman was charged with eighteen felonies, almost all attributed to the Red Light Bandit. The most important counts came under the state's so-called Little Lindbergh Law, one of many such statutes enacted around the country after the kidnapping of the aviator's son in 1932. California's law provided for the death penalty if an abduction was committed in the course of a robbery and if it involved bodily harm. Kidnapping was broadly defined, and the Red Light Bandit's two sex crimes qualified: The women had been moved during the attacks, and any movement against a person's will, no matter how minor, met the kidnapping statute.

Pride and penury caused Chessman to represent himself at trial, a disastrous decision that was only worsened when he drew a sixty-six-year-old trial judge named Charles F. Fricke, whose favoritism for prosecutors and penchant for long prison terms had earned him the courthouse nickname "San Quentin Fricke."[5] Chessman staggered through the trial as best he could, but he made one mistake after another on technical matters, and he was hamstrung by Fricke's procedural rulings, which consistently supported the prosecution. On May 21, 1948, the jury convicted Chessman and, in the two cases involving sexual assaults, sentenced him to the gas chamber.

A month later the case took a strange twist that eventually became critical. Ernest R. Perry, a visibly decrepit old man who had served as the court reporter, died of a massive heart attack. Chessman pointed out at his formal sentencing, which came two days after Perry's death, that Perry had yet to transcribe most of his notes. That was a major concern—before the days of reporting machines, clerks used old-fashioned shorthand, which could be difficult to read—but the judge waived off the issue and accepted the prosecutor's promise that the district attorney's office would help finish the task. The man chosen for the work did nothing to inspire confidence. He had a long history of drunkenness and was the prosecutor's uncle to boot. The result was a dubious product—a judge later ordered hundreds of corrections—and in the years to come the quality of the trial transcript, on which Chessman had to rely for his appeals, became the main appellate issue over which the two sides wrangled. Without it, Chessman's appeals might have run their course before Brown became governor, or perhaps even before Chessman became famous.[6]

The renown came from neither his crimes nor his legal tactics but from his writing. He had long dreamed of a literary career, and in prison he began to pursue it with zeal. The result was *Cell 2455, Death Row,* a dramatized, exaggerated, occasionally fabricated account of Chessman's life. It appeared on May 3, 1954, just eleven days before the scheduled date for the author's execution, and from the beginning the book caused a sensation. The *New York Times* praised it, as did the *Saturday Review.* There were even comments from Negley Teeters and Harry Elmer Barnes, the famous criminologists whose book Pat Brown, as a young district attorney, had praised as a forward-thinking tome of modern penology. Chessman should be spared, they said, so that scholars might study him, the better to understand criminal inclinations and successful rehabilitation.[7]

The condemned man's popularity quickly spread to more than book reviewers and academics. Chessman became a celebrity. Movie stars began to agitate on his behalf. Writers proclaimed him an artist. Women wrote to those who knew him to ask about his personal qualities. Several female fans mentioned marriage; one enclosed a picture of herself.[8] It was said that eventually *Cell 2455* sold more than five hundred thousand copies and was translated into more than a dozen languages.[9]

With fame came riches, and Chessman began hiring a series of lawyers and investigators to work on his appeals. The result was that the battle to save Chessman's life stretched forward until it would snare California's most powerful politician.

———

Capital punishment was the open wound of Pat Brown's soul. Years as a prosecutor notwithstanding, he never came to comfort with the idea that the state might rightly take a life. In part his objection was professional. He believed that the death penalty was no deterrent, that it wasted time and money in the justice system, and that it sometimes made heroes of the very criminals it sought to punish with finality. But there was a personal side too: Brown's Catholic faith, an innate belief in the goodness of people, a naturally sympathetic nature. By training and temperament, Brown was a man of mercy.

As early as 1942, even before he was elected district attorney, Brown found a pending execution an occasion for compassion. He wrote to Culbert Olson, who had just lost his bid for a second term as governor, and asked him to commute the sentences of three young men scheduled to die in San Quentin's gas chamber. It was true that the men had "a long record of crime behind them," but Brown added cryptically that his knowledge of the case, presumably gleaned from his contacts as a lawyer, led him to conclude that "fate has played a terrible part in putting these boys in the gas chamber." If only Olson were to search the case sufficiently, he could find a reason to spare their lives. "This act of mercy," Brown wrote, would "live with you the rest of your days." Two days later, the day of the scheduled executions, Olson's chief of staff, Stanley Mosk, the bright young lawyer who would go on to succeed Brown as attorney general, wrote back. In an odd foreshadowing that no one could then have understood, Mosk explained that because the condemned men had prior felony convictions, the governor could offer no clemency without the approval of the state supreme court, and the justices had refused.[10]

Sympathy was always Brown's reaction in the face of the death penalty. Once, when he was district attorney, he personally handled a capital case but found himself so moved by the defense attorney's closing argument that he stood up and asked the jury to convict the defendant but return a sentence of life in prison. "Even at that time I was a softy on the death penalty," he said later. "I just couldn't kill those people. . . . I did believe in the death penalty then, I really did. But when I was the prosecutor, I just couldn't do it."[11]

On another occasion, he wisely passed up the chance to witness an execution, heeding the advice of two police detectives who told him that if he did he would never again prosecute a capital case. (More than forty years later, Brown finally visited San Quentin's death row for the first time but did not see anyone put to death.)[12]

As attorney general, Brown's beliefs only deepened, and he began to speak about the issue more often. Capital punishment offended his most basic sense of decency. Executions "cheapen human life." They reflected simplistic, ancient beliefs that were better abandoned. "We would consider it revolting to actually take an eye for an eye or a limb for a limb," he wrote once, yet executing a man was considered acceptable by many. Nor was the law fair: In some California counties death sentences were sought regularly, in others hardly at all. The effect was to "bring the whole of law enforcement into disrepute." And it was for naught: Capital punishment failed to deter crime "in any way, shape or manner." He repeatedly supported bills in the legislature to impose a moratorium on executions, which failed as regularly as they were introduced.[13]

Brown first bumped into the Chessman case in May 1954, just days after *Cell 2455* was published and a few months before Brown would easily be re-elected to a second term as attorney general. Less than twenty-four hours before he was scheduled to die, Chessman won a temporary reprieve from a judge in Marin County, where San Quentin was located. Although an opponent of the death penalty, Brown was furious. However unwise or immoral, capital punishment was the law in California, and Brown believed it should be enforced, quickly and without the circus the Chessman case was fast becoming. In a speech to law students at Loyola University in Los Angeles, Brown attacked the judge for interfering in a case that had already gone to both the state supreme court and the U.S. Supreme Court. He told the students that the stay was an "unwarranted intrusion" that threatened the "integrity of the judicial process," intemperate language that caused the judge to threaten him with contempt. Ever the conciliator, Brown called and apologized.[14]

But Brown did not lessen his objections to the death penalty or to the protracted courtroom maneuvering. Weeks later on a San Francisco television show, *What's Your Opinion?* he complained that the Chessman case, with its famous defendant and endless appeals, was making a felon into a hero and the legal system into a laughingstock. The squalid scene, he insisted, was yet another argument for abolishing the death penalty altogether.[15]

After another stay—in this case one of Chessman's lawyers rode a burro into the Trinity Alps to track down a California supreme court justice on a camping trip and convinced him to sign the order—Brown grew so frustrated that he asked Gov. Goodwin Knight to postpone the deaths of two other men who had been scheduled to go to the gas chamber the same day as Chessman. "I want to make it clear that I'm doing this simply because a stay has been granted to Chessman," Brown told reporters. "There's no reason why a man who can write a book should have an advantage that these two other apparently friendless people do not have."[16]

Brown eventually regretted his role in whipping up public indignation at Chessman's legal struggle, but at the time the length of the case was extraordinary. Beginning in the mid-1960s, opponents of the death penalty habitually used the courts to delay executions, often for years. But before that, the focus was instead on abolishing capital punishment politically, or winning executive clemency in individual cases. Decade-long appellate campaigns, soon to be a staple of American capital cases, were extremely rare. By 1954, after just six years, Chessman had been on death row longer than any other man in California history.[17]

So it was no surprise that in the Department of Justice Brown's deputies were doing what they could to shorten the courtroom machinations and put Chessman in the gas chamber. Clarence Linn, a holdover from the previous attorney general and a man distrusted by some of Brown's inner circle, became Chessman's primary antagonist. On behalf of the Department of Corrections—like most state agencies, the prison system was represented by the attorney general's office—Linn opposed every attempt at delay, fighting to lift judicial stays and move forward with the execution.

Linn even tried to cut off Chessman's source of funding—his writing. After the success of *Cell 2455* San Quentin officials prohibited inmates from outside publishing. Chessman, clever and resourceful as always, managed to smuggle out additional manuscripts and get them to his publisher in New York, infuriating his prison keepers. Linn threatened to take legal action to prevent publication. That was too much for Brown, who had to publicly rein in his own deputy. The smuggling, Brown said, was "the damnedest thing I've ever seen." But he forbade further attempts to block publication. "Once books get out, I am not going to act as a censor," he said. "I am not going to fool around with that sort of thing."[18]

———

Brown's election to the governorship put him at the heart of the capital punishment debate—and in an intense new way. As in most states, California's constitution granted the governor a broad power of clemency. Ruled largely by conscience and judgment, the governor could pardon inmates of their crimes or commute their sentences to a lesser term, for example, from death to life in prison. Yet the death penalty also remained the law of the state, and Brown took seriously his sworn oath to uphold the law, disagree with it though he might. If the legislature were to abolish capital punishment, so much the better, but in the meantime he had no intention of implementing an abolition by fiat, commuting every case that came before him. The result was a man left to struggle with individual cases, deciding, based on little more than his gut, whether a person should live or die.

There was no grace period. The day after the inauguration, Cecil Poole, the governor's clemency secretary, walked into Brown's office with the first of many torments for his spirit. Poole, who would play a critical role in all of Brown's early clemency decisions, including Chessman, had been hired as a deputy district attorney by Brown in the old San Francisco days. In his new job he was the governor's chief aide on death penalty cases, although he was much tougher than his boss. Poole was so hard-line a prosecutor that his office nickname was "Ropes"—a macabre half-joke intimating that he wanted to hang everybody. But he was also a fierce defender of the governor. Dealing as he did with an emotional issue, Poole sometimes encountered passionate criticism of Brown, and he invariably returned it, decibel for decibel and adjective for adjective. Some law enforcement officials grew to dislike Poole so intensely that they gave him a second nickname, "Cesspool," a play on his name that surely reflected racism—Poole was black—as well as animosity.[19]

Poole's unpleasant message on Brown's first full day as governor was that an execution was scheduled at San Quentin in ten days, and if Brown wished to hold a clemency hearing he would have to say so quickly. It was hardly what Brown wanted to hear—no politician hopes to begin a new job with a leap into the churning emotional waters of the death penalty—and he told Poole to do nothing.

But at the mansion that night, talking with Bernice about his new duties, the case nagged at him. He called for the file the next day and began reading about John Russell Crooker, the man scheduled to die in little more than a week. Crooker was a law school student who had killed his former lover, a woman for whom he had once worked as a houseboy. Jilted, Crooker went to her home and hid, then confronted her and tried to convince her to continue their affair. She refused and eventually fell asleep. Crooker took a knife he found in the room and stabbed her to death. It was a gruesome crime—one of her young children found the mangled body the next day—but there was no evidence of premeditation or profit, and the trial judge wrote a note saying that he thought Crooker might someday be rehabilitated into a useful citizen. Brown told Poole he had changed his mind; he would hold a clemency hearing after all.

The meeting lasted an hour—Crooker's sister pleaded his basic decency; a psychiatrist described past mental problems—but Brown made up his mind before it was over. Always inclined toward second chances, Brown decided to commute Crooker's sentence to life in prison without the possibility of parole. Nothing could bring back the victim, Brown told Poole, and executing Crooker seemed unlikely to deter others from killing a former lover in a fit of rage. The hearing was on a Friday; the following Monday Brown signed Crooker's commutation. (Eight years later, as Brown was leaving office, he commuted Crooker and some other inmates again, revising their sentences to allow for parole. Crooker got out in 1972 and went on to a productive life, at least until 1978, when he visited Brown briefly in his law office.)[20]

Over the next nine months Brown held ten more clemency hearings. In three cases judges issued stays, delaying the executions and saving Brown from a decision. Four times he denied clemency and allowed the execution, each time a murderer, two of them convicted of sex crimes as well. Of the three cases in which he commuted a sentence, two stood out: Eddie Wein and Harold Langdon.[21]

Wein had been convicted of raping eight women, all by employing a ruse that earned him a nickname. He answered newspaper ads offering items for sale or rooms for rent. Feigning interest, he talked his way into the house to see if the woman placing the ad was alone. If so, he grabbed her, bound her, and raped her. The papers dubbed him the "want-ad rapist." Langdon had a less distinctive criminal past: He had gone into a Western Union office, ordered a clerk into the back room, and raped her.

The two cases drew attention because they were so analogous to Chessman's. None of the three men—Wein, Langdon, Chessman—had killed anyone, and yet they had been sentenced to die. All had committed sexual assaults on their victims. All had been convicted under the Lindbergh law, although in each case the kidnapping charge was somewhat technical, the result of moving a person a relatively short distance for a relatively short time. Because the cases offered so many similarities to Chessman's, in other words, the Wein and Langdon commutations seemed to suggest that Brown might consider clemency for the world-famous inmate with whom he was about to deal.

———

By fall 1959, as Brown basked in the acclaim of his first legislative session and approached his one-year anniversary in office, Chessman's long fight was waning. The old conflicts about the trial transcript had finally been resolved.

The California supreme court upheld the convictions. The U.S. Supreme Court rejected yet another petition. With the legal avenues closing, it seemed clear that the case would turn soon toward the issue of gubernatorial clemency. This had happened before. Over the years Chessman had twice been denied clemency, most recently by Goodwin Knight and, before that, by Earl Warren, who indulged a rare poetic impulse and penned a handwritten rejection that referred to Chessman's "abandoned heart."[22]

For Brown, the issue came to a head in early October. Chessman's execution was set for October 24, and the governor's office informed his lawyers that any request for a clemency hearing would have to be made quickly. Following precedent, Brown had decided that he would hold a hearing only if the inmate requested it. Some men sought no mercy. In the ten months Brown had been governor, two murderers had already gone to the gas chamber without appealing for clemency.[23]

At first it appeared that Chessman would take the same path. Poole wrote to Chessman's attorneys and told them that if they sought a hearing, there would be no need to argue their client's innocence. Brown had dealt with the case for years, of course, and was convinced that Chessman was guilty. An appeal for clemency would need to be based on a plea for mercy, not vindication.

Ever prickly, Chessman fired back an obstreperous letter denouncing the governor's conditions as a "coercive ultimatum" that would force him to effectively admit his guilt, something he had steadfastly refused to do.[24] Maintaining that he was an innocent man who should be set free, Chessman insisted he would never beg for a sentence of life rather than death. His lawyers were more practical, and the day before the governor's deadline they won Chessman's grudging permission to ask for a hearing. The request was granted and the hearing set for October 15, a Thursday, just nine days before the scheduled execution.

Brown dealt with the Chessman case amid a public mood strikingly different from that of later years. The United States, along with much of the developed world, experienced in the wake of World War II an increased opposition to the death penalty, perhaps a reaction to the state-sanctioned murder perpetrated by Nazi Germany.[25] In California, polls showed that about 50 to 55 percent of the population supported capital punishment, far lower than before or after.[26] In the late 1950s and early 1960s, denunciations of capital punishment came not just from liberals and intellectuals, but from law enforcement circles as well. Richard McGee, longtime director of the state Department of Corrections, openly opposed the death penalty, calling frequently for its elimination. Clinton Duffy, famous as the reformer warden at San Quentin, hated capital punishment so vehemently that he advocated public executions so as to foment revulsion at the practice.[27] Far more than their successors, Duffy and his contemporaries believed that prisons might reform the men within their walls. At San Quentin, Duffy improved the library, authorized production of a radio program, and started the first prison chapter of Alcoholics Anonymous.[28] Brown was a fellow disciple of gentler treatment for convicts. At a time when such things were nearly unheard of, he quietly told his staff to push for an early study of conjugal visits for inmates.[29]

Such forgiving public attitudes, combined with Chessman's popularity as a writer, resulted in an extraordinary campaign to save his life. Since Brown took office, pleas for mercy had been deluging the Capitol, and the volume only increased with the announcement of a clemency hearing. Letters, cards, and telegrams numbered in the hundreds, then the thousands, initially running to inches of file space, then to feet, finally to drawer after drawer. Clerks needed a separate folder just for letters from Brazil, where interest in the case was particularly high. One Brazilian petition was as thick as an unabridged dictionary.[30]

Brown's private advice—less massive but more influential—ran against clemency. For one thing, people who knew Chessman simply did not like him. He was arrogant, condescending, abusive, at times rude and obnoxious even to those who were trying to help him. Given the letters he would send to his attorneys, it is remarkable that he didn't end up representing himself again. Even one of the San Quentin chaplains thought Chessman had "not one redeeming feature in his person," an extraordinary remark coming from a clergyman.[31]

Political considerations mattered too. Even with opposition to the death penalty at a historic high, a slight majority of Californians still favored executions, and Brown might be seen as meddling with the legal system if he effectively overturned Chessman's sentence. From the start the governor was warned that the Chessman case was too hot to handle. McGee was openly political in his assessment. Saving Chessman would exact too great a price, he told the governor in a letter. "I frankly do not think," he wrote, "that the Chessman case or Chessman as an individual is important enough to jeopardize even in the smallest way the great confidence that the people of California have in you and [the] progressive policies which you sponsor, which far transcend the importance of any one single human being's welfare, to say nothing of one of the character of Caryl Chessman."[32] In effect, McGee was telling Brown to trade Chessman's life for other achievements, an honest and not unreasonable recommendation.

Poole was wary. To ready the governor for the clemency hearing, Poole wrote a long memorandum summarizing the case. He avoided a direct recommendation but left little doubt where he stood. He finished by saying that the governor must search his conscience and balance the needs of justice against the safety of society. "This society includes Caryl Chessman," Poole wrote. "It also includes the rest of us."[33]

The hearing was held in the governor's suite of offices on the Capitol's first floor, the windows letting in the light from an unseasonably warm fall day. Brown presided personally, as he would at all clemency hearings (unlike governors before and after), and the room was crowded with Chessman's attorneys, the prosecutors, prison officials, psychiatric experts, and reporters. Brown began by telling Chessman's lawyers that he knew the case well, was convinced of Chessman's guilt, and saw little point wasting time with claims of innocence. "I don't think that a governor should try to second guess the courts as to whether or not the man is guilty or innocent," Brown said. "I want to know from the standpoint of society why I should act one way or the other."[34]

Chessman's primary lawyer was George T. Davis, a flamboyant San Francisco defense attorney with a long record of celebrated cases. In the 1930s he helped win a pardon for Tom Mooney, a labor activist who had been convicted, probably wrongly, of bombing a patriotic San Francisco parade in 1916 as the country readied itself for World War I. After World War II Davis went to Germany and helped munitions magnate Alfred Krupp recover part of his fortune, which had been stripped away by the Allies.[35] By chance Davis also had old ties to Brown. He had once been a deputy district attorney under Brown in San Francisco and was appointed Truman's 1948 Northern California campaign manager largely at Brown's behest.[36]

Like any good lawyer, Davis focused on his strongest point—a comparison of the Chessman case with those of Wein and Langdon, whose sentences had been commuted by the governor earlier in the year. Like Chessman, Wein and Langdon were not murderers but had been sent to death row by a fatal elixir of circumstance, a kidnapping that involved both robbery and bodily harm. Davis admitted that all the cases included sex crimes, offenses sure to outrage but not normally subject to the death penalty. He was making headway. "You have addressed yourself to the things that bother me," Brown said.[37]

But it was almost at the end of the hearing that the governor revealed his deepest feelings, suggesting that there simply was no need for putting a man to death. Talking with Chessman's prosecutor, who was there to argue against clemency, Brown asked, "Eleven and a half years on Death Row, plus we are assuming now life imprisonment from here on out, would that not satisfy the ends of justice in this matter rather than to have the Roman Holiday next Friday at San Quentin?"[38] Then, after hearing arguments for hours, Brown said he would have a decision within four days. "I will do a little praying," he added.[39]

That night the governor was tormented. In his diary he wrote that he faced the "toughest decision" he would make. As always, personal opposition to capital punishment conflicted with sworn duty. "[T]hey are still crying for blood. It seems barbaric to me but I must, like everyone, obey the law. . . . Open mind, but leaning toward clemency."[40]

But the next day, Friday, Brown learned that his hands might be tied. Broad though it was, the governor's power to commute was not absolute. Clemency for a twice-convicted felon required the approval of the California supreme court, and Chessman had six felonies on his long record. Brown talked with Phil Gibson, the chief justice, but the news was not what the governor wanted to hear. Reluctantly, Gibson agreed to go along with the governor, but he said that only two other justices on the seven-member panel were willing to vote for clemency. Unless something changed, Brown would lose the vote 4–3 and be blocked from meaningful action. For all that he had anguished over the case, the critical fact was that Brown had no power to reduce Chessman's sentence.[41]

Knowing he had little choice, Brown decided he would formally deny clemency Monday morning. Yet the decision vexed him. Trying to draft a public statement, he was up until 3:30 A.M. Sunday. After a few hours' sleep he left to catch a flight to Chicago, where he planned to meet with his old hero, Adlai Stevenson, but his mind remained on Chessman. Just before boarding the plane Brown called Poole with a few changes to the statement, and then called from Chicago on Monday morning with another set of minor edits.[42]

The final version reiterated Brown's opposition to the death penalty and offered a mishmash of reasons for the refusal to commute Chessman's sentence, such as the nature of the crimes and Chessman's "contempt for society and its laws." There was only a glancing reference to the need for supreme court approval, although that issue was critical. Had Brown been able to do as he pleased, he almost surely would have issued a commutation—just as he had with Wein and Langdon—and the trouble that was to follow would have been avoided.

Brown's statement closed with a simple declaration of finality. The governor would "not intervene in the case of Caryl Chessman."[43] That echoed a comment at the clemency hearing. "Once this hearing is over with, this will be my action one way or another," Brown had said. "There will be no further action by me at all."[44] How he must have wished later that he had heeded his own words.

———

As Brown sauntered through his first year as governor, his son was struggling with the rigors of the Jesuit seminary. After three years at Sacred Heart, Jerry Brown felt increasingly constricted. The stern lifestyle—little talking, not much connection with the outside world—now seemed removed from reality for the boy who had grown up in a household where politics and current events were constants. Along with two friends in the seminary, Brown had begun privately visiting the priest who taught them Latin, unburdening himself with long, frank talks. By December 1959, when one of his friends left the order, Jerry was seriously considering the same option.

Five days before Christmas, on one of Pat's Sunday visits, father and son had a long walk together through the grounds of the novitiate, and Jerry said that he was likely to abandon clerical studies. Pat was ambivalent. He cherished the idea of seeing his son more often, yet as a believing Catholic he considered the priesthood the highest form of service. He made no recommendation, and said merely that he would support Jerry's decision, whatever it might be. In January 1960, a few weeks short of his twenty-second birthday, Jerry decided firmly that he would abandon both Sacred Heart and his desire to be a priest.

The governor was out of town when it became official, just as he had been gone when Jerry left for the novitiate more than three years earlier. In Pat's absence Bernice, who had been even less enthusiastic than Pat about their son's ecclesiastical ambitions, issued a brief statement from the governor's office disclosing the news. "I think he has his feet on the ground and knows what he wants to do," she said of her son.

What Jerry wanted to do first was start life as a college student. He enrolled at the University of California's Berkeley campus, moved into the school's International House, and registered as a classics major.[45]

Two days after Brown denied Chessman clemency—and three days before the scheduled execution—U.S. Supreme Court justice William O. Douglas issued a stay, allowing Chessman to go before the high court once again. Even without the governor's help, Chessman had avoided yet another date with the gas chamber.

It was a development that gave Brown no worry. Chessman was now a litigant in federal court rather than a clemency applicant in the governor's office, and California's chief executive was taking advantage of the season— the legislature was out of session—to get away from the office a bit. On one such jaunt, he nearly encountered his demise even before Chessman. Hunting ducks on the San Joaquin River south of Sacramento, Pat and Bernice were in a blind with Ed Pauley, the oilman who was a big donor to the governor's campaigns, and Pauley's wife, Bobbie. Unforgivably, Pauley somehow dropped his shotgun, and it went off. By pure luck no one was hit.[46]

There was political traveling to be done as well. In Oklahoma Brown spoke at a Democratic fund-raising dinner. In Massachusetts he defended social programs and derided Republicans—Vice President Nixon was a "well-mended political windsock"—at Harvard Law School. After the holidays, in January 1960, Brown took off again, spending several days in Washington, D.C., tending the political garden by meeting with national Democratic figures.[47]

Then, just after his return from the Washington trip, the Chessman case suddenly and unexpectedly crept back toward the governor's office. Earlier, the U.S. Supreme Court had denied Chessman's request for a delay, lifting the Douglas stay, and an execution date had been set for February 19. Now U.S. District Court judge Louis Goodman rejected yet another Chessman bid for more time but added that "extra-judicially" he was impressed by Chessman's claim that nearly twelve years on death row amounted to cruel and unusual punishment. Although legally without merit, Chessman's claim might be deserving of executive clemency, the judge insisted.[48]

With less than three weeks to go before the execution, the judge had put the governor in a terrible spot. Goodman was refusing to act but hinting broadly and publicly that Brown should save Chessman's life. As he invariably did in a capital case, Brown wanted to spare the condemned man, but he also knew there was nothing new in Chessman's pleadings. The claim of cruel and unusual punishment had been raised often, and Brown had considered it when denying clemency back in October. This time he waited a few days after Goodman's comments, then settled squarely on the fence. "I don't know if I'll ever look at the case again, but I am not foreclosing it," Brown told reporters.[49]

Brown was wavering badly, forgetting his earlier vow that the October decision would be final. Swayed by Goodman's remarks and a nettling conscience, the governor began to mull the ways that Chessman might be saved. He called Gibson, the chief justice of the state supreme court, at home one evening to discuss the case. Brown knew he needed the court's approval to commute Chessman's sentence, but he said he wanted to wait until every possible legal action had been exhausted before making up his mind. Gibson advised against delay. Brown should tell Gibson immediately if he wanted to commute so that Gibson could poll the court—perhaps with a little arm-twisting—in the hope that a majority might be found to support the governor. "We could get into a hell of a worldwide tragedy on this thing if we let it go to the last minute," Gibson told one of Brown's aides.[50]

By Wednesday, February 17—just forty-eight hours from the scheduled execution—it was clear that Chessman's best chance to stay alive was a commutation from the governor rather than another judicial stay. The result was an ever brighter spotlight on the Capitol. Members of a Southern California religious sect—robed, bearded, and barefoot despite the winter temperatures—picketed outside, demanding mercy. Mail to the governor's office reached a volume not seen even in October, just before the clemency hearing. The woman who had been in charge of the governor's office mail room for more than seventeen years, stretching back to Earl Warren's first term, could recall nothing like it.[51] The Vatican urged clemency, as did activists from Scandinavia to Argentina. In London Queen Elizabeth was about to give birth, yet most of the morning papers devoted more space to Chessman.[52] International press interest was so acute that the wire services worried about a three-second edge in reporting new developments.[53]

Hoping to increase pressure on the governor even more, Chessman's lawyers formally requested that the state supreme court recommend clemency. That forced the justices to take a stand, but the plan backfired. In the afternoon, after deliberating just under two hours, the justices voted 4–3 against a commutation, the same tally that Brown had encountered informally back in October, and almost surely the same one Gibson would have found if he had privately queried his colleagues after Judge Goodman's remarks. The governor, by now secretly hoping to spare Chessman's life, was especially frustrated that one of his two recent appointees to the court voted to deny clemency, but there was nothing he could do. At sundown the governor's office issued a statement saying that Brown was powerless unless the court reconsidered.[54]

The next day, Thursday, February 18, 1960, was already fated to be a day on which the world's attention turned toward California—even without the Chessman case. By sheer fluke it was the opening day of the 1960 Winter Olympics at Squaw Valley, a ski resort near the north end of Lake Tahoe. Hosting the games was a coup for the state. Squaw Valley was only twelve years old—ski resorts proliferated amid America's post–World War II boom—and the Olympics had not been held in the United States since 1932. The opening ceremonies were to be a day of California pride, another example of the state's star power, with the governor welcoming the world's athletes to the Sierra Nevada.

But Brown canceled his appearance, insisting he should stay by his desk in the event there were new developments in the Chessman case. It was an easy decision. Just three years before, as an ambitious Democratic attorney general looking to score political points against the Republican governor, Goodwin Knight, Brown had sharply criticized Knight for leaving his office on the morning of a controversial execution. Knight was touring an aircraft carrier, a decision highlighted all the more when he eventually decided to grant one more stay and delay the execution. His phone call from the ship came seconds too late, and the next day Brown held a news conference to pillory Knight for "gallivanting on an aircraft carrier" at such a time. The governor should have remained at his post, Brown said, available to "anybody and everybody" for last-second developments.[55] With twenty-four hours remaining before the execution of a world-famous inmate, Brown could hardly repeat the behavior he had criticized, so he canceled his Olympics trip and sent Bernice in his stead.

Brown called off his normally scheduled news conference too, the first time he had done so since taking office, and spent the day working. Chessman's lawyers returned to the supreme court to ask again for a recommendation of clemency, but nothing had changed from the day before. Chessman lost by the same vote, 4–3, and the governor issued a terse three-sentence statement saying there was nothing he could do. Chessman, it appeared, would finally meet his end at ten o'clock the next morning.[56]

Still, those around Brown were worried. They knew that he was agonizing, that he believed it was wrong to take a life, and that he wanted desperately to do something to save Chessman. He had been convinced that there was nothing he could do—the supreme court's objection tied his hands—

and he would have to let Chessman die. But Brown was never the firmest of men, and everyone worried that he might falter at the last moment.

Dutton, who was accompanying Bernice to Squaw Valley, stopped on his way out of the office to talk with the governor and remind him to stay the course.[57] Bernice was sufficiently worried that after she arrived in the mountains, she tried to call the mansion so she too could buck up her husband. But the vast international press corps covering the Olympics had tied up all the phone lines, so at the urging of friends she went out to dinner, resolving to call Pat later in the evening.[58]

She might not have reached him anyway. Champion, Poole, and Dick Tuck, another staff member, took Brown to dinner at the Mansion Inn, the hotel near the governor's residence where he had liked to swim before his private pool was built. The staff members wanted to provide both reassurance and diversion, get the governor out of the house, and make sure he was not alone. It seemed to work. They talked a little about Chessman, but it was not their only topic, and Brown seemed resigned to the inevitable.[59]

After dinner they walked back across the street to the Governor's Mansion and said good night. Champion remembered later that the staff members were sure they had done everything they could to stiffen Brown's resolve. There was nothing Brown could do anyway, and no one who could try to sway him in the few hours that remained.[60]

But they had forgotten one person whose opposition to the death penalty was as strong as the governor's—his son. For more than three years, during his father's campaign and first year as governor, Jerry Brown had been in the novitiate, literally locked away from the world, without telephones or television or newspapers. When Champion and Poole and Dutton tried to think of people who might influence the governor, Jerry had quite naturally slipped their minds.

Of course, Jerry had left Sacred Heart only weeks before. Now he was as free as anyone to use a telephone, and he did. He called his father at the mansion and urged that Chessman's sentence be commuted. Pat responded that the supreme court would never approve. Undeterred, Jerry suggested the one idea that apparently no one had considered, perhaps because it was politically naive. Couldn't the governor, Jerry asked his father, issue a temporary reprieve and then ask the legislature to impose a moratorium on executions? Pat told his son there wasn't one chance in a thousand that the legislators would pass such a bill. "But Dad," Jerry responded, "if you were a doctor and there was one chance in a thousand of saving a patient's life, wouldn't you take it?" It was a naive argument, but the governor needed little convincing. He thought about it only a moment and then, in a decision that would affect the rest of his career, agreed to grant a stay. "He was plowing very fertile ground," the older man wrote later, referring to his son. "I had been searching my soul for an excuse to do something."[61]

Alerted by a phone call from the governor, Poole and Champion rushed back to the mansion to head off what they were sure was a disastrous idea, but by the time they arrived, Brown's mind was set: He would give Chessman a sixty-day reprieve and ask the legislature to abolish the death penalty. A little before midnight, ten hours before Chessman was scheduled to die, Brown phoned officials at San Quentin and called off the execution. Told the news, Chessman asked the warden, "You're not kidding, are you?"[62]

Insiders were less surprised. Later that night Bernice finally got through from Squaw Valley. Learning what her husband had done, she replied simply, "I knew I shouldn't have gone." Years after, she wondered what would have happened if she had been able to talk with Pat before he acted. "I don't know whether I would have been able to prevail, or whether Jerry would have prevailed," she said. "That would have been an interesting thing, to see who would have been the most persuasive. But [Pat] was sitting there alone in that mansion. It's a big house, and he was sitting there alone and pondering this thing. Then Jerry called, and Jerry can be persuasive, and he persuaded him to do this."[63]

The immediate problem for the governor and his men was a public explanation. The truth was rejected. It sounded feeble to say that after months of consideration, after an earlier refusal of clemency, after repeated public declarations that the supreme court's stance closed all options, the governor changed his mind a few hours before the execution because of a phone call from his twenty-one-year-old son.

Fortunately, secretaries sorting through the thousands of letters and telegrams received on the last day had found one from a State Department official warning that if Chessman were executed, protests might occur in Uruguay during an upcoming visit by President Eisenhower. Nobody really cared—in fact, by most accounts the governor did not even know of the State Department telegram when he made his decision—but a concern over the president's international standing seemed a substantive explanation, so it was offered up as the reason for the stay. Brown knew better; he wrote later that the State Department telegram was a convenient "public excuse."[64]

He used it the next morning when he called a press conference to explain his last-second decision the night before. He made no mention of Jerry, but held up the telegram for reporters to see. He cited other reasons too, mainly the comments of the federal judge that he was impressed by Chessman's arguments and the fact that the supreme court had split so narrowly in refusing to recommend clemency. It was a sad performance. It was even clear the governor had not thought through his decision carefully. At first he insisted that the death penalty abolition bill he would send to the legislature would have no direct effect on Chessman since he was already under sentence. Brown said he hoped that if the legislature passed the bill one of the supreme court justices might be inspired to change his position, thus allowing the governor to commute Chessman's sentence to life in prison. Poole had to correct his boss, noting that the bill could in fact commute the sentences of all current death row prisoners, simply by statute, which is the way the bill was eventually drafted. Brown joked away his mistake. Poole, he said, was a lawyer; "I have only been attorney general."[65]

The public response to the last-second reprieve was a fury. Letters poured in criticizing Brown for extending the life of a heinous criminal. Before the decision the mail had been largely supportive of Chessman. Now the trend reversed. The governor's decision was "shameful," "foolish," "a black day." "I demand protection for my three daughters," wired one woman, "now that rape and kidnapping can freely be practiced by perverts." A Los Angeles County group calling itself the California Defense Committee started a recall petition. A Republican assemblyman said the governor should be impeached. Even the *Sacramento Bee*, normally the friendliest of California's big newspapers, was critical. The legislature should ponder the death penalty amid something other than the hysteria of the Chessman case, the paper insisted. Linking the two, as the governor had done, was a "grave error in judgment."[66]

Legislative leaders were equally enraged. In the previous few years, legislators had considered and rejected bill after bill to abolish capital punishment. In his first news conference as governor, Brown had tacitly acknowledged the issue's futility, saying he would sign an abolition bill if it reached his desk but would not push for it.[67] Now, thanks to the governor, the legislature would have to repeat the entire unnecessary bloodletting, warring under media klieg lights over an issue that touched emotions like few others. Worse, it would be for nothing. In the Capitol support for the death penalty was as strong as ever, perhaps stronger: Some lawmakers who had previously supported abolition said they would vote against it this time, because they did not want to seem to support Chessman. Hugh Burns, the senate leader who often bucked the governor, made clear the fate of the new proposal: "We'll just kick it out the window and go home."[68]

It took little time to prove Burns right. The administration's bill, which would have abolished the death penalty and commuted the sentence of every man on death row, was introduced in the state senate by Fred Farr, a former legal aide lawyer and a tireless opponent of the death penalty. Set for a hearing in the Senate Judiciary Committee on March 9, a week after it was introduced, the bill was a dead letter from the start. Brown's proposal, wrote the *Bee,* had no more chance "than a mid-summer snowfall in the Sahara."[69]

For show, legislators dragged out the hearing. In the Capitol's biggest committee room, four hundred onlookers packed the gallery. Thousands more watched a live broadcast on public television. Both sides offered an array of witnesses, ministers, and law professors for the bill's proponents, prosecutors and policemen for the opposition. The testimony took sixteen hours, finally concluding at 1:00 A.M.[70]

Knowing he was short of votes, Farr tried desperately to salvage something, amending his own bill from complete abolition to a three-year moratorium. Even that was a loser. The committee was overwhelmingly Democratic, but six members of the governor's own party defected, joining the two Republicans in voting no. The final tally was 8–7 to kill the bill, but it could have been a bigger margin. Democrats staged a close vote to soften the blow to the governor's political fortunes. "They could have made it any number they wanted," Poole remembered. "They tried to let him down as easy as they could."[71]

Unable to resist, Brown made one last, halfhearted try at saving Chessman, whose execution had now been reset for early May. When Brown signed the February reprieve and threw the issue to the legislature, he insisted that if lawmakers retained the death penalty he would let Chessman die. But as the date neared, the governor and his clemency secretary quietly approached the supreme court one more time. Brown hoped that Thomas P. White, his most recent appointee to the court and a clemency opponent, might change his mind, at least partly in recognition that Brown had given him the job. But White refused—he was right to disregard the identity of the requester—and the governor remained one vote short.[72]

There was nothing left to do but concede. Dutton worried seriously that if Brown continued to issue temporary stays of the execution he would lose all credibility, perhaps even risk impeachment. Had the whole thing continued indefinitely, Dutton remembered later, "it would not have been Pat Brown, a conscience-stricken man, but Pat Brown, buffoon."[73] Six days before the new execution date, the governor issued a long statement saying there was nothing new in the case and adding that since the supreme court had refused to budge, "the most important single fact is that [he was] constitutionally now prohibited from extending clemency." He insisted he would have nothing more to say about Chessman. In his diary Brown bemoaned his unhappy duty: "I tried my best to get the Legislature to modify the law with respect to capital punishment. They wouldn't do it. They are wrong but I have sworn to uphold all the laws of this state, and they will be."[74]

The day before the scheduled execution, a Sunday, the governor went to mass, then sat around the mansion all day, unable even to distract himself with reading. He spoke with the chief justice three times, although nothing about the supreme court's position had changed.[75]

The following morning, May 2, execution day, the governor sat at his desk in the Capitol. With ten minutes to go, he took up his pen and made a brief diary entry: "I feel that it is better now to get it over. Up until now I have had a terrific sympathy for Chessman, but now that it's almost over I feel quite calm." He noted that opponents of the death penalty still wanted him to issue another temporary reprieve, although in the long run it would do no good. Then he added an exculpatory expression of his own powerlessness: "There is nothing I can do. I am happy that I have not the responsibility."[76]

Poole sat a few feet away on an open phone line to San Quentin. There wasn't much to say. From time to time Brown would ask if anything had happened, and Poole would say no, and they would return to waiting in silence. Finally the warden told Poole that the little gauze bags of cyanide had been lowered into the sulfuric acid, creating the poison gas that would kill Chessman in minutes, and there was nothing more anyone could do to stop it. Poole told the governor, who got up and walked out.

Brown told his driver to take him to Folsom Lake, about fifty miles up the American River, east of Sacramento. The governor got out and took a long walk along the shore, his hands folded behind his back, and did not return to the office all day.

The next morning Poole tried to buoy his boss a little, telling him that at least he had tried to save Chessman's life. Brown shook his head and then said simply, "Do you suppose anybody thinks that this is a better world now?" Poole had no answer.[77]

A good many Californians felt the world was emphatically not a better place, and they let the governor know about it. Politicians are like all service-industry workers: They hear loudest from the disenchanted. Just as mail to the governor's office had once attacked Brown for denying Chessman clemency and then for granting him a reprieve, now letters flooded in insisting that somehow the governor should have prevented the execution. The state had become a symbol of "institutionalized barbarity." It was a "mockery" of justice. One Floridian said he had planned to move to California but now would not. A New Yorker called it "the slaughter state." A letter from Reading, Massachusetts, contained only one word, printed neatly in block letters: "Killer." Telegrams were especially pithy: "I hope you sleep well tonight." "I hope you enjoy your dinner." "It is you who are the moral degenerate." "Are you proud of yourself for murdering Caryl Chessman? You are a disgrace to the world."[78]

Closer in, people around Brown—those who shared and protected his political interests—were angry not that he had let Chessman die, or even that he had tried to keep him alive, but that, at different times, he had done both. The trouble was not so much the final outcome as the governor's wandering route to get there. Weakened by his own hand, Brown lost an opportunity to build on his early successes.

Dutton was especially livid. The man who had helped Brown become governor and then served as his chief aide once in office—who had been by Brown's side both when they climbed the mountain and when they stood at the summit—sensed that at the acme of his power the governor's uncertain performance had wounded horribly both his political future and his policy goals. Ignoring decorum, Dutton told the governor point-blank that he had violated the public's trust, that he had been given an opportunity to help "the blind and the crippled and the disabled and the poor" and had thrown it all away "for a foul man like Chessman." Brown thought he lost Dutton's respect because of the Chessman case, never to regain it fully. In time Dutton would mellow a bit, but he never got over the belief that Brown had lost so much to gain so little. "He had won big in '58," Dutton remembered. "He had won a great legislative record in '59. He was being thought about at least a little as a presidential possibility. He was developing as a major figure nationally. Chessman splattered all that. . . . Humpty Dumpty never got put back together as strong again."[79]

Home offered no refuge, for Bernice, always a sterner personality than

Pat, was almost as critical as Dutton. Months later the governor was still loath to discuss with his wife—"the daughter of a police captain," as he put it—his plans to commute another inmate's sentence, lest it remind her of the Chessman debacle.[80]

Brown was miserable. He was depressed, "very bad and very low," as he put it. It was, he remembered, "one of the worst periods" of his life. It seemed that his career might be wrecked. If he attended a sporting event, boos rained down when the governor's name was announced.[81]

To some degree the venom was unfair. Brown's personal bedrock—the conviction that it was morally wrong for government to kill people—never moved. He fought nobly, proposing that capital punishment be abolished, and he surrendered honorably, enforcing the law when the legislature refused to change it. But it was also true that in the long Chessman melodrama, Brown created for himself the worst of all possible situations, angering everybody. First he denied Chessman clemency, disappointing the condemned man's supporters. Then he stopped the execution, enraging those who thought justice required a death. Then he oversaw Chessman's demise, and although he had no power to stop it, the very fact that Brown was governor when the execution occurred made him once again a villain to capital punishment opponents. At various points he had raised, then dashed, the hopes of both sides, those who wanted Chessman put to death and those who wanted him kept alive. By turns, Brown made himself the target of every critic's catcalls.

In the human sense it was the most understandable of failures. From the beginning Brown wanted to save Chessman's life, as he did that of every condemned man. Yet everyone around him told him not to, told him that it could not be done, that it would not be prudent, that it was a waste. Slowly he was pushed to accept what seemed to him a horrible wrong. Then, at last, he found someone who told him to heed his instincts, to do what he believed was right, not what was prudent and reasonable and unavoidable. And it was his own son. It would have taken a hard man to reject both his child and his conscience—to discipline himself and stay the course—and Brown was rarely a hard man.

Therein lay the greatest tragedy, for it was a disaster born of his best qualities wrongly applied. All his life Pat Brown's personality had been his great weapon. Friendly and charming and affable, he saw the best in other people and made them see the best in him. His was the world of useful benevolence. Getting along with people, showing a genuine and sincere ability to sympathize with them, liking them and being liked, trying earnestly to be a decent fellow—these traits had brought him success, had made him the yell leader and the community organizer and the respected prosecutor and, finally, the governor of his state. They had brought him power and prestige.

Now, in a moment of trial, he did the same thing. He looked for the best in people: He saw the appeal of his son's youthful optimism, hoped for a spark of mercy in the legislature, perhaps even dreamed of some remaining virtue in Chessman himself. He sympathized, went along, felt compassion. He tried to do the right thing. His conscience told him that it was wrong for the state to kill someone, his son told him it was wrong for the state to kill someone, and he had the chance to put things right. For all that it cost him, he never fully changed his mind. Years later he wrote a book about the death penalty—by far the best of the three books he wrote in retirement—and ended his chapter on the Chessman case by saying that given the passions of the day, it would have been politically impossible for any elected official to stop the execution. "I firmly believe all of that," he added. "I also believe that I should have found a way to spare Chessman's life."[82]

But the reality was that saving Caryl Chessman's life was impossible. In his mind, if not his heart, Brown knew the legislature would not repeal capital punishment. He told Jerry so. He knew the supreme court would not let him commute Chessman's sentence. The justices had refused twice. Chessman was going to die, and the governor had a responsibility, just as Dutton would later tell him, to think about the millions of people he might help in other ways. Civil rights bills and better schools were real accomplishments that affected everyday Californians. It may sound cold to balance a man's life against pieces of legislation, but that was Brown's responsibility—and he knew it. In his first week in office, reading through the first clemency appeal he faced, he consciously weighed the impact of the case on his newly introduced legislative program. The year after the Chessman affair he refused clemency in another case partly to win the support of a key legislator on an agricultural bill, a bill that Brown believed would improve the lives of migrant workers.[83] As well as anyone, Brown knew that the life-and-death decisions of clemency did not happen in a vacuum.

And yet at the crucial moment of the most famous capital case he would ever face, Brown's resolution flickered. Bernice Brown was right: Her husband was alone in a great big house, talking to his only son. But being in charge is about being alone, even at night, even in a great big house, even when your own son calls.

What Pat Brown needed that night was not a desire to abolish capital punishment or sympathize with his son or even listen to the futile admonitions of his own conscience. What he needed that night was a hard, rigorous self-discipline, an acceptance of an unpleasant reality, and a willingness to see it through. His wife knew it. His friends knew it. Even he knew it. And he didn't have it.

9   CIGAR SMOKE

AFTER CHESSMAN, BROWN NEEDED, for once, to escape his beloved state. Public events, normally a source of great joy, had become nightmares. Crowds hooted at the mention of his name. "I was really blasted and booed from one end to the other," he remembered. "The Walls of Jericho fell down on me."[1]

Fortunately, he had a trip planned. Two weeks after the execution, in the middle of May 1960, he traveled to Bainbridge Island, near Seattle in Puget Sound, for a conference of western governors. Combining people and politics, such trips were usually a balm for Brown, but at this one he found himself in a partisan exchange with Gov. Mark Hatfield of Oregon. Gary Francis Powers, the pilot of a U-2 spy plane, had just been shot down and captured by the Soviet Union. President Eisenhower initially denied the existence of espionage flights, then admitted it, and the resulting furor derailed a Paris summit meeting scheduled between Eisenhower and Soviet Premier Nikita Khrushchev.

Brown told reporters that the incident had damaged Eisenhower and that spillover from the affair would hurt Eisenhower's vice president, Richard Nixon, the Republicans' presumptive presidential nominee. The GOP might abandon Nixon in favor of New York Gov. Nelson Rockefeller, Brown insisted. Hatfield, who had been elected the same year as Brown and would go on to a long career in the U.S. Senate, disagreed. The Soviets knew Nixon would be a tough-minded president, Hatfield said, and that fact would only strengthen his campaign.[2]

The importance of the mini-debate was not in the details, but the topic. It was a presidential election year, and as Brown and Hatfield demonstrated, the political crowd was focused on the events of the nation and the world. The governor of California was no exception; he was involved. For a year, as he soared through the early days of his administration and struggled through the morass of the Chessman case, Brown had been eyeing a bigger venue. Like California governors before and after, Pat Brown was suffering from presidential fever.

It had taken little time for the disease to incubate. At the beginning of 1959, after his election as governor but before his inauguration, Brown wrote to Adlai Stevenson to say that he enjoyed their recent meeting. It was a meaningless letter of courtesy, but Brown added a handwritten postscript that revealed his thoughts: "How do you deny you are running for president and make it seem true?"[3] The night of the inaugural Brown joked publicly about getting to the White House, and the idea never completely left his mind.

Barely two months later, in March, Brown spoke at the Gridiron Club banquet, an annual spoof of Washington officialdom organized by the capital's press corps. Hoping to use the affair as something of a coming-out party for his national ambitions, Brown and his staff spent hours crafting his talk. Brown thought he held his own against House Republican leader Charles Halleck, the GOP speaker, and toward the beginning he threw in a witty line that went over well. "I will use this very important forum to declare," he said, "courageously and unequivocally, I am not a candidate for president in 1960. Now that I am back in the thick of the race . . ."[4]

Before leaving town, Brown telephoned Drew Pearson, a fixture in the political gossip of the day. It was too early for definite moves toward the presidency, Brown said, but he made no bones that he was hoping. "I'm going to be as good a governor of California as I can," Pearson remembered him saying, "and then see what happens." Pearson thought his old friend might have a chance. "It could be," he noted in his diary, "that the two nominees will be from opposite ends of the country—Rockefeller of New York and Brown of California."[5]

If there was any prospect of winning the nomination, more than a year of maneuver lay ahead, and after he returned from the East, Brown got a memo from Dutton laying out a strategy. For now, Brown would run for president only in his own state, entering the California primary as a "favorite son."

Favorite sons still mattered because national political conventions still mattered. Only sixteen states held presidential primaries, and together they offered only a fraction of the delegates needed for the nomination. Most states still chose their delegates the old-fashioned way—in closed caucuses or secret meetings of local political bosses—and it was those states that made the final decision at the convention. Although the era was closing, running for president remained a combination of electioneering and negotiation, a far murkier process than it would become in later years. Some men ran for president without ever saying they were doing so. In 1960, for example, Adlai Stevenson insisted to the end that he did not want the nomination, although in the final hours he pushed hard for it. Lyndon Johnson never entered a single primary and officially declared his candidacy only days before the Democratic National Convention, although he finished second to John Kennedy in the voting for the nomination.

The system lent importance to favorite sons, a term that would eventually mean little more than a figure of regional popularity but which at the time still represented a specific kind of campaign. As a favorite son, a governor or senator entered his state's primary, or seized control of the delegates at the state caucuses or convention if the state held no primary, even though he had no real hope of becoming president. Assuming that he won, the state's delegates would go to the convention pledged to him. On the convention floor favorite sons had two alternative strategies, which often overlapped. Sometimes they dreamed of snatching the nomination if none of the serious candidates could find a majority and the convention deadlocked. If not—and this was the more common outcome—they used their delegations as bargaining chips in dealing with potential nominees. Once the favorite son withdrew, the delegates were not legally obligated to follow his lead in voting for another candidate, but often, through a combination of intimidation and affection, a favorite son could lead his followers to one camp or another. In return for the votes, the favorite son often secured for himself or his state promises of the vice presidential nomination, cabinet posts, or just more control over federal appointees.

As Dutton wrote his memo to Brown in spring 1959, he was focused most on the second strategy, using the California delegation as a bargaining chip. He wanted Brown to run as a favorite son in the state's primary, but he also wanted him to leave open the possibility of seeking delegates in other states. This would only strengthen Brown's hand, making him appear a national figure. With luck, it might lead to a serious bid for the White House. In execution the plan was simple: If reporters asked the governor about his ambitions, Dutton suggested, Brown should say he was only a favorite son but take care never to rule out a serious candidacy. The listener could infer what he might.[6]

Brown found it easy advice to follow. He did not think of himself as a serious presidential candidate, but he believed his appearance as a potential national figure would only strengthen his hand in controlling the California delegation. He told reporters that he was merely a California candidate but then allowed for the possibility of something more: "How serious that is, we will wait and see."[7]

With time, he began to be tempted by the idea of a truly serious bid. Attention and approval were tonics to Brown's soul, and the mention of his name as a possible president, however unlikely, generated public interest. Some of the attention would have touched anyone. A little girl from Illinois—she identified herself as "age 12¾"—wrote to offer a contribution to a Brown presidential campaign: the $76.55 she had saved to buy a horse. (Brown wrote back to politely decline the largesse; even high office was not reason enough to separate little girls from equine dreams.)[8]

What was more, Brown found himself increasingly at the heart of national political calculations. On their trips to California, presidential candidates now made time to stop and see the governor. Massachusetts Sen. John F. Kennedy came by the mansion for breakfast, the first time he and Brown met. They shook hands and sat down to eat, and Brown, characteristically, began the conversation by blurting out, "I understand you've got Addison's disease."[9]

By the end of July Brown was thinking about discarding the favorite son mantle and making a real run for the White House, seeking delegates not just in California but in other states as well. On his way to Puerto Rico for a conference of governors in July, he stopped in Washington for a series of political consultations that signaled a newfound seriousness. He had dinner with the California House delegation, then the next day had lunch with Senate Majority Leader Lyndon Johnson and a bevy of Democratic senators and met separately with House Speaker Sam Rayburn. One appointment was particularly revealing: Brown talked with Truman's former secretary of state, Dean Acheson, "to sharpen my focus on international affairs," he said—not an aptitude he needed to expand if he intended to remain a governor.[10]

Talking with reporters, Brown came closer than ever before to declaring that he was in the race to win, not merely to control his home state's delegation. Favorite sons, he said, were "historically put in with some hope . . ."

He let the sentence trail off and then added, "I think I'll leave it that way." The papers got the message. "Gov. Brown Stirs Speculation on '60," read a headline the next day in the *New York Times*.[11]

In many respects, running for president—doing it seriously, across the country, not just in California—seemed like a risk worth taking. The Democratic nomination was there to be seized: The party had neither incumbent nor heir apparent. Like a lot of Democrats, Brown thought about the field of potential candidates—most of them senators—and was not dazzled. Kennedy was young and inexperienced. Hubert Humphrey was too liberal. Lyndon Johnson was a regional candidate. Stuart Symington was a nice man and a competent one, but Brown thought he lacked fire in the belly. The one nonsenator, Adlai Stevenson, remained an idol, but he was playing a coy game, feigning disinterest, and he had lost twice. In politics losers cannot be long tolerated.[12] Brown was a new governor, but his first legislative session had been a great success, a generator of national press coverage that would be the envy of any candidate. New Yorkers had long dominated American presidential politics, so why not now the new titans, Californians?[13]

There were two big problems, the first of which Brown had created for himself. During the race against Knowland, he had promised to serve a full term if elected governor. In fact, he had savaged his opponent for trying to use the governorship as a stepping-stone to the presidency. Now, before a year was out, Brown was thinking of doing exactly the same thing. Asked about the issue, he performed his about-face abruptly and openly, for there was not much else he could do. Yes, he admitted to reporters, he had said he would not run for president, had even said that if elected he would refuse to serve. "That was a very accurate quote, and I did say that," Brown acknowledged, "but upon meditation I just feel it sounds unpatriotic."[14]

The second issue was the need to generate support outside California for a man still largely regarded as a home state figure. The solution was an informal Brown campaign, Lilliputian though it may have been. Two California supporters, John Purchio and Leonard Dieden, began traipsing around the West. Ostensibly traveling on behalf of California Democratic chairman Bill Munnell to investigate the feasibility of a western bloc at the national convention, their real goal was to both judge and generate interest in a Brown presidential campaign.[15] Only days after Purchio and Dieden finished their trip, Brown used yet another governors' summit to push for a regional coalition, a development sure to benefit any western candidate.[16]

Brown as a baby with his father, the man who taught him to hustle. (Courtesy of the Bancroft Library, University of California, Berkeley)

Brown in 1939, at thirty-four, the first time he ran for district attorney. (Courtesy of the Bancroft Library, University of California, Berkeley)

The Browns in 1950, when Pat was running for attorney general. From left, in front, are Jerry, Pat, Kathleen, and Bernice. Behind their parents, from left, are Cynthia and Barbara. (Courtesy of the Bancroft Library, University of California, Berkeley)

During a break at a conference of attorneys general in 1957 at Sun Valley, Idaho, Brown shows his ability at a low style of politics. (Courtesy of the Bancroft Library, University of California, Berkeley)

President Eisenhower and Sen. William F. Knowland, Brown's Republican opponent in the 1958 gubernatorial race. Of Knowland, Eisenhower wrote in his diary, "In his case, there seems to be no final answer to the question, 'How stupid can you get?'" (Courtesy of the Bancroft Library, University of California, Berkeley)

Election night, 1958: The governor-elect is all smiles as the *San Francisco Chronicle* proclaims his victory. It was the Democrats' largest landslide in California since the turn of the century. (AP/Wide World Photos)

A family portrait at the Governor's Mansion, 1959. From left, behind Pat and Bernice, are their four children: Jerry (note his liturgical collar), Kathleen, Cynthia, and Barbara. (AP/Wide World Photos)

As governor, vacations were never really vacations. Even in the California backcountry cameras followed a governor's every move. (Courtesy of the Bancroft Library, University of California, Berkeley)

Agony on the golf course was a familiar experience for Brown, a committed duffer. He played on election day whenever he was on the ballot, killing time between voting and awaiting the returns. (Courtesy of Maryalice Lemmon)

Brown and Earl Warren after duck hunting, a diversion Brown loved whenever the chief justice returned to California. (Courtesy of the Bancroft Library, University of California, Berkeley)

At San Quentin Prison on April 30, 1960, Caryl Chessman holds one of the books he wrote on death row. Two days later he was executed. During the long and wrenching case, Brown offended both the supporters and the opponents of capital punishment. (AP/Wide World Photos)

Hollywood stars Marlon Brando, Steve Allen, and Shirley MacLaine (center, left to right) visit the Governor's Mansion to ask that Brown spare kidnapper Caryl Chessman's life. The celebrities are flanked by university professors Richard Drinnin on the left and Eugene Burdick on the right. The three stars may have been among Chessman's most famous advocates, but they were far from alone. The case drew worldwide attention. (AP/Wide World Photos)

The president and the governor during one of Eisenhower's golfing trips to Palm Springs. The first time the two men met after Brown's election, the governor so loved the national spotlight that he discarded his schedule and stayed around to chat up the White House press corps. (Courtesy of the Bancroft Library, University of California, Berkeley)

The presidential politics of 1960 proved a troublesome whirl for Brown. At a fund-raising dinner in Beverly Hills on May 31, the governor and three of the contenders hoping to capture the presidential nomination at the Democratic National Convention later that summer in Los Angeles. From left: John F. Kennedy, Brown, Lyndon Johnson, and Stuart Symington. LBJ, as always, is a little pushy. (AP/Wide World Photos)

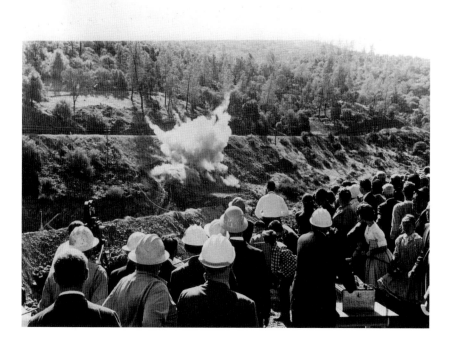

On October 21, 1961, Brown (in hard hat at lower right) sets off an explosion to start construction of the State Water Project's dam on the Feather River, near Oroville. He told the crowd that the sound from the three hundred pounds of dynamite "will echo in California history for generations to come." (Courtesy of the Bancroft Library, University of California, Berkeley)

At San Francisco's Fisherman's Wharf in 1962 during the race against Richard Nixon. Campaigning was always a joy for Brown. So was sampling local fare. In this case it's crab, but sometimes it was more exotic. In retirement, Brown once saw expatriate hippies smoking hashish in Nepal and thought about joining them. (He decided against it.) (Photo: *San Francisco Chronicle*)

Richard Nixon concedes defeat—inelegantly—in the 1962 gubernatorial race. Brown watched the performance on television, then laughed about it on the phone with President Kennedy the next day. "He's an able man," Brown said of his vanquished opponent, "but he's nuts." (AP/Wide World Photos)

Brown with Jesse Unruh, once a brilliant ally and later a bitter enemy. The smiles here are purely for the cameras: The picture was taken at a preconvention meeting of the California delegation to the 1964 Democratic National Convention, long after the two men had grown to distrust one another. (Courtesy of the Bancroft Library, University of California, Berkeley)

On Brown's orders, students are dragged from Sproul Hall during the Free Speech Movement sit-in at the University of California, Berkeley. The protests launched the student protests of the 1960s—and revealed a new social turbulence that would mark the rest of Brown's tenure as governor. (Photo © Ron Enfield)

Brown greets President Johnson. In public, LBJ hailed the governor. In private, he disparaged him. Flanking the two men, left to right, are California Democratic Chairman Charles Warren, Brown fund-raiser Gene Wyman, and the president's daughter Lynda Bird Johnson. (Courtesy of the Bancroft Library, University of California, Berkeley)

National Guard troops stand guard in Watts on August 14, 1965, the fourth day of rioting and the day Brown arrived in California after a rushed return from Greece. In all, thirty-four people were killed and more than one thousand injured. One magazine said the riots showed that in Los Angeles, "the easy life is coming to an end." (Photo by John Malmin, AP/Wide World Photos)

Brown shares a rare laugh with Los Angeles mayor Sam Yorty, who challenged the governor in the 1966 Democratic primary. A conservative who appealed to disgruntled blue-collar Democrats, Yorty presaged Ronald Reagan's appeal to the same voters. (Courtesy of the Bancroft Library, University of California, Berkeley)

Former San Francisco mayor George Christopher and Brown share an awkward moment in June 1966, during a news conference after Brown apologized for his campaign's role in publicizing Christopher's old conviction for violating milk-pricing laws. (Photo: *San Francisco Chronicle*)

Governor-elect Reagan and Governor Brown shake hands during a meeting at the Capitol, November 21, 1966. It was the first time they had met since the Republican's landslide victory. (AP/Wide World Photos)

Two versions of Gov. Edmund G. Brown. Pat and Jerry at State Water Project aqueduct carrying water from Northern California's Feather River to Southern California's farms and cities. Pat built the artificial river; Jerry renamed it in honor of his father. (Courtesy of the Bancroft Library, University of California, Berkeley)

Brown in his retirement years. (Courtesy of the Bancroft Library, University of California, Berkeley)

By the fall Brown was riding a wave. Supporters created Brown for President Clubs. At a big fund-raising dinner at the Fairmont Hotel in San Francisco, young Hawaii congressman Daniel Inouye said that his state, which had entered the Union only weeks before, would back the California governor as a serious candidate, the first concrete sign of spreading support. Brown was invited to appear on *Meet the Press,* where he took advantage of the national television audience to declare that he no longer thought the Senate was the best place to find future presidents, citing instead—wonder of wonders—the "many Democratic governors who would make good candidates." As Brown wrote later, "I loved every minute of it."[17]

He basked in the newfound spotlight whenever he could. On a trip to Palm Springs to meet with President Eisenhower, Brown discarded his schedule—which called for him to return to Sacramento immediately after the meeting—and stayed around chatting with members of the White House press corps for hours. Some reporters thought, probably rightly, that they were as much the target of the trip as the president.[18]

By late October Brown was writing in his diary that he would make as good a president as any of the prominent candidates, perhaps better. Yet he knew also that strategically he was at a disadvantage. He was most likely to emerge with the nomination if there were a deadlock and then a brokered convention, but he expected that after eight years out of power Democrats would avoid a messy public display.[19]

Two weeks later he sounded uncertain about his national ambitions. "I feel my prime duty outside of my family is to the people of this state," he mused in the diary. "Is the presidential thing helping or hurting that objective? I don't know."[20]

Publicly, the chatter about a Brown candidacy culminated in early December with a flattering profile in the *New York Times Magazine.* Brown had come to the governorship as "the seemingly bemused beneficiary" of a Democratic landslide, the piece said, but since then had proved himself "a man with a knack for surmounting obscurity and obstacles." The writer had no illusions about Brown. The governor resembled the "friendly community optometrist," but he was also "virtually undislikable." Not among the front-runners, the story concluded, Brown might be a compromise candidate if the Democrats could settle on no other.[21]

It was just the kind of national acclaim for which presidential candidates pine, but ironically it marked the beginning of the end for Brown's dream. The same weekend the piece ran there was a huge banquet staged by the

Democratic Advisory Council, a talking shop designed to give the party a public face different from that of the conservative southern leadership in Congress. The dinner doubled as a beauty contest for the possible Democratic presidential candidates, and nearly everyone showed up. Each man was to give a short talk, limited to three or four minutes so that the program would not drag on all night. Gabby as ever, Brown felt constricted by the tiny window of time. His speech was a dud, a brief but wandering mishmash that excited nobody. Faced with an audience that included the party's most important figures, and relying on slim hopes that required him to seize every opportunity, Brown had flubbed his chance.[22]

The odds had been long anyway, even at the height of his boom. His early assessment of the other candidates was wishful thinking. Kennedy was young, but he was buttressed by his father's fortune. Humphrey was a liberal from a small state, but he had been a national figure since he led the civil rights forces at the 1948 Democratic National Convention, when Brown was a mere foot soldier. Johnson was a southerner, but he was also the majority leader of the U.S. Senate—and a tactical genius to boot. As presidential candidate, Brown was trying to play in a league where he did not belong. Even his supporters recognized it. Although it had been kept quiet, the early soundings had produced bad news: Brown's big financial donors did not want him to run. A campaign without money was virtually impossible, a fact Brown knew as well as anyone. "I just felt," he said later, "that I had better stick to my knitting."[23] At his last press conference of the year, the governor made his decision public. He would be only a favorite son, he told reporters, and planned to seek no delegates outside California.[24] The presidential campaign—always more wish than reality—was over.

Often a little disgruntled, Dutton was once again mad at his boss as 1960 began. In time Brown's brief flirtation with a serious presidential campaign would increase his national stature, Dutton believed, but in the short run the governor's inconsistencies had only hurt. This was somewhat disingenuous, since Dutton himself had counseled a two-pronged strategy—Brown should insist he was a California candidate while never foreclosing a meaningful bid—but it was also true that Brown had sometimes hedged a bit too much in his pronouncements, insisting almost in the same breath that he was merely a favorite son, but might be a serious candidate, but probably would not be. "The least adept thing we did," Dutton wrote in a memo summarizing Brown's first year as governor, "was the handling of the favorite son–national politics problem, and I still think that the deficiency was in the on-again, off-again way it was juggled."[25]

Pat was not the only Brown to start off the new year with a memo from Dutton. The chief of staff wrote to the governor's wife as well. Dutton believed that if Brown's political fortunes were to continue to rise, a more human public face was needed. For that, Bernice was a key ingredient. Dutton wanted her to keep the governor's press office informed about birthdays and family gatherings, and he tried to reassure her that hordes of reporters would not descend on her. The coverage could be orchestrated, he insisted, "in a dignified, restrained way." To expand her public role, he urged two trips to generate publicity, one to mental hospitals, the other to a women's prison. "We can arrange all of the details of the travel, provide written briefings in advance, and assure dignified news coverage by some of the women of the press," Dutton told her, not by accident using the word *dignified* twice in the same missive.[26]

It was a reminder that as Pat's profile grew, so too did the spotlight on the rest of the Browns—who did not always share his unbounded exuberance for public life. Much was expected of Bernice and the children, and Pat's relentless love of a crowd sometimes made him impervious to the strains on the family. Each of the Browns dealt with the stresses differently, but the differences were perhaps most marked between the children at either end of the birth order.

Barbara, the Browns' oldest daughter, disliked politics intensely. She hated the command performances at public events, where she and her sisters were introduced as a trio, a pretty sideshow to their father's endless politicking. "I felt like I had no identity and it was really important to me to do something different," she said later. She almost skipped her father's inauguration as attorney general. Later in life she became a family therapist. Pat never understood. After his retirement, when he would call, he would ask why she didn't enter politics.[27]

Kathy, the baby of the family, never knew a different life. She could not remember a time when her father did not have an official car. But even for her, politics sometimes intruded painfully. When she was a little girl, her father would take her to Sunday brunch after church at the Cliff House, a restaurant overlooking the beach at the western edge of San Francisco. Their father-daughter time would be interrupted by a radio host setting down microphones and interviewing Brown right at the table. Kathy was disappointed; her father loved it. Other times, he would suggest a trip for the day as if it were a lark. When they arrived at their destination, Kathy would see the ranks of waiting Democrats and understand that their family outing was a political rally. After Pat became governor, Kathy had to be driven to school by a police officer, an embarrassment she loathed so much that she talked the driver into letting her out a block from the building so the other children would not see. Once on a Friday when she was to leave school and go somewhere with her parents immediately, she walked out to find her father's black limousine waiting right in front. Never one to ignore an audience, the governor was outside talking to a group of kids who had gathered to gawk. Kathy, as any child would be, was horrified.[28]

Like her children, Bernice was at best ambivalent about politics, with its constant chitchat and glad-handing and backslapping. Proper and restrained, she lacked her husband's gregarious buoyancy. At golf he was a joyous hacker; she took up the game and practiced for six months before setting foot on a course, the better to ensure her competence when she actually ventured a round. Their differences showed in their attitudes toward publicity too. Pat loved seeing his name in print or posing for pictures. Except when posing for an official shot, he grinned hugely at every photographer he saw, as if the camera were a long-lost friend come back to greet him. Bernice was often guarded, scrutinizing the lens with care, as if it might assault her.

But she had a toughness that Pat lacked and needed. "My mother held people to far greater account than my father ever did," Kathleen Brown remembered later. "My father was much quicker to forgive and forget than my mother ever was. It was just his nature. It's who he was. It was one of his greatest strengths and it was one of his greatest weaknesses. I mean I remember my mother never speaking to people again. If someone crossed my father, she just cut them off and she'd walk right by them. They'd be off the list. My father just wasn't that way. It wasn't in his nature."[29]

Aware of her husband's undisciplined tendencies, Bernice helped to rein him in. Once on a trip to Washington, at a time when the whole 1960 electoral picture remained unclear, reporters pressed Pat for a more definitive statement of his plans: Would he run for president or not? Bernice whispered something to him, and, evidently repeating her counsel, he announced: "I smiled modestly and said nothing."[30]

Aside from good advice, Bernice was also capable of a dry remark that was wittier than her husband's corny gags. Years later she told an interviewer about the family's time in the mansion and noted that Pat was driven by the California Highway Patrol, while she and Kathy were chauffered around by the less distinguished State Police. "They're two different breeds really," she said in trying to explain the difference between the two agencies. "I have sometimes thought some of the state police shouldn't be allowed to carry guns."[31]

Dutifully, Bernice accepted Dutton's recommendation for a more public presence and began speaking to Democratic women's groups. She typically stayed away from political issues, offering instead charming tidbits about the governor and his family. Still, a governor's office press release emphasizing her added responsibilities made no claim that she found it a pleasant task: "Mrs. Brown frankly admits she never would have chosen a political career for her husband if the choice had been hers to make."[32]

———

Ironically, Brown's departure from the presidential race as a serious candidate made his political life more difficult. Had he actually mounted a campaign for the nomination, entering primaries around the country, he would have been out seeking votes, his refuge and joy. Instead he faced 1960 not as an overt and gleeful warrior but as a player in the Byzantine world of secret meetings and backroom promises.

First, Brown needed to ensure that he would be the only major candidate in the state's presidential primary in June. California would send to the Democratic National Convention one of the biggest delegations in the country, and all eighty-one votes would be pledged to the winner of the primary. If someone else entered the California race and beat the governor—an unlikely scenario but not impossible—he would be humiliated, and would lose all potential influence at the convention.

Kennedy was the biggest threat to run in California. His entire campaign strategy revolved around strong showings in nearly every state with a primary, thus building a delegate count and a sense of momentum that made his nomination seem inevitable. Kennedy's great fear was a deadlocked convention. The only other Catholic ever to be nominated by a major party, New York Gov. Al Smith in 1928, had been trounced, and Kennedy worried that if given the chance delegates might rush toward the safety of a more traditional candidate.

Speaking at the National Press Club in mid-January, Kennedy went public with the idea of competing in California, admitting that he might enter the state's primary against the governor's wishes, an aggressive maneuver.[33] Privately, Kennedy's father made the case. An intermediary was dispatched to contact Tom Lynch, Brown's old friend and deputy and now his successor as San Francisco district attorney. Lynch remained a confidant, perhaps Brown's closest, the kind of man people sought when they wanted to talk to the governor without talking to the governor. Reached by the Kennedys' emissary, Lynch agreed to meet with Joe Kennedy at a mutual friend's cabin near Lake Tahoe.

Kennedy launched into a lecture about how his son planned to contest and win California. The message was clear: The governor should consider dropping out of his own state's primary. But Lynch was not one to be intimidated, even by Joe Kennedy. He insisted that a primary battle in California would be a bloody affair. Brown was popular, and Californians did not like being told what to do by political bosses, let alone those from the East. What was more, Lynch suggested that Brown was secretly leaning toward supporting the younger Kennedy at the convention and bringing most or all of the California delegation with him. If that was true, Kennedy might not need to slog through the state's primary; he would eventually have the state's delegates anyway.[34]

Lynch had talked with Brown and knew he was leaning toward Kennedy, but the decision to back the young senator was not an obvious one. In one sense it ran counter to the whole idea of the favorite son candidacy, which was to maintain and maximize negotiating flexibility at the convention. But Brown desperately wanted to keep Kennedy out of California, and in any event Kennedy had the smell of a winner. It was still an age when some candidates disdained campaigning, but Kennedy was out on the hustings, logging thousands of miles, entering primary after primary and visiting state after state. Brown, the inveterate glad-hander, liked the younger man's ceaseless stumping, not to mention his charm and intelligence. Once at a dinner party Brown spent much of the evening talking with Kennedy, then walked over to the host, businessman Bart Lytton, and said, "Damned attractive fellow, isn't he?"[35]

Lynch and Joe Kennedy could talk, but a firm agreement required the two principals. So after a Democratic dinner in Washington, D.C., Brown and John Kennedy met at Kennedy's house to discuss the presidential race. Kennedy left no doubt about what was on his mind. He pulled out a poll suggesting that if he entered the California primary, he would win. But Kennedy insisted he preferred to stay out of California. He feared a bruising battle, perhaps in the end a losing one. Pleasing polls are no guarantee of victory. If Kennedy entered, so would the other candidates. Kennedy and Brown might split the Catholic vote, allowing Humphrey or Symington to win. Kennedy offered Brown a deal: Kennedy would stay out of California, so long as the governor agreed not to accept an offer of the vice presidential nomination. Kennedy made no bones about the reason. Two Catholics could not share the ticket, and if Brown thought he had a chance at the second spot he would work to deny Kennedy the first one. Brown agreed, promising he would not accept the vice presidency. Then, in an impulsive moment that would determine much that was to come, Brown went a little further. Although he had not strictly made it a part of their agreement, Kennedy had asked for Brown's support, and the governor now gave it to him—conditionally. Brown promised that if Kennedy started to win primaries, he would have the support of California's governor on the convention floor.[36]

Although it remained a secret, the agreement was significant. Kennedy won important primaries in Wisconsin and West Virginia.[37] The public impact was to drive Hubert Humphrey from the race. The private impact was to put Brown on the hook as a supporter. In the short run, the Brown-Kennedy deal worked to the advantage of both men. Kennedy avoided the time and expense of running in California but had the inside track on the delegation's support. Brown was assured he would be the sole candidate in the primary and thus have the state's delegates pledged to him. But in the long run, the critical issue remained unsettled: On the convention floor, when the grand business of picking a presidential nominee was distilled down to a head count of delegates, how much would Brown's support be worth? Once the governor released the California delegates from their obligation to vote for him as a favorite son, they were not required to follow his lead and vote for Kennedy for the nomination. Any sway Brown still held over his troops at that point would be amorphous, based on suasion rather than command. Thus, regardless of the candidate, it was crucial to know the delegates—their preferences, their loyalties, their vulnerabilities, the pressure points at which they might yield. And as Brown and Kennedy shook hands on their agreement, all of that remained a mystery, because nobody knew who the delegates would be.

––––––––

On February 26 ten California Democrats met in the wedding chapel of the Carmel Highlands Inn. They were there not to unite a couple in matrimony but to bring together in harmony—so they hoped—the various factions of the Democratic Party.

The idea was to pick the delegates who would go to the national convention in support of Brown—and who Brown planned eventually to steer toward Kennedy. The governor had selected the ten people invited to the meeting, who in turn were to appoint the delegates, mostly from names of party activists submitted by local caucuses and Democratic leaders. The strange location was picked because it was out of the way and thus safe from reporters and cameras, but leaks are inevitable, and the supposedly secret meeting was recounted in the papers.[38]

In a way the meeting showed how favorite son candidacies frustrated the purpose of party primaries, which had been adopted as Progressive reforms to reduce the power of political bosses and increase the say of common voters. When a favorite son ran and all other presidential candidates avoided a given state's primary—the situation in California in 1960—the whole purpose of the primary election was frustrated. California voters would not have a chance to pick among slates of delegates dedicated to the real candidates, such as Kennedy, Humphrey, or Symington. Instead voters would face only one major slate of delegates, pledged to Brown. Sitting in the wedding chapel, the political pros of California were about to pick the state's delegates as surely as if the primary did not exist, a fact recognized by the nickname quickly given to the little meeting: "the smoke-filled sanctuary."

Because Brown hoped to control the delegates even after they had no formal obligation to him, the obvious preference would have been to pick only hidebound Brown loyalists. That might have been impossible, for California produced few such creatures. The state's political structure did not allow it. Patronage jobs were scarce, almost nonexistent. Party lines were blurry, and thus so was the power of party officials. Even California's growth contributed. In more static places like Chicago, the machine's precinct and ward workers were expected to know every family in their area and to provide the kind of everyday help—jobs or legal assistance, for example—that commanded loyalty and respect. Postwar California was growing so fast that nobody could keep track of the neighborhoods.

But in any event Brown made no effort to pack the delegation. He tried to be nicer than that. Brown wanted a "fair and democratic method" for picking delegates, and he wanted the actual slate of names to represent every wing of the party, almost as if he were engaged in a good-government exercise rather than hardball politics. "I tried to be absolutely fair," he said later.[39] That was true. The delegation included supporters of all the major presidential possibilities—Kennedy, Johnson, Stevenson, even some Humphrey loyalists. And it crossed ideological lines, encompassing, at least by Democratic standards, liberals, moderates, and conservatives.

Ironically, the diversity was an attempt at unity: a more cohesive group might have opened wide the divisions of the party, precisely because it would have been devoted to one faction or another, and some people would have felt left out. But the ideological stew was also typically Brown. He wanted to bring people together, to unify them, and he was sure he could convince everybody to get along.[40] When it was announced the delegation was said to be "broadly based."[41] In fact, it was too much so. Everyone had been satisfied but no one truly pleased, and Brown was stuck with leading a slate of delegates who agreed on little but their registration. It was a disaster waiting to happen, and in the months to come the most basic fact about the group—the way in which it had been created—would prove the fault line buried deep in its geology, a fissure that became more dangerous as pressure increased.

Still, there is no evidence that anyone objected at the time. The ugly and divisive infighting that would have occurred with a contested primary had been avoided, and California Democrats, still new to power and fearful of a fratricide, had come together.

The Kennedys were satisfied too. They had been skeptical of the process, as they were skeptical of most things about California politics, so they dispatched Larry O'Brien, one of their bright young aides, to monitor the Carmel meeting. He did so from a motel room nearby and returned East to report that the arrangements were acceptable. The Kennedys guessed that at least 25 percent of the delegation would be loyal to JFK once released, perhaps as much as half. On March 2, only days after the meeting in the chapel, Kennedy talked over the California situation with his factotum and speechwriter, Ted Sorensen, and declared himself satisfied. A few hours later, he announced he would skip the California primary.[42] In effect, the Brown-Kennedy deal, though still confidential, had been ratified. Kennedy would not enter the California primary, which ensured that the other serious candidates would stay away too. Running as a true favorite son, Brown would win, and take his state's delegation to the convention.

Victory was never in doubt, but the vote totals from the primary gave Brown pause. A political maverick and old-age pension advocate named George McClain cobbled together a rival slate of delegates and appeared on the ballot as a candidate for president. Brown won easily, but McClain captured almost 650,000 votes, almost a third of the total and far too high a figure. The results made clear that in the wake of the Chessman case—the execution had finally occurred about a month before the primary—Brown had been weakened, just one more encouraging sign for California delegates who might be tempted to buck their leader. In his diary the governor excoriated himself: "It is obvious that I am in deep trouble when one out of every three Democrats will vote for a political faker like McClain. I am not doing things right."[43]

In Sacramento ten days later, less than a month before the convention was to open, the California delegation met for the first time. It was immediately obvious that the carefully constructed group was destined to rupture. Every four years the state's delegation to the national convention picked California's two members of the Democratic National Committee. Paul Ziffren, who held one of the seats, was up for reelection to the post, and he had made enemies. Northern Californians bore a traditional grudge against him, for he was from Los Angeles. The congressional delegation never liked Ziffren. Ed Pauley was angry with Ziffren because of a nasty spat over tickets to the convention. Perhaps worst of all, Ziffren was originally from Chicago and thus an outsider, and there had even been attempts to tie him vaguely to the mob. Brown decided it was time for Ziffren to go, and convinced Attorney General Stanley Mosk to run against him for the DNC seat. Mosk won easily, but there were a lot of hard feelings. After the meeting Brown invited everybody over to the Governor's Mansion, but his normal charm could not smooth the waters. People stood around in little groups, glaring at one another, sullen and brooding.[44]

Hoping to avoid trouble from the supporters of other presidential candidates, Brown was trying to keep his preference for Kennedy a secret—later he referred to himself as a "damn liar" for maintaining a phony public neutrality—but he could not hide his real feelings.[45] Brown kept letting on that Kennedy was really his man, which raised even further the likelihood of trouble in the delegation and drove another wedge between the governor and his chief aide. After Brown hinted at a news conference that he preferred the Massachusetts senator, Dutton fired off a hectoring memo, full of underlining and scratch-outs, attacking Brown for making his position too obvious. "Showing last week that you are leaning toward Kennedy at this time is a serious mis-timing, if not mistake," Dutton lectured. "*You will lose an appreciable amount of effectiveness with your own delegation* if you appear to identify yourself with a particular candidate at an illogical time."[46]

Dutton was right. Given Kennedy's big lead in the delegate count—the result of repeated primary victories—the only hope for other candidates was simply to slow down his momentum and deny him a first-ballot victory. Kennedy and his opponents agreed on one thing: If the convention deadlocked, Kennedy's chances fell dramatically. So supporters of the possible Kennedy rivals—Johnson, Stevenson, and Symington—adopted the same strategy. They wanted the favorite sons to hold their delegations for at least one ballot. They were especially worried about Brown, fearful that he might release the California votes before the convention began, and they struggled to ratchet up the pressure on the governor.

Clair Engle, one of the state's two U.S. senators and a Kennedy opponent, privately threatened to quit as chairman of the delegation if Brown withdrew as a favorite son and formally endorsed Kennedy. Word of the threat got back to the governor, who had to take it seriously.[47] Dick Berlin, the president of Hearst newspapers and a Johnson friend, approached Brown more directly. If Brown held the California delegation for himself for just one ballot, Berlin insisted, he would be one of only two people considered for the vice presidency. It wasn't really much of an offer. Berlin refused even to confirm the obvious—that he was speaking for LBJ—and he did not guarantee a spot on the ticket, only consideration for it. Brown, who had no great fondness for Johnson, said no.[48]

More appealing to Brown was a growing enthusiasm for Stevenson, who still claimed he did not want to run but was sounding and acting more and more like a candidate. Among the California delegates, there was a buzz for Stevenson. The California Democratic Council had grown out of the Stevenson Clubs of 1952, and to many the two-time nominee remained a hero. Only days before Brown was to leave for the convention, Lt. Gov. Glenn Anderson, not a man for whom Brown had much respect but a good liberal nonetheless, announced he would vote for Stevenson once the governor released the delegation. Brown resisted any urge to switch candidates and join the Stevenson bandwagon, but on the key question—when exactly did the governor intend to free his delegates?—he openly dithered. "I'm not sure what I'm going to do," he told reporters just before leaving for the convention. "Kennedy wants it now. The other three want me just to be a favorite son as long as I can be."[49]

———

Brown faced a short journey to the convention. For the first time in twenty years, the Democrats were staging their quadrennial meeting in the West.

It was scheduled to be the first event ever held at the new $6 million Los Angeles Memorial Sports Arena.[50]

The symbolism of the site was not overlooked. Ziffren had conceived the idea of a Los Angeles convention in part as a regional statement of pride, although it was not a universal sentiment. Southerners, in particular, never fully recovered from their suspicions that the party's showcase had been hijacked by kooky sun-worshippers from Hollywood.[51] Californians didn't mind; the presence of a national convention was just one more sign of their state's clout.

The governor felt the same way, naturally, and he missed no chance at the glory that accrues to the host. He wrote to prospective delegates, staged a big party featuring California wines, and even erected billboards welcoming his fellow Democrats to town. One effort by the Brown camp was truly innovative. Before the delegates began arriving, Dutton suggested contacting Los Angeles taxi drivers to urge them to act as the governor's stand-in hosts. "Basically, this would be an indirect means of getting the taxi drivers to mention the name Brown often in their contacts with fares during the convention," Dutton wrote.[52]

Brown arrived in Los Angeles on July 8, a Friday—the convention was to open the following Monday—in slightly better style than a taxicab. He flew down on his official plane, the *Grizzly*. Originally bought during Warren's administration, it was replaced later in Brown's term by a state-of-the-art plane that had previously been owned by the entertainer Arthur Godfrey. In either incarnation—the *Grizzly I* or the *Grizzly II*—the gubernatorial plane was a favorite Brown perk.

The *Grizzlies* were propellor planes and flew lower and slower than jets, so they offered the governor a chance to survey his great domain. Often he instructed the pilots to alter course so that he might see and assess a problem—floods were the cause of frequent detours—but typically the scene below was a source of pride. The governor liked to boast about his state as he flew over it. Once when the writer Stuart Alsop was traveling with Brown to research an upcoming profile, the governor spent much of the flight squatting down in the aisle next to Alsop's seat to point out the passing sights, all the while "shouting like a hog caller" over the drone of the engines.[53]

Both *Grizzlies* were large enough to accommodate staff members—the first plane seated about fifteen people, the second nearly twenty—and often Brown worked while he flew. He liked to dictate letters in the air, so much so that Mickey Bailey, who took the fastest shorthand of all the governor's secretaries, became something of a regular on the plane.[54] Other aides often came along as well. As governor, Brown always traveled with an entourage of some kind. He was accompanied on most out-of-town trips by his "travel secretary," usually a bright and promising young fellow who served as a man Friday, handling tasks large and small. A California Highway Patrol officer was there as driver and bodyguard. Often there was a member of the press office staff.

To the convention, Brown took family as well as employees. Bernice went along, as did fourteen-year-old Kathy, who remembered the event chiefly because somebody arranged for her to have lunch with Ricky Nelson, the teen-idol star of television's *Ozzie and Harriet.*[55]

As soon as he arrived in Los Angeles, Brown came face-to-face with the heat of national politics. Bobby Kennedy, who was running his older brother's campaign, met with the governor and demanded that he set free the California delegates immediately and declare himself finally and publicly as a Kennedy supporter. Brown said he wanted to wait until Sunday, when he hoped that Engle might back Kennedy too. Brown remembered Kennedy snapping at him, "I don't care about that. You're not going to get Engle. I know you're not going to get him. I want you to come out for [JFK] right now." The tone offended Brown, who did not like receiving a caustic lecture from an insolent young man in his mid-thirties who was, after all, nothing more than the younger brother of one of the candidates, a "punk kid," as Brown called him later. The governor was neither the first nor the last person to find Bobby arrogant and cheeky, and he refused to budge, but the exchange served notice that Brown and the Kennedys would sustain a sometimes touchy alliance.[56]

California's delegates caucused on Sunday, the day before the convention opened.[57] The pressure on Brown had only increased. Favorite son governors in Kansas and Iowa were safely delivering their delegations to Kennedy, and Brown was expected to do the same.[58] But from the meeting's first moments, things went badly. Brown announced his formal endorsement of Kennedy—a surprise to no one—and dispatched his press aide to distribute to the waiting reporters a copy of his remarks. "I want to make it absolutely clear that every delegate has to exercise his own independent judgment," the speech said. "You are now in a position to exercise that independent judgment." Not unreasonably, reporters read that to mean that

Brown was finally abandoning his favorite son status and releasing the delegation, an interpretation included in stories that moved over the wires almost immediately. Brown's remarks were a little disingenuous—he didn't really want the delegates to exercise independence, but to follow his lead and vote for Kennedy—but it was soon obvious there was a far bigger problem. Candid or not, the governor's comments were apparently premature.

Back inside the room, Johnson and Stevenson supporters were enraged. The governor had promised to hold the delegation as a favorite son for at least one ballot, they insisted. Now he had broken his word. The congressmen were especially livid. Most favored either Stevenson or Johnson—as Senate majority leader, Johnson had tremendous power over their bills— yet they had avoided a public endorsement. Brown had promised, they said, that if they endorsed no one before the convention's official opening, neither would he. Uniformly neutral, they would find safety in numbers and shield one another from candidate pressure. Chet Holifield, a congressman from Los Angeles, stood up and accused Brown to his face of reneging on the deal, the bitterness of his feelings so evident that years later Brown recalled the speech vividly.[59]

Brown tried to back down, emerging from the meeting and telling reporters that he had not technically released the delegation after all. His earlier statement, he said, had been intended merely to suggest that delegates should exercise their own judgment *eventually*, but not yet. It was a sad performance, and most of the reporters, based on their sources in the delegation, disputed the accuracy of the explanation. Brown had intended to release the delegates, several stories said, but was rebuffed, in effect forced to stand by his own candidacy against his will.

The delegation was in tatters, more divided than when it had arrived in Los Angeles, which once would have seemed impossible. Holifield took his anger into the hallway and openly described the rift to reporters. He was not alone. John Moss, a congressman from Sacramento, called the situation "ridiculous." Harry Sheppard, a congressman from San Bernardino, said the governor had been "morally wrong." Delegates could not agree on the basic facts of what had occurred. Some insisted they had been released and would vote for whom they pleased on the first ballot. Others said they were still obligated to Brown as a favorite son. Stevenson supporters announced they had at least thirty-two votes in the delegation, far too many if the governor was to deliver the great bulk of California's support to Kennedy. Even Engle, the delegation chairman, admitted publicly that he was bewildered. "I am more confused than ever after this meeting," he told reporters. Only one thing was settled: the delegation would meet again Tuesday, the day before the convention was to pick a nominee, and try to hash things out.

For the governor, disaster had struck. California's top Democrats had struggled to ensure a unified face at the convention. That had been the whole idea behind keeping the real candidates from entering the primary in favor of Brown's favorite son bid. Now, through a mix of unavoidable circumstance and inadequate leadership, California was offering not a solid team ready to bargain to the state's advantage but, even in public, a bickering, squabbling mob.

———

When the convention opened the next night, it offered Brown a chance to briefly trade the afflictions of inside politics for the pleasures of the podium. As governor of the host state, he greeted the delegates, throwing both arms up over his head in a big, wild wave, beaming out at the packed hall and drinking in the cheers. Blessed with a national television audience, he did his best to sound like a national figure, delving more deeply than usual into foreign affairs. It was good liberal stuff: The United States must "stop pretending that Communist China does not exist[,] . . . that neutrality is always immoral[,] . . . [and] that just being anti-Communist is a foreign policy." In the Eisenhower years the country had been "drifting in the shadow" of nuclear war; now it needed the vigor of a Democratic president. "We must dare to dream, to do and to build," he said, finishing with one of his favorite verbs.[60]

Brown's more immediate dream was still to deliver the bulk of his delegation to his chosen presidential candidate, who now looked like a sure thing. Kennedy was picking up delegates in a flood, people rushing to the side of the presumptive nominee. When Brown got up Tuesday morning, the day of the California delegation's all-important meeting, he was greeted with headlines suggesting that Kennedy had the nomination in hand. The situation only made Brown look worse. Not only had favorite son governors in small states like Kansas and Iowa announced for Kennedy, big-state delegations that had come to Los Angeles officially undeclared, such as Illinois and Pennsylvania, were producing overwhelming majorities for the front-runner. The men in charge of those states—Chicago Mayor Richard Daley and Pennsylvania Gov. David Lawrence—had delivered.[61] Yet California remained a mess.

The delegation was scheduled to meet in the afternoon. Some delegates had objected to the fact that Sunday's caucus had been closed, so remarkably the Tuesday session was public. It was even moved to accommodate the huge number of reporters and cameramen who wanted to watch the bickering. Because the Knickerbocker Hotel, where the delegates were staying, was too small for the expected press corps, the meeting was shifted to an NBC studio at Sunset and Vine.

As the meeting began, Brown released the delegates from their obligation to vote for him on the first ballot—exactly the thing he had tried to do on Sunday. This time it stuck: The convention was under way, and few delegates wanted to fool with a symbolic gesture toward a favorite son while the real decision was being made. Still, the meeting grew contentious almost immediately. Brown did not want to poll the delegation right away. By now it was clear that Stevenson support was strong, and the best hope for Kennedy was to delay an official tally and continue twisting arms. But the Stevenson forces, led by Brown's erstwhile ally, state senator George Miller, started shouting for a roll call. At one point Engle, the delegation chairman and thus the man with the gavel, ruled that a motion to adjourn had carried, but he was greeted with such boos from the Stevenson forces that he reversed himself and allowed the proceedings to continue.

At 4:00 P.M., the starting time for the convention's evening session at the Sports Arena, the California delegates were still shouting at each other at their television studio across town. Unable to control much of anything, Brown and the other Kennedy forces eventually lost their efforts to delay a roll call, and the clerk started ticking off the names. The result was a nightmare for Brown, who had staked his prestige on handing Kennedy a victory: 31½ votes for Stevenson, 30½ for Kennedy, 9 for Symington, 6½ for Johnson, the others scattered.[62]

There was still a full day left before the convention actually picked the nominee, and Brown and his subordinates went to work trying to shift delegates into the Kennedy column. They won a few converts, but it was tough going. The liberals stood by Stevenson. Johnson supporters stuck with their man, or, in some cases, switched to Stevenson as a ruse, trying to build momentum for any candidate with a chance to stop Kennedy.[63] In the end, when the roll of the states was called Wednesday night, Kennedy managed to eke out the narrowest of victories among the California delegates, picking up 33½ votes to 31½ for Stevenson.[64]

Overall, Kennedy sailed to a first-ballot victory, precisely the goal toward which his campaign had struggled for months. But as insiders analyzed the voting state by state, the buzz the next day was not that Kennedy had won the California delegation, which he had, but that Brown had lost control of it. Heading into the convention, the governor had talked of "at least 40 votes" for Kennedy, double the total for Stevenson.[65] That had been Bobby Kennedy's hope too.[66]

Instead Brown had produced only a tiny plurality for Kennedy—and that only after messy public bloodletting. The papers were full of stories about Brown's damaged reputation.[67] Russell Baker, then a young reporter and eventually a Pulitzer Prize–winning columnist and memoirist, wrote in the *New York Times* that Brown's failure to control his delegation "is the scandal of the cigar-smoke set."[68] The governor was mocked even by his own aides. After the final roll call somebody told a *Time* magazine reporter that Brown was out on the sidewalks conducting a poll of passersby. "He wants to find out," said the aide, who ambushed his boss from the safety of anonymity, "whether we should support Albert Schweitzer or Fidel Castro for the vice presidency." The *Time* writer coined an epithet that Brown would never quite shake. The governor had seemed like a "tower of jelly," the magazine said, "because he could not make up his mind which game to play—'Back-Jack' or 'Favorite Son.'"[69] Public reaction followed the press coverage: letters poured in to the governor's office complaining that Brown had botched the convention.[70]

As if that were not enough, another blow hit. Kennedy asked Dutton to come over to his hotel suite, where Dutton found the newly nominated candidate still in his pajamas at midmorning. Kennedy asked him to leave Brown's office and join the presidential campaign, an offer that excited Dutton immediately. Leading up to the convention, he and Brown had grown further apart, first because of Chessman, which infuriated him, then because of the convention, which disappointed him. Perhaps he would have left anyway—national politics held a powerful attraction for a man of Dutton's abilities and ambitions—but Brown's stumbling performance in the previous months had done nothing to help. Dutton told Kennedy he would take the job. Brown and Dutton had a charged relationship, filled with good moments and bad, but that was part of its value to the governor. Dutton had no fear about contradicting his boss. "You and I have not always agreed on specifics," Brown wrote to Dutton years later, "but I know our ultimate goals have always been the same." Now, amid all his other troubles, the governor had lost his most candid and important aide, the man who had engineered his election victory and been at his side for his first eighteen months in office.[71]

In some ways the criticism of Brown was unfair. The California delegation had not splintered as badly as it seemed, or at least not much worse than should have been expected. Nor was the trouble Brown's fault alone. Tom Rees, a legislator from Los Angeles and a delegate, blamed Jesse Unruh, the powerful member of the state assembly, for the disastrous Tuesday caucus. Rees, who was friendly with Unruh, remembered that at a critical moment Unruh tried to seize control, a much-resented move that only added strength to the pro-Stevenson rebellion. As things collapsed, Rees told Unruh, "You screwed this up."[72]

But for all the excuses, the fact remained that Brown had been the leader. The delegates traveled to Los Angeles as his delegates, no one else's. Right or wrong, the Kennedys expected him to deliver, as the leaders in other states did, and instead more than half the Californians voted for other candidates. It was a failure the Kennedys, hard-chargers to a man, never quite forgot or forgave. John Kennedy wondered if he should have slugged it out with the governor in the California primary. Brown lost face, and Unruh, who had mostly been a loyal servant to the governor, became the Kennedys' lieutenant in California. Ever eager to please, Brown had instead damaged his own reputation in the eyes of the man who was now the most important Democrat in America.[73]

Unintentionally, Brown had set himself an impossible task months before. To keep Kennedy from entering the Democratic primary, the governor had promised his support. To keep the various factions of the Democratic Party intact, he had created a delegation so diverse that it made the first goal nearly impossible. Secretly bound to support one candidate, Brown was leading a group that was loyal to many. Inclusive to a fault, California's delegation was a collection of adversaries, briefly bound together in a truce but certain—sooner or later—to quarrel. Brown described it as "not an easy team of horses to drive."[74] Controlling so unruly a band would have been arduous work, and in 1960 California had neither the politics nor the politician for the job.

Politically, the state's free-form system allowed little in the way of control. Without patronage or strong parties, there was almost nothing with which to punish and reward the delegates. This was what the Kennedys failed to understand. Although they may once have been satisfied with a quarter of the California delegation, as the convention approached and the pressure for a first-ballot win increased, they came to expect that California's governor would command his troops in the way that men did in other states. It was more than simply a misunderstanding at the convention; it was a difference in the political cultures of a country still regionalized. Although the perception was beginning to change, California remained for many Americans an exotic locale, "a strange land across the mountains" in the words of one contemporary writer, and nowhere was the bewilderment more evident than in politics.[75] Easterners kept looking for California's machines, the bosses, the guys who called the shots. Once at a dinner party in San Francisco, Connecticut Gov. Abe Ribicoff, a devotee of old-time politics, asked Brown who decided that he should run for governor. Mystified, Brown responded, "I did."[76]

If anyone was to impose order and unanimity on California's 1960 delegates, Brown was not the man to put down the iron hand. As always, he had been friendly and well intentioned, but in the snake-pit world of national politics, that was not enough. At the delegation's first meeting in Los Angeles, he had told the delegates that they should devote a "clear majority" to one candidate, so that California "will have a strong voice" on the convention floor. The consensus, he continued, "should only come through individual judgment and decision" by the delegates.[77] It was a nice thought but a hopeless one. Delegations maximized their strength not through individuality but through sheeplike obeisance to a strong leader. Mayor Daley, a Kennedy man, held the Illinois delegates with such martial rigor that poor Adlai Stevenson could collect only a pathetic two votes out of sixty-nine from his own home state. Years later, at another Democratic convention, another California politician named Brown—the legendary assembly Speaker Willie Brown—would discipline a young dissenter by threatening to boot him off the delegation's plane, stranding him in Miami Beach without a way to get home.[78] For good or ill, Pat Brown was the kind of fellow who invited people on to planes, not kept them off.

Even Brown's friends were critical. Weeks after the convention, when things had cooled down a bit, Brown's aide Hale Champion wrote to a political science professor who had studied the delegation and offered an appraisal. "I might add as a side note, and all this is, of course, private comment to you, that the governor's personality enters heavily into this problem. If he were a tough guy in Warren's pattern some of the things that took place just simply would not have happened. . . . The fact is that a tough governor, one known to be ready with reprisals, can do a lot more than you appear to believe he can. Pat just is not a whipcracker at heart and people know it and like him for it. This time, however, this reputation for being a nice guy hurt instead of helped."[79]

As with the Chessman case, Brown had managed to anger everybody.

The Kennedys were mad that he had failed to produce a big majority among the California delegates. Stevenson supporters were equally mad that he had abandoned his favorite son bid before the roll call, allowing any first-ballot votes at all for Kennedy. When Brown announced the state's totals, Stevenson fans in the galleries rained down boos—a painful reminder of the hooting that had been Brown's constant companion only months before, after the Chessman debacle. Brown was so devastated that two nights later, when the convention met in the massive Los Angeles Coliseum to hear Kennedy's acceptance speech, the governor of California tried consciously to slink into the stadium, in the hope that an unnoticed entry might spare him another bout of public derision.[80]

Brown had endured all he could take. In the course of a few months he had nearly ruined himself. Again and again, voters who had once elected him had booed him. Now, fresh from what should have been a moment of splendor—his home state hosting the national convention of his own political party—Brown was at one of the low points of his life. He told Bernice that he was thinking about resigning as governor.[81]

There was only one slight bit of consolation. It was an election year, and since it was summer, the campaign was soon to begin. The governor was not on the ballot, but fortunately one of his favorite causes was—a massive project to provide water for farms in the Central Valley and cities in Southern California. Voters were being asked to approve a bond issue to pay for the work, and thus a little stumping was in order. Blessedly, the governor could flee the confusing, vicious maze of secret meetings and convention halls, and head back to rallies and crowds and speeches. Laid low by his own mistakes, Pat Brown had the chance to seek redemption by doing the one thing he loved most: shaking hands.

10 BUILDING A RIVER

OF ALL THE STRANGE IRONIES of the California experience, two of the most striking are physical: Southern California holds one of the world's great metropolises, and the Central Valley has become the most agriculturally productive place on earth. Sit down with a map of the United States and data about the natural climate of each region, and you will mark off large sections of the southwestern corner as wasteland, good for growing neither plants nor people. The Southern California coast receives little rainfall—it is far drier than any place in the eastern half of the United States—and much of the Central Valley receives even less, so little as to be classed a desert.[1]

Long before Pat Brown was born, Californians began examining such natural arrangements and thinking they should be changed. California's farmers and city dwellers wanted more water, and in the early decades of the twentieth century they began to reach across extraordinary distances to fetch it. Farmers in the Imperial Valley, in the deserts southeast of Los Angeles, tapped the waters of the Colorado River through a canal that dipped down into Mexico and then ran back north into California. Twice, Los Angeles built aqueducts across the desert to draw from rivers more than 200 miles away: first the Owens, in the Sierra Nevada, and then the Colorado. San Francisco reached almost as far, damming Hetch Hetchy Canyon in Yosemite National Park and channeling the waters 155 miles to the city. The suburbs on the east side of San Francisco Bay appropriated their own river, the Mokelumne, and built their own aqueduct. In the 1930s, with the Great Depression constricting state finances, the federal government took control of a massive state scheme called the Central Valley Project. Dams blocked a series of rivers in the north, principally the Sacramento near Mount Shasta, and diverted the water into long canals toward what soon became irrigated farms.

Yet even those projects did not sate California's thirst. In the years after World War II, farmers in the Central Valley and dreamers in Southern California continued to search for more water, looking for additional rivers to dam and rechannel. They thought of taming the Feather, wildly tumbling out of the Sierra Nevada in the north. They eyed the Eel, along the coast near Eureka. In the most outsized vision of all, they contemplated tapping the Columbia, pouring into the ocean at Oregon's northern border, as far from Los Angeles as St. Louis is from the Atlantic Ocean. As Brown fled his troubles at the Democratic National Convention in summer 1960, it was this environment into which he was ready to leap, a political world in which more water was never enough.

———

In the early years of his career, Brown had largely ignored his state's great water disputes. Big-city lawyers had little contact with the troubles of farmers, and San Francisco's water supply had been secured decades earlier, in Brown's youth, when the city dammed Hetch Hetchy. In law school Brown took a course in water law, but the next two decades gave him few opportunities to put his learning to use.[2]

That changed when he ran for attorney general. Campaigning statewide for the first time, stopping at ranches and farms and small towns, he encountered as never before the worries of rural California. The biggest of these was water. For decades, farmers in the Central Valley had been pumping so much water out of the ground that the land was literally sinking, huge patches of earth bellying down toward bedrock as the water beneath was sucked away. If irrigated farming was to continue—and in the Central Valley that was understood as a given—more water would be needed from somewhere.[3]

In fall 1950, in the days and weeks after he won the attorney general's race, Brown sensed that water might dominate his future, and he began carrying around a primer. Stuffed into the briefcases he invariably lugged was the new edition of the *California Law Review,* the entire soporific issue devoted to the topic and filled with articles that were as useful as they were dry: "Background of California Water and Power Problems," "Developing a New Philosophy of Water Rights," "The Central Valley Project and the Farmers."[4]

Such knowledge was put to use quickly, for almost as soon as he took the oath of office Brown faced a major decision on water. Like all systems operated by the U.S. Bureau of Reclamation, the Central Valley Project allowed its water to be used only on farms of 160 acres or less. The Progressives who had created the bureau at the beginning of the century had adopted the limit to ensure that the agency would help to preserve family farms, and in subsequent decades the law became both cherished and hated. In time the bureau would become almost laughably lax about enforcing the 160-acre limitation, but as Brown moved into the attorney general's office it was still a bitterly contested issue.

Large agricultural interests were in the midst of a legal battle to invalidate the 160-acre limit, arguing that California law prohibited a water district from signing a contract containing the federal restriction. If successful, the suit would greatly enrich big agriculture, which for the first time would be able to buy cheap, federally subsidized water from the Central Valley Project and then use it to irrigate huge corporate farms, some of which sprawled across thousands of acres. The argument fostered an internecine struggle in rural California, with small farmers supporting the acreage limit and big ones opposing it with equal vehemence. Under Howser, Brown's predecessor, the state Department of Justice had argued that the acreage limit should be overturned. Brown, now the attorney general, had to decide if the state should stick with Howser's position or reverse it.

Political payback suggested a reversal. Most of California's biggest farmers—actually large corporations running fiefs the size of small states—were Republicans. They had no sympathy for Brown, nor he for them. "They had supported the opposition to me, so I wasn't about to do anything for them anyway," he said years later. "Now, that may sound like a small-gauge guy—that he would let politics interfere with his judgment on a thing like this, but that happens to be true."[5]

On substantive grounds as well, Brown was inclined to abandon Howser's position. Brown recognized that the water project was fundamentally a subsidy from taxpayers to agriculture. Considering the astronomical cost of water projects—the huge dams, the river-sized canals—farmers paid a fraction of the real cost of bringing the water to their fields. The 160-acre limit effectively capped the subsidy that one farmer could enjoy, a stab at equality that appealed to Brown's instincts. Without the acreage limit, people who owned the most land would receive the biggest subsidy. Or there might be a worse outcome. If giant corporate farmers were allowed to use as much of the water as they wished, Brown feared that the Bureau of Reclamation might postpone for years the building of additional diversion systems to channel water from the main canals to local fields, a delay he regarded as a near-disaster. Bureau of Reclamation water, Brown said in one statement, "makes possible new fertility to parched lands . . . [and] more food for California's sensationally expanding population." He wanted to keep the federal water coming, and he was convinced the 160-acre limit made that more likely.[6]

Thus doubly motivated—by both politics and policy—Brown considered the matter briefly, and then, two months after taking office, announced that the state was changing its legal mind. The new attorney general and his Department of Justice would argue that the acreage limit should be sustained, the reverse of Howser's old stance. The U.S. Supreme Court eventually upheld the limit, though there is no reason to think Brown's position swung the case. Still, in his first battle in the California water wars, Brown had at least fought on the winning side.

––––––

If the Great Depression had once rendered California too poor to shoulder the financing of the Central Valley Project, the booming postwar years restored both the state's finances and its ambitions. In May 1951, only weeks after Brown's decision on the 160-acre limit, the state's chief water engineer, Arthur Edmonston, unveiled a bold new plan that the state would pursue alone, without federal help. Owing much to the dreamers of previous decades, the new proposal was as grand in scope as any existing water project in the American West. Near the little town of Oroville, north of Sacramento, the state would dam the Feather River, one of a dwindling number of untamed waterways in the state. Held in the resulting reservoir, water would be released at the thoughtful judgment of humans rather than the capricious whim of nature. Once out the spillway, the water would travel down the Sacramento River to the Delta, where the two most important rivers in the state—the Sacramento and the San Joaquin—join, turn west, and head toward San Francisco Bay and the Pacific. Because it would flow into the Delta at well-regulated intervals, the fresh water from the reservoir would push back saltwater from San Francisco Bay, which in drought years could surge alarmingly far inland.[7]

Edmonston had no intention of stopping there. He did not wish to dam rivers only to let them run to the sea. Instead, he would effectively reverse part of California's geography. South of the Delta, the San Joaquin River drains the Central Valley from south to north, swallowing up rivers as they come out of the Sierra Nevada and steering the combined flow northward. The problem, from the perspective of Edmonston and his ilk, was that the water was needed farther south, at farms along the southwestern edge of the Central Valley and in the great metropolises of the southern coast. So Edmonston proposed building an artificial river. Huge intake valves would suck water from the Delta and pump it into the new concrete channel, which would run roughly parallel to the San Joaquin but in the opposite direction. The new river would run southward down the western side of the valley, eventually bringing irrigation water to farms that received little rainfall, had no natural rivers, and were not served by the federal government's Central Valley Project. At that point, geology presented a barrier, the Tehachapi Mountains. Although nearly as far south as Phoenix, the sheer face of the Tehachapis rises high enough that in the winter snow can snarl traffic on the highway through one of the passes. But Edmonston proposed that California's artificial river defeat its natural mountains: The water would be pumped almost three thousand feet uphill to the top of the range, then pour down into huge new reservoirs in the Los Angeles basin.

Taken as a whole, the idea was staggering. The dam on the Feather River would be the tallest in the country, and the proposed dam site was almost as near to Seattle as to San Diego. The aqueduct that would move the water south would instantly become California's longest river; if built in the East, it would stretch from Boston to Virginia. The climb over the Tehachapis was the equivalent, in height at least, of making a river run up the side of Niagara Falls fifteen times. For a while, there was serious talk of putting a nuclear reactor at the base of the Tehachapis, just to generate the power needed to make the new river flow uphill.

———

By the time Brown became governor, in January 1959, Edmonston's plan had been lying around for the better part of a decade, the subject of much talk and little action. Brown's predecessor, Goodwin Knight, managed an administrative advance—knitting together the state's many water-related agencies into a single Department of Water Resources—but actual construction was a goal that eluded him. Brown was partly to blame. As an ambitious Democratic attorney general angling for personal and partisan advantage, he conspired with Democrats in the legislature to ensure that the Republican governor could not pass a bill launching the great project.[8]

Brown had resolved that he would be the governor to build the greatest California waterworks of all. Water would be a hallmark of his career, as it had been a hallmark of California history. That Brown set his sights on the issue was a sign of both personal ambition and political liberalism. In later years, damming rivers came to be seen as the act of conservatives, an accommodation to industrial concerns heedless of environmental damage. In Brown's era, it was exactly the reverse. Dams represented progress for the little man. Woody Guthrie, the consummate left-wing show business activist of his day, wrote a whole suite of odes to the Bonneville Power Administration in the 1930s. "Roll on Columbia," the title of one Guthrie song, meant not that the river should roll unfettered to the sea but that it should roll through the turbines that sent light and heat across the land. "Your power is turning our darkness to dawn," he sang. "So roll on, Columbia, roll on!"[9] The spirit of Guthrie's ideas was still alive in the 1950s. When Brown made water a centerpiece of his 1958 gubernatorial campaign, he did it as a sign of concern for the workingman. Appearing on television to answer questions phoned in by voters, he was introduced by an announcer asking, "Should corporate interests and nature run their course at your expense, or should the government solve the water problem?"[10] It was no accident that corporations and nature were paired as enemies of the public interest. The great California water projects represented nothing if not government's conquest of nature, and to Brown and most of his contemporaries, they were unquestioned achievements. Abbott Goldberg, a water lawyer and one of Brown's top aides on the issue, once used language of biblical grandeur to describe the great dams and canals. "By bringing water to the thirsty land," he said, summarizing the prevalent view among water experts, "you were in effect doing the Lord's work."[11]

To Brown, opponents were simply timid people who lacked the vision and courage to embrace a grand effort. "What are we to do?" he wrote to one newspaper publisher. "Build barriers around California and say nobody else can come in because we don't have enough water to go around?"[12] And then there was just raw hubris. Brown once said that he wanted to build the water project for the same reasons he wanted to win cases as a lawyer.

"You've got to remember that I was *absolutely determined* that I was going to pass this California Water Project," he said years later. "I wanted this to be a monument to *me*." At the time Brown told Ralph Brody, one of his chief water aides, that success in the grand project would put Brody in the cabinet—and Brown in the White House.[13]

He unveiled the details of his proposal three weeks after taking office, a special appearance before a joint session of the legislature heralding the moment's import.[14] He began by noting the failures of the recent past—omitting any discussion of his own role—and suggesting the need for a bolder approach. "We have brooded over the expense and become lost in a forest of fear," he said, adding that the result had been "delay and frustration." The problem was straightforward: "We do not have enough water when and where we need it. We have too much water when and where we do not need it." To a man of Brown's era and inclination, the solution was equally simple: move water. The north was not so much a victim of flooding as it was a supply of overabundant fresh water. The Delta was described as a natural holding pond, "the tap from which the water can flow."

In broad outline he described the project Edmonston had envisioned: a massive dam on the Feather River in the north and then a long aqueduct south to farms and cities, with spurs along the way for deliveries to smaller areas. To pay for it all, the governor suggested that the state's revenues from offshore oil drilling be devoted to the water project and that the state float a bond issue of at least $500 million, larger than any single act of borrowing in state history.

Brown's greatest innovation was political rather than financial. Through the previous decade, as the state contemplated its own version of the massive western water projects, proposals had always foundered on the shoals of regional mistrust. The north wanted dams to control floods, and the south wanted water, but both sides worried about what would happen after the project was built. Northern California legislators worried that the south would take an ever-increasing draw from the northern rivers. The north would be reduced to colonial status, providing the south with the state's most valuable raw material—water. With the pumps and canals sucking away the north's birthright, future growth in the northern counties might be precluded for the most ironic of reasons, lack of water. For precisely the same reasons in reverse, Southern California mistrusted the north, fearing that as they grew, northern counties would claim back the water they had once agreed to ship south. The great economic engine of Southern California would have helped to pay for the north's desired dams, but the south's benefit would be erased. In trying to solve this stalemate, the assumption had always been that any potential agreement would have to be written into the state's constitution, where it could not be changed by the legislature alone. Thus encased in legal stone, the two regions could assume that the deal would stick. The problem was that a constitutional amendment had to be agreed to—word for word—by both sides, a task that had proved impossible. Knight had always treated a constitutional amendment as a prerequisite for approval of the water project, which is why he probably would have failed to win its approval even without the obstructionism of Brown and his fellow Democrats.

Brown's insight was simply to bypass this nettlesome issue. If he could convince both sides to go along for the short run, specific problems of water allocation could always be hammered out later, after the project was built. This left the potential for a future of wrangling, but wrangling about California water was inevitable anyway, and in the meantime the project would be built. He could even offer some intermediate comfort for both regions. For the north, he could point to his own legal opinion, issued when he was attorney general, that interpreted the state constitution as offering a guarantee of future water rights for the "counties of origin," the places where the rivers rose.[15] For the south, Brown insisted that water deliveries from the proposed state project would be guaranteed at least until the bonds were paid off, which would take decades. Thus neither side had the absolute security of a constitutional amendment, but both had some form of reassurance. As he spoke to the legislature to unveil the program, Brown announced that one of the largest past obstacles to a water deal had simply disappeared: The administration would not push for an amendment to the state constitution, so nobody had to worry about how to word it.[16]

Along with omitting a constitutional amendment, Brown's plan lacked the federal 160-acre limit. In 1958, as Brown was running for governor against William Knowland, the U.S. Supreme Court had upheld the limit for the federal government's Central Valley Project. It was the case in which Brown had changed the state's position years before, and now his view had prevailed. But an unanticipated side effect was to refocus the attention of the state's large agricultural interests. Having failed to win approval for using federal irrigation water on their massive holdings, the farmers turned toward supporting a state-built project—as long as it carried no acreage limitation. Brown thought that in some ways large-scale farming made sense, just as other industries found efficiency in size. But more important was the straightforward political calculation. If the water project was to pass the legislature, Brown needed the support of large landowners. To get their support, he could not possibly propose that the state mimic the federal government's 160-acre cap. So as he outlined his program to the legislature, he included no limit on the size of the farms that might use the water, though he had just spent years in court defending such a law. "I wanted to build a water project," he said later, in utter candor, "and worry about the philosophy of land use later on."[17]

Even with Brown's concessions to political reality—the willingness to forgo the acreage limitation, the elimination of a call for a constitutional amendment—the odds remained long against his proposal.[18] Apportioned by geography rather than population, the state senate was dominated by northerners, many of whom viewed Brown's project as little more than a theft of their region's water by the south. As much as they wanted new dams to control floods, they were unwilling to give away their counties' water, which they saw as both a birthright and a precondition for future growth and development. The northerners began to meet weekly at the Senator Hotel, across the street from the Capitol, to plan strategy for fighting off Brown's plan. Confident they had the upper hand, they concluded that the governor's proposal was dead. Brown, they decided, should satisfy himself with a more modest accomplishment—diverting the state's oil revenues toward possible use for some other water project, one out in the future and not yet designed.[19]

But far from surrendering, Brown expanded his ambitions. His proposal for a $500 million bond issue grew to $960 million and then to an astonishing $1.75 billion, a figure more than three-fourths the size of the total state budget for the year. The need for water was critical, he insisted, and it must be completed no matter the cost. In mid-May the governor jumped on a state report predicting water shortages and insisted that by midsummer some communities might face rationing. At times he sounded almost apocalyptic: "The needs are desperate. We are in trouble now. Unless we act now to take care of that trouble, the growth and future of California is in mortal danger."[20]

Privately, Brown was collecting votes one at a time, legislator by legislator. Fred Dutton, Brown's top aide, remembered that to get the support of Hugh Burns, the senate president pro tem, the governor agreed to retain an industry-friendly Republican appointee as the state's insurance commissioner. Gene McAteer, Brown's fellow San Franciscan, insisted that one of his friends be appointed a judge, a condition Brown met and later regretted. Assemblywoman Pauline Davis insisted that a series of small lakes be built in her district for boating and fishing. She got them, although Capitol insiders quickly dubbed them "Pauline's Puddles."[21]

Often Brown was at odds with friends, as many of the northern Democrats fighting him so bitterly were men he had known for years. George Miller, the senator who so often had been a point man for the administration's programs, broke sharply with the governor. Miller's district included the Delta—the broad, alluvial area at the confluence of the Sacramento and San Joaquin Rivers—and he was rightly concerned that the pumps sucking away water for the south would cause incomprehensible environmental damage, not to mention the loss of water for local farming. The administration's assurances that the Delta would not be damaged were "so much pap," Miller declared.[22]

By late May the critical bill—the measure that would put the bond issue on the ballot the next year—was ready for a vote on the senate floor. Against the governor's wishes, northerners began offering amendments to guarantee their region's right to keep its water in the future, which obviously would have reduced deliveries to the south and thus undercut support for the bonds in Los Angeles. With one amendment in danger of passing, the senate took a long lunch recess, and the governor called to his office at least two wavering supporters. Brown somehow brought them back into the fold—it isn't clear exactly how—and when the senate reconvened the amendment died narrowly. Returned to the pristine state the governor wanted, the bill passed 25–12, supported by an odd coalition of legislators representing Southern California, the farm counties at the southern end of the Central Valley, scattered areas anticipating some specific local benefit (such as the construction of the primary dam or a spur canal), and northerners displaying little more than a personal allegiance to the governor. "We are still climbing up hill," Brown wrote, "but it looks pretty good."[23]

———

As the bill moved across the Capitol Rotunda to the assembly, Brown faced a new set of political dynamics. Although northerners were far more numerous in the senate, southerners dominated the assembly, where apportionment reflected the huge population in and around Los Angeles. The result was that while the governor again faced the prospect of hostile amendments, this time the goal of the opponents was reversed. Just as northerners had once tried to amend the bill to ensure that they could keep the water if it was needed, southerners now hoped to add an iron-clad guarantee that the water would be shipped south. Brown desperately wanted to avoid changes of any kind. If the assembly approved even a minor amendment, the measure would have to be voted on again by the senate, a prospect not relished by the administration.

Less than a week after the bill passed the senate, Brown tried to head off possible assembly amendments at the source and met with members of the Los Angeles County Board of Supervisors to convince them his plan was sound. For three hours he struggled to win them over, arguing that water deliveries were already effectively guaranteed to the south and that the bill needed no additional safeguards. The proposal was fair to all sections of the state, Brown insisted, and he would accept no changes. The supervisors backed off a little, but only days later the Metropolitan Water District openly rejected the governor's stance, urging Southern California legislators to alter the bill.[24]

The measure was taken up on the assembly floor in mid-June, with only days remaining before the session adjourned. Southerners offered the amendments to strengthen their region's claim on the water, but, as it had in the senate, the administration fought them off. The bill had to be passed as it was, the governor insisted, lest the entire project collapse. Jesse Unruh, the powerful assemblyman and Brown ally, acknowledged that the measure, like many practical legislative achievements, was a collection of compromises. As he fought off an amendment popular with many Democrats, Unruh said, "At times we have to rise above principle."[25] In the end the amendments were defeated, and the final vote reflected a relatively easy victory, 50–30. The project's careful geographic balance had won again, as it had in the senate, but so too was the governor himself a factor. Thomas MacBride, an assemblyman from Sacramento, wrote later to Ralph Brody and said that he thought a major reason for the program's passage was simply "unequivocal loyalty to Pat." Democrats wanted a major achievement for their new Democratic governor, a task made all the more enjoyable by his native affability. MacBride admitted such feelings played a role in his aye vote: "I wanted to help Pat."[26]

The governor celebrated the bill's final passage with an appropriate victory toast—a glass of water—and then signed the measure the following month.[27] But of course that was merely a procedural step. For though Brown had won a great achievement in the legislature, his signature on the bill's final page did not ensure that dams would be built or aqueducts dug. It meant only that the huge proposed bond issue would be put to the voters, and thus that the governor would need to convince Californians to approve a project like no other in their history.

———

Given the long delay between the passage of the bill and the next statewide election, Brown did not come face-to-face with his new task for a year, until summer 1960, just after the Democratic National Convention. In the intervening months he had worked to organize the campaign on behalf of the water bonds, but now it was time to move from planning to execution. Four months remained before the November election, when voters would decide the fate of the bond issue and thus of the entire project.[28]

Brown began by pitching the bond issue to his friends in organized labor, a constituency that was of mixed mind. On the one hand, the state project lacked the federal rule limiting irrigation water to farms of 160 acres and thus would enrich the big corporate farmers who had long been hostile to unions. On the other hand, it would require a massive construction effort that would create thousands of jobs, many for union members. By one estimate 40 percent of the money spent on the water project would go toward wages. For construction workers, the governor told one union convention in Long Beach, the water plan offered "an immediate and personal stake." But the bid for labor support was an uphill fight. Worried about a huge subsidy for big landowners, the executive board of the state AFL-CIO voted to oppose the bonds, and the governor could do little but try to win the hearts of rank-and-file union members. He recalled the glory days of their alliance—fighting Bill Knowland's right-to-work proposal two years earlier—and urged a revitalized unity: "Let us continue to fight together."[29]

Taking on enemies was more fun. When Republicans at a state convention failed to endorse the bond measure, Brown insisted that the GOP "ducks the real tough, hard problems that we have to face." He noted that Earl Warren and Goodwin Knight, his two Republican predecessors, had both talked about building a big state water project, but added playfully that their only shortcoming was a failure to actually get something done.[30]

More than at any time since becoming governor, Brown was back on the campaign trail, making stop after stop, perhaps a news conference in one town, a luncheon in another, a dinner speech somewhere else. The topics sometimes alternated: a speech on behalf of the water bonds, the next in support of Kennedy's presidential bid. Campaigning always energized Brown, and this time was no exception. Even in the north, where many people viewed the water project as little more than southern theft, Brown made an enthusiastic pitch. At a stop in Willows, a small farm town near Oroville, the site of the proposed dam, he argued that the water to be sent south was unneeded in the north. In fact, it was not even used by northerners; it was simply flowing to the ocean. "We must bear in mind that there is plenty of water for everyone," he said. "California does not have a shortage of water. The problem is that the water is in the wrong places." And in any event, even if northerners were being robbed now, they might need help finding more water later. The Eel River could someday be rechanneled back over the coastal mountains, eastward down into the Sacramento River valley, where the water would irrigate crops. To do that, Brown told his listeners at Willows, the northern half of the state might need the political help of southerners, just as the southerners now needed the help of the north. In California's endless game of moving rivers to suit the needs of people, allies were good to have.[31]

But the governor's strongest appeal to northerners was based on a more immediate brand of self-interest. Whereas Southern California was arid, Northern California was occasionally cursed by a deluge of water—winter floods that poured down from the Sierra Nevada and swept aside all in their path. This knowledge was fresh. Only four years earlier, in winter 1955–56, the worst California flooding in years had inundated vast reaches of the state and killed sixty-four people. The worst damage had come from the Feather River, which would be tamed by Brown's proposed dam.[32]

The only problem with the argument was that increasingly experts were suggesting the Feather River should be left untouched, at least in the short run. Just months before voters would decide the fate of the bond, two consulting companies hired by the state delivered reports that were deeply troubling to the administration. The bond issue of $1.75 billion—an amount decided on primarily for practical political reasons—would provide too little money to complete the entire project, the consultants said. Even without inflation, the project was simply too costly, and if costs escalated during the long years of construction, the state could find itself seriously short of money. In the worst-case scenario the southbound aqueduct would not be completed, the equivalent of a bridge built halfway across a canyon. To finish the job, the state would have to find more money, maybe by floating another bond issue, maybe by raiding tax coffers. The alternative was to delay construction of the Oroville Dam. In the consultants' view, the dam wasn't needed anyway, at least not to accomplish the main purpose of the project, which was shipping water to the San Joaquin Valley and Southern California. Demand could be met for years merely by building the intake valves that would suck water from the Delta, the aqueducts that would carry it south, and the pumps that would push it up and over the intervening hills. The Feather River could be left for later, when finances allowed or the need arose.[33]

Brown toyed with the idea. For months he had known privately that the entire project relied on questionable financing. Fred Dutton, his closest aide, thought the administration was too focused on water—thought there were other things on which to spend precious political capital—and had been warning since the spring that the bond issue would produce too little cash. In April, after a long briefing by staff members from the Department of Water Resources, Dutton sat down and wrote a memo suggesting that the governor's greatest dream was in fact a reckless gamble. "Baldly stated, *the program is economically unfeasible*," Dutton began, underlining for emphasis. Inflation would push up costs by $335 million, he estimated, an additional cost unaccounted for in the state's planning. Revenues from offshore oil drilling were to be diverted to the water project, but they had been overestimated initially by $175 million. Combined, the two fiscal holes meant that the state would be short by half a billion dollars, a quarter of the project's cost. And there was more: Farmers would be unable to pay the full cost of the water and thus would have to be subsidized by urban dwellers, both an economic injustice and a political death knell. In the end, Dutton wrote, the state might need to subsidize the project out of income tax revenues, something taxpayers would not stand for. The problems were serious enough, he said, that Brown should escape from the office for a day with top advisers and think through a possible solution, perhaps a drastic scaling back of the project. If nothing were done, Dutton predicted, the consultants hired by the state would conclude that the project was unfeasible, and their reports would be released just before the election, a political disaster.[34] Brown had ignored Dutton's worries, but now, months later, he was facing advice strikingly similar to that of his chief of staff. The state's own consultants had found problems with the project's financing, and Brown was scrambling to answer pointed questions.

Confronted by reporters about the embarrassing new report, he initially fell back on an old political dodge and said he had not read it, then later declared that he could make no promises about when the Feather River dam might be built. Worse still, he declared it likely that no decision about the dam would be made before November 8, when voters were scheduled to decide the entire project's fate.[35]

That response proved disastrous. The Feather River Project Association, which had been backing the plan since the early going, suddenly threatened to withdraw its support, an about-face that would likely have doomed the bond issue at the polls. Administration officials knew they could ill afford to lose their major supporters so close to the election. With less than two months to go, they leaked a decision to effectively ignore the financial warnings. If the bonds were approved and the project launched, the Oroville Dam would be built immediately. If the money ran out later, more could be found. It was a blithe assertion, but in the world of California water projects, optimism had always been the way.[36]

In early October Brown took a break from the water wars to spend a few days campaigning for John F. Kennedy in the East. Election day was less than a month away, a time when Brown might normally have been on the hustings in California. But the swing for Kennedy gave him the chance to show his loyalty to the Democratic nominee, who had been displeased by Brown's performance at the Democratic National Convention.

In Washington, D.C., Brown held a news conference, indulging one of his favorite pastimes by comparing California to New York and himself to Nelson Rockefeller. Brown insisted he was in the East campaigning for Kennedy because Rockefeller had been in California campaigning for Nixon. As for the Republican nominee, Brown told reporters that California Republicans neither liked nor trusted Nixon, the easy implication being that voters shouldn't either.[37] Four days later in Newark, New Jersey, Brown's language of attack was more direct. In his presidential campaign, Nixon was employing "the same adroit cynicism, the same ruthless ambition" he had shown in his early Red-baiting campaigns in California. "California remembers too well our fellow Californian," Brown said. The state, he added, would not vote for Nixon again.[38]

Back home by the middle of the month, Brown faced the final weeks of the water bond campaign with a challenge that was both critical and ironic. The governor was proposing to build a massive waterworks that would transport the most important commodity of the American West from the northern half of the state to the southern half, and yet the project was endangered by southern opposition. For all that he had shored up support in the north, Brown knew that many voters, probably most, would still vote no. He had insisted on building the Oroville Dam immediately to hold whatever northern support he could, but if the bonds were to pass the critical factor was to run up huge vote totals in the south. And to do that the governor needed the backing of a huge public bureaucracy that had, in the decades since its founding, become a legend in the power circles of Southern California: the Metropolitan Water District.

The Met, as it was often known, had been created in 1928 to oversee Southern California's endless search for water from afar, beginning with the supply from the Owens Valley, two hundred miles away in the Sierra Nevada. For decades the Met had been a regional powerhouse of Southern California, and Brown needed its endorsement of the water bonds. But in a touch of irony the agency that would eventually receive much of the Feather River's water was opposed to the bond issue that would pay for the system. Locked in a legal dispute with Arizona over rights to the water of the Colorado River, the Met feared that its case might be weakened if the state of California provided an alternative source. Assuming it could continue to take water from the Colorado, Southern California had enough for the time being. If water were needed from the north later, the Met could always get it, without state help, just as it had done in the Owens Valley. In the meantime, there was no reason to support Brown's extensive state plan.[39]

For months Brown worked both publicly and privately to reverse the Met's opposition, and finally cracks began to show in the board's normally solid front. Some members spoke out against the agency's official position and endorsed the bonds. Joseph Jensen, the chairman of the Met board and a vehement opponent of the water project, fought back by preparing a public statement attacking the water plan on a whole series of points, among them that it was poorly planned and financed. The governor's office got a copy a day early, and Brown attacked Jensen's statement even before it was released. After months of complicated negotiations, Brown claimed, the Met chief had raised new objections, "a striking demonstration of bad faith."[40]

The governor was relying on the inevitability of Southern California's thirst. The region always wanted more water, even if the need was more in the future than the present, and Brown was sure that sooner or later the Met would endorse the plan. With days left in the campaign, his confidence was rewarded. Rebelling against its own chairman, the Met's board of directors voted to reverse its position. The Met agreed to endorse Brown's bond issue and to sign a contract to buy water from the project once it was built, a valuable recommendation as Southern California voters went to the polls.[41]

———

Less than two weeks before the election, the problem of financing resurfaced. The reports of the administration's two consultants, released as drafts months earlier, were completed and released again in final form. Not much was new. Read by wishful eyes, the reports could offer succor to both supporters and opponents of the water project. The studies said the engineering was sound, and the water would eventually be needed. Paying off the bonds would pose no problems for the state's finances. However, the reports pointed out yet again that the administration had calculated stagnant costs, without inflation. Assuming that prices rose—a safe bet for a project that would take decades to complete—the bond issue and the oil revenues would not produce enough money to finish all the work. The state would eventually have to pony up more cash, either through future borrowing or from general tax revenues. The next day's headlines proved that in California water disputes were always seen through the favored interpretation of the analyst, even in newsrooms. Working from exactly the same material, the *Los Angeles Times* (which favored the water project) said the reports gave a "sound rating" to the plan, while the *San Francisco Chronicle* (which opposed the project) reported that the plan had been "called impossible."[42]

At a news conference the next day the governor took the optimistic side. He touted the bond issue to the voters and reiterated his determination that the dam would be built as soon as possible. Arguments about the cost were of little consequence to Brown, for he had decided that the state would push ahead regardless of accountants' warnings. Two weeks before, anticipating the release of the final reports, he had insisted that the water would eventually be needed, so the project must be built. "I know we will never be able to do it cheaper than we can now," he said. "Whatever the cost of the program may be, it has to be paid for."[43]

———

Brown finished the water bond campaign on a triumphant note, formally signing the contract with the Metropolitan Water District on November 4, the Friday before the Tuesday election. Impressed by his own achievement, he called it the most important document he had signed as governor.[44] Over the weekend he was confident, privately predicting the water bonds would pass by 325,000 votes, not a landslide, but a comfortable margin nonetheless.[45]

On election night, however, the result was a cliffhanger. Democrats held their big party at the Beverly Hilton, where a twelve-foot-high paper banner proclaimed "Water!" The vote for the bond issue teetered at about the 50 percent mark all night, although by late in the evening the lead was large enough for the governor to claim victory. Voters, he said, had taken "bold and decisive action."[46] But as late returns trickled in through the wee hours of Wednesday morning, the tide turned. Northern counties were reporting, and their big negative margins began to narrowly top the aye votes from Southern California. At one point the bonds were trailing by more than 200,000 votes, a small fraction of the 4 million counted but still a deficit. By the time Brown went to bed at 3:00 A.M., he thought the measure would fail, although publicly he did nothing to indicate a reversal of his earlier optimism.[47]

Brown slept a little, then boarded a plane for San Francisco, keeping up appearances as he talked with reporters. "I know that the opponents have tried to count the water bonds out," he said, "but I advise them to take another look."[48] In the late afternoon the governor's hopes began to be vindicated. Los Angeles County was still reporting late precincts, and the returns were overwhelmingly in favor of the bonds. The deficit narrowed to 140,000 votes, then kept shrinking. At the *Sacramento Bee,* still an afternoon paper, compositors made up the front page with a story saying the water bonds were behind, with only "a mathematical chance" they would pull ahead. But just as the newspaper was going to press—so late that there was no time to change the headline, "Water Bond Issue Trails"—wire service bulletins were slapped across the top of the story: The latest returns from Los Angeles had pushed the bond issue ahead by 20,000 votes statewide.[49] The lead only grew as the day wore on, and by that evening, twenty-four hours after the polls had closed, it was clear the bonds had passed. The margin was thin—fewer than 174,000 votes, or less than 3 percent of the total—but it was certain. In his diary Brown celebrated the victory with an entry that must have been as joyous as it was sparing: "Water wins."[50]

On an issue that centered inherently on the state's physical qualities, the results predictably reflected geography. The bond issue carried in only fourteen of California's fifty-eight counties, but they were the areas where the water project promised a local benefit. Only two counties in Northern California voted aye: Butte and Yuba, where the Oroville Dam would be built and the resulting flood protection was most needed. Support was strong in the Central Valley. In Kern County, where big agricultural landowners anticipated cheap, subsidized water, support ran three to one. Most important was the South Coast, with its huge cache of people and hence of votes. City dwellers from Los Angeles to San Diego believed that someday they would need more water. In Los Angeles County alone the margin was more than 300,000 votes. To win the support of the Metropolitan Water District, Brown had relied on the agency's ceaseless desire for water. The returns proved that the trait ran deep in voters too.[51]

———

The other great issue on the ballot was the choice between Kennedy and Nixon, and in California the results were even closer for the presidential contest than they had been for the water bonds. Kennedy took a narrow lead on election night, but during the next few days the counting of absentee and overseas military ballots whittled at the margin. It was clear that Kennedy had won nationwide; his electoral college margin was large enough to stand regardless of the California outcome. But the state returns remained a source of curiosity and concern for California politicos, the governor included.

The outcome was still uncertain the week after the election, when Brown left the state for a tour of Argentina. With more than two dozen other American governors, he had been invited to celebrate the 150th anniversary of the country's independence, a refreshing jaunt after the rigors of the campaign. By November 16, eight days after the election, workers back in California were still counting the final ballots, but Brown had heard the trend was bad for the Democrat. En route from the seaside resort of Mar del Plata to the northern town of Cordoba, he wrote that "fragmentary reports" suggested a Nixon victory. Perhaps looking to explain away the likely defeat, Brown told reporters after the plane landed that Kennedy's Catholicism had hurt him—and not just in the Deep South. Even in California anti-Catholicism had been "really bad," Brown said.[52]

If he was setting the stage for bad news, he got it the next day. The final count of absentee ballots gave Nixon the slimmest of victories: barely 35,000 votes out of more than 6.5 million cast. The presidential result slightly tarnished the election for Brown, for he had been unable to deliver his state to the Democratic nominee. But it was by no means debilitating. California was Nixon's home state, after all, and the Republican had been struggling to avoid the ignominy of rejection by the voters who knew him best. Brown was neither pleased nor devastated. While visiting a wine-making region at the foot of the Andes, the governor took the time to note in his diary that Kennedy had lost California, but added no other comment about the election.[53]

Regardless of the presidential outcome, Brown's great victory remained. He had advocated the greatest public works project in the history of his state, and now it would be built. He had wooed the legislature with skill and patience, the voters with enthusiasm and hustle. The problem that had stumped Earl Warren and Goodwin Knight had been conquered. After the tribulations of 1960—the Chessman case and the Democratic National Convention—Brown had bounced back. On a trip to Washington to visit the president-elect, Brown pronounced the governorship "the second biggest job in the United States, a rough one but enjoyable," the final word a description he might not have used just a few months before.[54]

Enthused by victory, Brown savored again the privileges of office. Earl Warren, who had sent a congratulatory note calling the water plan "a great step forward," made his usual holiday trip to California, and the chief justice and the governor met for duck hunting.[55] On holiday break from his senior year at the University of California, Jerry went along, and Warren brought his three sons, a stag vacation Brown loved. The met at a Colusa County farm owned by Wally Lynn, a San Francisco businessman who was always their host, and bagged their limit. Brown described it as a "wonderful shoot." "It not only gave me an opportunity to be with my son," he wrote Lynn later, "but also an opportunity to be with some of the finest men I have ever met." Of course, there was a political bonus too, a fact not missed by the governor. The *Bee* ran a big front-page picture of Brown and Warren flanking their host, a full line of birds slung over each man's shoulder, the governor still holding his shotgun. It was an image, Brown thought, worth more than $100,000 in political advertising.[56]

In January Brown headed east to enjoy the biggest Democratic celebration in a long time: Kennedy's inaugural. Democrats had last installed one of their own as president in 1949, when Brown was still the district attorney of San Francisco, so the ceremony was not to be missed. Undoubtedly to his joy, the governor rode in the inaugural parade down Pennsylvania Avenue, standing in the back of an open car, smiling and waving, bareheaded despite the freezing temperatures. The three bands that followed symbolized California: the St. Mary's Chinese Girls Drum Corps from San Francisco, their red and gold silk costumes redolent of Chinatown, then two high school bands, one of them led by baton twirlers who insisted on disregarding the eastern winter and, although they had brought long pants, sporting short skirts. On the viewing stand, Bernice was more practical than either her husband or the high school students. She passed out plastic bags for people to put around their feet to ward off the bitter cold and wind.[57]

At the end of the night some of the Californians went back to the Browns' hotel suite and watched television reports on the inauguration. As the station signed off for the night, the "Star Spangled Banner" was played. Everyone stood, almost jokingly at first, Brown puffing out his chest with playful patriotism. But as the anthem went on, the mood shifted, everyone sensing the drama and moment of the day's events, becoming more serious, unabashedly standing at attention. By the final bars, no one—least of all the governor of California—was hamming it up.[58]

———

In the years that followed, construction of the water project proceeded apace. The dam on the Feather River was completed in 1967, and the following year the aqueduct reached the farmers of the San Joaquin Valley. In the early 1970s the project crossed the Tehachapis, and Brown's artificial river began flowing into new, man-made reservoirs around Los Angeles. The linchpin of the system remained the dam on the Feather River, but eventually, including ancillary facilities along the route, the entire system came to encompass 32 reservoirs, 17 pumping plants, and 662 miles of canals and pipelines.[59]

The old worries about the project's finances proved neither completely groundless nor completely warranted. Some of the bonds initially authorized to pay for the Central Valley Project had never been sold, and that borrowing authority was eventually transferred to the State Water Project, in effect expanding the size of the debt for the state project beyond Brown's $1.75 billion. To sell some of the original bonds in an inflated market, the state also had to raise the interest rate it paid, again increasing costs. Yet in large measure the project eventually paid for itself. Revenues from the sale of water and power paid off the bonds, meaning that users of the system covered the great bulk of its cost.[60]

Among the various groups of water users, however, there was one striking subsidy, and it enriched people who had no real need of help—some of California's biggest landowners. When the water began flowing over the Tehachapis, Los Angeles and its suburbs did not need the extra supply. The entire project had been built to supply water for population growth that was a prediction rather than a reality. In the meantime, with no need for water, the Metropolitan Water District decided to sell its supply to the farmers of the San Joaquin Valley. Because there was no way to move the water to other potential buyers, the farmers along the aqueduct route knew they had the upper hand: The Met had only one potential customer and no other use for the water. So the Met agreed to sell the water to agricultural users at a cut-rate price, well below what the Met was paying to the state. The net result was an extraordinary subsidy, worth millions of dollars a year, from Southern California city dwellers to Central Valley farmers.[61]

These were not the yeoman farm families of myth and legend. The landowners of the western San Joaquin Valley were some of the biggest corporations in the state. Foremost among these was the Kern County Land Company, which had been created in the nineteenth century by one of California's earliest real estate schemers, James Ben Ali Haggin. In the area served by Brown's new water system, Kern owned more than 220,000 acres, an empire five times the size of the District of Columbia, or fifteen times as large as Manhattan Island. The giant Tejon Ranch was owned principally by the parent company of the *Los Angeles Times*. Among other big corporate "farmers" drawing off subsidized water were Standard Oil and the Southern Pacific Railroad.[62]

To lessen the impact of the subsidy and placate liberal Democrats, Brown announced a stair-stepped pricing plan whereby the big landowners would pay a surcharge for water, but even he recognized that as a halfmeasure. "We threw them a bone in the thing," he remembered later. "It wasn't very substantial and it had no effect upon big or small farms either."[63] The subsidy effectively ended in the late 1980s, when the Metropolitan Water District began using its full water allotment, but the fact remains that for nearly two decades Brown's beloved water project provided enormous wealth for some of the state's largest agricultural interests, corporations with no legitimate claim to assistance. If that bothered him greatly, he never let on.[64]

Ultimately, the central fact about the water project was not so much that it was a good idea or a bad idea, but simply that it reflected its era. Providing water for cities and farms seemed an obvious benefit, like supplying electricity or gas. More water would be needed so long as the state grew, and nobody knew how to stop the state's growth, or particularly wanted to. Brown's aide Abbott Goldberg once put the matter bluntly: "The only solution to the water problem was birth control."[65] But those attitudes changed swiftly, for the world soon changed in fundamental ways. The political climate turned against massive expenditures by government. Awareness grew that much of the precious water transported down the length of the state simply disappeared along the way, evaporating into the California sun. The water project neither delivered as much water as had been predicted nor generated as much electricity as was needed to operate the pumps. Most important, the modern environmental movement took root, and people began to cherish rivers not as tame sources of power and water but as wild environments of beauty and ecological importance. They began, in other words, to question the old belief, often expressed by Brown, that a river running its timeless course to the sea was "wasting" water.[66]

That is why the Feather River project was both the culmination and the death knell of a certain chapter in California history. It was the most extraordinary of the many efforts to do the Lord's work and bring water to the thirsty land, as Goldberg had put it. But it was also the last grand effort to be completed. The state's most ambitious water engineers had long envisioned a host of other staggering projects—tapping the Eel River, for example, or skirting the Delta with a massive canal—but none has ever been built. For now at least—and for reasons that seem quite convincing to the modern mind—Brown's era was the last time Californians attempted so audaciously to remake their natural landscape.[67]

————

In the immediate wake of the election, just after the bonds had passed, such issues were far on the horizon. In the short run the achievement seemed obvious, as much for symbolic as practical reasons. Until that time all the existing California water projects had been pursued independently by the state's great regional rivals—Southern California and the San Francisco Bay Area—or they had been the handiwork of the federal government. The new system would be, remarkably, the first waterworks ever built by the state. To men like Brown, it was the physical proof of California's unity, a connection between north and south more tangible than any other. "This is California's own product," he told reporters just before construction was set to begin, in early fall 1961. "It is the expression of our faith in our future."[68]

That was the mood three days later, at a ceremony near Oroville to mark the great event. The band from Oroville High School played, and a local politician said it was a day for which the town had been waiting. Then the governor donned a hard hat and touched off the first blast, pushing buttons that ignited three hundred pounds of dynamite laid at the site of the main diversion tunnel, through which the river would run during the six years needed to construct the dam. A burst of earth and rocks shot into the sky, and Brown told the crowd that the sound "will echo in California history for generations to come."[69]

He hoped so. For all that it was an engineering achievement or a political marvel, the water project also remained, for Brown, a personal legacy. He wanted to enjoy the accolades it would bring. Years later someone suggested that the project's aqueduct should be named in his honor. Jerry Brown, who was then the governor, suggested that it would be better to wait until his father's death. Aghast, Pat replied, "Hell, I won't know anything about it then!" Fortunately for his ego, Brown lived long enough to see his son relent, and in 1982 the artificial river Brown had built was renamed the Edmund G. Brown California Aqueduct. In his expansive moments, he liked to speculate that it might be visible from the moon.[70]

11   "BY GOD, I CAN BEAT THAT SON OF A BITCH"

IN SEPTEMBER 1961 PAT BROWN hunkered down in front of a television set to watch an announcement he did not wish to hear. Richard Nixon, the former vice president of the United States and a man who had come within a hairbreadth of winning the Oval Office, was standing before dozens of reporters and cameramen in the Statler Hilton Hotel in Los Angeles. The state government in Sacramento, Nixon declared, was "a mess." California's government was too big, its crime rate too high, its economy too sluggish. As for the "amiable but bungling man who presently is governor," he was incapable of finding the solutions. So Richard Nixon would take the job. He would run for governor of California in 1962. Republicans, Nixon vowed, would "beat Pat Brown to a pulp."[1]

The would-be pulp watched with dread. Brown's first term had featured an ironic combination of policy successes and political setbacks. His achievements—the water project, the new college campuses, the tax increase that helped to pay for it all—were more deeply appreciated with the passing of time. The failures, by contrast, were immediately obvious. His debacles in dealing with the death penalty and national politics had left many Californians believing their governor a weak and vacillating figure, the amiable bungler described by Nixon. Nearly a third of voters thought Brown was doing a poor job. Even among those who approved of his work, more than half were unable to cite anything specific as a major accomplishment.[2]

Polls suggested Brown would lose to Nixon badly, and that was not the worst news. At least Nixon was a national figure. The governor's numbers were little better against far weaker opponents. He trailed former Gov. Goodwin Knight, who was contemplating a comeback. He was tied with San Francisco Mayor George Christopher, a local figure. Most ignominious of all, the governor polled only five points better than William Knowland, the man he routed so easily in 1958. Knowland was out of politics, yet one in five Californians said they did not know how they would mark a ballot in a potential Knowland-Brown race. The cold fact was that with less than fourteen months to election day, the governor was the most unpopular major politician in California.[3]

Brown's self-confidence was a fragile thing in the best of times, and as he watched Nixon's announcement, his courage gave way completely. Frightened that he might be on the losing end of a rout, Brown called key Democrats and told them to find someone else to carry the party's banner against Nixon. Brown had spent his life in the pursuit of political office. Now, cowed by bad circumstances and a bold opponent, he was ready to quit.[4]

———

In many ways Nixon cut a daunting figure. Born and raised in Whittier, east of Los Angeles, he had been elected to Congress at thirty-three, to the Senate at thirty-seven, to the vice presidency at thirty-nine, an age when Brown was still in his first year as San Francisco district attorney. Politically, he was said to be brilliant, knowledgeable, strategic—and ruthless. Many people in California politics hated Nixon, especially his fellow Republicans, but nobody thought him a boob.

Brown first met him in 1950, on a hot day in Bakersfield when both were campaigning, Nixon for the U.S. Senate and Brown for attorney general of California.[5] From the beginning, Brown got glimpses of Nixon as a schemer. Later in the same campaign, both men found themselves in Sacramento at the same time. They met at the Senator Hotel, and Nixon proposed a pact. If Brown avoided an endorsement of Helen Gahagan Douglas, the actress and congresswoman who was Nixon's opponent for the Senate, Nixon would refuse to endorse Brown's Republican opponent in the attorney general's race. Brown was already keeping his distance from Douglas, who was well to his left politically, but he found Nixon's proposal slick. He offered a characteristically noncommittal answer, and the two men went their separate ways.[6]

Two years later, Brown watched on television as Nixon, accused of having a slush fund, gave his famous Checkers speech, invoking the family dog as emblem of his honesty and preserving his place on the Republican ticket. Brown was not convinced. He found the vice presidential candidate reminiscent of the con men he had prosecuted as district attorney.[7]

In 1955 came one more troubling episode related to Nixon. Brown met with Goodwin Knight, then the governor, to discuss water issues. When they finished with those matters, Knight began discussing Nixon. Knight said he believed Nixon to be, as Brown later remembered it, "one of the most dangerous men in the world." Nixon had double-crossed Knight twice, and the state's other major Republicans—Warren, Knowland, and U.S. Sen. Thomas Kuchel—had been treated the same way, Knight insisted. The vice president, Knight said, was "the worst man imaginable for the presidency of the United States." It was a surprising moment, a Republican sharing such confidences with a Democrat, and about a man who was next in line for the most powerful job in the world. Brown was accustomed to the rough-and-tumble of politics, but Knight's comments struck him as noteworthy. The next day in his office, Brown dictated a memo, intended solely for his confidential political files, describing his conversation with Knight and noting carefully the time and circumstances.[8]

At the time Nixon posed no immediate threat to Brown, for they played on different stages. Nixon spent the 1950s in Washington, Brown in Sacramento. That changed in November 1960, when Nixon narrowly lost the presidency to John Kennedy and suddenly snapped into focus as a potential rival for Brown. Within days of the election Brown's new chief of staff, Hale Champion, was urging the governor to find a friendly congressman who could push for an investigation of a potentially juicy scandal, a large loan to Nixon's brother from the reclusive tycoon Howard Hughes. A public inquiry would be nice, Champion said, "just to keep Nixon off balance." The Brown team also squirreled away a film on Nixon provided by the Kennedy campaign. "We may need it in 1962," Champion wrote.[9]

Nixon was less certain about his future. Depressed after the loss to Kennedy, he decided to return home to California. Nixon and his wife, Pat, opted to build a new home in Los Angeles, and while construction was completed she and their two daughters remained in Washington. Nixon moved into an apartment on Wilshire Boulevard, in part because he had taken a job with a California law firm and in part because solitude allowed him to lick his wounds in private. Alone and happy about it, he settled into a routine of TV dinners and work but soon found politics drawing his attention. On a speaking tour in spring 1961, he focused mostly on international issues but insisted he had no plans to run for president again. By summer speculation was rampant that Nixon would return to politics even before the next presidential election. The rumors said he would seek California's governorship.

For Nixon, the attraction was not the job but the potential. By the early 1960s California's sheer heft—it was home to almost one in every eleven Americans—meant that the governors of today might be the presidents of tomorrow. New York had once held that status; stints in Albany had put Theodore and Franklin Roosevelt on the path to national prominence. In the postwar world it was California's turn. Every presidential election since World War II had featured a Californian on the Republican ticket: Earl Warren as the vice presidential nominee in 1948 and then Nixon three times, in 1952 and 1956 as Dwight Eisenhower's running mate and in 1960 as his own man. In 1964 the GOP's nomination would be wide open, and there were those in the party who believed that a short turn as governor would prove a useful interlude for Nixon, keeping him in the public eye and reestablishing his reputation as a winner. Eisenhower felt that way and wrote to his former vice president to say as much. Winning election as governor would "offset to a large extent the razor-thin margin by which you lost the presidential race," Ike wrote. And it would still allow Nixon to seek the presidency in 1964.[10]

Nixon hesitated. He was writing a book. He did not especially want to be governor of California. His wife was adamantly opposed to another campaign. But the decision could not wait forever, and so finally, in September 1961, he sat down with his family to discuss the issue. There was little doubt where Nixon's inclinations lay: He was a political animal to the bone. But family sentiment prevailed, and, at least by Nixon's account in his memoirs, he decided to skip the race. Upstairs in his study, he was drafting a statement to that effect when his wife appeared. Drained and stressed, Pat Nixon told her husband that she would support whatever decision he might make. She reversed what she had said only minutes before and promised that she would join him on the campaign trail. "You must do whatever you think is right," Nixon remembered her saying. "If you think this is right for you, then you must do it." Nixon threw out the draft speech announcing that he would not run and began working on the statement of candidacy that would cause Brown such trepidation.[11]

———

Attacks of self-doubt may have been common in Brown's psyche, but usually they were also mercifully brief. So it was with his anxiety over Nixon's announcement. The governor regained his equilibrium quickly—fellow Democrats helped by insisting that he was their man—and returned to the realization that he loved being governor too much to quit. To insiders, that was no surprise. Deep down, he always wanted to hang on to the job as long as possible.

Barely a week into his first term, Brown had been talking about a second. At his first cabinet meeting, he said he was trying to limit public appearances during his first six months in office, when the legislature would be in session. "As soon as that is over, I will start campaigning for governor again," he added, only half-joking.[12] In the years since, nothing had changed his mind, and once he recovered from the initial shock of realizing that his opponent would be a former vice president, Brown launched into a reelection training regimen.

The first goal was physical. He went on a diet, swearing off potatoes and cocktails. For exercise, he and Bernice played golf every morning—up at 5:00 A.M., then eighteen holes quickly, carrying their own clubs. The result was the loss of almost twenty pounds from his customarily roly-poly frame. Second, for a less corporeal brand of rejuvenation, he spent three days in silent retreat at a Jesuit center south of San Francisco, giving him "the chance and the peace for prayer and spiritual awareness." Last—and least needed, given Brown's familiarity with his state—was a week spent with staff at the desert home of a supporter. Isolated from meetings and distractions, the governor boned up on issues. Two staff members were assigned to play devil's advocate and argue with whatever position Brown took, the better to prepare him for the hurly-burly of a campaign.[13]

Preparations were needed at home too. Given Nixon's reputation as a Red-baiter and a rhetorical brawler, the Browns expected a tough, perhaps vicious, struggle. Kathy, now fifteen and the only child remaining at home, might find more shelter in a private boarding school than the public high school she had been attending in Sacramento. So Pat and Bernice sat down with Kathy in the Governor's Mansion and explained they thought it best if she switched to a Catholic school in Monterey. They heard no objections—Kathy was ready for a new challenge—and in fall 1961 she headed off to a new life. Pat and Bernice looked ahead to a year that featured one old constant of their lives, campaigning, and one new circumstance: For the first time since the earliest months of their marriage more than three decades before, they presided over an empty house.[14]

Looking ahead, Nixon knew he faced a fundamental disadvantage. By 1962 Democrats outnumbered Republicans in California by more than a million. To win in the fall, Nixon had to broaden his appeal and reach across party lines. Doing so required that he distance himself from the right wing of the state's Republican Party, especially the conspiracy theorists of the John Birch Society. Named for an American soldier killed in China ten days after the end of World War II, the fiercely anti-Communist Birchers were at the outermost fringe of reason. The group's founder, Robert Welch, had taken to declaring that Dwight Eisenhower was not merely a weak-willed moderate—a view held by many Birchers—but an active and knowing agent of an international Communist conspiracy. The former president, Welch maintained, was guilty of treason.

But Nixon had to be careful. He needed to separate himself from Welch's nuttiness without completely alienating conservative Republican activists, who formed the grassroots of any GOP campaign. That was made more problematic by the presence of a conservative opponent in the Republican primary, a state assemblyman named Joseph Shell. Young and handsome, Shell was square-jawed conservatism in the flesh. He had captained the University of Southern California football team to the Rose Bowl in 1939, married his college sweetheart, served as a pilot in World War II, gotten rich in the oil industry, and won election to the assembly in a special election in 1953. After the 1960 census, Democrats redrew the boundaries of his Los Angeles legislative district so that it was far less favorable to a Republican. Faced with a nearly impossible reelection bid, Shell decided instead that he might as well go down fighting for a big prize, so he ran for governor.[15] Shell's candidacy complicated Nixon's. If Nixon moved toward the center too far and too fast, Shell would provide a haven for disgruntled conservatives.

The issue came to a head at the annual meeting of the California Republican Assembly, an independent group whose endorsement was a prize sought after by GOP candidates. Hoping to distance himself from the Birchers without alienating them, Nixon offered a resolution denouncing Welch but not the group as a whole. Instead, he demanded that Republicans leave the John Birch Society only if Welch was not expelled. It was a nice idea. Given his connection to Eisenhower, Nixon had to denounce Welch in some fashion, but he also needed the support of the society's members, many of whom thought Welch too extreme. But Shell sensed an opportunity to win conservative hearts, and he condemned the Nixon proposal. It was no business of the convention, he insisted, if people were involved with outside organizations.

The Nixon forces pushed the resolution through committee, but on the convention floor its fate seemed in doubt. Nixon agreed to modify the measure so that it merely denounced Welch, without any mention of whether Republicans should belong to the John Birch Society, and it passed easily. The full convention endorsed Nixon for governor, although Shell did well in the voting.

In a sense Nixon had accomplished his purpose, authoring a resolution that derided Welch and his ludicrous conspiracy theories about Eisenhower. Democrats would face a tougher task portraying Nixon as an extremist. But the incident revealed the depth of bitterness and discord in the Republican Party. The convention's final session was snarling and combative, and at the end the moderates and conservatives were as divided as ever. When one middle-of-the-road delegate insisted, "Let's get one thing straight: We are all opposed to communism," members of the Birch contingent laughed derisively.[16] Patricia Hitt, then a member of the Republican National Committee and an ardent Nixon loyalist, said that if somehow Shell won the primary she would campaign for him in the general election out of solemn partisan duty, but that after giving a pro-Shell speech she would have to go to the ladies' room and vomit.[17]

Nixon was never in danger of losing the nomination; he was too big a name for that. But at the June 5 primary, Shell managed to beat him in seven counties, and statewide the challenger took a third of the Republican vote, a portion big enough to suggest a serious split in the party.[18] Two weeks later Nixon and Shell met at midnight at the home of Henry Salvatori, a rich Republican businessman who would later play a critical role in the rise of Ronald Reagan. Shell agreed to endorse Nixon, but the hard feelings festered. Months later, just before election day, conservatives grew so displeased with Nixon that they mounted a write-in effort for Shell.[19]

The primary results offered no great solace to Brown either. He had no serious Democratic challenger, but more than one hundred thousand Democrats wrote in either Nixon or Shell, compared to only a handful of Republicans who voted for the governor. Fortunately, reassurance was at hand. Earlier in the year, a newspaper editor who was a friend of Jack Burby, the governor's new press secretary, had asked if Brown would make a joint appearance with Nixon at a statewide editors' meeting sponsored by the Associated Press. By traditional norms of campaign management, it was far from obvious that Brown should participate, but Burby urged that he do so. Burby knew that Brown's years of constant one-on-one politicking had left him with a remarkably personalized view of the world. To take the measure of an opponent, Brown had to meet him, shake hands, inhabit the same room, sense the reaction of those around him. Yet nothing like that had occurred with Nixon. To Burby's thinking, the joint appearance would give his boss a chance to sum up Nixon personally and, Burby hoped, to find him wanting.

The plan worked. At the editors' meeting, Brown was charming and friendly, yet substantive and experienced in discussing the state's big issues. To Brown's ears, Nixon sounded grim, almost bitter, using his speech to criticize the press, an odd choice given the venue. The governor knew he had done well and thought his opponent had come off poorly. Afterward, he and Burby walked out to a waiting car. As soon as they got in, Brown reached across the seat and joyfully whacked his aide on the thigh. "By God," he exclaimed, "I can beat that son of a bitch."[20]

––––––

In July, with the indolence of summer sapping interest from the race, Brown found time for some travel. Much of it was for pleasure, although as always there was politicking too. Washington came first. On the morning of July 5, he played golf at Burning Tree, the course that had once been favored by President Eisenhower. In the afternoon, he went to the White House, where Kennedy offered detailed pointers about debating Nixon, even discussing whether Brown should use notes.[21]

He returned to Sacramento but soon was off again, this time for four days of hiking, fishing, and swimming in Kings Canyon National Park, a vast area of the Sierra Nevada south of Yosemite. Brown made a side trip to the General Sherman, a great redwood reputed to be the world's largest tree.[22]

But the highlight of the summer's sightseeing may well have been a weekend at Wyntoon, the Hearst family estate near Mount Shasta. Like most things connected to William Randolph Hearst, Wyntoon was a fanciful world unto itself. The McCloud River ran through the estate's fifty thousand acres of forest. The main buildings were three four-story mansions: Cinderella House, Fairy House, and Bear House. There was a swimming pool, of course, but also stables, a croquet court, and a huge stone lodge, called the Gables, with a dining room for sixty and a private movie theater. As a guest of the Hearsts, the governor enjoyed the weekend amid such splendor, and when he got back to the office used the excuse of a thank-you note to George Hearst Jr., then running the *Los Angeles Herald Examiner,* to make a carefully crafted pitch for the paper's support. "I sometimes get discouraged when members of the Republican Party say that the Democratic Party is anti-business," Brown wrote. "Certainly, there are some who are socialistic or even worse, but the average Democrats in California government . . . are people who realize that only when business makes money and employs people and pays good salaries do we have the sources of taxes that permit us to do the things government should do in a great state like California."[23] Nobody knows if the entreaty did any good, but the paper stayed neutral, a surprise for a paper that typically backed Republicans.

Summer vacation over, the Browns made their annual fall move to Los Angeles and readied themselves for the heart of what the governor predicted would be the toughest campaign of his life.[24] It was already going well. Nixon, it turned out, had entered the race at precisely the wrong moment. Through spring and summer 1961, as Nixon was deciding whether to run, California was suffering the aftereffects of a brief national recession. The state's unemployment rate was higher than it had been since Brown took office. When he announced his candidacy, Nixon cited joblessness as "most important of all" among California's problems. Then that fall, just after Nixon jumped in, things began to improve. By the time Brown returned from his romp at Wyntoon and jumped into the fall portion of the 1962 campaign, the unemployment rate was a full percentage point lower than the year before, and falling. The nation's economy as a whole had surged into an expansion that would last the rest of Brown's tenure. The entire time Nixon was out on the hustings urging a change of leadership, Californians' pocketbooks were getting fatter.[25]

It would have taken a mighty challenger to overcome such obstacles, and, at least that year, Nixon was not the man. For one thing, too many people did not believe he wanted the job he was seeking or would keep it if he got it. Nixon insisted from the day he entered the governor's race that he would not seek the presidency in 1964, but voters refused to take him at his word. After all, Nixon had once vowed he would not run for governor, then changed his mind.[26] Polls found that 40 percent of voters thought Nixon was "very likely" to abandon the governorship midterm and run for president, and the Brown team was happy to foster the impression. "It is obvious that our job," noted one strategy memo, "is to keep alive the belief that Nixon's real goal is the presidency."[27] Only minutes after Nixon announced his candidacy, the Brown campaign issued a nicely quotable statement suggesting the opponent's ulterior motive: The former vice president had decided to "enter a contest he tried to avoid, seeking an office he does not really want, under a four-year contract he does not intend to fulfill."[28]

There was something disingenuous about the claim. Brown had promised in 1958 to serve a full term as governor and then almost immediately after winning the election launched a fleeting bid for the presidency. But in political terms that was ancient history, and in any event Nixon's fellow Republicans—some of them potential 1964 competitors—were happy to join Brown in implying that the former vice president might have something up his sleeve. Before Nixon's announcement was in the papers, Oregon Gov. Mark Hatfield was telling reporters that Nixon might still run in 1964. The next day New York Gov. Nelson Rockefeller said the same thing.[29]

Even Nixon inadvertently dropped hints that his dreams remained elsewhere. When he declared his candidacy, he said not that he longed to be governor but that he wanted to be in public service and that governor of California was the most interesting job he could hold, "next to being president of the United States."[30] At a rally in Sacramento later in the campaign, he said that he would win because he wanted to take power from government "and give it back to 180 million individuals," although of course that was the population of the entire country, not the state he supposedly wanted to govern.[31]

An excess of ambition was not the only thing that made voters wonder about Nixon. Often they simply did not like him. When pollsters asked people for their thoughts about both Brown and Nixon, they got strikingly different answers. Complaints about Brown dealt mostly with policy: too much spending, taxes too high, capital punishment. The only personal trait cited frequently was indecisiveness. The list of common complaints about Nixon was a far more intimate indictment: He was a dirty campaigner, offensive, aloof, opportunistic, and hot-headed.[32]

The result was that one candidate had many friends, the other many enemies. When a Brown operative surveyed the northern coast in preparation for a gubernatorial trip through the area, he reported back that the publisher of the *Eureka Times-Standard,* a major paper in the region, had been charmed by a recent phone call from the governor. The man was a Republican so committed to the GOP that he kept an autographed copy of Nixon's new book on his desk, but he had been going around town for days taking every opportunity to mention, "Pat called me," and then recounting the conversation in detail. A hundred miles inland, in Redding, the editor of the *Record-Searchlight* remembered that ten years earlier Nixon had visited the town and criticized the paper's political coverage without reading the stories in question. The sting was so deep that the Redding editor still bore Nixon nothing but enmity. The lesson was easy to see: Pat Brown made people like him; Richard Nixon had a knack for the opposite. Harry Truman once told Brown that he should never mention Nixon's name. "Let him go to hell on his own hook," the former president said.[33]

Nixon's supporters recognized their man's weakness. Toward the end of the campaign, at a big Nixon fund-raising dinner where Eisenhower spoke, a Nixon backer presiding over the event announced, in an almost unbelievable gaffe of candor, that too many people had been saying, "I don't like Nixon, but I don't know why."[34] Maybe Nixon sensed the issue himself. Years later, writing his memoirs, he thought about Brown and noted, with what must have been envy, that the governor was a politician "whom no one particularly disliked."[35]

———

Nixon's lead—the cushion that encouraged him to run and nearly scared off Brown—shrank from the day he announced his candidacy. Back in summer 1961, when Nixon was deciding what to do, his margin was a stunning 16 points. Then it was 10 in the fall, then a meaningless 2 points by February 1962. In April, with only weeks until the primary, Brown finally pulled ahead for the first time.[36] The governor held his lead through the summer, but there was cause to worry. A month before election day, both sides faced the Russian roulette of politics, a televised debate.

Debate negotiations had dragged on for weeks. At the Associated Press meeting earlier in the campaign—the event that gave Brown a boost of confidence—the two men had simply given speeches in sequence, with no questions from reporters or each other. Nixon had pressed hard for another encounter, this time a true debate with the candidates interrogating one another, or at least facing unpredictable questions from journalists.

Brown feared a true debate. He knew Nixon had been a college debater, and the old insecurities of a man who had never attended college came rushing back. What was more, Brown had seen Nixon debate during his first bid for Congress, in 1946, and had thought him dangerously clever. Against such a foe, the governor thought he would lose. But he also felt obliged to meet Nixon head-on. If he ducked a confrontation altogether, voters might think him cowardly, and cowards do not win elections.[37] So the two sides struck a deal: one debate, televised live, with questions from journalists but no direct exchange between the candidates. It was to be held at another meeting of newspaper editors, this one sponsored by United Press International, at San Francisco's Fairmont Hotel, the grand address atop Nob Hill that was so often the site of Brown fund-raisers.

Both men began with opening statements, brief and polished and predictably dull. The action came, as everyone expected, when the editors started asking questions of the candidates. The greatest excitement boiled down to just two moments, both of them instances when Nixon, who believed it was easier to attack a position than to defend one, confronted Brown.[38] Early in the question-and-answer session, Nixon was asked if he supported the reelection campaigns of two California congressmen who had admitted their membership in the John Birch Society. He replied that he was endorsing no congressional candidates. Then, hoping to turn the tables, he faced Brown and asked if the governor supported two liberal state legislators "who helped to lead the riots against the Committee on Un-American Activities when it met in San Francisco."

The rules specified that the candidates were not to query one another, but Nixon's question actually offered Brown a great opportunity. The protests to which Nixon referred had occurred in 1960, when Berkeley students and other young people objected to the committee's hearings at San Francisco's City Hall. To break up the protest, police used fire hoses to wash the students down the building's marble steps, and they dragged away others by the hair. It seemed to many liberals that the misconduct had been more on the part of the authorities than the demonstrators. But regardless of opinions on that point, Brown had an opening: Nixon simply had his facts wrong. The two lawmakers he referred to were not present when the trouble occurred. The previous day and at a different location, they had given speeches objecting to the committee hearings, but they were never at City Hall and had nothing to do with the so-called riot.

Wisely, Brown noted that the question was against the rules but said he would answer it anyway. But then he missed the opportunity to catch Nixon in a straightforward factual error. Either the governor did not know the legislators' whereabouts on the day of the committee hearing or he forgot, so he simply said that he did not always agree with the two lawmakers but thought they did "excellent" work and knew that they had led the fight in Sacramento "for the blind and the lame and the aged." He said he supported them "unequivocally."[39]

It was a notable exchange, but a few minutes later the fireworks got louder. Tom Braden, the publisher of the Oceanside paper and a Brown appointee to the state Board of Education, asked Nixon if he thought the old loan from Howard Hughes to Nixon's brother had been "morally and ethically" proper. There had long been rumors about the loan. Nixon had been vice president at the time. Collateral for the loan was skimpy—a piece of property owned by Nixon's mother—and there seemed to be some evidence that Nixon himself must have been involved in securing the money. One of the documents had been signed by his mother in a Senate office building in Washington, D.C., for example. Given the massive defense contracts that fed the Hughes empire, the matter raised serious questions. Had the vice president, for example, offered any special treatment to Hughes's companies in return for a friendly loan to the Nixon family?

But the rules restricted inquiries to matters of current public policy, not personal issues, and the moderator ruled Braden's question out of order. Nixon saw an opportunity amid the attack, however, and dramatically insisted that he be allowed to answer. He ran through the details of the loan, declaring that Brown "and his hatchetmen" had been spreading rumors about the story. The governor was guilty of a cowardly ambush, Nixon said, because he had been accusing Nixon of wrongdoing "privately" and "slyly." With growing indignation, Nixon went on: "All the people of California are listening on television. The people of this audience are listening. Governor Brown has a chance to stand up as a man and charge me with misconduct." Then he turned to face Brown directly: "Do it, sir!"

Across the stage, standing at his own podium, Brown was dumbfounded, as if he had been caught with a clean punch to the jaw. Nixon was glaring at him, waiting for an answer. Brown started with a flat denial: "I have said nothing about it to anyone whatsoever." Then, perhaps realizing that what he had just said was neither truthful nor believable, he immediately backpedaled.[40] He conceded that he might have mentioned the Hughes loan "in casual conversation from time to time," a comment that drew titters from the crowd.

It was a weak response, and standing there beneath the klieg lights of television, Brown thought to himself that he had been badly hurt. As he left the stage, it seemed that the governor's fears had come true. He had suffered the worst of the debate, failing to point out Nixon's inaccuracies and then contradicting himself about the loan.

But later that night, after flying to Hollister to give a speech, Brown watched the debate replayed on television and suddenly felt buoyed. Brown thought that Nixon seemed mean, overaggressive, too nasty. Brown's answers might have won few points with debating judges, but voters like their leaders to be friendly, decent fellows. Sitting in front of the television set—the exact place and posture in which most Californians would have experienced the debate—Brown was reassured to think that, if nothing else, he came across as the nicer man.[41]

———

Out on the trail Nixon could get no traction. He tried the old conservative broadsides—taxes too high, regulations too restrictive—but big government was not yet the enemy for Californians. He fell back on the Old Faithful of his career and argued that Brown did not know how to deal with the threat of Communism, but the day of the Red scare in California was fading fast. Hugh Burns, the conservative Democrat who was president of the state senate and chairman of its Un-American Activities Committee and who had not always been a friend to the governor, declared that no new anti-Communist laws had been enacted while Brown was governor because none were needed.[42] Besides, the Nixon campaign seemed almost absurd on the topic. At the rally where he announced his candidacy, cheerleaders led the crowd in chanting "Nixon is blue hot!" so as to avoid the use of the word *Red*.[43]

Then in the final weeks the campaign went deeper in the gutter. It had always been an aggressive fight—on both sides. Brown personally instructed his staff to plant hostile questioners at Nixon events[44] and kept on his payroll a prankster named Dick Tuck, a Brown aide with a flair for mischief. Tuck became a legend in politics, in part because his brand of gamesmanship seemed funny and clever rather than nasty, but he was still a burr in the side of his opponents. Once during a Nixon campaign stop in Chinatown, Tuck arranged to have people there holding a big banner in Chinese, ostensibly to welcome the Republican candidate. Neither Nixon nor any of his aides had any idea what it said, but the candidate dutifully posed in front of it. Only when a Chinese supporter rushed up did they learn that the banner read, "What About the Hughes Loan?"[45]

Toward the end the tricks got dirtier. Democratic voters began receiving postcards from something called the Committee to Preserve the Democratic Party in California. The cards claimed that extremists had seized control of the Democratic Party and that Brown and his fellow candidates were in league with the left-wingers. It was a fake, orchestrated by Republicans rather than Democrats. Nixon campaign officials later admitted they were behind the ruse.[46]

Meanwhile, Don Bradley, Brown's campaign manager, had dispatched

Democratic workers to visit Republican offices and collect whatever extremist material was being distributed so that Democrats could then accuse the Republicans of pandering to the far right.[47] On one such hunting trip, the Democratic troops found some GOP offices distributing a booklet titled "California Dynasty of Communism," a play on the initials of the California Democratic Council. The booklet featured a picture of the governor bowing slightly, his head down and hands together, as if in supplication. On the facing page was a picture of Khrushchev, as if Brown were showing subservience to the Soviet leader. In fact, the picture of the governor had been carefully cropped. The uncropped picture showed that Brown was greeting a young Laotian woman who, on an official visit, was greeting him the same way. Khrushchev, obviously, was not there at all. Nixon had repudiated the booklet, but Democrats claimed that it was being distributed at Republican offices.

Another pamphlet, this one titled "Pat Brown and the CDC," also began appearing. In this case the picture showed the governor applauding joyfully, but it was another cropped shot. The full picture showed Brown applauding a little girl who had made her way onto the assembly dais despite the leg braces she wore because of polio, but in the Nixon brochure the girl was gone, and the picture was placed in such a way that it appeared Brown was applauding the idea of admitting the People's Republic of China to the United Nations. The CDC had in fact endorsed that idea, but Brown had opposed it for years. H. R. Haldeman, Nixon's campaign manager and later his White House chief of staff, admitted that the Nixon forces were behind this pamphlet, and he defended the use of the picture. It was "illustrative" of the governor's stands, he said.[48]

The Nixon campaign answered with its own charges, alleging that Democrats were distributing two pamphlets that falsely claimed the former vice president was anti-Semitic and a crook. The Brown camp, for what it was worth, denied any connection with the pamphlets. Both sides traded lawsuits, and although they got restraining orders prohibiting the distribution of some materials, they knew the legal action was largely a stunt. The election would be over before a court case could work its way fully through the legal system.

The specter of dirty tricks played on Brown's mind, however. One morning he awoke in a motel room and realized through the blur of fatigue that there was a woman in bed beside him. His mind leaped instantly to Nixon's hardball reputation, and he assumed in horror that the Republicans had somehow slipped a girl into the room to cause a scandal. He braced himself for the flashbulbs of news cameras, but then remembered that amid the exhaustion of a campaign schedule, he had forgotten one critical fact: Late the previous night Bernice had flown in and met him.[49]

Perhaps the voters were as affected as the governor. Anti-Communism may have faded as an issue, but the idea that the governor of California might bow to Khrushchev was too much to take. As the anti-Brown pamphlets began to appear, Nixon enjoyed a burst of momentum. It soon became apparent that the debate had helped too. Brown may have concluded that he seemed the nicer man, but voters were telling pollsters that Nixon enjoyed the best of the exchange.[50]

Just as Nixon got rolling, another boost: a visit by Eisenhower, who remained immensely popular. The former president never liked Nixon, but now he came through for his old subordinate. "I can personally vouch," Ike told a Nixon fund-raising dinner crowd at San Francisco's Cow Palace, "for his ability, his sense of duty, his sharpness of mind and his wealth in wisdom."[51] One Nixon aide recalled Eisenhower's traditionally tepid support and griped, "If he'd only given that speech two years ago, Dick Nixon would be president today."[52]

In the wake of Eisenhower's visit, poll takers hit the streets again. The results were released in mid-October, with less than three weeks left in the campaign. The pamphlets and the debate and the former president had taken their toll: Brown's lead was down to just three points. Among those people most likely to vote, the race was tied.[53]

———

Three days later, a Monday, the campaign changed dramatically—along with the rest of the world. President Kennedy announced that he had ordered a naval blockade of Cuba to halt the importation of Soviet nuclear missiles. Brown rushed back to the Governor's Mansion from his temporary residence in Los Angeles and then at the end of the week headed to Washington for a meeting of nine key governors on civil defense issues. Interest in the California campaign, keen before the missile crisis, faded. Kennedy's support surged—people rallying round the flag—and by extension so did support for incumbents everywhere, especially Democratic ones. Politically, the Cuban Missile Crisis was good news for Brown, bad news for Nixon.[54]

Still, neither man stopped campaigning. In fact, the rhetoric on both sides only grew more heated in the final week. Nixon claimed that the state's civil defense programs were inadequate and that Brown was trying to "hoodwink the people of California into a false sense of security"—emotionally charged accusations with the world at the brink of nuclear war.[55] Brown, who was always a tougher campaigner than people gave him credit for, finally blew up at Nixon's insinuations that he was soft on Communism, including the pamphlets with the misleading photos. "I know you're not going to let this fellow get away with this thing," Brown told one crowd. "We're going to retire him to private life where he belongs." Getting a little carried away, Brown even insisted that he was "every bit as good of an American as Mr. Richard Nixon and a whole lot better." Three days later, the governor called his opponent "a man without heart, a man without feeling for the people."[56]

On November 5, the day before the election, Brown awoke to find the morning papers containing the final poll. It was good news. Brown was ahead by seven points overall, four among people who were likely to vote.[57] After his one brief downward blip—the poll three weeks earlier that had suggested a possible tie—he had rebounded. With both candidates sprinting toward the finish, Brown was back in front with a solid lead, exactly the position he had held for most of the campaign.

The last day was a whirlwind. Brown flew the length of the state, from San Diego to Eureka, then turned around and retraced half his route back down to San Francisco. In all, he gave eleven speeches in eleven hours. At the last one, he spoke to twenty-five hundred people at an outdoor rally in his hometown and predicted a victory. Then, confident but exhausted, he went home.[58]

Characteristically, Nixon spent the final day in lonelier circumstances, canceling his scheduled appearances and instead preparing himself for a final statewide television broadcast that night. Even with the practice, he botched the big moment. In a Freudian slip that only reinforced lingering doubts about his vow of disinterest in the White House, he said at one point, "When I become president . . . " He caught himself and started over, only to stumble again: "governor of the United . . . "[59]

On election day, both candidates rose early so that they and their wives could be photographed voting. The Browns played their traditional election day round of golf—Bernice winning as usual—and then flew to Los Angeles. They were renting a house there to use during the campaign, but as a kind of staging area that night they took the Presidential Suite at the Sheraton West, where they got together with friends to have dinner and await the results. It was a large and jovial party: From room service they ordered tournedos of beef for eighteen.[60]

Across town at the Beverly Hilton, Nixon dined alone on a pineapple milkshake and coffee. He had spent the day in his office, and although that evening he was in surroundings similar to Brown's—Nixon too was in the Presidential Suite—his experience was much different. Much of the time he remained alone, recording his thoughts on a yellow legal pad as the night wore on. "Only God & people know who is winning," he wrote at one point. Then a little later: "This race will be 50½–49½ somebody will win by a noze—only hope my noze is longer." (Apparently he spelled *noze* that way as a personal joke.) When the first returns arrived, he thought he was ahead but noted, "No trend as yet." With time, however, it became apparent that things were turning against him. In county after county, he was running well behind his 1960 performance, when he carried California only because of absentee ballots counted the next day. Brown's margin was growing too big to overcome. Late that night, on his yellow pad, Nixon summed up in one word his chances to be elected: "Never."[61]

At about midnight Nixon encountered his press secretary, Herb Klein, and declared that he was ready to concede. Klein talked him out of it. They went over the numbers one more time, and while they agreed that the odds were long, it was by then too late for a concession speech to make the morning papers. Some conservative areas remained uncounted, so Nixon decided that he might as well wait until the next day on the outside chance of a miraculous comeback. Klein went down to the press room and told the fatigued reporters that there would be a news conference at 10:00 A.M.[62]

While Nixon was talking with Klein, Brown's motorcade was heading from his hotel over to the Hollywood Palladium, a Big Band–era ballroom where Democrats had gathered for the traditional election night party. The governor knew that things were running in his favor, but he remained a little cautious. Leaving the hotel, he claimed to be carrying two statements, one declaring victory and another that he refused to describe but which presumably was noncommittal.[63]

He arrived at the Palladium and spent some time working his way through the big crowd. By the time he reached the dais it was nearly 1:00 A.M., and all doubt was gone. The lead was well over 100,000 votes and growing. Eventually the margin would grow to almost 300,000 votes—not a rout but a good solid victory. "I want to tell you," Brown told his cheering supporters, "I'm re-elected governor of California."[64]

It had been an emotional night for everyone. At her boarding school in Monterey, the nuns let Kathy Brown stay up past curfew, listening to the radio for the returns. Somehow she concluded from the early tallies that her father had lost. She sneaked down to the phone booth in the dormitory hallway, called his hotel, and, in tears, told him that she still loved him and thought he was a great dad. He told her that it wasn't over and tried to buck up her spirits, but she wasn't cheered until two nuns tapped on her door later in the night and, handing her a cupcake with a lone candle, said that her father had won a second term.[65]

Not even a teenager, however, could match the inner turmoil that gripped Richard Nixon in those hours. After losing the presidency of the United States, he had disregarded the fervent wishes of his wife and spent more than a year running hard for an office he did not truly want—all thanks to his own grinding ambitions. Now it had come to nothing. Just two years after winning his party's presidential nomination, he had been rejected for the governorship of his home state. Losing the state election after losing the presidential race was, he said, "like being bitten by a mosquito after being bitten by a rattlesnake."[66]

By the time he went to bed, in the wee hours, Nixon was gloomy and drained. When he emerged from his suite the next morning he was in no better shape, perhaps worse. He had gotten little sleep. His appearance was haggard. He was unshaven. His eyes particularly showed exhaustion. By some accounts he had been drinking.[67] The defeated candidate and his advisers huddled, and it was quickly decided that Nixon was in no condition to make a statement. Klein, the press secretary, would face reporters, reading the candidate's congratulatory telegram to Brown and answering a few questions. As this was going on, Nixon would slip out a back door of the hotel and be driven home.

What happened next is a little unclear, for the recollections of participants vary. Some people claimed that Nixon, watching Klein's news conference on television, was bothered by what he considered the reporters' impertinence; others said he was goaded into making a statement by distraught supporters. Whatever the details, Nixon decided he would face the press and rushed downstairs. He suddenly appeared onstage and took the podium from Klein. From the first words, it was clear that his talk would be a doozy.

He started off aggressively, intimating that the people to whom he was speaking—people who took pride in fairness and objectivity—took great joy in seeing him lose. "Now that Mr. Klein has made his statement," he said, "and now that all the members of the press are so delighted that I have lost, I would just like to make a statement of my own." Switching gears, he tried to be gracious, saying he had "no complaints" about the press coverage of the campaign and praising Brown. Then, back to grievance: the governor had called Nixon heartless and a bad American, while Nixon had defended his opponent's patriotism, comments he said had gone unreported by the press.

"I want that—for once, gentlemen—I would appreciate if you would write what I say, in that respect. I think it's very important that you write it—in the lead, in the lead." He singled out Carl Greenberg of the *Los Angeles Times* as the one fair reporter at that newspaper, embarrassing Greenberg, whose stories had been, like those of most reporters, impartial. Moving on, Nixon rambled through other topics: his pride in his volunteers, the national election results, Cuba, the proliferation of defense contracts in California.

Then he began to close. "One last thing," he said, and added that he planned to take a vacation and spend more time with his family. Again he said, "One last thing," and noted that people had asked him "about losing in '60 and losing in '64." (This was yet another Freudian slip about the presidency.) "The answer is that I'm proud to have run for governor. . . . [Voters] have chosen Mr. Brown. I can only hope that his leadership will now become more decisive."

Then for the third time: "One last thing." He said he thought the reporters looked "a little irritated" by the beginning of his talk and hinted that perhaps this was due to a misunderstanding: "My philosophy with regard to the press has really never gotten through. And I want to get it through." That opened the psychological floodgates, and Nixon's bitterness toward the press poured out. Reporters could write what they like, but, he said, "I wish you'd give my opponent the same going over that you give me." He complained that his recent gaffe—"governor of the United . . ."—had been reported in the *Los Angeles Times,* but a flub by Brown the same day had not been. Then came what appeared to be a stunning declaration of retirement:

I leave you gentlemen now and you will now write it. You will interpret it. That's your right. But as I leave you I want you to know, just think how much you're going to be missing. You won't have Nixon to kick around any more, because, gentlemen, this is my last press conference. . . . I believe in reading what my opponents say and I hope that what I have said today will at least make television, radio, the press first recognize the great responsibility they have to report all the news and, second, recognize that they have a right and a responsibility, if they're against a candidate, give him the shaft, but also recognize if they give him the shaft, put one lonely reporter on the campaign who will report what the candidate says now and then. Thank you, gentlemen, and good day.

He stalked away, pausing once he was out of earshot of the reporters to tell Klein, "I know you don't agree. I gave it to them right in the ass. It had to be said, goddammit. It had to be said."[68]

To be fair, a few of Nixon's comments had been kind, others at least truthful. Brown had indeed said that Nixon lacked a heart. In a moment of foolish exuberance he had also claimed to be a better American than his opponent. Brown was a tougher campaigner than people thought, but in that moment he was offering little more than rash and unnecessary insults.

But the bulk of Nixon's talk was a sad performance. Given the tone and contents, it was easy to forget that he was there to give a concession speech. Rather than graciousness, he offered rambling belligerence. It was spiced with the famous Nixon paranoia, which by the end of the 1962 campaign was running at a high pitch. A few days before the election a Nixon staff member overheard Richard Bergholz, a reporter for the *Los Angeles Times* whom Nixon disliked, place a phone call to Brown's press secretary. There was nothing suspicious about that—reporters call campaign officials all the time for countless reasons—but the Nixon campaign, including the candidate himself, was swept up with the feeling that Bergholz might be a spy.[69]

More important, Nixon's critique of the campaign was plainly inaccurate. His entire talk, not to mention his parting comment to Klein, reeked of bitterness toward the press, as if Nixon were a wronged man, the victim of vicious journalistic criticism. In fact, Democrats in California had struggled for decades against the fact that most of the state's major newspapers favored Republicans, both in the news sections and in the editorial pages. In the 1940s and 1950s, almost all California papers covered politics with ham-handed prejudice, touting their own candidate and virtually ignoring the opposition. For years Nixon had benefited from this. In his early career, he was for all practical purposes the creation of the *Los Angeles Times,* then as avidly Republican as any newpaper in the country. On the editorial pages, the *Times* remained a Nixon supporter during the gubernatorial campaign. One of the ironies of Nixon's screed was that the paper he attacked so vigorously had endorsed him.[70]

It was true that by 1962 political coverage on the news pages had begun to change, nowhere more than at the *Los Angeles Times.* Otis Chandler, the scion of the family that owned the *Times,* had taken over from his father and vowed to improve what had always been one of the worst newspapers in the country. But that change resulted not in an anti-Nixon prejudice but in an almost pathological fairness. Editors at the *Times* had announced that they would measure the stories on Nixon and Brown throughout the campaign, ensuring that both men received equal coverage. Day after day, the paper ran one story on Nixon, one on Brown, both of almost precisely equal length, sometimes with headlines of exactly the same size. Nixon, coddled for years, was stunned by the sudden neutrality. He praised television coverage as particularly fair, when the truth was that KTTV, a Los Angeles station, had aired so many commentaries favorable to Nixon and critical of Brown that the Federal Communications Commission ordered the station to provide Democrats with more time. Standing before the reporters on that weary postelection morning, Nixon was annoyed, not because the *Times* and other newspapers had covered the campaign of 1962 unfairly, but because he yearned for the pro-Nixon bias of a bygone day. In many respects the 1962 gubernatorial campaign was the first time in California history that a political race had been covered in a reasonably evenhanded way. Nixon's complaints looked and sounded like sour grapes.[71]

His supporters knew their man had come off poorly. Standing next to him on the stage, Klein desperately tried to think of some way to stop the proceedings, but could not. Had it been a prize fight, he noted later, he would have thrown a towel into the ring and led Nixon back to the locker room. After the debacle Klein drafted a statement for Nixon saying his remarks had been "inappropriate and ungraceful," but it was never issued.[72]

Like Klein, Brown thought Nixon had disgraced himself. The governor watched it all on television and felt sorry for his defeated foe. Still a young man by the standards of national leaders, Nixon seemed to be throwing away a promising career. A gracious defeat might have left open other paths, but instead Nixon had chosen to go down in ugliness and vitriol. "That's something that Nixon's going to regret all his life," Brown told Bernice as they watched it. "The press is never going to let him forget it."[73] To reporters, Brown said the former vice president might have a political future. Privately, his view was different. The day after the election the president called to offer congratulations, and the two men mused over Nixon's political obituary.

"God, that last farewell speech of his!" Kennedy said.

"Wasn't it terrible?" Brown responded. "I don't see how he can ever recover. . . . This is a peculiar fellow. . . . I really think he's psychotic. He's an able man, but he's nuts."[74]

———

If it was a low point for Nixon, it was the opposite for Brown. At fifty-seven, he was at the top of his world. Despite mistakes, his first term as governor had been, on balance, successful beyond all hopes. On his watch, California had done more to address its ceaseless growth than during any similar period in its history. University campuses had been built. Schools had been opened. Roads had been laid. Air pollution had been targeted more aggressively than in any other part of the country. The social programs that provided a safeguard for California workers—unemployment insurance and workmen's compensation—had been strengthened. To pay for it, Brown had had the guts to raise taxes and had seen it pay off. The economy was roaring along. Most important, California's Gordian knot of public policy—water—had been untied, the legislature and the voters convinced to approve a massive project that would ensure water for farms and homes for decades to come. It was an accomplishment that had eluded all of Brown's predecessors.

Voters had confirmed the success. In successive races, Brown had defeated two of the country's most famous Republicans, the former majority leader of the U.S. Senate and the former vice president of the United States. He was the "Giant Killer," a nickname first used after his rout of Bill Knowland and set in stone by his defeat of Nixon. In winning reelection, Brown was certain he had not merely beaten an ideological opponent, he had ended the career of a shady figure, a "bad man" hunting for power.[75] The governor's old hero Adlai Stevenson wrote him a note the day after the election and expressed the pervasive sentiment that Brown had done the country a favor: "Everyone has you to thank."[76] Better still, the victory was not only grand, it was individualized. Brown won with the handiest and most natural weapon, his personality. A fundamental friendliness and a boundless infatuation with his state had always been the twin cornerstones of his demeanor. Now in the greatest political battle of a long career, the nice-guy smile and the California enthusiasm had served as two of his best weapons, for he was running against a man who possessed neither. For Pat Brown, 1962 proved to be the perfect campaign because he was facing the perfect opponent.[77]

In the wake of victory, few obstacles remained. No Republican threats were standing. Knowland was history. Knight was washed up. Nixon was a bitter loser dishonored by his own lack of grace. In the twentieth century, Brown was only the third California governor elected to a second term, and the first Democrat. In the legislature, his party's margin of control was bigger than ever. In the most dynamic state in the most important country in the world, Brown was supreme.

But the problem with summits is that they are deceptive places to stand. The exaltation generated by the view overwhelms the hard reality that there is nowhere to go but down.

PART III
FALLING

12   RACE AND POLITICS

EVEN BEFORE BEATING RICHARD NIXON, Pat Brown decided it was time for a celebration. In the middle of October, with the campaign at full throttle, Brown declared he would follow through on an idea he had nurtured privately for a year. California was about to pass New York in total population—taking "its rightful place on top," in Brown's words—and he wanted to mark the great day.[1]

The result was a three-day bash just before New Year's, 1963, including an extra day off for state employees and an oddball collection of observances for the public. In San Diego the mayor asked motorists and ship captains to blow their horns in a single, cacophonous moment of glee. In the Bay Area a savings and loan company erected an electric sign that flashed population estimates showing California ahead of New York. In Truckee, high up in the mountains near the Nevada line, the town fathers went out to the highway, where they found a family of newcomers driving into California and pounced on them with an official welcome.[2]

The ballyhoo was a little phony. The Census Bureau insisted for months afterward that New York remained bigger than California, and even the governor admitted he might have been premature. "I have told the people of the world that we passed New York on December 21," he wrote to Adlai Stevenson's son, "but no one can really be sure."[3]

Even if it were true, not everyone thought demographic preeminence was worth celebrating. The public events drew slim crowds, and in Brown's hometown of San Francisco—a city born of a boom in the nineteenth century but slowly being eclipsed by one in the twentieth—the establishment was positively grumpy. City administrators rejected a proposal that their workers get an additional day off, and the *San Francisco Chronicle* complained that the whole affair was a commemoration of failure. Rather than take extra holidays, the paper editorialized, Californians should work to lessen "the blight and the miseries that planless growth has brought to this golden state."[4] Almost nobody had been saying such things four years earlier, when Brown started his first term, and the dissent was an early sign that some Californians had begun to commit heresy, to question the old certitude that bigger is always better.

———

Barely a week later, on January 7, 1963, Brown stood in front of the Capitol on an unseasonably warm winter's day and took the oath of office for his second term. It was the first time in thirty-two years that a California governor had been inaugurated outside, but location was not the important novelty. In the state's entire history, Brown was the first Democrat to serve a second term as governor. He swore fealty to the constitution and then, reflecting the fevers of the Cold War, also had to promise that he was not a subversive, had not been one for five years, and did not plan to become one during his term. When he finished, National Guard howitzers stationed nearby let loose a nineteen-gun salute.[5]

The ensuing speech took fifty minutes. The opening was pure boast. In the first four years, he said, his administration had laid plans to build an artificial river down the spine of the state, had started a vast expansion of the greatest system of public colleges and universities in the world, and had vowed that race would be no bar to work. Promising a second term like the first would have been foolish valor, so Brown focused most of his talk on smaller hopes. He wanted strict controls on the placement of billboards, for example, and said he would insist on top-flight architecture in state buildings. Only toward the end did he come around to his most powerful theme. A century had elapsed since Lincoln promised the slaves they would be "forever free." The country had fallen short. "In conscience," Brown said, "we cannot say today that we have redeemed Lincoln's promise." The answer lay in an aggressive civil rights agenda, and the governor outlined the particulars. Housing discrimination would be outlawed. Bias in state agencies would be eliminated through muscular use of the governor's executive powers. Anyone seeking a state license of any kind should have to promise fair treatment for all. The crowd pounded out its approval.[6]

That night a black-tie ball marked the occasion—and featured entertainment that emphasized California's unique place among the states. Nowhere else in the country could a governor's inauguration draw such stars. Frank Sinatra, the most famous entertainer in the world, headlined the show. Dean Martin did his drunk act and sang "Volare." Gene Kelly danced a soft-shoe. Steve Allen told jokes, including one with an ironic prescience he could not possibly have comprehended. It was a good thing the Democrats had triumphed, he told the crowd. "If Dick Nixon had won, you'd be sitting here listening to Roy Rogers and Ronald Reagan."[7]

———

Brown began his second term by returning to an issue that had caused him much heartache in his first, the death penalty. Knowing that outright abolition was impossible, he proposed a four-year moratorium on executions. Even that measure failed; it passed the assembly by one vote but died in committee in the senate.[8]

Rebuffed by the legislature, Brown turned to his own powers. The month of his second inaugural there was one execution at San Quentin, but thereafter he began commuting every death sentence that came before him. Brown never said he had adopted a blanket policy of commutation, but that was the effect: No more executions occurred while he was governor. As he was leaving office, he was urged by death penalty opponents to make an even more sweeping gesture, to commute the sentences of all sixty-four men on California's death row. He considered it, but returned to his old stance that capital punishment was the law, whether he liked it or not, and in the end commuted just four of the men still facing execution.[9]

Over the long run, Brown's second-term commutations made him by far the most vigorous gubernatorial opponent of the death penalty among his California contemporaries. During his eight years in office, he issued twenty-three commutations and allowed thirty-five executions, meaning that he spared about 40 percent of the convicts who came before him. By contrast, Goodwin Knight issued commutations less than 15 percent of the time, Earl Warren less than 10 percent.[10]

———

But the dominant thread of the early months of Brown's second term was not the death penalty. The greatest focus was on civil rights, in particular, a fair housing law.

By later standards, Brown was far from perfect in his dedication to tolerance and equality. As a kid, he joined other neighborhood boys in throwing bricks at Chinese laundry wagons.[11] As a prosecutor, he bemoaned the presence of gays in his city, which he described forlornly as "the Mecca of all homosexuals of the Pacific Coast." "This type of individual," he insisted, caused crime and sometimes became "addicted to this form of activity by reason of contacts with others of the same nature." More and more minors, he thought, were engaged in "this vice." Until well into his adult life, Brown had no sense that women struggled against hard odds in America. "I never even actually thought about women with respect to equal rights, between you and me," he said years later to a female interviewer. "It didn't occur to me till after I became governor that you gals were really in a secondary position."[12]

But in Brown's day, civil rights largely meant the fight against racism and anti-Semitism, and on those issues—most of the time and for most of his life—he had been one of the good guys. In high school he had responded to a fraternity's anti-Semitism by organizing his own group, where both Jews and Gentiles were welcome.[13] As a young district attorney, he wrote to legislators and urged them to pass a bill banning racial discrimination in hiring, a change that would only be made years later when Brown himself was governor. "I agree with those who say you cannot make people good by law," he wrote, "but sometimes it helps."[14] As attorney general, he pushed for integration of the Los Angeles Fire Department by the simple method of issuing a legal opinion that segregated firehouses were unconstitutional.[15] And he joined the attorneys general of Massachusetts and New York in refusing to stay at the Camelback Inn in Phoenix, the site of a national conference, because it barred Jews. The next year, when his counterparts in southern states were giving speeches with titles like "The Ugly Truth about the NAACP," Brown promised the resources of his office to protect black families moving into previously all-white neighborhoods. After the launch of Sputnik shocked the country into a stunned and fearful anxiety, Brown used the occasion to urge the death of Jim Crow. To catch the Soviets in the space race, he said, America must use "all our human resources without regard to race, creed or color."[16]

As governor, he kept the faith. Once when Martin Luther King Jr. came to California to speak in Los Angeles, Brown donated $100 to help fund the

Freedom Riders, the courageous protesters who had challenged the segregation of southern buses and bus stations—and been savagely beaten as their reward. Months later at a governor's conference, southern colleagues accused Brown of funding troublemakers, but he never backed down or said he regretted it. For another King trip, Brown agreed to send out the invitations for a fund-raiser at the Beverly Hills home of the actor Burt Lancaster. The governor was hardly the linchpin of the evening's success, but he played whatever small role he could in a night that brought huge rewards for King's Southern Christian Leadership Conference: $1,000 from Paul Newman, $5,000 from Marlon Brando, $20,000 from Sammy Davis Jr.[17]

On policy matters, Brown's record had been a mix of activism and practicality, as it was on almost everything. His first year as governor, he advocated and then signed the state's landmark measure creating a Fair Employment Practices Commission. In the later years of his first term, his million-vote landslide growing more distant, he grew more cautious. In 1961, the year before he would be up for reelection, Brown backed a bill extending the state's protections against housing discrimination, but he did it with no great zest, and the measure failed. But by 1963 the governor's fortunes had revived. A second term was safely in hand, and the Democratic majorities in the legislature were larger than ever. Even on controversial issues like civil rights, the governor was back in fighting trim.

————

Brown began the battle armed with the findings of a special commission created to study housing and minorities. The report was a plea for action. Californians liked to think of their state as a bulwark of tolerance, a beacon of light and justice by comparison to unenlightened parts of the country. The reality was less exalted. Blacks and whites were sharply divided in California, a divide so complete that it might as well have been decreed by law, as it was in the Deep South. In most cities whites and blacks simply did not live near one another. In San Diego more than a quarter of the city's census tracts had no blacks at all. In Fresno half the city's blacks huddled in just two small sections. In the sprawling new suburbs—the emblem of postwar California—the statistics were sharper still. One study found that during a period in which 350,000 new homes were built in Northern California, fewer than 100 had been bought by nonwhites. Orinda, a suburb east of San Francisco, had 1,600 households; 4 were nonwhite.[18]

Economics played a role—as a rule minorities were poorer than whites and thus were concentrated in older, cheaper neighborhoods—but so did bigotry. Blacks had trouble getting loans even when they could afford them. The Los Angeles Realty Board refused to accept black members. Houses repossessed by the Veterans Administration, and thus up for resale at bargain prices, were simply made unavailable to potential buyers who were black.[19]

Some of this should have been illegal even under existing law. California already prohibited racial discrimination in publicly financed housing and in "all business establishments," a phrase interpreted by the courts to include real estate brokers and most apartment owners. But the statutes were piecemeal, and more important they lacked an enforcement mechanism. To avail themselves of the law's protection, the victims of discrimination had to hire a lawyer, then wait months while the case slogged its way through the courts. Cost alone—not to mention the emotional strain and the practical constraints of time—meant that for most people the remedy to discrimination simply did not exist.[20]

Brown's commission concluded that the solution was a new and formidable fair-housing law—with teeth. The Fair Employment Practices Commission established in the governor's first term should be expanded so that its mandate included housing, the panel said. If a complaint of housing discrimination arose, the FEPC should be able to investigate, try to mediate a solution, and, if need be, punish those in the wrong.[21] Brown grabbed hold of the idea and, in his second inaugural speech, made it his own.

———

Even if he had possessed no personal commitment, Brown needed to push forward on civil rights for political reasons. Black Californians had begun to wonder if the Democrats who received so much black support could do more for their supporters. On inauguration day, while Brown was giving his speech, protesters from San Francisco's black community paraded nearby with pickets. "You Have Our Votes," read one sign, "Where Is Our Representation?"[22]

Fighting the same war on a quieter front, a group of San Francisco ministers hammered out an eleven-page memo urging Brown to move briskly on civil rights. They offered plenty of ideas—a human relations commission, stronger laws restricting job discrimination, better counseling to help minority kids get into apprenticeships—but their principal goal was the housing bill. The preachers knew their audience. To the governor who took pride in California's prominence, they noted that New York, "under a Republican administration," was still ahead in enacting civil rights measures. It was time to "make California No. 1 in human relations," just as it was in human beings. A month after the inauguration speech, with his administration's proposal still in the works, Brown used the ministers' lobbying to reenergize his own staff. "I like this program," he wrote in a memo to one of his aides. "How much of it are we working on?"[23]

As Brown knew, his staff was already hard at work. Assistants had surveyed existing housing laws to see what worked—the best of the bunch was a local ordinance in New York City—and they had been coordinating efforts with the assemblyman who would actually introduce the measure, Byron Rumford.[24] Rumford, a black pharmacist from Berkeley, had known both discrimination and the courage to fight it. Born in Arizona in 1908, when the region was not yet a state, he watched his maternal grandmother fight against segregated schools decades before the Supreme Court found them objectionable. Encouraged by a mentor who had graduated from the University of California, Rumford moved west after high school and worked his way through pharmacy school by parking cars at a San Francisco nightclub. He graduated in the midst of the Great Depression and started taking civil service exams for state jobs. Often the tests were a ruse, since state agencies had no intention of hiring a black man. Silly questions were routine. During an oral exam for a job as a food and drug administrator, Rumford was asked what he thought of Joe Louis as a fighter, an inquiry of no relevance that was presumably designed merely to throw Rumford off-stride. (He said he thought Louis was a fine boxer; the examiner flunked him.) He finally found a job at an Oakland hospital, where he and other African Americans were not allowed to eat in the dining room with white employees. In time he was able to save up enough money to buy a small pharmacy in Berkeley, where, as the owner, he faced no bigoted bosses. By 1948 he was a sufficiently respected local figure that he was elected to the state assembly, doubling its black membership.[25] In his first year in the legislature he sponsored a bill to desegregate the National Guard, and ten years later he carried the Fair Employment Practices Act signed into law by Brown. By 1963 Rumford's focus was on a fair housing bill, although he recognized the long odds against it. Walking the halls of the Capitol in a hunt for cosponsors, he warned Democrats from marginal districts that their support might endanger their reelection bids.[26]

Within weeks there was proof that Rumford was right to predict anger. In Berkeley, Rumford's hometown, voters rejected a fair housing ordinance that had been passed by the city council. Opponents argued the law would have infringed on private property rights, but even in a college town with a growing reputation for liberalism, racism was plain to see: During the campaign, someone burned a cross on the front lawn of a prominent local black man.[27]

That spring, as the Rumford bill was starting its journey through the legislature, the struggle for racial justice invaded Brown's world far more directly. His son, Jerry, had graduated from the University of California and enrolled at Yale Law School, but he was still showing the kind of social conscience that led him to the seminary and inspired him to encourage his father's opposition to the death penalty. Civil rights protests were in full flower in the South, and along with a lawyer who was organizing student volunteers, Jerry traveled to Mississippi.

He finagled a meeting with Mississippi Gov. Ross Barnett, a staunch segregationist, and tried to convince Barnett to allow a black student named Dewey Greene Jr. to enroll at the University of Mississippi. Barnett got on the phone to his visitor's father and told Pat that Jerry was associating with the wrong crowd, by which Barnett meant activists working for racial justice.

The Deep South was a volatile place to be in spring 1963, especially if you were a white, northern college kid who sympathized with civil rights activists. Pat and Bernice were understandably worried, but within days Jerry had left Mississippi safely. Brown wrote Barnett, diplomatically trying to balance his gratitude as a father with a desire to distance himself from a notorious defender of American apartheid:

Dear Ross,
Just a note to tell you that I very much appreciated your thoughtfulness in calling me about my son. Although you and I disagree vehemently on certain things, I am quite confident that we both are trying to carry on the traditions of our great country.[28]

The last sentence must have made Brown cringe—he had no use for a man like Barnett—but a father's duties came first.

In the legislature Rumford's fair housing bill was moving forward. It passed the assembly, although not without worrisome developments. Assembly seats were determined by population, which meant that urban liberals dominated the chamber. Yet even there Rumford had to accept amendments that limited the bill's scope. That suggested bleak prospects in the senate, where seats were still determined by geography—no county could have more than one senator—which meant that rural conservatives dominated.[29]

Hopes did not rise when the bill was sent to the senate's Governmental Efficiency Committee, often a killing field for liberal legislation. The chairman was Luther Gibson, a newspaper publisher from Vallejo, a navy town northeast of San Francisco. Gibson was a Democrat, but an extremely conservative one.[30] The committee's vice chairman was no improvement: It was senate president pro tem Hugh Burns, the conservative Fresno lawmaker who often differed with the governor. Neither Gibson nor Burns saw much need for more civil rights legislation, and from the start they suggested amendments to weaken the bill even more. Rumford believed Gibson's real goal was to dilute the bill into oblivion, chipping away with amendments until the final measure, if it passed at all, would amount to "almost nothing."[31]

The governor was worried too. In late May, two days before Gibson's committee was to open hearings on the bill, Brown used a ceremony commemorating the centennial of the signing of the Emancipation Proclamation to renew his highly public push for the Rumford bill. Segregation was "the heritage of slavery," he said, and it was not limited to the South. Blacks were the targets of prejudice in California, not just in Alabama or Mississippi. The fair housing law would help, at least a little, to put things right. "No man should be deprived of the right of acquiring a home of his own because of the color of his skin," Brown insisted.[32]

But the message was not getting through to the senate. Burns was stalling, looking for ways to kill the Rumford bill with slow poison. He suggested sending the whole issue to a commission for more study and insisted that the legislature should "move cautiously," because most Californians opposed "this type of legislation."[33] Gibson relied on more direct action. The chairman scheduled a hearing for Rumford's bill, then canceled it. The following week he did the same thing again. For supporters, this was too much to take. The bill had passed the assembly and stood at least a slim chance in the senate, but it looked as if the chairman of a single committee might block a vote. With the end of the legislative session only weeks away, Gibson showed no sign of relenting.

Turning up the pressure, members of the Congress of Racial Equality marched into the Capitol, put down air mattresses around the Rotunda, and declared they would not leave until they were assured a fair housing bill would pass. There had been a bomb scare at the building, but authorities still showed a wise tolerance. The supervisor of the State Police declared that as long as the demonstrators did nothing "improper," no one would ask them to leave. The governor plainly agreed with the policy. The next day, while leading two of his grandchildren around the Capitol, he came across the demonstrators plopped down on the floor. He chatted with them a bit, thanked them for supporting his civil rights bills, and then moved along.[34]

Unfortunately, Rumford's bill was proving no more mobile than the demonstrators. With ten days remaining in the legislative session—and on the same day that Alabama gov. George Wallace stood in the door of the University of Alabama in a grandstanding attempt to stop the school's integration—Gibson postponed yet another scheduled hearing on Rumford's bill, the third time in less than a month he had found reason for delay. Three days later Gibson's committee finally met, but the chairman declared negotiations at an impasse and refused to let the committee vote. Fed up, Rumford finally abandoned his diplomatic pose and verbally slugged it out with Gibson in public. "I no longer care to discuss this with you personally," Rumford snapped. The CORE demonstrators were even less decorous. Their spirits boosted by a recent visit from Paul Newman and Marlon Brando, they lay down in front of the huge main doors leading to the senate chamber, insisting that since the senate had blocked the fair housing bill, they would block the senate. Police dragged them away, but as soon as possible they returned to their mattresses in the Rotunda.[35]

On the last day of the legislative session, Burns and Gibson decided they had stalled long enough. If the committee never voted at all, their tactics would appear crude and heavy-handed. So they consented at last to take a roll call in Gibson's committee. Rumford had agreed to a few more weakening amendments, and the bill passed and was sent to the senate floor. But Burns and Gibson had no intention of seeing the measure enacted; the committee vote was for show. Opponents knew that with less than twenty-four hours before a constitutional deadline for the legislature's adjournment, hundreds of bills remained on the calendar. Burns declared that no measure would be taken out of order, so, as one of the last to get out of committee, Rumford's bill would be among the last to come up for a vote on the floor. Almost surely, the midnight adjournment would come first, and the bill would die for lack of time.[36]

Buttressing the strategy, another opponent objected to the senate's "consent calendar," a list containing dozens of noncontroversial bills usually voted on all at once. Unanimous agreement was required for bills to be on the "consent calendar"; any member's objection removed them all. They would have to be voted on one at a time, the roll of the forty senators called member by member, bill after bill. Hours would be wasted, exactly the goal of the Rumford Act opponents. As the day dragged on, the strategy worked. By evening, after hours of plodding work, there seemed little hope the senators would reach the bill.

From across the Capitol, assembly speaker Jess Unruh tried to help. Just before 10:00 P.M., with two hours left before adjournment, the speaker declared that his chamber would consider no more senate bills until the senate dealt with all the pending assembly bills, including the Rumford Act. The idea was to hold hostage the senate bills that Unruh controlled. If senators wanted to see their own measures acted on by the assembly, they would have to take up Rumford. It was a good try, and it helped to increase the pressure, but still Burns would not budge. The senate continued working its calendar, in order, one bill at a time, a slow form of execution for the housing measure.[37]

Supporters thought that if they could force a vote, they had a decent chance of winning. Brown had been working the legislature, promising favors for supporters and trouble for opponents, and Rumford backers were predicting a close but probably successful final roll call—if they could ever get one.[38] Fortunately, a new strategy was being hatched on the senate floor. The key conspirator was Democrat Joseph Rattigan, a man with a deeply personal motive for pushing the Rumford bill. Rattigan had grown up in Washington, D.C., in the 1920s and 1930s, when the city was still both southern and segregated. The only time the races mixed in Rattigan's boyhood was on District of Columbia buses, and even that was a practice at the edge of acceptance. On the lines that crossed into Virginia, the buses stopped at the end of the bridges over the Potomac so that black passengers could move to the back. This racism troubled Rattigan, but as a youth he rarely objected. His friends saw segregation as normal, and he did not want to mark himself as different, and in any event there was nothing a boy could do.

Now redemption was at hand, but it was mired deep in the mud of a senate schedule that offered little hope. Rattigan gathered other supporters and launched a last, desperate scheme. They would move to schedule debate on the housing bill at a specific time, in effect pulling the bill out of order and insisting that it be dealt with. Such a motion had one critical advantage: Under the legislature's rules, it could not be debated, and thus if the opponents were caught off guard, they would have no time to rally their troops.

Just after 10:30 P.M., less than ninety minutes before adjournment, the conspirators fired their first shot. Edwin Regan, a rural Democrat who was also Rattigan's seatmate, moved to schedule debate on the Rumford Act at exactly 11:00 P.M. Burns was furious, and he rose to speak. He began defending tradition—the senate always took up measures in order, he said—which was exactly the kind of stalling tactic the Rumford supporters needed to squelch. Rattigan jumped to his feet, called out a point of order, and insisted that Regan's motion could not be debated. The roll should be called instantly, he demanded. Glenn Anderson, the lieutenant governor and a liberal committed to civil rights, was presiding over the senate, one of the few duties a lieutenant governor has. Anderson upheld Rattigan's point and told the clerk to call the roll. Burns had been outsmarted in the body he supposedly ruled. Short of members on the floor—during the marathon sessions that precede adjournment, senators come and go constantly—Burns was suddenly unable to gather his forces.

The result was a narrow victory for Regan's motion, setting debate on the housing bill for 11:00 P.M., and, at long last, guaranteeing there would be a vote. In the intervening twenty minutes, Regan and Rattigan worked the floor, going from desk to desk to shore up wavering supporters and hunt for last-minute converts. In the forty-member senate they needed 21 votes to pass the bill, and when the roll call came, there was just one vote to spare. The bill passed 22–16, all the ayes coming from Democrats, all but two of the no votes from Republicans.

Staff members rushed the bill across the Capitol to the assembly, which had to agree to the senate's amendments. There was plenty of support in the lower house, and with minutes to go before adjournment, in one of the final roll calls of the session, the assembly approved the bill, sending it to a governor who was sure to sign it into law. For supporters, it was a joyful moment of release. In the Rotunda the demonstrators who had been sleeping on the floor for a month broke into song, although amid the fatigue and emotion the mood was better remembered than the details: Some people recalled hearing "The Battle Hymn of the Republic," others "We Shall Overcome." Rattigan enjoyed a less public moment of elation. He was nearly overcome with emotion, but he found Byron Rumford. The two legislators—one a white man who had resented racism, the other a black man who had overcome it—embraced. In tears, Rattigan said he had just atoned "for a Jim Crow boyhood."[39]

The governor signed the bill a month later, full of pride. From the first day of his second term, he had proposed a law against housing discrimination, had even made it the linchpin of his reborn administration, and now it was a reality. It was, he said years later, "one of the great victories" of his career.[40] He soon set out to expand on it, signing an executive order prohibiting discrimination by anyone holding a state license and requiring state government managers to "positively encourage Negroes and other minority group members to apply for jobs in state government." "Simply not discriminating is not enough," he declared.[41]

Righteous victory put Brown in a mood to speak plainly about bigotry, which in turn offered a hint of the vehemence the topic could arouse. Three days after signing the Rumford Act, he was at a national conference of governors in Miami Beach. Reporters asked about the 1964 presidential campaign, still a year off. Brown said that Barry Goldwater, the front-runner for the Republican nomination, could not carry California, where voters would not "support a segregationist." The reporters gave him a chance to back down, asking if he really meant to say that Goldwater favored separation of the races. "I certainly do," Brown said flatly. The blunt talk touched off a fury. Reporters scurried around the conference asking other governors what they thought of Goldwater's racial views, then filed front-page stories about the controversy. (George Wallace said he didn't know about Goldwater, but he was happy to declare himself a segregationist.) Letters from people enraged at his comments about the likely Republican nominee flooded Brown's office. Wrote one voter: "As long as it's the vogue to express your opinion about people as exemplified by your statement that Senator Goldwater is a segregationist, I would like to express my own opinion concerning you—namely that I think you are a SOB."[42]

———

Freed from the rigors of the legislative session, Brown made one of his periodic pilgrimages to Washington, although this one was unusual for what happened both before he got there and after he left. His plane from San Francisco was delayed by mechanical troubles, and he reached the capital only after an all-night flight that landed at 8:15 A.M. Unshaven, he headed directly to a meeting on western water issues with Interior Secretary Stewart Udall and the governors of Arizona and Nevada.[43]

It was an inauspicious beginning to an ambitious trip, because from Washington, Brown was leaving the country for his longest foreign journey as governor—a six-week Grand Tour of Europe. Part vacation, part booster trip for California business, Brown's excursion was also a reflection of his state's special status. As he boarded the jet to cross the Atlantic, he was slated for meetings with foreign leaders, international business executives, even the pope, honors not always received by mere state officials.

The traveling party was small. Brown's press secretary, Jack Burby, went as an aide-de-camp. Burby's wife took advantage of the chance to tag along. Bernice went, of course. The Browns' older daughters, Barbara and Cynthia, were busy with their own families back at home, but Kathleen went, and Jerry, who was working in Paris that summer, joined the group from time to time.

They stopped briefly in Ireland, where Brown visited County Tipperary, the home of his grandfather, and then two days later they headed for London. The governor met with both Prime Minister Harold Macmillan and Labour leader Harold Wilson, but he also gleaned what information he could about Britain's national health insurance system, in the hope that it might offer lessons for the United States.[44]

By the end of the week, they were in Paris. On their first night in town, the governor and his party went to dinner at a nice restaurant near the Champs Elysees—and by amazing happenstance were seated three tables from Richard Nixon and his family, who were completing their own European trip. The wounds from the previous year's campaign had yet to heal; the two groups did not exchange a word.[45]

Brown promoted his home state, as he would almost everywhere he went during the long trip. He tried to sell the French on California prunes, raisins, and chickens and boasted that he was served California wine at Maxim's, a Parisian culinary landmark.[46] Escaping the city, the Browns lolled around the Riviera for a few days.

Then they headed for Rome, where the governor's official duties intruded. Staff members had been sending newspaper clippings to his various stops, trying to keep him abreast of California events, but in Rome Brown found a more extensive and troubling update. Hale Champion, the governor's closest aide, had sent a long letter summarizing the home front. The legislature was meeting again, this time in a special session to deal with some budgetary matters that had not been resolved during the regular session. Unruh had overplayed his hand in parliamentary maneuvers and come off poorly in the papers, potentially damaging the Democrats. Brown was not entirely free of blame. Rather than stay at home and tend to the legislature, he had flown off to Europe, knowing he could always sign or veto bills after his return. Still, even if he had been present, it is doubtful he could have prevented Unruh's troubles. As it was, he could do nothing, and Champion recommended that the governor steer clear of the flap until he got back to California. It was easy advice to follow: Reporters in Europe were unlikely to ask about trouble in the California legislature.[47]

In St. Peter's Square at the Vatican, Brown posed for photographers in the driver's seat of a horse-drawn carriage. In meetings he suggested that Fiat might want to build a plant in California. He listened politely when one local official suggested that San Francisco might need a marble statue of Saint Francis of Assisi on Alcatraz Island, site of the just-vacated federal prison.[48] On a Saturday the Browns were hustled off to Castel Gandolfo, the papal summer residence, for an audience with Pope Paul VI. Ushered into an ornate waiting room, the governor and his family were left to cool their heels for hours. Bernice was furious. The governor, who unlike his wife was a practicing Catholic, took the delay in stride. Finally they were led into the pope's presence, which clearly awed Pat. "I've never seen my father so sheepish," Kathleen Brown remembered later. The governor gave the pope a picture book about California and invited him to visit the state. The pope, who spoke little English, replied that his future travel plans were "in the hands of God."[49]

In Yugoslavia two days later, Brown spent forty minutes with Marshal Tito. The two men had a gentle dispute about the nature of a free press. Tito said criticism was fine so long as it was "constructive and concrete, not political." Brown asked who decided such things. Then they shared a working politician's laugh when the governor allowed that sometimes the newspapers in California annoyed him.[50]

After Belgrade it was time for a vacation within a vacation, a few days' rest at the seaside resort of Dubrovnik. As always, Brown talked with everybody. When a singer in a nightclub learned that the prominent visitor was from California, he praised Frank Sinatra as the greatest man in the world, better even than Tito. Then he seized his chance and asked the governor to pass along a demo tape. Once he was back in the States, Brown dutifully sent the tape to Sinatra.[51]

With the trip winding down, relaxation became the norm. In Venice, the film festival was under way, and Brown lounged around on the beach with the producers.[52] In Germany, he visited Soest, the town in Westphalia from which Brown's maternal grandmother had emigrated. Finally, in their last days in Europe, they reached Berlin. They climbed an observation platform and stared across the barbed wire atop the wall separating East from West. A practical man confronted by an ideological divide, Brown reached for familiar mental handholds. He localized one of the world's most famous symbols: "Imagine if they put up a wall between Northern and Southern California." And as always, he empathized: The East German border guards staring back at them were simply "innocent victims of circumstances."[53]

The Browns headed home the next day. In all, the governor had visited eight countries, met with leaders both national and religious, boasted of California's every product, and made a pilgrimage to the roots of his family tree. The pope had exacted what was for Pat Brown a rare form of tribute—reticence—but elsewhere the governor had chatted up everyone he could find, from Marshal Tito to a nightclub singer hoping for the biggest break of his life. Thousands of miles from home, Brown had been his usual friendly self. He did not know it, but the trip was a final respite before a series of battering storms. Brown may have been unchanged overseas, but he was about to return home to a state where almost everything seemed in flux.

13   REJECTION

HOME AT LAST AFTER six weeks in Europe, Brown found it difficult to readjust.[1] Returning to workaday concerns was not the only adaptation he faced, for that fall he and Bernice passed a milestone of aging: Their last child enrolled in college. Kathleen's choice baffled and frustrated her father, for she decided to attend Stanford. The builder of campuses for the University of California could not understand why his daughter would snub the state's great public university. But he agreed to let her go, swayed by the advice of the nuns who ran her boarding school and the willingness of Lou Lurie, a rich businessman and supporter, to pay her tuition. Coming to peace with some of her decisions once she reached the campus proved impossible. She dropped French for art history, which seemed absurd to the practical graduate of a night law school. When she told him about the switch, he hung up the phone.[2]

He made time to visit, and as always, he sought attention. Amazingly, he seemed genuinely mystified that his children found the trait embarrassing. He wrote to Kathleen afterward:

> I couldn't understand the other day why you were so quick to get me out
> of the dining room where you were with all of those girls. I wish you
> would explain to me what is wrong with being the governor of California.
> I thought you would show me off to those young ladies instead of giving

me the bum's rush out of the dormitory. Next time I will come earlier, blow the siren in front of both the men's and women's dorms, have the red light on, and I'll have three highway patrolmen with me instead of just one.[3]

The trip to Palo Alto was followed by a brief return abroad: Brown stood in for Kennedy at the inauguration of Argentina's new president. Brown's official car—adorned with the Stars and Stripes on the front fender—was pelted with gravel and coins by demonstrators chanting "Castro sí, Yankee no." "I don't consider it very important," the governor told reporters as he arrived back in the United States, "because no harm was done."[4]

But perhaps it was an omen. Second terms are often a grinding chore, and, in that fall of 1963, Brown was marching toward trouble. In the coming months, he would face a complicated and perplexing swirl of events with intertwined story lines of presidential politics, bitter personal rivalries, race relations, even life and death. At varying times and with varying degrees of justification, he would be portrayed as an extraordinarily decent man, a conniving politician, a dedicated liberal, a compromising moderate, a sharp tactician, a bumbling dolt. More than at any other time in his career, success would blend with failure, although in the long run his world would slowly disintegrate from the joy of political triumph to the bitterness of political rejection. Worse, it was only the beginning of his woes.

———

On November 22 Brown was working in his office on the first floor of the Capitol when an aide came in to tell him that President Kennedy had been shot. They waited a time to get more news, but as the situation clarified horrifically, Brown decided he should make some comment.[5]

His voice laden with emotion, he spoke haltingly, searching for words, a rare thing for him. "One of the great American presidents has died," he began. He hoped that Kennedy's death might bring about "a lessening of some of the hatreds not only in our own country but in the world." He mentioned his personal feelings of loss, extended his condolences to the family, and asked Californians to pray for the new president and the country. "I've asked everyone to go home," he said. "I don't think it's fitting that there be any more work today, and I myself, I'm going to cancel everything else today." Then he added simply, as if he did not know what else to do, "Now that's all I want to say."[6]

It was decided immediately that he would attend the funeral. Brown's back had been hurting him, but that was nothing under the circumstances, so he boarded the *Grizzly* for the short flight to San Francisco and then transferred to a faster commercial jet for the long, grim ride to Washington, D.C. He was accompanied by two California Highway Patrol officers in plainclothes, one seated behind him, one in front, although he did not know it. Brown had told his chief of staff, Arthur Alarcon, that he did not want extra security at such a time, for fear of the message it might send to a frightened citizenry. Alarcon sent the officers along anyway, but he did not tell the governor.[7]

Three days later, the night of the funeral, the new president called the attending governors to the Executive Office Building, across the street from the White House. With plain and sparing words, Lyndon Johnson sketched both the tribulation the country had just endured and the challenge that lay ahead:

> Here is our president shot in the head and his wife holds his skull in her lap as they drive down the street. Here is our governor [John Connally of Texas] who looked around and said, "Oh, no, no, no," and because he turned, a bullet just missed his heart. It went down through his lung into his leg and tore his left hand off. And then, yesterday, they take the law into their own hands. We have to do something to stop that hate, and the way we have to do it is to meet the problem of injustice that exists in this land, meet the problem of inequality that exists in this land, meet the problem of poverty that exists in this land, and the unemployment that exists in this land.[8]

Brown had never been a Johnson man. They had nothing in common personally, and southerners held little appeal for California liberals. But sitting in the audience as Johnson spoke, the bite of a November evening mixing outside with the restless energy of a distraught city, Brown was touched by the speech. It was obviously an emotional night, and Brown went away convinced that the new president had answered the call.[9]

————

As Brown flew home, California's conservatives were determined to undo his greatest achievement of the year. Within days of the Rumford Act's passage, opponents had resolved to destroy it, either by blocking its enforcement or by repealing it altogether. Led by the real estate industry, they settled on an initiative petition, collecting voter signatures for a measure that not only would repeal the Rumford Act but also would prohibit the legislature from enacting other antidiscrimination housing laws in the future.[10]

The governor's office was quietly plotting strategy against the initiative, coordinating declarations of opposition from various state officials and collecting the names of real estate agents "who have a healthy point of view," meaning that they wanted to keep the Rumford Act on the books. The approach was a three-step sequence. First, convince the real estate industry to abandon the whole idea of an initiative petition. Second, if that failed, discourage voters from signing it in the hope that it might be kept off the ballot. And third, if need be, defeat the initiative at the polls.[11]

By New Year's Day 1964, the first goal was a dead letter, since it was clear the industry was pushing forward. Brown switched gears and encouraged people not to sign the petitions. At a news conference, he told reporters it would be "against the best interests of the people of this state" to repeal the Rumford Act before it had "a fair chance to work."[12] A month later that portion of the governor's strategy died too. Initiative supporters submitted their petitions to county clerks around the state. Not only had Californians disregarded Brown's suggestion that they refuse to sign, they had signed in such numbers that the measure was ensured a spot on the November ballot. In time it was designated Proposition 14, the name by which it would become famous.[13]

Brown was left with only the final leg of his plan: defeat the initiative at the polls. For the governor, that meant being at the center of another long and emotional campaign, and he took to it with characteristic gusto. The day after the signatures were submitted, he declared that the initiative would involve Californians in a "war between races." Rumford Act opponents, he said, were motivated by fear and would produce "a bad day for California."[14]

One day later his passion over the issue flared again, this time in private. At the urging of his staff, Brown had called Otis Chandler, the young and reformist publisher of the *Los Angeles Times* who had lessened the paper's traditional fetish for hard-core conservatism. The governor had hoped California's largest paper would editorialize against the initiative, and he was bitterly frustrated when he picked up the *Times*'s editorial page and saw that his appeal had been rejected. In a letter to Chandler, Brown let loose his rage:

I believe you should know that I am deeply disappointed in your editorial support of the initiative repealing the Rumford Act. Your editorial in Sunday's Times puts property rights over human rights. You freeze into the Constitution bigotry and discrimination. If you had opposed the initiative and asked the Legislature to repeal or modify the Rumford Act, I would differ with you but could understand it. But in this day and age when the non-Caucasian is striving so valiantly to find his place in the sun, I can only say that I am very, very sorry.

Brown closed with biblical fury, even instructing his secretaries to underline the words for emphasis: *"You know not what you do."*[15]

If Chandler was an object of wrath for the governor of California, Brown was the cause of a headache for the president of the United States. Lloyd Hand, a Johnson loyalist, was monitoring the California delegation to the Democratic National Convention scheduled for the following summer. Aware of the 1960 troubles with the California group, the Johnson forces wanted to make sure everything went smoothly this time. The president was assured of his own nomination, but he wanted to avoid any dissension at all, especially on the vice presidential pick. But on the phone, Hand told Johnson that there was already trouble in California. Brown was chafing that on a recent trip to Washington he did not get a one-on-one meeting with LBJ.

Johnson and Brown had never been close. They were completely different—Johnson a genius schemer, Brown a friendly glad-hander—and during the 1960 presidential campaign, they had been driven further apart when Brown said he doubted the Texan could attract much support in California. Johnson had been furious, and he was not the kind of man to forget such things. Now, as the president listened to Hand, his frustration erupted and revealed the brilliant, manipulating, self-pitying whirlwind that was Lyndon Johnson.

"I've talked more to that son of a bitch than all the governors in the United States put together," Johnson raged. "He's taken more of my time than all of them put together. . . . Tell him I'm not handling any of it. I'm not talking to a human being about it. I don't want the presidency that much. I'm not that interested in it. I cannot handle the things I've got and be playing with every city councilman that wants to come see me. When one of them do, all of them do, and I just can't possibly do it." The presidency was a consuming burden, he insisted. He had too much to deal with already: Cuba, a tax bill, civil rights, Panama, Cyprus. It would be "cruel and inhuman punishment" to force on him mere domestic politics. As for Brown, "I've seen him about three times since I've been in here and each time he has to tell me what a great man he is and how he defeated Nixon. I listened to him patiently . . . but there comes an end when you just can't do it."

Caught between the president and the governor he was supposed to be courting, Hand tried to explain Brown's insecurities to Johnson: "He feels you're not interested in him." "How can he feel that way when I've seen the son of a bitch three times?" Johnson asked. "He's just toting up my time— 30, 40 minutes. I haven't been in here but two months and I've seen him three times."

Hand tried again. The president should call Brown, he said, and offer some meaningless flattery. Brown was "such an insecure man" that the slightest acclaim from the president would win undying devotion. If praised, Brown would assemble a California delegation of true Johnson followers. Why, Hand said, the governor might even let the Johnson campaign dictate the names.[16]

Five days later Johnson was on the phone with the governor, his voice all honey and compliments for the man he had just disparaged privately as an annoying son of a bitch. "I wouldn't do anything that you didn't want done because I'm relying on you completely," the president told Brown. "You're the man that's demonstrated over the years that you're the fellow who can get the job done in California."[17] Three weeks after that, Brown announced the names of California's delegates—Johnson loyalists all.

———

As Johnson and Brown danced their minuet of presidential strategy, California politics was offering a more transcendent dilemma. It had begun the previous fall, almost as soon as Brown returned from the long trip to Europe in September 1963. President Kennedy disclosed to Brown what should have been private information: Clair Engle, California's colorful and engaging U.S. senator, had developed a brain tumor. Doctors at Bethesda Naval Hospital, where Engle had been treated, had told the White House of his condition, and now Kennedy was telling the governor. Brown needed to know because Engle's health presented a delicate problem. He had been elected to the Senate in 1958, in the Democratic landslide that made Brown governor, and thus he was up for reelection in 1964. If he was unable to campaign Democrats had to find another candidate quickly.[18]

In late December, as the world was celebrating the holiday season, Engle's plight was confirmed sadly in public. After weeks as an invalid, he returned to the Senate floor to vote on a foreign aid bill. He struggled to walk to his seat despite the use of a cane. After the roll call two senators helped him up the aisle as he left the chamber, but the few small steps were an ordeal he negotiated with difficulty. An appearance designed to showcase a man carrying on with his duties had instead raised added doubts as to whether Engle was capable of public life.[19]

Privately, Brown knew the situation was nearly hopeless. The governor's aide Roy Ringer had been told that doctors were more concerned with saving Engle's life than his political career. And shortly before the Senate appearance, Brown got definitive word that Engle's doctors had said he would be unable to campaign until summer, far too late to begin the race.[20]

For Brown and the Democrats, the best practical outcome was for Engle to resign. The governor would appoint a successor, who would have the advantage of incumbency over a Republican challenger in November. Given the cold realities of politics, the worst alternative was for Engle to seek reelection. Engle might die before election day, leaving the party with a dead candidate. He might live until the election, but, as a visibly dying man, lose the race and hand a valuable Senate seat to the Republicans. Even if he lived long enough and won reelection, he was likely to die soon thereafter, leaving his appointed successor as the Senate's most junior member, which would weaken California's influence. Democratic leaders had been hinting for weeks that Engle should get out of the race, throwing open the competition for the party's nomination. But far from quitting, Engle announced he would run again, a prospect that Democrats increasingly saw as a disaster. So in a moment of uncharacteristic steeliness, California's most prominent Democrat flew east to confront the issue personally just after New Year's Day 1964. No one would have relished the task, and certainly not a man like Brown. The governor who found it nearly impossible to fire a bad employee was planning to tell a dying man he should stand aside and let someone else take his job.

Ushered into the senator's sickroom, Brown began gently. Nobody, not even Engle himself, would want a man reelected to the Senate if he could not carry out his duties, Brown said. Before Engle could respond, his wife,

Lucretia, who had been pushing to keep him in the race, abruptly said that her husband was going to run. Perhaps she could not bring herself to accept the truth about his condition, perhaps she did not know, perhaps it was simply her way of clinging to some hope for a miracle. In any event, Brown could not let her decide the issue, so he simply went on. He made it clear again that Engle should not run if he could not serve, that Democrats needed a strong candidate, that perhaps Engle should think about stepping aside. It was a ghastly duty, and Lucretia Engle hated Brown for it, then and for years to come. But Brown was right: Engle was incapable of running, and the Democrats needed to find another candidate. Hard reality required an emotional toughness, and, atypically, Brown found it.

Somehow reporters had heard about the meeting and staked out Engle's house. Understandably, Brown lied, or at least dissembled, saying simply that he and the senator had enjoyed a good meeting and that Engle "looks fine physically." Asked if the senator would be able to campaign, Brown hedged: "I just can't say. I'll leave that to the doctors." Then the governor and his aide Irv Sprague got into the car, and the governor let himself sink into the awfulness of the day's mission. "That," he said to Sprague, "was the worst thing I ever had to do in my life."[21]

———

Even amid the excitement of the victory over Nixon, Brown had recognized the potential for trouble. Talking with Kennedy the next day, he noted that the Republicans who had dominated California only a decade before now held almost no major offices. "Of course," he added, "now we'll start fighting amongst ourselves."[22] Within months Brown was proved right, as an old lingering rivalry exploded into open warfare between the two most powerful Democrats in the state: the governor and the assembly speaker, Jesse Unruh.

Unruh was already becoming a legend. The fifth of five children born to an illiterate farmer and his wife, Unruh grew up so poor that the family bathed in their horse troughs and had neither underwear nor socks. After spending his youth in Kansas and Texas, he bounced around a bit after high school—for a time he lived in a chicken coop—and then eventually talked his way into the navy during World War II despite flat feet and low blood pressure. He got married just before shipping out, then spent the war stationed in the Aleutian Islands, where he was so bored he memorized a self-help book called *Thirty Days to a Better Vocabulary*. Discharged in 1945, he enrolled at the University of Southern California mostly because his wife, a Californian, was working there at the time. At USC, he ran for the student senate and discovered that politics was the love of his life.[23]

Unruh was so gifted politically that just four years after he was elected to the legislature, Fred Dutton, the manager of Brown's gubernatorial campaign, tapped him to run the Southern California operations. When Brown was elected governor, Unruh was named chairman of the powerful Ways and Means Committee, which wrote the state's budget. Perhaps because he had so little as a boy, Unruh grew into a man who wanted more of everything: more fame, more power, more adulation, more food, more liquor, more women. At the peak of his career, he weighed more than three hundred pounds and was famous for his nighttime excursions around Sacramento. By day he built a dedicated following in the assembly. Unruh was brilliant, aggressive, hardworking, brash, often obnoxious, the kind of man who relished confrontation as much as Brown dreaded it. But, like Lyndon Johnson, Unruh was a son of a bitch on the side of the angels. His favorite causes were social programs and civil rights, and in the early years of the Brown administration he was an indispensable ally in the legislature.

By the second half of Brown's first term, Unruh had managed to get himself elected speaker of the assembly and was intent on cementing his own power, independent from the governor. Unruh built close ties to the Kennedy administration, where feelings remained ruffled over Brown's poor performance at the 1960 national convention. When Brown ran against Nixon, Unruh convinced the White House the governor could win only if Unruh was allowed to oversee a precinct-by-precinct ground operation in Los Angeles County, paying thousands of workers $10 each to get out the vote. Under pressure from Kennedy operatives, the governor's campaign reluctantly agreed. After the election Unruh's followers began whispering, without much justification, that the speaker's effort had been crucial to the governor's victory. Brown and his staff bristled at the implication of political impotence, and the two men grew even more alienated.[24]

Within months the feud was in the open, details of the bickering published in the papers.[25] An almost comical low point came when Brown met with Republican lawmakers and referred to Democratic legislative leaders—obviously including Unruh—as "bastards." The Republicans pretended they were appalled and insisted to reporters that the governor had offended their frail sensibilities.[26]

By winter 1964, as Engle struggled to keep both his life and his career, the relationship between Brown and Unruh had ruptured completely. At the beginning of a messy battle for one of the choicest jobs in politics—a seat in the U.S. Senate—California Democrats were led by two men fighting each other at least as much as the common enemy.

———

Engle tried to hang on as a candidate, but it was hopeless. Speaking by telephone to the convention of the California Democratic Council, he stammered weakly, able to utter only a few words. Even his strongest supporters admitted he was in no condition to campaign, and he eventually withdrew.[27]

Privately, Brown was tempted to run for Engle's seat himself. "In my secret heart I would like to flirt with the idea of going to the Senate," he wrote, but the timing was wrong. He did not want to be on the ballot again so soon after the bitter Nixon battle, and of course there was always the possibility of a third term as governor.[28]

Still, even as a noncombatant, Brown remained at the center of the maneuvering. Stanley Mosk, the attorney general elected when Brown won the governorship in 1958, wanted to seek Engle's seat, but he was beset by a dicey problem. Around Sacramento it was well known that Mosk, who was married, had a girlfriend. Rumors spread quickly that there were embarrassing pictures showing the attorney general with the woman on a trip to Mexico. In later years some people remembered Brown helping to spread the gossip, which may be true.[29] What is certain is that the governor heard the rumors and like many Democrats was worried that if Mosk became the party's nominee, Republicans might use the information against him in the fall campaign. So he encouraged Mosk to pass up the race, perhaps even promising a seat on the California supreme court, to which Mosk was appointed a few months later. Whatever happened, Brown was reluctant to talk about it in a context that might be recorded for history. "One of these days I'll tell you what I did to get Mosk out of it," Brown told the president. "I don't want to tell you over the telephone." The president, who always had his ear to the ground for political gossip, had heard anyway, or at least wanted Brown to think he had. "Yeah," LBJ drawled, "but I know."[30]

With Mosk out, Alan Cranston, the state controller and an old liberal activist from the California Democratic Council, seemed a shoo-in for the nomination. But with only a day before the filing deadline, the old Brown-Unruh feud suddenly invaded the Senate campaign. Pierre Salinger, a former *San Francisco Chronicle* reporter who had served as President Kennedy's press secretary, flew to California and announced he was entering the race. Salinger had never held elective office, but he was nonetheless a formidable candidate: His work in the White House had earned him national fame as one of the early stars of televised politics. The idea to run was Salinger's, and he made the final decision himself, but Unruh had a hand in it too. Cranston was an old Brown ally, and Unruh did not want to see him in the Senate. So the speaker encouraged Salinger's inclination to run and later convinced Lucretia Engle to record a commercial endorsing Salinger as her husband's successor.[31]

To the governor, who had already endorsed Cranston, Salinger's candidacy was an annoyance. "Pierre is really making some real headway out here, but he's causing me a lot of embarrassment," Brown told LBJ. "Even though I like Pierre I want you to know that I think it was a selfish thing for him to do to come into this state."[32]

In the new battle of surrogates, Unruh had the upper hand, for his candidate was tied to the nation's martyred leader. Just before the primary, Salinger's campaign mailed cards to Democratic voters in Los Angeles showing a picture of Kennedy topped by the phrase "In his tradition" and accompanied by a mock ballot checked off for Salinger. The resulting margin in the behemoth county offset Cranston's edge in the rest of the state, and Salinger won narrowly. After a long and emotional struggle that dragged them through Engle's health, Mosk's sex life, and the ongoing war between Brown and Unruh, California Democrats at last had a nominee for the U.S. Senate.[33]

Engle had within him one last heroic moment of national service. In early June the Senate was waiting out the longest filibuster in American history, as southerners tried to block enactment of President Johnson's Civil Rights Act, which barred discrimination in public facilities. On the morning of June 10, after enduring 534 hours and 10 million words of delay, the Senate voted on a motion of cloture, which would stop the stonewalling speeches and allow a vote. Engle recognized the majesty of the day. Not since Reconstruction had the country enacted so important a civil rights bill. Now, led by a southern president, Congress was about to begin the long work of redress. Engle could no longer walk or speak, but he insisted that he be wheeled into the chamber. When his name was called, he voted aye by pointing to his eye.[34] Less than two months later, he was dead.

———

In late July, with barely a month to go before the Democratic National Convention in Atlantic City, Brown took a phone call at the Governor's

Mansion. When he heard a White House operator announce that the president of the United States was calling, Brown's heart leapt. Everybody in politics knew that Johnson, who had served without a vice president since taking office, was mulling over his choices for a running mate. Brown dearly wanted the job. He had even campaigned for it—a little too plaintively—in public. Introduced to graduating medical students as their "first choice," he responded with an ill-advised ad lib: "I just hope that when the president of the United States is asked for his first choice for vice president that he'll make the same choice as you. I'll be as available then as I was tonight."[35] Now, with Johnson coming on the telephone line, Brown thought he was about to be tapped as the president's running mate. The governor was temporarily an invalid, working from home because of a broken ankle suffered when he stepped in a hole on the golf course. After days of being cooped up in the mansion, it suddenly appeared he might be headed for a national stage.

Brown checked his enthusiasm for the initial pleasantries: the governor was at work appointing judges; the president was well; the problems of the world seemed manageable. Finally, Johnson got to the point of the call, although he did it in a roundabout way that must have caused Brown's hopes to soar. "Say Pat, I want to ask you to do something," he began. "You've been mighty faithful and I think awfully effective. When nobody else could do anything in California, you've done [things]. And they're always talking about Democrats are going to lose and we're going to be in a hell of a shape, but you take Nixon to the cleaners and I think you knocked him off or he'd be giving us all hell right now."

Brown seemed one sentence from national office—and then the bubble burst: "So I gave a little thought to Sunday and came to the conclusion that I wanted to ask you and [Texas Gov.] John Connally to take my nominating time and I want you to make one of the nominating speeches and John to make one, kind of the principal ones. We'll have a few seconding, but I want to see if you wouldn't place my name in nomination."

The governor was crushed. He knew the president would not want to be nominated by his own running mate. The governor of California was clearly out. "Well I can't think of anything that would give me greater pleasure," he said without a trace of joy. "I'll take whatever role you want me to in that."

Almost immediately, he bounced back gamely. He would start to work on the speech right away, he said a few moments later, regaining a little of his usual zest. Johnson helped him along. The governor's recent talk to the

Gridiron Club in Washington had been, the president said, "one of the best I ever heard." He wanted the nominating speech to be its equal, or maybe better. "I want you to come out there looking fresh as a daisy and I want you to have that speech in hand and I want it to be the best speech that's ever made. And California's entitled to it and you can do it if you just get away from all these damn fellas harassing you." Perhaps the broken ankle would help. "You stay out there with that wife of yours and get that lead pencil and an ol' yellow tablet and you get that speech worked out." He had great confidence in the governor, or he would not have asked him to be a nominator. "It's like a man selecting his wife."

Brown was temporarily dumbstruck at an analogy that rendered him Lyndon Johnson's intimate life partner. Then, his habitual cheeriness now fully restored, he managed to recover. "Well, uh . . . You put it very funny but I like it."[36]

Just two days later Brown was back on the phone with the president, but this time it was the governor who was looking for help. The feud with Unruh was worsening just as the national convention approached. An Unruh loyalist named Carmen Warschaw—"this dame," as Brown called her—had the governor worried. Heiress to an aluminum fortune, Warschaw was a big name in California Democratic circles. At one time she had been close to Brown, who had appointed her to the Fair Employment Practices Commission when it was first created. But Warschaw had since migrated to the Unruh camp. The month before Brown's phone call to the president, the governor had played hardball to stymie Warschaw's bid for the Democratic National Committee.[37] Now she was running for chair of the Southern California branch of the party, and Brown was worried she might win, weakening his own clout. "This will really have a very bad effect on California unless you vest your authority in me in this thing and have the White House back me up in it," Brown pleaded with the president. "It's really reaching serious proportions."

It was a local quarrel, and a minor one at that, and the president was not about to rescue the governor of California from his own subordinates. So Johnson said nothing, a silence so long that eventually Brown asked "Hello?" as if he feared the two men had been disconnected. Finally they moved on to the portion of the Democratic infighting that interested LBJ: how it might affect his own reelection campaign. Both Brown and Unruh wanted to control the Johnson campaign in Southern California, and the president was refusing to settle the dispute. In an ominous beginning for Brown, Johnson said he understood that Unruh had always run Democratic operations in Southern California.

"And lost it. And lost it," the governor said quickly, sounding almost desperate. "Don't ever forget that. He lost it for Kennedy. I won it in Southern California against Mr. Nixon."

When Johnson mentioned that he was troubled that Unruh might support Bobby Kennedy for the vice presidency, something the president did not want, Brown leapt in to assure the president of his unswerving loyalty: "Let me tell you this: When you pick up that telephone and you tell me this is my man, that's your man." LBJ, who knew enough to avoid a brawl when he could, told Brown to give Unruh a lecture but never really took a side.[38]

———

Atlantic City, where the Democrats planned to hold their 1964 national convention, was at the low point of its life. The heady days of the 1920s were a wasting memory; the revival of the 1980s, a dreamer's vision. No major hotel had opened in thirty-five years. In the Californians' rooms plaster and doorknobs fell off at the touch, windows refused to open, sinks and showers emitted no water. Delegates from the state where so much was new and shiny were warned before they arrived: "Welcome to Appalachia by the Atlantic."[39]

In contrast to the accommodations, the convention itself was to be an example of modern efficiency. President Johnson dominated the landscape of the Democratic Party, and for months the administration had worked to ensure a graceful coronation. Johnson was to be nominated by acclamation, and most delegations, including California's, had been structured to accept his nominee for vice president just as willingly. On the phone with Georgia Gov. Carl Sanders, LBJ noted the futility of arguing about precise vote counts on the convention floor: "We're not gonna have any votes to begin with."[40]

Brown flew east ahead of the large delegation he was leading. Along with other Democratic governors, he had been invited to a dinner at the White House, a show of party unity just before the convention opened.[41] The symbolism was nice, but on one topic dissension was already marring the careful convention planning. Mississippi had sent two delegations, and the convention would have to choose which one to seat. The regular delegation was all-white, a product of strictly segregated Jim Crow politics. The second delegation was that of the Mississippi Freedom Democratic Party, a product of the civil rights movement that had held its own, integrated convention and chosen its own, integrated delegation.

On Saturday, two days before the convention officially opened, the debate over who represented the true Democrats of Mississippi went before the nation, courtesy of a televised hearing of the party's Credentials Committee. It was an extraordinary event, more for what it said about life in Mississippi than about politics in Atlantic City.

At the same time that Brown and the other governors met with Johnson at the White House, an unlettered farmwoman from Sunflower County, Mississippi, offered moving testimony to the moral starkness of the Deep South in 1964. Fannie Lou Hamer described her attempts at registering to vote, which earned for her a jailhouse beating overseen by a state highway patrolman and administered by two black prisoners. "After the first Negro had beat until he was exhausted," Hamer recounted, "the state Highway Patrolman ordered the second Negro to take the blackjack." In response to the agony, she began to move her feet, so the patrolman directing the torture ordered that the first attacker sit on her feet to immobilize them. When she began to scream, another man beat her in the head.[42]

Testimony like that stirred hearts in the California delegation, many of whose members had flown to Atlantic City determined to recognize the Freedom delegation as the true voice of Mississippi Democrats. On Monday, the convention's opening day, the Californians caucused for the first time, and liberals tried to push for a formal vote declaring the state's support of the Freedom Party forces.

For Brown, it was a critical moment. He had no sympathy for the segregationist views of the regular Mississippi delegates, nor for their obvious disloyalty to the president and the national Democratic Party. Most of the "regular" Mississippi delegates openly scorned LBJ as a traitor to his region, despising him for having signed the Civil Rights Act. The truth was that Mississippi's official party had dispatched a Goldwater delegation to the convention that would nominate Johnson. Brown knew all of this, but he was also a practical politician. In the White House, LBJ was worried that if the Freedom Party delegation were seated, the entire South might walk out of the convention. That could spark a backlash among white voters everywhere, not just in Dixie. Brown knew that if there was any hope of convincing Californians to reject Proposition 14 that fall—to retain the fair housing law, in other words—white voters had to support the civil rights movement, not fear it.

To find his way through such a thicket, the governor had decided to take the lead of the president, another realistic pol worried about the November election. Four years earlier Brown had lost control of his delegation at the national convention and as a result had damaged his relationship with the Democrat in the White House. He was determined that no such thing would happen again. He would hold the delegation together and await word from the White House as to how the Mississippi dilemma should be solved.[43]

To keep control of the Californians, Brown conjured a firmness that was not always his demeanor. When liberal San Francisco congressman Phil Burton moved that California formally support the seating of the Freedom delegation, Brown arbitrarily ruled him out of order. The Credentials Committee had yet to send a recommendation to the convention floor, he insisted, so nothing could be decided. "We can't fight about it until we know what we are fighting about," he said.[44]

The next day, Tuesday, the administration finally imposed a compromise: Two of the Freedom Party members would be seated as at-large delegates, although the Mississippi seats would be retained by the regulars, so long as they were willing to sign a pledge of support for the party's nominee and platform. (In the end, almost all the regular Mississippi delegates refused to promise they would support Johnson and left the convention.) With an hour to go before the convention's evening session got under way, the California delegates caucused at their hotel, four blocks from the main convention hall, to consider the compromise proposal. There was no repeat of 1960. This time Brown had the delegation firmly in hand. Liberals pleaded to support the Freedom Party members, but the governor insisted on the president's compromise. Late in the meeting, trying to stall for time, Unruh, who was there as a delegate, moved for a fifteen-minute recess, and Brown ruled out of order the man who prided himself on parliamentary genius. After an emotional debate, the delegates voted overwhelmingly— 114–59—to support the compromise backed by LBJ.[45]

In a way it didn't matter at all. The California caucus dragged on so long that while the Californians were still locked away in their own debate, the full convention approved the compromise by voice vote. But the show of support from a huge and powerful state was not to be overlooked, and the president was grateful. Pierre Salinger called LBJ, his old boss, to report the huge margin of support among California delegates. The governor, Salinger said, had been a "real pillar" in supporting the administration's Mississippi compromise. "One hell of a job," Salinger said in reference to Brown's work.[46]

The president told his aide Walter Jenkins to call Brown and express his gratitude, but the governor of California could not be reached. Because of the long California caucus, Brown had been late to arrive at the convention hall. Now he was stuck outside, unable to get past protesters insisting that the entire Freedom Party delegation should be seated.[47] The irony was obvious. Pat Brown, who had often found national conventions so difficult, had finally handled the politics of such an event with hard-nosed tactical maneuvering and delivered the solid majority of his state's delegation to the cause of his choice. The only problem was that he couldn't get through the door to celebrate.

———

Brown had done more than earn Johnson's gratitude. So far as the public view was concerned, the governor had even bested his old rival Unruh. The speaker had failed in his effort—in many respects a noble one—to seat the Mississippi Freedom Party delegation. Brown had held the Californians in support of the president's compromise, and the president had let it be known that Brown would run his campaign in California. Reporters filed stories describing the governor's performance as a victory. The *Los Angeles Times* said he was the "unquestioned winner" in the feud with Unruh.[48] The *Sacramento Bee* said it was "unmistakably clear" that Brown had bested the speaker.[49] In fact, the feud was far from over, and there were plenty of California Democrats who privately favored Unruh over Brown, but for now, at least in the public eye, Brown was the waxing power.

The next night he bathed in the warmth of victory when he rose to nominate Johnson. Walking onstage to deliver the second nominating speech—Connally had given the first—Brown was conscious to maintain a steady gait. The cast from his broken ankle had only recently come off, and he did not want to be seen limping to the podium. The television networks still filled the airways with gavel-to-gavel coverage of the conventions, and Brown, who loved an audience above all else, cherished the brief moment of national glory. He had been practicing his speech over and over again in his hotel room.[50]

But he had barely begun his ten-minute talk when CBS and NBC, the two most important networks, abruptly switched their coverage to the Atlantic City airport, where LBJ was arriving from Washington. The rest of Brown's speech brought the delegates to their feet repeatedly, but across the country nobody saw it. It was, the governor told a reporter later, one of life's little tragedies.[51]

By tradition the heart of the fall campaign began on Labor Day. Brown was focused on defeating Proposition 14, the measure to repeal the Rumford fair housing law. He may have been too focused. All summer long he had been attacking supporters of the initiative as bigots. Prop. 14, he said at one typical stop, was a "vicious" measure mounted by a "vigilante committee" and would be a "blow to decency" and a victory for "prejudice and bigotry."[52] Often he mingled his comments about the housing law with attacks on Republican presidential candidate Barry Goldwater, denouncing what Brown saw as dangerous zealotry. When Goldwater accepted the Republican nomination by claiming that "extremism in the defense of liberty is no vice," Brown told reporters, "The stench of fascism is in the air."[53]

He was enjoying the straight talk. All his life he had tried to make people like him, and he discovered a certain liberation in abandoning caution and letting loose his real feelings. Brown was convinced in his soul that extremists were dangerous and especially that the people who wanted to repeal California's fair housing law were bigots, plain and simple. He took pleasure in saying so.[54]

The problem was that he needed to attract votes, not chase them away. His strength as a politician had always been that he was a positive, friendly, unifying force. "Politics is addition," he once told Lyndon Johnson, "not division."[55] Now, in one of the most emotional campaigns of his career, he seemed to have forgotten it.

Jack Burby, Brown's press secretary and by now a trusted and close adviser, sat down at the beginning of the fall campaign and composed a memo urging his boss to soften the attacks. Burby warned Brown against "extreme language" and the use of the words *bigot* and *hate.*

> Had we consulted a good psychologist early on we would have known—as is now obvious—that most of the people we are talking to don't regard themselves as bigots, even if they do discriminate against Negroes. . . . So I would urge a softening of the language, but not a retreat when it comes to making specific charges. Surely our friends and your best supporters love it when you really let Goldwater or someone else have it. So do I. But I begin to question whether it is helping your own cause in the long run.[56]

In the calm of his office, Brown agreed. He sent back a handwritten note to Burby: "Jack, I want to become more temperate." But self-discipline was never the governor's strong suit, and back on the campaign trail, he reverted to old habits. The same day he sent Burby the scribbled vow of moderation, Brown said again that Prop. 14 supporters were bigots. To the Council of Mexican-American Affairs a few days later, he said the proposition was "aimed" at blacks and Latinos and backed by a coalition of "radical right" forces who were engaged in a "shameless campaign of distortion." In mid-October he said flatly that the California Real Estate Association, the sponsor of Prop. 14, was "favoring segregation." Days later the governor declared the initiative the most dangerous measure ever to appear on a California ballot, a threat to the state's "tranquility and safety."[57]

Voters did not agree. For much of the year, polls had shown support for the proposition hovering at about 50 percent, with a fifth of voters refusing to take a stand one way or the other. But with only days left in the campaign, a new poll showed a spike in support, and suddenly it seemed almost certain the proposition would pass.[58]

For Brown and his fellow liberals, fissures of future trouble snaked through the data. Republicans supported Prop. 14 overwhelmingly, but even among Democrats a narrow majority backed the measure. The campaign in favor of the initiative stressed the threat the law supposedly posed to home owners, but half of renters supported the initiative too. The old blue-collar reliables who helped to put Brown in power were now a question mark; labor union members supported Prop. 14 in greater numbers than nonlabor voters. Most stark of all, not surprisingly, was the racial divide. Whites favored the measure almost three to one; blacks opposed it nine to one.[59]

Brown had taken great pride in the Rumford Act. During the law's first year, dozens of complaints had been reviewed, most alleging discrimination in the rental of apartments. In about half the cases the Fair Employment Practices Commission—the enforcer of the law—had found the complaint justified. Almost invariably the matter had been resolved through negotiation rather than a formal hearing.[60] The measure was certainly no cure-all, yet it represented a noble statement that the state did not intend to sit idly while black residents were shunted away from entire neighborhoods. Now, faced with the brutal realities of public opinion, Brown had to accept the fact that many Californians were ready to abandon one of his greatest accomplishments.

On election day, the results were overwhelming. Prop. 14 passed by more than two million votes, twice the size of the landslide that had made Brown governor six years before. Only in barren Modoc County, where there were more acres than people, did voters heed the governor's call and reject the initiative, and there the margin was a mere nineteen votes. In every other county in the state, Prop. 14 passed. Even in liberal San Francisco, the governor's hometown, voters balked at his advice.[61]

———

Two days after the election Brown got a call from the president. LBJ had slept most of the previous day, but now, recovered from the exhaustion and joy of his rout over Barry Goldwater, he was sitting in his bathrobe, unshaven and belching his way through conversations as usual, calling supporters around the country to express his thanks.

With Brown, Johnson reviewed the California scene. Pierre Salinger had lost the Senate race to George Murphy, the Republican song-and-dance man from Hollywood. "You'll have trouble with this Murphy," Brown told the president. "He's as stupid as stupid can be." Democrats had held their comfortable majority in the state's house delegation, and LBJ urged Brown to soften the congressmen with a little flattery before they headed for Washington. "Just tell 'em they're all great," he counseled. "Kind of honor them a little bit and send 'em up in a good frame of mind."[62]

Most of all, the president wanted to discuss his own overwhelming victory. "Patrick," he began the conversation, using a name that did not apply. "You ought to be a banker, Pat." Brown had predicted that the president would carry California by a million votes, Johnson said. Instead, the margin was about 1.4 million. "Well," the president said, turning on the Texas charm, "why don't you go into the banking business, and go to lending money—a fella that's that conservative?"

Brown was already thinking ahead to the next election, and he seized the moment to plead for the support of the country's most powerful politician. "We want to talk about keeping this governorship here in California," he told the president. "Between you and me, running for a third term is not going to be an easy thing in this state—and I need all the help I can get."[63]

They avoided the one issue that had consumed much of the governor's campaign time, Prop. 14. The wound was still raw, and for Brown it was a topic better left to more personal communications. Four days later, while riding in the limousine from San Francisco to Sacramento, he found time to answer an old letter from his daughter Kathleen and offered a blunt assessment of what Californians had just done:

> You could draw but one conclusion from the vote on 14 and that is that the white is just afraid of the Negro. The Negroes have a long way to go

before there is any acceptance by the white majority in our state. There is absolutely no reason to feel this way about it, but it is something that all of the eloquence in the world cannot change.[64]

For a man like Brown, it was the saddest of defeats to close the strangest of years. In the world of small-scale maneuver that often flummoxed him, he showed a sturdy spine. Faced with emotional pleas from a dying man's wife and a group of black Mississippians struggling against their state's legalized racism, Brown looked past their claims in favor of bigger goals. He held his ground and displayed an uncharacteristic discipline that was rigorous, calculating, perhaps even a little cold.

He found trouble, however, where success had been his norm. Elections had always been his salvation, the campaign trail his haven. In 1958 he led the Democrats to their greatest landslide of the century. In 1960 he convinced voters to approve the biggest public construction project in the history of the state. In 1962 he had freed the body politic from the curse of Richard Nixon. But in 1964 he turned to the part of politics he loved most—campaigning, meeting people, shaking hands—and was rejected. Pat Brown's old friends and saviors—the voters of California—had slapped aside some of the most heartfelt appeals of his career.

14   BERKELEY

AT 3:00 A.M. on December 3, 1964—exactly one month after election day—Edward Strong, a philosophy professor who had become chancellor of the University of California's flagship Berkeley campus, walked into the school's main administration building carrying a bullhorn. "May I have your attention?" he called to hundreds of students occupying the building, Sproul Hall. "I have an announcement."

The students' sit-in, a protest against rules that restricted political activity on campus, was unlawful, Strong said. The functioning of the university had been "materially impaired." Patience had been exercised, but now that time had passed. "I urge you, both individually and collectively, to leave this area," he said. "I request that you immediately disperse. Failure to disperse will result in disciplinary action by the university." Then, in a remark that may have reflected plain courtesy or forlorn hope or just utter desperation, Strong added simply, "Please go."[1]

Few did. The students had prepared for confrontation. Pitchers of water had been distributed so that handkerchiefs might be soaked and pressed to the face as a defense against tear gas. Objects that might cause injury if someone was dragged across them had been pushed to the corners. Limp, passive resistance had been practiced. The protesters were going nowhere. Strong's plea was a final effort, one last attempt by the university to clear its own students from its own building peacefully—and avoid the use of the police.

By that time Strong and others knew what was next. The governor of California, a former district attorney and attorney general, a "responsible liberal" who liked law and order and followed the rules and rose to greatness through the most conventional of paths, was not going to tolerate the forced occupation of public buildings. His California Highway Patrol officers, reinforcements for the overwhelmed local sheriff's department, were massed outside, and the governor had already told them to clear the building by force if necessary. Less than an hour after Strong spoke, they went in.

It took more than twelve hours to empty the place, students dragged or carried out one by one, some interviewed by reporters along the way. They were taken to a temporary booking station in the building's basement, then to waiting police buses, then to jail. Sproul Hall was still being cleared when faculty members and other students arrived for morning classes.

For a world that had yet to experience the turbulent decade that was to come, it was a shocking scene: students at one of America's most prestigious universities hauled off to jail by the score. And there was no doubt where the responsibility lay. Whether from courage or a mistaken political calculation or simple necessity—or more likely all three—Pat Brown had announced that it was his decision. "I felt it was the right thing to do," he said a few hours later.[2]

Perhaps. But for the people involved that night—and for many who were not even there—things would never be the same. Not for the students, who would flex their political muscles by bringing down the campus hierarchy. Not for the university, which would come to be viewed as the home of American radicalism. Not for Californians, who would shudder at the thought that a mob might capture their vaunted citadel of learning. Not for young people across the country and around the world, who would see the protests as a template for rebellion. And not, most emphatically, for Pat Brown, who would be marked as the man who let it all happen.

———

After nearly six years as governor, Brown had grown to love the University of California. At first wary of its enormous financial demands, he now saw it as one of the jewels that distinguished his glittering state. At meetings of governors, his counterparts asked how California had created so great a public institution.[3] Brown could legitimately boast that he had played a role; he supported the creation of the higher education Master Plan that protected the university's supremacy and, more important, provided enough money in his budgets to build three new campuses and vastly expand others. The cash had poured in, not only at the infant sites, but also at Berkeley and UCLA, where relentless expansion meant constant building. There were new lecture halls, dining commons, student housing projects, buildings for everything from biology to space sciences to drama. In Berkeley alone there were new radiation labs, a greenhouse, parking structures, even tennis courts and bowling lanes. By July 1964 the university's president, Clark Kerr, could report that the school had awarded more than $260 million in construction contracts in the previous five years. On a per capita basis, state support of the university was at its highest level ever.[4]

Nor did Brown flinch when college students began questioning authority figures such as himself. In 1961, as student activists risked mayhem and death by challenging Jim Crow oppression in the South and protested lesser injustices elsewhere, Brown used his commencement speech at the University of Santa Clara to defend young catalysts of change:

> I say thank God for the spectacle of students picketing—even when they are picketing me at Sacramento and I think they are wrong—for students protesting and freedom-riding, for students listening to society's dissidents, for students going out into the fields with our migratory workers, and for marching off to jail with our segregated Negroes.

"Passive conformity," the governor warned in words that might have been written later by student activists, would produce only "the Organization Man" but never "the responsible political agent who saves his country." The good news was that the campuses had become "boot camps for citizenship—and citizen leaders are marching out of them."[5]

———

If the governor wanted an example of the new breed of young activists, he might have pointed to a gangly, twenty-one-year-old philosophy student who would soon epitomize the youthful unrest of his time: Mario Savio. A machinist's son, Savio grew up in New York, a good Italian Catholic kid who served as an altar boy and later worked for a Catholic relief agency in Mexico. He started college back home, then transferred to Berkeley when his parents moved to Los Angeles. By spring of his junior year, in 1964, he was hanging around on the fringes of an activist crowd that was trying to force Bay Area businesses to hire more minorities. Demonstrators staged sit-ins in the lobby of San Francisco's posh Sheraton-Palace Hotel. They picketed automobile dealers, a restaurant chain, and the powerful and conservative *Oakland Tribune*. They even invented an ingenious form of commercial blockade for grocery stores, the shop-in. Protesters would fill shopping carts, unload them at the checkout stand, then announce impishly that they had forgotten their money and walk out, leaving the store with a cluttered and temporarily useless register line. Arrested in the Sheraton-Palace demonstration, Savio ended up in jail with other activists, who told him about a civil rights campaign being planned for the summer in Mississippi. Volunteers, including many college students, would lead "Freedom Schools," summer tutorials designed to teach the victims of Jim Crow about their rights, their history, and their culture—and to encourage them to register to vote.[6]

Savio didn't much impress his initial interviewer when he volunteered. The civil rights activist who talked to Savio described him as "not a very creative guy altho *[sic]* he accepts responsibility and carries it through if you explain to him exactly what needs to be done; not exceedingly perceptive on the movement, what's involved, etc.; not very good at formulating notions with which one moves into the Negro community."[7] Perhaps because of the early doubts about him, Savio spent the first half of the summer in relatively safe Holmes County. But by summer's end, Savio was shifted to McComb, a small town with perhaps the most beleaguered outpost of the entire Freedom Summer. McComb had, as one writer later put it, "the reputation of a rabid dog."[8] The Ku Klux Klan was even stronger there than in the rest of Mississippi, bombings more common. Local authorities offered little protection for civil rights workers. In July night riders lobbed dynamite into a house that had been rented for the volunteers. The next morning, a local police officer examined the damage, smiled, and said, "Looks like termites to me."[9]

In McComb, Savio sat down amid the heat of a southern July and penned an earnest, handwritten letter to a politician he saw as sympathetic to liberal dreams: the governor of his home state of California. "The stands you have taken on questions on equality in housing and employment encourage me in the belief that you are a good friend of the work we are trying to advance in Mississippi," Savio wrote to Brown. Part of that work, he said, was to seat the Mississippi Freedom Party delegation at the Democratic National Convention. The regular delegates should be rejected. The "Democratic Party" of Mississippi was not a "democratic party." The state's "Negroes are systematically excluded" from politics. The "yoke of oppression falls almost as heavily upon the poor whites of Mississippi." In the end, of course, Brown would offer only partial support to the Freedom Party delegates, by supporting the compromise brokered by Lyndon Johnson. But in McComb, the evidence of racism abundantly around him, Savio turned for rescue to the man he would soon oppose. "You have the power" to help seat the Freedom Party delegates, he wrote to Brown. "Please help free Mississippi."[10]

Weeks later Savio returned to Berkeley a changed man. The summer in the South had galvanized his passion and outrage into commitment and determination. Sometimes a private stutterer, he began to show a surprising talent for public speaking. Given a microphone, he was ardent, lyrical, dynamic. He had a cocky self-assurance that drew followers instantly. Over the course of the coming months, Savio would prove again and again that none of his elders on the Berkeley campus—from the university president to the faculty members—could even remotely approach his skills with a crowd.

———

Savio returned from the South determined to avoid the "sandbox" politics of student government and fraternity councils—and he was not alone. The Berkeley campus was changing in ways that distanced students from traditional college life and gave them a greater sense of involvement with the outside world. The campus was bigger and busier than ever before; the student body had swelled by almost ten thousand in the previous ten years. The nature of the student body was changing along with its size. California's Master Plan for Higher Education, enacted in Brown's first term as governor, was beginning to work, which meant that freshmen and sophomores were increasingly shunted to the state colleges and community colleges. At Berkeley a higher proportion of the students were in graduate school, and even among the undergraduates, more were juniors and seniors. Compared to their predecessors, they were older, more independent, less connected to campus traditions. More were living in off-campus apartments, flocking to bohemian coffeehouses rather than fraternity dances. Their college years would not be spent picking the "Soph Doll"—there actually was such a contest for second-year women—or worrying about who got to paint the big *C* on one of the hills behind campus.[11]

As the students wandered back to Berkeley in September 1964, they suddenly discovered a changed environment for their newfound activism. For years, dating back to the 1930s, the university had tried to insulate itself from outside controversies by prohibiting students from using the campus for real-world politicking. Races for student government were obviously another matter, but with few exceptions, money could not be raised for outside causes, nor activists recruited. Students were prohibited from publicly speaking out in favor of specific candidates or ballot propositions. For many years candidates could not even speak on the campus. The rule had been usefully circumvented by an odd, somewhat legalistic arrangement in which political battles were waged just off the edge of campus. At times the situation became almost bizarre. In 1956 presidential candidate Adlai Stevenson spoke from a flatbed truck parked a few feet off the campus, loudspeakers aiming his words at a huge crowd standing on university property. By the 1960s Kerr had loosened some of the rules, but he still forbade much student political activity on campus.[12]

As a result, students for years had erected card tables on the sidewalk at the southern edge of campus, distributing literature and raising money and recruiting activists for a dizzying array of causes. The problem was that some of those tables were actually on university property. Visually, the campus seemed to begin when one passed a series of chest-high posts that separated the sidewalk from Sproul Plaza, a broad, open square between the administration building and the student union. But in fact a property line split the sidewalk outside the posts: an eight-foot-wide strip running along the street was owned by the city; the inside twenty-six feet, the territory nearest the posts, were owned by the university. Nothing marked the dividing line, save two small bronze plaques—embedded in the ground—which noted that one was now entering the territory of the regents of the University of California and added that "permission to enter or pass over is revocable at any time."

Campus administrators had known for years that some of the students' tables were on university property and thus technically were violating the rules against political activity, but they had let the matter slide. Now, troubled by the increasing hubbub along the narrow strip of sidewalk, administrators decided to crack down. As the students returned to campus to begin classes, university administrators announced that the little strip of sidewalk would no longer be treated as if it were exempt from university regulations. Political activity there, like everywhere else on campus, would be prohibited. Given the students' increased activism, the timing could not have been worse: Administrators were capping a valve just as the pressure increased.[13]

Student activists, some of whom had spent the summer standing up to the ugly racism of the Deep South, launched a counterattack immediately. The university was attempting to prohibit activity on campus that would be allowed, even constitutionally protected, only a few feet away, off the campus. The U.S. Constitution, they insisted, applied with as much force at the university as anywhere, and they vowed to protest the new restrictions with a campaign of picketing, vigils, rallies, and civil disobedience.

Wisely, they maintained a coalition united across ideological divides. The student groups that objected to the new rules ranged from the Young Socialist Alliance to the University Society of Individualists, a conservative group that would, the following spring, contribute a footnote to Bay Area history when one of its members, wearing a button announcing "I am a right-wing extremist," became the first woman to insist on her right to ride a San Francisco cable car while standing on the running board.[14]

Within days the protests spread, as students began insisting on their right to political activity not just on the strip of contested sidewalk but throughout the campus.[15] With geographic expansion came intellectual stretch too. No longer was the quarrel just about distributing handbills. Students began to portray their campaign as a moral conflict in which they were battling for their individual rights against a massive institution, a huge and unfeeling machine, a "factory" designed to produce men and women who could work usefully in the country's economy. It was the kind of view that can appeal to twenty-year-olds, especially at a university that was in fact larger and more bureaucratic than before. Kerr fell into that trap nicely. He liked to talk about the new knowledge-based economy and the merging of interests between scholarship and industry. And he did believe that universities must become more connected to the workaday world. The "knowledge industry," he had said a few years before, should be "the focal point of national growth" in the second half of the twentieth century, comparing it to the automobile industry or railroads of earlier eras. A phrase like "knowledge industry" infuriated the students. "UC Manufactures Safe Minds," read one sign carried by a protester.[16]

The simmering dispute first drew widespread public notice, and thus the governor's attention, in early October. On the morning of October 1, a

Berkeley mathematics graduate named Jack Weinberg was driven to campus by two friends, a big door balanced on top of their car. Weinberg, who would eventually coin the credo of the student movement by saying that no one over thirty should be trusted, set the door on trestles in front of Sproul Hall, the main administration building on the campus, and used it as a table from which to distribute material for the campus Congress of Racial Equality. In short order, two deans and a campus police officer appeared and told Weinberg he was violating university regulations. When he refused to take down his makeshift table and leave, they arrested him.[17]

Immediately, a series of things went wrong for the administration. By chance, it was a few minutes before noon, the time set by student leaders for a rally in front of Sproul. So a crowd began pouring into the plaza, yelling at the authorities and encouraging Weinberg. The lone police officer went for help, leaving the deans to stand guard over Weinberg. The wait gave him the opportunity for an impromptu speech to the swelling crowd, which added to the mob interest and enthusiasm. The policeman returned with reinforcements, but Weinberg declined to go quietly. Schooled in the tactics of southern civil rights demonstrators, he went limp, forcing the police literally to carry him away. They got him to a squad car that had been driven onto the plaza moments before, but by then the police were in serious trouble.[18]

As officers had begun to carry Weinberg, someone in the crowd—it was never clear exactly who—yelled "Sit down." Within seconds hundreds of people did, and it proved a stroke of utter tactical genius. The police car was trapped, surrounded by hundreds of peaceful protesters doing nothing more provocative than sitting.[19] For the moment the students had won. The car was going nowhere, and the officers were flummoxed. They kept the motor running for about ten minutes, then shut it off, then started it up again, then shut it off. A student let the air out of at least one tire, and Savio climbed on top of the car and began to speak.[20]

It was a remarkably friendly stalemate. Police allowed the car to be used as a speaker's platform, provided only that would-be orators remove their shoes before climbing up. After one demonstrator rented a microphone so that speakers could be better heard by people at the edge of the crowd, students put down newspapers so that the base of the microphone stand would not mar the paint on the car's roof. When the roof began to sag, students took up a collection to pay for repairs. A speakers' list was devised, and people from all sides of the issue began holding a serial debate from the top of the vehicle. Professors stopped by to offer their views. At one point, in an effort to calm what was becoming an unruly crowd, police let Weinberg climb on top of the car and speak. Another time, Weinberg was allowed to go inside Sproul Hall to use the bathroom, and then, under a prearranged deal between protest leaders and police, to return to his four-wheeled cell.[21] He also conducted interviews. The failing roof had worried him a bit, he confessed to one reporter, but he had simply moved to the other side of the car, and now was confident it would hold. The students were bringing him food and he was able to lie down on the seat from time to time when he tired. All in all, he said, the car was not as uncomfortable as a southern jail where he had once been locked up for his civil rights work.[22]

A captured police car was big news, and for the first time the quarrels of the campus snared the governor. By chance he was just across the bay, giving a speech at the Sheraton-Palace Hotel in San Francisco, where earlier in the year Berkeley students had protested the lack of black employees. Ironically, the governor's talk focused on the need for unfettered freedom of thought on campuses. Education was being threatened, he said, by "those who would clamp the lid on intellectual inquiry." "And I can assure you that in California we are determined to counter that effort with all the force we can muster."[23]

But freedom of thought was one thing, surrounding a police car was another. After the speech Brown's office issued a written statement aligning him with the hard-liners. "This is not a matter of freedom of speech on the campuses," Brown's declaration read. "This is purely and simply an attempt on the part of the students to use the campuses of the university unlawfully by soliciting funds and recruiting students for off-campus activities. This will not be tolerated. We must have—and will continue to have—law and order on our campuses."[24]

The problem was that nobody knew how to impose law and order, and so as the afternoon turned into evening, then night, the car remained on the plaza, with Weinberg inside and student protesters still tightly packed around. By the next morning, nothing had changed, and the university administration was at sea. Passing the problem up the chain of command, Kerr talked with the governor directly. In private Brown struck a more conciliatory tone than in his statement the day before. When Kerr raised the possibility of using the National Guard to clear the plaza, Brown refused. He did not want the kind of violence that had accompanied civil rights demonstrations in the South, he told Kerr. If absolutely necessary, the California Highway Patrol might be used, Brown said, but first Kerr should try to resolve the situation peaceably.[25]

To that point, Kerr had left the direct negotiating to his underlings, but now he stepped in and agreed to meet personally with Savio and other student leaders. Kerr's background as a labor negotiator came in handy, and the two sides struck a deal: Weinberg would be booked and released; the students would free the police car; the thornier long-term issues, such as political activity on campus, would be referred to committees for future study, an age-old method of delay. About fifteen minutes after the bargain was made, Savio climbed onto the car and read the written provisions of the truce to his troops. "I ask you to rise quietly and with dignity, and go home," he told the demonstrators. It had been thirty-two hours since the car had been seized.[26]

In the aftermath the governor was relieved. He thought the university's Board of Regents, of which he was the president, might loosen restrictions at the campus. But he was also annoyed. "My real concern in this whole matter was the manner in which the students protested the rules and regulations," he wrote in a letter. "Once the students kidnapped the police car, they went far beyond the field of civil disobedience and into an outright area of total disrespect for the law. . . . If every group of outraged citizens took it upon themselves to correct these injustices by civil disobedience and violation of the law, you can imagine what America would be like today."[27]

Brown could not have known it, but he would need no imagination. Much to his dismay, he was destined soon enough to again see a campus where outraged people took it upon themselves to reject the rules.

———

The day after the police car incident the crisis seemed to have passed. The next day, a Saturday, was Family Day on campus, and the celebrations brought out more traditional students and visitors, many of them alumni whose interests ran more to fraternity and sorority life than protests. "The university put on its raccoon coat for the old-timers," as one newspaper put it.[28]

But almost immediately it became obvious that the hastily negotiated settlement that freed the police car was a flawed peace. It was open to varying interpretations, vague on critical points, and even referenced committees that did not exist.[29] Frustrated, the students looked to Brown as a sympathetic figure. Now officially coalesced into a group called the Free Speech Movement, they flooded his office with letters seeking help. Savio dispatched a youthfully earnest telegram asking that the governor arrange for five student leaders to meet with the regents. If they received no answer, Savio wired, the students would conclude their request had been denied and must "consider alternative action. Please understand the matter is grave."[30]

There was no meeting, and by early November the leaders of the Free Speech Movement deemed progress too slow. They urged students to resume their political activities, which caused Kerr to declare the truce void, and both sides returned to stalemate. Over the Thanksgiving break, the university sent letters to the homes of protest leaders threatening fresh punishments.[31] Furious, the FSM announced that if the administration did not back down, the protesters would once again employ "direct action."[32] Nobody doubted what that meant: Sproul Hall was about to be invaded.

———

On Wednesday, December 2, university administrators could foresee by 10:00 A.M. that they were headed for a long day. The students had scheduled another rally in front of Sproul Hall, and this time it was said that the folk singer Joan Baez would attend. That was sure to excite the crowd, and it had Kerr worried. In a morning strategy session, the university president asked if the Baez rumor were true. Strong, the chancellor of the Berkeley campus, said that apparently it was, and that it looked as if the students planned to force the administration's hand, baiting the authorities into martyr-producing arrests. Kerr urged restraint. Unless violence broke out, he said, police action should be delayed at least until the evening, when some of the regents planned to meet. Even the regents were thinking about passing the buck: Ed Carter, a department store magnate and one of the most conservative members of the board, was already trying to reach the governor.[33]

From the start, the noon rally had a different air from earlier protests. The feel was edgier, more ardent, an atmosphere that reminded one observer of a preacher's altar call.[34] Savio, by now a well-known figure at the school, took to the Sproul Hall steps to deliver the critical sermon. The university, Savio said, resembled a corporation churning out a product. The Board of Regents was the board of directors, the faculty the employees, the students mere "raw material." But the students would not be processed, would not be "made into any product," not "bought by some clients of the university, be they the government, be they industry, be they organized labor, be they anyone."

Then he began an eloquent peroration:

There is a time when the operation of the machine becomes so odious, makes you so sick at heart, that you can't take part; you can't even tacitly take part, and you've got to put your bodies upon the gears and upon the wheels, upon the levers, upon all the apparatus and you've got to make it stop. And you've got to indicate to the people who run it, to the people who own it, that unless you're free, the machine will be prevented from working at all.[35]

It was a great speech, the idea borrowed from Thoreau, the cadences simple and inspiring.[36] Baez, who had fulfilled her promise to appear, began singing "We Shall Overcome," and more than a thousand people followed Savio into the building.

They had come prepared for a long stay. Food was brought in, and after police closed the building more supplies were hauled up by ropes lowered from a second-story window. There was a sense of excitement. Movies were shown, a Laurel and Hardy picture and another intended to be a laugher: *Operation Abolition*, a horrible bit of propaganda produced by the House Un-American Activities Committee to discredit protesters at the panel's San Francisco hearings a few years before. There was a Hanukkah service on one floor, dancing on another. Baez gave an impromptu concert. Two girls, it is said, lost their virginity on the roof.[37]

————

The governor was far away from such scenes, insulated by both atmosphere and distance from campus histrionics. Brown was in Southern California, where he often spent the fall, either to campaign or to nurture connections. That evening he was driven to Beverly Hills, where he listened to Frank Sinatra sing songs and Bob Hope tell jokes at a $5,000-per-couple fund-raising dinner for the Cedars-Sinai Medical Center.[38]

Brown's aides had been keeping tabs on the situation all day, talking with Kerr by phone and tracking the key meetings, but it was only that evening that Brown himself was dragged into the troubles.[39] Amid the serenity of a black-tie affair, he was told there was a call from Kerr.

Throughout the day Kerr had opposed using the police to clear the students out of Sproul. He argued that the demonstrators would eventually recognize how much they had already won, for the regents had in fact liberalized some of the campus rules at a meeting two weeks before. Kerr was worried about charges of police brutality, and he had little confidence in the Alameda County sheriff's department, an agency then viewed by liberals as a hotbed of authoritarian belligerence. As a labor negotiator, Kerr had seen tense situations worsened by a single split-second of rash judgment. "Somebody," he said years later, "can pull a pistol at the wrong time or slap somebody with a baton." Even personal conviction played a role: Kerr was a practicing Quaker and thus a man devoted to pacifism and moral suasion.[40]

So Kerr devised a novel alternative to force: He and the governor would walk into Sproul Hall the next day and try to reason with the students and convince them to leave. Not all would go, but some might, Kerr believed, and if the police were eventually used, at least the university could point to its extraordinary efforts at peacemaking. In many ways it was an absurd idea. If Kerr and Brown walked into Sproul, the students would surely try to engage them in an impromptu debate, generating media coverage that would put the governor on an equal footing with tired, smelly, irreverent undergraduates.

But Brown trusted his extraordinary talents at personal politics. One on one, he could win over almost anyone, maybe even mouthy college students. "The governor always thought," one of his closest aides said years later, "he could solve anything if only he could get in the room and look them in the eye."[41] Amazingly, as Kerr lobbied for his plan by phone, the governor agreed. He told Kerr that they would walk into Sproul together the following morning and try to talk their way into a peaceful resolution.[42]

But Kerr would not be the last person to contact the governor that night. Two months earlier, when the police car had been captured, officers had been called to the campus and then sent away by university administrators reluctant to order action. That did not sit well with the police. In their minds they had been prevented from freeing a kidnapped police car while educators haggled with a mob.[43] This time authorities on the scene decided to take their case directly to the governor. In turn, that meant that Brown would make the final decision after talking not with a soft-spoken pacifist university president, but with a tough Irish cop from Oakland.

———

Supervising Inspector Daniel O'Connell of the California Highway Patrol was convinced the sit-in should not be tolerated. O'Connell liked law and order. Although he reached the upper echelons of his organization, he would later pride himself on the number of regular street cops who attended his retirement party. As he met that night with other law enforcement officials in the campus police headquarters in the basement of Sproul Hall—literally underneath the protesters—O'Connell regarded the events two months earlier with lingering dismay, convinced that the failure to haul away the protesters and free the police car by force had only encouraged more brazen demonstrations later. He had little sympathy with either the students, whom he regarded as foul-mouthed hooligans, or the university administrators, who in his view "couldn't administer their way to the bathroom."[44]

If the building was to be cleared, O'Connell's men would be needed. The campus police, the Berkeley city police, and the Alameda County Sheriff's Office—the other three agencies involved that night—lacked the manpower to arrest hundreds of people and haul them off to various jails while also controlling crowds outside. As the highest-ranking CHP officer in the Bay Area, on the other hand, O'Connell could mobilize hundreds of men within a few hours. The problem, at least as O'Connell perceived it, was that the California constitution granted special independence to the university. It is far from clear that he was legally correct, but O'Connell believed that without the approval of either the university authorities or the governor—who was the president of the Board of Regents—his men lacked authority to move in.

O'Connell decided to contact his ultimate boss, the governor. He called CHP headquarters in Sacramento, which always knew the governor's whereabouts because its officers served as drivers and bodyguards when Brown was not in the Capitol or the Governor's Mansion. O'Connell found out who was assigned to the governor's detail that night, then called the Beverly Hilton, where the fund-raising banquet was being held. He told the officers to get Brown, and—for the second time—the governor was brought to the phone to deal with the controversies of Berkeley.

Brown had known O'Connell for years. When the CHP man had made sergeant in 1948, he had been assigned to the agency's Bay Bridge office, the outpost closest to San Francisco, where Brown was the district attorney. From time to time they would run into each other at social events or business functions involving law enforcement folks, and they struck up an acquaintance. Three years later, the same year Brown became attorney general, O'Connell became the CHP's lobbyist at the Capitol. Working on legislation, their paths intersected even more. They served together, for example, on a committee that evaluated bills for the state peace officers' association. Although never close, the two men knew each other well enough that, when not on official business, they were "Danny" and "Pat."

O'Connell told the governor that "anarchy" reigned in Sproul Hall, and he asked for permission to use the CHP to restore order. In later years, O'Connell would also say that he told Brown the students had begun setting small bonfires with records looted from offices—something he insists he saw but that is not supported by other evidence. In any event, the governor asked a few questions about the details of O'Connell's proposal, then wanted to know if anyone from the Alameda County District Attorney's Office was present.[45]

There was. District Attorney Frank Coakley had sent over a bright young deputy named Ed Meese, who would soon come to the attention of California's next governor, Ronald Reagan, and eventually go on to serve in Reagan's presidential cabinet as attorney general of the United States. Meese had been celebrating his birthday that night with a dinner at his parents' house in Oakland but had hustled over to campus after receiving a call from Coakley. O'Connell handed the phone to Meese, who spoke briefly with the governor. As with the CHP man, the governor had at least a passing acquaintance with Meese. A few years earlier Meese had spent some time lobbying the legislature on behalf of the state district attorneys association, an assignment that put him in a few meetings with the governor. Now he reconfirmed what Brown had already heard: The students should be hauled out, and the highway patrol's manpower would be needed for the job.[46]

Brown was getting that advice from many quarters. At the banquet he ran into Franklin Murphy, the chancellor at UCLA. Murphy and Kerr did not get along. Before taking the UCLA job in 1960, Murphy had run the ship at the University of Kansas, and he did not much like the idea that he now had a boss. Kerr, on the other hand, liked to make it plain that he was in charge. Almost from the beginning, either directly or through subordinates, the two men argued over a series of almost laughably picky issues: who would control the UCLA secretarial staff, whether the phone operators at the Los Angeles campus would answer the lines by saying "University of California" or "UCLA," whether the southern campus would have its own song.[47] Now, at the banquet, Murphy had a chance to both disagree with his nemesis in the president's office and urge that proper authority be upheld. He had little tolerance for the protesters—he later described them as "charged up with drugs and irrational and so on"—and he told Brown the police should be sent in.[48]

The governor needed little convincing. Brown had spent his life as a liberal, not a rabble-rouser. University officials had announced at 7:00 P.M. that Sproul Hall was closing, just as it did every night, so the demonstrators were clearly trespassing. Faced with a cop on the scene making a point-blank request to enforce the law, Brown thought he must concur. "You've got to remember, I was a former district attorney and a former attorney general and I was a law enforcement man," he said years later. "I'm really a conservative on law enforcement, but a liberal economically and in civil rights. But on law enforcement, I have a reverence for obeying the law."[49] Brown told Meese to give the phone back to O'Connell and then told the CHP man what he wanted to hear: Give the students a chance to leave, but if they refuse, haul them out.[50]

Then the governor called Kerr, who had met with key regents that evening in San Francisco but had now returned to his home high in the hills of El Cerrito, just north of Berkeley. He was telling his wife about the day's events—and about his hopes to defuse the situation peacefully the next morning—when the phone rang. It was a quick, straightforward conversation. The governor said only that he was sending in the police and he expected the university to cooperate. Then he hung up.[51]

———

In their basement redoubt inside Sproul Hall, O'Connell and the other top police officials huddled to plan their massive operation. Off-duty officers were told to report at 1:00 A.M. for a briefing on what to expect. At 3:05 Strong went in and offered his bullhorn warning. Then officers began to make arrests.

Because there was never a precise count of those who walked into Sproul that day and throughout the evening police allowed students to leave, it is impossible to know the number that remained when Strong came in. About eight hundred people were eventually arrested, although the chaos of the night is reflected in the fact that the exact number has never been settled. Some students left after the chancellor's announcement, but it is obvious that most demonstrators stayed, even those who feared a police record. One wobbler phoned his parents, and when they told him to leave the building immediately, he returned to his spot on the floor, sat down, and waited for the inevitable arrest.[52]

The first person taken into custody was the protesters' lawyer, Robert Treuhaft, whose wife, Jessica Mitford, had the year before made a splash by publishing *The American Way of Death,* a scathing exposé of the American funeral home industry. Then the police moved on to the students, who wanted to delay things as long as possible. Conscious as always of public opinion, protest leaders wanted to make sure that students and professors arriving for classes the next day saw people being hauled off the campus by uniformed police officers. Such a scene, FSM leaders believed, would generate more support for their cause. So they implemented their earlier practice sessions, telling demonstrators to go limp as they were arrested. That meant the police would have to carry out the protesters one by one, a process that would drag on glacially.[53]

Demonstrators were given a chance to leave, then, if they refused, hauled away. Some walked and were led along, some were carried, some were dragged. Arms were twisted and heads were bumped, particularly as people were dragged down staircases, but by the standards of what might normally be called police brutality, things stayed peaceful. In the end, it took twelve hours, long enough that passersby saw the arrests not only as they arrived on campus in the morning but even as they headed to and from lunch.

The protesters were searched, loaded into buses and paddy wagons, and distributed to various jails to be held on charges of failing to disperse, refusing to leave a government building after being ordered to do so, and resisting arrest. They didn't stay behind bars for long. Within hours of the mass arrest, sympathizers—many of them faculty members—raised $8,500 in contributions and posted bail. Within a day, all the protesters were out, except for one poor fellow who had been caught with a little marijuana.[54] Months later they were convicted of varying combinations of trespassing, unlawful assembly, and resisting arrest. The most common sentence was probation and a $150 fine.[55]

———

Even before the last protester had been dragged from Sproul Hall, more than eight hundred members of the university's faculty and teaching staff met to consider the crisis. The governor's action angered many. Almost half the educators signed a wire to Brown: "Punitive action taken against hundreds of students cannot help to solve our current problems, and will aggravate the already serious situation."[56]

Other complaints were more direct. About forty students and instructors from the university's Davis campus arrived at the Capitol to show solidarity with their Berkeley colleagues. Led by a political science professor, they picketed for an hour and then, amazingly, were ushered in to see the governor while reporters looked on. In "soft and sympathetic tones," as one of the newspapermen put it, Brown said he approved of the goals of the Free Speech Movement but not its methods. The sit-in had represented "complete defiance of law and order," and that could not be tolerated. As for Savio: "He said he was going to stop the wheels of the university. He unilaterally made a judgment of what was right or wrong."[57]

Savio was trying to reach the governor, hoping that the state's chief executive would put pressure on the regents to loosen the campus rules. He called on a Saturday a few days after the arrests and by chance got through to Brown, who was in the office catching up on work. The governor told the student leader to obey the law and work through university officials, a response so dissatisfying that two days later Savio called again. This time he got Winslow Christian, Brown's chief of staff, who put the phone down on the desk while Savio railed on excitedly.[58]

Savio's lobbying failed, but it was the university that was seeking an escape from the crisis. The university could not arrest its students every time there was a protest, and the thrill of battle had only heightened the protesters' enthusiasm. There was little doubt that the students would, if necessary, return to their sit-down tactics. At least as important, large chunks of the faculty were siding with the students, and the university could not quarrel endlessly with its own professors.

At a news conference the day after Savio's call to Christian, the governor tried to calm the waters. The whole dispute was the "most unnecessary quarrel I've ever seen in my life," he said. He defended the rights of faculty members to denounce him, downplayed the suggestion that Communists were behind the troubles, and expressed confidence in Kerr as "a man of seasoned judgment and intelligence." Playing to conservatives, Jess Unruh, the assembly speaker with whom Brown was feuding, had raised the possibility of a legislative investigation, but the governor said he saw no need. Such an inquiry might just "stir this thing up again."[59]

At another point Brown called the district attorney in Alameda County, which included Berkeley, to ask if the charges might be dropped.[60] That was never a real possibility, but on the broader issue of campus speech, officialdom was ready to surrender. Only days after the Sproul arrests, the faculty took a formal vote and supported the students. Then, a week before Christmas, the Board of Regents met and settled the issue. With Brown and his liberal appointees leading the way, the regents adopted a four-point statement. It began with an insistence on "law and order" and a reminder that they, not the faculty, ran the university. But the last sentence amounted to capitulation: "The policies of the regents do not contemplate that advocacy or content of speech shall be restricted beyond the purview of the First and Fourteenth Amendments to the Constitution."[61] That was what the students had sought all along, a declaration that the content of speech would be no more restricted on campus than off.[62]

The Berkeley campus became an open forum, home to countless causes proclaimed by polite students and crazed street preachers alike. Decades later the striking thing about the school's regulations was their similarity to the Free Speech Movement's platform. Where student protesters had once demanded that "civil liberties and political freedoms which are constitutionally protected off-campus must be equally protected on campus," the university administration eventually acknowledged that on "university grounds open to the public generally, all persons may exercise the constitutionally protected rights of free expression, speech and assembly."[63] The Free Speech Movement had won.

———

The protests and their ending—especially the arrests—changed the nation nearly as much as the campus. The events in and around Sproul Hall put Berkeley on the front pages as never before, its fame spreading across the country and then around the world. At San Francisco State five hundred people turned out for a rally to support the Berkeley protesters. At Harvard fifty diehards stood silently in a freezing rain to show their solidarity.[64] When Kerr received an honorary degree from Scotland's University of Strathclyde the following spring, students boycotted the ceremony.[65] The Free Speech Movement launched the student dissent that came to typify the sixties. Before Berkeley, student protests had been either small and brief, like the San Francisco demonstrations against the House Un-American Activities Committee in 1960, or limited regionally, like the civil rights work that prepared Savio for leadership. But here was a model for young people everywhere: claim the moral high ground, employ the tactics of civil disobedience, do not back down even if the police arrive. A sociologist wrote later that Berkeley set "the tone for an entire college generation's confrontation with authority."[66] The very name of the city became a shorthand, a symbol condemned by conservatives and celebrated by liberals.

The man who ordered the police to act waffled a little in the years that followed, always hunting for a way that he might have unified people rather than arrested them. Once, he said that if he had to do it over again, he would not order the building cleared.[67] On another occasion, he said that if given a second chance, he would wait twenty-four hours in the hope that the protesters might drift away.[68]

There had been still other options. Brown could simply have refused to take the phone call from the police, effectively insisting that the university solve its own problems. Or he could have lied about his role. Surely Lyndon Johnson would have taken the call, made the decision, overseen the details—and then denied everything publicly. For good or ill, Brown was a simpler man. By and large, he had neither the inclination nor the self-discipline for secrecy, and the night of the Sproul arrests was no exception. In the midst of the turmoil, at 3:45 A.M. while the arrests were still taking place, Brown issued a statement assuming responsibility. He had ordered the police to act, the governor said, "as a demonstration that the rule of law must be honored in California."[69]

In the end, when he thought about the Free Speech Movement, Brown always returned to the simple bedrock belief of his wee-hours declaration: As governor, he had a duty to enforce the law. Faced with the students' frank trespass, Brown saw himself as a man with a clear and binding duty. Soon after the arrests, the governor received a letter from an old friend who sided with the students. As he dictated an answer, Brown's frustration poured out, sometimes even teetering toward self-pity. He insisted he had worked night and day for the university, and now the students had "blatantly" brought it to a halt:

> Never did these young men and women complain to me about the rules on the campus and never did they tell me they had no opportunity to discuss their grievances with the dean of the school or the president of the university. . . . Even our own revolutionary war was accompanied by some negotiations and only as a last resort did it result in the Boston Tea Party. . . .
>
> I assure you that these young people did nothing but embarrass the university and my administration. If we had had meetings I am sure we could have made substantial progress. . . .
>
> I must confess that I am amazed that a person of your intelligence, exemplified by your letter, would approve of almost a thousand students occupying, without permission, a building belonging to the state and, when asked to leave, flatly and bluntly refusing to do so. They probably thought that by mere numbers they would avoid arrest. However, when the gover-

nor is called upon by the legal authorities of the state for assistance, it is mandatory that he act or turn in his badge.[70]

Brown had stayed true to himself, and in a strange way that was the problem. In a situation in which the rules were wrong and in which he was challenged by people breaking the rules so as to change them, Brown stuck by his simple and straightforward view of the world. At each turn he did what seemed honest and responsible. When the police called to seek his guidance, Brown willingly took the phone. When a cop on the scene recommended action, Brown granted the request. When reporters wanted to know what had happened, he truthfully said the decision had been his.

Unintentionally, Brown had placed himself visibly at the center of the controversy, creating for voters an association that need not have existed. Almost everybody in California knew what had happened in Berkeley—an astonishing 92 percent of adults told pollsters they had heard or read something about the demonstrations—and the governor became a focal point of the debate.[71] In the deluged mailroom of the governor's office, fatigued aides tallied more reaction to the Sproul arrests than anything since Caryl Chessman's execution almost five years earlier. In the first week alone, more than forty-five hundred messages poured in: postcards, telegrams, letters short and long.[72] The flood of mail overwhelmed the governor's staff, and people were soon getting the wrong form letter in reply. One Brown critic from Berkeley wrote back to say he was "grateful for the privilege of viewing the garbage that you feed your loyal supporters" and then asked that he be sent the response intended for the governor's opponents. Brown's staff dutifully sent along "the other form letter you requested."[73]

The vast majority of Californians disapproved of the students, and often the letter writers mirrored that view.[74] The head of an American Legion post in Santa Monica urged that everybody involved in the protests be expelled from the university, "faculty included."[75] A man who said he was a small-time landlord complained about high taxes and attached to his letter a newspaper picture of Savio being dragged away by police. "For this I suffer a confiscatory tax of 40 percent of my gross?" he asked.[76]

But for all the venom directed toward the students, some of the letters contained a secondary strain, one that should have worried Brown. "Even though I was tough, I was looked upon as soft," Brown once said about the Berkeley protests.[77] He was right, and it was the second part of the sentence that mattered. To some letter writers, it did not matter that Brown had ordered the arrests, had earned the enmity of protesters who found him the embodiment of authority and convention. To some people, and it was no small number, all that mattered was that a great university had become the playground of a mob—and it had happened on Pat Brown's watch. It raised their ire as few things had and changed the view of their friendly governor. "On two occasions I have supported you for election," one voter wrote to Brown. "I will not err again in '66."[78]

15

WATTS

ON AUGUST 13, 1965—by weird happenstance a Friday the thirteenth—Pat Brown spent the evening in Athens, Greece, attending the World Congress of the American Hellenic Educational Progressive Association. Attended by thirteen thousand Greek Americans, the conference offered Brown a chance to burnish his connections with an important ethnic constituency. It was the kind of event Brown liked, but he was also looking ahead a few hours. His Greek political chores completed, he and Bernice were scheduled that night to begin a monthlong tour of Europe, a reprise of the rambling vacation they had enjoyed the year before. Their bags were packed, and they were assured a dramatic start: a midnight cruise on the Aegean Sea.[1]

But at the convention banquet Brown was suddenly told he had a call from America. His closest aide, Hale Champion, was on the phone, and the news was horrific. Massive rioting had erupted in Watts, a predominantly black section of Los Angeles, and the violence had mushroomed beyond control. Overwhelmed, the mighty Los Angeles Police Department was asking for help from the California National Guard. The request was not going smoothly. Glenn Anderson, the lieutenant governor and the state's acting chief executive in Brown's absence, could not be found. He was flying from Sacramento to Los Angeles, but in the meantime the request for the National Guard was awaiting action as the crisis escalated. There were rumblings that federal troops might be needed before order could be restored.[2]

It seemed a stunning development. The tensions that accompanied the Civil Rights movement had occasionally required soldiers in American cities, but that happened in the South, in backward places like Arkansas and Alabama, not in progressive California. Brown justifiably thought of himself as a good guy on racial questions. He was the governor who had signed more civil rights bills than any other chief executive in California history. He had pushed for laws to ensure fair housing and fair employment and had fought like hell when conservatives pushed for the repeal of the housing law. He was confident that black Californians knew their state was a decent place to live, and there was reason for his belief. Only months earlier the Urban League had rated sixty-eight American cities and concluded that blacks enjoyed more opportunities in Los Angeles than anywhere else.[3]

And yet now Brown's most trusted adviser was on the phone with news of an urban apocalypse in the land of endless sunshine. It was California's greatest emergency since Brown had been governor—and he was halfway around the world.

———

For Brown, 1965 had been a hard year from the start. Deep into the sixties socially as well as chronologically, California was now a place of division as much as dreams. The acid battles over the Rumford Act and the Free Speech Movement the previous fall had split the state, and the rifts were reflected in opinions about the governor who played so crucial a role in both controversies. Regarding Brown, fewer people than ever before were neutral. More voters thought the governor was doing a good job, and more a poor one. Only the dispassionate percentages—people who gave him a middling "fair" rating or who had no opinion at all—had dropped.[4]

The Democrats Brown supposedly led were more deeply divided than ever, a fact that haunted the governor through the early months of the year. In January he headed a big California delegation that went east to attend the inauguration of Lyndon Johnson, but the Democratic politicos took along their battles from home. From the start the Californians sundered into peevish and competing camps devoted to Brown and his rival, Speaker Jess Unruh. There were separate airplanes and hotels, even separate social events once the group reached Washington. One newspaper chronicled the hostility and headlined the story "State Sends a Civil War."[5]

The year's legislative session was equally frustrating, both because of the Democratic bickering and because of Brown's own shriveled policy ambitions. Once, the governor had pushed the legislature toward big steps, massive engineering projects or major civil rights bills or large tax increases needed to fund an activist government. Now, at the start of his seventh year in office, his administration fatigued and sagging, Brown's chief complaint was that lawmakers were doing too little to save money.[6]

Even after months of slogging, the legislature's product was an unbalanced budget, and although the books were eventually squared with a series of minor tax increases, disappointment saturated the Capitol. By the end, Democratic feuds were completely public, their insults daily fare for the papers. Unruh accused the governor of "blackmail" during a dispute over the budget. Brown accused the speaker of "fiscal irresponsibility." George Miller, the powerful state senator who hated Unruh as much as Brown did, referred to the "alleged leadership of the Assembly," which he flatly accused of lying.[7] The *Sacramento Bee* surveyed the legislative situation and termed it "nightmarish."[8]

As if that were not enough, the old reliable of trouble—Berkeley—provided yet another source of public uproar. In an almost comic epilogue to the Free Speech Movement, a young man named John Thompson, who was not a student at the university, walked onto the campus and held up a sign reading "FUCK." Quickly arrested on a charge of outraging public decency, Thompson found himself a new martyr for the cause of free expression, which this time was dubbed the Filthy Speech Movement.[9]

Within a day, students were back in front of Sproul Hall, rallying on Thompson's behalf, although this time there was the air of a party or an undergraduate stunt, not the serious complaint of the first FSM the previous fall. Signs advertised the "Fuck Rally" and the "Fuck Defense Fund" (after the organizer was arrested the latter was changed to the "Phuque Defense Fund"). One young man was arrested for reading *Lady Chatterly's Lover* to a police officer. The Cal Conservatives offered a unique brand of support: They ordered one thousand "Fuck Communism" signs. Students at the rally, one of Kerr's assistants informed the president in a memo, "seemed more amused than shocked."[10]

Neither the public nor the governor were so blithe. Brown got on the phone to Kerr and demanded that the university president do something about the vulgar impudence of his students.[11] To Brown, this was something altogether different from the Free Speech Movement, when he had sympathized with the students' goals if not their methods. Public obscenity was another matter. Here was no misguided-but-honest campaign for the cherished liberties of the First Amendment. This was simply a bunch of kids spewing foul language. The governor, a man whose era did not abide such things, could not see that as an acceptable expression of free speech. He would eventually rally to the defense of a professor who supported the students, but the open vulgarity still enraged him. The students involved deserved to be expelled, he railed, for they were merely "thoughtless troublemakers" with "sick minds." As for the Filthy Speech Movement: "I agreed with neither its goals nor its methods."[12]

Voters shared his rage. The Berkeley campus, one fumed, had degenerated into an "atmosphere of filth and degradation." The protesters were "bearded hoodlums" and a "dirty little pack of beatniks and communists who want only to create trouble." Added a Southern Californian: "I do not believe anything has ever provoked me more than the situation at the University of California."[13] Californians were back in high dudgeon, and the real trouble of 1965 had not even begun.

———

Brown's trip to Greece offered a breather from such rancor, but even that was not without controversy. George Papandreou had been forced from office as the prime minister of Greece by King Constantine, and the ensuing crisis had spiraled downward into street demonstrations and violence. The Johnson administration was worried that Brown, intentionally or not, might allow himself to be used as a symbol of American favoritism for one side or the other. George Ball, the undersecretary of state, told Brown that the trip was ill advised, but the governor insisted on going anyway.[14] It occurred to no one that the real danger of Brown's journey might be that California, not Greece, was ready to explode with mayhem in the streets.

Yet beneath the surface there had long been a quiet sense that trouble was possible even in California. As early as 1963, with racial tensions rising across the country, Brown instructed National Guard officials to contact Los Angeles authorities and discuss what would happen if soldiers were needed to keep order in California's largest city.[15] Then for six weeks in summer 1964, from the middle of July through the end of August, urban rage swept across black communities in the East. A series of riots broke out, first in New York City, then Rochester, then down through the grit of northern New Jersey—Jersey City, Paterson, Elizabeth—and finally to Chicago and Philadelphia. By comparison with what was to come, they had been small affairs—Rochester was the worst, but even there only four people died—but they still hinted that the old fifties calm was fading.[16]

Rising racial tensions in Los Angeles were spotted by an astute deputy in the attorney general's office, Howard Jewell, who wrote a prescient memo warning of poor relations between the black community and the Los Angeles Police Department. The department was led by a bombastic and controversial chief named William Parker, and Jewell contrasted the Los Angeles situation with that in San Francisco:

> Negro leaders in San Francisco and Los Angeles do not naturally differ in their outlook or in their techniques. The demonstrators do not differ naturally—the attitudes of the white community of San Francisco and Los Angeles do not differ naturally. What does differ is the attitude of the respective police departments. Chief Cahill of SF has met every effort to convince San Francisco and his own police department that the civil rights struggle is not between the demonstrators and the police, but that in fact the police department is a third and neutral force. Chief Parker, by contrast, has made it clear that the struggle is between the police department and the demonstrators. . . . One cannot contemplate the personalities and emotional makeup of the chief antagonists to the struggle—the civil rights leader on the one hand and Chief Parker on the other—without being struck by the similarities. Each is independent and strong-willed. Each regards himself as a champion of a beleaguered minority. Each has an almost Oriental regard for "loss of face." Each is determined to prevail no matter what the cost to the community generally. Each is currently embarked upon a course of conflict which is designed not to avoid violence, but to place the blame for violence upon the opposing parties. Neither is willing to take any steps to reduce the possibility of violence. Each has as his motto, "Not one step backward."

Jewell did not think Parker was actually a bigot, and he believed the department was well run, but he was coldly analytical about public perceptions: "Chief Parker personifies the frustrations of Negroes and gives focus to their activities. I am not saying that this is fair or justified, but I am saying that this is a fact."

The result of such strains could be cataclysmic, warned Jewell, whose memo was forwarded to the governor's staff but apparently never reached Brown personally. "In Los Angeles, if demonstrators are joined by the Negro community at large, the policing will no longer be done by the LA Police Department but by the state Militia. If violence erupts, millions in property damage may ensue, untold lives may be lost and California would have received an unsurpassed injury to her reputation."[17]

If Jewell had focused his worries geographically, he would undoubtedly have centered on the south-central section of Los Angeles, home to much of the city's black community. And if he had telescoped his concerns even more, he would have fixed on a small area within south-central, a place that would soon become a byword for urban rage: Watts.

The history of Watts was California in microcosm. Settlement in the area stretched back to the era of Mexican rule. A real estate developer was important in the town's history. Controversies over water played a role. Explosive population growth followed.[18]

The area began as part of a great Mexican rancho south of Los Angeles and in the nineteenth century was still called Tajuata. Over time it transformed into a collection of houses on small lots and gained a new name when the Pacific Electric railroad dedicated the local station to a property owner and developer named Julia A. Watts. By 1907 it was incorporated as an independent city, and, although never rich, was a busy little place. In 1911 the first streets were paved. In 1912 Carnegie money paid for a public library. By 1920 there were two local grammar schools. In 1926 it was willingly subsumed by Los Angeles, a marriage that provided something for both communities: Watts got even better public services; Los Angeles acquired more customers for the water brought via the new aqueduct from the Owens Valley, on the eastern side of the Sierra Nevada.

As late as the 1920s Watts still had a white population large enough to support an active Ku Klux Klan contingent, but in parts of the town blacks had carved out places of their own. Land was cheap, and a rural area south of the main business district had long been a destination for blacks migrating from the South. Known as Mudtown, perhaps for the dusty wagon roads that still served as streets, the area was one of the settings for the writer Arna Bontemps's novel *God Sends Sunday:*

> Mudtown was like a tiny section of the deep south literally transplanted. . . .
> In the moist grass along the edges [of the streets], cows were staked. . . .
> Ducks were sleeping in the weeds, and there was on the air a suggestion of
> pigs and slime holes. Tiny hoot-owls were sitting bravely on fence posts
> while bats hovered overhead like shadows.

As Los Angeles grew, restrictive covenants and informal discrimination often prohibited blacks from moving to many of the burgeoning suburbs.

As late as the 1950s Lynwood identified itself as "the friendly Caucasian city." The result was that Watts and the south-central neighborhoods that surrounded it became the soul of black Los Angeles. The population boomed during World War II, when defense industry factory jobs lured blacks west. At the same time whites moved out. By 1950 nearly three-quarters of Watts's population was black. By 1960 more than 86 percent was.[19]

Racial isolation was joined by neglect. Watts had little industry and few jobs, and it became an island of poverty amid California's postwar boom. From 1959, the year Brown took office, to 1965, when the riots occurred, the median income in Watts declined, the local people getting poorer just as their fellow Californians grew richer. Other than a public housing project, virtually no new housing was built, so neighborhoods grew more crowded. Easterners sometimes saw the bungalows of Watts and, comparing it to places like Harlem, described a comfortable village. But the residents of Watts wanted no comparison to Harlem. They were Californians; they wanted the California life. And by that comparison, they could see, quite literally all around them, the comfortable and roomy neighborhoods they knew they did not have. They were right: By the mid-1960s Watts was more than three times as crowded as the rest of Los Angeles.[20]

City officials did not seem to care. Some streets remained unpaved. Streetlights were rare. Schools lagged behind those in the rest of the city. The library that had once been the pride of an independent community was now a neglected branch of the vast Los Angeles behemoth. Local landlords almost all lived elsewhere, and houses and apartments had fallen into disrepair. Residents charged that grocery stores sold rotting food rejected by suburban outlets, often at gouging prices. The local movie theater was so decrepit that rats ran beneath the seats nibbling at dropped popcorn. Beset with racial segregation and poverty and despair, Watts residents knew they had been walled off from the glitter of postwar California. The governor once dispatched his aide William Becker to meet with people in Watts. Becker summed up their complaints in one honest, striking sentence: "We want the kind of life the white man has."[21]

Brown's first duty in Greece was minor but intimidating. On the flight over, a traveling companion, Sacramento restaurateur and Greek American leader George Johnson, told the governor how thrilled the welcoming crowd would be if he said a word or two in Greek. Brown begged off, noting accurately that foreign pronunciations were an enemy he could not conquer. But Johnson persisted. He said that just one word would suffice: *efharisto*, Greek for "thank you." Terrified, Brown said it would be impossible for him to pronounce such a thing.

So Johnson took out a business card and jotted down on the back, "F. Harry Stowe," a rough phonetic approximation of the Greek pronunciation. Brown glanced at the familiar-looking name and read it aloud easily: "F. Harry Stowe." Now say it quickly, he was told. He charged through it, compacting all the syllables into one word: *FHarryStowe*. It was good enough, reasonably close to *efharisto*, and everyone agreed that Brown would, after the welcoming ceremony, say thank-you in Greek.

By the time the plane landed, the governor looked nervous, but he stuck with the plan. A group of waiting schoolchildren serenaded him on the tarmac, and a local official welcomed him to the country. Brown walked to the microphone, wiped his brow, then leaped into his brief linguistic performance: "Harry F. Stowe!"[22]

As Brown waited for the opening of the convention he was there to attend—killing time by touring the ancient sites of Greece[23]—Los Angeles suffered through a muggy mid-August heat wave. The evenings were warm, and so at 7:00 P.M. on Wednesday, August 11, there were people milling around outside—sitting on their porches or walking to the corner store or tending the yard—when a California Highway Patrol officer stopped twenty-one-year-old Marquette Frye along Avalon Boulevard, a few blocks from the central business district of Watts.[24]

Seconds before, another motorist had flagged down the CHP motorcycle officer and said that Frye was driving erratically, and the reason soon became obvious. His sobriety in doubt, Frye staggered through a straight-line walking test, missed his nose and touched his upper lip instead, and lost his balance while trying to stand with his feet together and his eyes closed. He told the police that he had consumed a pint and a half of vodka that night, and admitted, "I'm drunk a little."

But none of that caused any trouble. Frye was cooperative, even joking with officers when they told him he was being arrested for drunken driving. Then his mother, Rena Frye, arrived. Rena Frye and her sons lived nearby, and she had been alerted by a neighbor that her son had been stopped. She spoke briefly with the officers and then with her son, who apparently put his arm around her and insisted he was not drunk. As one of the police officers remembered it, Rena Frye told her son that he was plainly drunk, that in fact she could smell the liquor on his breath.

Drawn by the minor excitement and fed by the presence of so many people outside, a crowd had been growing rapidly, from 25 or 30 people as the first officer wrote the citation, to 50 or 60 by the time a backup unit arrived, to perhaps 150 when mother and son had their exchange. Berated by his mother on the streets of his own neighborhood, Marquette Frye shoved her aside and then transferred his anger from one authority figure to another. He began shouting at the police officers that they should not touch him, that he would not be arrested or taken to jail.

A scuffle broke out, and the tensions of Watts began to transform a drunk-driving arrest into a broader conflict. Worried about the potential for trouble, one of three officers at the scene got on his radio and called an "11-99," the police code for an officer who needs assistance. Patrol cars and motorcycles began pouring into the area.

To many in the crowd, meanwhile, it seemed that officers were using excessive force in their scuffle with Frye, which quickly grew to include his mother and brother as well. Bystanders later said they saw officers kick Frye as they put him in a patrol car, and even three Los Angeles police officers said they saw a highway patrol officer punch Frye twice after he was handcuffed. People began to shout about police brutality.

Suspicion and distrust between the police and the crowd now multiplied exponentially, fueled by old antagonisms and ignited by odd coincidence. As officers began to leave the scene, one thought that he was spat on. He turned and went into the crowd to arrest a young woman he believed had done it. She denied it, and there was more scuffling, finally even a tug-of-war between officers on one end and male members of the crowd on the other, with the young woman in the middle. Worse still, the woman had just come from a beauty shop where she worked. She wore a loose-fitting barber's smock, which some people in the crowd took for a maternity dress. Word spread through the crowd and then the neighborhood that white police officers had roughed up a pregnant black woman, adding to the indignation.

By the time the final police unit left the scene at 7:45 P.M., forty-five minutes after the stop, the crowd was wild and enraged, heaving rocks and bottles at the last police car as it drove away. Thinking their presence was inciting people, officers had decided to clear the area in an effort to calm it, but by now emotions were too high to be controlled. The crowd milled around and soon began to throw things at passing vehicles. Police made some arrests and tried to establish a perimeter, then had to pull back because they were outmanned.

By midnight the area around Watts was out of control. The racial tensions of America had erupted. Cars driven by white drivers had been not only stoned but also overturned and burned. A white reporter was dragged from his car and beaten. The police command post was under such heavy attack that it had to be moved. Firefighters were stoned when they tried to douse a burning car. A police officer was stabbed. Looting began.

Fatigue and morning sunlight dispersed the crowds hours later, but by then parts of Watts looked like a wasteland. At the intersection of Imperial Highway and Avalon Boulevard, the wreckage of five burned automobiles sat in the street, surrounded by rubble.

———

That morning, Thursday, August 12, someone in the governor's office ripped a news story from the wire service teletype and took it to Winslow Christian, the chief of staff. It was worrisome but not disastrous. From Sacramento, the previous night's disturbance seemed strictly a local Los Angeles affair. Late that morning—it was well into the evening in Greece—Christian talked by phone with Brown and mentioned the trouble, but neither man viewed it as critical. It failed even to dominate their attention: Much of the conversation dealt with other issues.[25]

But throughout the day the situation worsened in Watts. Even noble efforts at reconciliation ended in anger. The Los Angeles County Human Relations Commission gamely organized a community meeting at a park near the scene of the trouble, intending to encourage calm and lawfulness. Rena Frye, whose son's arrest had started the trouble, was among those counseling peace. Then after several speakers urged restraint, a teenager took the microphone and suggested that not only would the streets turn violent again that night, this time the rioters would spread trouble to white neighborhoods.[26]

By early evening angry crowds had gathered again and started to stone passing cars. By 7:15 P.M. violence was significant enough that police officers had been ordered to maintain a perimeter but stay out of the interior of the riot area unless absolutely necessary. Fifteen minutes later the LAPD asked for help from the county sheriff's office. An hour after that police abandoned the heart of the area altogether.[27]

Before the night was over Watts would descend almost to chaos, the previous night's activities repeated and magnified. Assaults and arson increased. Looting was rampant. Firefighters, shot at and stoned as they tried to extinguish blazes, eventually refused to respond. A police command post had to be moved. Later, flashes of rioting erupted outside the lines, and the police abandoned their perimeter and resorted to running street battles, sometimes even hand-to-hand fighting between officers and residents. The comedian and social activist Dick Gregory courageously convinced police to let him enter the area. Armed only with a bullhorn, he began urging calm. Grazed in the thigh by a bullet, he insisted on trying yet again to break up the crowds.[28] Mervyn Dymally, a black assemblyman who represented the area, also walked the streets to counsel peace. When he refused a rioter's command that he prove his mettle by throwing a bottle, the youngster denounced him: "You're with The Man."[29]

Watts was now too dangerous for white reporters—a soundman for ABC was beaten so severely that initially it was thought he might be blinded—but Robert Richardson, a black advertising salesman for the *Los Angeles Times,* spent hours in the riot area. "It was the most terrifying thing I've ever seen in my life," his account began. "I went along with the mobs, just watching, listening. It's a wonder anyone with white skin got out of there alive."[30]

———

In Greece it was already Friday morning. Brown checked the *Athens Daily Post,* but the paper carried only a brief item on the Los Angeles troubles. Written before the latest outbreak, the story offered no hint of doom, so the governor went about his plans for the day. That night he was to give a speech at the convention, and then he and Bernice would leave on their cruise.[31]

Had Brown known the extent of the trouble in Watts it might have made little difference, for he was governor in title only. The powers were not his. California's constitution contained a nineteenth-century clause declaring that when the governor leaves the state, his full powers are assumed by the lieutenant governor. In theory, every time Brown traveled across the state line to the other side of Lake Tahoe, his lieutenant governor, Glenn Anderson, could do anything Brown normally could do: sign bills into law, call a special session of the legislature, appoint judges, hire and fire state officials, commute a condemned man's sentence. With Brown in Greece as Watts began to burn, Anderson was the acting governor, as fully endowed with the powers of the office as any man elected to it. Among California politicos, it was not a situation that made hearts pound with confidence.

Anderson had been elected mayor of his hometown of Hawthorne when he was just twenty-seven, the youngest man in the country to hold such a post. He was elected to the legislature after World War II and became active in the California Democratic Council, the grassroots group that helped to build the party. In 1958 he won the Democratic nomination for lieutenant governor and in November rode Brown's coattails into the job, where, like lieutenant governors before and after, he had virtually nothing to do.[32]

Considered a nice man and well meaning—a good liberal to be sure—Anderson was hardly a brilliant or decisive figure. Some people, including Brown, thought him a bit of a bumbler. Occasionally, the governor joked privately that he and Anderson should always ride in the same plane, because if anything happened to him he did not want to leave the state in Anderson's hands.[33] Now, unintentionally, Brown had done exactly that in a crisis.

As the riots worsened Thursday night, Anderson could literally see the trouble. He had been in Santa Barbara most of the day attending a local festival, but he arrived home that night in Hawthorne, only a few miles from the scene of the riot. Against the night sky, the fires in Watts were plainly visible.[34] It seemed obvious that the city might need help keeping order, and ranking National Guard officers were in touch with police commanders. But the police insisted repeatedly that the situation was either under control or close to it. Anderson consulted with the Guard officers under his command, who kept echoing the police belief that state assistance would not be needed.[35]

In the wee hours Anderson went to sleep for a while, then rose early and told an aide to check in once again with the police. By then—about 6:45 A.M. Friday—the situation on the streets of Watts had calmed, perhaps because of simple exhaustion. Police counted dozens of stores and vehicles either burned or looted, and they had made seventy-seven arrests.[36]

Weary after a few hours' sleep, Anderson now faced a critical decision. The University of California's Board of Regents was scheduled to meet that day in Berkeley, and Anderson wanted to attend. Ironically, he thought he should be in the Bay Area in part because there was a possibility of large-scale trouble there too. For days, antiwar protesters had been trying to stop troop trains as they pulled into the Oakland shipping terminal, standing on the tracks in a human blockade, and authorities were predicting more problems with the arrival of another train that day. In a decision that would mark the rest of his career, the lieutenant governor, now also the acting governor, boarded a United Airlines flight for Oakland. Sadly for him, the looting in Watts resumed even before he landed.[37]

———

When the looting started again early Friday, with a long summer day yet to come, the Los Angeles police finally admitted that they needed help. Parker, the police chief, decided to ask for one thousand National Guard troops. What followed was a chaotic and yet critical series of phone calls, largely among various members of the police department, the National Guard, and the governor's office. A general consensus emerged quickly that Los Angeles wanted and needed help, but the precise format of the request seemed confused. Parker was apparently under the impression that no formal request was needed, and he even seemed to think that National Guard troops could be placed directly under his command. Guard officers knew they needed the approval of Anderson, as acting governor, and they knew a formal legal request would have to be made. Communication swirled around, but for at least an hour nobody actually managed to reach Anderson and tell him the Guard had been requested. It did not help that Sam Yorty, the mayor of Los Angeles, left town at 10:05 A.M., after the rioting had resumed that morning and after he and Parker had agreed that the National Guard would be needed. Given the circumstances, Yorty's decision to fly to San Francisco was unforgivable and astonishing, all the more so since he had no pressing engagement—merely a luncheon speech to a civic club.[38]

The request for the Guard finally reached Anderson at 11:00 A.M., relayed by Winslow Christian, Brown's chief of staff. Anderson was in Berkeley attending the meeting of the university regents, and he told Christian over the phone that he did not have enough information to decide whether the Guard should be called out. He insisted on flying to Los Angeles so he could meet with Parker and assess the situation personally. It was an unnecessary delay—what would be prudence in everyday life becomes timidity in a crisis—and then Anderson compounded his mistake. Picked up by a National Guard plane in Oakland, he decided that before flying south, he would head northeast to Sacramento, where he would meet with Lt. Gen. Roderic Hill, commander of the National Guard. Hill would then fly with Anderson to Los Angeles.

As Anderson was on his roundabout journey south, the situation in Watts was worsening by the minute. Police estimated that three thousand people were mobbed around one intersection, stoning cars as they passed. Looting was widespread, people carrying away food, clothing, televisions, in one case a fishing rod and a fifth of whiskey. Fires were so numerous— and the crowds so hostile to any official figure—that firefighters were no longer able to respond. Police officers had been reduced nearly to hostages inside their own stations, guarding at least one station with shotguns or making only an occasional sally into the streets.[39]

Yet Anderson could not be found, not even contacted. The normal gubernatorial plane, the *Grizzly,* had not been available. With Brown out of the country, nobody expected the need, and the plane had been dispatched on other business. Anderson had been put aboard a substitute aircraft, and although it had a radio, no one in the governor's office knew how to raise the pilots. In the bustle and confusion, nobody asked the Guard officers about it, and apparently nobody in the Guard raised the issue with the governor's staff. In the midst of a crisis that was now drawing national attention, the man in charge of California's government was, through no fault of his own, shut off from the world.[40]

Frustrations mounted almost everywhere. There was some talk, perhaps inaccurate, that Anderson wanted to meet with law enforcement officials and black leaders once he reached Los Angeles. A Brown staff member told Parker, who blew up at the idea. The police chief yelled that his men were struggling through one of the most violent situations he had ever seen. He needed armed soldiers, not a talking shop with community activists. If Anderson wanted more information about what was happening, Parker insisted, he could go to the emergency command post at police headquarters and read the log.[41]

Concerns were building in the governor's office too. By chance, Hale Champion, Brown's director of finance and top aide, had been in Los Angeles when the trouble broke out. He quickly took command of the administration's response. Champion doubted Anderson's ability to make decisions in a crisis, and now it seemed that his worries were coming true. Parker had asked for the National Guard two hours earlier, and yet Anderson had apparently done nothing.[42]

Looking for help, Champion called Tom Lynch, Brown's former deputy in the district attorney's office and the man Brown had picked to replace Stanley Mosk as attorney general when Mosk went on to the state supreme court. Champion knew that Lynch was also in Los Angeles; the two men had eaten dinner together earlier in the week. Now Champion tracked down Lynch at the Hillcrest Country Club, where he was having lunch. As attorney general, Lynch gave some quick legal advice about using the National Guard to suppress the riot, then rushed toward the office. Like everyone else, Lynch was exasperated about the inability to find the acting governor. Overtaken by frustration, he threatened briefly to sign the necessary papers himself, though legally he had no power to do so.[43]

Lynch's help was welcome, but Champion knew the state was tumbling toward catastrophe. So as Anderson's plane finally headed south from Sacramento and the business district of Watts went up in flames, Champion decided to call the elected governor rather than the acting one.

In Athens, Brown was summoned from the convention and at last took a phone call that told him of the depth of the crisis back home. The previous day Winslow Christian had described the Watts uprising as a local matter—which it had been at the time—but now Champion told Brown that the National Guard would be needed. Brown agreed immediately. As acting governor, Anderson should get the Guard into the streets as soon as possible, Brown said, and he suggested that a curfew might be a good idea, the first time anybody had mentioned such a thing. Before hanging up, Brown said he would check on transportation back to the United States and return as soon as possible.[44]

Champion waited eagerly for Anderson's plane to land, then got the acting governor on the phone immediately and told him the situation was bad—and worsening. Brown wanted the National Guard activated and put into the streets as soon as possible, Champion said. Anderson concurred and announced to waiting reporters that he was sending soldiers to Los Angeles. In effect, Brown had made the decision, even though he had no legal authority. Perhaps Anderson would have decided to call out the Guard on his own, but the fact was that he had done it only after Brown, relaying commands through Champion, told him to. Often too vacillating in the exercise of power he possessed, Brown had displayed a rare strength in the use of power he technically did not have.[45]

———

Brown's long trip home began with a delay. There were no more flights out of Athens that night, so the governor sweated out a twelve-hour wait before catching the first plane. Just before boarding, he talked again with Champion in Los Angeles, where it was now the wee hours of Saturday morning, just a little after midnight. The update was not good news. The first Guard units had reached Watts, mustering at a playground and then fanning out for their assignments, helping police to sweep the streets for looters. Along 103d Street, a business district so badly burned that it became known as "Charcoal Alley," the Guardsmen took up positions every few feet, guns at the ready, looking more like figures from a war zone than a major American city. Two thousand soldiers were in the riot area already, and more were likely to be needed.[46]

The plane made a brief stop in Rome, where Brown's initial reaction to reporters amounted to little more than staccato bursts of dismayed wonderment. "Terrible . . . unbelievable . . . absolutely beyond my comprehension," he told reporters. He recovered enough to combine a dose of alarmism with wishful thinking about California racial history: "From here, it is awfully hard to direct a war. That's what this is. It is mob rule at its worst. I cannot understand. Relations between different races have always been excellent in California."[47]

Brown boarded the plane again for the long leg to New York's Kennedy Airport, where the gravity of the situation in Watts was revealed by the greeting committee: two White House aides sent to brief the governor. The news, bad enough when he left Rome, was worse now. Rage and fear had permeated a huge area of south-central Los Angeles, and it had turned deadly. At the Do-Rite Market, clerks decided to defend the store even after looters smashed the windows and ransacked the liquor section. When an eighteen-year-old walked in and made for the beer box, a clerk shot him in the head with a 12-gauge shotgun and killed him.[48] At times the violence was random or mystifying. A bystander was shot in the heart and killed. Another man died when a ricochet struck him in the head. A woman died in a burning building—and her body was not found for a week.[49]

The chaotic mood touched the police, who toughened their tactics. They had begun to make large numbers of arrests, sweep the streets clean with shoulder-to-shoulder marches, and shoot people who failed to obey their commands. Daryl Gates, later the chief of police but then a midlevel commander, remembered officers firing "indiscriminately," sometimes "blasting away" so freely that he had trouble convincing them to cease fire.[50] Officers shot and killed one man as he fled a looted shoe store. Another man was killed when officers fired at looters who were pelting them with liquor bottles. In one fifteen-minute period, officers shot and killed four people said to be looting.[51]

When Brown left Europe, the latest reports were that only one person had died. When the governor landed in New York, presidential aide Lee White told him that the death toll had reached seventeen. "Boy, that really sobered him," White reported in a phone call to LBJ confidant Jack Valenti.[52]

But if the ugly news jolted Brown, it did not debilitate him. Perhaps more than at any other time in his career, he responded with a decisive, consistent hand. He agreed to expand the call of the National Guard to whatever degree was needed, advocated a curfew, and said that if necessary he would declare martial law on his return to California, a step already advocated by some black leaders in Los Angeles who trusted the National Guard more than the police department. The Johnson administration was not normally a hotbed of admiration for Brown, but White, talking to Valenti, praised the governor for "taking charge." On every issue, White said, Brown had "exactly the reaction I would have had and the one that I think is correct."[53]

On the most dramatic potential development, however, the administration kept the governor in the dark. If the National Guard failed, the next step would be a request for federal troops. The idea that the U.S. Army might be needed to keep order in California was striking but not far-fetched. In the governor's office, Champion was reasonably sure that the Guard could handle Watts, but he worried that if trouble broke out elsewhere in the state, federal help would be needed. Already there were hints that a wider disturbance was possible. The night before, minor riots had broken out across Southern California: in Pasadena, Monrovia, Compton, and Venice.[54] But when Brown discussed the issue with White during their airport meeting in New York, the governor was left hanging. Brown said he believed the most populous state in the nation should handle its own problems, but he still wanted to know if federal help might be forthcoming. White refused to make a firm commitment. Only the president could make that decision, he said. White was so pessimistic that Brown came away convinced that White had effectively told the state to fend for itself. In fact, the administration knew that regular soldiers might be needed, but officials did not want to reveal their greatest worry to Brown. The military said it would take sixteen hours to get units into Los Angeles, and administration officials were concerned about so long a delay. The president believed that if the riots went on unabated federal authorities would have no choice but to intervene, and so in the hope of shortening the lead time, Johnson secretly ordered troops and planes to be readied. He told an aide he would decide the soldiers' destination later: "I'll let 'em know whether they're going to Los Angeles or Vietnam."[55]

————————

Still hopscotching his way home, Brown switched in New York from a commercial flight to an air force jet provided by the president. The plane stopped to refuel in Omaha, where Brown again called Champion and urged a curfew.[56]

The governor finally reached Los Angeles at 10:45 P.M. on Saturday. He had returned as quickly as possible, but it was three days after the riots started and twenty hours after he left Greece. Champion and Anderson drove to the airport and briefed Brown on board the jet, and then reporters mobbed Brown even before he cleared the steps of the plane, Bernice stranded above him on the stairway. There wasn't much new to say, so he tried for bland reassurance: He had confidence in law enforcement authorities and planned to stay in Los Angeles "until this situation is completely cleaned up."[57] He went directly to the office, then to a hotel where the governor's staff, many of whom had rushed south from Sacramento, had set up camp.[58]

Legally, the riot area should have been empty by the time Brown arrived. Anderson had declared an "extreme emergency," the most drastic gubernatorial power available. Ruling almost by fiat, he had imposed a curfew on a huge swath of south-central Los Angeles. In one-tenth of one of the biggest cities in the country, it was illegal to be on the streets between 8:00 P.M. and sunrise.[59]

But Los Angeles did not calm. When firefighters responded to a blaze along Broadway, snipers forced them to retreat three times, once abandoning some of their equipment. Firemen finally reached the blaze only under cover from National Guard rifles.[60] Shortly after the governor landed Guardsmen shot a man they said was running a roadblock. Almost at the same time two men were shot and killed while allegedly looting liquor stores. At a sheriff's department station in the riot area, commanders ordered that external lights be turned off and those inside be dimmed whenever possible, to make the building less a target. At the police headquarters downtown, an old-time reporter for the *Los Angeles Times* claimed that for the first time in his career he saw policewomen take handguns from their purses and strap them on.[61]

Still, the combination of a curfew—which allowed authorities to chase people off the streets—and the massive National Guard presence had begun to make a difference. By Sunday morning more than thirteen thousand Guardsmen were patrolling the riot area, a massive show of force that was working. One writer noticed a strange indicator of returning order: The local prostitutes were back in business.[62]

Yet no major official toured the area or consulted in any meaningful way with black leaders in Los Angeles. Mayor Yorty had flown over Watts in a helicopter. Chief Parker had flatly refused to attend a meeting with black leaders. A deputy chief of the police department had rejected the efforts of a delegation of black leaders, telling them at one point during the rioting that he would not consult with them because they were "part of the problem."[63] Now the governor who had played the tough guy earlier—urging that the Guard be mustered quickly and expanded as necessary, insisting on a curfew, even considering martial law—switched gears and became a conciliator. He insisted that he would go to Watts and meet both regular folks and the National Guard troops standing watch. Yorty offered the helicopter for an aerial inspection, but the governor who loved personal contact more than anything insisted that his trip would be on the ground and face-to-face, a handshaking enterprise.[64]

The convoy included fifteen vehicles, civilian cars and Jeeps from the National Guard. Brown stopped first at a high school in the riot area, standing around outside to shake hands and talk with local residents. He heard a litany of complaints about life in Watts, many of them justified. Jobs were rare. Stores gouged customers who had no cars and thus no way of shopping elsewhere. Police harassment was said to be so common that some residents wanted the National Guard to remain permanently, as a counterbalance to the Los Angeles police.[65]

From the high school the convoy headed for the central business district of Watts, although it stopped briefly at a fire station being used as a National Guard command post. The governor went inside to talk with the unit's commander, but when he emerged the vehicles had all been turned around, ready to leave the area rather than plunge deeper in. Shots had just been fired a half-block ahead, the governor was told, and live electrical wires were lying across the street. The dangers were too great, Guard officers insisted. Brown should leave. He returned to the office downtown and met with fifty leaders of the black community. He promised that the State Disaster Office would start distributing food to the riot area, where grocery stores had been looted.

Viewing the trouble personally for the first time, Brown managed to combine toughness with fantasy. He insisted that the riots had been caused by "a hoodlum gang element that took advantage of a situation."[66] Blacks complained about rough treatment from the police, Brown knew, but the prosecutor in him had trouble processing that idea. "As an old district attorney," he said the next day, "I know . . . the police have a difficult job to do."[67]

The fantasy was a laudatory dream about his state. Stunned and bewildered by what had happened, Brown suggested that racial strife was nearly impossible in California. "Here in California," he said, "we have a wonderful working relationship [between whites and blacks]. We got along fine until this happened. This is the first trouble we have had."[68] That was utter nonsense, as Brown should have been the first to notice. The previous year he had spent months denouncing as plain bigotry a ballot measure eventually approved by a majority of the voters. If the repeal of the Rumford Act did not reveal a racial fissure, nothing could.

But the governor also understood that in Watts he had glimpsed a California he knew little about. The following day he seemed genuinely bewildered:

> I don't think any of us had any idea this would happen. No one advised me that Los Angeles was in a turbulent situation. We were all aware of the fact that there is a great deal of Negro unemployment and we have all been trying to help, working out ways of getting jobs for youths and unemployed adults. . . . The poverty, the frustrations and the conditions they live in[,] . . . the Negroes feel very strongly about this.[69]

Brown's tour was not the reason, but as the governor returned to his office the situation in Watts had calmed almost completely. He expanded the curfew for Sunday night, but that was an abundance of caution. The desperate rage of the first few nights had faded. By Tuesday, six days after the violence began, it was over. Brown lifted the curfew at 11:15 A.M., and utility crews soon set about the daunting task of restoring service to the area. Less than an hour later buses to and from Watts began running again.[70]

The final tally of destruction was horrific: 34 dead, more than 1,000 injured, almost 4,000 arrested. Property damage was estimated at $40 million, an enormous figure for the day.[71] At the peak, more than 13,000 National Guard troops were on riot duty, roughly the same number of soldiers that the United States had used a few months before to put down an insurrection in the Dominican Republic.[72]

———

Watts laid bare the nightmare possibilities of America's struggle with race in the 1960s. Other cities would soon endure similar calamities, but Watts came first. Not since World War II, two decades earlier, had an American city exploded with such violence.

To many whites, the riot was simple crime, and ungrateful crime at that. Watts erupted just as the country was moving to right old wrongs. Only five days before the rioting began, President Johnson signed the Voting Rights Act he had pushed through Congress. The day before the trouble in Watts the first federal registrars had been dispatched to the South to enroll black voters, the president himself directing the attack county by county.[73] Asked to identify the causes of the violence in Watts, whites cited "lack of respect for law and order" and "outside agitators."[74]

Blacks, by contrast, cited unemployment and poor living conditions. To many blacks, 1965 had been a year not of progress but of violence and strife. They remembered not only the Voting Rights Act but also the protests that helped to lead to its enactment, protests often met with raw savagery from the white power structure. Through the early months of the year, a campaign to register black voters in Selma, Alabama, was met with brutality sanctioned by the local sheriff, who regularly sported on his lapel a button offering to the hopes of black Americans a one-word rebuff: Never. Deputies kicked and clubbed peaceful protesters, even jabbed them with electric cattle prods as they were forced out of town. When protesters attempted to publicize their plight by marching the fifty-six miles from Selma to Montgomery, the state's capital, authorities blocked them at the Edmund Pettis Bridge, just at the edge of town. When the marchers refused to turn back, deputies on horseback charged forward, swinging bullwhips and rubber tubing wrapped in barbed wire, some hollering the rebel yell of the Civil War. John Lewis, standing firm at the front of the column, had his skull fractured by a billy club.[75]

Official violence and racism were less dramatic in Watts than in Selma, but they were not unknown, and even the worst of the accusations were readily believed by local residents. It was said in the black community that in one of the police substations there was a picture of Eleanor Roosevelt inscribed with the words "nigger lover." Officers were said to call their billy clubs "nigger knockers" and to begin each night shift with a ritualized invocation to mayhem: "LSMFT," short for "Let's shoot a motherfucker tonight."[76]

The resulting bitterness and rage fueled the events of that August. For many in Watts, throwing rocks or lighting fires was closer to sensible revenge than senseless riot. When the trouble broke out, one young man stuck to the old ideals of service and community and headed to an emergency meeting of a local civic improvement group. But along the way, surrounded by looters, he surrendered to a mix of grievance and assertion. Taking something from the white merchants who had gouged the locals seemed to be replacing one kind of thievery with another, he said, capturing the mood that underlay Watts, and much that was to happen across the country in the years ahead. "Going into a store," he said, "was uplifting yourself."[77]

––––––––

Martin Luther King Jr. arrived the day the curfew was lifted. Brown threw up the walls of regionalism. "I prefer that we handle this ourselves," the governor said. "I'm not criticizing Dr. King. I think he's a great man, but I don't think this is the time for any civil rights demonstrations. Even legal demonstrations could be misunderstood at this time."

King came anyway and pled his case for peace in a series of meetings: the governor, the mayor, the police chief. The reception varied. The session with Brown went well. The governor had already announced that he was interested in the "underlying" as well as the "immediate" causes of the riot, phrasing that obviously signaled a willingness to investigate the poverty and despair felt so deeply in Watts. King thought Brown's response had been "marvelous." But Yorty and Parker were a different story. When King met with Parker, Parker flew into a tirade about "black agitators." The conversation left King pessimistic. "I just felt that [Yorty and Parker] are absolutely insensitive to the problem and the need to really cure the situation," King told President Johnson later. Watts had put the Nobel laureate in an apocalyptic frame of mind. If nothing were done to redress the deeper grievances of the ghetto, King said, he feared a "full-scale race war."[78]

From the other side of the great social divide, whites in California were thinking equally cataclysmic thoughts. A month after the riots, the governor attended a cocktail party at a suburb in the northern part of the state, far from Watts, and heard a litany of fear. One guest boasted of a new Smith

& Wesson. Another noted that her pistol was small enough to fit in her purse. A third said that rioters should be shot.[79]

Brown knew he could not belittle such dread, but, privately, he was also hoping for reconciliation, or at least understanding. "The white backlash is understandably very severe and a governor must in every utterance he makes maintain the rule of law," he wrote to the columnist Drew Pearson. "On the other hand, I have a deep and, I hope, understanding sympathy for the Negro and would rather not be reelected governor than to let them think some of the white people do not appreciate the terrible problems of poverty and prejudice."[80]

Brown appointed a blue-ribbon commission to examine the causes of the riots, promising that it would not merely assess blame but also recommend steps to avoid a repetition. It was a good beginning, but Brown picked as the panel's chairman a former director of the Central Intelligence Agency named John McCone. He proved a poor choice, even if merely for cosmetic reasons. A political conservative, McCone lacked credibility with the black community, where the reputation of the panel soon dipped so low that some people refused to cooperate.[81]

The panel had two black members—a judge and a minister—but from Watts they looked like establishment figures, their color trumped by class. That was a thread running through the whole experience of Watts. After the riots, the governor's civil rights aide, Bill Becker, held a series of meetings with local residents and came away struck by "an almost universal *bitterness* toward the 'establishment,' both white and Negro." In the wrong way and for the wrong reasons, Parker was right when he said that in Watts, black leaders couldn't lead. They knew it too. The national leadership of the Civil Rights movement consisted mostly of southerners, often men who grew up in positions of prestige or influence in the black community. Nobody, said James Farmer of the Congress of Racial Equality, had any roots in Watts. Even Martin Luther King Jr. held little sway. When Dick Gregory tried to calm rioters during some of the worst violence, someone in the crowd shouted back at him, "We don't want Martin Luther King down here either." When King finally visited, he was openly mocked, his most famous moment of oratory turned to ridicule. "I had a dream, I had a dream," one man shouted, "hell, we don't need no damn dreams. We want jobs."[82]

When the McCone Commission issued its report in December, after three months of hearings, doubters were not reassured. Recognizing that poverty underlay much of the trouble, the panel recommended job training and better schools in inner cities. And there was even a veiled suggestion that Los Angeles police should build a better relationship with the residents of Watts, rather than merely arrest them. "Law enforcement agencies," the commission wrote, should "place greater emphasis on their responsibilities for crime prevention" and "institute improved means for handling citizen complaints and community relationships."[83] But there seemed to be only a glancing treatment of the racism that fomented so much of the anger in Watts, and there was no criticism at all of Parker or Yorty, men blamed by many black Californians for allowing an atmosphere of fear, anger, and bigotry to permeate much of Los Angeles.

More important, almost nothing changed in the lives of Watts residents. More than a quarter century later, when a jury acquitted four police officers in the videotaped beating of black motorist Rodney King, the ensuing riots were touched off at the intersection of Florence and Dalton, an intersection well within the curfew area of 1965 and only four miles from the spot where the first bottle was thrown after Marquette Frye was arrested.

More than any other single event, the Watts riot took the bloom off California. That spring and summer the state had still been celebrated as the acme of modern productivity and achievement. One story asked if California was both the "biggest and richest" of the states.[84] The *New Republic* praised the "uncommon sophistication" of California's government.[85] Less than a month before the rioting broke out, *Newsweek* featured a big story on the San Francisco Bay Area's plan for a new system of commuter trains, called BART, for Bay Area Rapid Transit. Touted as "Transit for Tomorrow," BART glistened with proof that California held the future. The cars would be "sleek" and "quiet," the result of wondrous new materials that would dampen shock and noise. Trains would be controlled by "electronic computers," devices so extraordinary that BART managers planned to place them behind picture windows at their Oakland headquarters so that passersby might gawk at the "flashing lights and spinning tape reels." The result would be the "most advanced rapid transit system in the world."[86]

In the wake of Watts, people suddenly saw a different image of California: armed soldiers patrolling in Jeeps through the streets of a major American city. "In the City of Angels last week," one writer said, "a 50-square-mile piece of the American dream had turned . . . into a nightmare."[87] There was no hesitancy in suggesting that Watts hinted at bigger troubles for the state. *U.S. News and World Report* began a long piece with a eulogy for the old California ecstasy:

> The massive outburst of rioting by Negroes here underscores this point: The easy life is coming to an end in the country's third-largest city.
>
> After 25 years of haphazard growth and unprecedented prosperity, Los Angeles now faces the same tough economic and social problems that confronted older cities years ago.

The writer cited a string of woes: rising crime, a sluggish economy, sprawl that transformed life into ceaseless traffic jams. California had once been celebrated in the national press for its great accomplishments. Now the state's biggest city was derided as a place with "king-size troubles."[88]

It was a pivot point for the state. The smoke from Watts blocked out the California sunshine, and it never shone quite so brightly again.

————

The governor had woes to equal those of his state. As was the case with the Berkeley protests the year before, what mattered to the voters was not so much the details of Brown's performance as the basic fact of the calamity. It had happened on his watch, so it was his responsibility. Three months after the riots, pollsters found that more than half the public disapproved of the governor. Some voters were creative in their disdain. One man, apparently convinced that liberal coddling of blacks had led to the trouble, wrote to Brown to say that he had sent $1 to the NAACP so Brown could consider himself an "honorary Negro."[89]

Compared with other politicians, the governor's popularity was abysmal. Among the California officials more popular than Brown were George Murphy, the song-and-dance man turned senator whom the governor thought a boob; Jesse Unruh, the assembly speaker and hated rival in Sacramento; Sam Yorty, the Los Angeles mayor who had fled his city as the riots worsened; even Glenn Anderson, the lieutenant governor widely thought to have botched the call-up of the National Guard. Brown was less acclaimed than a group of men he viewed as a rogue's gallery of idiots and scoundrels.[90]

The governor's waning popularity was ironic, for he had handled Watts as well as possible, given the sad accidents of timing and geography. Out of state, Brown was technically out of power too, reduced from governing to advising. Yet his advice was both sound and effective. Anderson formally called out the Guard only after arriving in Los Angeles and hearing from Champion that Brown wanted soldiers in the streets. Probably Anderson would have acted anyway, but Brown's counsel undoubtedly helped. The curfew, which Brown advocated earlier and more forcefully than anyone else, helped significantly to calm the streets.[91] Once he returned, Brown had the common decency to go to Watts and talk to people, local resident and law enforcer alike. It was symbolism, to be sure, but it was the right kind of symbolism at the right time. From start to finish, the governor's natural impulses were dead-on: Use the force needed to restore order quickly, get people off the streets to limit violence, and, as soon as possible, go to the area to show the flag of honest concern.

There was an irony involved there too. Brown's physical distance from the events was a help, not a hindrance. His advice was sound because his instincts were right, but it was steady because he was too far away to get conflicting counsel. Too often in Brown's career, a second phone call led him to countermand his previous decision. A determination to let Caryl Chessman be executed gave way to a plea for mercy. A conviction that the Free Speech Movement protesters should be left in Sproul Hall was overwhelmed by a policeman's arguments that arrests were in order.

Had Brown been in California during Watts, he would have heard opinions that were just as much in opposition. He would have spoken to Los Angeles officials who wanted the National Guard, but he also would have heard the counsel of several junior gubernatorial staff members who wondered if soldiers were really needed. Filled with good liberals, the governor's staff included an element that was distrustful of Parker, the bombastic Los Angeles police chief. When Parker asked that the Guard be activated, some of those aides told Anderson that the chief might be exaggerating things, that perhaps the lieutenant governor should wait and go to Los Angeles and see for himself. If Brown had been there, he would have heard the same advice.

As it was, physical distance was the governor's shield. At the height of the crisis, he was flying halfway around the world and thus virtually out of touch. His primary sources of information were the periodic phone calls to Champion and the New York briefing from the White House aides, who had been in touch with Champion and relied on his assessments. This time nobody could call Brown back with a different opinion, and thus he was saved from one of the characteristic failures of his career—agreeing with the last person to whom he spoke.

Yet none of that mattered as the governor tried to regain his footing after Watts. Once, California had led the nation into the sunny postwar optimism of the 1950s. Now, in less than twelve months, it had set the tone for the turbulence of the sixties. If the Free Speech Movement launched the era of student protest, Watts opened another chapter: massive urban riots fueled by racial injustice, bitterness, and despair. The pattern would repeat with equal ferocity in Newark and Detroit just two years later. As was so often the case, California had been America's proving ground of the future.

For Brown, there was a special misery. All that he had once fought for was coming down around him. He had built universities; now the campuses were hotbeds of rebellion. He had signed civil rights laws; now black California was rising up in rage. He had counseled justice and inclusion; now whites were buying pistols and threatening vigilantism. Brown's second term, launched with an affirming victory, was ending with a horrifying thud. Worst of all—for a working politician—it was only weeks from the start of the next campaign.

16   TIRED OLD GOVERNOR

ONLY DAYS BEFORE WATTS EXPLODED, Pat Brown summoned his top lieutenants to a little-noticed meeting at the Governor's Mansion. It was a powerful and well-connected group. Perhaps closest to the governor was Tom Lynch, his old friend and confidant from youthful romps at Yosemite, later his deputy in the district attorney's office, now the attorney general of the state of California. Among others, there was also Hale Champion, Brown's top aide as governor; Don Bradley, the architect of the victory over Richard Nixon; Gene Wyman, a Los Angeles lawyer with a Midas touch at fund-raising; Alan Cranston, the politically ambitious state controller and a favorite of the left; and Warren Christopher, the brilliant and self-disciplined jack-of-all-trades helper to the administration. They were some of the men who had helped Brown through his first two terms as governor. Now they hoped to devise a strategy for winning a third.[1]

That he intended to run again was a foregone conclusion. Like all performers, politicians fear the day the cheering stops, and Brown was no exception. Being governor, he said once, was "like being married to a beautiful shrew." It could be unpleasant during the day—"You take all the shit," is the way he phrased it—"but then you go out at night and everybody just stands up and looks at what you've got on your arm and thinks you're the greatest guy in the world. And you feel as if you are."[2]

He could not be forced to relinquish such adulation, for California had no limit on the service of its chief executives. Earl Warren had been elected three times, a record Brown yearned to equal, and in any event another turn as governor would keep his career alive. Reelected, he might someday be appointed attorney general of the United States or a Supreme Court justice. If the stars aligned just right, perhaps he could even run for president.

So almost from the day he came up the loser in the competition to be Lyndon Johnson's running mate, Brown turned his attention toward a third term. Denied promotion to a national job, he would seek to keep his state one. Two days after Johnson's landslide victory over Barry Goldwater, the president and Brown talked on the phone, and the governor mentioned nonchalantly that he would run again.[3]

The serious planning did not start, however, until the hot August Monday when Brown met with Lynch and the others. Optimism prevailed in one sense. Less than a year had passed since Johnson routed Goldwater by portraying the Republican as a dangerous extremist, and the strategy now seemed as replicable for Brown as it had been effective for Johnson. California was home to some of the most conservative Republicans in the country—the crusading editor of the *Santa Barbara News-Press* had won the Pulitzer Prize for exposing the local strength of the John Birch Society—and thus the state offered tempting targets for Democratic moderates warning of right-wing kooks.

But worries abounded too. Debating fundamental strategy, the Brown team differed as to whether, after eight years in office, the governor should run on his record or offer a new agenda, should boast of what he had done or what he would do. No resolution could be reached. They were deeply concerned about the feud between Brown and his fellow Democrat, assembly speaker Jess Unruh, although ultimately other Democratic rifts would prove more debilitating in the months to come. There was even a sense around the table that Brown needed to shore up support among poor, urban white voters, which was worrisome simply because it was a group that should already have been firmly in the governor's grasp.[4]

By chance, another meeting in Sacramento that day offered a different kind of insight into the upcoming governor's race. At the Hotel El Dorado a thousand people packed the ballroom, and hundreds more were turned away. They were there to hear a talk about politics, but the speaker had never held office, never even run for anything. Ronald Reagan, an aging actor transformed into a conservative star by a famous speech for Barry Goldwater's presidential campaign, was on a statewide tour to gauge the public mood and see if he should seek the governorship the following year.

Reagan offered a stern conservative philosophy—he warned of ominous "aerial surveys" used by the government to control farmers' planting—but mostly he proved himself a talker's talker, charming and funny and not as harsh as Goldwater. Somebody asked if he regarded a career in Hollywood as adequate training to lead the state, and he joked it away—"I don't know, I never played a governor"—before turning serious and painting himself as the victim of a snobbish attack. No group, he said, "should be relegated to second-class citizenship by reason of their occupation."[5]

The polished delivery drew attention from the real significance of the night, which was not the speaker but the audience. The Brown team should have sensed trouble, for the crowded hall and the disappointed latecomers heading home early proved that Reagan's celebrity was an advantage rather than a handicap. His fame did not cause Californians to ridicule his big ambitions. It brought them out on a Monday night to listen to a political speech.

———

Reagan was neither new to the political scene nor an experienced politician. In his younger days he was a liberal. He idolized Franklin Roosevelt, campaigned for Harry Truman, and joined a starry-eyed group called the United World Federalists. Already a famous movie star, he campaigned for Helen Gahagan Douglas when she ran for the Senate against Richard Nixon in 1950, siding with the congresswoman even as Nixon Red-baited her mercilessly.[6]

Then, in the early 1950s, Reagan began a long march rightward, an ideological journey aided by ties both personal and professional. Divorced from his first wife, the actress Jane Wyman, he married Nancy Davis, a conservative herself and the daughter of a wealthy and conservative doctor from the Midwest. At the same time, Reagan's star quality was giving way to advancing age, so he signed on as a spokesman for General Electric. He hosted the company's weekly television show, but also traveled the country to speak at GE plants, an induction to corporate culture that nurtured a growing personal conservatism. He supported Dwight Eisenhower over Adlai Stevenson and in 1960 offered public testimony to his conversion by joining Democrats for Nixon. Two years later, when Nixon ran for governor against Brown, Reagan finally changed his registration and formally became a Republican. In the public mind he was sufficiently identified with the GOP that at Brown's second inaugural Steve Allen could joke that had Nixon won, the crowd would be listening to Ronald Reagan.

True conservative renown came to Reagan in 1964, when he agreed to record a speech on behalf of Goldwater's faltering presidential campaign. Shown on television, Reagan's eloquent call to anti-Communism and the free market excited the Republican faithful and sparked a burst of donations to the campaign. Almost overnight Reagan and Goldwater seesawed in the eyes of political strategists—Reagan rising as Goldwater fell—and the actor was hailed as the new conservative flag-bearer.

Lack of experience did not dissuade either the would-be candidate or his backers. He spent 1965 probing public sentiment—the task that took him to Sacramento on the day Brown met with advisers—and then, a few days after New Year's 1966, officially declared that he was running for governor. Reagan staked out conservative ground from the start, refusing to reject the John Birch Society as Nixon had done four years earlier. If someone chose to support his campaign, Reagan said, he would accept, no matter what group they might associate with. On economics, he offered standard conservative fare: government was too big and taxes too high. He saved his sharpest rhetoric for the emotional issues that would prove his best weapon. At night city streets had become "jungle paths," a racially laden reference to Watts that no one could possibly misconstrue. In Berkeley a great university had been "brought to its knees by a noisy, dissident minority," the mob's "neurotic vulgarities" met only with "vacillation and weakness."[7]

In the office of the alleged vacillator, Reagan caused little trepidation. Brown's previous opponents had been a former majority leader of the U.S. Senate and a former vice president. In contrast, an inexperienced actor hardly seemed worrisome. Somebody once sent a magazine clipping about Reagan to Jack Burby, Brown's press secretary. In a moment he must later have rued, Burby scrawled across the bottom, " 'Bring him on' is our motto."[8]

———

A month after Reagan's announcement, Brown answered with his own. He flew almost the length of the state for a series of press conferences declaring that he wanted another term as governor. President Johnson, he noted, had declared the intention to create a Great Society. "We call that same vision California," he said.[9]

Toward the end of the day, there was a problem. Brown was scheduled to stop in Santa Barbara, and local Democratic leaders had mustered crowds to greet him. But as the plane approached the airport the pilot announced that he could not land: The runway was too short for the big DC-7 the campaign had rented. They circled for ten minutes but could think of no alternative. Finally the plane banked eastward and headed for the next stop, in Fresno, leaving behind the governor's loyal supporters, disappointed and abandoned.[10]

The logistical flub was a bad omen, for California Democrats were starting the campaign year plagued with bitter divisions. For most of his career Brown had enjoyed the flexible moderate's great advantage in politics, unifying disparate forces into a working coalition, pleasing no group entirely but all of them enough. To activists, he was a liberal who could win. To blue-collar workers, he was a bread-and-butter politician. To blacks, he was a champion of civil rights legislation. To the moderate establishment, he was a former district attorney and attorney general, a reliable fellow. But as he headed into the 1966 campaign the old asset turned to a curse, and Brown began to experience not the strength of political moderation but its weakness: He was under attack from all sides.

On the left, trouble had been raging for months. Throughout 1965 the Johnson administration escalated the war in Vietnam. The campus at Berkeley, already riled up by the Free Speech Movement, was the site of early antiwar protests, their intensity increasing along with the war. By summer opposition to the war was often a defining point of pride for American liberals, and it was a cause taken up eagerly by the head of the California Democratic Council, a newspaper publisher from San Diego County named Si Casady.

Brown had picked Casady to head the CDC, but Casady began to attack the Johnson administration's Vietnam policies publicly, his objections growing more strident with time. Privately, Brown shared Casady's doubts about the war's effectiveness. Through back channels the governor told LBJ that Vietnam was a tightening noose. White House aide Joe Califano talked to Brown, then summed up the governor's view succinctly: "Believes we should get out as fast as we can with some honor."[11] But publicly Brown was the loyal Democratic foot soldier, supporting the president, and he expected Casady to do the same.

Convinced as always that personal interaction could solve problems, the governor tried to bring Casady into line by urging him to visit Washington and meet with Johnson administration officials. The plan didn't work. Casady described a briefing at the State Department as a "3-hour bull session" and said the only thing of value provided by the trip was a brief booklet explaining the administration's policy. To save time and money, he said, the material could have been mailed to him.[12]

By the time Brown officially announced his reelection campaign, he was openly declaring that Casady should resign as president of the CDC. Liberals were enraged. Letters poured in to the governor's office from people declaring they would not vote for Brown because of his treatment of the CDC chief. One came from Casady's wife, Virginia, who insisted she was writing without her husband's knowledge. Brown wrote back, as always trying to preserve both his personal relationships and his political career:

> I differ with Si on Viet Nam, but do not quarrel with his right to speak as he has. I quarrel with the words he used and the accusations he has made against the president, the congress and myself. I think he is still my friend, and I am his, but I don't want him as president of an organization that I worked so hard to build. I think that his words, not his beliefs, make more difficult the achievement of objectives that we both desire.[13]

The wounds would not heal. Vietnam would eventually end Lyndon Johnson's career, destroy Democratic hopes of holding the White House, and divide the American left for years to come, but its power as a political issue went on display first in California. At the CDC convention in February Casady was forced out as president by moderates loyal to the governor, but Brown's brief victory hardly offered the picture of unity one hopes to present at the start of a tough campaign. When the governor spoke to the organization whose hero he once had been, two hundred delegates rose and walked out in protest.[14]

———

The liberal catcalls at the CDC convention barely died away before Brown faced another Democratic insurgency, this one on his right. In early March, Sam Yorty, the acerbic mayor of Los Angeles, announced that he would challenge Brown for the Democratic nomination for governor.

Like so many Californians, Yorty was from somewhere else.[15] Born in Nebraska in 1909, he caught a train west at the age of eighteen to seek his fortune in Los Angeles. He got a job as a salesman in a clothing store, but from the beginning politics drew his eye. A bantam of a man, he liked to boast about his thick neck and strong voice, and he took to public speaking with zest, first as a volunteer on behalf of others and then for himself.

"I would rather give a speech than eat," he once said. He was not an easy man to get along with: It was sometimes said that Yorty was the proof that Will Rogers did not meet everybody.[16]

Elected to the state assembly in 1936, Yorty began his career as a liberal, if not a left-wing radical, but moved slowly rightward, inspired at first by extravagant fears about Japanese spies and Communists and later by political expediency. He was out of office for a time, but in 1950 was elected to Congress, where he served two terms in the House before losing a bid to move up to the Senate. By 1960 he had broken so completely with his liberal roots that, although still a Democrat in name, he endorsed Richard Nixon over John Kennedy.

In 1961 he ran for mayor of Los Angeles, portraying himself as a rebel against a "downtown machine" that did not really exist. He won and then four years later won a second term by routing Jimmy Roosevelt, son of the former president. Along the way he became the champion of the white Los Angeles working class, partly by defending the police unquestioningly during and after the Watts riot. By 1966 liberals regarded Yorty at best as an apostate, at worst as a stalking horse for Republicans. Brown was convinced that Yorty's campaign was secretly funded by the GOP as a way to split the Democrats.[17]

The rivalry between the governor and the Los Angeles mayor was an open secret. Both personally and politically, Yorty thrived on conflict with more liberal Democrats, and he feuded with Brown constantly and publicly. Once, they appeared together to dedicate a new building in Los Angeles's Little Tokyo section. At one point in the ceremony a girl appeared with a samurai sword. "Don't give that knife to Yorty," Brown quipped.[18]

———

In retirement, Brown would say that Yorty was one of only two people he truly despised. The other was Jess Unruh.[19] By 1966 the relationship with Unruh, always strained, had ruptured completely. Unruh had been ambitious his whole life—the trait had pulled him up from dirt-poor childhood to political legend—and he had no intention of tempering his drive. Once, out on the town in Sacramento, another legislator mused idly that he might seek the state's top office. What, he asked, would Unruh like to be when he was governor? "President," Unruh answered.[20]

But the intermediate step for the speaker was to become California governor, and he dearly wanted to run in 1966. Brown had had his chance, and now Unruh was the rightful heir. What was more, he claimed to have the governor's word. The two men had talked, Unruh said, and Brown promised to stand aside. Even if true, it was a promise not worth the paper it wasn't written on. Brown did not intend to quit, not for anyone, but most emphatically not for Unruh. The speaker had been "such a mean bastard," as the governor remembered later, that Brown was determined to block his rise.[21]

Even if Brown had stayed out of the race, Unruh might have lost the primary. A poll put him fourth in the Democratic field.[22] But that was of little moment to the speaker. He wanted to run, and he thought himself the victim of a double-cross. Brown said he would stay out, then jumped in. Unruh, who had a loyal following among many Democratic legislators, grew even more antagonistic toward Brown, and the governor headed into battle more isolated than ever.

———

By 1966 the buoyant California mood that Brown once knew was fading fast. The Vietnam War kindled tensions everywhere. Race relations had exploded. College students had rebelled. And increasingly there was even a hint that Californians were losing their mania for growth, until then perhaps the state's most consistent characteristic.

When Brown became governor, few people questioned the need for more dams, more roads, more schools. Almost without exception, development was seen as the way of the future, in California and across the country. Then in 1962, as Brown was winning a second term, Rachel Carson published *Silent Spring,* a book that changed the world by helping to launch the modern environmental movement. Three years later, as Brown was gearing up to run for a third term, a Humboldt State College professor named Raymond Dasmann published *The Destruction of California,* a book that echoed Carson's environmentalism but tied the issue specifically to the state.

Like Brown, Dasmann was a San Francisco boy, but after that their lives diverged. Dasmann went into the army during World War II, met and married a local girl while stationed in Australia, then took a Ph.D. in wildlife biology from the University of California, where he studied deer populations. He went to Africa for a time to study wild game, but by the mid-1960s he was teaching at Humboldt State, along California's northern coast. In time he became an icon of the environmental movement, settling in the liberal college town of Santa Cruz and building his own vacation cabin in the Sierra Nevada.[23]

Dasmann was no absolutist. He objected to the title of his own book—imposed on him by the publisher—because he thought it too negative. And he tempered his message with a likable candor. He wrote that people should cut down fewer trees but admitted that he would "howl loudly" if his book could not be published for lack of paper.[24]

But he left little doubt that he found California's apparent future a frightening prospect. Since his ten-year-old daughter was born, Dasmann noted in the book, California's population had grown by six million people. The state accommodated them, brought them water and electricity and roads and schools, but now the booming population threatened the very qualities that drew people westward. For $5.95, readers got a shot across the bow of California progress:

What is the threat to California, and from whom does it stem? . . . The enemies are those who have looked so long into the blast furnaces of civilization that they can no longer appreciate a sunset—those to whom growth is progress and progress is good, regardless of its direction—those to whom money is the single standard against which all else must be measured. California has been hacked and battered by the forces of ignorance and greed, and is today being forced in a direction that few would want to travel if they could see what lay ahead.[25]

Dasmann never mentioned Brown by name, and there was much on which the two men would have agreed, but no careful reader could miss the political implications of the author's complaints. Brown liked to boast that the state was building "a 500-mile artificial river" to carry water to the people who needed it. Dasmann found that idea crazy. "We insist that water must be shipped to the places where people and industry have located," he wrote. "We could equally well insist that people and industry should locate in the areas where water is available." And he was quick to lay blame at political feet: "Why encourage further industrial and population growth in Southern California through shipping that water over hundreds of miles? The only answer to this is political. Southern California has the votes."[26]

The true significance of Dasmann's book, however, lay not in its contents but in its reception. It did well, at least for a book of its type, and drew attention to the idea that California had as many problems as possibilities.

Newsweek devoted a story to the book, headlined "Overcrowd." Dasmann, the magazine said, had caught the front edge of a wave. With his book, California's "self-congratulations turned to agonizing criticism."[27] Californians had once praised the growth Brown so loved. Now they read books saying it was all a big mistake.

———

Six weeks after opening his campaign, Brown paused for a quick trip to Washington, D.C. He gabbed about the campaign with President Johnson and tried to convince the national press corps that he had momentum, but the most revealing moments touched on policy rather than politics. On Capitol Hill, Brown endorsed a package of bills to help farmworkers, including a proposed law to recognize their collective bargaining rights and the creation of a federal minimum wage for agriculture.[28] It sounded good, but in fact Brown's stance was one more reflection of an administration grown weary, for he was asking the federal government to do things he had failed to do at home.

Brown took office determined to help California's farmworkers, a group much in need of aid.[29] Descended from Spanish land grants and the glory days of the Southern Pacific Railroad, which owned huge portions of the state, California's agricultural industry became not only the most productive in the world but also one of the most centralized. In 1959, the year Brown became governor, 6 percent of California farms accounted for 75 percent of the state's agricultural acreage.[30] Such vast operations required not a hardy farm family but large numbers of hired workers. For decades the backbone of the agricultural labor force had been California newcomers, who enjoyed few options and worked for penurious wages. Successive waves of immigrants were used—Chinese, Japanese, Mexican, and Filipino—and then during the Dust Bowl, farmers turned to the internal American migrants portrayed by John Steinbeck in *The Grapes of Wrath*. During World War II, with much of the domestic labor force in the military and potential Japanese American workers locked away in prison camps, farmers convinced Congress to begin a formal program for temporarily importing workers from Mexico, who were known as braceros. The bracero program, continued long after the war emergency passed, became a target for labor unions and Latino groups, who argued persuasively that it flooded the labor market, depressing the natural economic demand for better wages and improved living conditions.

In his early years as governor Brown sided with the liberals. Wielding the state's regulatory power, Brown appointees made it harder for employers to replace striking American farmhands with braceros, which gave the native workers a better hand at bargaining. More important, in his first legislative session as governor, Brown supported a state minimum wage for agriculture, a milestone proposal.

But the minimum wage bill lost badly, and in the years that followed Brown rarely challenged California agriculture. By his second term he abandoned his support for a state minimum wage, instead favoring the federal bill he endorsed in Washington. When the bracero program grew too unpopular to be continued, Brown recommended a phase-out rather than simple repeal.[31] Never did the governor seriously push for a state law recognizing the collective bargaining rights of farmworkers, who were excluded from the provisions of the National Labor Relations Act.[32]

By the time Brown traveled to Washington in spring 1966, California agriculture was ready to present him with a serious dilemma. Led by a dynamic young organizer named César Chávez, grape pickers in the San Joaquin Valley town of Delano were engaged in a historic strike to seek recognition of a farmworkers' union. Three days after Brown appeared on Capitol Hill, the strikers began a 250-mile march to Sacramento to publicize their struggle, encourage consumers to boycott grapes, and call for a state law recognizing collective bargaining rights. They planned to arrive on the steps of the Capitol on Easter Sunday, and they were demanding a meeting with the governor.

Brown's support of big agriculture had not gone unnoticed. The workers saw him as their enemy. He was known to be a personal friend of the Di Giorgio family, whose farming operation was one of those being struck and which was seen by Chávez as a particularly difficult, even dishonest foe. Along the route of the march, in night camps, the farmworkers entertained themselves with a set-piece skit that reflected their anger about Brown—and their hopes that he might yet come to their aid. At first, a man playing the governor was portrayed as the Di Giorgios' hapless puppet, hauled onto the stage so that he might do the farmers' bidding. But then, in midskit, the Brown character switched sides and by the end of the piece was shouting out his support for the strike—"Huelga! Huelga!"—as a Di Giorgio character dragged him away.[33]

Brown eventually took some steps to help the union. The Di Giorgio grape ranch staged a vote to see if the workers wanted representation, but the rules were set to benefit the Teamsters, who were competing with

Chávez and who were widely seen as friendly to the farmers. Pressured by the Mexican American community and eager to hold his traditional Hispanic support, Brown appointed an arbitrator who recommended and then oversaw a second vote, this one conducted under fair conditions. Chávez won and hammered out a contract with Di Giorgio.[34]

But as the workers marched toward the Capitol, that was in the future. In the meantime Brown was wary of a high-profile Easter Sunday meeting. Politically, he had no desire to antagonize either the workers or the farmers in the midst of a campaign. And personally, he was scheduled to spend Easter with his family in Palm Springs. Frank Sinatra, still a devoted Democrat, had loaned the Browns the use of his vacation home, and the governor was looking forward to the trip. He had missed much family life in his career and decided that on this occasion he would stand his ground. "By golly I wasn't going to leave my family on Easter," he remembered later. "I was going to church with them." So he hedged. Brown sent word to the marchers that he would meet with their leaders Saturday or Monday but not on Easter.[35]

Chávez said no. The meeting should be held on Sunday, the final day of the march, when a big rally was planned, or not at all. If the governor tried to approach the column on another day, the marchers would walk past, Chávez declared.[36] The reality was that Chávez had no need of a meeting with the governor. The most important goal of the march was to generate publicity for the strike and its accompanying grape boycott, and the marchers were already front-page news. Whether Brown showed or not, Chavez had succeeded. Perhaps that is why at the rally, the union leader was magnanimous about the governor's absence. "We are not mad," he said. "But I guess we had wanted him so much to be here that we are very saddened."[37]

As Chávez spoke on the steps of the Capitol, the governor was four hundred miles to the south, in Palm Springs. He attended Easter mass, then watched his grandchildren hunt for Easter eggs on Sinatra's lawn.[38]

———

If Brown paused to take stock of his personal life, he must have felt content. He was days from his sixty-first birthday, a prime age for a man in high office. He was in good health, although fighting a paunch as always. Avuncular in both attitude and appearance, his face was so round and pleasant-looking and his dark glasses so visibly pronounced that he was invariably described in newspaper profiles as "owlish."

The previous fall he and Bernice had celebrated their thirty-fifth wedding anniversary, a landmark for a marriage that seemed to work despite the obvious differences of the partners. Politics often takes its toll on marriages, and in a union that would eventually last sixty-six years anything is possible, but if Pat philandered, there is no evidence of it.

Their children were not only grown but started on the trajectories of their own lives. All three daughters were married and had children, eight gubernatorial grandchildren in all. Jerry had finished law school at Yale, passed the bar on his second try, and completed a clerkship for Mathew Tobriner, the man who years before convinced Pat to become a Democrat and who was now, thanks to Pat's appointment, a justice of the California supreme court. After the clerkship Jerry took a job with a prestigious firm in Los Angeles, a move that some of his friends saw as evidence of an early interest in politics.[39]

Pat's mother, Ida, was still alive and still the intellectually curious woman who had taken her sons to brainy lectures in San Francisco decades earlier. On a visit, her granddaughter Kathleen Brown once found volumes of Freud and Marx and the Bible, all lying open and obviously in the midst of a comparative inspection. "There's a connection here," the old woman said. Pat phoned her often, and she loved her frequent trips to see him in Sacramento. She lived alone in a small walk-up apartment near Golden Gate Park in San Francisco, having sold the flats where her children grew up. Independent by nature, she liked to fend for herself. One of the governor's aides realized at one point that Ida should be signed up for Social Security, which had not existed when she was young. Thinking they would handle the chore for her, staff members checked the records but found that she had already gone down to the San Francisco office and completed the necessary forms. The year of the race against Reagan, Ida was eighty-eight, or as Pat liked to say, the same age as the Governor's Mansion but in better shape. She had a sense of humor about her advancing years. For one of her mother-in-law's birthday celebrations, Bernice suggested chartering a bus to bring her and her friends to the mansion for a dinner party. Pat loved the idea and called to suggest it. His mother replied that he had the wrong mode of transportation in mind. For her friends, she said, they would need a fleet of ambulances.[40]

———

Back on the campaign trail after his Palm Springs vacation, Brown found the governor's race more labyrinthine than ever. Two days after Brown dashed off a note thanking Sinatra for the loan of his house, a new poll suggested conflicting results in prospective general election races. The governor led Reagan, albeit narrowly, but was now a shocking fifteen points behind the other major Republican candidate, former San Francisco Mayor George Christopher. The basic dynamic was not new—earlier polls had shown Brown beating Reagan but losing to Christopher—but the size of the gap by which Brown trailed Christopher had almost doubled, and was now so large that it seemed nearly inerasable. Anyone contemplating the pollsters' unforgiving numbers would have concluded that if Christopher emerged as the Republican nominee, the governor's hopes for a third term were doomed. Against Reagan, Brown at least stood a fighting chance.[41]

Reagan led Christopher for the Republican nomination, as he had from the beginning of the race. But his lead had shrunk, and almost a fifth of GOP voters remained undecided. If Reagan faltered in the closing weeks— always a possibility with an untested candidate—Christopher could storm back to take the nomination.[42]

So the governor, already feuding with anti-Vietnam activists on his left and fighting Yorty to his right, decided to meddle in a campaign in which he was not even a candidate, the Republican primary. Secretly, he approved a plan aimed at derailing Christopher's campaign. Brown's old friend and campaign operative, Harry Lerner, launched an operation to dig out the records of a 1940 case in which Christopher, who then owned a dairy, had been convicted of violating milk-pricing laws. Lerner fed the information to Drew Pearson, the Washington columnist who had helped Brown often in the past.[43]

Christopher's conviction was almost to his credit. New to the business and struggling to gain a toehold against larger and more established dairies, he had undercut an anticompetitive price floor and thus probably did consumers a favor. The case certainly involved no moral failings, and by 1966 the events were more than a quarter century old. The same information had been used against him before, without success.[44] But the Christopher campaign blundered badly, trying to suppress the column Pearson wrote and thereby inadvertently publicizing its existence. Several papers recognized the story as a Democratic plant and refused to run it, but finally it saw print, and the news was out.[45] Christopher sank well behind Reagan in the polls, but ironically the real loser was Brown. Word soon leaked that his campaign was responsible for passing the information to Pearson, tarnishing the governor as a conniver, a reputation he had always managed to avoid. Before the whole incident Brown trailed Christopher but at least led Reagan. After it the governor trailed both men.[46]

The June primary results revealed much about the race. Reagan more than doubled Christopher's vote total, laying to rest permanently any thoughts that an actor could not be a serious candidate. Against Brown, Yorty took almost 40 percent of the Democratic vote and actually beat the governor in five counties.[47] For Brown, it was far too weak a showing, and it renewed his ever-present self-doubts. In a note to Hubert Humphrey a few days later he tried to sound optimistic—"I was a little bit low right after the primaries, but my spirits have somewhat escalated"—before admitting with candor that the basic structure of the race was still a problem: "We haven't solved it yet."[48]

Brown knew the key to the general election race would be the Yorty voters, the conservative Democrats who had deserted him in the primary, and he doubted he could win them back. After the voting, he took advantage of the lull in campaigning and escaped to Mexico for a few days of relaxation and reflection. One day he and George Fleharty, an old partner on the hustings and one of the leaders of Brown's Northern California campaign, went out in a little boat to do some fishing. The governor said he wanted to take Fleharty into his confidence. It had been a mistake to run for a third term, he said, but it was too late to get out now. He would keep fighting— somebody needed to make a good public effort to advance the Democratic platform with verve—but he had no illusions about the outcome. He expected to lose.[49]

———

Brown and Reagan both followed the primary with some careful political maneuvering, trying to befriend Christopher, the man one of them had just attacked and the other had just defeated. Both nominees met with Christopher to seek his endorsement. In Brown's case, the idea was that in return for Christopher's backing, the governor would criticize the Pearson column that had publicized Christopher's milk conviction—the very story that had been planted by Brown's campaign. Pearson, loyal friend to the core, told associates that he did not mind.[50] But Christopher, deeply wounded by the bloodshed of the primary, was wary of both men. Eventually he announced his support for all the Republican ticket, which obviously included Reagan, although it was at best a cold embrace.[51]

The truth was that Reagan needed no help. By summer his campaign centered on a few basic themes, and, adept at following a script, he clung to them tenaciously. He accused the Brown administration of "fiscal irresponsibility" for taxing workers too heavily while paying welfare benefits that were too generous. He criticized protesting students at Berkeley and said that Mario Savio should not be readmitted. He emphasized rising crime rates and insisted that race riots had been dealt with too leniently. And he argued for the repeal of the Rumford Act. That was once again a live issue, because the California supreme court had overturned Proposition 14. The justices ruled that the ballot measure, which invalidated the fair housing law, violated the equal protection clause of the U.S. Constitution by allowing discrimination. The decision meant that the Rumford Act was back on the books—and back in the political arena. Reagan insisted the law benefited "one segment of our population" while restricting "one of our most basic and cherished rights," the ability to sell property to anyone.[52]

Left to defend all that had happened in California in the previous eight years, Brown could offer only complicated responses ill suited to the hurly-burly of a campaign. Tom Braden, the newspaper publisher Brown had appointed president of the state Board of Education, once ran into *Los Angeles Times* reporter Bill Trombley in an airport. "What's the 30-second answer to the 'mess in Berkeley,'" Braden asked, employing one of Reagan's favorite phrases to describe the protests. Trombley replied that he didn't think there was one.[53]

On race, Brown's task was harder still. He was happy that the supreme court had overturned Prop. 14 and said so, but that merely put him at odds with the majority of voters, who had supported the measure. Hoping to put Reagan on the defensive, he accused the Republican of playing to white anger over the fate of Prop. 14, urban riots, and the upheavals of the civil rights era. Reagan was "riding the backlash," Brown said, "and perhaps even subtly contributing to it."[54] That line of attack failed too. Reagan's denials were indignant, and the whole effort did nothing to increase Brown's appeal to conservative white voters, many of whom were in fact troubled about racial tumult.

Whether Reagan contributed or not, Brown was right about the basic point: White backlash was real. As the campaign wore on, evidence of it increased. Gallup pollsters found that most Americans thought the Johnson administration was pushing too fast on civil rights, the first time a majority said yes in the four years Gallup had been asking such a question. Among Californians, opinions about the governor's race were mirrored in views on the Rumford Act. People who opposed the fair housing law overwhelmingly favored Reagan; those who supported it overwhelmingly favored Brown. The governor knew the mood was cutting against him. As he said years later, "People always felt that I was too friendly with the blacks anyway."[55]

———

On July 1, less than a month after the primary, Brown wrote a letter to the publisher of the newspaper in Bakersfield, at the southern tip of the Central Valley. Meant to boost his campaign, the missive did more to reveal just how bewildered the governor was, how he was boasting about the accomplishments of his first term while his opponents were noting the problems of the second.

Recalling his glory days, Brown wrote about the bond issue that funded the State Water Project, coaxed past the legislature with statesmanship and the voters with persistence, he said. He remembered making "at least 200 speeches," a dogged effort of which he was justly proud. The farmers around Bakersfield, he noted accurately, would benefit as much as anyone, perhaps more. And yet in the primary the county had voted for Yorty, a man "who did absolutely nothing for the water bonds."[56] The situation dumbfounded Brown. Never mind that it was years before, never mind all that had happened since, he had delivered the goods, and now the voters were turning their backs.

Almost at the same time, Brown wrote to another newspaperman, Dick Berlin, the president of the Hearst chain, publishers of a grand old dinosaur in American journalism, the *Los Angeles Herald-Examiner.* If television was in its youth as a political medium, big-city afternoon newspapers were in their dotage. Once, afternoon papers had lorded over the media world, the preferred reading of workingmen who started the workday early, ended it early, and read the news on the homeward-bound train or while their wives readied dinner. But by the 1960s afternoon papers were in trouble. Television offered a competing source of news. Cities and their suburbs sprawled farther and farther outward, making newspaper distribution through midday traffic nearly impossible. The emerging shift toward a postindustrial economy meant blue-collar workers constituted a declining share of the workforce.

The *Herald-Ex,* as it was universally known in Los Angeles, was the biggest relic still standing from the old days: It was the largest afternoon newspaper in the country. Like most Hearst publications, it traditionally supported Republicans, but Brown wrote to Berlin and made his pitch anyway. The governor suggested that Hearst corporate headquarters could send out a reporter from the East to cover the governor's race, so the old conservative California biases would be overcome.[57] The paper stuck with its normal reporters, but Berlin did the best he could. Days before the election, he ordered up an editorial endorsing Brown. "Am praying for you," Berlin wrote in a short note to the governor. "Do hope you make it."[58]

———

The lone bit of good news came just before Labor Day, the traditional starting date for heavy fall campaigning. Brown had closed to within three points, a remarkable recovery from the massive fifteen-point deficit he faced right after the primary. Over the summer he had positioned himself for the battle against Reagan by moving toward the center. He signed a controversial bill that toughened the penalties for inciting a riot and even said he might support amendments to the Rumford Act.[59] As a result, he won back some of the conservative Democrats who had deserted him for Yorty in the primary.[60] With luck and momentum, it seemed, the governor might yet pull through. Unquestionably an underdog, he wrote hopefully to a friend: "Ronnie . . . is beginning to wear a little bit thin."[61]

Buoyed by the closer race, Brown jumped into a five-day tour, barnstorming frantically. At a labor union picnic, he boasted about the economy. In farm country, he promised more help for agriculture. Standing in an alfalfa field soon to be the site of a new state college, he touted the importance of education.[62]

Then, almost as soon as it began, the comeback was halted. The circumstances initially seemed beyond the scope of the governor's race. Chasing a sixteen-year-old boy suspected of stealing a car, a San Francisco police officer pulled his gun and fired. Shot in the back, the boy died on the spot. Versions of the shooting differed. The officer said he first fired warning shots into the air. Witnesses disagreed. It was a moot point in one sense, because police policy at the time allowed officers to use any force available, including gunshots, to capture a fleeing suspect thought to have committed a felony. But the shooting occurred in a tough San Francisco neighborhood called Hunters Point, which like Watts was mostly black and mostly poor. In Hunters Point the idea that a running teenager had been shot in the back by a white policeman stirred deep pools of anger. Within hours the area looked like a small-scale Watts: vandals broke windows, locals turned to looting, police officers wearing riot helmets and carrying shotguns marched through the streets, raucous crowds retreating before the show of force.

When the mayor asked for the National Guard, Brown granted the request immediately, then abandoned a campaign trip and ordered that the *Grizzly* head directly for San Francisco. "Anything can happen when things break loose," he said after arriving. "The mayor and the chief needed help, and I wanted to help. We're going to have law and order in California."

He admitted that he knew no cure-all for the riots' causes. Jobs existed, he said, but given the complexities of a modern economy, poor youngsters were often ill equipped for the work. Over the long haul education would be the key, but that was of no help now. "It's going to take years," he said. Asked if he thought Reagan would make political hay of the trouble, he said emphatically that he did not care.[63]

Shrewdly, Reagan did look for an advantage. By the following day the streets of Hunters Point had calmed almost completely, but Reagan declared that the brief flare of violence showed that Brown had learned nothing from Watts. The governor had failed to take steps that might have prevented outbursts like Hunters Point, Reagan said, adding that black leaders "who have urged civil disobedience have forfeited their right to leadership."[64] Genuinely miffed, Brown spat back that with soldiers in the streets he would not quarrel with "that actor." Reagan was more to be "pitied than condemned," Brown said, because he was commenting on matters "he never has had to deal with . . . in his entire life."[65]

But voters neither pitied nor condemned Reagan. Instead, Hunters Point served only to remind them that barely a year earlier much of Watts had burned, that Brown had been governor while almost three dozen people died in the middle of Los Angeles, and that the current campaign was a choice between a liberal Democrat presiding over a state adrift and a conservative Republican who promised to chase the thugs from the "jungle paths" of urban streets. Two weeks after the trouble in Hunters Point, a new poll showed the race returning to its old form. Conservative Democrats had fled Brown, and Reagan was once again comfortably in the lead. The results so delighted Reagan that he found himself hoping not only to win but also to lead a Republican landslide down the whole of the ticket.[66]

———

Brown fought to the end, but there was not much more to do than endure the harsh realities of politics. With ten days to go, his efforts backfired. The campaign paid to air a half-hour film, which included a brief scene in which the governor was shown speaking to some children. At one point, he noted that he was running against an actor and then added, "An actor shot Lincoln." To those who were there, or who saw the clip as the movie was being made, it seemed a jocular remark, harmless and funny. It was Brown in his element, dishing up the old charm and making people chuckle and like him. Viewers at home apparently thought the same thing. When the film first aired in San Francisco, only one person called the television station to complain. More people phoned to object that it had bumped one of their favorite shows, *Car 54—Where Are You?* Brown's crack about the actor assassin was thought so benign that it was included in shorter commercials excerpted from the film. But in print, without the context of merriment, it seemed the cheapest of shots. It made Brown look petty, almost silly, and it angered people in a rich and influential California industry that had long been filled with Brown fans: show business.[67]

Gaining confidence by the day, Reagan was talking openly of staffing his future administration. He scored psychological victories by drawing big crowds, even on the governor's home turf. Stopping in San Francisco, Reagan rode through downtown in an open car, standing and soaking in the cheers. Reaching to shake his hand, people pushed forward with such frenzy that one woman was almost crushed beneath the wheels of the motorcade. Old-timers in the press corps said that Brown, even in his heyday in his own hometown, had never enjoyed such treatment.[68]

Few friends rushed to the governor's defense. People recognized a dead campaign, and they avoided the corpse. Flying home from a presidential trip to Asia, White House aides telephoned Brown from Air Force One to cancel LBJ's planned swing through California. They cited his need for minor surgery, but the governor—aware that the operation was no emergency, indeed was merely needed sometime in the next three weeks— thought he was being side-stepped.[69]

Unruh too had dubious commitments. Brown asked for his help, but the speaker begged off in favor of an "educational study mission" to Latin America, a weak excuse for a working politician in the midst of campaigning season. Twisting the knife, Unruh offered the cold comfort of a half measure. He would return to California a week before the election, he said, and would be happy to make some speeches for the governor in the final days.[70]

Swallowing his pride, Brown even sought help from Yorty, the man who had wounded him so grievously. Brown called the White House and asked that LBJ convince Yorty to endorse him. It was a hopeless request, and more than that it was sad—the governor pleading for help from a president who had snubbed him and a mayor he despised.[71]

The difficulties finally overwhelmed even Brown's election-year buoyancy. On a night flight after a day of campaigning—one more day in a lifetime of shaking hands and seeking votes—the fatigue and futility hit him so deeply that he projected the mood even to his spouse. Clutching a scotch, he looked across the little aisle of the plane to Bernice, seated opposite. "Tired old governor," he said. "Tired old wife."[72]

———

Brown began citing the patron saint of all trailing candidates—Harry Truman—and vowing he would pull off an upset similar to the president's great victory in 1948. Reagan vowed to keep campaigning, answering Brown's analogy with a clever one-liner: "President Tom Dewey told me not to pay too much attention to polls."[73]

The pace was furious at the end. The day before the election, Brown had breakfast with precinct workers in Los Angeles, spoke to a noon rally in San Francisco, shook hands at a factory gate in the afternoon in Santa Clara. That night, hoarse from the final push, he barked out one last speech at a hastily arranged rally in Sacramento. He asked the crowd if Reagan had ever done anything for California, still astonished, even after months of campaigning, that the voters did not care if Reagan had never built a campus or a dam or a freeway.[74]

The following night, the returns were brutal. Brown carried only three counties out of fifty-eight. Voters stuck by him in San Francisco, where he was still a hometown boy. Across the bay, he took Alameda County, home to the Berkeley students who had caused him such heartache, although even there, amid the liberals of Berkeley and the big African American community of Oakland, Reagan came within two thousand votes of victory. Somehow Brown carried Plumas County, a patch of mountains with only a few thousand residents.[75]

But everywhere else he lost, often by big margins. In Kern County, where the farmers had benefited so greatly from the State Water Project, he failed to get 40 percent of the vote. In Orange County, south of Los Angeles, then emerging as the center of right-wing America and a place that would one day name its airport after John Wayne, Brown could not even reach 30 percent. Statewide, he lost by nearly a million votes, almost exactly the margin by which he had beaten William Knowland to win the governorship eight years earlier.[76]

Democrats sank together. Republicans won all but one of the statewide races and cut deeply into Democratic margins in the legislature. White backlash was obvious. Although appointed by the governor, California supreme court justices must run for reelection, and three justices who had voted to overturn Proposition 14 were up for new terms. Although each was reelected, each received a surprisingly large negative vote.[77]

Brown's friend Ben Swig found the governor almost in a daze on election night. At a downcast campaign headquarters in Los Angeles, supporters shouted "No, no!" as Brown acknowledged Reagan's victory. "I don't like to say it either, but that's the situation," the governor said. When the crowd sang, "For He's a Jolly Good Fellow," Brown seemed near tears.[78] Writing to President Johnson a few days later, he blamed the loss on nature's inevitability: "We fought hard, but the tide was just going out."[79]

———

Brown had always been the regular guy of California politics, a little overweight, a little befuddled, an average Joe with a wife and some kids and an honest desire to do the right thing. He triumphed over grander opponents—a rich publishing heir like Bill Knowland and a boy wonder like Richard Nixon—in part by being the average candidate for average voters.

Repeating the trick seemed an easy task, for Reagan was anything but average. He was Hollywood, literally and figuratively. He was a rich actor with movie star friends and a fan club and a famous ex-wife. But remarkably Reagan in 1966 managed to become the candidate of the common man. Blessed with a showman's sense of audience, he felt his way toward his listeners' worries. Ahead of his advisers, Reagan realized that Berkeley was a source of deep resentment for working Californians. When he spoke people kept asking him about the troubles at the campus, so he added the issue to his regular spiel. In time the pollsters' science confirmed the candidate's intuition. Voters said the antics of Berkeley students posed a greater problem for the state than unemployment, pollution, or transportation.[80]

Berkeley was just one of the issues that cut deeply with Californians, and Reagan was a master at sensing them all. In the end he won the war because he shrewdly selected the battlegrounds on which he fought. Complaints about the high cost of welfare appealed to struggling working families. Denunciations of the Rumford Act won sympathy both from home owners who sincerely thought the law overreaching and from bigots who simply wanted to keep blacks from the neighborhood. Perhaps most vivid of all, warnings about urban jungles fanned the fears of people who had sat in their suburban homes and watched the smoke rise from Watts.

It was a set of issues that appealed most vividly to the voters Reagan needed: blue-collar workers. People who carried a lunch bucket or wore a hard hat were the most likely to resent the tumult of the sixties. They had the least sympathy for disobedient college students and protesting blacks.[81] Not every potential convert could be won, of course, but Reagan drew far more working-class support than Republicans normally did, and it was enough. In 1958, when Brown won his first term as governor, he had the backing of 78 percent of white union members and their families. Eight years later, against Reagan, that figure dropped to just 57 percent.[82] In the dozen most heavily working-class towns in California—most of them ringed around Los Angeles and filled with workers from the aeronautics factories—the change was especially striking. Against Nixon four years earlier Brown had carried all twelve. Against Reagan, he lost all but one.[83]

That was the real genius of the Reagan campaign—the recognition that Democrats were weakest where they once had been strongest. Outnumbered both in California and across the country, Republicans knew they had to appeal to Democrats and independents if they were to win. Nelson Rockefeller and his ilk tried to do that by winning over wavering moderates of the establishment. Sensing an underlying anger and resentment among voters, Reagan appealed instead to blue-collar workers, a group that had long been a bastion of Democratic loyalty.

Because he did it successfully, he changed American politics. When working-class Californians abandoned the old labor lawyer Pat Brown for the Hollywood actor Ronald Reagan, the heart was cut from Franklin Roosevelt's New Deal coalition and transplanted to an emerging conservative force. It was in 1966 that Reagan found the Democrats who would one day put him in the White House.

Brown and his men saw it coming. Charles Guggenheim, the eastern filmmaker hired to produce Brown's commercials, got a glimpse of this insight almost as soon as he set foot in California. He came out right after the primary and on his first night in the state went to a party filled with Brown loyalists, including Don Bradley, the old Democratic strategist and warhorse. Not knowing anyone, Guggenheim wandered out to the patio and looked down on Los Angeles, a string of headlights visible in the distance as homeward-bound commuters crept along. Suddenly he realized that Bradley was standing next to him, at once both thoughtful and talkative, delivering a little lecture not only about the big protests and problems but also about the everyday woes of regular folks, about the fact that life does not always provide a happy ending, even in California.

"You see all those people down there?" Bradley asked. "You know where they're from, Guggenheim? They're from Peoria. They're from Kankakee. They're from Pittsburgh. . . . You know why they're here? Well, they're back in Peoria and their kids are on drugs and their wife is unhappy because there's all kinds of crap in the streets and there's all kinds of problems and the schools are no good and the blacks are coming in.

"So they move. They move west. . . . Their kids are still on drugs. There's still violence in the schools. There's still problems with blacks. . . . . They can't go any further. The ocean is there. And they're still unhappy. And you know something? That's why we're going to get our ass beat."[84]

————

Defeat stung, but Brown tried to keep his chin up. He wrote to another outgoing governor—Robert Smylie of Idaho—to commiserate. "It may not be a happy club but it is not an unhappy club either," Brown insisted. Forcing a figurative smile, Brown suggested that answering to the voters, which had always been a joy, might really have been a burden better tossed aside. "And, also," he added gamely, "if we are not able to take it on the chin, we shouldn't have been in politics in the first place."[85]

Earl Warren, now completely broken from his Republican roots, sent a kind, handwritten letter. The chief justice said he had voted for Brown and in the days after marking his absentee ballot had been "praying that there would be enough thinking voters in California to insure [his] re-election." Defeat was "unjustified," Warren wrote, and left him feeling glum.[86]

Using the status he would soon lose, Brown wrote to the president to ask for a final audience as governor. The relationship between the two men—never good—had not improved. After the primary Brown had been unhappy that LBJ had neither called nor written to express congratulations on the victory over Yorty. A White House aide wrote to the president that Brown was "fussing" about the matter, precisely the kind of pouty demand for attention that annoyed Johnson.[87] In the wake of Brown's loss to Reagan, LBJ agreed to receive the governor, although he was grumpy about it. "I'll see him," the president dictated to an aide, "but only if he can get in and out without getting it in the paper that he sees me. I doubt he can. But if it gets out, it's off. If the governor of California gets in, then I know I'll have requests from a bunch of other people."[88]

The meeting was set for December 15, little more than a month after Brown's defeat, and he flew east as a lame duck waiting for his term to end. As LBJ had feared, word of the meeting leaked out, even though presidential aides had imposed what one reporter called "an atmosphere of unusual secrecy" about the day's events. For once Brown kept his mouth shut, insisting that he could not say anything about his conversation with the president. His only comment was an inaccurate claim that Johnson had requested the meeting.[89]

Inside the White House the two men talked for forty-five minutes, the president graciously asking if there was anything he could do for Brown. The governor cited only one last request, although it was a big one—a seat on the Supreme Court. He said he understood that such an appointment might be difficult if Warren remained on the court; two former California governors might seem a bit much. But if the opportunity somehow arose, Brown said, it would be a job to cherish. As it turned out, Warren resigned in the waning days of the Johnson administration, but Brown got no call, perhaps because, whether he realized it or not, the president had not always been his biggest fan.[90]

———

The last day in the office was a short one. Photographers were summoned for the inevitable photographs: Pat dictating a last letter to his secretary, Bernice overseeing the packing of family belongings at the Governor's Mansion. The governor made no effort to hide his melancholy. "It's sad," he said. "Don't ever think it isn't." But he did a little work, meeting with a remaining judicial candidate and making some final appointments. One had a lasting impact on American politics. He filled an unpaid slot on an obscure drug-policy panel by picking a young Los Angeles lawyer for whom the appointment was the first low rung on the ladder of politics, Edmund Gerald Brown Jr.[91]

At midday the governor milled around with the staff, a clutch of people soon to be out of work, all trading memories of the past and best wishes for the future. It was a woebegone affair; some people cried. Then at last Hale Champion burst the sadness. Perhaps they should all stick together and go overseas, he joked, and offer themselves as a package government for some distant and troubled land.[92] Everybody seized the chance to laugh, but beneath the humor the little gag hinted at the alienation they all felt. The governor and his team had been cast aside so thoroughly that they might as well leave the country. Then at last Brown was ready to go. He said good-bye a final time, and left. Almost immediately, painters came in to touch up the office for Reagan.[93]

Brown was leaving the city as well as the Capitol. Reagan wanted to be sworn in at the earliest possible moment—just after midnight on January 2, 1967—and Brown wanted no part of the ceremony. There was no tradition in Sacramento of the outgoing governor attending the inaugural, and the Browns were eager to leave a town that was no longer theirs. Pat and Bernice were driven to San Francisco to attend the wedding of a family friend and then, because they had decided to make a new home in Los Angeles, boarded the *Grizzly* the next day for the final time. Faces drawn with sadness, they flew south.[94]

Brown had spent his whole adult life seeking office, only to be booted from the job he loved the most. After nearly a quarter century as a public figure, he was again a private citizen.

17   DYNASTY

ON THE DAY REAGAN was sworn into office Brown spent the afternoon in the winter sunshine of Pasadena, watching Purdue nip Southern California 14–13 in the Rose Bowl. The pleasant weather was one of the reasons he and Bernice had decided to move south, but so was the shifting balance of the state. In Brown's lifetime, his famous hometown had faded in importance, passed by its gauche southern rival. Los Angeles, not San Francisco, was now the imperial city of the West. As governor, Brown spent a month there every year, and the buzz of the place was attractive. Joe Ball, an old Democratic loyalist who ran a powerhouse law firm in Los Angeles, offered Brown a job as the quintessential rainmaker, and Pat and Bernice decided they would, like so many Americans before them, migrate to Southern California.

Bernice found a house they liked high above Beverly Hills, with views of the Los Angeles basin spread out beneath them. Best of all for Pat, there was a small pool just out the back door. Unabashed as always, he began each morning with a quick skinny-dip.

Brown could play golf when he liked, the office was a short drive down the canyon, and business at the law firm was as good as anyone could have wanted. On the night Brown was defeated for reelection, his old friend Ben Swig, the owner of the posh Fairmont Hotel in San Francisco, promised a sizable amount of legal work once Brown got settled in private practice, a gesture Brown found "a very consoling thing." Joe Allbritton, a businessman who later bought the *Washington Star*, did the same, and Brown was soon making more money than ever before in his life.[1]

Early on, Brown's name remained in the news. He bequeathed to Reagan a bare fiscal cupboard, mostly because he lacked the political power in his second term to enact a substantial tax increase, even as the state grew rapidly and the need for spending mushroomed. In his final year as governor, he kept the books in balance with an accounting maneuver that further straitened the circumstances Reagan would inherit.[2] There was nothing particularly new in any of this. When he became governor, Brown inherited a fiscal crisis from Goodwin Knight and had been forced to expend political capital enacting a big tax increase during his first year in office. Now Reagan did the same, and he was not shy about blaming his predecessor.

Nor was Brown shy about answering, both about tax issues and Reagan's performance generally. A few weeks into the new administration, as Reagan boasted that he would cut items from the state budget, a process known as "blue-lining" in Sacramento parlance, Brown declared that his successor "has used a blue pencil where his heart ought to be." Weeks later he decried the governor's leadership as "empty slogans" offered by a "pleasing television personality." By the end of the year Brown was blunt in saying that Reagan as politician was an experiment gone bad. "His lack of governmental background has caused him and the people of the state great harm," Brown said.[3]

Such feelings did not fade. Brown wrote two books about Reagan, the first timed to damage the Republican's chances for reelection as governor in 1970 and the second to hurt his 1976 campaign for the presidency. A loser's wails make poor reading, and the books were the most unfortunate episodes of Brown's retirement, both little more than churlish screeds. In Brown's better moments the anger mellowed to humor. For the rest of his life he would disclose that he was heading for the bathroom by announcing that he needed to cast a vote for Ronald Reagan.

———

When Brown was not engaged in partisan rhetorical combat, he revealed his lack of direct power by lobbying others, sometimes for odd causes. He tried to get President Johnson to pardon Artie Samish, once a legendary Sacramento lobbyist who had lorded over the legislature in the 1940s before going to prison for corruption and was now an old man living a quiet life.[4] Another time, Brown wrote directly to LBJ to urge that the president meet with one hundred college students in the hope of convincing them that the Vietnam War was a just and prudent cause. "I am sure your personal magnetism will convince them," Brown wrote, a charming if ill-advised echo of his own willingness to meet directly with student protesters at Berkeley during the Free Speech Movement years before.[5]

Relegated to the sidelines, Brown missed the real action. After two years of private life, he took time on Christmas Eve to write to Drew Pearson, his old columnist friend. "The first two years out of public service have been interesting and stimulating," Brown wrote, "but I would be less than frank if I didn't tell you that I miss the challenge of public office."[6]

A path back to lost glory opened while he was on a business trip to Japan in 1970, as Reagan was preparing his bid for a second term. Gene Wyman, Brown's friend and best fund-raiser and a sworn enemy of Jesse Unruh, told Brown that Democratic contributors were ready to fund a new Brown campaign for governor. After a difficult first term Reagan might be vulnerable, and plenty of Democrats still hated Unruh, the party's likely nominee. Brown was eager to avenge his loss, but he preserved domestic harmony by calling Bernice to see what she thought.

As he surely expected, the response could not have been more negative. Never a political creature, Bernice was glad to be free of the grind and happy that Pat was making a good living. Still, those objections might not have won the day were it not for her final argument: There was already going to be an Edmund Gerald Brown on the 1970 ballot.

Jerry had been elected to the Los Angeles community college board the year before and now was running for secretary of state. Owing largely to his famous name and his family connections, political oddsmakers gave him a good chance at winning. The biggest potential problem, Bernice told Pat, was the possibility of two Browns on one ballot. Sickened by dynastic ambitions, voters would revolt. Pat knew she was right, so he turned down Wyman's offer and, once and for all, declared his political career dead.[7]

———

Brown soon found his business interests more lucrative than he could have expected. Indonesia's state-run oil company, Pertamina, retained Brown's firm for its American legal work and later gave Brown a franchise to import twenty thousand barrels a day to the American market. It was an arrangement that put Brown into business with military dictators but also made him, for the first time in his life, a truly rich man. Eventually he was able to donate $1 million to the University of California—and note proudly that it was not his last million. If the unsavory nature of his business partners bothered him, he did not say so.[8]

Still, even with all his newfound wealth, the fiscal habits of the civil servant died hard. Brown remained a frugal man if not occasionally a cheapskate. He refused to abandon golf balls in water hazards whenever it was possible to fish them out and chided a grandson for not doing the same. Once, in Washington, the former governor and his wife went out to dinner with their old friend Tom Braden. In the midst of the meal Brown said with wide-eyed wonder, "You know, Tom, I've got a million dollars—a million dollars!" But when the check came, he made no move for his fattened wallet, and Braden ended up paying. A week later Braden's phone rang. Brown was on the line, sheepish that he had followed up financial bragging with parsimony. "Bern's been giving me hell," he told Braden.[9]

The international legal work required frequent business trips, often to Asia, occasionally elsewhere, and in retirement the Browns traveled the world. Since Pat was both a former governor and the lawyer for a major oil company, first-class treatment was standard. In Bali they once spent the weekend at cottages owned by Pertamina and then on Monday played golf at the resort's course. The weekend crowd had cleared out, leaving the place mostly empty, and the pins had been removed from the greens. The golfers needed something to aim at, so a local man was instructed to stand at the holes, a human flagstick for the visiting nabobs.[10]

Brown enjoyed such treatment but did not require it. In fact, he was the same man overseas as he was at home: unpretentious, gabby, always looking to connect with regular folks. In the South Pacific on a family Christmas trip, he became so engrossed chatting with islanders that he missed a flight. Lack of English proved no bar to sociability. The world over, he pointed to a mark on his hand and entertained children with his old and apocryphal story that he had caught a bullet, if necessary resorting to mime.

Always he loved the local flavor. In Paris he insisted on visiting a true café rather than a tourist joint. In Hong Kong he went on an uncharacteristic buying binge in the tailor shops: a suit, two sport coats, two pair of pants, four shirts, and a pair of shoes. In China he determined that he would reach the top of a nearby rise on the Great Wall, huffing and puffing alongside his grandchildren long after his aging contemporaries had quit. In Nepal, where expatriate hippies were openly and legally smoking hashish, the sixty-seven-year-old former governor wanted to join the gang and have a few puffs. On reflection, sad to say, he decided against it.[11]

————

Jerry enjoyed a rise in politics far more rapid than that of his father. Father and son may have been Pat and Jerry to those who knew them, but officially, on the ballot, they were both Edmund Gerald Brown. The familiarity helped. Jerry won his race for secretary of state in 1970 and acknowledged his debt at the swearing in. "I want to thank my mother for naming me after my father," he said. "I grew to like that name during the campaign."[12]

His tenure as secretary of state was successful, and after only one term, in 1974 he was elected governor. (Perhaps learning from the elder Brown's mistake, Reagan declined to seek a third term.) Jerry, who was only thirty-six, was inaugurated in the assembly chamber in the Capitol on January 6, 1975, almost eight years to the day since his father left office. Pat watched from the visitors' gallery and cried.[13]

Asked what he planned to do after the ceremony, Pat said he wanted to head over to the governor's office and see what changes had been made since he left, a sign of how much he longed to be back at the center of events, both figuratively and literally.[14]

But Jerry did not want paternal advice. He had always been more like his serious mother than his gregarious father, and he clearly bore scars from a childhood during which his father was often absent. Once an interviewer for *Playboy* mentioned to Jerry that some politicians successfully combine family and career. Jerry responded, "Do they?"[15]

Like a lot of children who enter their parents' line of work, Jerry was determined to be his own man, a natural and understandable desire. His inaugural speech disclosed a style far different from his namesake's—it was eight minutes long—and once Jerry was in office he continued, in various ways, to separate himself from the old era. As governor he declined to be driven in a limousine or to live in the new Governor's Mansion Reagan had built, preferring a regular car from the state motor pool and an apartment near the Capitol.

By turns, Pat was confounded and frustrated. Again and again he forwarded names to his son for possible appointment, only to admit later that he had little sway. "I have sent my high recommendation of you to Jerry," he wrote one job seeker. "I haven't the slightest idea what he will do about it, but you may rest assured you have the old man's support." "Jerry is very independent and has his own screening process," he told another prospective appointee, "but I will certainly put in a good word for you." Even Jerry's aides grew to feel for the former governor. "I have really enjoyed talking with you over the last three years," the appointments secretary once wrote to Pat, "and I am only sorry that I have not been able to make your batting average better."[16]

Pat kept at it, sending along ideas, urging appointments, recommending public appearances, but he was shouting into a hurricane. He had spent his whole life trying to become the man at the center of affairs—the bride at every wedding and the corpse at every funeral, to use the line about Teddy Roosevelt—and now he could not even get a meeting with his son the governor. "I really think I can make some contributions," he wrote to Jerry two months into the new administration. "Please give your father a chance to meet with you alone." Then a few months after that: "Please let me know your plans." And later still: "My eight years as attorney general and eight years as governor have given me some insight into California government. . . . I still believe that you should discuss tough decisions with me."[17] Through Jerry's eight years as governor, the dynamic did not change, and Pat learned a hard lesson of political life: Build a career so successful that it launches a dynasty, and you may miss out on developing a relationship with the heirs.

Disappointment never trumped parental loyalty, however. The elder man fired off angry letters to newspapers and talk show hosts when his son was attacked and distributed clippings when he was praised. In 1976, when Jerry was making a surprisingly strong run for the presidency, his parents visited the Philippines, where Pat found Imelda Marcos "charming" and Ferdinand Marcos curious about the future of his American patrons. Who, Ferdinand asked, would be elected to the White House later that year? Pat replied that someone else would probably win, but the best man for the job was his son.[18]

Pat defended Jerry even at the cost of friendships, a high price for a garrulous man to pay. Ed Hills had known Pat since they were boys together in the same San Francisco neighborhood. Later Hills ran Pat's early campaigns. When Pat filed the papers to run for attorney general, Hills went with him to the clerk's office, literally standing by him as the papers were signed, like the best man at a wedding. But when Jerry ran for secretary of state, Hills supported a rival. Both a loving father and a political warhorse, Pat could not abide the betrayal, and he stopped speaking to Hills. "I turned his picture to the wall," he said.[19]

As Brown grew old quietly, his former opponents led extraordinary lives. Richard Nixon and Ronald Reagan went on to be president, of course, but it may be Brown's first opponent for the governorship, William Knowland, who experienced the most startling personal journey.

After losing the 1958 election to Brown, Knowland retired from politics and returned to running the family newspaper, the *Oakland Tribune*. But he gave play to the self-destructive tendencies that had plagued his personal life for years. He continued the womanizing that caused his wife to push him away from the U.S. Senate and into the gubernatorial race against Brown. In 1972, after forty-five years of marriage, he divorced her to marry a young mistress he had met on a gambling trip to Las Vegas. It was a disastrous match. His new wife drank her way through their honeymoon, sometimes making embarrassing public scenes, and when they got home her behavior only became more erratic. In less than a year Knowland was again contemplating divorce.

At the same time he ran up huge gambling debts, and although in many respects a rich man, Knowland was soon scratching around for ready cash. In January 1974 he asked the *Tribune* to pay his entire year's salary up front and then spent the money almost immediately. By the following month there seemed to be few options left, and so on a winter's morning in 1974 Knowland drove to his vacation home along the Russian River, north of San Francisco. He retrieved a pistol he kept at the home, walked down to the water's edge, fired one round into the river as a test, and then shot himself in the right temple.[20]

Brown and Knowland had never been close. They were vastly dissimilar people, personally as well as ideologically. But when reporters called after the suicide Brown was understandably gracious. The 1958 campaign had been tough but clean, he said, and in defeat Knowland had been "a real gentleman." Displaying both the kindness of the eulogist and his own penchant for expansive affection, Brown told one writer, "I have lost a friend."[21]

———

In January 1977 the Browns paid a call at the White House. Jimmy Carter, the first Democrat elected president since Brown left office, had just been inaugurated, and the former governor of California was welcomed as a distinguished visitor. Gossips claimed Brown might be considered for a post in the new administration, but it was loose talk. He had no connections to Carter and was in any event the father of a man who had run against the new president.

Still, the White House meeting showed that by now Brown was a Democratic elder statesman, trotted out for ceremonial occasions or called by reporters looking for a quick quote. He liked talking, and he was accessible, so he spoke out on many topics: taxes, elections, the perennial idea that perhaps California should be split in two. He was vocal in defending his ties to the oil industry, which increasingly came under attack by young activists of the growing environmental movement. Once in Santa Barbara he was ready to make a speech in the Biltmore Hotel when he saw a group of protesters. Alone, he walked down the sidewalk, crossed the street, and waded into the yelling, sign-waving crowd. The pickets were there to protest the planned construction nearby of a plant to handle liquefied natural gas imports from Indonesia. There was a lot of youthful anger and indignation, people yelling at the governor, sometimes using language that local reporters were reticent to repeat. But Brown stood his ground. In a face-to-face impromptu street debate, he acknowledged his ties to the Indonesian oil industry but denied he would make any money off the plant and defended it as a way to meet California's energy needs. Instinctively honing his argument to appeal to his audience, he even said the state's reliance on nuclear power might be reduced by more natural gas. Nobody seemed convinced, but he tried.[22]

On one matter, however, Brown kept a notable silence. He took no stance on the last major proposal to build a dam across a California river, the Auburn Dam on the American River east of Sacramento. There were efforts to win his support for the controversial project, but Brown was quietly lobbied by the most effective of advocates, one of his own grandchildren.

Charles Casey, the eldest son of Brown's eldest daughter, Barbara, shared a bond with his grandfather. They both loved the outdoors, and as a boy Casey had gone on trips with Brown to the high country of Yosemite. But as an adult Casey had made choices different from those of his dam-building grandfather. Casey went to work for a group called Friends of the River, fighting to stop construction of the Auburn Dam.

At one point, Casey got wind that his grandfather was being pressured to endorse the dam's construction, so he sat down and wrote a long letter that was both a personal communication between grandfather and grandson and a reflection of the changing times in California. "I'm not sure how many people would celebrate California being the most populous state in the nation anymore," Casey wrote to the man who had once led the celebrations. "Years ago, California's greatness was based to a certain extent on all the people living here. We were better because we were bigger." But all those people proved a mixed blessing. The more people who came, the more the state had to deal with their presence. Now there were forces at work demanding yet another dam, one that would flood yet another canyon, and it was time to stop. The state could find other ways, conserving more water or diverting it from unneeded agriculture. If more dams were needed they could always be built, Casey said, but the state could never again "create anything so sublime as a wilderness river and canyon."[23]

Much to Casey's relief, Brown took no side in the Auburn controversy, the great California dam builder silencing himself in deference to a much-loved grandson, a child of a different era who had decided to protect natural rivers rather than create artificial ones.

———

Although never truly a writer, Brown was drawn to writing, for it was the one way that he could communicate as widely in retirement as he had in office. For a few months early in 1978, he produced a weekly column for the *Los Angeles Herald-Examiner*, "the old reactionary Herald-Examiner," as he called it. Ghostwritten by a former staff member, the columns offered few surprises. He objected to Proposition 13, the pending ballot measure to sharply limit property taxes, noting that the real beneficiaries would be apartment owners rather than average folks. He urged that the state "go slow on nuclear power," but more for economic reasons than environmental ones. He suggested tougher regulation of handguns, "relics of our violent past." The column was canceled by spring, perhaps because it was only mediocre but also because the writer's son was readying his bid for reelection to the governor's chair, and the paper could not allow its editorial pages to be transformed into a cheering section for family members.[24]

A more serious writing project came later, when Brown agreed to produce—again with much help—a book about his experiences dealing with the death penalty. Dick Adler, a magazine writer hired to ghost the volume, drove down to Brown's legal office several times a week and tape-recorded interviews in which they roamed back to what had been for Brown the most deeply troubling aspect of being governor. The result, *Public Justice, Private Mercy,* was by far the best of Brown's three books, a cry against the death penalty as ineffective and wrong but also an honest and at times touching account of his own struggles with a governor's power of commutation, a power literally of life and death. "It was an awesome, ultimate power over the lives of others that no person or government should have or crave," he concluded. "Each decision took something out of me that nothing—not family or work or hope for the future—has ever been able to replace."[25]

On a flight from Los Angeles to San Francisco one of the old capital cases reached forward from history to take still another piece from Brown's soul. The man in the seat next to him pointed out a story in that morning's *Los Angeles Times,* and Brown began to read about Eddie Wein.[26] It was the same Wein who had been convicted of raping eight women in Los Angeles in the mid-1950s and sentenced to death because he moved some of his victims a few feet and thus qualified for the state's Lindberg law, which made kidnapping a capital offense. Twice denied a commutation by Brown's predecessor, Goodwin Knight, Wein was eventually scheduled for execution in June 1959, half a year after Brown took office. By the time of the clemency hearing, four days before Wein's scheduled death, Brown had made up his mind. Troubled that Wein would be executed for a largely technical violation of the kidnapping statutes while someone who committed the same sex crimes would merely serve time in prison, Brown commuted the sentence to life without parole.

He intended to do nothing further on the case, but as he prepared to leave office after losing to Reagan, he once again considered Wein's fate. Wein had been in prison for ten years, by most accounts a good prisoner who had come to accept responsibility for his crimes, which he had once denied. The head of the state prison system, a former warden at San Quentin, recommended that in light of Wein's development his sentence should be changed to allow for the possibility of parole. Ever optimistic about people, Brown agreed. As he closed his gubernatorial career, he issued a second commutation, this one creating the potential that someday Wein might be released. "I left office on the last day of 1966 with some regrets," Brown later wrote, "but Eddie Wein wasn't one of them."

The serenity vanished on the flight to San Francisco. Brown read that Wein had been paroled in 1974, after serving seventeen years in prison, and had now raped again. He had attacked two women, brutally assaulting one and murdering the other, stabbing and strangling her and then drowning her in the bathtub. For Brown, it was an extraordinarily painful lesson in the unintended consequences of his own forgiving spirit. As governor, he had commuted the death sentences of twenty-three people, including Wein. Later he remembered the anguish he felt sitting in that airplane and thought that if, at that moment, he could have traded all twenty-three of the lives he saved in exchange for that of the woman Wein murdered, he would have done so.

———

Brown turned seventy-five the year his nemesis, Ronald Reagan, was elected president of the United States, and eighty-five the year his daughter Kathleen became the third member of the family to win statewide office, as treasurer of California. For fun, Pat accepted a temporary appointment as a deputy district attorney, thereby again becoming an officer of the law, and administered the treasurer's oath to his daughter.[27]

Since leaving the governor's office Brown had endured the typical curses of age. Doctors diagnosed glaucoma just five years after he left office. He underwent prostate surgery five years after that. One shoulder bothered him occasionally.[28] But he kept going, if not always at his old pace. Once, in Sacramento, he ran into Jerry Harrell, who had covered the Capitol for the Associated Press when Brown was governor. Harrell thought Brown was slowing down, but he was still at heart the same old guy, still ebullient, still working the crowds, still asking questions—How you doing? What have you been up to?—the friendly pol reduced to half-speed.[29]

With time, though, he grew doddering. It came on him bit by bit. The interviews for *Public Justice, Private Mercy* had to be done first thing in the morning, for by midday Brown began to ramble and forget. A day in his honor at the Capitol in 1992 worried some family members, for he had to give a speech, but he pulled it off, catching a boost from the adoring crowd and charming them as the genial old man they all remembered.[30]

Weeks later he spoke at the Richard Nixon Library, paired up with H. R. Haldeman to discuss the 1962 race for governor, thirty years after the fact. Brown was charming there too, regaling the crowd with the old stories, but he forgot some of the lines now and then, though he had told them all a thousand times before. From time to time during the discussion, he seemed to lose his place, and Haldeman, surely sensing a weakened foe, went easy on him.[31] Brown's public appearances grew more seldom, then stopped altogether.

———

If Jerry Brown was wary of the family mantle, Kathleen Brown embraced it. She talked often about her father's political career and its effects on her life, and she was far more solicitous toward his crowd than Jerry had ever been. Naturally, the old-timers came to like her more than they liked Jerry, and soon she was being touted, not entirely accurately, as her father's replica and final legacy. By 1994 she was finishing her first term as the state's treasurer and was ready to try to succeed both her father and her brother as governor.

The family patriarch was only dimly aware of such things. As he approached his ninetieth birthday, he was fading fast. Bedridden and senile, he was unable to give political counsel to the child who would have taken it, even as he had once been willing to offer guidance to a child who refused.

Kathleen tried to visit him once a week, and he would always ask what she was running for, even when no campaign was under way. When her bid for governor finally began, she at last had an answer, but Pat could no longer hold it in his mind. At every visit he would ask what office she was seeking, and she would tell him, and they would discuss it a little. For months the conversation repeated itself, visit after visit.

In November Kathleen was defeated in a rout and afterward went again to see her father. As always, he asked what she was running for. "Dad," she said, "the election's over. I lost." His eyes opened with a clarity she had not seen in months, and he asked by how much. She told him the ugly numbers, and a lifetime of ballot boxes and tally sheets and election returns came flooding back to his crippled brain. "That's a *loss*," he said, and never again asked her about politics.[32]

———

He died on a winter Friday in February 1996, two months before his ninety-first birthday. Earlier in the day a maid had come to Bernice and told her that Pat would not eat. She went in and tried to convince him that he should take a little nourishment, but he did not respond. She sat with him, and as she did so, he stopped breathing. The doctors said he had a heart attack, but it was only the latest in a long string of ailments. His death was, Bernice remembered, "a very peaceful event."[33]

Three days later there was a public viewing at the funeral home, attended by the elites of Southern California politics. Brown would have loved that, but he would have loved too the presence of a black woman who recalled his support of racial justice, of a UCLA student who knew of the governor's fondness for the university, of a couple who thought back to a time for which they longed, of regular folks who remembered Brown as the embodiment of better days.[34]

The funeral mass was said two days later in San Francisco, at St. Cecilia's, the Catholic church near the comfortable home that Pat and Bernice had bought decades before. The day's memories were both sweet and perceptive. Kathleen Kelly, Brown's eldest granddaughter, gave a eulogy and said it was just the kind of event her grandfather would have loved, for he was the center of attention, surrounded by family, friends, "and hundreds of voting Democrats."[35] The monsignor celebrating the Mass, a priest who had known the former governor for years, said simply that Brown "loved people genuinely. . . . He cared for their needs, their welfare, their pain." Talking to a reporter, a childhood friend named Michael Tilles remembered the inverse of Brown's honest concern for others: He wanted people to love him back. "He used to say to me, 'I wonder if people will ever remember me?'"

On that day there was no question that people remembered. Almost one thousand strong, the crowd filled the huge church. When the pallbearers marched the casket from the sanctuary, police honor guards saluted and helicopters from the National Guard flew past, one peeling off to symbolize a missing man. Draped in the state's Bear Flag, the casket was taken to a waiting hearse and then driven along freeways that had been cleared of traffic, until the motorcade reached the cemetery south of San Francisco. A small group of family and close friends gathered around the gravesite, near the front gate and just down a gentle hillside from the grave of Brown's father, and, in the waning California afternoon, laid Pat Brown to rest.

EPILOGUE

BERNICE BROWN OUTLIVED HER HUSBAND by six years. Her health declined until she was blind and bedridden, yet she upheld the tradition of a nightly cocktail and complained when her attendants watered down the drink. She died in 2002, at ninety-three.

The political dynasty that she and Pat created had faded by then. Always looking toward the future, the West is inhospitable territory to ambitions based on a link with the past. After losing her race for governor, Kathleen Brown abandoned politics and settled into a career in high finance. Two of Pat's nephews held local offices, but neither moved on to statewide prominence. Although there were occasional rumors that at least one of the grandchildren might join the game, nothing came of it.

Only in Jerry Brown did the family business truly live on, and even there the path was rocky. As he left the governor's office, he lost a bid for the U.S. Senate and then went overseas to work with Mother Teresa in India and study Zen Buddhism in Japan. He returned to California to begin a series of extraordinary personal reinventions, by turns giving play to competing traits in his complicated personality. For a time he sought a conventional role, becoming chairman of the state Democratic Party. But he grew disgruntled with that and sought the 1992 Democratic presidential nomination as an insurgent who complained about corporate influence and raised money through a toll-free telephone line. Later he abandoned the Democratic Party altogether and hosted a left-wing radio talk show. In 1998 he won election as mayor of his adopted hometown of Oakland, where he cozied up to real estate developers and ordered the police to get tough with criminals. Publicly, he did not talk often about his father, but occasionally observers could catch a glimpse of his private feelings. When he was inaugurated as mayor, he held a meditation session at the former warehouse he had converted into a communal living space for himself and his most loyal aides. In one corner he had built an altar, a table decorated with things dear to him. One was a picture of his father.[1]

———

Pat Brown was by then an icon of California politics, but his reputation had not always enjoyed so happy a status. In the years just after he was thrown from office, Brown's style seemed increasingly anachronistic. Campaigning became less personal, the pitch for votes inexorably tipping more toward the wholesale than the retail. Television seized preeminence, and the handshaking that Brown so adored receded to a matter of little concern. In many respects Brown was the last of his breed, a fact made plain by his final defeat. Contemporaries, Brown and Reagan both spent the 1920s and 1930s learning how to communicate, but in vastly different ways. Brown trooped to meetings of the Kiwanis or the Knights of Columbus, booming out a politico's oration audible to the man in the back row. Reagan honed a different skill, talking to microphones and cameras to win over radio listeners, movie audiences, and television viewers. Brown's skill was once the more valuable political talent, but by 1966 a new day had dawned. Politics never reverted to the style Brown loved.

In substance too voters rejected much that had been dear to Brown's heart. Californians became ambivalent about their state's enormous growth. The newcomers who had once signaled the state's importance seemed merely to bedevil everyday life. Freeways that had been the epitome of modern efficiency became bottlenecks choked with traffic. Suburban tract homes once hailed as offering the good life to the working class were attacked as ugly sprawl. Dams once celebrated as admirable controls on the brute force of nature were said to be environmental disasters.

The antigovernment rhetoric with which Reagan attacked Brown became the animating force of American politics. The evils of taxation—an argument that Brown found unappealing—took hold as the central focus of the Republican Party, which dominated both the presidency and the California governorship for much of Brown's retirement. Led by Reagan, voters rejected Brown's steadfast belief that government was part of the solution to society's woes. By 1982 the Democratic candidate for governor, Los Angeles Mayor Tom Bradley, declared that he was "running to bring state government under control," an echo more of Reagan than of Brown.[2]

But in the 1990s, as Brown's life waned, his reputation revived. Measured against his successors—and remembered with the generosity of nostalgia—Brown's folksy style resonated with honesty and humanity. And in a state that continued to grow at an astonishing pace, Brown's investments in grand public projects took on the air of prudent planning rather than wasteful government bureaucracy. For all the crises that beset the Brown years, the state built things that lasted into the future and served the multitudes that kept arriving in California. The state's schools were amply funded. Brown's artificial river delivered water to farms and cities. The public colleges and universities experienced a golden age of expansion. In Brown's time as governor the University of California built three campuses from scratch. In the ensuing three decades no campus opened.[3]

What was more, Brown's era emerged as a central chapter in the great drama of California and thus of the country. If the twentieth century was the American century on a global scale, it was the California century on a national one. In 1900—the last census before Brown's birth—California had the same population as Kansas, a middling-sized state. In 2000—the first census after Brown's death—California was home to one of every eight Americans, the greatest proportion of any state since before the Civil War. With size came influence. California may still occasionally be ridiculed as the home of oddballs, but the fact is that American life is redolent with the products of the state's experience: popular culture, computers, increasing ethnic diversity, Reaganite conservatism. For good or ill, California has often provided the template of American life, and it was during the postwar period that the state most vigorously seized that role. As the leader of the time, Brown became the symbol of what many people remembered as California's glory days.

If there was a moment when that new image crystallized, it was early in March 1992, just before the start of spring, when the state was suffering the double curses of recession and drought. Hungry for happy memories of better days, the California legislature paused from its workaday chores for a ceremony in honor of the eighty-seven-year-old former governor.

There was a reception and a lunch, but the high point of the day came in the ornate chamber of the state assembly, where Brown was to give a little talk and receive a plaque. He shuffled down the chamber's long center aisle, shaking hands with legislators, and then had to be helped up the few short steps to the dais. The greeting had already been warm, but when he rose to speak, the applause and cheers were thunderous. The legendary speaker of the assembly, Willie Brown, had introduced the former governor, and as Brown stood at the rostrum enjoying the ovation, the speaker leaned in and whispered an acknowledgment of the roar. "Do you want to run for president?" he murmured in Brown's ear. "Accept their nomination."[4]

In part, it was a private joke. Jerry Brown was in the midst of his latest bid for the presidency and had skipped the ceremony to stay on the campaign trail. There was more to the speaker's remark, however. Willie Brown was an African American leader of a different generation than Pat Brown, but both men shared an appreciation for the feel of a crowd, and the speaker surely sensed in the reception something more than polite applause for an aging figure of yesteryear. The Californians rising to cheer their former governor were saluting not only the old man before them, but the era he symbolized, and the accomplishments of his time, and what that day had meant for California and America.

ACKNOWLEDGMENTS

WRITING A BOOK IS at once solitary and communal, solitary in that at some point the entire matter boils down to the author and the intimidating glare of a blank computer screen, communal in that the help of many people is nonetheless required. In my case, countless people provided countless favors.

Pat Brown died more than two years before I began work on the project, yet he assisted in two ways. First, his oral history is among the most candid of the hundreds I have read. He did not always remember things accurately—who does?—but there seems to have been no effort at whitewash. Second, Brown donated his gubernatorial papers to a public institution—the University of California—where they are available to all. Succeeding governors did not always follow suit, and more recently the California legislature has enacted a needlessly restrictive statute governing access to gubernatorial papers. The study of California history will suffer as a result. It says much about Brown that he left open the historical record of his tenure, and I am grateful for his candor.

Many members of the immediate and extended Brown families shared their memories. Bernice Brown, who died while the book was being written, agreed to be interviewed extensively when I first began the project. She was in her nineties and both blind and bedridden, yet we talked for two hours a day for the better part of a week. It was remarkably gracious of her. She had never met me and really had no idea who I was or what I was doing or even if there might eventually be a tangible result. However, she answered question after question. Pat's lone surviving sibling, Connie Carlson, provided wonderful memories, as did all four of the Brown children, Barbara, Cynthia, Jerry, and Kathleen. Jerry Brown provided access to his gubernatorial papers, at the University of Southern California. Kathleen Brown allowed me to see private family materials never before available to researchers, including letters from Pat to Bernice and Pat's diary. Of the other interview subjects, I particularly thank Fred Dutton and Hale Champion, Brown's two most important assistants during his time as governor, who were both generous with their time.

In light of such help, I should make one thing clear. No one had any control over the research or writing, or sought to. I provided no portion of the manuscript to any member of the Brown family or the extended Brown political circle. The book is entirely my own, especially the inevitable errors and lapses in judgment.

For critical financial support, I thank the Henry J. Kaiser Family Foundation, of Menlo Park, California, and the Koret Foundation, of San Francisco.

In many ways, my home base for the project was the University of California. The university's extraordinary research resources are a treasure of which the state's taxpayers should be proud, and three branches of the vast institution were of particular help to me.

At the Institute of Governmental Studies (IGS), two directors, Nelson Polsby and Bruce Cain, appointed and then repeatedly reappointed me as a visiting scholar, providing access to many resources. They also read the manuscript and provided keen observations and analysis. Others at IGS who helped in various ways include Terry Dean, Marc Levin, Jerry Lubenow, Carole Page, Louise Salazar, and Liz Wiener. A student research assistant, Abel Talamantez, did excellent work researching the chapter on the 1962 campaign against Nixon.

Brown's gubernatorial papers are at the university's Bancroft Library, which became my home away from home. I visited dozens of libraries and archives during my research, and the Bancroft is simply the best research facility in the country for those of us interested in California history and one of the friendliest and most useful on any topic. The staff provided countless forms of help, often well beyond the normal call of duty: processing previously uncataloged items so that I might see them, transferring audio recordings to modern media, allowing me to borrow old film footage. The Brown Papers are a massive collection—more than one thousand cartons—and much of the material had never before been used by researchers. Navigating such waters was a challenge, and I could not have asked for more or better assistance. I cannot name everyone at the Bancroft who helped, but my particular thanks to Emily Balmages, William Brown, Iris Donovan, James Eason, Franz Enciso, Amy Hellam, David Kessler, Jenny Mullowney, Erica Nordmeier, William Roberts, Theresa Salazar, Dean Smith, Susan Snyder, Elizabeth Stephens, Baiba Strads, and Jack Von Euw.

At the University of California Press, my editor, Naomi Schneider, was an invaluable supporter from beginning to end, providing both steady encouragement and a countless supply of free lunches. Sierra Filucci helped with many issues of production. I also thank Sue Heinemann, project editor, and Sheila Berg, copy editor.

Aside from the Bancroft and the other libraries at the university's Berkeley campus, I received wonderful help at many institutions around the country. In some cases material was opened for the first time at my request. Among the archivists, I thank Robert Marshall (California State University, Northridge), William A. Jones and Mary Ellen Bailey (California State University, Chico), Jenny Sternaman (Ronald Reagan Presidential Library), Kirsten Tanaka and Lee Cox (San Francisco Performing Arts Library and Museum), Claudia Anderson (Lyndon Baines Johnson Library and Museum), John L. Morton (Colusa County Archives), Abby Bridge (California Historical Society), Diana Shenk (University of Washington), Karen Jean Hunt (California State University, Dominguez Hills), Dace Taube (University of Southern California), and Sarah Cooper and Alexis Moreno (Southern California Library for Social Studies and Research). At the San Francisco Law School, the dean, Mark Owens, gave me access to old yearbooks, applications, and other materials.

A joy of this book was the opportunity to talk often with people who spend their time thinking and writing about California. Special thanks to Peter Schrag, who somehow found time in his busy schedule to read each chapter as the drafts emerged from the printer, providing invaluable comments, advice, and encouragement. Among others who helped in various ways, I thank John Anderson, Sherry Bebitch Jeffe, Bill Boyarsky, Gray Brechin, Lou Cannon, John Aubrey Douglass, Philip Fradkin, the late John Jacobs, and Susan Rasky.

Of the many colleagues from my journalistic career, I owe particular thanks to two editors. John Armstrong, my former boss at the *Contra Costa Times,* approved a leave of absence that allowed me to get started and a severance package that helped me to keep going. Clay Haswell has played a critical role in my career twice: He hired me to come to California more than a decade ago and later repeated the mistake by hiring me at the Associated Press at a key moment. My friend and former colleague Karl Mondon sacrificed his day off to take my picture for the dust jacket.

Bill and Helena Klitz provided wonderful diversions—Bill with our racquetball games, Helena with her concerts—but because they were my landlords as well as my friends, they added one other form of help any writer needs: cheap rent. It went neither unnoticed nor unappreciated.

My daughter, Ellie, brought joy and perspective, although she currently prefers Dr. Seuss to political biographies. My brother and his family—Jeff, Patty, Micah, and Carl Rarick—provided support, encouragement, and the chance to spend Christmas in subzero temperatures.

Last, I must thank a network of incredible friends. Some of them read chapters or discussed the book, but far more important, they went out for drinks, sent me encouraging e-mails, and graciously understood when I hunkered down at the computer and turned antisocial for months on end. Their ceaseless support saw me through crises personal and professional, often in ways for which I am inexpressibly grateful. I am a lucky man; my friends are too numerous for an exhaustive list. But with apologies to those left out, my deepest thanks to Dan Borenstein, Isabel Breskin, Hal Brunette, Yvonne Condes, Tom Dresslar, Allison Ellman, Hallye Jordan, Sonia Krishnan, Mike Lewis, David Long, Anthony Loveday, Katie Oyan, Ellen Quain, and Carrie Sturrock.

Without their help, and that of the other people and organizations listed above, and that of many more unfortunately omitted, the book you hold now would not exist.

Ethan Rarick
Berkeley, California

NOTES

Most references to archival collections and oral histories are by surname and are self-explanatory with reference to the bibliography. In a few cases, where several archival collections or several oral histories relating to the same person might cause confusion, other citations have been used as follows:

All references to "JFK" or "LBJ" oral histories are to histories conducted by the respective presidential libraries, as listed in the bibliography.

All references to "LOC" oral histories or archival collections are to materials in the Library of Congress, as listed in the bibliography.

EGB Papers—Edmund G. Brown Papers, 68/90 c, Bancroft Library, University of California, Berkeley

Kenny SoCal Papers—Robert Kenny Papers, Southern California Library for Social Studies and Research

EGB oral history—Edmund G. Brown, "Years of Growth, 1939–1966: Law Enforcement, Politics, and the Governor's Office," by Regional Oral History Office, University of California, Berkeley

EGB AG oral history—Edmund G. Brown, "The Governor's Lawyer," in "Earl Warren: Fellow Constitutional Officers," by Regional Oral History Office, University of California, Berkeley

EGB CSU oral history—Edmund G. Brown, by the archives of the California State University

Hawkins oral history #1—Augustus Hawkins, by the State Government Oral History Program, California State Archives

Hawkins oral history #2—Augustus Hawkins, "Black Leadership in Los Angeles," by the Oral History Program, University of California, Los Angeles

Kent oral history #1—Roger Kent, "Building the Democratic Party in California, 1954–1966," by Regional Oral History Office, University of California, Berkeley

Kent oral history #2—Roger Kent, "A Democratic Leader Looks at the Warren Era," in "California Democrats in the Earl Warren Era," by Regional Oral History Office, University of California, Berkeley

Poole oral history #1—Cecil Poole, "Executive Clemency and the Chessman Case," by Regional Oral History Office, University of California, Berkeley

Poole oral history #2—Cecil Poole, "Civil Rights, Law and the Federal Courts: The Life of Cecil Poole, 1914–1997," by Regional Oral History Office, University of California, Berkeley

PROLOGUE

1. "California Tells World It Is Now—Officially—No. 1 State," *Sacramento Bee,* December 28, 1962, p. 1; "State Honoring Itself as 'California First,'" *Los Angeles Times,* December 29, 1962, p. 1.

2. In the end, the predictions were probably too optimistic. Other demographers said later that the state surpassed New York in 1964 or 1965. See "Governor Plans Big Party for Day California Is Tops," *San Francisco Chronicle,* January 7, 1962, p. 2.

3. Schrag, *Paradise Lost,* p. 23; Maharidge, *The Coming White Minority,* p. xviii; Lewis Lapham, Foreword to Carey McWilliams's *California: The Great Exception* (1949; rept., Berkeley: University of California Press, 1999), p. xiii.

4. Gunther, *Inside U.S.A.,* pp. 1, 16.

5. "California Revolution," *Nation,* January 30, 1967, p. 133.

6. "Edmund G. Brown Is Dead at 90; He Led California in Boom Years," *New York Times,* February 18, 1996, p. 1.

7. "The Wonder Years," *Los Angeles Times,* February 21, 1996, p. 3.

CHAPTER 1: GO-GETTERS

1. Hill, *Dancing Bear,* pp. 14–15.

2. *Grandfather August Schuckman and the Mountain House,* pamphlet of stories by Gilbert Allenn, privately published and provided to the author by Kath-

leen Brown, pp. 2–5; Harold Brown oral history, pp. 1–4; EGB oral history, pp. 1–15; Constance Brown Carlson oral history, pp. 1–10.

3. *Grandfather August Schuckman,* pp. 2–7; Harold Brown oral history, p. 4.

4. Family genealogical records provided to the author by Kathleen Brown; San Francisco city directories, 1887–1900; Rapoport, *California Dreaming,* pp. 20–21; Constance Brown Carlson interview, May 10, 2000.

5. Family genealogical records provided to the author by Kathleen Brown; San Francisco city directories, 1887–1900; Rapoport, *California Dreaming,* pp. 20–21; Constance Brown Carlson interview, May 10, 2000.

6. EGB oral history, p. 2; Constance Brown Carlson interview, May 10, 2000; San Francisco city directories, 1889 onward.

7. EGB oral history, pp. 1–29; Harold Brown oral history, p. 13; Constance Brown Carlson oral history, pp. 3–35.

8. Kahn, *Imperial San Francisco,* pp. 128–37; Bronson, *The Earth Shook,* pp. 24–31; Dolan, *Disaster 1906,* pp. 11–27.

9. Constance Brown Carlson interview, May 10, 2000.

10. Constance Brown Carlson interview, May 10, 2000; San Francisco directories, 1889 onward.

11. Harold Brown oral history, p. 21; EGB oral history, p. 8.

12. In his oral history, Brown said his father bought the flats rather than built them. This appears to be false, since all other sources say he had them built, and Spring Valley Water Company records, available at the San Francisco Public Library, show service began at that location on January 17, 1909, roughly the time the Browns were moving in. Other information from Constance Brown Carlson interview, May 19, 2000; Constance Brown Carlson oral history, pp. 1–2; Harold Brown oral history, pp. 10–21; EGB oral history, p. 8.

13. EGB oral history, p. 11; Harold Brown oral history, pp. 39–40.

14. EGB oral history, p. 11; Harold Brown oral history; Constance Brown Carlson oral history; Constance Brown Carlson interview, May 10, 2000.

15. EGB oral history, p. 11; Harold Brown oral history; Constance Brown Carlson oral history; Constance Brown Carlson interview, May 10, 2000.

16. EGB oral history, p. 6. Details on the fair from Ewald and Clute, *San Francisco Invites the World.*

17. EGB oral history, pp. 15–18; Constance Brown Carlson interview, May 10, 2000; Harold Brown oral history, p. 4.

18. EGB oral history, p. 6.

19. EGB oral history, pp. 23–25.

20. Constance Brown Carlson oral history, p. 7.

21. Constance Brown Carlson interview, May 10, 2000; EGB oral history, pp. 22–25.

22. EGB oral history, pp. 4–5; Issel and Cherny, *San Francisco, 1865–1932,* p. 144.

23. EGB oral history, pp. 30–40.

24. EGB oral history, pp. 30–40.

25. EGB oral history, pp. 30–40.

26. EGB oral history, pp. 6–18.

27. Constance Brown Carlson oral history, pp. 21–24; Constance Brown Carlson interview, May 10, 2000; EGB oral history, pp. 9–14.

28. Constance Brown Carlson interview, May 10, 2000; EGB oral history, pp. 14–15.

29. Letters from EGB to Bernice Brown, July 8, 1929, and July 15, 1929, provided to the author by Kathleen Brown.

30. EGB oral history, p. 51.

31. EGB oral history, pp. 26–29, 40–47.

32. EGB oral history, pp. 44–55.

33. EGB oral history, p. 44.

34. Copies of Brown's applications and various historical material, San Francisco Law School archives; EGB oral history, pp. 44–47.

35. EGB oral history, pp. 46–49; "M. L. Schmitt Funeral Today," *San Francisco Examiner,* May 16, 1928, p. 1; "Milt Schmitt, Once Political Leader, Dead," *San Francisco Chronicle,* May 16, 1928, p. 8.

36. EGB oral history, pp. 47–50.

37. Minutes of the student body meeting, October 7, 1926, San Francisco Law School archives; *The Barrister,* San Francisco Law School yearbook, 1927 ed., p. 15; EGB oral history, pp. 40–50.

38. EGB interview with Flynn, pp. 64–66, contained in supplementary material to EGB oral history; State Bar notice of admission contained in EGB Papers, Carton 154, folder 19, "Brown, Edmund G."; "St. Mary's Trims Stanford, 16–0," *San Francisco Chronicle,* October 2, 1929, p. 1H.

39. EGB oral history, pp. 32–35.

40. EGB oral history, pp. 36–37.

41. Letter from EGB to Bernice Layne, July 2, 1923, provided to the author by Kathleen Brown.

42. Letter from EGB to Bernice Layne, September 10, 1924, provided to the author by Kathleen Brown.

43. Letter from EGB to Bernice Layne, June 30, 1925, provided to the author by Kathleen Brown.

44. For an example, letters from EGB to Bernice Layne, September 20, 1927, and September 27, 1927, provided to the author by Kathleen Brown.

45. EGB oral history, pp. 54–55.

46. Letter from EGB to Bernice Layne, April 10, 1928, provided to the author by Kathleen Brown.

47. Letter from EGB to Bernice Layne, February 3, 1928, provided to the author by Kathleen Brown.

48. Letter from EGB to Bernice Layne, March 13, 1928, provided to the author by Kathleen Brown.

49. EGB oral history, pp. 58–62.

50. State Roster, Secretary of State's Office, 1927.

51. EGB oral history, pp. 58–62; Bernice Brown interview, February 21, 1999.

52. The second-place finisher, Frank M. Goodban, outpolled Brown nearly 2–1, recording 1,156 votes. Statement of Vote, 1928 primary election, Secretary of State's Office.

CHAPTER 2: A NEW RELIGION

1. "Capt. Layne's Daughter Weds," *San Francisco Chronicle,* November 1, 1930, p. 15.

2. "Capt. Layne's Daughter Weds," *San Francisco Chronicle,* November 1, 1930, p. 15; "Police Captain's Daughter Elopes with Attorney," *San Francisco Examiner,* November 1, 1930, p. 15; "Daughter of Police Captain Elopes to Reno, Married There," *San Francisco Call-Bulletin,* November 1, 1930, p. 13.

3. Letter from EGB to Bernice Layne, July 19, 1929, provided to the author by Kathleen Brown. For a sampling of Brown cases from those years, see many files, EGB Papers, Cartons 146–54, and 1930 court register, EGB Papers, Carton 103. For dump trucks' work, see letter from EGB to Glenn Newton, December 11, 1933, Carter Papers, Box 4, folder "Brown." Also see EGB oral history, pp. 34, 63–77, 120–21; and Harold Brown oral history, pp. 22–25.

4. The Christmas card list is in EGB Papers, Carton 155, folder 32, "miscellaneous lists." For Brown's other civic activities, see various documents, EGB Papers, Carton 149, folder 56, "miscellaneous"; Carton 154, folder 19, "Brown, Edmund G."; and Carton 183, folder 2, "Brown, personal, 1941." See also EGB oral history, pp. 74–75.

5. "Supervisors Selected by Cincinnatus," *San Francisco Chronicle,* July 12, 1935, p. 4.

6. *New Order of Cincinnatus,* vol. 1, no. 1, October 27, 1935.

7. EGB oral history, p. 108; "7,000 S.F. School Children Join Lincoln Day Exercises," *San Francisco Examiner,* February 13, 1936, p. 3; "City Suspends Activities to Honor Lincoln," *San Francisco Chronicle,* February 13, 1936, p. 8.

8. Letter from EGB to Mitchell Bourquin, September 16, 1940, EGB Papers, Carton 183, folder 1, "Brown, personal."

9. Sascha Rice interview, February 24, 1999.

10. EGB oral history, p. 107.

11. EGB oral history, pp. 71, 108; letter from EGB to Raymond Haight, October 27, 1938, EGB Papers, Carton 154, folder 19, "Brown, Edmund G."

12. In 1928, when Brown ran for the legislature as a Republican, San Francisco Republicans outnumbered Democrats more than two to one. By 1936, the first

election in which Brown voted as a Democrat, the proportions had almost reversed. Newcomers cannot account for the Democratic surge. During those years, San Francisco's total number of registered voters increased 63,302, while Democratic registration increased 125,433, meaning that Brown joined thousands of other people in switching parties. Statewide, the Democratic increase occurred but not as rapidly. Statement of Vote, Secretary of State's Office, various years.

13. The exact date of Brown's partisan switch is unknown, although he later mistakenly put it in 1934. In fact, it was sometime between September 1935, when he was still registered as a Republican, and March 26, 1936, when he appeared on the rolls for the first time as a Democrat. Great Registers of San Francisco, available in the California Room, California State Library. For Brown's feelings about the partisan switch, see EGB AG oral history, p. 2; and draft of a foreword for an unpublished book by Brown, contained in Brown family materials made available to the author.

14. Tobriner oral history, pp. 270–71.

15. See various documents, including letter from EGB to John Clark, November 26, 1938, EGB Papers, Carton 154, folder 19, "Brown, Edmund G.—personal file."

16. Letter from EGB to Kennett Dawson, December 31, 1938, EGB Papers, Carton 154, folder 19, "Brown, Edmund G."

17. Burke, *Olson's New Deal for California,* p. 37.

18. Letter from Ivan Sperbeck to Melvin Belli, September 18, 1940, EGB Papers, Carton 183, folder 1, "Brown, personal."

19. Letter from EGB to Kennett Dawson, May 29, 1939, EGB Papers, Carton 154, folder 19, "Brown, Edmund G."

20. Letter from EGB to Mr. and Mrs. Norval Fast, July 6, 1939, EGB Papers, Carton 183, folder 1, "Brown, personal."

21. Letter to Howard Ellis, February 13, 1940, EGB Papers, Carton 154, folder 19, "Brown, Edmund G." For details of Brown's job hunt with the Olson administration, see many other letters also in this folder.

22. Letter from EGB to Franck Havenner, February 22, 1940, EGB Papers, Carton 183, folder 1, "Brown, personal."

23. The description of Brady's career is based principally on many newspaper accounts from his long tenure, but see especially "Brady's Office Investigated," *San Francisco Chronicle,* September 6, 1939, p. 30; "Bar Lays $53,000 Fund Misuse to Brady," *San Francisco Chronicle,* August 10, 1927, p. 1; "Brady, Layne Fire Shot at Each Other," *San Francisco Chronicle,* February 21, 1923, p. 6; "Layne Hit as Aid of Bail Bond Brokers," *San Francisco Call,* February 20, 1923, p. 1; "Brady in Defi [sic] to Women," *San Francisco Examiner,* April 6, 1923, p. 17; "Brady's 'Disbeliefs' Invalidate Proper Punishment for Murder," *San Francisco Chronicle,* October 28, 1930, p. 24.

24. EGB oral history, pp. 64–67.

25. "Brady Faces 2 Opponents," *San Francisco Chronicle,* October 8, 1939, p. 11.

26. "Reisner Wins Ruling," *San Francisco Chronicle,* October 17, 1939, p. 8.

27. "New Warning Given against Vote Stalling," *San Francisco Examiner,* November 5, 1939, p. 1; EGB oral history, pp. 93–99.

28. EGB oral history, p. 94.

29. EGB oral history, pp. 111–14.

30. Letters from EGB to Bernice Brown, July 11, 1940, and July 17, 1940, provided to the author by Kathleen Brown.

31. Letter from EGB to Bernice Brown, July 15, 1940, provided to the author by Kathleen Brown.

32. Letter from EGB to Bernice Brown, July 16, 1940, provided to the author by Kathleen Brown.

33. Letter from EGB to Bernice Brown, July 17, 1940, provided to the author by Kathleen Brown.

34. Letter from EGB to Bernice Brown, July 17, 1940, provided to the author by Kathleen Brown.

35. EGB oral history, pp. 111–14; letter from EGB to Bernice Brown, July 17, 1940, provided to the author by Kathleen Brown.

36. EGB oral history, pp. 9–10, 20–21, 77–89.

37. EGB oral history, pp. 77–92.

38. EGB oral history, pp. 9–12, 77–92; Kathleen Brown interview, December 11, 1998.

39. FBI documents in Brown's FBI file, obtained by the author under the Freedom of Information Act.

40. Letter from EGB to Milton Morris, December 23, 1941, EGB papers, Carton 156, folder 2, "Associated Home Builders."

41. Cynthia Kelly interview, November 12, 2001.

42. Letters from EGB to Kennett Dawson, December 13, 1941, EGB Papers, Carton 183, folder 2, "Brown, personal, 1941"; and from EGB to Milton Morris, December 23, 1941, EGB Papers, Carton 156, folder 2, "Associated Home Builders."

43. Letter from Y. Bepp to EGB, June 14, 1942, EGB Papers, Carton 150, folder 28, "Bepp."

44. Letter from Y. Bepp to EGB, October 28, 1942, EGB Papers, Carton 183, folder 9, "Brown, personal, 1942."

45. Letter from EGB to Navy Secretary Frank Knox, 3–23–42, EGB Papers, Carton 183, Folder 10, "Brown, personal, 1942."

46. Letter to Y. Bepp from EGB, November 3, 1942, EGB Papers, Carton 183, folder 9, "Brown, personal, 1942."

47. Letter from EGB to Y. Bepp, January 26, 1943, EGB Papers, Carton 149, folder 56, "miscellaneous."

48. Letter from EGB to "To Whom It May Concern," January 26, 1943, EGB Papers, Carton 149, folder 56, "miscellaneous."

49. Brown died July 8, 1942. Rapoport, *California Dreaming,* p. 30; EGB oral history, pp. 26–29.

50. For the story of Brown's meeting with Clarvoe here and in the paragraphs that follow, see EGB oral history, pp. 95, 119–20.

51. "Grand Jury Report Blasts Matt Brady, Liquor Board," *San Francisco Chronicle,* December 19, 1942, p. 1; "Grady Jury Ex-Foreman Attacks Brady's Defense, Last Year 'He Did Exactly Nothing,'" *San Francisco Chronicle,* February 3, 1943, p. 12.

52. EGB oral history, p. 123; "Brown Files for District Attorneyship," *San Francisco Chronicle,* September 23, 1943, p. 8.

53. "A Working Prosecutor, Brown Vows," *San Francisco Chronicle,* October 25, 1943, p. 5; "Brown: Has Brady Ever Tried a Case?" *San Francisco Chronicle,* October 26, 1943, p. 6.

54. EGB oral history, p. 124.

55. EGB oral history, p. 123.

56. "Brady Blasts Opponent's Record," *San Francisco Examiner,* October 29, 1943, p. 1; "Brown Revealed as Counsel for 2 S.F. Gambling Clubs," *San Francisco Examiner,* October 31, 1943, p. 1.

57. "Brown Replies to 'Unfair Attack,'" *San Francisco Examiner,* November 2, 1943, p. 10.

58. "Notorious," *San Francisco Chronicle,* November 1, 1943, p. 14; EGB oral history, p. 120.

59. Bernice Brown interview, February 23, 1999.

60. EGB oral history, p. 125.

CHAPTER 3: THE CHAIRS OF POLITICS

1. Physical description of Brown at his swearing in based on pictures in the *San Francisco Chronicle* and *San Francisco Examiner,* January 9, 1944.

2. EGB oral history, p. 127.

3. "Chinese to Join District Attorney Staff," *San Francisco Chronicle,* December 10, 1943, p. 7.

4. Information on appointments based on various newspaper reports, December 1943, but see especially *San Francisco Chronicle,* December 2, 10, and 25, 1943. For the investigator's background, see EGB oral history, p. 102.

5. Letter from EGB to Frank Clarvoe, March 1, 1950, EGB Papers, Carton 1020, folder 10.

6. "Brown Plans Changes in Office Routine," *San Francisco Chronicle,* January 8, 1944, p. 7; Lynch oral history, pp. 22–36; Levit oral history, pp. 3–7.

7. "Four Named as Deputies by Brown," *San Francisco Chronicle,* December 2, 1943, p. 6.

8. Various legal files, EGB Papers, Cartons 156 and 161. For the quote, see letter from EGB to Ruth Plant, May 28, 1945, EGB Papers, Carton 161, folder 6, "Hockadey, Ruth v. Hockadey."

9. Not until his second term, in 1948, was Brown finally able to ban outside legal work by himself and his deputies. "Brown Bans Outside Jobs," *San Francisco News,* April 28, 1948, p. 3. For Brown's income from outside work, see 1944 financial records, EGB Papers, Carton 105, records in black, unlabeled notebook.

10. "Brown's Speech: 'I Will Act on Behalf of All—Not a Few,'" *San Francisco Chronicle,* January 9, 1944, p. 6.

11. EGB oral history, pp. 131–35.

12. EGB oral history, p. 101.

13. Letter from EGB to George Keefe, September 5, 1945, EGB Papers, Carton 97, folder 7, "correspondence—personal."

14. "S.F. Bookies Closing," *San Francisco Call-Bulletin,* December 22, 1943, p. 1.

15. EGB oral history, p. 101.

16. EGB oral history, p. 28.

17. Author's interview with William Newsom Jr., who was told about the incident by his father, November 14, 1998.

18. "Youth, Don't Be a Chump," copy provided to author by Jeff Brown, EGB's nephew.

19. "Curb Divorce to Cut Crime, Brown Urges," *San Francisco Chronicle,* March 4, 1945, p. 7.

20. Letter from EGB to Harry Elmer Barnes and Negley Teeters, September 5, 1945, EGB Papers, Carton 97, folder 7, "correspondence, personal."

21. "Brown Assails 'Soft' Judges and Juries," *San Francisco Chronicle,* December 30, 1949, p. 3; "Pat Brown's Umbrage," *San Francisco Chronicle,* December 31, 1949, p. 8.

22. By far the best account of the Burns case, and the source for much of this version, is Stephen G. Bloom, "San Francisco's Worst Kept Secret: The Untold Story of Millionaire Abortion Queen Inez Brown Burns," *The Californians* 13, no. 2 (1995): 40. See also Lynch oral history, pp. 57–62; Elkington oral history, pp. 15–19.

23. EGB oral history, pp. 111–14.

24. EGB oral history, p. 113.

25. EGB oral history, p. 113.

26. EGB oral history, p. 113.

27. Kenny oral history, p. 266; EGB oral history, p. 137.

28. EGB oral history, p. 137; EGB AG oral history, p. 77.

29. Sherry oral history, pp. 123–24.

30. Various campaign memos, EGB Papers, Carton 107, folder 53, "Interoffice Political."

31. "Brown to Return May Pay to City," *San Francisco Examiner*, May 7, 1946, p. 5.

32. Various newspaper stories, especially "Brown Still Holds Lead over Howser," *San Francisco Chronicle*, June 8, 1946, p. 1; for Brown's views on election night, see EGB oral history, p. 138.

33. "Gambling Ship Charges Enter Attorney Race," *Sacramento Bee*, October 4, 1946, p. 1.

34. Someone, apparently the Brown staff, even prepared the text of a radio speech containing a partial retraction, although it is undated and it is not clear if it was ever delivered; EGB Papers, Carton 122, folder 7, "speeches—attorney general—1946."

35. Letter from EGB to George Keefe, August 9, 1945, EGB Papers, Carton 97, folder 7, "correspondence, personal."

36. "Ex-Manager for Brown Backs Howser," *Los Angeles Times*, October 25, 1946, p. 2.

37. "Brown Hopes to End Violence in Labor Disputes," *Sacramento Bee*, October 30, 1946, p. 4; "Edmund G. Brown Has Sports Program," *Sacramento Bee*, November 2, 1946, p. 1.

38. "Brown Promises Non Partisan Policy as Attorney General," *Sacramento Bee*, November 2, 1946, p. 4.

39. Letter from EGB to Glenn Anderson, November 19, 1946, Anderson Papers, Carton 54, folder "Brown, Edmund G."

40. Letter from Janet Aitken to EGB, May 1, 1947, EGB Papers, Carton 134, folder 1, "Housing in SF." For the overall issue, see also "Third and Final Report on Housing Conditions in San Francisco," San Francisco District Attorney's Office, 1948.

41. "Brown Report Links S.F. Housing Crisis to Crime," *San Francisco Examiner*, May 8, 1947, p. 4.

42. Letter from EGB to Ralph Swing, May 16, 1947, EGB Papers, Carton 134, folder 1, "Housing in SF." See also "Brown Angry at Senators," *San Francisco Examiner*, May 20, 1947, p. 3.

43. Letter from EGB to the editor of the *San Francisco Call-Bulletin*, August 25, 1948, copy at EGB Papers, Carton 134, folder 1, "Housing in SF." "Housing Outlook," editorial, *San Francisco Call-Bulletin*, August 19, 1948, p. 24.

44. News conference transcript, February 1, 1966, EGB Papers, Carton 997, folder 9, "Jan.–Mar. 1966."

45. Memo to Brown's staff, October 2, 1947, EGB Papers, Carton 107, folder 53, "Interoffice Political."

46. For NLG endorsement, see National Lawyers Guild papers, Box 86,

folder "San Francisco Guild Lawyer." For *Examiner,* see the paper of October 31, 1947, p. 11.

47. Letter from EGB to Roosevelt, January 19, 1948, EGB Papers, Carton 127, folder 9, "Roosevelt."

48. Letters from EGB to Roosevelt, January 19, 1948, and February 11, 1948, EGB Papers, Carton 127, folder 9, "Roosevelt."

49. Brown was rewriting history a little. Actually, four years earlier he had let the pro-Truman voices influence him, agreeing beneath the podium of the convention to desert Wallace's vice presidential bid after a single ballot. Letter from EGB to Roosevelt, March 29, 1948, EGB Papers, Carton 127, folder 9, "Roosevelt."

50. "Roosevelt Snub of Truman," *San Francisco Chronicle,* April 14, 1948, p. 2.

51. "Pat Brown Center of State Demo Row," *San Francisco News,* April 15, 1948, p. 21.

52. Letter from EGB to Roosevelt, April 15, 1948, EGB Papers, Carton 127, folder 9, "Roosevelt." See also EGB AG oral history, p. 69.

53. Arthur Caylor column, *San Francisco News,* April 16, 1948, p. 21.

54. Letter from EGB to Frank Mackin, July 22, 1948, EGB Papers, Carton 156, folder 6, "Brown, E. G."

55. Letter from EGB to Frank Mackin, July 22, 1948, EGB Papers, Carton 156, folder 6, "Brown, E. G."

56. Letter from EGB to Frank Mackin, July 22, 1948, EGB Papers, Carton 156, folder 6, "Brown, E. G."

57. Letters from EGB to Jerry Brown, July 21, 1948, EGB Papers, Carton 156, folder 6, "Brown, E. G.," and to Frank Mackin, August 12, 1948, EGB Papers, Carton 32, folder "Democratic Plans."

58. Copy of a card, Kenny SoCal Papers, Box 4, folder 30.

59. EGB AG oral history, pp. 1–3; Jones oral history, pp. 16–17.

60. The description of Howser's troubles is based on many contemporary reports, but for a good summary, see "Howser Office Record Piles Up," *San Francisco News,* July 2, 1948, p. 1. See also Sherry oral history, pp. 106–15. For his medical problem, see "Crime Board Chief Blasts Howser Aide," *San Francisco News,* July 8, 1948, p. 1.

61. For Brown's thinking during this period, see especially his letter to Eugene Horton, April 18, 1949, EGB Papers, Carton 128, folder 31, "Howser."

62. Speech in San Jose, August 4, 1958, copy at EGB Papers, Carton 142, folder 5, "misc."

63. "Brown May Run Again for State Attorney General," *San Francisco Chronicle,* January 5, 1950, p. 7.

64. "Brown Announces His Candidacy for Attorney General," *San Francisco Chronicle,* February 13, 1950, p. 2.

65. EGB oral history, p. 147.

66. Kent oral history #2, p. 10.

67. EGB oral history, pp. 142–61, 174–80; letters from EGB to Harry Bridges Victory Committee, January 30, 1945, and February 5, 1945, EGB Papers, Carton 1020, folder 3, "B misc."

68. "Brown Asks Voters to Check His and Shattuck's Records," *Sacramento Bee,* November 4, 1950, p. 4.

69. Author's interview. Still worried about the reaction of friends to his wife's past, the man asked that the couple's identities be concealed.

70. Letter from EGB to Fritz Marquardt, October 16, 1950, EGB Papers, Carton 128, folder 15, "M misc."

71. EGB oral history, pp. 148–49; Pearson's column can be found, among other places, in the *San Francisco Chronicle,* October 21, 1950, p. 10.

72. Warren, *Memoirs of Earl Warren,* p. 199; EGB oral history, p. 148.

73. "Warren Landslide Indicated by Poll," *Los Angeles Times,* November 6, 1950, p. 16.

74. EGB oral history, p. 178.

CHAPTER 4: WAITING

1. The phrase was probably written by Warren's collaborator, but it appeared under the governor's byline in "California's Biggest Headache," *Saturday Evening Post,* August 14, 1948, p. 20. The headline, doubtless written by an uncomprehending easterner, is misleading; the piece brims with optimism.

2. Farrelly and Hinderaker, *The Politics of California,* p. 3.

3. Gunther, *Inside U.S.A.,* p. 1.

4. "California's Centenary," *New York Times,* September 6, 1950, p. 28.

5. McWilliams, *California: The Great Exception,* p. 18.

6. California Department of Justice Biennial Report, 1950–52, p. 5.

7. EGB AG oral history, p. 90.

8. Letter from EGB to Alfred W. Robertson, July 23, 1951, EGB Papers, Carton 110, folder 2, "Brown, personal."

9. Letter from EGB to Glenn Anderson, January 4, 1951, Anderson Papers, Carton 54, folder "Brown, Edmund G."

10. EGB AG oral history, pp. 5–6; "Warren, Attorney General Brown Work on Joint Approach to Crime Problem in State," *Sacramento Bee,* January 17, 1951, p. 10.

11. EGB AG oral history, p. 8.

12. The opinions of Brown's Department of Justice are summarized in the department's regular reports for the Governor's Council. For the opinions cited here, see the reports dated March 1952, January–February 1953, and November–December 1955.

13. Memo from EGB to William O'Connor, April 18, 1951, EGB Papers, Carton 17, folder 10, "William O'Connor."

14. Department of Justice Report for Governor's Council, June 1955. For Brown quote, see "Bible as Art Wins a Role in Schools," *New York Times,* June 13, 1955, p. 25. For other useful background, see "Brown Ruling against Bible Bill Reported," *San Francisco Chronicle,* March 27, 1955, p. 15; "Brown: Constitution Forbids Bible Reading in Public Schools," *San Francisco Chronicle,* June 12, 1955, p. 22; "State Attorney Rules Out Bible Reading for Religious Purposes in Public Schools," *Sacramento Bee,* June 13, 1955, p. 3; Senate Bill 1152, 1955 session.

15. Letter from EGB to Pearson, February 4, 1952, Pearson Papers, Box G263, 1 of 3, folder "Brown."

16. McCullough, *Truman,* p. 889.

17. Abell, *Drew Pearson Diaries,* p. 194.

18. EGB statement, May 29, 1952, EGB Papers, Carton 31, folder 2, "Brown slate."

19. EGB oral history, p. 170. The overall description of the 1952 presidential campaign from EGB oral history, pp. 162–84a; Heller oral history, pp. 366–67; Bradley oral history, pp. 17–25.

20. Stone, *Earl Warren,* p. 91.

21. Another factor that probably led to Republican advantage, although a minor one, was pointed out in a nonpartisan context by James Q. Wilson. Since California had few patronage jobs, poor residents stood little chance of receiving some kind of material payback from political involvement. The noneconomic nature of California patronage, such as appointments to boards of commissions, skewed political reward toward people with relatively less need for extra income. See Wilson, *The Amateur Democrat,* p. 203.

22. Letter from EGB to Nathan B. McVay, December 21, 1953, EGB Papers, Carton 109, folder 28, "MC–Pol., 51–54."

23. Elliott was also something of a political visionary. As early as 1948, Elliott complained that national political conventions had become "super-colossal circuses with great noise, fanfare, disorder and loud oratory" and suggested they be replaced with a nationwide primary to formally select the nominees of both parties. Letter from Elliott to James Roosevelt, January 29, 1948, Clifton Papers, Carton 1, folder "Roosevelt—1948."

24. "Authorities Reveal Anti-Crossfiling Plan Could Be Voted, Still Not Become Law," *Sacramento Bee,* July 26, 1951, p. 8.

25. Much of the history of the founding of the California Democratic Council is based on Wyatt interview, August 9, 2001; Bradley oral history, pp. 22–39; Shirpser oral history, pp. 237–48; Wilson, *The Amateur Democrat,* pp. 96–125; Carney, *The Rise of the Democratic Clubs,* pp. 1–16; Richards oral history, pp. 22–30. See also pamphlet titled "California Democratic Council: The First Eight Years," in Cranston Papers, Carton 11, folder 2.

26. Tobriner oral history, pp. 286–89; exchange of letters between EGB and Frank Jordan, December 22, 1948, and November 16, 1948, EGB Papers, Carton 32, folder 3, "Associated Democrats."

27. "Demos Plan for '54, Urge New Approach to Local Politics," *San Francisco Chronicle*, February 1, 1953, p. 4.

28. Bradley oral history, pp. 23–34, quote on 34; EGB oral history, pp. 203–10.

29. Letter from EGB to Robert Strauss, October 7, 1955, EGB Papers, Carton 166, unnumbered binder labeled "PO, 1955–1956."

30. Bernice Brown interview, February 23, 1999.

31. Much has obviously been written about Jerry Brown's life and personality. For his childhood, see particularly "Jerry Brown's School Days," *San Francisco Chronicle*, June 26, 1977, magazine, p. 8. See also letter from EGB to Jerry Brown, March 1, 1957, EGB Papers, Carton 17, folder 6, "Personal—Brown."

32. Letter from EGB to Jerry Brown, July 21, 1948, EGB Papers, Carton 156, folder 6, "Brown, E. G."

33. Letter from EGB to Kathleen Brown, July 18, 1957, EGB Papers, Carton 17, folder 6, "Personal—Brown."

34. Exchange of letters between EGB and Barbara (Brown) Casey on October 10, 1951, and October 15, 1951, EGB Papers, Carton 110, folder 2, "Brown, personal."

35. "Brown Won't Run against Warren," *San Francisco Chronicle*, May 5, 1953, p. 1.

36. For Knight background, see especially *Nation*, "Knight over California," May 29, 1954, pp. 461–65; and "California's Excellency Excels at Jokes as Well as Politics," *Life*, March 29, 1954, pp. 116–27.

37. EGB oral history, p. 190.

38. Florence Clifton oral history, p. 53

39. Graves oral history, pp. 137–59; EGB oral history, p. 190.

40. "Democrats Suffer California Blow," *New York Times*, December 13, 1953, p. 58.

41. In the end, the *Los Angeles Times* endorsed Brown anyway, although the paper noted that it normally supported only Republicans. The attorney general was, the paper said, perhaps a little tepidly, "an honest, able, energetic administrator." "Brown Makes Good as Attorney General," *Los Angeles Times*, June 3, 1954, pt. II, p. 4.

42. Statement of Vote, 1954.

43. EGB oral history, p. 191.

44. Translation of a story from the Lima paper *La Crónica*: "California Attorney General Last Night at Country Club Awaited His Reelection," November 3, 1954, p. 1, found in EGB Papers, Carton 1021, folder 18.

45. Letter from EGB to Pat Frayne, November 6, 1954, EGB Papers, Carton 1021, folder 18.

46. List of 1956 Christmas gifts, EGB Papers, Carton 17, folder 6, "Personal—Brown."

47. Letter from EGB to Warren Erickson, August 28, 1956, EGB Papers, Carton 109, folder 4, "D Pol., 56–57."

48. Letter from EGB to Clara Shirpser, August 3, 1955, Shirpser Papers, Box 2, folder "Brown."

49. "I Won't Run for Senate, Brown Says on TV," *San Francisco Chronicle,* October 18, 1955, p. 6.

50. For general background on Jerry's decision to enter the novitiate, see especially Pack, *Jerry Brown,* pp. 1–27; but also Bollens, *Jerry Brown,* pp. 22–43; Rapoport, *California Dreaming,* pp. 44–53; Schell, *Brown,* pp. 55–76; and Jerry Brown interview, *Playboy,* April 1976, p. 69.

51. Letter from EGB to Jerry Brown, May 20, 1957, EGB Papers, Carton 17, folder 6, "Personal—Brown."

52. Letter from EGB to Jerry Brown, March 1, 1957, EGB Papers, Carton 17, folder 6, "Personal—Brown."

53. Letter from EGB to Jerry Brown, April 26, 1957, EGB Papers, Carton 17, folder 6, "Personal—Brown." In an interview with the author on February 23, 1999, Bernice Brown said she did not object to her son's decision but acknowledged, "I didn't like it."

54. EGB oral history, pp. 235–36.

55. EGB oral history, pp. 212–32; EGB AG oral history, pp. 63–64; Heller oral history, pp. 378–82; Bradley oral history, pp. 54–55; Shirpser oral history, pp. 480–82; Martin, *Ballots and Bandwagons,* pp. 373–455; Dutton oral history, pp. 63–69; Rees oral history, pp. 286–88; Gatov oral history, pp. 188–96.

56. Beard interview, January 6, 2003.

57. Years later, Brown thought the struggle with Knight occurred over conditions at Camarillo State Hospital rather than Modesto, but the Camarillo investigation came much later, after Knight was no longer running for governor. In any event, Brown spoke candidly twice about his political motivations vis-à-vis the state mental hospitals; EGB oral history, p. 243, and EGB AG oral history, pp. 60–61. Other details from "Brutal Handling Charged in State Hospital Deaths," *San Francisco Chronicle,* September 7, 1956, p. 1.

CHAPTER 5: VICTORY

1. Lynch oral history, pp. 97, 123.

2. Montgomery and Johnson, *One Step from the White House,* pp. 1–19, 278.

3. Montgomery and Johnson, *One Step from the White House,* pp. 10–54.

4. Montgomery and Johnson, *One Step from the White House,* pp. 80, 220; Ambrose, *Eisenhower: Soldier and President,* p. 334.

5. Montgomery and Johnson, *One Step from the White House,* pp. 220–27; Abell, *Drew Pearson Diaries,* pp. 487–88.

6. Montgomery and Johnson, *One Step from the White House,* pp. 228–54.

7. "Knowland Plan to Bow Out in '58 Jolts Capitol," *Sacramento Bee,* January 8, 1957, p. 1.

8. Letter from EGB to Jerry Brown, July 11, 1957, EGB Papers, Carton 17, folder 6, "Personal—Brown."

9. Fred Dutton, as close as anyone to Brown's political plans at the time, remembers no such meeting and doubts it occurred. Brown, however, recounted it in detail in his oral history, pp. 234–35, and Irv Sprague, then an aide to another California congressman and later a Brown aide, told the author about the meeting in an interview, May 23, 2000. See also "Brown Says '58 State Demo Slate Will Be Best in Years," *Sacramento Bee,* March 8, 1957, p. A6.

10. Letter from EGB to Jerry Brown, April 26, 1957, EGB Papers, Carton 17, folder 6, "Personal—Brown."

11. EGB oral history, pp. 239–41; Dutton oral history, pp. 108–10.

12. Letters from EGB to Jerry Brown, July 11, 1957, and August 13, 1957, both in EGB Papers, Carton 17, folder 6, "Personal—Brown."

13. Letters from EGB to Kathleen Brown, July 18, 1957, and to Jerry Brown, August 13, 1957, both in EGB Papers, Carton 17, folder 6, "Personal—Brown."

14. EGB oral history, pp. 251–55; Dutton interview, May 22, 2000; Burch interview, May 22, 2000; Dutton oral history, pp. 1–61.

15. Dutton interview, May 22, 2000.

16. Dutton interview, May 22, 2000; Burch interview, May 22, 2000; Dutton oral history, pp. 108–13.

17. "Brown One Step Nearer Candidacy," *San Francisco Chronicle,* August 24, 1957, p. 5.

18. Montgomery and Johnson, *One Step from the White House,* pp. 232–34.

19. Kossen oral history, pp. 33–34.

20. Montgomery and Johnson, *One Step from the White House,* pp. 228–54; Halberstam, *The Powers That Be,* pp. 261–66; Caldecott oral history, pp. 29–37.

21. Anderson, *Campaigns,* p. 283, also in *Christian Science Monitor,* November 7, 1958.

22. EGB oral history, p. 245.

23. "Brown Almost Says It's Governorship," *San Francisco Chronicle,* September 4, 1957, p. 7; "Brown to Tell Plans after State Tour," *San Francisco Examiner,* September 4, 1957, p. 12.

24. Introduction letters from EGB, September 27, 1957, and October 7, 1957, EGB Papers, Carton 1026, folder 2, "Demo Matters."

25. Letter from Dutton to Christopher, October 3 ,1957, EGB Papers, Carton 1026, folder 1, "Frederick Dutton—Personal."

26. Memo from Frank Mackin to EGB, October 3 ,1957, EGB Papers, Carton 49, folder 24, "campaign planning."

27. "Brown Announces for Governorship," *Los Angeles Times,* October 30, 1957, p. 1; "Demo Brown Will Seek Governorship," *Sacramento Bee,* October 30, 1957, p. 1; "Coast Democrat to Fore," *New York Times,* October 31, 1957, p. 24.

28. Abell, *Drew Pearson Diaries,* p. 403.

29. Various California Polls taken throughout the race. To see the change after the Knowland-Knight switch, see polls dated September 19, 1957, and November 20, 1957.

30. Press release, February 12, 1958, EGB Papers, Carton 47, folder 8, "press releases, Feb. 4–28, 1958."

31. For Brown's candid admission that this is what happened, see EGB oral history, pp. 345–46.

32. Press release, December 10, 1957, EGB Papers, Carton 47, folder 5, "press releases—December 1957."

33. Press release, February 12, 1958, EGB Papers, Carton 47, folder 8, "press releases, Feb. 4–28, 1958"; Montgomery and Johnson, *One Step from the White House,* p. 249.

34. EGB oral history, p. 233.

35. Montgomery and Johnson, *One Step from the White House,* pp. 240–41.

36. Recording of speech in Santa Barbara, Phonotape 3118c, Bancroft Library, UC Berkeley; "Brown Calls for Positive 'Economic Leadership,'" *Humboldt Times,* May 4, 1958, p. 1; "Brown Attacks GOP Policies, Hits Knowland," *Modesto Bee,* May 14, 1958, p. 1.

37. "California: Just Plain Pat," *Time,* September 15, 1958, pp. 18–21.

38. "Mrs. Pat Brown Campaigns," *Sacramento Bee,* October 14, 1958, p. B1.

39. Press release, February 21, 1958, EGB Papers, Carton 47, folder 8, "press releases—Feb. 4–28, 1958."

40. EGB oral history, p. 254.

41. McHenry oral history, p. 157.

42. For Stegner's involvement, see especially letter from Bill Coblentz to EGB, June 11, 1958, EGB Papers, Carton 1023, folder 6, "Coblentz file." For McHenry and Burdick, see memo from Dutton to EGB, February 17, 1958, EGB Papers, Carton 45, folder 10, "Dutton correspondence to Brown."

43. Text of ads in EGB Papers, Carton 51, folder 19, "radio and TV spots."

44. Letter from EGB to Joe Wyatt, January 28, 1958, EGB Papers, Carton 38, folder 8, "CDC."

45. Graves oral history, p. 150.

46. Dutton oral history, pp. 81–85.

47. "Brown Charges Knowland Deceit in Knight Switch," *Los Angeles Examiner,* November 2, 1957.

48. Press releases, August 30, 1958, August 28, 1958, August 27, 1958, August 4, 1958, EGB Papers, Carton 47. Release dated August 4, 1958, in folder 18, "press releases, Aug. 1–15," all others in folder 20, "press releases, Aug. 16–31."

49. EGB speech on September 2, 1958, copy in EGB Papers, Carton 50, folder 2, "editor mailings." See also text of Brown campaign commercials, EGB Papers, Carton 51, folder 19, "radio and TV spots."

50. Summary of the interviews, EGB Papers, Carton 50, folder 14, "interview analysis"; various California Polls.

51. Copies of the ads, MP 320C, Bancroft Library, UC Berkeley.

52. Dutton oral history, pp. 86–94.

53. EGB oral history, p. 245.

54. For the general incident, see Montgomery and Johnson, *One Step from the White House,* pp. 248–51; Schuparra, *Triumph of the Right,* pp. 38–39. For Brown releases, September 14, 1958, September 15, 1958, and September 16, 1958, see EGB Papers, Carton 47, folder 22, "press releases, Sept. 11–20."

55. Estelle Knowland Johnson oral history, p. 9.

56. "Demo Landslide, Record Vote in State Forecast," *San Francisco Examiner,* November 4, 1958, p. 1.

57. EGB victory statement, Phonotape 3117 C, Bancroft Library, UC Berkeley. The general account of election day and the celebration is based on many sources, including coverage the next day in the *San Francisco Chronicle, San Francisco Examiner,* and *Sacramento Bee;* Dutton interview, May 22, 2000; Kathleen Brown interview, September 7, 2000; recording of EGB victory statement, Phonotape 3117 C, Bancroft; and recorded EGB interview on election night, Phonotape 3249 C, Bancroft.

58. "Brown Charges Knowland Trying to Take Over GOP," *Los Angeles Examiner,* August 10, 1958.

59. "Governor-Elect Has Hectic Morn," *San Francisco Examiner,* November 6, 1958, p. 1.

CHAPTER 6: THE BIG WALLOP

1. Burch interview, May 22, 2000.

2. Levit oral history, pp. 17–18.

3. Champion interview, May 19, 2000; Champion oral history, pp. 1–27.

4. "Brown Asks All Appointees of Knight to Quit," *Sacramento Bee,* December 5, 1958, p. 1.

5. "The New Year Rides a Donkey," *Sacramento Bee,* January 3, 1959, p. D14.

6. The text of the inaugural was published in the *Sacramento Bee,* January 5, 1959, p. 6.

7. It was a dumb thing to say—during the campaign he had promised to serve a full term as governor—so an hour later he denied it. He maintained somebody else must have said it, which was ludicrous. In any event, that same day his nephew Jeff asked him who the 1960 presidential front-runner was, and the new governor said, "Me." "Inauguration Fires Up Demos; Less Exuberant GOPers Wish Them Luck," *Sacramento Bee,* January 6, 1959, p. 6; Jeff Brown interview, August 13, 1998.

8. California Department of Finance and U.S. Census Bureau population estimates. The state estimates are available in the state budget; the Census Bureau numbers are at "Nevada's Census Up 69% since 1950," *New York Times,* December 7, 1959, p. 24.

9. 1960 census, vol. 1, pt. A, pp. 6–23.

10. "California Fears Industry Pirates," *New York Times,* May 17, 1959, p. 80.

11. "Shifts in California's Industrial and Employment Composition," *Monthly Labor Review,* May 1959, pp. 509–17.

12. Michener material from introduction to Morgan, *Westward Tilt,* p. vii; "That California Way of Life," *Changing Times,* January 1960, pp. 27–32.

13. Ward and Burns, *Baseball,* pp. 347–52.

14. "78,672 See Dodgers Win; City Gives Team Big Welcome," *Los Angeles Times,* April 19, 1958, p. 1.

15. "Fans Here Mourn Loss of Two Clubs," *New York Times,* April 16, 1958, p. 43.

16. "Giants Beat Dodgers in Coast Debut; Games Everywhere But Here," *New York Times,* April 16, 1958, p. 1; "Big League Curtain Rises," *Christian Science Monitor,* April 16, 1958, p. 1.

17. "Parade for Giants Tomorrow," *San Francisco Chronicle,* April 13, 1958, p. 1, and various stories, April 16, 1958, p. 1; "Fans Here Mourn Loss of Two Clubs," *New York Times,* April 16, 1958, p. 43; "Crowd of 78,672 Sets Four Major Attendance Records," *Los Angeles Times,* April 19, 1958, p. II-4.

18. Constance Brown Carlson interview, May 10, 2000.

19. Bernice Brown interview with Governor's Mansion docents, January 9, 1959, Mansion archives.

20. Letter from EGB to Jerry Brown, January 21, 1959, EGB Papers, Carton 352, folder "gov.'s personal/family."

21. Bernice Brown interview, February 24, 1999.

22. EGB diary, January 19, 1959.

23. EGB oral history, pp. 278–300.

24. The "budget" in this case is defined as the state's "General Fund," the basic pot of tax dollars the legislature spends every year. Deficit figures from "New Estimate Puts State Deficit at $282 Million," *Sacramento Bee,* December 12, 1959, p. 10. Budget figures from 1959–60 proposed state budget, California Department of Finance.

25. The 1959–60 proposed state budget, pp. xx–xxiv and Schedules 1 and 2. For the administration's thinking regarding the tax package, see Levit oral history, pp. 16–23.

26. EGB oral history, p. 278; EGB diary, January 28, 1959; Dutton interview, May 22, 2000.

27. EGB diary, January 28, 1959; 1959–60 proposed state budget, p. xxiii.

28. EGB diary, January 20, 1959, January 29, 1959, March 3, 1959.

29. Burby interview, May 15, 2000.

30. EGB AG oral history, pg. 84.

31. Champion interview, May 2, 2000; Kathleen Kelly interview, November 29, 2001.

32. Letter from EGB to Jerry Brown, January 21, 1959, EGB Papers, Carton 352, folder "Gov.'s Personal/Family."

33. "First Bill," *Sacramento Bee*, January 30, 1959, p. 1. For general information throughout this chapter about the 1959 session of the legislature, the best sources are the contemporary press accounts, and the best of these are from the *Bee*. For a good summary, see Tuttle, *The California Democrats*, pp. 141–73.

34. Excerpts of the Urban League report are included in Rumford Papers, Carton 3, folder 5.

35. FEPC First Annual Report, p. 7, in Rumford Papers, Carton 3, folder 6.

36. Hawkins oral history #1, pp. 133–35; Rumford oral history, pp. 42–55; Crouchett, *William Byron Rumford*, pp. 59–63.

37. Brown's role, about which virtually nothing has been written, is documented in various communications among FEPC supporters. See memo from William Becker to the officers of the California Committee for Fair Employment Practices, March 17, 1959, in Rumford Papers, Carton 3, folder 8. In Rumford Papers, Carton 5, folder 3, see various documents: telegram from Rumford to Terry Francois, April 3, 1959; letter from Franklin H. Williams to Rumford, March 19, 1959; and letter from Rumford to Adrien Falk, April 3, 1959.

38. For the role of the business community, see "Emasculated FEPC Bill Is Advanced," *Sacramento Bee*, April 2, 1959, p. 1.

39. News conference transcript, EGB Papers, Carton 996, folder 3.

40. "Senate Backs Brown, Votes for Stronger FEPC Measure," *Sacramento Bee*, April 7, 1959, p. 1.

41. Text of remarks by John Anson Ford, first chairman of the commission, at FEPC third anniversary luncheon, September 27, 1962, in Rumford Papers, Carton 3, folder 1.

42. Letter from EGB to John Canterbury, November 30, 1953, EGB Papers, Carton 31, folder 3, "campaign planning."

43. EGB diary, March 27, 1959; "Governor Snaps His Whip over the Legislature," *San Francisco Chronicle*, March 25, 1959, p. 1.

44. "Brown Takes Poke at Tax Bill Critic," *Sacramento Bee*, May 26, 1959, p.

12; "Brown Assails Hypocrites in Legislature," *Sacramento Bee,* March 24, 1959, p. B4.

45. "Governor Warns Tax Plan Foes: Beer, Races, Oil," *San Francisco Chronicle,* April 18, 1959, p. 1.

46. EGB diary, April 21, 1959.

47. EGB diary, May 25, 1959.

48. Burns oral history, pp. 13–31.

49. "Lid's Off Old State Secrets," *Contra Costa Times,* November 11, 1999, p. 1.

50. For example, see letter from Brown to Miller, December 23, 1957, appointing him Contra Costa County chairman. Similar letters to other campaign appointees contain no such request for oversight. EGB Papers, Carton 1026, folder 4.

51. George Miller III interview, May 25, 2000; Keith Sexton interview, October 29, 1999; Fred Dutton interview, May 24, 2000.

52. George Miller III interview, May 25, 2000; Pope interview, January 16, 2003; EGB diary, January 29, 1959.

53. Report of the Senate Fact-Finding Committee on Revenue and Taxation, 1965, pt. 1, p. 11; "Cigarette, Income Tax Hikes Vetoed," *Los Angeles Times,* May 27, 1959, p. 1; "3 Cent Cigaret, Income Tax Boost Bills Pass State Senate," *Sacramento Bee,* May 27, 1959, p. 1.

54. *The Reporter,* February 21, 1957, p. 18.

55. "Pat Brown for President," *Newsweek,* June 8, 1959, p. 29.

56. The reporter was C. K. McClatchy, heir to the paper and destined to be its publisher. "Rapid Growth of California Is Reflected by Drastic Expansion in MVD Quarters," *Sacramento Bee,* April 12, 1959, p. 3.

57. Jones, *California's Freeway Era,* p. 53. Note also that Bottles refers to the Aldrich plan as "the basis of today's existing freeway system," Bottles, *Los Angeles and the Automobile,* p. 220.

58. Jones, *California's Freeway Era,* pp. 37–54. By comparison, Moses had built 325 miles of parkway in New York. For Moses comparison, see Jones, but also "The Comprehensive Parkway System of the New York Metropolitan Region," *Civil Engineering,* March 1939, pp. 160–62.

59. "The California Freeway System," California Department of Public Works, 1958. Also see Jones, *California's Freeway Era,* pp. 227–51; Senate Bill 480, 1959 California Legislature; "Thirteenth Annual Report to the Governor of California by the Director of Public Works," 1960; and Report of the Joint Interim Committee on Highway Problems, California State Senate, 1959, including in Appendix to the Journal of the Senate, 1959.

60. California has less than six thousand miles of freeway and expressway, compared to more than twelve thousand in the original plan; "1998 Assembly of Statistical Reports," California Department of Transportation, p. 58.

61. "S.F. Is Given the Word by Brown," *San Francisco Examiner*, February 25, 1959, p. 12; "Freeways a Must, Brown Tells S.F.," *San Francisco Chronicle*, February 25, 1959, p. 2.

62. In every year that Brown was governor, federal highway aid through the interstate program was exceeded by state taxes paid by highway users. There was even an argument to be made that the interstate system, also funded by gas taxes, might be a net loser for California. For the 1960 fiscal year, California received 8.9 percent of all federal highway expenditures, yet consumed, and thus paid taxes on, 9.5 percent of motor fuel. For this, see Report of the Joint Interim Committee on Highway Problems, California State Senate, 1959, p. 39. For the annual funding totals, see "Statistical Reports of the Department of Public Works pertaining to the Division of Highways," California Department of Public Works, 1972, pp. 15–16.

63. Over the life of the freeway program, state highway taxes were forecast to produce four times as much money as federal aid. Report of the Joint Interim Committee on Highway Problems, California State Senate, 1959, p. 42.

64. "Minimum Wage Bill Loses; Two-Year Study Is Ordered," *Sacramento Bee*, April 28, 1959, p. 1.

65. "Oil, Gas Tax Bill Is Rejected, Brown Warns of Budget Peril," *Sacramento Bee*, May 29, 1959, p. 1; "Brown Hopes for Revival of Tax Bill," *Sacramento Bee*, May 29, 1959, p. 6.

66. "6 Hour Battle Kills Oil, Gas Tax in Assembly; Backers Give Up," *Sacramento Bee*, June 7, 1959, p. 1; "43–29 Vote Ends Hope of Oil Tax," *San Francisco Chronicle*, June 7, 1959, p. 1.

67. "Giant Firecrackers Blast as Sound and Fury of Legislative Session Ends," *San Francisco Bee*, June 20, 1959, p. 5.

68. "Brown Proud, Pleased with Legislature," *Los Angeles Times*, June 21, 1959, p. 1; "Brown Praises Legislature for Good Job," *Sacramento Bee*, June 20, 1959, p. 4.

69. Memo from Richardson to EGB, January 21, 1959, EGB Papers, Carton 353, folder 10, "legislative program Jan.–Feb."

70. For specifics on labor issues, see "Governor Brown's Legislative Achievements for California Workers," EGB Papers, Carton 1025, folder 10, "political mailings."

71. In addition to the specific sources cited above and elsewhere in this chapter, a good summary of the session's achievements is in "Precedent Shattering Legislature Nears End," *Sacramento Bee*, June 19, 1959, p. 1.

72. "Big Daddy of California," *Nation*, March 9, 1963, pp. 199–207.

73. EGB oral history, p. 316.

74. California Poll, April 8, 1959.

75. As to Californians' increasing wealth, the state's after-tax per capita personal income rose by more than the state's inflation rate every year of the Brown

era. See California Statistical Abstract, 2000, pp. 64, 72. For poll results, see California Poll, June 11, 1959.

76. "Precedent Shattering Legislature Nears End," *Sacramento Bee,* June 19, 1959, p. 1.

77. The comments came in a letter but one which, according to contemporary press accounts, Chandler knew would be leaked to reporters. See "Norman Chandler Sizes Up Brown," *San Francisco Call-Bulletin,* June 3, 1959, p. 13.

78. EGB diary, June 20, 1959.

CHAPTER 7: ALL THESE STUDENTS

1. "From the Chancellor's Desk," UCLA newsletter, January 1959 and April 1959, EGB Papers, Carton 337, folder 13, "UC, Jan.–May, 1959." Quoted material from April edition.

2. Smelser and Almond, *Public Higher Education in California,* p. 34.

3. *A Master Plan for Higher Education in California, 1960–1975,* California State Department of Education, 1960, pp. 56–57.

4. Kerr interview, fall 1999.

5. Douglass, *The California Idea,* pp. 230–31.

6. Douglass, *The California Idea,* pp. 223–35.

7. Kerr interview, fall 1999.

8. Dumke oral history, p. 7.

9. Coons, *Crises in California Higher Education,* p. 20.

10. "Edmund G. Brown Is Dead at 90; He Led California in Boom Years," *New York Times,* February 18, 1996, p. 1.

11. The anecdotes were related to the author in many interviews and were part of the vast Brown storytelling repertoire.

12. Stadtman, *The University of California,* pp. 257–80; Douglass, *The California Idea,* pp. 248–52.

13. Kerr, *The Uses of the University,* p. 69. The poem, by the way, was cited to illustrate the fact that modern universities had been willing to accept increasing federal oversight in return for precious research dollars: There was a young lady from Kent / Who said that she knew what it meant / When men took her dine / Gave her cocktails and wine / She knew what it meant but she went.

14. Stadtman, *The University of California,* pp. 13–21.

15. Stadtman, *The University of California,* pp. 380–81; Douglass, *The California Idea,* p. 112; Kerr, *The Gold and the Blue,* vol. 1, pp. 56–62.

16. Letter from Clark Kerr to EGB, May 27, 1959, EGB Papers, Carton 337, folder 14, "UC, June–Sept., 1959."

17. Bean and Rawls, *California: An Interpretive History,* p. 398.

18. "Master Planner," *Time,* October 17, 1960, pp. 58–69.

19. Stadtman, *The University of California,* pp. 381–82.

20. Kerr interview, fall 1999.

21. John Aubrey Douglass, "Californians and Public Higher Education: Political Culture, Educational Opportunity and State Policymaking," *History of Higher Education Annual,* 1996, p. 93.

22. Kerr interview, fall 1999; Kerr, *The Gold and the Blue,* vol. 1, pp. 176–77; Dumke oral history, p. 12.

23. EGB oral history, p. 478; Kerr, *The Gold and the Blue,* vol. 1, pp. 176–77.

24. News conference transcript, May 12, 1959, EGB Papers, Carton 996, folder 3.

25. The university had requested an 8 percent increase in general state support, compared with the previous year. In the end, the final budget increased general support by .2 percent. The university also received $5 million for salary increases, although that was less than administrators had requested. Details on the UC budget are from an excellent budget summary, transmitted to the regents on July 20, 1959, by UC vice president James Corley, EGB papers, Carton 338, folder 2, "Board of Regents, July–Sept., 1959."

26. EGB diary, June 25, 1959; news conference transcript, February 17, 1959, EGB Papers, Carton 996, folder 2.

27. Memo from Ralph Richardson and William Coblentz to EGB, March 17, 1959, and memo from Fred Dutton to Ralph Richardson, March 24, 1959, both in EGB Papers, Carton 338, folder 5, "Board of Regents, March 1959"; memo from Dean McHenry to "Gloria," March 14, 1959, UC President's Papers, Series 5, Box 5, folder 10, "McHenry confidential materials."

28. Memo from Clark Kerr to regents, April 10, 1959, EGB Papers, Carton 338, folder 4, "Board of Regents, April 1959"; letter from Dean McHenry to Ralph Richardson, April 8, 1959, EGB Papers, Carton 338, folder 4, "Board of Regents, April 1959"; memo from Dean McHenry to Clark Kerr, March 31, 1959, UC President's Papers, Series 5, Box 5, folder 10, "McHenry confidential materials"; memo from Clark Kerr to Harry Wellman, April 9, 1959, UC President's Papers, Series 5, Box 5, folder 10, "McHenry confidential materials."

29. Memo from Dean McHenry to Clark Kerr, March 31, 1959, UC President's Papers, Series 5, Box 5, folder 10, "McHenry confidential materials."

30. "Brown Warns Colleges, UC to End Feud," *San Francisco Chronicle,* April 15, 1959, p. 1.

31. Minutes of the joint meeting, April 15, 1959, Office of the Board of Regents; "Brown Prods Colleges into Peace Action," *San Francisco Chronicle,* April 16, 1959, p. 1.

32. Exchange of letters from Eugene Burdick to Fred Dutton, July 6, 1959, and from Fred Dutton to Eugene Burdick, July 9, 1959, EGB Papers, Carton 337, folder 14, "UC, June–Sept. 1959."

33. Memo from Dean McHenry to Clark Kerr, May 27, 1959, UC President's Papers, Series 5, Box 5, folder 10, "McHenry confidential materials."

34. "Negotiating the California Master Plan for Higher Education," speech by Dean McHenry, February 9, 1993, UC Santa Cruz.

35. Letter from Fred Dutton to John Carr, November 25, 1959, EGB Papers, Carton 337, folder 15, "UC, Oct.–Dec., 1959."

36. "Brown Asks Master Plan for College," *San Francisco Chronicle,* November 11, 1959, p. 8.

37. "Brown Asks Action on College Issue," *Berkeley Daily Gazette,* November 30, 1959, p. 5.

38. This description of the crucial negotiations is based on handwritten notes made during the meeting by Dean McHenry, who sought to create almost a verbatim transcript and did a remarkably fine job. Notes labeled "summit meeting," December 8, 1959, UC President's Papers, Series 5, Box 5, folder 10, "McHenry confidential materials."

39. For the provisions of the Master Plan, the best source is the plan itself. *A Master Plan for Higher Education in California, 1960–1975,* California State Department of Education, 1960. An excellent summary is at Douglass, *The California Idea,* pp. 309–10.

40. "UC, State Boards Okeh Higher Education Plan," *Sacramento Bee,* December 19, 1959, p. 1; EGB news conference transcript, December 18, 1959, EGB Papers, Carton 996, folder 5.

41. "UC, State Boards Okeh Higher Education Plan," *Sacramento Bee,* December 19, 1959, p. 1; EGB news conference transcript, December 18, 1959, EGB Papers, Carton 996, folder 5.

42. "Brown Will Call Session on Schools, Smog," *Sacramento Bee,* January 6, 1960, p. 1.

43. EGB news conference transcript, January 29, 1960, EGB Papers, Carton 996, folder 6.

44. Memo from Don Leiffer to EGB, January 8, 1960, EGB Papers, Carton 380, folder 7, "Education, Jan. 1960." Leiffer, it should be noted, was going to be under the ceiling: He was on leave from a teaching job at San Diego State College.

45. EGB news conference transcript, February 12, 1960, EGB Papers, Carton 996, folder 7.

46. Dumke oral history, p. 20; "Legislature's Joint Budget Committee Backs Plan for Higher Education," *Sacramento Bee,* March 8, 1960, p. 6.

47. Letter from James Corley to Clark Kerr, January 15, 1960, UC President's Papers, Series 5, Box 4, folder 20, "Master Plan Survey #3."

48. Letter from James Corley to Clark Kerr, January 29, 1960, UC President's Papers, Series 5, Box 4, folder 20, "Master Plan Survey #3."

49. Memo from Dean McHenry to Clark Kerr, March 18, 1960, UC President's Papers, Series 5, Box 5, folder 1, "Master Plan Survey #4."

50. "Negotiating the California Master Plan for Higher Education," speech by Dean McHenry, February 9, 1993, UC Santa Cruz.

51. Memo to campus chief executive officers from Clark Kerr, February 3, 1960, UC President's Papers, Series 5, Box 4, folder 20, "Master Plan Survey #3."

52. Sexton oral history, p. 48.

53. "Solons Dislike Mixing School Plan, Constitution," *Sacramento Bee,* March 20, 1960, p. 1.

54. Memo from Dean McHenry to Clark Kerr, March 18, 1960, UC President's Papers, Series 5, Box 5, folder 1, "Master Plan Survey #4."

55. Heilbron oral history, pp. 66–67; Kerr interview, fall 1999.

56. "Brown Endorses Key Education Plan," *Sacramento Bee,* March 24, 1960.

57. *San Francisco Chronicle,* March 27, 1960, p. 14; "Senate OK's Master Plan for Colleges," *San Francisco Chronicle,* March 30, 1960, p. 1.

58. Letter from Clark Kerr to George Miller, March 31, 1960, UC President's Papers, Series 5, Box 5, folder 1, "Master Plan Survey #4."

59. "Agreement Near on School Master Plan," *Bakersfield Californian,* April 5, 1960, p. 2; "House Votes 70–0 for 'Donahoe Act,' Senate Action Next," *Bakersfield Californian,* April 6, 1960, p. 2; Sexton interviews, July 17, 1999, and October 29, 1999.

60. Smelser and Almond, *Public Higher Education in California,* p. 70; Lemann, *The Big Test,* p. 134. For several general discussions of the legacy of the Master Plan, see Douglass, *The California Idea,* pp. 314–25; Smelser and Almond, *Public Higher Education in California,* pp. 9–141; Kerr, *The Gold and the Blue,* vol. 1, pp. 172–91.

61. Douglass, *The California Idea,* p. 320. For attendance rates and enrollment figures, see Douglass, *The California Idea,* pp. 314–25, 358; Smelser and Almond, *Public Higher Education in California,* pp. 34–51.

62. California State Budget, Department of Finance, 1959–60, 1961–62, 1966–67, and 1968–69, schedules 3 and 4.

63. "Governor Signs Education Plan," *Sacramento Bee,* April 27, 1960, p. 1.

CHAPTER 8: ANGUISH

1. Kunstler, *Beyond a Reasonable Doubt?* p. xi; Hamm, *Rebel and a Cause,* p. 136.

2. Dutton oral history, p. 121.

3. Machlin and Woodfield, *Ninth Life,* pp. 13–40; Kunstler, *Beyond a Reasonable Doubt?* pp. xi–xvi; Hamm, *Rebel and a Cause,* p. 3; Parker, *Caryl Chessman,* pp. 18–21.

4. Kunstler, *Beyond a Reasonable Doubt?* pp. 3–268; Machlin and Woodfield, *Ninth Life,* pp. 41–161.

5. Machlin and Woodfield, *Ninth Life,* p. 76.

6. There are three principal books that recount the Chessman trial in detail, and the foregoing description is based on all three. They are Kunstler, *Beyond a*

Reasonable Doubt? Parker, *Caryl Chessman,* and Machlin and Woodfield, *Ninth Life.*

7. Hamm, *Rebel and a Cause,* pp. 36, 78–79.

8. Davis and Hirshberg, *The Desperate and the Damned,* p. 181.

9. Kunstler, *Beyond a Reasonable Doubt?* p. xv.

10. Letters from Brown to Culbert Olson, November 11, 1942, and from Stanley Mosk to Brown, November 13, 1942, both at EGB Papers, Carton 183, folder 9, "E. G. Brown, Personal '42."

11. EGB oral history, pp. 131–35. Brown and Adler, *Public Justice, Private Mercy,* pp. x–xi.

12. Brown and Adler, *Public Justice, Private Mercy,* pp. ix–x.

13. See in particular a Brown press release, January 19, 1955, EGB Papers, Carton 11, folder 2, "capital punishment"; "Brown Urges Suspending Executions," *San Francisco Chronicle,* November 14, 1956, p. 1.

14. "Brown Flays Marin Court on Chessman," *San Francisco Examiner,* May 19, 1954, p. 12; Brown and Adler, *Public Justice, Private Mercy,* p. 26.

15. "Brown Assails Handling of Death Penalty," *San Francisco Chronicle,* August 11, 1954, p. 15.

16. "Chessman Granted Another Reprieve by State Justice," *San Francisco Chronicle,* July 30, 1954, p. 1. Machlin and Woodfield, *Ninth Life,* pp. 195–96.

17. "Marin Judge Stays Death of Chessman," *San Francisco Examiner,* May 14, 1954, p. 1. For other evidence that Chessman's stay on death row was extremely long, see Parker, *Caryl Chessman,* pp. 130–35. For the changing strategy of capital punishment opponents, see Hamm, *Rebel and a Cause,* p. 152. For Brown's regrets, see Brown and Adler, *Public Justice, Private Mercy,* p. 52.

18. Eventually a California appellate court would throw out an indictment charging Chessman's publisher, literary agent, and lawyer with smuggling. Justice Matthew Tobriner, Brown's old friend and the man who convinced him to become a Democrat, denounced the concept that the state should control the product of a prisoner's mind, saying that it carries "an odor of totalitarianism." For Brown quote, see "Brown, Linn Differ on Chessman Book," *San Francisco Chronicle,* March 22, 1957, p. 5. For Tobriner, see Kunstler, *Beyond a Reasonable Doubt?* p. 282.

19. Dutton interview, May 22, 2000; Alarcon oral history, p. 106.

20. The description of the Crooker hearing and Brown's feelings about it is based on Brown and Adler, *Public Justice, Private Mercy,* pp. 3–19.

21. Summary from a memo from Cecil Poole to EGB, October 20, 1959, EGB Papers, Carton 1000, folder 19, "capital punishment."

22. Warren's handwritten notes on memo from James Welsh to Warren, May 26, 1952, EGB Papers, Carton 207, "Chessman Book, 2–19–60."

23. Memo from Cecil Poole to EGB, October 20, 1959, EGB Papers, Carton 1000, folder 19, "capital punishment."

24. Brown and Adler, *Public Justice, Private Mercy*, pp. 32–33.

25. For a general discussion of these issues, see Hamm, *Rebel and a Cause,* pp. 11–37.

26. By 1969 support was up to 65 percent and rising. Hamm, *Rebel and a Cause,* p. 151. For Brown-era numbers, see California Poll summary dated September 22, 1966.

27. Duffy and Hirshberg, *88 Men and 2 Women,* pp. 5–27.

28. Hamm, *Rebel and a Cause,* p. 23.

29. In 1968 California became the third state in the nation to allow conjugal visits. For Brown's role, see memo from Fred Dutton to Cecil Poole, October 9, 1959, EGB Papers, Carton 378, folder 3, "corrections—Jan.–April 1960." For conjugal visit information, see "Conjugal Association in Prison: Issues and Perspectives," *Crime and Delinquency,* January 1982, pp. 52–71.

30. For a sampling of letters, see EGB Papers, Carton 208, various folders. For petition, see EGB Papers, Carton 212.

31. Leibert and Kingsbery, *Behind Bars,* p. 147. For Chessman letters to his attorneys, see EGB Papers, Carton 204.

32. Letter from McGee to EGB, October 8, 1959, EGB Papers, Carton 207, "Chessman Book, 5–2–60."

33. Memo from Poole to EGB, October 14, 1959, EGB Papers, Carton 207, "Chessman Book, 2–19–60."

34. The description of the hearing, here and in the paragraphs that follow, is based on the transcript, available at EGB Papers, Carton 206, folder 4, "clemency hearing." Only the pages of the quotations are cited specifically; this one is at pp. 1–2.

35. Machlin and Woodfield, *Ninth Life,* p. 205.

36. George T. Davis oral history, p. 57.

37. Hearing transcript, p. 38.

38. Hearing transcript, p. 97.

39. Hearing transcript, p. 110.

40. EGB diary, October 15, 1959.

41. EGB diary, October 16, 1959.

42. The last changes were not actually made; Brown had called too late. Poole oral history #1, p. 2; Brown and Adler, *Public Justice, Private Mercy,* p. 35; EGB diary, October 18, 1959.

43. Brown and Adler, *Public Justice, Private Mercy,* pp. 35–36.

44. Hearing transcript, pp. 17–18.

45. Pack, *Jerry Brown,* pp. 15–30; Bollens and Williams, *Jerry Brown,* pp. 31–37; EGB diary, December 20, 1959. For Bernice Brown quote, see "Governor's Son Will Quit Study for Priesthood," *Sacramento Bee,* January 26, 1960, p. 3.

46. "Brown Drops Ducks after Close Call," *Sacramento Bee,* October 25, 1959, p. 3.

47. *San Francisco Chronicle:* "Brown Says Flatly: Not Running Yet," November 15, 1959, p. 12; "Brown Talks at Harvard of U.S. Aims," December 5, 1959, p. 6; "Truman Blasts Demo Liberal Snobs," December 8, 1959, p. 10.

48. "Brown Hints He Would Review Chessman Case," *Sacramento Bee,* January 30, 1960, p. 1.

49. "Judge Would Give Life to Chessman," *San Francisco Chronicle,* February 6, 1960, p. 1.

50. Memo from Cecil Poole to EGB, February 16, 1960, EGB Papers, Carton 207, "Chessman Book, 2–19–60."

51. "Pro, Con Chessman Letters to Brown Reach New Heights," *Sacramento Bee,* February 16, 1960, p. 1.

52. "Chessman Execution Protests Mount around World," *Sacramento Bee,* February 18, 1960, p. 1; Kunstler, *Beyond a Reasonable Doubt?* p. xi.

53. Memo from Hale Champion to governor's staff, February 17, 1960, EGB Papers, Carton 207, "Chessman Book, 2–19–60."

54. The Supreme Court order is at EGB Papers, Carton 207, "Chessman Book, 2–19–60." For Brown frustration with his appointee, see Mosk oral history, p. 37. Various press accounts provide details; see especially "Chessman's Fate Hinges on State High Court Rehearing," *Sacramento Bee,* February 18, 1960, p. 1.

55. "Brown Attacks Knight Handling of Abbott Case," *San Francisco Chronicle,* March 20, 1957, p. 1.

56. EGB, February 18, 1960, EGB Papers, Carton 207, "Chessman Book, 2–19–60."

57. Dutton oral history, p. 117.

58. Bernice Brown oral history, pp. 51–59.

59. Brown's aides were not the only people worried about him that night. Walking home from the Capitol, Democratic Sen. Joseph Rattigan, an opponent of the death penalty who empathized with Brown's plight, thought about stopping by the mansion to commiserate with the governor. Not wanting to intrude on a man wrestling with his moral stance, Rattigan decided instead to go home, and straight to bed. For staff events, see Champion interview, May 19, 2000; Poole oral history #1, pp. 3–6; Champion oral history, pp. 54–56. For Rattigan story, Rattigan interview, September 26, 2000.

60. Champion interview, May 19, 2000.

61. Brown and Adler, *Public Justice, Private Mercy,* pp. 39–40.

62. Poole oral history #1, pp. 3–6; Poole oral history #2, pp. 47–58; Champion oral history, pp. 54–56; Brown and Adler, *Public Justice, Private Mercy,* pp. 40–41; "The Quality of Mercy," *Time,* February 29, 1960. For the time of the call, see transcript of EGB's February 19, 1960, news conference, EGB Papers, Carton 207, folder "transcript of governor's press conference."

63. Bernice Brown oral history, pp. 51–59.

64. Brown and Adler, *Public Justice, Private Mercy,* p. 40.

65. Press conference transcript, February 19, 1960, EGB Papers, Carton 207, folder "transcript of governor's press conference." For the language of the bill as introduced, commuting all existing death sentences, see Senate Bill 1xx, 1960 legislative session.

66. For letters, see "Messages Run about 3–1 Denouncing Governor for Reprieving Chessman," *Sacramento Bee,* February 20, 1960, p. 1. For the petition and impeachment, see "Senate Will Get Death Penalty Bill Tomorrow," *Sacramento Bee,* March 1, 1960, p. 1. For editorial, see "Death Penalty Session Would Be Grave Error," *Sacramento Bee,* February 20, 1960, p. B20.

67. "Brown Will Not Press for Death Penalty Ban," *Sacramento Bee,* January 9, 1959, p. 10.

68. "Bill Is Planned," *Sacramento Bee,* February 19, 1960, p. 1. For an example of legislators changing their position, see Jesse Unruh's comments in "Burns Opposes Brown on Capital Punishment," *Sacramento Bee,* February 20, 1960, p. 1.

69. "Senate Will Get Death Penalty Bill Tomorrow," *Sacramento Bee,* March 1, 1960, p. 1.

70. "Bill to Abolish Death Penalty Dies in Senate Committee," *Sacramento Bee,* March 10, 1960, p. 1.

71. Poole oral history #2, p. 58.

72. Poole oral history #2, p. 59.

73. Dutton oral history, pp. 119–21.

74. EGB diary, April 26, 1960; EGB statement, April 26, 1960, EGB Papers, Carton 1000, folder 18, "Chessman."

75. EGB diary, May 1, 1960.

76. EGB diary, May 2, 1960.

77. Description of May 2 based on Poole oral history #1, pp. 6–7; Poole oral history #2, pp. 60–62; Brown and Adler, *Public Justice, Private Mercy,* pp. 50–51; and, for description of Brown at Folsom Lake, Lemmon interview, June 12, 2000.

78. Sampling of correspondence from EGB Papers, Carton 209, folders 1 and 11.

79. Dutton oral history, p. 118; EGB oral history, pp. 283–84, 300–301, 395–98.

80. Brown and Adler, *Public Justice, Private Mercy,* p. 67.

81. EGB oral history, pp. 301–2, 396–98.

82. Brown and Adler, *Public Justice, Private Mercy,* p. 52.

83. Brown and Adler, *Public Justice, Private Mercy,* pp. 10, 72–84.

CHAPTER 9: CIGAR SMOKE

1. EGB LBJ oral history, pt. 1, p. 5.

2. "Western Governors Differ on Summit's Import," *Sacramento Bee,* May 17, 1960, p. 2.

3. Letter from EGB to Adlai Stevenson, December 16, 1958 (mistyped on the letter as December 16, 1968), Stevenson Papers, Box 14, folder 11, "Edmund Brown."

4. EGB oral history, pp. 291–92; "Gridiron Club Has Gibes at Nepotism," *Washington Post,* March 15, 1959, p. 1. Text of speech is at Reagan Gubernatorial Papers, Box C31, folder 20, "EGB1." For other evidence that Brown's speech went well, see letter from Earl Warren to Thomas Storke, Warren LOC Papers, Box 112, folder 1, "Chief Justice—Personal S, 1958–1959."

5. Abell, *Drew Pearson Diaries,* p. 511.

6. Memo from Fred Dutton to EGB, April 23, 1959, EGB Papers, Carton 429, folder 10, "political misc., March–April 1959."

7. "Hands Off Primary, Brown Tells Rivals," *San Francisco Chronicle,* June 24, 1959, p. 13; EGB diary, June 24, 1959.

8. Letter from EGB to Alexis Ulfig, April 27, 1959, EGB Papers, Carton 429, folder 10, "political misc., March–April 1959."

9. O'Donnell, Powers, and McCarthy, *Johnny, We Hardly Knew Ye,* p. 103.

10. "Close Mouthed Brown Has Busy Sessions in East," *Sacramento Bee,* August 1, 1959, p. 4.

11. "Gov. Brown Stirs Speculation on '60," *New York Times,* July 31, 1959, p. 21; "Brown Hints at Serious Bid for '60 Nomination," *Sacramento Bee,* July 31, 1959, p. 1.

12. EGB oral history, p. 396; EGB LBJ oral history, pt. 1, pp. 7–8.

13. Remarkably, in thirteen out of the twenty-one presidential elections between the Civil War and 1948, at least one of the major parties nominated a New Yorker. White, *The Making of the President 1960,* p. 68.

14. "Brown Says He'd Run in 1960 If . . . ," *San Francisco Chronicle,* August 19, 1959, p. 8.

15. "Demos Show Big Interest in Brown," *San Francisco Chronicle,* September 17, 1959, p. 23; letter from Leonard Dieden to Francis J. Byrnes, September 22, 1959, EGB Papers, Carton 429, folder 6, "political misc., Sept. 1959."

16. "Brown Proposes a Demo Summit," *San Francisco Chronicle,* September 25, 1959, p. 7.

17. "Governor Won't Help (or Block) Building of Brown for President Clubs," *San Francisco Chronicle,* September 28, 1959, p. 9; "Not a Candidate, Brown Says—Now, That Is," *San Francisco Chronicle,* October 12, 1959, p. 21; "Brown Now Called Real Candidate for Nomination," *San Francisco Chronicle,* November 7, 1959, p. 8; Brown and Adler, *Public Justice, Private Mercy,* p. 31.

18. "Brown Sees Ike, Plugs California as Site for Winter White House," *Sacramento Bee,* October 6, 1959, p. 2.

19. EGB diary, October 28, 1959.

20. EGB diary, November 12, 1959.

21. "That Dark Horse Named Brown," *New York Times Magazine,* December 6, 1959.

22. EGB LBJ oral history, pt. 1, pp. 6–7; EGB oral history, pp. 395–96; Ziffren oral history, pp. 105–20; Martin, *Adlai Stevenson and the World,* p. 466.

23. EGB LBJ oral history, pt. 1, p. 7.

24. "Brown Bars Active Drive for '60 Bid," *Sacramento Bee,* December 29, 1959, p. 1.

25. Dutton did note that in the long run the national exposure would help Brown. Memo from Fred Dutton to EGB, January 5, 1960, "Summary of Progress and Operations during 1959" (one of two memos from Dutton to Brown that date), Champion Papers, Carton 3, folder 8.

26. Memo from Fred Dutton to Bernice Brown, January 15, 1960, EGB Papers, Carton 428, folder 2, "gov personal—Mrs. Brown."

27. Casey interview, November 17, 1998; Pack, *Jerry Brown,* pp. 6–7.

28. Kathleen Brown interviews, December 11, 1998, and September 7, 2000.

29. Kathleen Brown interview, September 7, 2000.

30. "Gov. Brown Stirs Speculation on '60," *New York Times,* July 31, 1959, p. 21.

31. Bernice Brown oral history, p. 14.

32. Press release, June 3, 1960, EGB Papers, Carton 428, folder 2, "gov personal—Mrs. Brown."

33. "Kennedy May Face Brown in California," *San Francisco Chronicle,* January 15, 1960, p. 1.

34. Lynch oral history, pp. 169–74.

35. EGB LBJ oral history, pt. 1, pp. 7–10; EGB oral history, p. 408; Lytton JFK oral history, pp. 5–7.

36. EGB oral history, pp. 400–405; EGB LBJ oral history, pt. 1, pp. 9–11; EGB JFK oral history, pp. 5–7; Sorensen, *Kennedy,* pp. 130–31.

37. The secrecy held for years. Dutton went with Brown on the trip to Washington but did not attend the meeting and did not know of the two men's private deal until the author informed him of it. Dutton interview, April 29, 2002.

38. For details on the meeting and the legal process of picking the delegation, see especially "Top 10 State Demos Huddle to Pick Pro Brown Convention Delegates," *Sacramento Bee,* February 26, 1960, p. 6; Tillett, *Inside Politics,* pp. 252–77; and the invitation to the meeting from William Munnell, February 19, 1960, Unruh Papers, LP236:435.

39. EGB LBJ oral history, pt. 1, p. 12; letters from EGB to Ronda Solomon, January 21, 1960, and Bert F. Corley Jr., January 21, 1960, both in EGB Papers, Carton 431, folder 5, "delegation, 1959–Feb. 1960."

40. For the intentional effort at a politically diverse delegation, see especially memo from Fred Dutton to EGB, September 28, 1959, EGB Papers, Carton 431, folder 5, "delegation, 1959–Feb. 1960."

41. Governor's office press release, March 10, 1960, EGB Papers, Carton 431, folder 4, "delegation, March–April 1960."

42. Letter from Theodore Sorensen to Paul Ziffren, March 2, 1960, EGB Papers, Carton 432, folder 11, "Kennedy, May June July 1960"; Bradley oral history, p. 116; Sorensen, *Kennedy,* pp. 130–31; memo from Steve Smith to John F. Kennedy, February 27, 1960, John F. Kennedy Pre-Presidential Papers, Box 927, folder 17, "California/Political"; "Kennedy Will Skip California Primary," *San Francisco Chronicle,* March 3, 1960, p. 6.

43. EGB diary, June 7, 1960.

44. Ziffren oral history, pp. 137–44; MacBride oral history, pp. 91–99; EGB oral history, pp. 408–11; letter from EGB to Orville Freeman, June 13, 1960, EGB Papers, Carton 431, folder 3, "delegation June 1960."

45. EGB oral history, p. 410.

46. Emphasis in original. Memo from Fred Dutton to EGB, undated, EGB Papers, Carton 1000, folder 20.

47. Exchange of letters between EGB and J. Edward Day, June 21, 1960, and July 7, 1960, EGB Papers, Carton 431, folder 8, "Demo. National Convention, July 1960."

48. EGB LBJ oral history, pt. 1, pp. 11–14. For other evidence that Brown remained loyal to Kennedy, see Dallek, *Lone Star Rising,* p. 566.

49. "Governor Ponders as Anderson Asks Delegate Support for Adlai," *Sacramento Bee,* July 7, 1960, p. 1.

50. *New York Times,* July 9, 1960, p. 8.

51. Ziffren oral history, pp. 131–45.

52. Memo from Fred Dutton to Jean Gildea, January 13, 1960, EGB Papers, Carton 431, folder 9, "Democratic National Convention, Jan.–June 1960."

53. Calkins interview, April 15, 2002; "California's Complex Governor," *Saturday Evening Post,* June 25, 1960.

54. Bailey interview, August 8, 2001.

55. Kathleen Brown interview, September 7, 2000.

56. EGB oral history, pp. 405–6; EGB LBJ oral history, pt. 1, pp. 14–15; EGB JFK oral history, pp. 10–11.

57. The description of the delegation meeting here and in the following paragraphs is based principally on contemporary news accounts. See especially "State Delegation Is Divided Despite Jump by Brown," *Sacramento Bee,* July 11, 1960, p. 1; "Kennedy's Rolling—Brown Joins Up," *San Francisco Chronicle,* July 11, 1960, p. 1; "Brown Backs Kennedy; Quick Victory Shaping Up," *San Francisco Examiner,* July 11, 1960, p. 1; "Gov. Brown for Kennedy," *New York Times,* July 11, 1960, p. 1.

58. "Kennedy, Johnson Vote Battle Seethes," *Sacramento Bee,* July 10, 1960, p. 1.

59. EGB oral history, pp. 410–16.

60. "Brown Calls for Demo Leadership," *Sacramento Bee,* July 12, 1960, p. 6.

61. Lawrence, a Stevenson man really, backed Kennedy reluctantly, but in the end the state voted overwhelmingly for the winner. White, *The Making of the President 1960,* pp. 158–68; McKeever, *Adlai Stevenson,* pp. 453–64.

62. Description of the Tuesday delegation meeting is based principally on various press accounts, including the following published on July 13, 1960: "Stevenson Tops California Caucus in Brown Rebuff," *Los Angeles Times,* p. A; "Adlai's Arrival Steals Show by Drawing Biggest Ovation," *Sacramento Bee,* p. 1; "Big State Vote for Adlai Gives Brown a Jolt," *San Francisco Chronicle,* p. 1; "California for Adlai," *San Francisco Examiner,* p. 1.

63. Champion interview, May 20, 2000; Dutton LBJ oral history, pp. 5–10; Gatov JFK oral history, p. 6.

64. "How the States Voted," *New York Times,* July 14, 1960, p. 14.

65. Letter from EGB to Orville Freeman, June 13, 1960, EGB Papers, Carton 431, folder 3, "delegation June 1960."

66. Memos from Robert Kennedy to Steve Smith, May 25, 1960, and to "files," June 8, 1960, RFK Pre-Presidential Papers, Political Files, Box 39, folder 12, "Memos, RFK, outgoing, 5–60 to 9–60."

67. For two examples, see "Brown Stature Apparently Is Hit by Failure to Hold Slate," *Sacramento Bee,* July 15, 1960, p. 1; and "Brown's Setback Surprises Party," *New York Times,* July 14, 1960, p. 17.

68. "Highlights and Chronology of Nominating Session of the Democratic Convention," *New York Times,* July 14, 1960, p. 18.

69. *Time,* July 25, 1960, p. 20.

70. EGB Papers, Carton 1007, folder 7, "post-convention, anti-Brown."

71. Dutton LBJ oral history, p. 14; Dutton interview, May 22, 2000; letter from EGB to Fred Dutton, March 15, 1974, EGB Papers, Carton 929, folder 2, "Edmund G. Brown Jr."

72. Rees oral history, pp. 253, 288–300. See also Bradley oral history, pp. 119–20; Gatov oral history, p. 349; "Big State Vote for Adlai Gives Brown a Jolt," *San Francisco Chronicle,* July 13, 1960, p. 1.

73. Sorensen, *Kennedy,* p. 159. For the Kennedy preference for Unruh, see O'Donnell, Powers, and McCarthy, *Johnny, We Hardly Knew Ye,* p. 178; O'Brien, *No Final Victories,* pp. 60–61; Champion oral history, p. 133; Salinger oral history, pp. 20–30.

74. "Governor Ponders as Anderson Asks Delegate Support for Adlai," *Sacramento Bee,* July 7, 1960, p. 1.

75. "Pat Brown—A Man to Be Reckoned With," *Reporter,* December 24, 1959.

76. Lynch oral history, p. 171; Rees oral history, pp. 262–63; Bradley oral history, p. 127: Houghteling JFK oral history, passim; Rose JFK oral history, pp. 121–27.

77. "Brown Backs Kennedy; Quick Victory Shaping Up," *San Francisco Examiner*, July 11, 1960, p. 1.

78. Richardson, *Willie Brown*, pp. 413–14.

79. Letter from Hale Champion to Eugene Lee, September 13, 1960, EGB Papers, Carton 431, folder 1, "political 60 delegation."

80. EGB oral history, pp. 397–98, 420–21.

81. EGB oral history, pp. 397–98, 420–21.

CHAPTER 10: BUILDING A RIVER

1. For a general overview of California's water history, the best single source is Norris Hundley's *The Great Thirst*, which is the basis for much of the background information throughout this chapter. For a sampling of other sources of general information on the topic, see Erwin Cooper's *Aqueduct Empire*, Robert Gottlieb's *A Life of Its Own*, William Kahrl's *California Water Atlas*, Marc Reisner's *Cadillac Desert*, and Donald Worster's *Rivers of Empire*.

2. EGB oral history, p. 333.

3. EGB oral history, p. 333; EGB AG oral history, pp. 23–26.

4. EGB oral history, p. 338.

5. EGB oral history, p. 342.

6. For a succinct statement of Brown's views on the manner in which water projects subsidized agriculture, see Appellants' Opening Brief, U.S. Supreme Court, *Ivanhoe Irrigation District v. All Persons*, pp. 52–54, a document that Brown would have personally approved. For his comments on the need for water to produce more food, see press release, March 7, 1951, Brody Papers, Carton 6, folder "Ivanhoe validation"; and also letters from EGB to the California Farm Bureau Federation, January 9, 1958, EGB Papers, Carton 1, folder "Ivanhoe," and to Harry Horton, June 12, 1957, EGB Papers, Carton 1, folder "water projects––1957."

7. "Report on Feasibility of Feather River Project and Sacramento–San Joaquin Delta Diversion Projects Proposed as Features of the California Water Plan," State Water Resources Board, May 1951. For other descriptions of the Edmonston plan, see Hundley, *The Great Thirst*, pp. 278–80; Kahrl, *California Water Atlas*, p. 51.

8. EGB oral history, pp. 345–46.

9. Lyrics from Lomax, *The Folk Songs of North America*, p. 443.

10. Phonotape 547–1, Bancroft Library, UC Berkeley.

11. Goldberg oral history, p. 51.

12. Letter from EGB to Franklin Payne, October 19, 1960, EGB Papers, Carton 419, folder 11, "water resources, bond campaign, Nov. 1–8."

13. EGB oral history, p. 360; Brody oral history, pp. 1–9.

14. Description of Brown's speech here and in the paragraphs that follow based on text of the speech, *Journal of the Assembly*, 1959, pp. 326–31.

15. Brown had spent years discussing his "counties of origin" ruling, maintaining when he was in the north that it was a crucial protection for the region, while deriding it as meaningless whenever he was in the south, a politic deceit he freely acknowledged. EGB AG oral history, p. 54.

16. EGB oral history, pp. 342–43. For other background on the decision to avoid a constitutional amendment, see Brody oral history, pp. 11–13; Banks oral history, pp. 56–59; Cooper, *Aqueduct Empire,* pp. 221–42.

17. EGB AG oral history, pp. 33–34. See also EGB oral history, pp. 337–39.

18. For general information on the progress of Brown's plan through the legislature, see Hundley, *The Great Thirst,* pp. 276–302; Cooper, *Aqueduct Empire,* pp. 221–42; Reisner, *Cadillac Desert,* pp. 341–55; Harvey P. Grody, "From North to South: The Feather River Project and Other Legislative Water Struggles in the 1950s," *Southern California Quarterly* 60 (fall 1978): 287–315.

19. Memos summarizing the meetings of the northern senators, April 13, 1959, April 20, 1959, April 17, 1959, EGB Papers, Carton 359, folder 9, "water resources—April."

20. Statement by EGB, May 13, 1959, EGB Papers, Carton 341, folder 3, "water resources, May 1959"; "State Water Needs Critical, Brown Warns Legislature," *San Francisco Chronicle,* May 14, 1959, p. 9.

21. EGB oral history, pp. 352–55; Dutton oral history, pp. 102–4; Cooper, *Aqueduct Empire,* pp. 224–25.

22. "Senators Hurl Wet Blanket on Brown's Water Plan," *San Francisco Chronicle,* May 20, 1959, p. 8.

23. Letter from EGB to Franklin S. Payne, June 4, 1959, EGB Papers, Carton 364, folder 35, "SB1106"; Fisher interview, January 5, 2003; "Water Bill Wins in Senate after Plea by Governor," *San Francisco Chronicle,* May 30, 1959, p. 1; "State Senate Approves Water Program, 25–12," *Los Angeles Times,* May 30, 1959, p. 1.

24. Governor's office statement, June 5, 1959, EGB Papers, Carton 364, folder 35, "SB 1106"; "L.A. to Ask Changes in Water Bill," *San Francisco Chronicle,* June 9, 1959, p. 16.

25. "Legislature Passes Giant Water Bill," *San Francisco Chronicle,* June 18, 1959, p. 1.

26. Letter to Ralph Brody from Thomas MacBride, August 7, 1959, EGB Papers, Carton 364, folder 35, "SB 1106."

27. "Brown Budget, Water Bond Victories Pave Way for FRP," *Sacramento Bee,* June 18, 1959, p. 1; governor's office press release, July 9, 1959, EGB Papers, Carton 364, folder 35, "SB 1106."

28. Brown raised money for the bonds campaign and at one point convinced a rich businessman friend to pay the salary of the campaign manager. For evidence of the governor's role, see memo from EGB to Ralph Brody, November 7, 1959, EGB Papers, Carton 341, folder 9, "water resources, bond campaign, Nov. 1959"; and letter from Fred Dutton to Thomas Page, April 12, 1960, EGB Papers,

Carton 420, folder 10, "water resources, bond campaign, April"; EGB diary, April 11, 1960. For other involvement by the Brown team in developing the campaign, see various documents, EGB Papers, Carton 420, folders 7–10.

29. "Brown Woos Labor for Water Bonds," *San Francisco Chronicle,* July 28, 1960, p. 21; "Brown Appeals to AFL-CIO for Water Backing," *San Francisco Chronicle,* August 16, 1960, p. 1.

30. "Brown Jibes at GOP on Water," *San Francisco Chronicle,* August 10, 1960, p. 7.

31. "Brown out Arguing for Water Bonds," *San Francisco Chronicle,* September 18, 1960, p. 18; EGB oral history, pp. 411–12; Brody oral history, pp. 37–38.

32. Hundley, *The Great Thirst,* p. 280.

33. "Consultants Suggest Delay on Oroville Dam," *Sacramento Bee,* July 21, 1960, p. 1; "State Water Plan Costs to Soar," *San Francisco Chronicle,* July 22, 1960, p. 1. For other information about the project's financing, see Senate Bill 1106, 1959 session, California Legislature; California Department of Water Resources, Bulletin No. 78, December 1959; and Hirshleifer, De Haven, and Milliman, *Water Supply,* pp. 289–357.

34. Memo from Fred Dutton to EGB, April 15, 1960, EGB Papers, Carton 420, folder 10, "Water resources—bond campaign—April."

35. "Brown Now Says Oroville Dam Is 'Set,'" *San Francisco Chronicle,* September 14, 1960, p. 1.

36. "Brown Now Says Oroville Dam Is 'Set,'" *San Francisco Chronicle,* September 14, 1960, p. 1.

37. "Brown, in NY, Recalls Rocky's Defense Attack," *Sacramento Bee,* October 6, 1960, p. 2.

38. "Brown Terms Nixon 'Same Adroit Cynic,'" *Sacramento Bee,* October 10, 1960, p. 2.

39. Hundley, *The Great Thirst,* pp. 278–91; Cooper, *Aqueduct Empire,* pp. 205–7, 237–38.

40. Governor's office press release, October 21, 1960, EGB Papers, Carton 419, folder 12, "water resources—bond campaign—Oct. 20–26"; "Brown Charges MWD Head with Bad Faith," *Sacramento Bee,* October 22, 1960, p. 4; "MWD Chief Bares Water Plan Blast Hit by Brown," *Sacramento Bee,* October 23, 1960, p. 15; Cooper, *Aqueduct Empire,* pp. 239–41.

41. EGB oral history, pp. 367–68; press release, November 1, 1960, EGB Papers, Carton 419, folder 11, "water resources, bond campaign, Nov. 1–8."

42. Hundley, *The Great Thirst,* p. 287.

43. "Brown Hopeful on Water Bond Study," *San Francisco Chronicle,* October 15, 1960, p. 4; "Gov. Brown Pledges High Oroville Dam Priority Despite Talk of Delay," *Sacramento Bee,* October 28, 1960, p. C1.

44. "MWD, Feather River Water Pact Is Signed," *Sacramento Bee,* November 4, 1960, p. 24.

45. EGB diary, November 5, 1960, and November 6, 1960.

46. "Brown and Democrats Jubilant over Lead," *Los Angeles Times,* Election Extra edition, November 9, 1960, p. 4.

47. EGB diary, November 8, 1960.

48. "Water Bonds Piling Up 50,000-Vote Lead," *Los Angeles Times,* November 10, 1960, p. 4.

49. "Senate Realignment Dies, Water Bond Issue Trails," *Sacramento Bee,* November 9, 1960, p. 1.

50. Statement of Vote, 1960 General Election, California Secretary of State's Office; EGB diary, November 9, 1960.

51. Statement of Vote, 1960 General Election, California Secretary of State's Office.

52. EGB diary, November 16, 1960; "Brown, on Argentina Visit, Says Kennedy's Religion Hurt Him Badly," *Sacramento Bee,* November 16, 1960, p. 4.

53. EGB diary, November 17, 1960.

54. "Kennedy Asks Stevenson to Head UN Delegation; Acceptance Is Deferred," *New York Times,* December 9, 1960, p. 1.

55. Letter to EGB from Earl Warren, December 10, 1960, Warren LOC Papers, Box 13, folder 1, "chief justice—personal, 1958–1960."

56. Letter from EGB to Wallace Lynn, January 13, 1961, EGB Papers, Carton 494, folder 15, "gov personal L"; "Chief Justice, Sons Bag Bird Limits," *Sacramento Bee,* December 29, 1960, pictures on p. 1 and p. C1.

57. Kathleen Brown interview, September 7, 2000; "Brown Leads State's Bands," *San Francisco Chronicle,* January 21, 1961, p. 4.

58. Kathleen Brown interview, September 7, 2000.

59. For a good general overview of the modern State Water Project, see the Department of Water Resources, "California State Water Project Atlas," published in June 1999. See also Hundley, *The Great Thirst,* pp. 291–302; Kahrl, *California Water Atlas,* pp. 55–56.

60. Hundley, *The Great Thirst,* pp. 294–300; Kahrl, *California Water Atlas,* pp. 50–56.

61. Hundley, *The Great Thirst,* pp. 294–300.

62. Hundley, *The Great Thirst,* p. 277.

63. EGB oral history, p. 374.

64. See Brown's discussion of this issue, EGB oral history, pp. 361–62, 374.

65. Goldberg oral history, p. 52.

66. For one example of Brown using the phrase, see transcript of his interview with the *San Francisco Examiner,* September 12, 1960, EGB Papers, Carton 420, folder 3, "water resources, bond campaign, Sept. 10–19."

67. To be sure, new dams and canals were built after Brown's tenure. The federal government completed New Melones Dam on the Stanislaus River in 1978,

for example. But none of the more recent projects approaches the State Water Project in size and scope.

68. News conference, October 9, 1961, EGB Papers, Carton 996.

69. "Blast at Oroville Dam Site Starts Water Project Work," *Los Angeles Times,* October 13, 1961, pt. III, p. 1; "Brown Fires Blast Marking Work Start on Oroville Dam," *Sacramento Bee,* October 12, 1961, p. 1.

70. EGB oral history, p. 355; Ringer oral history, p. 101.

CHAPTER 11: "BY GOD, I CAN BEAT THAT SON OF A BITCH"

1. The text of Nixon's comments is in the *Los Angeles Times,* September 28, 1961, p. 2.

2. California Polls, March 10, 1961, and October 21, 1961.

3. In March 1961 the California Poll found that only 21 percent of Californians thought Brown was doing a "good job," compared to 32 percent who said he was doing a "poor job" (35 percent said "fair"). Although they were not nearly so well known, Senators Tommy Kuchel and Clair Engle both received far better marks. California Poll, March 10, 1961. For head-to-head matchups, see California Poll, March 13, 1961.

4. EGB oral history, pp. 424–28.

5. Letter from Richard Nixon to EGB, November 7, 1958, Nixon Pre-Presidential Papers, Laguna Nigel archives, Series 320, Box 106, file "Brown."

6. EGB oral history, p. 177.

7. EGB oral history, p. 183.

8. Memo to "political files," April 20, 1955, EGB Papers, Carton 116, folder 7, "confidential."

9. Memos from Hale Champion to Andy Barrigan, November 21, 1960, and to EGB, November 30, 1960, both in EGB Papers, Carton 434, folder 9, "Nixon."

10. Letter from Eisenhower to Nixon, September 11, 1961, Nixon Pre-Presidential Papers, Document #PPS 324.162.1, Nixon Library and Birthplace.

11. For Nixon's reaction to his loss in 1960 and his subsequent entry into the 1962 race, see Nixon, *Memoirs,* pp. 237–41; Brodie, *Richard Nixon,* pp. 443–56; Ambrose, *Nixon,* pp. 626–49; Aitken, *Nixon,* pp. 294–98.

12. Transcript of January 14, 1959, cabinet meeting, p. 5, EGB Papers, Carton 1007, folder 1, "governor's council meeting minutes."

13. Brown, *Reagan and Reality,* pp. 9–10; EGB oral history, pp. 80, 424–62; "Brassy Fight for a Golden Prize," *Life,* October 19, 1962.

14. Kathleen Brown interview, September 7, 2000.

15. Schuparra, *Triumph of the Right,* pp. 62–63.

16. "GOP Group OK's Nixon Anti-Birchers Resolution," *San Francisco Ex-*

aminer, March 4, 1962, p. 12; "Tough Battle—Nixon Wins," *San Francisco Examiner,* March 5, 1962, p. 1; "Shell Blasts Nixon on Welch Issue," *San Francisco Chronicle,* March 3, 1962, p. 1; "GOP Picks Nixon and Christopher," *San Francisco Chronicle,* March 5, 1962, p. 1.

17. Hitt oral history, p. 102.

18. The seven counties where Shell beat Nixon were in the north: Nevada, Placer, Plumas, Sacramento, Shasta, Sierra, and Trinity. Statement of Vote, California Secretary of State, June 5, 1962.

19. Schuparra, *Triumph of the Right,* pp. 68–76.

20. Interview with Jack Burby, May 15, 2000; Burby oral history, pp. 92–94; "The Big Hello by Brown, Nixon," *San Francisco Examiner,* June 22, 1962, p. 1; EGB oral history, p. 428.

21. "Kennedy Visit—A Dilemma for Gov. Brown," *San Francisco Chronicle,* July 6, 1962, p. 1; "Brown, Kennedy Discuss State Race," *San Francisco Chronicle,* July 10, 1962, p. 31.

22. "Brown Hikes, Works in the Woods," *San Francisco Chronicle,* July 31, 1962, p. 2.

23. Letter from EGB to George Hearst Jr., July 18, 1962, EGB Papers, Carton 583, folder 13, "political governor July 1–22"; Nasaw, *The Chief,* pp. 425–26.

24. Letter from EGB to Simeon Van Derslice, July 20, 1962, EGB Papers, Carton 579, folder 23, "governor's personal V."

25. During Brown's tenure as governor, California's unemployment rate would never again hit the levels of 1961, and personal income would continue to grow. For seasonally adjusted monthly unemployment levels, see California Statistical Abstract: 1965, p. 80; 1966, p. 31; 1967, p. 31. For per capita disposable income figures, see California Statistical Abstract, 1978, p. 47.

26. "Governor Race Is Out—Nixon," *San Francisco News-Call Bulletin,* March 6, 1961, p. 4.

27. Memo from Harry Lerner to Charles O'Brien, February 14, 1962, EGB Papers, Carton 584, folder 14, "political—Harry Lerner." California Poll, February 15, 1962.

28. "Nixon Announces He's in Governor Contest," *Los Angeles Times,* September 28, 1961, p. 1.

29. "Gov. Hatfield Doubts Nixon Will Shun '64," *Los Angeles Times,* September 28, 1961, p. 2; "Knight-Brown Blasts Hurled against Nixon," *Los Angeles Times,* September 29, 1961, p. 1.

30. "Text of Nixon Talk on Plans," *Los Angeles Times,* September 28, 1961, p. 2.

31. "Nixon Says He Will Clean up Capitol, Remove Warne," *Sacramento Bee,* September 13, 1962, p. 1.

32. California Poll, August 6, 1962, and August 7, 1962. Similar differences in the public perception of Brown and Kennedy were also found in another

poll, by Louis Harris, in December 1961. In fact, the Harris Poll supports not only this aspect of the California Poll but also many conclusions of California Polls throughout the campaign, as cited in this chapter. The Harris Poll is at Kennedy Presidential Office Files, Box 105, folder 1, "Polls, 1962 elections in California."

33. Memo from Tom Saunders to EGB, July 12, 1962, EGB Papers, Carton 588, folder 21, "Committee to Re-Elect Governor Brown"; "Truman in LA Blasts Nixon's 'Innuendo Trick,'" *Sacramento Bee,* September 13, 1962, p. 8.

34. Brodie, *Richard Nixon,* p. 460.

35. Nixon, *Memoirs,* p. 239.

36. California Poll, February 14, 1962, and April 10, 1962.

37. He may also have been shamed into it. Bernice, presumably trying to be funny, had offered to debate Pat Nixon. EGB oral history, pp. 438–44; "California Day at World Fair," *San Francisco Chronicle,* June 16, 1962, p. 6.

38. The details of the debate are taken principally from a transcript, available at EGB Papers, Carton 1024, folder 1, "Nixon—TV debates." For other details and observations, see contemporary newspaper accounts, especially "Nixon, Brown Argue over Hughes Loan," *Sacramento Bee,* October 2, 1962, p. 1; "Nixon and Brown Take Off Gloves in TV Meeting," *San Francisco Chronicle,* October 2, 1962, p. 1. For Brown's perceptions and thoughts, see EGB oral history, pp. 428, 446. See also Ambrose, *Nixon,* pp. 650–74; Nixon, *Six Crises,* p. 323.

39. For an excellent summary of the anti-HUAC demonstrations, see Jacobs, *Rage for Justice,* pp. 81–84.

40. In fact, the Brown campaign worked consistently to dig up proof that the loan was corrupt. See, as one example, Champion oral history, p. 43.

41. Brown was not the only person who thought the debate played differently on television. A number of Brown aides watched the event in the auditorium and thought it went poorly, but Jack Burby, then the press secretary, watched on television and said immediately that it was, from Brown's perspective, a draw at worst. Burby oral history, pp. 95–96.

42. "Nixon Vows Anti-Red State Drive," *Los Angeles Times,* September 14, 1962, p. 1.

43. In another example of the fading importance of anti-Communist feeling, an initiative that would have allowed a wide array of government officials to declare a group "subversive" failed badly at the polls. For the Nixon chant, see "Brassy Fight for a Golden Prize," *Life,* October 19, 1962.

44. Memo from T. N. Saunders to Jack Burby, March 22, 1962, EGB Papers, Carton 1024, folder 1, "Nixon—TV Debates."

45. "Merry Prankster Tuck Is Back," *Los Angeles Times,* January 31, 1990, p. 3.

46. Memo from Roger Kent to Democratic State Central Committee, January 1963, supplementary material to EGB oral history, folder 14, "Pat Brown—Gov. and After"; "Nixon's Way to the Top," *New Republic,* June 9, 1973, p. 15.

47. Bradley oral history, p. 135.

48. Both anti-Brown publications are described in "Brown Picture Fakes Blamed on Nixon Aides," *Los Angeles Times,* October 19, 1962, p. 28; "Nixon Aide Admits GOP Prepared Booklet Demos Say Is New Smear," *Sacramento Bee,* October 19, 1962, p. 8. See also Brown campaign poster, Committee to Re-Elect the Governor Papers, Carton 1, folder 3, "Anti-Nixon Material."

49. Brown, *Reagan and Reality,* p. 39.

50. California Poll, October 18, 1962.

51. "Eisenhower Here—All Out for Nixon's Election," *San Francisco Chronicle,* October 9, 1962, p. 1.

52. "Will It Be Brown or Nixon?" *Newsweek,* October 29, 1962.

53. California Poll, October 19, 1962.

54. "Winning and Losing the 1962 Race for Governor of California," symposium on March 21, 1992, taped by the Richard Nixon Library and Birthplace, Yorba Linda; "Brown Pledges Radio, TV Talks to People on Civil Defense Measures," *Sacramento Bee,* October 28, 1962, p. 12.

55. "Nixon Claims State CD Lags," *Sacramento Bee,* October 30, 1962, p. 1; "Hoodwinking Is Laid to Brown," *Sacramento Bee,* November 2, 1962, p. 6.

56. "Better American Than Nixon, Brown Declares," *Los Angeles Times,* November 1, 1962, p. 1; "Brown Says Nixon Has No Heart," *Los Angeles Times,* November 4, 1962, p. 1.

57. "California Poll Shows Brown Leading Nixon," *Los Angeles Times,* November 5, 1962, p. 1.

58. "Coast Race Close," *New York Times,* November 7, 1962, p. 1; "The Final Day of a Hot Campaign," *San Francisco Chronicle,* November 6, 1962, p. 1.

59. "Both Brown, Nixon Do Twist—of Tongue," *Sacramento Bee,* November 6, 1962, p. 1; "The Final Day of a Hot Campaign," *San Francisco Chronicle,* November 6, 1962, p. 1.

60. "Brown, Extra Cautious, Carries 2 Statements," *Los Angeles Times,* November 7, 1962, p. 2.

61. Klein, *Making It Perfectly Clear,* pp. 46–64.

62. Klein, *Making It Perfectly Clear,* pp. 46–64.

63. "Brown, Extra Cautious, Carries 2 Statements," *Los Angeles Times,* November 7, 1962, p. 2.

64. "Coast Race Close," *New York Times,* November 7, 1962, p. 1; Statement of Vote, 1962, California Secretary of State's Office.

65. Kathleen Brown interview, September 7, 2000.

66. "Losing Like Mosquito Bite—Nixon," *Los Angeles Times,* November 8, 1962, p. 13.

67. The account of Nixon's famous "last press conference," here and in the following paragraphs, is based on contemporary news accounts and also Aitken, *Nixon,* pp. 304–6; Ambrose, *Nixon,* pp. 668–74; Brodie, *Richard Nixon,* pp.

461–63; Hill, *Dancing Bear,* pp. 163–78; Klein, *Making It Perfectly Clear,* pp. 46–64; Nixon, *Memoirs,* pp. 244–46; Rather and Gates, *The Palace Guard,* pp. 123–30; Witcover, *The Resurrection of Richard Nixon,* pp. 13–24; and Wills, *Nixon Agonistes,* pp. 403–16. There are various transcripts of Nixon's statement, but the differences are minor. The quotes here are from the *New York Times* transcript, November 8, 1962, p. 18.

68. David, *The Lonely Lady,* p. 124.

69. Klein, *Making It Perfectly Clear,* pp. 59–60.

70. Understandably aggrieved, the *Times* even published a front-page statement the next day noting its support of Nixon.

71. The bias of California political coverage in the 1940s and 1950s is plainly evident to anyone reading the stories today. It should be noted that this bias included favoritism toward Democrats in the state's few Democratic papers, principally the McClatchy-owned *Bees.* There are many sources describing Nixon's traditionally friendly treatment, especially from the *Los Angeles Times.* See, for example, Ambrose, *Nixon,* pp. 117–40; Halberstam, *The Powers That Be,* pp. 360–71; Mitchell, *Tricky Dick and the Pink Lady.* For a more scientific measure of favorable coverage of Nixon, see Galen Rarick, "California Daily Newspaper Reporting of the 1950 U.S. Senatorial Campaign—A Content Analysis," master's thesis, Stanford University, 1951. For the FCC order regarding KTTV, see "Station Is Told to Give Demos More Time," *Sacramento Bee,* October 29, 1962, p. 8.

72. Klein, *Making It Perfectly Clear,* pp. 57–58.

73. "Nixon Denounces Press as Biased," *New York Times,* November 8, 1962, p. 1.

74. Recording of the phone call, November 7, 1962, Kennedy Presidential Recordings, Item 6A.2. For Brown's thoughts on Nixon, see also EGB oral history, pp. 461–62.

75. EGB oral history, p. 422.

76. Letter from Adlai Stevenson to EGB, November 7, 1962, Stevenson Papers, Box 14, folder 11, "Edmund Brown."

77. Louis Harris, Kennedy's pollster, took a detailed survey of the California political scene as the race was getting under way and concluded that Nixon was simply disliked. "The governor's chief asset has always been 'Pat Brown,'" Harris wrote. "For Nixon, his chief deficit has always been 'Dick Nixon.'" Harris survey, December 1961, Kennedy Presidential Office Files, Box 105, folder 1, "Polls, 1962 Elections in California."

CHAPTER 12: RACE AND POLITICS

1. "Governor Plans Big Party for Day California Is Tops," *San Francisco Chronicle,* January 7, 1962, p. 2.

2. "California Tells World It Is Now—Officially—No. 1 State," *Sacramento Bee,* December 28, 1962, p. 1; "San Diego Marks California First," *Los Angeles Times,* December 29, 1962, p. 9; "Who's Biggest in the Land?" *San Francisco Chronicle,* December 29, 1962, p. 1.

3. Letter from EGB to John Fell Stevenson Jr., February 26, 1963, EGB Papers, Carton 666, folder 8, "governor's personal S" (jokingly addressed to Adlai's grandson, Stevenson Jr., who was an infant, the letter is really to John Fell Stevenson, Adlai's son). For Census Bureau, see "U.S. Demotes California to No. 2," *San Francisco Chronicle,* October 5, 1963, p. 3.

4. Schrag, *Paradise Lost,* p. 50; "Who's Biggest in the Land?" *San Francisco Chronicle,* December 29, 1962, p. 1.

5. "Brown Takes Oath Before Big Crowd, Guns Roar Salute" and "Governor's Speech Draws Bursts of Applause," *Sacramento Bee,* January 8, 1963, p. 6.

6. The text of Brown's second inaugural is in the *Los Angeles Times,* January 8, 1963, p. 10.

7. "Crowd, Stars Open Stops at Inaugural," *Sacramento Bee,* January 8, 1963, p. 1.

8. Brown and Adler, *Public Justice, Private Mercy,* p. 154; Hamm, *Rebel and a Cause,* p. 145.

9. Brown and Adler, *Public Justice, Private Mercy,* pp. 141–52; Hamm, *Rebel and a Cause,* pp. 144–48; McInerny interview, September 5, 2000.

10. Court rulings spared Brown's two successors—Ronald Reagan and Jerry Brown—from directly facing the issue of commutation in a substantial number of cases. More recent governors have all been staunch proponents of the death penalty. Commutation rates from Joseph A. Spangler, "California's Death Penalty Dilemma," *Crime and Delinquency* 15 (January 1969): 147.

11. At the time anti-Chinese feeling in San Francisco was so strong it seemed normal. Years later, during an interview, Brown recalled his brick-tossing exploits but then only minutes later declared that a high school encounter with anti-Semitism was the "first touch [he] ever had with discrimination." EGB oral history, pp. 21–36.

12. For comments about gays, see memo outlining operations in the district attorney's office, from EGB to Thomas C. Lynch and Alvin E. Weinberger, May 27, 1949, EGB Papers, Carton 1019, folder 10. For comments about women, see EGB AG oral history, p. 86.

13. EGB oral history, pp. 35–36.

14. Letters to various legislators, May 28, 1945, EGB Papers, Carton 97, folder 7, "correspondence, personal."

15. At the time there were 81 blacks among Los Angeles 2,600 uniformed firefighters. Of those, 75 were assigned to just two firehouses, one of which did maintenance work. Department of Justice Report for Governor's Council, Sep-

tember 1954. Brown certainly did not single-handedly end segregation in the firehouses. Newly elected Los Angeles Mayor Norris Poulson had been campaigning for months for a change. But Brown's opinion came at a critical moment in the debate, after the Los Angeles city attorney had essentially dodged the question. The attorney general's opinion, by contrast, flatly declared the existing segregation unconstitutional, closely followed the reasoning of NAACP lawyers working on the case, and gave Poulson added ammunition to push for integration. Los Angeles firehouses were not integrated fully for another two years, but the change was clearly due—in part—to Brown's opinion. See Bock, *State and Local Government,* pp. 109–34, esp. 125–29.

16. For the Camelback Inn incident, see various documents, especially a letter from Jack Stewart to Arnold Forster, October 20, 1954, in EGB Papers, Carton 11, folder 1, "Camelback Inn." For 1955 incident, see copy of speech by Georgia Attorney General Eugene Cook and various clippings, EGB Papers, Carton 11, folder 9, "civil rights." For Sputnik quote, see copy of Brown speech, December 19, 1957, EGB Papers, Carton 52, folder 11, "speech—Dec. 19, 1957."

17. "Brown Hit for Help to Riders," *San Francisco Chronicle,* June 27, 1961, p. 7; Branch, *Parting the Waters,* p. 805.

18. "Report on Housing in California," Governor's Advisory Commission on Housing Problems, January 1963, pp. 6, 38–42, 67–68.

19. "Report on Housing in California," Governor's Advisory Commission on Housing Problems, January 1963, pp. 6, 38–42, 67–68.

20. For useful summaries regarding fair housing law in California, see Casstevens, *Politics, Housing and Race Relations;* "Report of the Governor's Commission on the Rumford Act," April 6, 1967; "Fair Housing in California," Assembly Committee on Governmental Efficiency and Economy, June 1967.

21. "Report on Housing in California," Governor's Advisory Commission on Housing Problems, January 1963, pp. 6, 38–42, 67–68.

22. "Negro Pickets Appear at Inauguration," *Sacramento Bee,* January 8, 1963, p. 6.

23. Memo from EGB to Sherrill Luke, February 6, 1963, and "Make California First in Human Rights" memorandum, both in EGB Papers, Carton 640, folder 5, "Civil Rights, thru Feb. 28, 63."

24. Memo from Sherrill Luke to EGB, January 11, 1963, and letter from Sherrill Luke to Byron Rumford, January 11, 1963, both in EGB Papers, Carton 640, folder 6, "Housing Discrimination, 12–26–62 to 3–29–63."

25. Rumford oral history, pp. 1–12.

26. Soto oral history, pp. 126–34.

27. Amerson oral history, p. 77.

28. Letter from EGB to Ross Barnett, April 10, 1963, EGB Papers, Carton 664, folder 5, "governor's personal—B." For other information on Jerry's trip, see also "Brown's Son Paid a Call on Barnett," *San Francisco Chronicle,* April 26,

1963, p. 1; "Governor Brown's Boy," *Esquire,* November 1974, p. 113; Pack, *Jerry Brown,* pp. 31–32; Rapoport, *California Dreaming,* pp. 76–79.

29. Details of the Rumford Act's progress through the legislature, as cited here and throughout this chapter, are nicely summarized in Casstevens, *Politics, Housing and Race Relations,* pp. 18–48; Dallek, *The Right Moment,* pp. 42–61; and "The Fight for Fair Housing," Friends Committee on Legislation, available at EGB Papers, Carton 982, folder 5, "Lu Haas." Also see contemporary news accounts, especially the ongoing coverage in the *Sacramento Bee.*

30. Former Sen. Joseph Rattigan, a liberal Democrat, referred to Gibson as "a registered Democrat—that's all." Rattigan interview, September 26, 2002.

31. Rumford oral history, p. 117.

32. "Brown's Defense of Negro Rights," *San Francisco Chronicle,* May 20, 1963, p. 1.

33. "Housing Bias Bill May Go to Study," *Sacramento Bee,* May 23, 1963, p. 5.

34. "Brown Thanks Sit-in Group," *San Francisco Chronicle,* May 31, 1963, p. 14.

35. *Sacramento Bee:* "Two Movie Actors Help Boost Morale of CORE Sitins in Capitol," June 12, 1963, p. 8; "Chances for Fair Housing Bill Collapse amid Verbal Battle," June 14, 1963, p. 1; "Capitol CORE Sitins Lie on Floor, Block Senate Doorway," June 15, 1963, p. 1.

36. For the maneuvering on the legislature's last day, see the materials cited in note 12 for general Rumford Act history, but also see *Journal of the Senate,* 1963 regular session, pp. 4797–99; *Journal of the Assembly,* 1963 regular session, pp. 6225, 6279–90; Rattigan oral history, pp. 30–50; Rattigan interview, September 26, 2002; Rumford oral history, pp. 115–19; and news accounts including "Housing Bill Passes in What Brown Calls Historic Step," *Sacramento Bee,* June 22, 1963, p. 1; "Housing Bias Bill Enacted," *San Francisco Chronicle,* June 22, 1963, p. 1.

37. Casstevens, *Politics, Housing and Race Relations,* pp. 35–36.

38. EGB oral history, pp. 492–93; Rattigan interview, September 26, 2002; "Housing—We Have the Votes," *San Francisco Examiner,* June 22, 1963, p. 1.

39. Rattigan oral history, p. 39; "Housing Bias Bill Enacted," *San Francisco Chronicle,* June 22, 1963, p. 1; "Racial Bias in Housing Outlawed," *Oakland Tribune,* June 22, 1963, p. 1.

40. EGB oral history, p. 493. For the date of signature, on which many sources differ, see Final Calendar of Legislative Business, 1963, California Legislature, p. 431.

41. "Equality and State Jobs," *San Francisco Chronicle,* July 6, 1963, p. 7; "Sweeping State Bias Ban," *San Francisco Chronicle,* August 4, 1963, p. 13.

42. Letter from Robert Kugel to EGB, July 22, 1963, EGB Papers, Carton 603, folder 4, "governor"; "Brown Says Goldwater Is a Segregationist," *Los Angeles Times,* July 22, 1963, p. 1.

43. "A Day Full of Troubles," *San Francisco Chronicle,* July 26, 1963, p. 11.

44. "Brown in Ireland for Tour's Start," *San Francisco Chronicle,* July 28, 1963, p. 11; "Brown, in Britain, Drumming up Business, Raps Nixon Remarks," *Sacramento Bee,* July 31, 1963, p. 3.

45. "Distant Countrymen," *New York Times,* August 12, 1963, p. 7; "Brown, Nixon Cool Paris in the Summer," *Los Angeles Times,* August 2, 1963, p. 2; "Two Unspeakable Days in Paris," *San Francisco Chronicle,* August 3, 1963, p. 1.

46. "Brown Will Talk Trade with French," *San Francisco Chronicle,* August 2, 1963, p. 12; "Brown Tells French to Think California," *Los Angeles Times,* August 3, 1963, p. 8; "Brown Deplores DeGaulle's Nuclear Policy as Tragic, Regrettable," *Sacramento Bee,* August 5, 1963, p. 3; "Brown Warns Paris Americans They May Not Recognize State," *Sacramento Bee,* August 3, 1963, p. 3.

47. Letter from Hale Champion to EGB, August 7, 1963, Champion Papers, Carton 1, folder 7, "Brown, Gov. Edmund."

48. "Brown and Family See Sights of Eternal City," *Los Angeles Times,* August 15, 1963, p. 3; "Brown's Interesting Mafia Talks," *San Francisco Chronicle,* August 17, 1963, p. 2.

49. "Pope Receives Gov. Brown, Asked to Visit California," *New York Times,* August 18, 1963, p. 3; "Brown Invites Pope to California, Makes Bid for Italian Auto Plant," *Sacramento Bee,* August 18, 1963, p. 4; Kathleen Brown interview, December 11, 1998.

50. "Brown and Tito Debate Censors," *San Francisco Chronicle,* August 20, 1963, p. 3.

51. Letter from EGB to Frank Sinatra, September 10, 1963, EGB Papers, Carton 666, folder 8, "governor's personal S."

52. "Film Fan's Intermission," *San Francisco Chronicle,* August 28, 1963, p. 11.

53. "Gov. Brown's Stand at the Wall," *San Francisco Chronicle,* September 5, 1963, p. 9.

CHAPTER 13: REJECTION

1. Letter from EGB to Kathleen Brown, October 1, 1963, provided to the author by Kathleen Brown.

2. Kathleen Brown interviews, December 11, 1998, and September 7, 2000; letter from EGB to Kathleen Brown, February 6, 1964, provided to the author by Kathleen Brown.

3. Letter from EGB to Kathleen Brown, October 1, 1963, provided to the author by Kathleen Brown.

4. "Brown's Car Was Stoned in Argentina," *San Francisco Chronicle,* October 16, 1963, p. 1.

5. EGB oral history, p. 532; "Tears and Quiet Greet News of JFK Slaying in State Capitol," *Sacramento Bee,* November 22, 1963, p. 1.

6. Phonotape 3582C, Bancroft Library, UC Berkeley.

7. Letter from Verne Inman to Dan Kilroy, November 21, 1963, EGB Papers, Carton 666, folder 26, "governor's personal—family"; "Brown Flies to Washington to Pay Respects," *San Francisco Chronicle,* November 23, 1963, p. 2; Alarcon interview, August 9, 2001.

8. Text of Johnson's remarks, which were censored for public release, is at LBJ Library and Museum, Diary Backup, Carton 1, folder "Nov. 25, 1963."

9. EGB oral history, pp. 532–34.

10. Memo from Bill Becker to Jack Burby et. al., August 26, 1964, and attachments, Rumford Papers, Carton 1, folder 11, "fair housing, April–Dec. 1964."

11. Memo from William Becker to EGB, November 6, 1963, Champion Papers, Carton 5, folder "housing."

12. News conference transcript, January 14, 1964, EGB Papers, Carton 997, folder 2.

13. "Rumford Act Foes Claim One Victory," *Sacramento Bee,* February 5, 1964, p. 1.

14. News conference transcript, February 5, 1964, EGB Papers, Carton 997, folder 2.

15. Letter from EGB to Otis Chandler, February 6, 1964, EGB Papers, Carton 706, folder 14, "housing discrimination, Feb. 1–14." For the editorial that so enraged Brown, see "Decision on Housing Initiative," *Los Angeles Times,* February 2, 1964, p. G6.

16. Conversation 1990/1991, February 9, 1964, tape WH6402.13, LBJ Library and Museum.

17. Conversation 2076, February 14, 1964, tape WH6402.15, LBJ Library and Museum.

18. EGB oral history, p. 517; Kent oral history #1, pp. 15–17, 224–38; Fowle, *Cranston,* pp. 159–63.

19. "Engle Casts Vote in the Senate," *San Francisco Chronicle,* December 20, 1963, p. 1.

20. Memo from Alice Clover to Hale Champion, Champion Papers, Carton 3, folder "Engle, U.S. Senator." Letter from EGB to Clair Engle, December 20, 1963, and attachments, EGB Papers, Carton 664, folder 16, "governor's personal—E."

21. Irv Sprague interview, May 23, 2000. Sprague was present throughout the conversation between Brown and Engle. See also EGB oral history, pp. 516–19; Lucretia Engle oral history, p. 34; "Brown Says Engle Looks Fine," *San Francisco Chronicle,* January 12, 1964, p. 26; "Mrs. Engle's Puzzling Role," *San Francisco Chronicle,* May 3, 1964, p. 9.

22. Recording of telephone conversation, November 7, 1962, Kennedy Presidential Recordings, Item 6A.2.

23. Cannon, *Ronnie and Jesse,* pp. 9–26.

24. Champion oral history, pp. 33–38; Cannon, *Ronnie and Jesse,* pp. 122–23.

25. For one example, see "GOP Chortling over Unruh Dig," *San Francisco Chronicle,* March 7, 1963, p. 8.

26. "Brown's Language Shocks Republicans," *San Francisco Chronicle,* May 26, 1963, p. 1B; "Governor Explains His Salty Words," *San Francisco Chronicle,* May 29, 1963, p. 1.

27. Kent oral history #1, p. 17; Fowle, *Cranston,* p. 166.

28. Letter from EGB to Kathleen Brown, February 6, 1964, provided to the author by Kathleen Brown.

29. Did Brown personally spread word of Mosk's personal troubles? The evidence is mixed. But in numerous interviews, many sources told the author that the gossip was extremely widespread, regardless of Brown's involvement. One person close to Brown, speaking on condition of anonymity, remembered being approached by law enforcement officials who had copies of the pictures. It is not clear who took the pictures or to what extent they were distributed among the state's politicos, and the man involved never showed them to the governor. Brown believed the photos were in the possession of the Los Angeles Police Department; others thought that various political groups had them. For Brown's recollection, see EGB oral history, p. 520A. For an account of the entire affair, see "The Judge, the Photos and the Senate Race," *LA Weekly,* March 4, 1994, pp. 15–28. For other evidence, see Cannon, *Ronnie and Jesse,* p. 281; Mills, *A Disorderly House,* pp. 161–66.

30. Conversation 2860/2861, April 6, 1994, tape WH6404.03, LBJ Library and Museum. See also Cannon, *Ronnie and Jesse,* p. 281; Warschaw oral history, p. 248.

31. EGB oral history, pp. 516–24; Salinger oral history, pp. 36–40.

32. Conversation 2860/2861, April 6, 1964, tape WH6404.03, LBJ Library and Museum.

33. EGB oral history, pp. 516–24; Gatov oral history, p. 327; Fowle, *Cranston,* pp. 169–80; Cannon, *Ronnie and Jesse,* pp. 280–82.

34. Branch, *Pillar of Fire,* p. 336.

35. The next day, Brown claimed implausibly that his comments had been a joke. "Brown's Little Joke," *San Francisco Chronicle,* June 6, 1964, p. 7.

36. Conversation 4371, July 28, 1964, tape WH6407.16, LBJ Library and Museum. For Brown's thoughts and hopes, see EGB oral history, pp. 510–11. For details on Brown's injury, see "Brown Breaks His Ankle," *San Francisco Chronicle,* July 22, 1964, p. 1.

37. For background on Warschaw's connection to the Brown-Unruh feud, see "Brown Victor as Women Vie for Party Job," *Los Angeles Times,* June 28, 1964, p. 1; "Bitter Clash over Democratic Post," *San Francisco Chronicle,* June 28, 1964, p. 1B; Gatov oral history, pp. 341–47.

38. Conversation 4422, July 30, 1964, tape WH6407.20, LBJ Library and Museum.

39. Note to delegates, EGB Papers, Carton 742, folder "national convention Nancy Sloss material."

40. Branch, *Pillar of Fire*, p. 471.

41. "State Delegates Take Off for Demo Conclave," *Sacramento Bee*, August 22, 1964, p. 1.

42. White, *Making of the President 1964*, pp. 278–79; Branch, *Pillar of Fire*, pp. 456–66.

43. For detailed evidence of Brown following Johnson's lead, see Kent oral history #1, pp. 238–43.

44. "Brown Stops Support for Negro Group," *Los Angeles Times*, August 25, 1964, p. 2.

45. "State Delegation OK's Mississippi Proposal," *Los Angeles Times*, August 26, 1964, p. 9; Kent oral history #1, pp. 130–32, 238–43.

46. Conversation 5205, August 25, 1964, tape WH6408.38, LBJ Library and Museum.

47. Conversations 5206/5210, August 25, 1964, tape WH6408.38, LBJ Library and Museum.

48. "Brown Given Complete Charge of State Drive," *Los Angeles Times*, August 27, 1964, p. 1.

49. "Governor Wins LBJ Okeh as Campaign Boss," *Sacramento Bee*, August 27, 1964, p. 3.

50. EGB oral history, p. 514.

51. "Brown Finds Life Is Full of Little Tragedies," *Sacramento Bee*, August 27, 1964, p. 3; Tomlinson interview, July 15, 2002; Kathleen Brown interview, September 7, 2000.

52. "Brown's View of Fight for Passage of Prop. 14," *San Francisco Chronicle*, August 12, 1964, p. 14.

53. "Brown Says Talk Has Fascism Stench," *Sacramento Bee*, July 17, 1964, p. 1.

54. EGB oral history, pp. 524–31.

55. Conversation 6237, November 5, 1964, tape WH6411.08, LBJ Library and Museum.

56. Memo from Jack Burby to EGB, September 17, 1964, EGB Papers, Carton 998, folders arranged chronologically.

57. *Sacramento Bee:* "Brown Says 14 Win Would Be Tragic," September 23, 1964, p. 3; "Brown Claims Prop. 14 Perils Rights of All," September 26, 1964, p. 2; "Governor Says Fair Housing Laws Do Work," October 18, 1964, p. 8; "Governor Calls Prop. 14 Most Perilous Issue," October 28, 1964, p. 7.

58. For a summary of the polling, see Casstevens, *Politics, Housing and Race Relations*, pp. 48–70.

59. Casstevens, *Politics, Housing and Race Relations,* pp. 71–84.

60. Casstevens, *Politics, Housing and Race Relations,* p. 47; "Report of the Governor's Commission on the Rumford Act," April 6, 1967, p. 22.

61. The Modoc County anomaly was the result of special vigor among local Prop. 14 opponents, especially an activist local minister. For Modoc County information, see "The Repeal of Fair Housing in California: An Analysis of Referendum Voting," *American Political Science Review* 62, no. 3 (September 1968): 753–69. For general vote totals, see Statement of Vote, 1964, California Secretary of State.

62. From California, of course, Washington, D.C., was not "up" but "back," but the president was a Texan to the core.

63. Conversation 6237, November 5, 1964, tape WH6411.08, LBJ Library and Museum.

64. Letter from EGB to Kathleen Brown, November 9, 1964, provided to the author by Kathleen Brown.

CHAPTER 14: BERKELEY

1. KPFA tape, as transcribed in Goines, *The Free Speech Movement,* p. 369. The general description of the events of December 3, here and in the next several paragraphs, is based on Goines, *The Free Speech Movement,* pp. 361–95; Heirich, *The Spiral of Conflict,* pp. 265–78.

2. "Chronology of Events: Three Months of Crisis," *California Monthly,* February 1965, pp. 35–74.

3. Kerr interview, fall 1999. Brown reported the conversations back to the university president.

4. Report from Clark Kerr to the regents, July 15, 1964, EGB Papers, Carton 724, folder "UC, July." A more mathematical version of Brown's support of the university: after four years of his administration, per capita state support of UC was $8.11, up from $5.98 in the last year of the Knight administration and by far the highest per capita level in state history. The numbers are from a report by the UC president's office, March 13, 1964, EGB Papers, Carton 724, folder "UC."

5. "Brown Hails Students' Active Political Role," *San Jose Mercury News,* June 4, 1961, p. 1.

6. Heirich, *The Spiral of Conflict,* pp. 78–89; Goines, *The Free Speech Movement,* pp. 83–102; Morgan, *The 60s Experience,* pp. 47–51.

7. McAdam, *Freedom Summer,* p. 165.

8. Harris, *Dreams Die Hard,* p. 61.

9. For details on McComb, see Branch, *Pillar of Fire,* pp. 493–95; Harris, *Dreams Die Hard,* pp. 61–63; McAdam, *Freedom Summer,* pp. 75–77; Goines, *The Free Speech Movement,* pp. 97–98.

10. Brown probably never saw the letter, for Savio was in no way noteworthy

at the time. It was answered, politely and without commitment, by a staff member. See Savio letter to EGB, July 24, 1964, and letter from William Becker to Savio, August 13, 1964, EGB Papers, Carton 742, folder "Democratic National Convention—Aug."

11. For a detailed description of changes to the university faculty and student body in this period, see Heirich, *The Spiral of Conflict*, pp. 49–89; Stadtman, *The University of California*, pp. 425–43. See also "Soph Doll Crowned," *Daily Californian*, March 15, 1965, p. 1.

12. For an internal history of the university's political restrictions, see "History of University Policy Regarding On-Campus Meetings and Distribution of Handbills," in McLaughlin Papers, Carton 20, folder 3, "Free Speech Movement, 1964." Also see Kerr, *The Gold and the Blue*, vol. 2, pp. 122–92; Heirich, *The Spiral of Conflict*, pp. 66–71; Rorabaugh, *Berkeley at War*, pp. 8–15.

13. For years, rumors circulated that the *Oakland Tribune*, owned by Brown's old adversary Bill Knowland, was behind the crackdown. It is true that the paper discovered that the strip of sidewalk was actually owned by the university, but no evidence suggests the paper was behind the university's decision. For the decision to enforce the rules on the controversial patch of sidewalk, see Heirich, *The Spiral of Conflict*, pp. 91–97; Stadtman, *The University of California*, pp. 443–47; Kerr, *The Gold and the Blue*, vol. 2, pp. 161–92; Williams oral history, pp. 91–95, 119, 235; Irving interview, March 10, 2000.

14. Memo from Edward Strong to Academic Senate, October 26, 1962, Free Speech Archives (CU-309), Carton 3, folder 52.

15. "Strong Yields to Political Groups," *Daily Californian*, September 29, 1964, p. 1.

16. "Bancroft Groups Refuse Conditions," *Daily Californian*, September 22, 1964, p. 1; Stadtman, *The University of California*, p. 447.

17. Heirich, *The Spiral of Conflict*, pp. 140–61; Goines, *The Free Speech Movement*, pp. 161–75; Stadtman, *The University of California*, pp. 449–52.

18. Supplementary UC police department report by Lt. Merrill F. Chandler, October 1, 1964, UC Berkeley Chancellor's Papers, Carton 66, folder 3, "Oct. 1–6"; Heirich, *The Spiral of Conflict*, pp. 140–61; Goines, *The Free Speech Movement*, pp. 161–75.

19. Supplementary UC police department report by Lt. Merrill F. Chandler, October 1, 1964, UC Berkeley chancellor's papers, Carton 66, folder 3, "Oct. 1–6"; Goines, *The Free Speech Movement*, pp. 161–75.

20. Summary of events in memo from George Murphy to Arleigh Williams, October 9, 1964, UC Berkeley Chancellor's Papers, Carton 66, folder 2, "Oct. 7–13."

21. Goines, *The Free Speech Movement*, pp. 161–204; Rorabaugh, *Berkeley at War*, p. 21.

22. "New 'Distinction' for Jack Weinberg," *Oakland Tribune*, October 2, 1964, p. 3.

23. "Gov. Brown's Comment on UC Strike," *San Francisco Chronicle*, October 2, 1964, p. 6.

24. Copy of the statement is in UC Berkeley Chancellor's Papers, Carton 66, folder 3, "Oct. 1–6"; "Students Plan New Protest of Ban on Politics," *Oakland Tribune*, October 1, 1964, p. 1.

25. Kerr oral history, pp. 21–22; Stadtman, *The University of California*, p. 450. Kerr is the only available source as to the governor's comments. No one else was involved in their telephone conversation, and Brown was not asked about the topic during his own oral history. The sources cited above seem the most reliable, as the interviews on which they are based occurred relatively soon after the events. Kerr has also been asked about these events two subsequent times, a 1978 interview by Bensch and Saeed and a 1999 interview with the author. Both times he recalled Brown's comment about the south but not necessarily his own reference to the National Guard. There is no reference to the National Guard in Kerr's memoir's, *The Gold and the Blue*, vol. 2, p. 197. The videotape of the 1978 interview by F. Bensch and F. Saeed is part of the Free Speech Movement Project, Media Center, Moffitt Undergraduate Library, UC Berkeley.

26. Stadtman, *The University of California*, pp. 450–51; Kerr, *The Gold and the Blue*, vol. 2, pp. 192–200.

27. Letter from EGB to Richard M. Schmorleitz, October 28, 1964, EGB Papers, Carton 673, folder 3, "Civil Rights, Oct. 21–31."

28. "UC's Morning After," *San Francisco Chronicle*, October 4, 1964, p. 1.

29. Stadtman, *The University of California*, pp. 452–57.

30. Telegram from Mario Savio to EGB, October 14, 1964, EGB Papers, Carton 673, folder 4, "Civil Rights, Oct. 1–20."

31. Heirich, *The Spiral of Conflict*, pp. 265–71; Stadtman, *The University of California*, pp. 456–57.

32. Stadtman, *The University of California*, p. 457.

33. Unaddressed memos outlining administrators' strategy sessions, 10:10 A.M., 11:00 A.M., and 11:50 A.M., all December 2, 1964, UC Berkeley Chancellor's Papers, Carton 66, folder 10, "Dec. 1–8."

34. Heirich, *The Spiral of Conflict*, p. 271.

35. KPFA tape, as transcribed in Goines, *The Free Speech Movement*, p. 361.

36. Savio sometimes cited Thoreau. From Goines, *The Free Speech Movement*, p. 361, here is Thoreau's less oratorical version of a similar, though not identical, thought:

If the injustice is part of the necessary friction of the machine of government, let it go, let it go: perchance it will wear smooth—certainly the machine will wear out. If the injustice has a spring, or a pulley, or a rope, or a crank, exclusively for itself, then perhaps you may consider whether the remedy will not be worse than the evil; but if it is of such a nature that it requires you to be the agent of injustice to another, then I say, break the law. Let your life be a counter friction to stop the machine.

37. Heirich, *The Spiral of Conflict,* pp. 273–74; Rorabaugh, *Berkeley at War,* pp. 32–33; Stadtman, *The University of California,* pp. 457–58; Irving interview, March 10, 2000.

38. "Cedars Sets $7,400,000 Pledge Mark," *Beverly Hills Citizen-News,* December 3, 1964, p. 2.

39. See memo from Ron Moskowitz to Winslow Christian, December 2, 1964, EGB Papers, Carton 675, folder 8, "Civil Rights—Berkeley—Dec."

40. Kerr's arguments to the regents from Stadtman, *The University of California,* p. 458; Kerr, *The Gold and the Blue,* vol. 2, pp. 211–15; Kerr interview, fall 1999.

41. Burby interview, May 15, 2000.

42. There is an enormous amount of conflicting evidence about Brown's exact role that evening, but Kerr, in an interview with the author, remembered the governor's agreement as coming during a phone call from the Hilton. Stadtman, *The University of California,* p. 458, working from a 1967 interview with Kerr, says the phone call was made after Kerr returned to his El Cerrito home but also says Brown agreed with the plan.

43. Memo from Berkeley City Manager John D. Phillips to mayor and City Council members, October 23, 1964, McLaughlin Papers, Carton 21, folder 16.

44. O'Connell interview, April 19, 2000.

45. The preceding paragraphs are based largely on the author's interviews with Daniel O'Connell, April 19, 2000, and April 20, 2000, although this account is also generally supported by other evidence, most notably the report from Berkeley Police Chief A. H. Fording to City Manager John Phillips, December 22, 1964, at UC President's Papers, Box 45, folder 1, "student demonstrations, Jan.–March, 1965." Fording's report indicates the call came from Brown, but both O'Connell and Brown (see oral history) remembered the call originating with the police, and this seems a more plausible scenario. Also, since Fording was not directly involved in the conversations, it seems possible that his report is simply mistaken. The only slim bit of evidence from Alameda County District Attorney J. Frank Coakley, although far from conclusive, also seems to suggest that the request originated with law enforcement authorities. In 1970 Coakley told interviewers, "First we cleared it with the governor; he was kind of reluctant for us to do anything about it." See separate interview with Coakley in the supplementary material to his UC Berkeley oral history. See also Coakley, *For the People,* pp. 230–31; "Gov. Brown Didn't Order the Arrests," *Daily Californian,* April 8, 1965, p. 1.

46. Meese interview, May 23, 2000.

47. Murphy oral history, pp. 13–117.

48. EGB oral history, pp. 474–75; Kerr interview, fall 1999; Burby interview, May 15, 2000; Heller oral history, p. 587. For the animosity between Kerr and Murphy, see especially previously sealed pages of Heller oral history, pp. 571a, 587a. See also Murphy oral history, p. 131.

49. EGB oral history, pp. 474–75.

50. Report from A. H. Fording, Berkeley police chief, to John D. Phillips, city manager, dated December 22, 1964, and attached memo from Earl Bolton to Clark Kerr, February 12, 1965, at UC President's Papers, Box 45, folder 1, "student demonstrations, Jan.–March 1965"; EGB oral history, pp. 474–75; O'Connell interviews, April 19, 2000, and April 20, 2000; Burby interview, May 15, 2000.

51. Kerr interview, fall 1999; Heirich, *The Spiral of Conflict,* p. 275.

52. Heirich, *The Spiral of Conflict,* p. 276.

53. Heirich, *The Spiral of Conflict,* pp. 265–78.

54. For the story of the arrests, see "Chronology of Events: Three Months of Crisis"; Heirich, *The Spiral of Conflict,* pp. 275–78.

55. Goines, *The Free Speech Movement,* p. 543.

56. Heirich, *The Spiral of Conflict,* pp. 280–84.

57. "No Amnesty, Brown Says," *Oakland Tribune,* December 4, 1964, p. 2.

58. Transcript of Brown press conference, December 8, 1964, EGB Papers, Carton 997, folder 4; "Brown Labels Uproar at UC 'Unnecessary,'" *Sacramento Bee,* December 8, 1964, p. B1; Christian interview, May 8, 2000.

59. Transcript of Brown press conference, December 8, 1964, EGB Papers, Carton 997, folder 4; "Brown Labels Uproar at UC 'Unnecessary,'" *Sacramento Bee,* December 8, 1964, p. B1.

60. Coakley, *For the People,* p. 232.

61. Heirich, *The Spiral of Conflict,* p. 319.

62. Amazingly, Savio tried to reject victory, suggesting that the regents had not gone far enough. But most students knew they had won, and the energy vanished from the Free Speech Movement. Administrators, who had once described rallies with a breathless excitement, switched to tones of ennui. A rally in January was said to be a "thoroughly lackluster affair." The crowd never topped two hundred, and even Savio left early. Report on FSM demonstration by David C. Fulton, January 7, 1965, UC President's Papers, Box 45, folder 1, "student demonstrations, Jan.–March, 1965." For other demonstrations, also see various memos to Kerr, same location.

63. FSM platform and the university's later regulations both quoted in "Constitutionally Interpreting the FSM Controversy," by Robert Post, in Cohen and Zelnick, *The Free Speech Movement,* pp. 411–15.

64. "Rallies at Colleges Back UC Protest," *Oakland Tribune,* December 5, 1964, p. 1.

65. "Students Boycott Kerr in Scotland," *Daily Californian,* April 30, 1965, p. 1.

66. Heirich, *The Spiral of Conflict,* p. 1.

67. EGB oral history, p. 554.

68. Videotaped interview with EGB, October 13, 1978, by F. Bensch and F. Saeed, Free Speech Movement Project, Media Center, Moffitt Undergraduate Library, UC Berkeley.

69. "Chronology of Events: Three Months of Crisis," *California Monthly,* February 1965.

70. Letter from EGB to George Hardy, December 15, 1964, EGB Papers, Carton 675, folder 8, "Civil Rights—Berkeley—Dec."

71. California Poll, February 2, 1965.

72. Memo from Vivian Porter to Winslow Christian, December 10, 1964, EGB Papers, Carton 675, folder 5, "Berkeley"; "Angry Reaction Greets Arrests," *Oakland Tribune,* December 4, 1964, p. 2.

73. Exchange of letters: from EGB to Glenn L. Stoner, January 12, 1965, and from Stoner to EGB, December 19, 1964, both in EGB Papers, Carton 752, folder 10, "Berkeley, Jan. 1–12."

74. For the general opinion, see California Poll, February 2, 1965.

75. Telegram from Jack Smythe to EGB, EGB Papers, Carton 673, folder 10, "Berkeley, civil rights, not answered."

76. Letter to EGB, signature unreadable, attached to newspaper clipping, December 11, 1964, EGB Papers, Carton 674, folder 10, "Berkeley, civil rights, not answered."

77. EGB oral history, p. 46.

78. Letter from John Elliss to EGB, December 7, 1964, EGB Papers, Carton 674, folder 10, "Berkeley, civil rights, not answered."

CHAPTER 15: WATTS

1. Champion deposition, pp. 40–41, Governor's Commission, vol. V; EGB deposition, pp. 7–9, Governor's Commission, vol. IV. Notes in this chapter referring to depositions, statements, formal reports, and the chronology from the Governor's Commission refer to the bound volumes published by the Governor's Commission on the Los Angeles Riots. Notes referencing archival materials in Governor's Commission Papers refer to collection BANC MSS 74/115c at the Bancroft Library, UC Berkeley.

2. Champion statement, p. 4, and Champion deposition, pp. 7–10, both in Governor's Commission, vol. V; EGB oral history, p. 557; EGB deposition, pp. 8–10, Governor's Commission, vol. IV.

3. *Violence in the City—An End or a Beginning?* Governor's Commission report, p. 3.

4. California Poll, February 4, 1965. The numbers: good job, 26 percent; fair job, 33 percent; poor job, 36 percent; no opinion, 5 percent. For comparison, the same categories, respectively, were 23, 39, 29, and 9 percent in October 1963.

5. "State Sends a Civil War," *San Francisco Chronicle,* January 21, 1965, p. 13.

6. "Brown Hits 'Do Nothing' Legislature," *San Francisco Chronicle,* May 19, 1965, p. 31.

7. "Solons Okeh Budget, Quit; Brown Plans Big Slash," *Sacramento Bee,* June 19, 1965, p. 1; "The Legislature Adjourns—Key Issues Unsettled" and "$4.18 Billion State Budget Is Adopted," both *San Francisco Chronicle,* June 19, 1965, p. 1; "Brown's Tax Ultimatum to Legislature," *San Francisco Chronicle,* June 20, 1965, p. 1; "Brown Gets Budget Cut List, Headed by Loss of Pay Raises," *Sacramento Bee,* June 22, 1965, p. 1.

8. "Solons Okeh Budget, Quit; Brown Plans Big Slash," *Sacramento Bee,* June 19, 1965, p. 1; "The Legislature Adjourns—Key Issues Unsettled" and "$4.18 Billion State Budget Is Adopted," both *San Francisco Chronicle,* June 19, 1965, p. 1.

9. Goines, *The Free Speech Movement,* pp. 480–508; Rorabaugh, *Berkeley at War,* pp. 38–41.

10. Memos from Dean Johnson to Kerr, March 3, 1965, and March 5, 1965, UC President's Papers, Bancroft Library, Carton 45, folder 1, "student demonstrations, Jan.–March 1965"; Goines, *The Free Speech Movement,* pp. 480–508; "Obscene Sign Causes Arrest; Protest Rally Called For," *Daily Californian,* March 4, 1965, p. 1; "More Arrested for Obscenity," *Daily Californian,* March 5, 1965, p. 1.

11. Kerr interview, fall 1999.

12. Letters from EGB to Mr. and Mrs. Karl Schwenke, April 2, 1965, and to F. S. Miller, May 6, 1965, EGB Papers, Carton 802, folder 14, "UC, May 1–12."

13. Letters to EGB from the following: Charles R. Davis, May 19, 1965; James B. Lee, May 11, 1965; Elizabeth Hayes, May 18, 1965; all in EGB Papers, Carton 802, folder 15, "UC, June 1–3."

14. Memo from R. W. Komer to Jack Valenti, July 29, 1965, LBJ Library and Museum, Confidential File, Box 90, folder "ST-5-California."

15. See various letters and memos describing the National Guard–Los Angeles contacts, all attached to letter from Robert L. Quick to John A. Mitchell, November 22, 1965, Governor's Commission Papers, Carton 5, folder 6A.

16. Governor's Commission Report, p. 2.

17. Memo from Howard Jewell to Stanley Mosk, May 25, 1964, EGB Papers, Carton 754, folder 6, "LA County riot, Sept. 11–30."

18. The history of Watts below is based largely on a paper produced in July 1965, before the riots, by Franklyn Rabow, a graduate student at UCLA, "Watts: A History of Deprivation." It is available at Governor's Commission Papers, Carton 7, folder 14, "History of Watts." For other Watts history, see also Horne, *Fire This Time,* pp. 23–42; McWilliams, *Southern California Country,* pp. 324–26.

19. Rabow paper, pp. 20–27, Governor's Commission Papers, Carton 7, folder 14, "History of Watts"; Horne, *Fire This Time,* p. 27.

20. Rabow paper, pp. 19–22, Governor's Commission Papers, Carton 7, folder 14, "History of Watts." For Watts median income, see Viorst, *Fire in the Streets,* p. 318. For population density figures, see LAPD records attached as exhibits to Reddin deposition, Governor's Commission, vol. XII.

21. Memo from William Becker to EGB, August 30, 1965, EGB Papers, Carton 754, folder 7, "L.A. Riots, Aug.–Sept. 9."

22. Alarcon interview, August 9, 2001, and Eppie Johnson interview, March 6, 2003. Alarcon heard the story from Bernice Brown, who was present. Eppie Johnson, son of George Johnson, heard it from his father.

23. For touring, see photograph, *Sacramento Bee,* August 11, 1965, p. 14.

24. The description of Frye's arrest and the following paragraphs describing the first night of rioting are based on many sources, including the Governor's Commission Chronology, pp. 1–34. For details of the arrest, see particularly the police reports of Officers Lee Minikus, Robert Lewis, and L. Bennett and the police Intoxication Report, all in Governor's Commission Papers, Carton 4, black untitled notebook, "Annex C." For general events of August 11, see also Horne, *Fire This Time,* pp. 45–63; Cohen and Murphy, *Burn, Baby, Burn!* pp. 23–84; Conot, *Rivers of Blood,* pp. 3–64. Some sources disagree on some details, but generally the descriptions of August 11 are fairly consistent.

25. EGB deposition, pp. 7–8, Governor's Commission, vol. IV; Christian deposition, p. 15, Governor's Commission, vol. V; letter from Winslow Christian to John A. Mitchell, October 15, 1965, Governor's Commission, vol. V.

26. Buggs deposition, pp. 33–63, Governor's Commission, vol. V; Governor's Commission Chronology, pp. 39–50; Cohen and Murphy, *Burn, Baby, Burn!* pp. 85–97.

27. Governor's Commission Chronology, pp. 56–72.

28. Governor's Commission Chronology, pp. 83–91; Cohen and Murphy, *Burn, Baby, Burn!* pp. 85–125.

29. Governor's Commission Chronology, pp. 88–89.

30. "Get Whitey, Scream Blood-Hungry Mobs," *Los Angeles Times,* August 14, 1965, p. 1.

31. EGB deposition, pp. 7–8, Governor's Commission, vol. IV; Christian deposition, p. 15, Governor's Commission, vol. V; letter from Winslow Christian to John A. Mitchell, October 15, 1965, Governor's Commission, vol. V.

32. Anderson JFK oral history, pp. 1–15.

33. Champion interview, May 19, 2000.

34. Anderson deposition, pt. II, p. 11, Governor's Commission, vol. III.

35. Governor's Commission Chronology, pp. 55–85.

36. Governor's Commission Chronology, pp. 90–95.

37. Governor's Commission Chronology, pp. 90–95; Anderson deposition, pt. I, pp. 67–69, Governor's Commission, vol. III.

38. Governor's Commission Chronology, pp. 96–110.

39. Governor's Commission Chronology, pp. 117–23; Conot, *Rivers of Blood,* pp. 202–25.

40. Champion interview, May 19, 2000; Champion deposition, pp. 1–22, Governor's Commission, vol. V.

41. Parker deposition on September 16, 1965, pp. 28–29, Governor's Commission, vol. XI; Governor's Commission Chronology, pp. 117–20.

42. Champion interview, May 19, 2000; Champion deposition, pp. 1–22, Governor's Commission, vol. V.

43. Governor's Commission Chronology, p. 122; Champion deposition, p. 18, Governor's Commission, vol. V; McDonald interview, January 8, 2003.

44. Champion statement, p. 4, and Champion deposition, pp. 7–10, both in Governor's Commission, vol. V; EGB oral history, p. 557; EGB deposition, pp. 8–10, Governor's Commission, vol. IV.

45. Hill deposition, pp. 63–67, Governor's Commission, vol. VIII.

46. Governor's Commission Chronology, pp. 155–61; "Eight Men Slain; Guard Moves In," *Los Angeles Times,* August 14, 1965, p. 1; EGB deposition, p. 10, Governor's Commission, vol. IV; Champion deposition, pp. 11–12, Governor's Commission, vol. V.

47. "Brown Returns, Says He Ordered Guard Call-Up," *Los Angeles Times,* August 15, 1965, p. 1.

48. Horne, *Fire This Time,* pp. 74–75; Conot, *Rivers of Blood,* pp. 256–57.

49. Conot, *Rivers of Blood,* pp. 245–61; Gentry, *The Last Days,* pp. 189–222.

50. Gates and Shah, *Chief,* pp. 100–102; Governor's Commission Chronology, pp. 171–76.

51. Conot, *Rivers of Blood,* pp. 245–61; Governor's Commission Chronology, pp. 171–76.

52. Conversation 8536, tape WH6508.04, LBJ Library and Museum.

53. Conversation 8536, tape WH6508.04, LBJ Library and Museum. See also EGB oral history, p. 557; Champion deposition, pp. 12–15, 35, Governor's Commission, vol. V; EGB deposition, p. 10, Governor's Commission, vol. IV; Anderson deposition, pp. 12–13, Governor's Commission, vol. III.

54. Champion mentioned this concern to White House aide Joseph Califano. See conversation 8538, tape WH6508.04, LBJ Library and Museum. See also Champion statement, pp. 10–11, Governor's Commission, vol. V. For other riots, see Governor's Commission Chronology, pp. 156–76.

55. Conversations 8536 and 8538, tape WH6508.04, LBJ Library and Museum. See also EGB oral history, p. 557; Champion deposition, pp. 12–15, 35, Governor's Commission, vol. V; EGB deposition, pp. 10, 31–32, Governor's

Commission, vol. IV; Anderson deposition, pp. 12–13, Governor's Commission, vol. III.

56. EGB oral history, p. 557; EGB deposition, pp. 10–11, Governor's Commission, vol. IV; Champion deposition, pp. 12–15, Governor's Commission, vol. V.

57. "Brown Returns, Says He Ordered Guard Call-Up," *Los Angeles Times,* August 15, 1965, p. 1.

58. Memo from Richard A. Kline to Edith Bellflower, September 2, 1965, EGB Papers, Carton 200, folder 2, "Carbons, Kline, Sept. 1965"; Champion statement, pp. 11–12, Governor's Commission, vol. V.

59. Governor's Commission Chronology, pp. 186–92.

60. Governor's Commission Chronology, pp. 200–201.

61. Governor's Commission Chronology, pp. 200–205; Horne, *Fire This Time,* pp. 112–15; Cohen and Murphy, *Burn, Baby, Burn!* pp. 201–32.

62. Conot, *Rivers of Blood,* p. 347.

63. Brookins deposition, p. 72, Governor's Commission, vol. IV.

64. EGB deposition, p. 38, Governor's Commission, vol. IV.

65. EGB deposition, pp. 48–53, Governor's Commission, vol. IV; Cohen and Murphy, *Burn, Baby, Burn!* pp. 249–51; "Brown's Riot Area Tour Curtailed by Sniper Fire," *Los Angeles Times,* August 16, 1965, p. 1.

66. "Brown's Riot Area Tour Curtailed by Sniper Fire," *Los Angeles Times,* August 16, 1965, p. 1.

67. "Brown Will Appoint 7-Man Investigative Panel," *Los Angeles Times,* August 17, 1965, p. 1.

68. "Brown's Riot Area Tour Curtailed by Sniper Fire," *Los Angeles Times,* August 16, 1965, p. 1.

69. "Brown Will Appoint 7-Man Investigative Panel," *Los Angeles Times,* August 17, 1965, p. 1.

70. Governor's Commission Chronology, pp. 220–30.

71. These numbers are from *Violence in the City,* the Governor's Commission report, p. 1. Some sources offer slightly different numbers. There are disputes even on the exact number of fatalities, depending on what is considered a riot-related death. Note also that some damage estimates have been wildly inflated. Even at the time officials knew that some public estimates were far above the actual amount. See memo to Bill Becker from Frank Cullen, August 20, 1965, EGB Papers, Carton 754, folder 7, "L.A. Riots, Aug.–Sept. 9."

72. Patterson, *Grand Expectations,* p. 611; Horne, *Fire This Time,* p. 3.

73. Conversation 8526, tape WH6508.03, LBJ Library and Museum.

74. California Poll, November 24, 1965.

75. Patterson, *Grand Expectations,* pp. 579–85.

76. Gentry, *The Last Days,* pp. 199–205.

77. Viorst, *Fire in the Streets,* pp. 333–34.

78. Conversation 8578, tape WH6508.07, LBJ Library and Museum; Gover-

nor's Commission Chronology, pp. 220–30; "Riot Declared Over But Snipers Still Hit and Run," *Los Angeles Times,* August 17, 1965, p. 1; "After the Blood Bath," *Newsweek,* August 30, 1965, p. 13.

79. Brown, *Reagan and Reality,* pp. 116–17.

80. Letter from EGB to Drew Pearson, August 20, 1965, EGB Papers, Carton 754, folder 7, "L.A. Riots, Aug.–Sept. 9."

81. Horne, *Fire This Time,* pp. 341–43.

82. Memo from William Becker to EGB, August 30, 1965, EGB Papers, Carton 754, folder 7, "L.A. Riots, Aug.–Sept. 9"; "After the Blood Bath," *Newsweek,* August 30, 1965, p. 13; Cohen and Murphy, *Burn, Baby, Burn!* pp. 18–19; Horne, *Fire This Time,* pp. 342. Emphasis in the original in Becker memo.

83. *Violence in the City—An End or a Beginning?* Report of the Governor's Commission, p. 8.

84. "Biggest and Richest?" *Newsweek,* July 19, 1965, p. 71.

85. "Researching Social Needs," *New Republic,* May 15, 1965, p. 7.

86. Some Californians had trouble adjusting. Thinking back to slower, more traditional trains, some commuters suggested that BART cars include bars, so that commuters might enjoy a cocktail between stations. "BART: San Francisco's Grand Design," *Newsweek,* July 19, 1965, p. 69.

87. "After the Blood Bath," *Newsweek,* August 30, 1965, p. 13.

88. "Troubled Los Angeles—Race Is Only One of Its Problems," *U.S. News and World Report,* August 30, 1965, p. 58.

89. Memo from Jim Alexander to Winslow Christian, September 29, 1965, EGB Papers, Carton 754, folder 6, "LA County riot, Sept. 11–30"; California Poll, November 30, 1965.

90. California Poll, November 30, 1965.

91. Interestingly, Parker, the police chief, was slow to see the need of a curfew but later acknowledged its benefits. Parker deposition on September 17, 1965, p. 153, Governor's Commission, vol. XI.

CHAPTER 16: TIRED OLD GOVERNOR

1. Discussion of the meeting here and in the paragraphs that follow is based on memo from Richard Kline to EGB, August 5, 1965, EGB Papers, Carton 200, folder 63, "political, general corr., 1965."

2. Champion interview, May 19, 2000.

3. Winslow Christian, who became Brown's chief of staff in 1964, remembered that "[f]rom day one, it was campaign time." Christian oral history, p. 47. For Brown conversation with LBJ, see tape of the conversation, November 5, 1964, tape WH6411.08, LBJ Library and Museum.

4. Memo from Richard Kline to EGB, August 5, 1965, EGB Papers, Carton 200, folder 63, "political, general corr., 1965."

5. "Reagan Again Attacks Growth of Government," *Sacramento Bee,* August 3, 1965, p. 14.

6. For general Reagan background, see especially Boyarsky, *Ronald Reagan: His Life,* pp. 46–86; Cannon, *Reagan,* pp. 71–97, and *Ronnie and Jesse,* pp. 67–88.

7. "Reagan Announces He's Candidate for Governor," *Los Angeles Times,* January 5, 1966, p. 3.

8. Boyarsky, *Rise of Reagan,* pp. 112–13.

9. "Brown Formally Opens Re-election Campaign," *Los Angeles Times,* February 2, 1966, p. 3.

10. Various letters, February 14, 1966, EGB Papers, Carton 923, folder 19, "political governor, Feb. 8–14."

11. Memo from Joe Califano to LBJ, July 29, 1965, LBJ Library and Museum, WHCF Name File, Box 499, folder "Brown, Edmund G.—6-1-65 to 12-31-65."

12. Exchange of letters, Simon Casady and EGB, October 20, 1965, and October 13, 1965, EGB Papers, Carton 290, folder 5, "Edmund G. Brown, correspondence, March 1966." See also memo to Marvin Watson from Chester Cooper, October 2, 1965, LBJ Library and Museum, WHCF Name File, Box 499, folder "Brown, Edmund G.—6-1-65 to 12-31-65."

13. Letter from EGB to Virginia Casady, February 18, 1966, EGB Papers, Carton 921, folder 7, "political Casady, Jan.–March."

14. Even in the CDC, the pro-Casady forces were never a majority. About sixteen hundred delegates remained and listened to the governor, some chanting "We Want Brown." But the booing from the liberals was loud, and reported by the papers. "CDC Will Support Brown, Cranston," *Sacramento Bee,* February 21, 1966, p. 1.

15. For general background on Yorty here and in the following paragraphs, see Ainsworth, *Maverick Mayor,* pp. 1–136; and Bollens and Geyer, *Yorty,* pp. 1–135.

16. Dallek, *The Right Moment,* pp. 158–59.

17. EGB oral history, p. 542.

18. "Gov. Brown Quips with Yorty, Unruh," *Sacramento Bee,* January 5, 1966, p. 4.

19. Jeff Brown interview, August 13, 1998.

20. Cannon, *Ronnie and Jesse,* pp. 165–66.

21. Did Brown promise he would not run and then break his word? Perhaps. Averse to conflict, he liked to tell people what they wanted to hear. Unruh should have known that. Unruh may also have listened hopefully, construing the governor's momentary inclination as a fixed promise. The exact conversation can never be known. For discussions of the event, see Dallek, *The Right Moment,* pp. 154–56; and Cannon, *Ronnie and Jesse,* pp. 121–22. For Brown quote, see EGB oral history, pp. 561–62.

22. The California Poll of April 22, 1965, showed Brown at 53 percent; Trea-

surer Alan Cranston, 16 percent; Lt. Gov. Glenn Anderson, 13 percent; and Unruh, 9 percent. It is impossible to know where the Brown voters would have gone if the governor had not been running. Nor did the poll consider a possible bid by Stanley Mosk, who was willing to leave the state supreme court for a return to politics.

23. Dasmann obituary, *Los Angeles Times,* November 9, 2002, p. B20.

24. Dasmann, *Called by the Wild,* pp. 122–24; Dasmann, *Destruction of California,* p. 214.

25. Dasmann, *Destruction of California,* pp. 20–21.

26. Dasmann, *Destruction of California,* p. 169.

27. "Overcrowd," *Newsweek,* September 6, 1965, p. 67.

28. "Gov. Brown, Christopher Visit D.C.; Both See Victory Despite Calif. Polls," *Washington Post,* March 15, 1966, p. 2; "Brown, Unionists Back U.S. Farm Labor Bills," *San Francisco Chronicle,* March 15, 1966, p. 1; "Brown's Crusade for the Redwoods," *San Francisco Chronicle,* March 23, 1966, p. 41.

29. For a general history of California agriculture and of the Delano grape strike described below, see McWilliams, *Factories in the Field;* Cottle, Maccaulay, and Yandle, *Labor and Property Rights;* Dunne, *Delano;* Meister and Loftis, *A Long Time Coming;* London and Anderson, *So Shall Ye Reap.*

30. Dunne, *Delano,* p. 34.

31. Congress let the overall bracero program expire at the end of 1964, although even then some workers were imported for specific areas.

32. Meister and Loftis, *A Long Time Coming,* pp. 92–109; transcript of Brown news conference, January 6, 1966, EGB Papers, Carton 997, folder 9.

33. Dunne, *Delano,* pp. 133–34.

34. Dunne, *Delano,* pp. 146–53; Taylor, *Chavez and the Farm Workers,* pp. 193–94; Levy, *Cesar Chavez,* pp. 231–32.

35. Letter from EGB to Joseph H. Skillin, April 26, 1966, EGB Papers, Carton 290, folder "April 1966"; EGB oral history, p. 319. For Sinatra, see Kelley, *His Way,* pp. 361–62.

36. "Grape March Ranks Swell," *Sacramento Bee,* April 10, 1966, p. 1.

37. "Capitol Protest Ends Grape March," *Sacramento Bee,* April 11, 1966, p. 1; Levy, *Cesar Chavez,* pp. 206–18.

38. Letter from EGB to Frank Sinatra, April 12, 1966, EGB Papers, Carton 290, folder 8, "Edmund G. Brown, correspondence, April 1966."

39. Pack, *Jerry Brown,* pp. 32–35.

40. Kathleen Brown interview, December 11, 1998; Carlson interview, May 10, 2000; Bernice Brown oral history, pp. 70–71; memo from Fred Jordan to Adrienne Sausset, December 7, 1965, EGB Papers, Carton 839, folder 32, "governor's personal family"; "Pat Runs Scared," *Look,* November 1, 1966, p. 42.

41. California Polls, February 16, 1966, and April 14, 1966.

42. California Polls, February 15, 1966, and April 17, 1966.

43. A variety of former Brown aides and associates have confirmed the role of both the campaign and the governor. For examples, see Bradley oral history, pp. 181–200; Champion oral history, pp. 71–74; and Ringer oral history, pp. 107–8. For a partly candid account by Brown, see EGB oral history, p. 566. For other accounts, see Dallek, *The Right Moment,* pp. 204–9; Cannon, *Ronnie and Jesse,* p. 78.

44. Dorsey, *Christopher of San Francisco,* pp. 49–57; Dick Nolan column, *San Francisco Examiner,* February 4, 1962, pt. II, p. 1.

45. Dallek, *The Right Moment,* pp. 204–9; Cannon, *Ronnie and Jesse,* p. 78.

46. California Poll, May 26, 1966. Although the "milk scandal" clearly had some effect, Christopher probably would have lost the Republican nomination to Reagan anyway. Christopher never led the race, and it is unclear precisely how much effect the milk story had. It has occasionally been reported that the story seriously damaged Christopher in the southern part of the state, where voters had never heard of it before. That is false. After the milk story, Christopher's support held roughly even in the south but continued a sharp decline in the north. California Poll, May 24, 1966.

47. Yorty carried Calaveras, Inyo, Kern, Mono, and Orange Counties. Statement of Vote, 1966, California Secretary of State's Office.

48. Letter from EGB to Hubert Humphrey, June 18, 1966, EGB Papers, Carton 290, folder 6, "Edmund G. Brown correspondence, June 1966."

49. Fleharty interview, July 22, 2002. Also see memo from Joseph Califano to LBJ, June 10, 1966, LBJ Library and Museum, WHCF Name File, Box 499, folder "Edmund G. Brown 1-1-66 to 6-30-66."

50. Memo from Robert Kintner to LBJ, June 28, 1966, LBJ Library and Museum, Confidential File, Box 76, folder "PL/ST political affairs."

51. "Christopher Says He's for Reagan," *San Francisco Chronicle,* July 19, 1966, p. 1.

52. There are many contemporary press accounts offering evidence of Reagan's basic campaign issues. For one example that touches on most of them, see "An Old Pals Lunch for Yorty, Reagan," *San Francisco Chronicle,* October 8, 1966, p. 7. For other examples, including the cited quotations, see the following stories, all *San Francisco Chronicle:* "Brown and Reagan Square Off," June 3, 1966, p. 1; "Reagan's Views on Readmitting Savio to UC," September 15, 1966, p. 8; "Reagan's View of Riots," September 30, 1966, p. 14; "Reagan Assails Rumford Act," October 7, 1966, p. 8; "Reagan Hedge-Hops State," October 23, 1966, p. 9; and "Reagan Hits Leniency to Rioters," October 24, 1966, p. 1.

53. Trombley interview, April 20, 2000.

54. Transcript of press conference, October 28, 1966, EGB Papers, Carton 997, folder 10. "Reagan Denies He's Riding Backlash," *San Francisco Examiner,* October 29, 1966, p. 4.

55. California Poll, October 12, 1966; "Politics: The White Backlash, 1966,"

Newsweek, October 10, 1966, p. 27; Statement of Vote, 1966; "Pollsters Call Backlash Big Factor in Elections," *Los Angeles Times,* November 6, 1966, p. 2. For Brown quote, see EGB LBJ oral history, pt. II, p. 20.

56. Letter from EGB to Walter Kane, July 1, 1966, EGB Papers, Carton 922, folder 18, "political governor, July 1–11."

57. Letter from EGB to Dick Berlin, June 23, 1966, EGB Papers, Carton 926, folder 13, "political publicity, June."

58. Letter from Richard E. Berlin to EGB, November 2, 1966, EGB Papers, Carton 922, folder 2, "political governor, Nov. 1–2."

59. "Governor Signs Controversial Anti-riot Measure, Negro Assemblyman Protests," *Sacramento Bee,* July 21, 1966, p. 4; "Brown Seeks Overhaul of Rumford Act," *Sacramento Bee,* August 13, 1966, p. 1.

60. California Poll, September 1, 1966.

61. Letter from EGB to Tom Storke, August 5, 1966, EGB Papers, Carton 918, folder 2, "Gov. Personal S."

62. "Governor's 5-Day Swing," *San Francisco Chronicle,* September 5, 1966, p. 6; "Governor Outlines His War on Crime," *San Francisco Chronicle,* September 6, 1966, p. 1; "Governor Cultivates Farm Vote," *San Francisco Chronicle,* September 7, 1966, p. 1; "Gov. Brown's Platform Shaping Up," *San Francisco Examiner & Chronicle,* September 11, 1966, p. 13.

63. "Brown Flies into S.F., Praises Shelley, Cahill," *San Francisco Chronicle,* September 29, 1966, p. 19.

64. "Reagan's View of Riots," *San Francisco Chronicle,* September 30, 1966, p. 14.

65. "Reagan's View of Riots," *San Francisco Chronicle,* September 30, 1966, p. 14.

66. Even then, no public pollster in the state anticipated the full dimensions of the rout. California Poll, October 11, 1966, and, for background, September 1, 1966. For Reagan's thoughts, see letter from Ronald Reagan to John McCone, Nixon Library and Birthplace, item PPS 501.13.2–4.

67. Guggenheim oral history, pp. 9–11; Guggenheim interview, May 22, 2000; "Mixed Reaction to Brown's Joke," *San Francisco Chronicle,* October 29, 1966, p. 9; "Finch Demands Brown Halt TV Jab at Actors," *Los Angeles Times,* October 30, 1966, p. B; Dallek, *The Right Moment,* pp. 234–36.

68. "Reagan Says He Would Choose Best Talent to Help Run State," *Los Angeles Times,* November 1, 1966, p. 1; "Tremendous Welcome Given Reagan by San Franciscans," *Los Angeles Times,* November 4, 1966, p. 1.

69. EGB LBJ oral history, pt. II, p. 19; "Brown on Johnson," *San Francisco Chronicle,* November 4, 1966, p. 1.

70. Exchange of letters, EGB and Jesse Unruh, October 13, 1966, and October 18, 1966, EGB Papers, Carton 922, folder 8, "political governor, Oct. 17–19."

71. Memo from Jake Jacobsen to LBJ, November 4, 1966, LBJ Library and

Museum, WHCF Name File, Container 499, folder "Brown, Edmund G., 1-1-66 to 6-30-66."

72. Boyarsky, *Ronald Reagan: His Life,* p. 104.

73. "Reagan Steps Up Tempo," *Sacramento Bee,* November 7, 1966, p. 1; "Brown Says Reagan Win Would Help GOP Unseat Johnson in '68," *Sacramento Bee,* November 7, 1966, p. 16.

74. "Brown Presses Late Drive," *Sacramento Bee,* November 7, 1966, p. 1; "Candidates Wait for Results after Furious Finishes," *Sacramento Bee,* November 8, 1966, p. 1.

75. Statement of Vote, California Secretary of State, 1966.

76. Statement of Vote, California Secretary of State, 1966.

77. Statement of Vote, California Secretary of State, 1966.

78. Letter from Ben Swig to Earl Warren, November 25, 1966, Warren LOC Papers, Box 119, folder 4, "Swig, Benjamin"; "Pat Brown, a Political Realist, Accepts His Defeat Graciously," *Los Angeles Times,* November 9, 1966, p. 3.

79. Letter from EGB to LBJ, November 21, 1966, LBJ Library and Museum, White House Confidential File, Box 90, folder "California."

80. California Poll, June 24, 1966.

81. Asked if blacks were denied job opportunities in California, union members were less likely than the population at large to say yes (California Poll, May 21, 1964). As to students, disapproval of the Berkeley protests was highest among people with only a high school diploma (California Poll, February 2, 1965). The same poll showed a particularly striking difference among people who said they approved of the demonstrations but "with reservations." Among college graduates, 29 percent put themselves in this category, almost three times the proportion for people with a high school diploma or less. This reflects especially Brown's vulnerability among blue-collar voters, because "approve with reservations" was essentially his position. He agreed with the students' underlying goal but not with the idea of staging a sit-in. That was a view that had little currency with blue-collar workers.

82. California Poll, October 12, 1966.

83. The twelve working-class cities are the only ones in which, at the 1970 census, at least 40 percent of workers were classified as being in "manufacturing industries." Ten were suburbs of Los Angeles: Bell Gardens, Commerce, Cudahy, Hawthorne, Huntington Park, Lawndale, Maywood, Paramount, South El Monte, and South Gate. Two were outlying suburbs of San Francisco: Milpitas and Sunnyvale. The list omits unincorporated areas and cities with populations of less than ten thousand. The 1970 census, the closest to the 1966 race, divided employment into three categories: "manufacturing industries," "white-collar occupations," and "government." 1970 U.S. Census, Table 41. For election results, see Statement of Vote, California Secretary of State, 1962 and 1966.

84. Guggenheim interview, May 22, 2000.

85. Letter from EGB to Robert Smylie, December 1, 1966, EGB Papers, Carton 918, folder 1, "governor personal S."

86. Exchange of letters, Earl Warren and EGB, December 9, 1966, and November 10, 1966, EGB Papers, Carton 918, folder "gov personal W."

87. Memo from Henry Wilson to LBJ, June 21, 1966, LBJ Library and Museum, WHCF Name File, Box 499, folder "Brown, Edmund G., 1-1-66 to 6-30-66."

88. LBJ response attached to memo from Marvin Watson to LBJ, November 29, 1966, LBJ Library and Museum, Diary Backup, Box 51, folder "Dec. 15, 1966."

89. "Brown May Have Briefed LBJ on Demo Defeat," *Sacramento Bee,* December 16, 1966, p. 10.

90. EGB LBJ oral history, pt. II, pp. 15–16.

91. *Sacramento Bee:* " 'It's Sad,' Says Governor on Last Day in Capitol," December 30, 1966, p. 1; "Quiet, Undramatic Farewells End Brown's Public Service Career," December 31, 1966, p. 3; "Brown Appoints Son to State Advisory Post," December 31, 1966, p. 3.

92. Burby interview, May 15, 2000.

93. "Quiet, Undramatic Farewells End Brown's Public Service Career," *Sacramento Bee,* December 31, 1966, p. 3.

94. "Nancy's Been Eager to Move in Before," *Sacramento Bee,* December 18, 1980; Calkins interview, April 15, 2002; Anthony interview, April 22, 2002.

CHAPTER 17: DYNASTY

1. EGB oral history, p. 575.

2. By switching the state's accounting system so that tax revenues were counted when they were owed to the state rather than when the cash actually arrived, Brown inflated the amount of money he could spend in his last budget while still keeping the books technically in balance. For a good running summary of fiscal issues throughout Brown's time in office, see the legislative analyst's summaries of legislative and executive action on the budget, various years.

3. *San Francisco Chronicle:* "The CDC Picks a New Target," March 11, 1967, p. 4; "Brown Charges Reagan Failure," May 6, 1967, p. 4; "Brown Grades Reagan after the First Year," December 22, 1967, p. 6.

4. Memo from DeVier Pierson to LBJ, December 5, 1968, LBJ Library and Museum, White House Central File, Name File, Box 499, folder for Brown, January 1, 1967, and onward.

5. Letter from EGB to LBJ, November 28, 1967, LBJ Library and Museum, White House Central File, Name File, Box 499, folder for Brown, January 1, 1967, and onward.

6. Letter from EGB to Drew Pearson, December 24, 1968, LBJ Library and Museum, Drew Pearson Papers, Box G263, 1 of 3, folder "Brown, Edmund G."

7. EGB oral history, pp. 575–82; Pack, *Jerry Brown,* pp. 118–22; "Pat Brown Almost Ran in 1970," *Los Angeles Times,* January 6, 1975, p. 3.

8. "Pat Brown at 80: Political Passions Still Run High," *Los Angeles Times,* April 22, 1985, p. 1.

9. Braden interview, May 26, 2000; Joe Kelly Jr. interview, January 14, 2003.

10. Letter from EGB to Ibnu Sutowo, December 19, 1974, EGB Papers, Carton 295, folder 32, "Far East thank you letters."

11. Letter from Bernice Brown to family members, September 2, 1972, EGB Papers, Carton 293, folder "Middle East trip"; letter from Bernice Brown to family members, April 12, 1969, provided to the author by Kathleen Brown; Charlie Casey interview, November 16, 2001; Kathleen Kelly interview, November 26, 2001; Sascha Rice interview, November 24, 1999.

12. "Doing It Up Brown," *Sacramento Bee,* January 5, 1971, p. 4.

13. Jeff Brown interview, August 13, 1998.

14. "Jerry Brown: Friends, Kin Appraise Him," *Los Angeles Times,* January 6, 1975, p. 1; "For Brown's Parents, Day of Great Pride," *Los Angeles Times,* January 7, 1975, p. 3.

15. *Playboy,* April 1976, p. 69.

16. Letters from EGB to Louis Baptista, January 9, 1975, and John Milovich, January 13, 1975, both EGB Papers, Carton 929, folder 6, "recommendations to Jerry from EGB." Letter from Carlotta Herman Mellon to EGB, April 24, 1978, Brown Jr. Papers, Carton D-6–7, folder "Edmund G. Brown Sr." For other examples of EGB forwarding names without result, see many letters, Brown Jr. Papers, Cartons D-6–7 and E-13–7, folders "Edmund G. Brown Sr."

17. Letters from EGB to Jerry Brown, March 12, 1975, and December 5, 1975, EGB Papers, Carton 939, folder 21, "correspondence, Jerry Brown"; letter from EGB to Jerry Brown, January 10, 1979, provided to the author by Kathleen Brown.

18. Letter from EGB to family members, January 9, 1976, provided to the author by Kathleen Brown. For other examples of Pat standing by Jerry, see various letters, EGB Papers, Carton 929, folder 1, "Edmund G. Brown Jr."; and letter from EGB to William F. Thomas, July 21, 1981, provided to the author by Kathleen Brown.

19. EGB oral history, p. 22.

20. Montgomery and Johnson, *One Step from the White House,* pp. 1–3, 280–307.

21. "Knowland Called 'Man of Convictions,'" *San Francisco Sunday Examiner & Chronicle,* February 24, 1974, p. 5.

22. "Pat Brown, Protesters Debate LNG Plant Issue Here," *Santa Barbara News-Press,* September 14, 1979, p. 1.

23. Letter from Charlie Casey to EGB, May 21, 1990, provided to the author by Casey; Casey interview, November 16, 2001.

24. See copies of the columns, EGB Papers, Carton 936, folder 8, "EGB column." For quote about the *Herald-Examiner,* see letter from EGB to future California Assembly Speaker Willie Brown, who is misidentified as Willie Barnes, March 10, 1978, same location.

25. Brown and Adler, *Public Justice, Private Mercy,* p. 163; Adler interview, March 3, 2003.

26. For Wein case, see Brown and Adler, *Public Justice, Private Mercy,* pp. 90–105.

27. Under California law at the time, only a judge or prosecutor could give the oath. "Deputy D.A. for a Special Day," *Los Angeles Times,* January 4, 1991, p. 3.

28. Letter from EGB to Seniors' Golf Association, January 18, 1973, EGB Papers, Carton 277, folder 4, "January 1973"; "Ex-Gov. Brown Undergoes Surgery," *San Francisco Chronicle,* June 24, 1977, p. 15; letter from EGB to family members, February 9, 1976, provided to the author by Kathleen Brown.

29. Harrell interview, January 11, 2003.

30. Adler interview, March 3, 2003; Barbara Casey interview, November 17, 1998.

31. Videotape of the event, "Winning and Losing the 1962 Race for Governor of California," Nixon Library and Birthplace.

32. Kathleen Brown interview, September 7, 2000.

33. Bernice Brown interview, February 25, 1999; Marcus interview, February 21, 1999.

34. "Hundreds Pay Respects to Brown," *Los Angeles Times,* Valley Edition, February 20, 1996, p. 3.

35. The description of the funeral and burial is from many interviews with family and friends and various contemporary press accounts. Quotations from "Brown Service Mourns Man, Era," *Sacramento Bee,* February 22, 1996, p. 1.

EPILOGUE

1. "Brown and Oakland Are Good Match," *Contra Costa Times,* January 5, 1999, p. 6.

2. Pettigrew and Alston, *Tom Bradley's Campaigns for Governor,* p. 14.

3. In the late 1990s the university began building a new campus at Merced, in the Central Valley.

4. Videotape of assembly floor session, March 2, 1992, California State Archives.

SELECTED BIBLIOGRAPHY

It would be impossible to list every source consulted in the research for this book. Below are those sources that are cited in the notes or used substantially. Sources fully identified in the notes are omitted.

ARCHIVAL COLLECTIONS

Bancroft Library, University of California, Berkeley

Gertrude Atherton Papers
Earl Bolton Papers
Edmund G. Brown Papers—BANC MSS 68/90 c
Phillip Burton Papers
Jesse W. Carter Papers—BANC MSS C-B 842
Hale Champion Papers—BANC MSS 67/98 c
Florence McChesney Clifton Papers—BANC MSS 80/116 c
Edmond Coblentz Papers
Committee to Re-Elect Governor Brown Papers—BANC MSS 67/34 c
Alan Cranston Papers
Charles A. DeTurk Papers
Margaret Greenfield Papers
Robert Kenny Papers—BANC MSS C-B 510
Roger Kent Papers
William F. Knowland Papers

Thomas H. Kuchel Papers
Mary Ellen Leary Papers
Donald H. McLaughlin Papers—BANC MSS 86/60 c
George Miller Papers
National Lawyers Guild Papers
Culbert Olson Papers
Julia Gorman Porter Papers
Records of the Governor's Commission on the Los Angeles Riots—BANC
    MSS 74/115 c
Records of the Office of the Chancellor, University of California, Berkeley—
    CU-149, Series 2
William Byron Rumford Papers
Clara Shirpser Papers—BANC MSS 74/41 c
Thomas M. Storke Papers—BANC MSS 73/72 c
University of California Office of the President Records—CU-5, Series 5

California State Archives

California Highway Patrol records (Accession files under "Highway Patrol")
Caryl Chessman Executive Clemency files (E 4622)
Jesse Unruh Papers
Earl Warren Papers

California State University, Chico

Clair Engle Papers

California State University, Dominguez Hills

Glenn M. Anderson Papers
Glenn Dumke Papers

California State University, Northridge

Julian Beck Papers
California Democratic State Central Committee Papers
Los Angeles County Federation of Labor Papers
Max Mont Papers

Charles E. Young Research Library, UCLA

Blasé Bonpane Papers
California Ephemera Collection
Ed Cray Papers
Philip Kerby Papers
Carey McWilliams Papers
Franklin D. Murphy Papers
Edward R. Roybal Papers

Institute of Governmental Studies Library, University of California, Berkeley

The California Poll (also known as the Field Poll)

John F. Kennedy Presidential Library, Boston, Massachusetts

J. Edward Day Papers
Elizabeth Smith Gatov Papers
John F. Kennedy Pre-Presidential Papers
Robert F. Kennedy Pre-Administration Papers
Presidential Office Files
Presidential Recordings
Theodore C. Sorensen Papers
White House Central Name File

Library of Congress, Washington, D.C.

Earl Warren Papers

Lyndon Baines Johnson Library and Museum, Austin, Texas

White House Central Papers
White House Confidential Papers
Pre-Presidential Papers
Presidential Daily Diary
Presidential Diary Backup
Presidential Recordings
John Macy Papers

Frederick Panzer Papers
Drew Pearson Papers
Irv Sprague Papers
Marvin Watson Papers

Mandeville Special Collections Library, University of California, San Diego

Joseph Mayer Papers

National Archives and Records Administration, Laguna Niguel, California

Richard Nixon Pre-Presidential Papers

Richard Nixon Library and Birthplace, Yorba Linda, California

Pre-Presidential Papers

Ronald Reagan Presidential Library, Simi Valley, California

Gubernatorial Papers

Archives, San Francisco Law School, San Francisco

Bound copies of student applications
Historical photographs
Minutes of student body meetings
Yearbooks

Seeley G. Mudd Manuscript Library, Princeton University

Adlai Stevenson Papers

Southern California Library for Social Studies and Research, Los Angeles

Harry Bridges Papers
California Democratic Council Papers

Robert Kenny Papers
Robert Shaw Papers

Stanford University, Hoover Institution Archives

Raymond Moley Papers

Stanford University, Special Collections

EPIC Campaign Materials (Saadi Papers)
Goodwin J. Knight Papers

University of Southern California Regional History Collection

Edmund G. Brown Jr. Papers
Craig Hosmer Papers

University of Washington Library, Special Collections Section

Henry M. Jackson Papers
Charles F. Luce Papers
Warren Magnuson Papers

Water Resources Center Archives, University of California, Berkeley

Ralph Brody Papers
Ivanhoe Irrigation District vs. All Parties legal records

INTERVIEWS

Individuals are identified in relationship to Edmund G. Brown.

Dick Adler, writer, by telephone, March 3, 2003
Arthur Alarcon, chief of staff, Los Angeles, August 9, 2001
Peter Anthony, *Grizzly* ground crew, by telephone, April 22, 2002
William Bagley, legislator, by telephone, April 17, 2002
Mickey Bailey, staff member, Orange County, August 8, 2001
J. William Beard, state senator, by telephone, January 6, 2003

Marcia Legere Binns, friend, by telephone, January 9, 2003

Coleman Blease, American Civil Liberties Union lobbyist, by telephone, October 7, 2002

Tom Braden, newspaper publisher, Woodbridge, Virginia, May 26, 2000

Bernice Brown, wife, Beverly Hills, February 21, 23, 24, and 25, 1999

Hal Brown, nephew, San Anselmo, September 4, 1998

Jeff Brown, nephew, San Francisco, August 13, 1998

Jerry Brown, son, Oakland, December 12, 1998

Kathleen Brown, daughter, Los Angeles, December 11, 1998, and August 9, 2001; Sun Valley, Idaho, September 7 and 8, 2000

Jack Burby, press secretary, San Luis Obispo, May 15, 2000

Meredith Burch, staff member, Washington, D.C., May 22, 2000

Richard Calkins, pilot of the *Grizzly*, by telephone, April 15, 2002

Lou Cannon, newspaper reporter, by telephone, November 4, 2002

Virna Canson, 1964 Democratic National Convention delegate, by telephone, September 29, 2002

Constance Brown Carlson, sister, San Francisco, May 10, 2000, February 1, 2001

Barbara Casey, daughter, Sausalito, November 17, 1998

Charlie Casey, grandson, Sacramento, November 16, 2001

Hale Champion, chief of staff, Fort Myers, Florida, May 19, 20, and 21, 2000; and by telephone, July 19, 2002, October 6, 2002, July 29, 2003

Marie Champion, wife of Hale Champion, Fort Myers, Florida, May 21, 2000

Robert Chick, staff member, by telephone, February 10, 2003

Winslow Christian, chief of staff, San Francisco, May 8, 2000

Carol Clark, granddaughter, by telephone, January 20, 2003

William Coblentz, staff member, San Francisco, March 27, 2001

Ed Costantini, staff member, by telephone, April 10, 2003

Frank Cullen, staff member, Los Angeles, February 23, 1999

Frederick Dutton, chief of staff, Washington D.C., May 22 and 24, 2000; and by telephone, April 29, 2002, July 29, 2003

Francesca Farr, daughter of state legislator, by telephone, May 30, 2000

Sam Farr, son of state legislator, Washington, D.C., May 26, 2000

Mervin Field, pollster, by telephone, March 6, 2003

Hugo Fisher, legislator and cabinet member, by telephone, January 5, 2003

George Fleharty, campaign supporter, by telephone, July 22, 2002

Karl Fleming, journalist, by telephone, March 6, 2003

Alvin Goldstein, lawyer in Department of Justice, by telephone, August 11, 2002

Charles Guggenheim, filmmaker, Washington, D.C., May 22, 2000

Lucien Haas, aide, Pacific Palisades, December 8, 2000

Jackie Habecker, staff member, by telephone, July 15, 2002

Jerry Harrell, journalist, by telephone, January 11 and 15, 2003
Louis Heilbron, state Board of Education member, San Francisco, February 11, 2000
Joseph C. Houghteling, newspaper publisher and supporter, by telephone, July 22, 2002
Carl Irving, journalist, Berkeley, March 10, 2000
Phil Isenberg, Democratic activist and legislator, by telephone, March 26, 2003
Lowell Jensen, prosecutor, by telephone, April 17, 2000
Eppie Johnson, Sacramento restaurant owner, March 6, 2003
Fred Jordan, staff member, Washington, D.C., May 24, 2000
Cynthia Kelly, daughter, San Francisco, November 12, 2001
Joe Kelly, son-in-law, San Francisco, November 12, 2001
Joe Kelly Jr., grandson, by telephone, January 14, 2003
Kathleen Kelly, granddaughter, San Francisco, November 26, 2001
Patricia Kelly Carlin, granddaughter, by telephone, February 7, 2003
Clark Kerr, University of California president, Berkeley, fall 1999; and by telephone, June 28, 2000
Quentin Kopp, former state legislator, by telephone, October 3, 2002
Mary Ellen Leary, journalist, Piedmont, September 8, 1998
Maryalice Lemmon, secretary, Sacramento, June 12, 2000
James Loebl, staff member, by telephone, January 8, 2003
Paul Lunardi, legislator, by telephone, January 6, 2003
Barbara Marcus, family aide, Los Angeles, February 21, 1999
Tom McDonald, Department of Justice staff, by telephone, January 8, 2003
John McInerny, staff member, Saratoga, September 5, 2000
Marie Moretti, aide, by telephone, March 15, 2003
Ed Meese, prosecutor, Washington, D.C., May 23, 2000
George Miller III, son of state legislator, Washington, D.C., May 25, 2000
John D. Monaghan, businessman and politico, by telephone, January 8, 2003
Helen Nelson, appointee, by telephone, January 14, 2003
William Newsom, son of Brown confidant, Dutch Flat, California, November 14, 1998
Daniel O'Connell, CHP commander, Sacramento, April 19, 2000; and by telephone, April 20, 2000
Eve Ostoja, secretary, by telephone, April 24, 2002
Frank Petersen, state senator, by telephone, January 8, 2003
Alex Pope, staff member, Berkeley, January 16, 2003
Joseph Rattigan, state senator, Santa Rosa, September 26, 2002
Thomas Rees, state legislator, by telephone, January 5, 2003
Joyce Rey, staff member, by telephone, March 26, 2003
Hilary Rice Armstrong, granddaughter, by telephone, January 11, 2003
Sascha Rice, granddaughter, Beverly Hills, February 24, 1999

Zeb Rice, grandson, Los Angeles, August 9, 2001
Charles Rickershauser, campaign aide, by telephone, February 13, 2003
Roy Ringer, staff member, Los Angeles, April 8, 2001
Jane Romney, family friend, by telephone, March 15, 2003
Thomas Saunders, campaign aide, by telephone, January 15, 2003
Keith Sexton, legislative aide, Moraga, July 17, 1999, October 29, 1999
Alex Sheriffs, University of California official, by telephone, April 12, 2000
Nancy Sloss, staff member, Washington, D.C., May 24, 2000
John Sparrow, University of California official, by telephone, April 11, 2000
Stuart K. Spencer, Reagan campaign aide, by telephone, February 28, 2003
Irv Sprague, staff member, Virginia, May 23, 2000
Howard Thelin, assemblyman, by telephone, January 8, 2003
Jack Tomlinson, staff member, by telephone, July 15, 2002
William Trombley, journalist, by telephone, April 20, 2000
John Vasconcellos, staff member, San Jose, September 3, 1998
Wilma Wagner, staff member, by telephone, January 10, 2003
Jerry Waldie, assemblyman, by telephone, January 6, 2003
Carmen Warschaw, Democratic activist, by telephone, September 30, 2002
Doug Willis, journalist, by telephone, January 9, 2003
Joe Wyatt, Democratic activist, Los Angeles, August 9, 2001
Walt Zebowski, photographer, by telephone, January 9, 2003

ORAL HISTORIES

Regional Oral History Office, University of California, Berkeley

Don A. Allen, "A Los Angeles Assemblyman Recalls the Reapportionment Struggle," in "One Man–One Vote and Senate Reapportionment, 1964–1966."
A. Wayne Amerson, "Northern California and Its Challenges to a Negro in the Mid–1900's."
Harvey O. Banks, "California Water Project, 1955–1961."
William Becker, "Working for Civil Rights: With Unions, the Legislature and Governor Pat Brown," in "The Governor's Office under Edmund G. Brown, Sr."
Earl C. Behrens, "Gubernatorial Campaigns and Party Issues: A Political Reporter's View, 1948–1966," in "Reporting from Sacramento."
Richard Bergholz, "Reporting on California Government and Politics, 1953–1966," in "Reporting from Sacramento."
John Roger Boas, "Democratic Party Politics and Environmental Issues in California, 1962–1976."
Don Bradley, "Managing Democratic Campaigns, 1954–1966."
Ralph M. Brody, "Devising Legislation and Building Public Support for the Cal-

ifornia Water Project, 1959–1960; Brief History of the Westlands Water District," in "California Water Issues, 1950–1966."

Joseph Brotherton, "The Di Giorgios: From Fruit Merchants to Corporate Innovators."

Bernice Layne Brown, "Life in the Governor's Mansion," in "Brown Family Portraits."

Edmund G. Brown Sr., "The Governor's Lawyer," in "Earl Warren: Fellow Constitutional Officers." Cited in notes as EGB AG oral history.

Edmund G. Brown Sr., "Years of Growth, 1939–1966: Law Enforcement, Politics and the Governor's Office." Cited in notes as EGB oral history.

Francis M. Brown, "Edmund G. Brown's Commitment to Lessen Social Ills: View from a Younger Brother," in "Brown Family Portraits."

Harold C. Brown, "A Lifelong Republican for Edmund G. Brown," in "Brown Family Portraits."

Meredith Burch, "Political Notes," in "Pat Brown, Friends and Campaigners."

Hugh Burns, "Legislative and Political Concerns of the Senate Pro Tem, 1957–1970," in "California Legislative Leaders, vol. 2."

Ronald Button, "California Republican Party Official and State Treasurer of California, 1956–1958," in "California Constitutional Officers."

Thomas W. Caldecott, "Legislative Strategies, Relations with the Governor's Office, 1947–1957," in "California Legislative Leaders, vol. 1."

Constance Brown Carlson, "My Brothers Edmund, Harold and Frank," in "Brown Family Portraits."

Judy Royer Carter, "Pat Brown: The Governorship and After," in "Pat Brown, Friends and Campaigners."

Oliver J. Carter, "A Leader in the California Senate and the Democratic Party, 1940–1950."

Hale Champion, "Communication and Problem-solving: A Journalist in State Government."

Winslow Christian, "The Human Side of Public Administration."

George Christopher, "Mayor of San Francisco and Republican Party Candidate," in "San Francisco Republicans."

Warren Christopher, "Special Counsel to the Governor: Recalling the Pat Brown Years," in "The Governor's Office under Edmund G. Brown, Sr."

Florence Clifton, "California Democrats, 1934–1950," in "California Democrats in the Earl Warren Era."

Robert Clifton, "The Democratic Party, Culbert L. Olson, and the Legislature," in "California Democrats in the Earl Warren Era."

Bertram Coffey, "Reflections on George Miller, Jr., Governors Pat and Jerry Brown and the Democratic Party," in "Political Advocacy and Loyalty."

Cyr Copertini, "Campaign Housekeeping, 1940–1965," in "California Democrats' Golden Era, 1958–1966."

James Corley, "Serving the University in Sacramento."

George T. Davis, "San Francisco Trial Lawyer: In Defense of Due Process, 1930s to 1990s."

May Layne Bonnell Davis, "An Appointment Secretary Reminisces," in "The Governor's Office under Edmund G. Brown, Sr."

Joseph A. Di Giorgio, "The Di Giorgios: From Fruit Merchants to Corporate Innovators."

Robert Di Giorgio, "The Di Giorgios: From Fruit Merchants to Corporate Innovators."

Donald Doyle, "An Assemblyman Views Education, Mental Health, and Legislative and Republican Politics," in "Education Issues and Planning, 1953–1966."

Glenn Dumke, "The Evolution of the California State University System, 1961–1982."

Frederick G. Dutton, "Democratic Campaigns and Controversies, 1954–1966."

Norman Elkington, "From Adversary to Appointee: Fifty Years of Friendship with Pat Brown," in "Pat Brown, Friends and Campaigners."

Lucretia Engle, "Clair Engle as Campaigner and Statesman," in "Political Advocacy and Loyalty."

Hugo Fisher, "California Democratic Politics, 1958–1965," in "California Legislative Leaders, vol. 1."

Elizabeth Gatov, "Grassroots Party Organizer to Treasurer of the United States."

Phil Gibson, "Recollections of a Chief Justice of the California Supreme Court," in "California Constitutional Officers."

B. Abbott Goldberg, "Water Policy Issues in the Courts, 1950–1966," in "California Water Issues, 1950–1966."

Richard P. Graves, "Theoretician, Advocate and Candidate in California State Government."

Charles Guggenheim, "The Use of Film in Political Campaigning," in "Pat Brown, Friends and Campaigners."

Jackie Habecker, "A View from the Reception Desk," in "The Governor's Office, Access and Outreach, 1967–1974."

Franck Havenner, "Reminiscences."

Louis Heilbron, "Most of a Century: Law and Public Service, 1930s to 1990s."

Elinor Heller, "A Volunteer Career in Politics, in Higher Education, and on Governing Boards."

Patricia R. Hitt, "From Precinct Worker to Assistant Secretary of the Department of Health, Education and Welfare."

Preston Hotchkis, "One Man's Dynamic Role in California Politics and Water Development, and World Affairs."

Martin Huff, "From Grassroots Politics to the California Franchise Tax Board, 1952–1979," in "California Democrats' Golden Era, 1958–1966."

Emelyn Knowland Jewett, "My Father's Political Philosophy and Colleagues," in "Remembering William Knowland."

Estelle Knowland Johnson, "My Father as Senator, Campaigner and Civic Leader," in "Remembering William Knowland."

Walter P. Jones, "An Editor's Long Friendship with Earl Warren," in "Bee Perspectives of the Warren Era."

Robert W. Kenny, "California Attorney General and the 1946 Gubernatorial Campaign," in "Earl Warren: Fellow Constitutional Officers."

Roger Kent, "Building the Democratic Party in California, 1954–1966." Cited in notes as Kent oral history #1.

Roger Kent, "A Democratic Leader Looks at the Warren Era," in "California Democrats in the Earl Warren Era." Cited in notes as Kent oral history #2.

Clark Kerr, "University of California Crises: Loyalty Oath and Free Speech Movement."

Richard Kline, "Governor Brown's Faithful Advisor," in "The Governor's Office under Edmund G. Brown, Sr."

William F. Knowland, "Republican Politics in the 1930s," in "Earl Warren's Campaigns."

Sydney Kossen, "Covering Goodwin Knight and the Legislature for the San Francisco News, 1956–1966," in "Reporting from Sacramento."

Thomas H. Kuchel, "California State Controller," in "Earl Warren: Fellow Constitutional Officers."

Frank Lanterman, "California Assembly, 1949–1978: Water, Mental Health, and Education Issues," in "California Legislative Leaders, vol. 1."

Maryalice Lemmon, "Working in the Governor's Office, 1950–1959," in "The Governor's Office under Goodwin Knight."

Bert W. Levit, "State Finance and Innovations in Government Organization, 1944–1959," in "Perspectives on Department Administration."

James Lowry, "California State Department of Mental Hygiene, 1960s," in "Perspectives on Department Administration."

Thomas C. Lynch, "A Career in Politics and the Attorney General's Office."

Paul Manolis, "A Friend and Aide Reminisces," in "Remembering William Knowland."

Robert McKay, "Robert McKay and the California Teacher's Association," in "Education Issues and Planning, 1953–1966."

Donald McLaughlin, "Reminiscences of a Dean, a Regent, and a Friend."

Frank Mesple, "From Clovis to the Capitol: Building a Career as a Legislative Liaison," in "The Governor's Office under Edmund G. Brown, Sr."

James R. Mills, "The Assembly, the State Senate, and the Governor's Office, 1958–1974."

Stanley Mosk, "Attorney General's Office and Political Campaigns, 1958–1966," in "California Constitutional Officers."

Helen Nelson, "The First Consumer Counsel in California," in "Pat Brown, Friends and Campaigners."

Franklyn Nofziger, "Press Secretary for Ronald Reagan, 1966," in "Issues and Innovations in the 1966 Republican Gubernatorial Campaign."

Warren Olney III, "Law Enforcement and Judicial Administration in the Earl Warren Era."

George Outland, "James Roosevelt's Primary Campaign, 1950," in "California Democrats in the Earl Warren Era."

Herbert L. Phillips, "Perspectives of a Political Reporter," in "*Bee* Perspectives of the Warren Era."

Cecil Poole, "Executive Clemency and the Chessman Case," in "The Governor's Office under Edmund G. Brown, Sr." Cited in notes as Poole oral history #1.

Cecil Poole, "Civil Rights, Law and the Federal Courts: The Life of Cecil Poole, 1914–1997." Cited in notes as Poole oral history #2.

Langdon Post, "James Roosevelt's Northern California Campaign, 1950," in "California Democrats in the Earl Warren Era."

Harold J. Powers, "On Prominent Issues, the Republican Party and Political Campaigns: A Veteran Republican Views the Goodwin Knight Era," in "California Constitutional Officers."

Joseph Rattigan, "A Judicial Look at Civil Rights, Education and Reapportionment in the State Senate, 1959–1966," in "California Legislative Leaders, vol. 2."

Ronald Reagan, "On Becoming Governor," in "Governor Reagan and His Cabinet."

Richard Richards, "Senate Campaigns and Procedures, California Water Plan," in "California Legislative Leaders, vol. 1."

William Roberts, "Professional Campaign Management and the Candidate, 1960–1966," in "Issues and Innovations in the 1966 Republican Gubernatorial Campaign."

Albert Rodda, "Sacramento Senator: State Leadership in Education and Finance," in "The Assembly, the State Senate, and the Governor's Office, 1958–1974."

Richard Rodda, "From the Capitol Press Room," in "*Bee* Perspectives of the Warren Era."

James Roosevelt, "Campaigning for Governor against Earl Warren, 1950," in "California Democrats in the Earl Warren Era."

William Byron Rumford, "Legislator for Fair Employment, Fair Housing and Public Health."

Pierre Salinger, "A Journalist as Democratic Campaigner and U.S. Senator," in "Political Advocacy and Loyalty."

Keith Sexton, "Legislating Higher Education: A Consultant's View of the Master Plan for Higher Education," in "Education Issues and Planning, 1953–1966."

Alex Sheriffs, "The University of California and the Free Speech Movement: Perspectives from a Faculty Member and Administrator," in "Education Issues and Planning, 1953–1966."

Arthur H. Sherry, "The Alameda County District Attorney's Office and California."

Clara Shirpser, "One Woman's Role in Democratic Party Politics: National, California, and Local, 1950–1973."

Nancy Sloss, "Political Appointees and Personalities," in "Pat Brown, Friends and Campaigners."

Elizabeth Snyder, "California's First Woman State Party Chairman."

Homer R. Spence, "Attorney, Legislator and Judge," in "Perspectives on the Alameda County District Attorney's Office."

Stuart Spencer, "Developing a Campaign Management Organization," in "Issues and Innovations in the 1966 Republican Gubernatorial Campaign."

Edward Strong, "Philosopher, Professor and Berkeley Chancellor, 1961–1965."

Stephen P. Teale, "The Impact of One Man–One Vote on the Senate: Senator Teale Reviews Reapportionment and Other Issues, 1953–1966," in "One Man–One Vote and Senate Reapportionment, 1964–1966."

Albert B. Tieburg, "California State Department of Employment," in "Perspectives on Department Administration."

Katherine Towle, "Administration and Leadership."

William E. Warne, "Administration of the Department of Water Resources, 1961–1966," in "California Water Issues, 1950–1966."

Earl Warren, "Conversations with Earl Warren on California Government."

Earl Warren Jr., "California Politics," in "Earl Warren: The Governor's Family."

Carmen Warschaw, "A Southern California Perspective on Democratic Party Politics."

John Wedemeyer, "California State Department of Social Welfare, 1959–1966," in "Perspectives on Department Administration."

Caspar W. Weinberger, "California Assembly, Republican State Central Committee and Elections, 1953–1966," in "San Francisco Republicans."

Arleigh Williams, "Dean of Students Arleigh Williams: The Free Speech Movement and the Six Years War, 1964–1970."

Rosalind Wyman, "It's a Girl: Three Terms on the Los Angeles City Council, 1953–1965; Three Decades in the Democratic Party, 1948–1978."

Samuel Yorty, "Samuel Yorty: A Challenge to the Democrats," in "Political Advocacy and Loyalty."

Institute of Industrial Relations, University of California, Berkeley

Mathew O. Tobriner, "Lawyer for Quasi-Public Associations."

Oral History Program, University of California, Los Angeles

Augustus Hawkins, "Black Leadership in Los Angeles." Cited in notes as Hawkins oral history #2.
Joseph Jensen, "Developing California's Natural Resources."
Robert W. Kenny, "My First Forty Years in California Politics, 1922–1962."
Dean McHenry, "UCLA Student Leaders: Dean E. McHenry."
Carey McWilliams, "Honorable in All Things."
Franklin Murphy, "My UCLA Chancellorship: An Utterly Candid View."
Paul Ziffren, "California Democrat."

State Government Oral History Program, California State Archives

William T. Bagley
Herbert M. Baus
David Brainin
John F. Burby
Frederick S. Farr
Roy Greenaway
Lucien C. Haas
H. R. Haldeman
Augustus Hawkins. Cited in notes as Hawkins oral history #1.
Paul J. Lunardi
Thomas J. MacBride
Carlos J. Moorhead
Charles O'Brien
Gerald J. O'Gara
Thomas M. Rees
Roy J. Ringer
Philip L. Soto
William Trombley
Jerome R. Waldie
Madale L. Watson
Clem Whitaker Jr.

Lyndon Baines Johnson Library and Museum, Austin, Texas

Edmund G. Brown
Fred Dutton

California State University, Fullerton

Robert H. Finch, "Views from the Lieutenant Governor's Office."

California State University Archives

Edmund G. Brown
Glenn S. Dumke
Lyman Glenny
Donald Leiffer
Dean McHenry
Walter Stiern

John F. Kennedy Library, Boston, Massachusetts

Glenn Anderson
Donald L. Bradley
Edmund G. Brown
Joseph Cerrell
Frederick G. Dutton
Elizabeth Gatov
John F. Henning
Joseph Houghteling
Bart Lytton
Donald Rose
Benjamin Swig

Library of Congress, Senate Historical Office Oral Histories

Roy L. Elson

Library of Congress, Association of Former Members of Congress Oral Histories

Chet Holifield
James Roosevelt

BOOKS

Abell, Tyler. *Drew Pearson Diaries, 1949–1959.* New York: Holt, Rinehart and Winston, 1974.
Ainsworth, Ed. *Maverick Mayor: A Biography of Sam Yorty of Los Angeles.* Garden City, N.Y.: Doubleday, 1966.
Aitken, Jonathan. *Nixon: A Life.* London: Wiedenfeld and Nicolson, 1993.

Ambrose, Stephen E. *Eisenhower: The President.* New York: Simon and Schuster, 1984.

———. *Eisenhower: Soldier and President.* New York: Simon and Schuster, 1990.

———. *Nixon: The Education of a Politician, 1913–1962.* New York: Simon and Schuster, 1987.

Anderson, Walt. *Campaigns: Cases in Political Conflict.* Pacific Palisades, Calif.: Goodyear Publishing Company, 1970.

Bartley, Ernest R. *The Tidelands Oil Controversy: A Legal and Historical Analysis.* Austin: University of Texas Press, 1953.

Bean, Walton. *Boss Ruef's San Francisco.* Berkeley: University of California Press, 1952.

Bean, Walton, and James J. Rawls. *California: An Interpretive History.* New York: McGraw-Hill, 1983.

Belfrage, Cedric. *The American Inquisition, 1945–1960.* Indianapolis: Bobbs-Merrill, 1973.

Belli, Melvin. *My Life on Trial.* New York: William Morrow, 1976.

Bock, Edwin A., ed. *State and Local Government: A Case Book.* Birmingham: University of Alabama Press, 1963.

Bollens, John C., and Grant B. Geyer. *Yorty: Politics of a Constant Candidate.* Pacific Palisades, Calif.: Palisades Publishers, 1973.

Bollens, John C., and G. Robert Williams. *Jerry Brown in a Plain Brown Wrapper.* Pacific Palisades, Calif.: Palisades Publishers, 1978.

Bottles, Scott L. *Los Angeles and the Automobile: The Making of the Modern City.* Berkeley: University of California Press, 1987.

Boyarsky, Bill. *The Rise of Ronald Reagan.* New York: Random House, 1968.

———. *Ronald Reagan: His Life and Rise to the Presidency.* New York: Random House, 1981.

Branch, Taylor. *Parting the Waters: America in the King Years, 1954–63.* New York: Simon and Schuster, 1988.

———. *Pillar of Fire: America in the King Years, 1963–65.* New York: Simon and Schuster, 1998.

Brodie, Fawn M. *Richard Nixon: The Shaping of His Character.* New York: W. W. Norton, 1981.

Bronson, William. *The Earth Shook, the Sky Burned.* Garden City, N.Y.: Doubleday, 1959.

Brown, Edmund G. *Reagan and Reality: The Two Californias.* New York: Praeger, 1970.

Brown, Edmund G., and Dick Adler. *Public Justice, Private Mercy: A Governor's Education on Death Row.* New York: Weidenfeld and Nicolson, 1989.

Brown, Edmund G., and Bill Brown. *Reagan: The Political Chameleon.* New York: Praeger, 1976.

Buchanan, William. *Legislative Partisanship: The Deviant Case of California.* Berkeley: University of California Press, 1963.

Bullock, Paul. *Jerry Voorhis: The Idealist as Politician.* New York: Vantage Press, 1978.

Burke, Robert E. *Olson's New Deal for California.* Berkeley: University of California Press, 1953.

Cain, Bruce E., and Roger G. Noll. *Constitutional Reform in California.* Berkeley: Institute of Governmental Studies, 1995.

California State Water Project Atlas. Sacramento: California Department of Water Resources, 1999.

Cannon, Lou. *Governor Reagan: His Rise to Power.* New York: Public Affairs, 2003.

———. *Official Negligence: How Rodney King and the Riots Changed Los Angeles and the LAPD.* New York: Random House, 1997.

———. *President Reagan: The Role of a Lifetime.* New York: Simon and Schuster, 1991.

———. *Reagan.* New York: G. P. Putnam's Sons, 1982.

———. *Ronnie and Jesse: A Political Odyssey.* Garden City, N.Y.: Doubleday, 1969.

Carle, David. *Drowning the Dream: California's Water Choices at the Millennium.* Westport, Conn.: Praeger, 2000.

Carney, Francis. *The Rise of the Democratic Clubs in California.* New York: Henry Holt, 1958.

Casstevens, Thomas W. *Politics, Housing and Race Relations: California's Rumford Act and Proposition 14.* Berkeley: Institute of Governmental Studies, 1967.

Caughey, John W., and Norris Hundley Jr. *California: History of a Remarkable State.* Englewood Cliffs, N.J.: Prentice-Hall, 1982.

Chessman, Caryl. *Cell 2455, Death Row.* Englewood Cliffs, N.J.: Prentice-Hall, 1960.

Christopher, Warren. *Chances of a Lifetime.* New York: Scribner, 2001.

Coakley, J. Frank. *For the People: Sixty Years of Fighting for Law and Order.* Orinda, Calif.: Western Star Press, 1992.

Cohen, Jerry, and William S. Murphy. *Burn, Baby, Burn!* New York: E. P. Dutton, 1966.

Cohen, Robert, and Reginald E. Zelnik, eds. *The Free Speech Movement: Reflections on Berkeley in the 1960s.* Berkeley: University of California Press, 2002.

Conot, Robert. *Rivers of Blood, Years of Darkness: The Unforgettable Classic Account of the Watts Riot.* New York: William Morrow, 1968.

Coons, Arthur G. *Crises in California Higher Education.* Los Angeles: Ward Ritchie Press, 1968.

Cooper, Erwin. *Aqueduct Empire: A Guide to Water in California, Its Turbulent History and Its Management Today.* Glendale, Calif.: Arthur H. Clark, 1968.

Cottle, Rex L., Hugh H. Maccaulay, and Bruce Yandle. *Labor and Property Rights in California Agriculture.* College Station: Texas A&M University Press, 1982.

Cray, Ed. *Chief Justice: A Biography of Earl Warren.* New York: Simon and Schuster, 1997.

Cresap, Dean R. *Party Politics in the Golden State.* Los Angeles: Haynes Foundation, 1954.

Crouch, Winston W., John C. Bollens, and Stanley Scott. *California Government and Politics.* Englewood Cliffs, N.J.: Prentice-Hall, 1952.

Crouchett, Lawrence P. *William Byron Rumford: The Life and Public Services of a California Legislator.* El Cerrito, Calif.: Downey Place Publishing House, 1984.

Dallek, Matthew. *The Right Moment: Ronald Reagan's First Victory and the Decisive Turning Point in American Politics.* New York: Free Press, 2000.

Dallek, Robert. *Flawed Giant: Lyndon Johnson and His Times, 1961–1973.* New York: Oxford University Press, 1998.

———. *Lone Star Rising: Lyndon Johnson and His Times, 1908–1960.* New York: Oxford University Press, 1991.

Dasmann, Raymond F. *Called by the Wild: The Autobiography of a Conservationist.* Berkeley: University of California Press, 2002.

———. *The Destruction of California.* New York: Macmillan, 1965.

David, Lester. *The Lonely Lady of San Clemente.* New York: Thomas Y. Crowell, 1978.

Davis, Bernice Freeman, and Al Hirshberg. *The Desperate and the Damned.* New York: Thomas Y. Crowell, 1961.

Davis, Mike. *City of Quartz.* New York: Vintage Books, 1992.

Day, Mark. *Forty Acres: Cesar Chavez and the Farm Workers.* New York: Praeger, 1971.

Delmatier, Royce D., Clarence F. McIntosh, and Earl G. Waters, eds. *The Rumble of California Politics, 1848–1970.* New York: John Wiley, 1970.

DeWitt, Howard A. *The California Dream.* Dubuque, Iowa: Kendall/Hunt, 1997.

Dolan, Edward F., Jr. *Disaster 1906: The San Francisco Earthquake and Fire.* New York: Julian Messner, 1967.

Dorsey, George. *Christopher of San Francisco.* New York: Macmillan, 1962.

Douglass, John Aubrey. *The California Idea and American Higher Education: 1850 to the 1960 Master Plan.* Stanford, Calif.: Stanford University Press, 2000.

Duffy, Clinton T., and Al Hirshberg. *88 Men and 2 Women.* New York: Doubleday, 1962.

Dunne, John Gregory. *Delano: The Story of the California Grape Strike.* New York: Farrar, Straus and Giroux, 1967.

Dvorin, Eugene P., and Arthur J. Misner, eds. *California Politics and Policies.* Reading, Mass.: Addison-Wesley, 1966.

Erie, Steven P. *Rainbow's End: Irish-Americans and the Dilemmas of Urban Machine Politics, 1840–1945.* Berkeley: University of California Press, 1988.

Eshelman, Byron. *Death Row Chaplain.* Englewood Cliffs, N.J.: Prentice-Hall, 1962.

Ewald, Donna, and Peter Clute. *San Francisco Invites the World: The Panama Pacific International Exposition of 1915.* San Francisco: Chronicle Books, 1991.

Farrelly, David, and Ivan Hinderaker, eds. *The Politics of California: A Book of Readings.* New York: Ronald Press, 1951.

Flamm, Jerry. *Hometown San Francisco.* San Francisco: Scottwall Associates, 1994.

Foster, Mark S. *Henry J. Kaiser: Builder in the Modern American West.* Austin: University of Texas Press, 1989.

Fowle, Eleanor. *Cranston: The Senator from California.* San Rafael, Calif.: Presidio Press, 1980.

Garrettson, Charles Lloyd. *Hubert H. Humphrey: The Politics of Joy.* New Brunswick, N.J.: Transaction Publishers, 1993.

Gates, Daryl F., and Diane K. Shah. *Chief: My Life in the LAPD.* New York: Bantam, 1992.

Gentry, Curt. *The Last Days of the Late, Great State of California.* New York: G. P. Putnam's Sons, 1968.

Gitlin, Todd. *The Sixties: Years of Hope, Days of Rage.* New York: Bantam Books, 1987.

Goines, David Lance. *The Free Speech Movement: Coming of Age in the 1960s.* Berkeley: Ten Speed Press, 1993.

Gottlieb, Robert. *A Life of Its Own: The Politics and Power of Water.* New York: Harcourt Brace Jovanovich, 1988.

Gunther, John. *Inside U.S.A.* New York: Harper and Brothers, 1947.

Halberstam, David. *The Fifties.* New York: Villard, 1993.

———. *The Powers That Be.* New York: Alfred A. Knopf, 1979.

Hamm, Theodore. *Rebel and a Cause: Caryl Chessman and the Politics of the Death Penalty in Postwar California, 1948–1974.* Berkeley: University of California Press, 2001.

Harris, David. *Dreams Die Hard.* New York: St. Martin's Press.

Harvey, Richard B. *Earl Warren: Governor of California.* New York: Exposition Press, 1969.

Heirich, Max. *The Spiral of Conflict: Berkeley 1964.* New York: Columbia University Press, 1971.

Hill, Gladwin. *Dancing Bear: An Inside Look at California Politics.* Cleveland: World Publishing Company, 1968.

Hirshleifer, Jack, James C. De Haven, and Jerome W. Milliman. *Water Supply: Economics, Technology and Policy.* Chicago: University of Chicago Press, 1960.

Horne, Gerald. *Fire This Time: The Watts Uprising and the 1960s.* Charlottesville: University Press of Virginia, 1995.

Hundley, Norris, Jr. *The Great Thirst: Californians and Water, a History.* Rev. ed. Berkeley: University of California Press, 2001.

Hyink, Bernard L., Seyom Brown, and Ernest W. Thacker. *Politics and Government in California.* New York: Thomas Y. Crowell, 1959.

Issel, William, and Robert W. Cherny. *San Francisco, 1865–1932: Politics, Power and Urban Development.* Berkeley: University of California Press, 1986.

Jacobs, Clyde E., and Alvin D. Sokolow. *California Government: One among Fifty.* London: Macmillan, 1970.

Jacobs, John. *A Rage for Justice: The Passion and Politics of Phillip Burton.* Berkeley: University of California Press, 1995.

Jones, David W. *California's Freeway Era in Historical Perspective.* Berkeley: Institute of Transportation Studies, University of California, Berkeley, 1989.

Jones, Landon Y. *Great Expectations: America and the Baby Boom Generation.* New York: Coward, McCann and Geoghegan, 1980.

Kahn, Judd. *Imperial San Francisco: Politics and Planning in an American City, 1897–1906.* Lincoln: University of Nebraska Press, 1979.

Kahrl, William L., ed. *The California Water Atlas.* Sacramento: State of California, 1979.

Katcher, Leo. *Earl Warren: A Political Biography.* New York: McGraw-Hill, 1967.

Kelley, Kitty. *His Way: The Unauthorized Biography of Frank Sinatra.* Toronto: Bantam Books, 1986.

Kennedy, David M. *Freedom from Fear: The American People in Depression and War, 1929–1945.* New York: Oxford University Press, 1999.

Kerr, Clark. *The Gold and the Blue, a Personal Memoir of the University of California, 1949–1967.* Vol. 1: *Academic Triumphs.* Berkeley: University of California Press, 2001.

———. *The Gold and the Blue, a Personal Memoir of the University of California, 1949–1967.* Vol. 2: *Political Turmoil.* Berkeley: University of California Press, 2003.

———. *The Uses of the University.* Cambridge, Mass.: Harvard University Press, 1964.

Klein, Herbert G. *Making It Perfectly Clear.* Garden City, N.Y.: Doubleday, 1980.

Klurfeld, Herman. *Behind the Lines: The World of Drew Pearson.* Englewood Cliffs, N.J.: Prentice-Hall, 1968.

Krier, James E., and Edmund Ursin. *Pollution and Policy: A Case Essay on California and Federal Experience with Motor Vehicle Air Pollution, 1940–1975.* Berkeley: University of California Press, 1977.

Kunstler, William M. *Beyond a Reasonable Doubt? The Original Trial of Caryl Chessman.* New York: William Morrow, 1961.

Largo, Andrew O. *Caryl Whittier Chessman, 1921–1960: Essay and Critical Bibli-*

ography. San Jose, Calif.: Bibliographic Information Center for the Study of Political Science, 1971.

Lee, Eugene C. *California Votes, 1928–1960.* Berkeley: Institute of Governmental Studies, 1963.

Lee, Eugene C., and Bruce E. Keith. *California Votes, 1960–1972.* Berkeley: Institute of Governmental Studies, 1974.

Leibert, Julius A., and Emily Kingsbery. *Behind Bars: What a Chaplain Saw in Alcatraz, Folsom and San Quentin.* New York: Doubleday, 1965.

Lemann, Nicholas. *The Big Test: The Secret History of the American Meritocracy.* New York: Farrar, Straus and Giroux, 1999.

Levy, Jacques E. *Cesar Chavez: Autobiography of La Causa.* New York: W. W. Norton, 1975.

Lomax, Alan. *The Folk Songs of North America.* Garden City, N.Y.: Doubleday, 1960.

London, Joan, and Henry Anderson. *So Shall Ye Reap.* New York: Thomas Y. Crowell, 1970.

Lorenz, J. D. *Jerry Brown: The Man on the White Horse.* Boston: Houghton Mifflin, 1978.

Machlin, Milton, and William Read Woodfield. *Ninth Life.* New York: G. P. Putnam's Sons, 1961.

Maharidge, Dale. *The Coming White Minority: California, Multiculturalism, and America's Future.* New York: Vintage Books, 1999.

Martin, John Bartlow. *Adlai Stevenson and the World.* Garden City, N.Y.: Doubleday, 1977.

Martin, Ralph G. *Ballots and Bandwagons.* Chicago: Rand McNally, 1964.

A Master Plan for Higher Education in California, 1960–1975. Sacramento: California State Department of Education, 1960.

Matusow, Allen J. *The Unravelling of America: A History of Liberalism in the 1960s.* New York: Harper and Row, 1984.

McAdam, Doug. *Freedom Summer.* New York: Oxford University Press, 1988.

McCullough, David. *Truman.* New York: Simon and Schuster, 1992.

McKeever, Porter. *Adlai Stevenson: His Life and Legacy.* New York: William Morrow, 1989.

McShane, Marilyn D., and Frank P. Williams III, eds. *Encyclopedia of American Prisons.* New York: Garland, 1996.

McWilliams, Carey. *California: The Great Exception.* 1949; rept., with a foreword by Lewis H. Lapham, Berkeley: University of California Press, 1999.

———. *Factories in the Field.* Santa Barbara, Calif.: Peregrine Publishers, 1971.

———. *Southern California Country: An Island on the Land.* New York: Duell, Sloan and Pearce, 1946.

———, ed. *The California Revolution.* New York: Grossman, 1968.

Meister, Dick, and Anne Loftis. *A Long Time Coming: The Struggle to Unionize America's Farm Workers.* New York: Macmillan, 1977.

Melendy, H. Brett, and Benjamin F. Gilbert. *The Governors of California: Peter H. Burnett to Edmund G. Brown.* Georgetown, Calif.: Talisman Press, 1965.

Miller, Michael V., and Susan Gilmore, eds. *Revolution at Berkeley.* New York: Dial Press, 1965.

Mills, James R. *A Disorderly House: The Brown-Unruh Years in Sacramento.* Berkeley: Heyday Books, 1987.

Mitchell, Greg. *Tricky Dick and the Pink Lady: Richard Nixon vs. Helen Gahagan Douglas, Sexual Politics and Red Scare, 1950.* New York: Random House, 1998.

Montgomery, Gayle B., and James W. Johnson. *One Step from the White House: The Rise and Fall of Senator William F. Knowland.* Berkeley: University of California Press, 1998.

Morgan, Edward P. *The 60s Experience: Hard Lessons about Modern America.* Philadelphia: Temple University Press, 1991.

Morgan, Neil. *Westward Tilt: The American West Today.* New York: Random House, 1961.

Muchnic, Suzanne. *Odd Man In: Norton Simon and the Pursuit of Culture.* Berkeley: University of California Press, 1998.

Nasaw, David. *The Chief: The Life of William Randolph Hearst.* Boston: Houghton Mifflin, 2000.

Nixon, Richard M. *The Memoirs of Richard Nixon.* New York: Grosset and Dunlap, 1978.

———. *Six Crises.* Garden City, N.Y.: Doubleday, 1962.

O'Brien, Lawrence F. *No Final Victories: A Life in Politics, from John F. Kennedy to Watergate.* Garden City, N.Y.: Doubleday, 1974.

O'Donnell, Kenneth P., David F. Powers, and Joe McCarthy. *Johnny, We Hardly Knew Ye: Memories of John Fitzgerald Kennedy.* Boston: Little, Brown, 1972.

Olin, Spencer C., Jr. *California's Prodigal Sons: Hiram Johnson and the Progressives, 1911–1917.* Berkeley: University of California Press, 1968.

Pack, Robert. *Jerry Brown: The Philosopher-Prince.* New York: Stein and Day, 1978.

Parker, Frank J. *Caryl Chessman: The Red Light Bandit.* Chicago: Nelson-Hall, 1975.

Parmet, Herbert S. *Richard Nixon and His America.* Boston: Little, Brown, 1990.

Patterson, James T. *Grand Expectations: The United States, 1945–1974.* New York: Oxford University Press, 1996.

Pettigrew, Thomas F., and Denise A. Alston. *Tom Bradley's Campaigns for Governor: The Dilemma of Race and Political Strategies.* Washington, D.C.: Joint Center for Political Studies, 1988.

Phillips, Herbert L. *Big Wayward Girl: An Informal Political History of California.* Garden City, N.Y.: Doubleday, 1968.

Putnam, Jackson K. *Modern California Politics.* San Francisco: Boyd and Fraser, 1984.

Rapoport, Roger. *California Dreaming: The Political Odyssey of Pat and Jerry Brown.* Berkeley: Nolo Press, 1982.

Rather, Dan, and Gary Paul Gates. *The Palace Guard.* New York: Harper and Row, 1974.

Reagan, Ronald. *An American Life.* New York: Pocket Books, 1990.

Reisner, Marc. *Cadillac Desert: The American West and Its Disappearing Water.* Rev. ed. New York: Penguin Books, 1993.

Richardson, James. *Willie Brown: A Biography.* Berkeley: University of California Press, 1996.

Robert, Myron, and Harold Garvin. *Glenn M. Anderson: Conscience of California.* Los Angeles: California State University Dominguez Hills Foundation, 2001.

Rolle, Andrew. *California: A History.* Wheeling, Ill.: Harlan Davidson, 1998.

Rorabaugh, W. J. *Berkeley at War.* New York: Oxford University Press, 1989.

Schell, Orville. *Brown.* New York: Random House, 1978.

Schiesl, Martin, ed. *Responsible Liberalism: Edmund G. "Pat" Brown and Reform Government in California, 1958–1967.* Los Angeles: Edmund G. "Pat" Brown Institute of Public Affairs, 2003.

Schrag, Peter. *Paradise Lost: California's Experience, America's Future.* New York: New Press, 1998.

Schuparra, Kurt. *Triumph of the Right: The Rise of the California Conservative Movement, 1945–1966.* Armonk, N.Y.: M. E. Sharpe, 1998.

Schwartz, Stephen. *From West to East: California and the Making of the American Mind.* New York: Free Press, 1998.

Seaborg, Glenn T., with Ray Colvig. *Chancellor at Berkeley.* Berkeley: Institute of Governmental Studies Press, 1994.

Sevareid, Eric, ed. *Candidates 1960: Behind the Headlines in the Presidential Race.* New York: Basic Books, 1959.

Severn, Bill. *Mr. Chief Justice: Earl Warren.* New York: David McKay, 1968.

Shirpser, Clara. *Behind the Scenes in Politics: The Memoirs of Clara Shirpser.* Portola Valley, Calif.: American Lives Endowment, 1981.

Smelser, Neil J., and Gabriel Almond. *Public Higher Education in California.* Berkeley: University of California Press, 1974.

Snyder, Elizabeth, with Gabriel Meyer. *A Ride on the Political Merry-Go-Round.* Los Angeles: Silverton Books, 1996.

Sollen, Robert. *An Ocean of Oil: A Century of Political Struggle over Petroleum Off the California Coast.* Juneau, Alaska: Denali Press, 1998.

Sorensen, Theodore C. *Kennedy.* New York: Harper and Row, 1965.

Stadtman, Verne A. *The University of California: 1868–1968.* New York: McGraw-Hill, 1970.

Starr, Kevin. *Embattled Dreams: California in War and Peace, 1940–1950.* New York: Oxford University Press, 2002.

Stevenson, Janet. *The Undiminished Man: A Political Biography of Robert Walker Kenny.* Novato, Calif.: Chandler and Sharp, 1980.

Stone, Irving. *Earl Warren: A Great American Story.* New York: Prentice-Hall, 1948.

Taylor, Ronald B. *Chavez and the Farm Workers.* Boston: Beacon Press, 1975.

Tillett, Paul. *Inside Politics: The National Conventions, 1960.* Dobbs Ferry, N.Y.: Oceana Publications, 1962.

Tuttle, Frederick B., Jr. *The California Democrats: 1953–1966.* Ann Arbor, Mich.: University Microfilms International, 1979. [Ph.D. dissertation, University of California, Los Angeles, 1975.]

Viorst, Milton. *Fire in the Streets: America in the 1960s.* New York: Simon and Schuster, 1979.

Voorhis, Jerry. *Confessions of a Congressman.* Garden City, N.Y.: Doubleday, 1947.

Walsh, James P. *The San Francisco Irish, 1850–1976.* San Francisco: Irish Literary and Historical Society, 1978.

Ward, Geoffrey C., and Ken Burns. *Baseball: An Illustrated History.* New York: Alfred A. Knopf, 1994.

Warren, Earl. *The Memoirs of Earl Warren.* New York: Doubleday, 1977.

Warshaw, Steven. *The Trouble in Berkeley.* Berkeley: Diablo Press, 1965.

Weaver, John D. *Warren: The Man, the Court, the Era.* Boston: Little, Brown, 1967.

White, G. Edward. *Earl Warren: A Public Life.* New York: Oxford University Press, 1982.

White, Theodore H. *The Making of the President 1960.* New York: Atheneum, 1961.

———. *The Making of the President 1964.* New York: Atheneum, 1965.

Wills, Garry. *Nixon Agonistes.* Boston: Houghton Mifflin, 1969.

———. *Reagan's America: Innocents at Home.* Garden City, N.Y.: Doubleday, 1987.

Wilson, James Q. *The Amateur Democrat.* Chicago: University of Chicago Press, 1962.

Wirt, Frederick M. *Power in the City: Decision Making in San Francisco.* Berkeley: Institute of Governmental Studies and University of California Press, 1974.

Witcover, Jules. *The Resurrection of Richard Nixon.* New York: G. P. Putnam's Sons, 1970.

Wolfe, Burton H. *Pileup on Death Row.* Garden City, N.Y.: Doubleday, 1973.

Worster, Donald. *Rivers of Empire: Water, Aridity, and the Growth of the American West.* New York: Oxford University Press, 1985.

MAGAZINES AND JOURNALS

American Political Science Review
Atlantic Monthly
The Californians

Commonweal
Crime and Delinquency
Esquire
Frontier
Harper's
History Today
Life
Nation
National Review
New Republic
New Times
New West
Newsweek
Playboy
Ramparts
Reporter
Saturday Evening Post
Southern California Quarterly
Time
U.S. News and World Report
Western Political Quarterly

NEWSPAPERS

Bakersfield Californian
Beverly Hills Citizen-News
California Eagle
Chico Enterprise-Record
Christian Science Monitor
Contra Costa Times
Eureka Times-Standard
Fresno Bee
Humboldt Times
LA Weekly
Los Angeles Herald-Examiner
Los Angeles Times
Modesto Bee
New York Times
Oakland Tribune
People's Daily World (San Francisco)
Sacramento Bee
Sacramento Union

San Diego Union
San Francisco Call-Bulletin
San Francisco Chronicle
San Francisco Examiner
San Francisco News
Santa Barbara News-Press
Santa Cruz Sentinel
Stockton Record
Ventura County Star
Wall Street Journal
Washington Post
Washington Star

INDEX

Note: EGB refers to Edmund G. ("Pat") Brown.

abortion clinics, 44–45
Acheson, Dean, 183
Adler, Dick, 375
aerospace industry, 116, 141. *See also* air
   travel
AFL-CIO, 216
agricultural industry, 350–51
air pollution, 133, 251
air travel, 29–30, 59. *See also* aerospace in-
   dustry
Aitken, Janet, 52
Alabama, racial violence in, 334
Alameda County, 49
Alameda County Sheriff's Office, 304, 305
Alarcon, Arthur, 273
Alcoholics Anonymous, 164
Aldrich, Lloyd, 128–29, 409n.57
Allbritton, Joe, 367–68
Allen, Emma (EGB's aunt), 12
Allen, Steve, 257, 343
Alsop, Stuart, 196
The American Way of Death (Mitford),
   307–8
Anderson, Glenn: as assemblyman, 51, 67;

popularity of, 338, 450n.22; and Rumford Act, 266; Stevenson supported
   by, 195; and Watts riots, 314, 324–28,
   331, 338–39
anti-Chinese feeling, 258, 432n.11
anti-Communist feeling, 242, 429n.43
antiwar protests (Oakland, 1965), 325
aqueducts, 205–6. *See also* State Water
   Project/bonds campaign
Arizona, water disputes with, 220
Atkinson, Maurice, 50
Atlantic City, 284
attorney general's office. *See* Department
   of Justice
Auburn Dam, 374–75

baby boomers, 52, 135–36
Baez, Joan, 302, 303
Bailey, Mickey, 196–97
Baker, Russell, 201
Ball, George, 317
Ball, Joe, 367
Barkley, Alben, 58
Barnes, Harry Elmer, 157

Barnett, Ross, 262
BART (Bay Area Rapid Transit), 337, 449n.86
baseball, 116–18
Bay Area Rapid Transit (BART), 337, 449n.86
Beard, Bill, 85
Becker, William, 320, 336
Bee, Carlos, 152
beer taxes, 121, 130
Belli, Melvin, 26
Bepp, Yoneo, 32–34
Bergholz, Richard, 249
Berkeley, 261–62. *See also* student protests; UC Berkeley
Berkeley city police, 305
Berlin, Dick, 195, 357–58
Berlin Wall, 269–70
Bidell's (Sacramento), 122
The Big Rock Candy Mountain (Stegner), 102
Big Sur, 129
Big Switch. *See* Knight, Goodwin; Knowland, William Fife
billboards, 256
blacks: in Los Angeles, 315; protests by, 260; rioting by, 317 (*see also* Watts riots); violence toward, 285; voting by, 334; westward migration of, 123. *See also* civil rights; racial discrimination/tensions
blue-collar workers, 362, 454nn.81–82
blue-lining, 368
Board of Education, 142, 143, 144–45, 146, 147, 151
Board of Regents, 142, 143, 144–45, 146, 147, 325
bonds campaign. *See* State Water Project/bonds campaign
Bonneville Power Administration, 210
Bontemps, Arna: *God Sends Sunday,* 319
Bottles, Scott L., 409n.57
braceros, 350–51, 451n.31
Braden, Tom, 240–41, 356, 370
Bradley, Don, 74, 77, 243, 342–43, 363–64
Bradley, Tom, 383
Brady, Matthew, 27, 28, 34–38, 39, 50

Brando, Marlon, 259, 264
Brennan, Jim, 24
Bridges, Harry, 62–63
Brody, Ralph, 125, 211
Brooklyn Dodgers (*later* Los Angeles Dodgers), 117–18
brothels, 42, 122
Brown, Barbara (EGB's daughter), 27, 74–75, 118, 187
Brown, Bernice Layne (EGB's wife): on Chessman case, 171, 176–77; children of, 27 (*see also* Brown, Barbara; Brown, Cynthia; Brown, Jerry; Brown, Kathleen); courtship by EGB, 17–18, 20; on EGB's death, 378; and EGB's political life, 74, 97, 101–2, 187–89, 365, 369; European trip by, 268, 269; golf played by, 97, 108, 188, 233; in Hawaii, 93; hunting by, 168; illness/death of, 381; on Jerry's religious life, 83, 167, 403n.53; at John Kennedy's inauguration, 225; at Lake Tahoe, 92; in Los Angeles, 366–67; marriage to EGB, 21–22, 353; and Pat Nixon, 429n.37; personality of, 188–89; in Philippines, 372; Sacramento home of, 118–19; in South America, 79; as teacher, 21
Brown, Constance ("Connie"; *later* Constance Carlson; EGB's sister), 10, 13, 14–15
Brown, Cynthia (EGB's daughter), 27, 74, 118
Brown, Edmund G. ("Pat"): absences from his family, 74–75, 371; ancestors' settling in California, 7–8; on anti-Semitism, 258, 432n.11; appearance of, 352; birth of, 9; business interests of, 369–70, 374; California cherished by, 7; ceremony to honor, 383–84; childhood home of, 10–11, 391n.12; childhood of, 9–14; children of, 27 (*see also* Brown, Barbara; Brown, Cynthia; Brown, Jerry; Brown, Kathleen); Christmas gift list of, 80; civil rights work of, 3; club/organizational activities of, 22, 62–63; courtship of/mar-

riage to Bernice, 17–18, 20–22, 353 (*see also* Brown, Bernice Layne); on crime prevention, 43–44; death/funeral of, 4, 138, 378–79; diary of, 119, 121; finances of, 91–92, 369–70; on gambling, 42–43, 49–50; gambling by, 15, 17, 50; on gays, 258; golf played by, 38, 97, 108, 188, 233, 236; at Gridiron Club banquet, 181, 282–83; in Grove Street Gang, 11; health/fitness of, 233, 377, 378; Hoover supported by, 24–25; hunting by, 168, 224; on Japanese Americans' internment, 32–34; on Jerry's religious life, 83; and John Kennedy's assassination/funeral, 272–73; at John Kennedy's inauguration, 224–25; on William Knowland, 373; law career of, 16, 18–19, 22, 24, 31, 41–42, 367–68; lobbying by, 368–69; in Los Angeles, 366–67; on mental hospitals, 85–86, 403n.57; nickname of Pat acquired, 13; on Richard Nixon, 230–31; personality of, 68, 82, 101, 177–78, 188, 203, 251–52; popularity of, 3–4 (*see also under* Brown, Edmund G., GOVERNORSHIP; Brown, Edmund G., POLITICAL CAREER); on population growth in California, 1, 255; *Public Justice, Private Mercy,* 375–76, 377; Ronald Reagan criticized by, 368; on religion in public schools, 69; religious upbringing/views of, 14, 30–31, 158; reputation of, 382–83; Sacramento home of, 118–19; at San Francisco Law School, 16–17; as student president, 17; success of, 79–80 (*see also* Brown, Edmund G., GOVERNORSHIP; Brown, Edmund G., POLITICAL CAREER); summer vacations in youth, 15, 18; writings by, 375–76
—GOVERNORSHIP: appointments, 113–14, 365; Berkeley protesters, 3, 293, 303, 309, 310–13, 442nn.42,45 (*see also* student protests); civil rights agenda, 256–60, 263, 315 (*see also* civil rights; Proposition 14); criticism of, 345–46, 450n.14; death penalty, 157–67,

168–75, 177–78, 257, 375–76, 417n.59 (*see also* Chessman, Caryl Whittier); debate with Richard Nixon, 239–42, 429nn.37,41; departure from office, 365–66; duties/travels around state, 122–23, 144; executions commuted, 376–77; goals/achievements, 115, 120, 126, 251, 256, 291, 315–16, 383; gubernatorial aspirations, 76–77, 87, 90–91, 94–95, 404n.9; gubernatorial bid (1958), 96–109; gubernatorial bid (1962), 3, 229–30, 232, 234–39, 242–47, 251–52; gubernatorial bid (1966), 341–42, 344–45, 353–64, 449n.3, 452n.43, 453n.66; higher education, 142–43, 144–45, 147–48, 151, 293 (*see also* education; Master Plan for Higher Education; University of California); inaugurations, 114–15, 256–57; legislation passed, 123–32, 133; news conferences, 121–22; popularity, 134, 272, 315, 338, 384, 445n.4, 450n.22; public works projects of, 3 (*see also* State Water Project/bonds campaign); reelection training regimen, 233; roads projects, 128–30; tax increases (*see* taxes); Unruh feud, 278–81, 283–84, 287, 315–16, 342, 347–48; Watts riots, 328–33, 335–36, 338–39; Yorty feud, 78, 347
—POLITICAL CAREER: as attorney general, 67–69; attorney general bid (1946), 47–49; attorney general bid (1950), 61–65; attorney general bid (1954), 77–78, 402n.41; campaigning/promoting style, 73–74, 77–78, 85, 168, 382; and communism, 62–63; and Democratic National Convention (1960), 191–95; at Democratic National Convention (1940), 28–29, 45; at Democratic National Convention (1944), 45–47, 399n.49; at Democratic National Convention (1948), 55, 58–59; at Democratic National Convention (1956), 83–85; at Democratic National Convention (1960), 195–204, 275; at Democratic National

Brown, Edmund G. *(continued)*
Convention (1964), 284–87; on Democratic speaker's bureau, 25–26; as
deputy district attorney, 377; as district attorney, 39–45, 49, 54–55, 67,
397n.9; district attorney bid (1939),
28, 34–35, 36; district attorney bid
(1943), 34–38, 50; district attorney bid
(1947), 54–55; and economy, 99,
100–101; as elder statesman, 373–74;
"Giant Killer" reputation, 251; housing subsidy supported, 52–54; Howser
attacked, 49–51, 61, 398n.34; John
Kennedy supported, 190–93, 195,
197–202, 203–4, 219, 420n.37; labor
funding of, 100, 102; liberalism of,
68–69, 115, 210; networking/cam-
paigning strategies, 24, 27–28, 34, 54,
62, 70–71, 100–101; New Order of
Cincinnatus founded, 23–24; and
Olson's election/governorship, 25–27;
popularity, 229–30, 238–39, 427n.3,
428n.32; presidential aspirations, 115,
181–86, 189, 407n.7, 420n.25; presidential candidacy (1952), 70–71;
Proposition 18 supported, 100, 102;
radio ads, 102–3; in Republican Party,
19–20, 23–25; state assembly bid,
19–20, 393n.52; switch to Democratic
party, 25, 393–94nn.12–13; television
ads/appearances, 81, 105–6, 107,
109–10, 121–22, 185; Truman sup-
ported/opposed, 55–59, 69–70,
399n.49; U.S. Senate aspirations,
80–81, 90–91, 280; vice-presidential
aspirations, 282, 437n.35; water project, 99, 204, 210–11, 216–17, 224,
227–28, 251, 349 (*see also* water). *See
also* Brown, Edmund G., GOVERNOR-
SHIP
—TRAVELS: by airplane, 29–30, 59, 196–97;
Argentina, 223, 272; Bainbridge Island, 180; in China, 370; Europe,
268–70; Greece, 317, 320–21, 324, 328,
446n.22; Hawaii, 93–95; Hong Kong,
370; Kings Canyon National Park,
236; Lake Tahoe, 92; Nepal, 370–71;
Palm Springs, 113; Paris, 370; Philippines, 372; South America, 78–79;
South Pacific, 370; Washington,
D.C., 236, 267–68; Wyntoon, 236–37;
Yosemite, 15

Brown, Edmund Joseph (EGB's father),
9–11, 12–13, 14–15, 30, 34, 391n.12,
396n.49

Brown, Frank (EGB's brother), 10, 34

Brown, Harold (EGB's brother), 10, 11, 12,
14, 30, 31, 33

Brown, Ida Schuckman (EGB's mother),
8–12, 14–15, 22, 30, 109, 353

Brown, Jeff (EGB's nephew), 407n.7

Brown, Jerry (Edmund Gerald, Jr.; EGB's
son): on aqueduct, 228; childhood
of, 27, 74–75, 371; civil rights activities in Mississippi, 262; on death
penalty/Chessman case, 171, 177; on
drug-policy panel, 265; European
trip by, 268; executions commuted
by, 432n.10; as governor, 371–72;
hunting by, 224; in India, 381; in
Japan, 381; as Jesuit novice, 82–83,
121, 167, 171, 403n.53; law career of,
353; as mayor of Oakland, 382; presidential bids, 372, 384; radio talk
show of, 381–82; relationship with
EGB, 372; at Santa Clara University,
82; as secretary of state, 369, 371; at
St. Ignatius, 82; at UC Berkeley, 167,
224; U.S. Senate bid, 381; at Yale Law
School, 262, 353

Brown, Joseph (EGB's grandfather), 8–9

Brown, Kathleen (EGB's daughter):
birth of, 59; at boarding school, 233;
business career of, 381; college education of, 91–92; on EGB's audience
with Pope, 31; and EGB's political
life, 108–9, 118, 187–88, 197, 247,
378; European trip by, 268, 269; gubernatorial bid (1994), 378; in
Hawaii, 93; relationship with EGB,
74–75, 247, 271–72, 378; at Stanford
University, 271; as state treasurer,
377, 378

Brown, Pat. *See* Brown, Edmund G.

Brown, Willie, 203, 384
Brown for President Clubs, 185
Bryan, William Jennings, 71
"bug housers," 86
Burby, Jack, 235–36, 268, 288–89, 344, 429n.41
Burch, Meredith, 94
Burdick, Eugene ("Bud"), 145; *The Ugly American,* 102
Burning Tree (golf course), 236
Burns, Hugh, 126–27, 174, 213–14, 242, 263–66
Burns, Inez, 44–45
Burton, Phil, 106, 286
buses, racial discrimination on, 265
Butte County, 223

Cal Conservatives, 316
Califano, Joseph, 345, 447n.54
California: accounting system, 368, 455n.2; budget, 120, 130, 268–69, 316, 407n.24; Democratic gains in, 26, 72–73, 81–82, 109, 278; Democratic losses in, 363; ethnic diversity, 4; as future, 2, 4, 65, 383; growth, 52, 348, 349–50; image, 337–38, 383; legislature, 124, 127, 131–32; migration to, 66–67, 116; Northern vs. Southern, 51 (*see also* water); political rifts in, 315; as political springboard, 232; political system, generally, 202–3; popularity, 66–67, 116; population growth, 1, 3, 66–67, 116, 255, 349, 375, 383, 390n.2; as rebel, 2–3; Republican dominance in, 19–20, 71, 99, 363, 401n.21; Republican losses in, 26, 72–73, 81–82, 109, 278; roads, 128–30, 409nn.57, 60, 410n.62; shipyards, 66; size, 4, 128, 383; unity, 227–28; as vacation spot, 66
California Defense Committee, 173
California Democratic Council. *See* CDC
"California Dynasty of Communism," 243
California Highway Patrol (CHP), 293, 304, 305. *See also* student protests; Watts riots
California Law Review, 206–7

California Real Estate Association, 289
California Republican Assembly, 234
California State University, 135–36
Cal-Neva (Lake Tahoe), 101
Camarillo State Hospital investigation, 403n.57
Camelback Inn (Phoenix), 258
capital gains taxes, 121
capital punishment. *See* Chessman, Caryl Whittier; death penalty
car culture, 128
Carlson, Constance Brown ("Connie"; EGB's sister), 10, 13, 14–15
carpetbagging, 74
car pollution guidelines, 127–28, 133
Carson, Rachel: *Silent Spring,* 348
Carter, Ed, 302
Carter, Jimmy, 373–74
Casady, Si, 345–46, 450n.14
Casady, Virginia, 346
Casey, Charles (EGB's grandson), 374–75
Cathedral of the Blessed Sacrament (Sacramento), 114
CBS, 287
CDC (California Democratic Council): Anderson in, 325; Si Casady as head of, 345–46, 450n.14; creation of, 73, 127, 195; criticism of, 126; on People's Republic of China, 243
Cell 2455, Death Row (Chessman), 157, 159, 160, 415n.18
Census Bureau, 255
Central Valley, dryness of, 205. *See also* water
Central Valley Project/160-acre limit, 206–8, 209, 212, 225
Champion, Hale: background of, 113–14; on Chessman case, 171–72; at EGB's and staff's departure from office, 365–66; and EGB's last gubernatorial bid, 341; on Richard Nixon, 231; on Unruh, 268–69; and Watts riots, 314, 327–28, 330–31, 339, 447n.54
Chandler, Norman, 134
Chandler, Otis, 250, 274–75
Chávez, César, 130–31, 351–52

Chessman, Caryl Whittier (Red Light Bandit): campaign to save life of, 164, 169; *Cell 2455, Death Row,* 157, 159, 160, 415n.18; clemency denied to, 163–67, 168–70; crimes/trial of, 154–57; criticism of EGB's role in case, 173–74, 176–77, 180; execution dates, 163, 168, 174; execution of, 175, 178, 194; fame/popularity of, 157, 164; stays of execution/delays for, 159–60, 167, 168, 171–73

Chicago Cubs, 29

Chicago riots (1964), 317

Chicago's Great Fire, 10

China, 100, 243

Chinese, attitudes toward, 258, 432n.11

Chow, William Jack, 40

CHP. *See* California Highway Patrol

Christian, Winslow, 309, 323, 326, 328, 449n.3

Christian Science Monitor, 117

Christopher, George, 230, 354–55, 452n.46

Christopher, Warren, 97, 341

cigarette/cigar taxes, 121, 128, 130, 133

civil rights, 256–70; and anti-Semitism, 258, 432n.11; Congress of Racial Equality, 264; of defendants vs. victims, 44; Fair Employment Practices Act, 261; Freedom Riders, 258–59; in housing, 256, 258, 259, 261–62 (*see also* Rumford Act); in New York, 260–61; preachers' lobbying for, 260–61; Rumford Act, 261–67, 289, 315, 356–57, 362–63 (*see also* Proposition 14); in state agencies/government, 256–57, 261, 267; in state licensing, 257, 267; student activism for, 262, 294–96; white support for, 285; for women, 258. *See also* Fair Employment Practices Commission; racial discrimination/tensions

Civil Rights Act (1964), 281, 285

Civil Rights movement, 336

Clarvoe, Frank, 34–35

clemency, 166, 178. *See also under* Chessman, Caryl Whittier

Coakley, J. Frank, 306, 442n.45

Coconut Island (Hawaii), 93

Cold War, 116, 256

collective bargaining, 100, 350, 351

colleges: admissions standards of, 147; growth of, 135–37, 143, 153, 383; independence of, 146–47, 148, 150; vs. universities, 136–38, 141–49

Colorado River, 205, 221

Columbia River, 206

Colusa County, 8, 11–12

Commission on Organized Crime, 60, 64, 68

Committee on Un-American Activities, 240

Committee to Preserve the Democratic Party in California, 242

communism, 62–63, 242, 429n.43

Congress of Racial Equality (CORE), 264

Connally, John, 282, 287

conservatism, 2, 4, 342, 363, 382–83

Constantine II, king of Greece, 317

Constitution, 69, 298, 356

consumer protections, 133

Coons, Arthur, 145

CORE (Congress of Racial Equality), 264

Corley, James, 149–50, 152

corruption, 60

Council of Mexican-American Affairs, 289

Court of Reconciliation (San Francisco), 44

Cranston, Alan, 77, 280–81, 341, 450n.22

crime prevention, 43–44

Crooker, John Russell, 161–62

cross-filing, 48, 71–72, 78, 81, 127–28

Cuban Missile Crisis, 244

Curtis, George, 54–55

Daley, Richard, 199, 203

dams, 206, 382. *See also* Central Valley Project/160-acre limit; *and specific dams*

Dasmann, Raymond: *The Destruction of California,* 348–50

Davis, George T., 165

Davis, Gray, 4

Davis, Pauline, 214

Davis, Sammy, Jr., 259

death penalty, 157–67, 168–75, 177–78, 257, 375–76, 416n.26, 417n.59, 432n.10. *See also* Chessman, Caryl Whittier

Democratic Advisory Council, 185–86
Democratic National Committee, 194
Democratic National Conventions: 1940
    (Chicago), 28–29, 45; 1944 (Chicago),
    45–47, 399n.49; 1948 (Philadelphia),
    55, 58–59, 186; 1956 (Chicago), 83–85;
    1960 (Los Angeles), 191–204, 275,
    422n.61; 1964 (Atlantic City), 284–87.
    See also individual politicians
Democratic Party: Credentials Committee,
    285, 286; feuding within, 316, 342 (*see
    also* Unruh, Jesse, EGB's feud with);
    funding of candidates for, 71, 77;
    gains in California, 26, 72–73, 81–82,
    109, 278; goals/ideology of, 25; losses
    in California, 363; national gains by,
    108; Republican dominance over,
    19–20, 71, 401n.21; and Stevenson
    Clubs, 72–73. *See also* CDC
Department of Corrections, 160
Department of Crime Prevention (San
    Francisco), 43
Department of Justice (California), 67, 68,
    85–86, 207–8
Department of Motor Vehicles (Califor-
    nia), 128
Department of Water Resources, 209–10,
    218
The Destruction of California (Dasmann),
    348–50
Detroit riots (1967), 340
Dewey, Thomas, 58–59, 60
Dieden, Leonard, 184
Di Giorgio family, 351–52
DiMaggio, Joe, 59
disability benefits, 133
district attorney's office (San Francisco),
    41, 43–44, 87, 397n.9. *See also under*
    Brown, Edmund G., POLITICAL CA-
    REER
divorce rate, 44
Dominican Republic, 333–34
Donahoe, Dorothy, 151–52
Donahoe Higher Education Act. *See* Mas-
    ter Plan for Higher Education
Douglas, Helen Gahagan, 29, 47, 62, 65,
    230, 343

Douglas, William O., 168
Douglass, John Aubrey, 153
drunk-driving legislation, 130
Duffy, Clinton, 164
Dumke, Glenn, 145–46, 149
Dust Bowl, 350
Dutton, Fred: and Bernice Brown, 187; on
    Chessman case, 171, 174–75, 176, 178;
    as EGB's chief of staff, 113; and EGB's
    gubernatorial campaign, 94–97,
    102–4, 106, 109, 404n.9; on EGB's
    presidential aspirations, 181, 182–83,
    186, 420n.25; on EGB's water project,
    213–14; on higher education, 143; and
    John Kennedy's presidential bid, 194,
    201, 420n.37; on Kerr and EGB, 145;
    personality of, 94; and Unruh, 279;
    on water project, 218
Dymally, Mervyn, 324

Edmonston, Arthur, 208–9
Edmund G. Brown California Aqueduct,
    228. *See also* State Water Project/
    bonds campaign
education, 135–53; Board of Education, 142,
    143, 144–45, 146, 147, 151; Board of
    Regents, 142, 143, 144–45, 146, 147;
    budget for, 153; colleges'/universities'
    growth, 135–37, 143, 153, 251, 383; col-
    leges vs. universities, 136–38, 141–49;
    junior colleges, 147, 153; Master Plan,
    138–39, 147–53, 293–94, 296; Ph.D.
    controversy, 136–38, 142–44, 146–48,
    150, 153; religion in schools, 69; re-
    search dollars for, 411n.13; school aid,
    131, 133; school desegregation, 261;
    universal access to, 147. *See also spe-
    cific schools*
Eel River, 206, 217, 227
Eisenhower, Dwight: golf played by, 236;
    and Khrushchev, 180; on William
    Knowland, 89; and Richard Nixon,
    232, 244; presidential bid of, 56, 57;
    refusal to run for president, 58;
    "under God" added to Pledge of Alle-
    giance by, 69; Welch's conspiracy the-
    ories about, 234, 235

elections/campaigns: betting on, 36; car-
    petbagging, 74; conventions vs. pri-
    maries, 182, 401n.23; cross-filing in,
    48, 71–72, 78, 81, 127–28; favorite sons
    in, 181–84, 192, 197–98; incumbents'
    advantage in, 71; newspapers' involve-
    ment in, 35–36, 50–51, 77–78, 402n.41
    (see also specific newspapers); New
    Yorkers as presidential candidates,
    184, 419n.13; party endorsements,
    72–73; polling in, 36, 63, 64, 98; voter
    education, 73; voting tally system, 49.
    See also individual politicians
Elliott, John B., 71–72, 401n.23
El Mirador Hotel (Sacramento), 122
El Retiro (Los Gatos), 30–31
employment commission (California),
    68–69
Engle, Clair: on Civil Rights Act, 281; and
    EGB's endorsement of John Kennedy,
    195, 197, 200; and EGB's gubernato-
    rial aspirations, 404n.9; illness/death
    of, 276–78, 280, 281; illness of,
    436n.21; popularity of, 427n.3; U.S.
    Senate bid/election, 91, 109
Engle, Lucretia, 277–78, 281
environmentalism, 227, 348–49, 374–75, 382
espionage, 180
Eureka Times-Standard, 238
Excavators and Dump Truck Owners' As-
    sociation of Northern California, 22
Executive Order 9066, 32

Fair Employment Practices Act (California,
    1958), 261
Fair Employment Practices Commission
    (FEPC), 123–26, 133–34, 259–60, 283,
    289
Fairmont Hotel (San Francisco), 92
Farley, James, 29
Farmer, James, 336
farmworkers, minimum wage for, 130–31,
    350, 351
Farr, Fred, 174
FBI, 63
Feather River dam, 206, 208–9, 211,
    217–19, 220, 223, 225, 227–28

Feather River Project Association, 219
Federal Communications Commission, 250
FEPC. *See* Fair Employment Practices
    Commission
Field, Mervin, 63, 98
Field Poll, 63, 64, 98
Filthy Speech Movement, 316–17
Finn, Tom, 19
Fleharty, George, 355
flooding, 217. *See also* water
Ford, John, 107–8
Fording, A. H., 442n.45
Frank Fat's (Sacramento), 122
Frankfurter Inn (San Francisco), 11
Freedom Riders, 258–59
Freedom Summer, 295
free speech and obscenity, 316–17
Free Speech Movement (FSM), 301–2, 308,
    309, 311, 315, 316, 443n.62
freeways/parkways, 128–30, 251, 382,
    409nn.57–58,60, 410nn.62–63
Fresno, housing segregation in, 259
Fresno State College, 141–42
Fricke, Charles F., 156–57
Friends of the River, 374
Frye, Marquette, 321–22. *See also* Watts riots
Frye, Rena, 321, 323
FSM. *See* Free Speech Movement
Fuck Rally (UC Berkeley, 1965), 316–17
Fulton Street Gang, 11

Gallatin, Albert, 118
Gallup, George, 98
gambling, 37, 42–43, 49–50
gasoline taxes, 130, 410n.62
gas prices, 129
Gates, Daryl, 329
General Electric, 343
General Sherman (redwood tree), 236
Gibson, Luther, 263, 264
Gibson, Phil, 167, 169
Gideon Bibles, 69
God Sends Sunday (Bontemps), 319
Goldberg, Abbott, 210, 227
Gold Rush, 8
Goldwater, Barry, 267, 288, 290, 342, 344
Goodban, Frank M., 393n.52

Goodman, Louis, 168, 169
Gould, Stephen Jay, 117
Governmental Efficiency Committee
    (Calif.), 263
grape boycott, 351–52
The Grapes of Wrath (Steinbeck), 350
Graves, Richard, 77, 78, 95, 103
Great Depression (1929–1939), 24, 155, 206
Great Society, 344
Greenberg, Carl, 248
Greene, Dewey, Jr., 262
Gregory, Dick, 324, 336
Gridiron Club banquet, 181
Grizzly I and *II* (airplanes), 196–97
Grove Street Gang, 11
Grunsky, Donald, 150
Guggenheim, Charles, 363–64
Gunther, John, 2; *Inside U.S.A.,* 66–67
Guthrie, Woody: "Roll on Columbia," 210

Haggin, James Ben Ali, 226
Haldeman, H. R., 243, 377
Half Dome (Yosemite), 15
Halleck, Charles, 181
Hamer, Fannie Lou, 285
Hammill, Pete, 117
Hand, Lloyd, 275–76
Harding, Warren, 88
Harlem, 320
Harrell, Jerry, 377
Harris, Louis, 431n.77
Harvard University, 140, 310
Hatfield, Mark, 180, 238
Havenner, Franck, 26
health care expansion, 127–28, 133
Health Maintenance Organization, 92
Hearst, George, Jr., 237
Hearst, William Randolph, 96, 236–37
Heller, Clary, 83–84
Heller, Ed, 77
Heller, Ellie, 77, 83–84
Hetch Hetchy Canyon, 205, 206
higher education. *See* colleges; education;
    universities; *and specific schools*
highways. *See* freeways/parkways
highway taxes, 410nn.62–63
Hill, Roderic, 326

Hills, Ed, 372
Hitt, Patricia, 235
Holifield, Chet, 198
Hollywood Palladium, 246
Hoover, Herbert, 24–25, 88, 104
Hope, Bob, 303
Horticultural Palace (San Francisco), 11
House Un-American Activities Commit-
    tee, 303, 310
housing, 52–54, 256, 258, 259, 261–62. *See
    also* Rumford Act
Howser, Frederick, 49–51, 60, 61, 78,
    207–8, 398n.34
Hughes, Howard, 231, 241
Humphrey, Hubert, 83, 84, 184, 186, 191
Hunters Point shooting (San Francisco),
    358–59

immigrant workers, 350–51, 451n.31
Imperial Valley, 205
income taxes, 120–21, 125–26, 128, 132, 133,
    134
Indians (American), 68, 69
inheritance taxes, 121
Inouye, Daniel, 185
Inside U.S.A. (Gunther), 66–67
Inter-American Congress of Public Law
    Administrators (São Paulo), 78
interest rates, 133–34
Interstate Highway Program, 130,
    410nn.62–63

Jackson (Calif.), 122
Japanese Americans, 32–34, 69
Jenkins, Walter, 286–87
Jensen, Joseph, 220
Jewell, Howard, 318–19
Jim Crow, 258
John Birch Society, 234–35, 240, 342, 344
Johnson, George, 320–21
Johnson, Hiram, 14, 88, 134
Johnson, Lyndon: and EGB, 275–76,
    280–84, 286–87, 290, 342, 360,
    364–65; on John Kennedy's assassina-
    tion, 273; personality of, 275; presi-
    dential bid (1960), 182, 184, 198; presi-
    dential bid (1964), 282–87, 290, 342;

Johnson, Lyndon *(continued)*
    and Vietnam War, 345–46; on Watts
    riots, 330–31
Jordan, Frank, 72, 109
junior colleges, 147, 153
juvenile delinquency/crime, 35, 43–44

Kaiser, Henry, 92
Kamp, Joseph: "Meet the Man Who Plans
    to Rule America," 106–7
Kefauver, Estes, 69–71, 83, 84
Kelly, Gene, 257
Kelly, Kathleen (EGB's granddaughter),
    379
Kennedy, Bobby, 84, 197, 201
Kennedy, Joe, 190
Kennedy, John F.: assassination/funeral of,
    272–73; Catholicism of, 223; and
    Cuban Missile Crisis, 244; and EGB,
    83–84; and EGB's gubernatorial race
    against Richard Nixon, 236; on Clair
    Engle, 275; inauguration of, 224–25;
    intellectuals relied on by, 102; on
    Richard Nixon, 251; popularity,
    428n.32; presidential bid, 182–84, 186,
    189–93, 195, 223–24, 422n.61; presi-
    dential bid, EGB's support of,
    190–93, 195, 197–202, 203–4, 219,
    420n.37
Kenny, Robert, 47–48, 49, 51, 60
Kern County, 223, 361
Kern County Land Company, 226
Kerr, Clark: on baby boom, 136; back-
    ground of, 140; limerick of, 140,
    411n.13; and Franklin Murphy, 306;
    and student protesters, 297, 300–304,
    307, 310, 441n.25, 442n.42; as Univer-
    sity of California president, 139–47,
    149–51; on university's growth, 294
Khrushchev, Nikita, 180
King, Martin Luther, Jr., 258–59, 335, 336
King, Rodney, 337
Kings Canyon National Park, 236
Kirkwood, Robert, 90
Klein, Herb, 246, 247, 249, 250
Knickerbocker Hotel (Los Angeles), 200
Knight, Goodwin: background of, 76;

Chessman denied clemency by, 163;
    Department of Water Resources cre-
    ated by, 209–10; executions com-
    muted by, 257; execution-stay snafu
    of, 170; as governor, 72, 76, 120; gu-
    bernatorial bid (1958), 90; and
    William Knowland, 86, 90, 93–98,
    107, 109; and mental hospital investi-
    gations, 86, 403n.57; on Richard
    Nixon, 231; popularity of, 230; on
    water project, 216
Knight, Virginia, 96, 118
Knowland, Helen, 89–90, 106–7, 373
Knowland, J. R., 88, 90
Knowland, Joseph, 87–88
Knowland, William Fife: background of,
    87–88; and EGB, 99–100, 103–8, 109;
    and Goodwin Knight, 86, 90, 93–98,
    107, 109; marriage to Helen, 89; *Oak-
    land Tribune* run by, 373; popularity
    of, 230; self-destructive lifestyle/sui-
    cide of, 373
Knudsen, Vern, 144
Krupp, Alfred, 165
KTTV, 250
Kuchel, Tommy, 80, 81, 427n.3
Ku Klux Klan, 295, 319
Kyne, Tom, 36

Lake Tahoe, 92
Lancaster, Burt, 259
Langdon, Harold, 162, 165, 166–67
LAPD. *See* Los Angeles Police Department
The Last Hurrah (film), 107–8
Lawrence, David, 199, 422n.61
Layne, Arthur D. (EGB's father-in-law), 21
Layne, Bernice. *See* Brown, Bernice Layne
Leiffer, Don, 148–49, 413n.44
Lerner, Harry, 64, 354
Levering, Harold, 125
Levit, Bert, 40, 113
Lewis, John, 334
liberty bonds, 13
Libertyville (Ill.), 80
Lincoln, Abraham, 256
Lindbergh, Charles, 156
Lindbergh Law, 156, 162, 376

Linn, Clarence, 160
loan rates, 127–28
Los Angeles: blacks in, 315; growth of, 66,
116; importance of, 116–17; racial ten-
sions in, 318–20; riots in, 337; water
supply of, 205. *See also* Watts riots
Los Angeles County, 223
Los Angeles County Board of Supervisors,
215
Los Angeles County Human Relations
Commission, 323
Los Angeles Dodgers (*formerly* Brooklyn
Dodgers), 117–18
Los Angeles Fire Department, 258, 432n.15
Los Angeles Herald Examiner, 237, 357–58,
375
Los Angeles Police Department (LAPD),
314, 318, 321–24, 325–27, 329–30, 333,
337
Los Angeles Realty Board, 260
Los Angeles State College, 135–36
Los Angeles Times: bias/fairness of political
coverage by, 51, 77–78, 103–4, 250,
402n.41; on EGB vs. Unruh, 287;
Richard Nixon's criticism of/support
by, 248, 249–50; on Rumford Act,
274–75; on water project, 221; on
Watts riots, 324
Los Angeles Urban League, 123
Love, Malcolm, 143
Lowell high school (San Francisco), 13
Lurie, Lou, 271
Lynch, Thomas Connor, 40, 45, 87,
189–90, 327–28, 341
Lynn, Wally, 224
Lynwood (Calif.), 320
Lytton, Bart, 190

MacBride, Thomas, 215
Machinery Palace (San Francisco), 11
Mackin, Frank, 97
Macmillan, Harold, 268
Malone, Bill, 46, 47, 58, 69–70
Mansion Inn (Sacramento), 119, 171
Marcos, Ferdinand, 372
Marcos, Imelda, 372
Marin County, 32

Marshall, John, 8
Martin, Dean, 257
Master Plan for Higher Education (Dona-
hoe Higher Education Act), 138–39,
147–53, 293–94, 296
Maxim's (Paris), 268
McAteer, Gene, 214
McClain, George, 193–94
McClatchy, C. K., 128, 409n.56
McComb (Miss.), 295–96
McCone, John, 336
McCone Commission, 336–37
McDonough brothers, 43
McGee, Richard, 163–65
McGrath, J. Howard, 56–57
McHenry, Dean, 102, 141, 143–46, 150–51,
413n.38
McWilliams, Carey, 2–3, 4
Meese, Ed, 306, 307
"Meet the Man Who Plans to Rule Amer-
ica" (Kamp), 106–7
Meet the Press, 107, 185
Memorial Sports Arena (Los Angeles),
195–96
Metropolitan Water District, 215, 220–22,
223, 226
Meyers, Louis, 50
Michener, James, 116
migrant workers, 350
Miller, George, Jr., 72–74, 127–28, 132, 137,
149, 151, 214, 409n.50
minimum wage, 130–31, 350, 351
minorities vs. whites, income of, 259–60
Mississippi, racism in, 262, 284–85, 295–96
Mississippi Freedom Democratic Party,
284–87, 295–96
Mitford, Jessica: *The American Way of
Death,* 307–8
Modesto mental hospital investigation,
85–86, 403n.57
Modoc County, 289, 439n.61
Mokelumne River, 205–6
Moody, Blair, 89
Moody, Ruth, 89
Mooney, Tom, 165
Moses, Robert, 129, 409n.58
Mosher, Clint, 96

Mosk, Stanley, 158, 194, 280, 437n.29, 450n.22
Moss, John, 198
Munnell, Bill, 125, 184
Murphy, Franklin, 306
Murphy, George, 290, 338
Murphy, Joe, 24

National Guard, 261, 317; and Watts riots, 314, 325, 326–32, 333–34, 339
National Labor Relations Act (1935), 351
National League, 117
Native Americans, 68, 69
Nazi Germany, 163
NBC, 200, 287
Nelson, Ricky, 197
Newark riots (1967), 340
New Deal, 104, 363
New Jersey riots (1964, 1967), 317, 340
Newman, Paul, 259, 264
New Melones Dam (Stanislaus River), 426n.67
New Order of Cincinnatus (San Francisco), 23–24
New Order of Cincinnatus (Seattle), 22–23
New Republic, 337
Newsom, William, 43
newspapers. *See* the press; *and specific newspapers*
Newsweek, 337, 349–50
New York (state): civil rights in, 260–61; importance of, 117; parkways in, 129, 409n.58; population of, 255, 390n.2
New York City, 261, 317
New Yorkers, as presidential candidates, 184, 419n.13
New York Giants (*later* San Francisco Giants), 29, 117
New York Times, 67, 77, 106–7, 117, 138, 157
New York Times Magazine, 185
Nixon, Pat, 231, 232, 429n.37
Nixon, Richard: ambitiousness/brilliance of, 230, 247, 251; Checkers speech, 231; criticism of the press, 248–50; debate with EGB, 239–42, 429nn.37,41; and Douglas, 343; and EGB, 230; European trip by, 268; farewell speech following gubernatorial defeat, 247–49, 250–51; gubernatorial race against EGB (1962), 3, 229–30, 232, 234–39, 242–47; and John Birch Society, 234–35, 240; and Goodwin Knight, 231; and William Knowland and Goodwin Knight, 95–96; paranoia of, 249; popularity of, 238–39, 431n.77; presidential bid (1960), 180, 219, 223–24, 231; press coverage as favorable to, 250, 431n.71; return to California, 231–32; scandals surrounding, 231, 241, 429n.40; and Shell, 234–35, 428n.18; U.S. Senate bid (1950), 62, 64, 65; as vice president, 80, 168
Nocturnes (fraternity), 13
Northern California flooding, 217. *See also* water

Oakland Tribune, 88, 295, 373, 440n.13
O'Brien, Larry, 193
obscenity and free speech, 316–17
O'Connell, Daniel, 304–5, 307, 442n.45
O'Connor, Bill, 77
oil industry, 374
oil/natural gas taxes, 121, 131–32
Olson, Culbert, 25–27, 47, 158
O'Malley, Walter, 117
OPEC oil embargo, 129
Operation Abolition, 303
Orange County, 116, 361
Orinda (Calif.), 259
Oroville Dam, 217–18, 219, 220, 223, 228. *See also* Feather River dam
Owens River, 205
Owens Valley, 220

Pacific Coast invasion fears, 31–32
Palmer, Kyle, 77–78, 96
Panama Pacific International Exposition (San Francisco, 1915), 11
Papandreou, George, 317
Parker, William, 318, 326, 327, 332, 335, 336, 337, 449n.91
parkways. *See* freeways/parkways
"Pat Brown and the CDC," 243
patronage, 114, 192, 202, 401n.21

Paul VI, pope, 269, 270
Pauley, Ed, 46–47, 93–95, 168, 194
Pearl Harbor attack (1941), 31
Pearson, Drew, 64, 70, 89, 94, 98, 181, 354–55
Pennsylvania, population of, 66
People's Republic of China, 100, 243
Perry, Ernest R., 156
Pertamina (Indonesia), 369–70, 374
Ph.D. controversy, 136–38, 142–44, 146–48, 150, 153
Philadelphia A's, 117
Philadelphia riots (1964), 317
philandering, 122
Pledge of Allegiance, 69
pollution, 133, 251
Poole, Cecil, 113, 161, 163, 165, 171–73, 175
Post, A. Alan, 145
potato famine (Ireland), 8–9
Powers, Gary Francis, 180
the press: bias in political coverage by, 35–36, 50–51, 77–78, 249, 402n.41, 431n.71; fairness of political coverage by, 250; newspapers vs. television, 121–22, 357; Richard Nixon's criticism of, 248–50. See also specific newspapers
Preston Industrial School (Ione, Calif.), 155
prison system, 160, 164, 415n.18, 416n.29
Proposition 13 (California), 375
Proposition 14 (California), 273–75, 285, 288–91, 315, 333, 356, 362, 439n.61. See also Rumford Act
Proposition 18 (California), 100, 102
prostitution, 42
Public Justice, Private Mercy (EGB), 375–76, 377
Purchio, John, 184

racial discrimination/tensions: bans on discrimination, 260; in Berkeley, 261–62; city ordinances against discrimination, 69; cross burning, 262; in hiring, 68–69, 123–25, 126, 133, 134; in housing, 256, 258–60; Jim Crow, 258, 284–85; in Los Angeles Fire Department, 258, 432n.15; and school desegregation, 261. See also civil rights; Watts riots

radio, 102–3
Rattigan, Joseph, 265–67, 417n.59
Rayburn, Sam, 183
Reagan, Nancy Davis, 343
Reagan, Ronald: conservatism of, 2, 4, 344, 363, 382–83; and death penalty, 432n.10; entry into politics, 342–44; as governor, 368; gubernatorial bid (1966), 354–62, 452n.46, 453n.66; media used by, 382; and Meese, 306; as president, 377; and Salvatori, 235
real estate industry, 274
Record-Searchlight, 238–39
Red China, 100, 243
Rees, Tom, 202
Regan, Edwin, 266
Reisner, John, 28
religion in public schools, 69
religious discrimination, 68–69
Republican Party: conservatives in, 342; Democratic Party dominated by, 19–20, 71, 401n.21; dominance in California, 19–20, 71, 99, 363, 401n.21; funding of candidates for, 71; goals/ideology of, 25; losses in California, 26, 72–73, 81–82, 109, 278; on taxation, 382–83; on water-project bond issue, 216
Reuther, Walter, 106–7
Revenue and Taxation Committee (California), 131, 132
Ribicoff, Abe, 203
Richardson, Robert, 324
Ringer, Roy, 277
riots, 317, 330, 340, 358–59. See also Watts riots
roads. See freeways/parkways
Rochester riots (1964), 317
Rockefeller, Nelson, 180, 219, 238, 363
"Roll on Columbia" (Guthrie), 210
Roosevelt, Franklin, 25, 29, 32, 45–47
Roosevelt, Jimmy, 55–58, 62, 65, 84
Rumford, Byron, 124, 261–62, 264, 266–67
Rumford Act (California, 1963), 261–67, 289, 315, 356–57, 362–63. See also Proposition 14

rush hour, 67
Russell, Richard, 89

Sacramento, 119, 122
Sacramento Bee: counties served by, 65; on
 death penalty/Chessman case, 173,
 174; as Democratic, 51; on EGB and
 Warren's hunting trip, 224; on EGB
 vs. Unruh, 287; on FEPC, 124, 134; on
 legislature, 316; McClatchy as publisher of, 409n.56; on road building,
 128; on water project, 222
Sacramento River, 12, 206, 208
Salinger, Pierre, 280–81, 286, 290
Salute to Young America Committee, 62
Salvatori, Henry, 235
Samish, Artie, 368–69
Sanders, Carl, 284
San Diego, housing in, 259
San Diego State College, 141–42, 143
San Francisco: anti-Chinese feeling in, 258,
 432n.11; Democratic dominance in,
 25, 393n.12; freeways in, 129–30; gam-
 bling in, 37, 42–43, 50; gays in, 258;
 housing in, 52–54; importance of,
 116–17; population growth in, 256;
 Republican dominance in, 19, 20,
 393n.12; riots in, 358–59; water supply
 of, 205, 206
San Francisco Bay Area, 208–9, 337
San Francisco Call-Bulletin, 42–43, 53
San Francisco Chronicle, 35, 37–38, 44, 51,
 117, 221, 256
San Francisco earthquake of 1906, 10
San Francisco Examiner, 35, 37, 96
San Francisco Giants *(formerly* New York
 Giants), 117
San Francisco Law School, 16–17
San Francisco News, 34–35, 36, 37, 57
San Francisco Police Department, 41
San Francisco State College, 141–42, 310
San Joaquin River, 208–9
San Joaquin Valley, 225, 226
San Jose State College, 141–42
San Quentin, 160, 164, 257
Santa Barbara News-Press, 342
Saturday Review, 157

Sausset, Adrienne, 113
Savio, Mario, 294–96, 299, 301–3, 309, 356,
 439n.10, 441n.36, 443n.62
Schmitt, Milton, 16, 18
schools: aid to, 131, 133; desegregation in,
 261; religion in, 69
Schuckman, Augustus (EGB's grandfa-
 ther), 8
Schuckman, Ida. *See* Brown, Ida Schuckman
Schuckman, Mrs. (EGB's grandmother), 8
Seaborg, Glenn, 144
secretaries, 122
Selma, racial violence in, 334
Senator Hotel (Sacramento), 122
settlers, 7–9
Sexton, Keith, 152
Shattuck, Edward, 61–64
Shell, Joseph, 234–35, 428n.18
Sheppard, Harry, 198
Sheraton-Palace Hotel (San Francisco),
 294–95, 300
shipyards, 66
shop-ins, 295
Silent Spring (Carson), 348
Silicon Valley, 4
Simpson, Roy, 143, 145, 151
Sinatra, Frank, 257, 269, 303, 352
Sinclair, Upton, 25, 104
ski resorts, 170
slums, 52–53
Smith, Al, 189
smog, 133, 251
Smylie, Robert, 364
snipe hunting, 12
Soest (Germany), 269
Sorensen, Ted, 193
Southern California: dryness of, 205, 217,
 220 *(see also water);* riots in, 330
Southern Christian Leadership Confer-
 ence, 259
Southern Pacific Railroad, 226, 350
Soviet Union, 180, 258
space race, 258
Sprague, Irv, 278, 404n.9, 436n.21
Sproul, Robert Gordon, 139
Sputnik, 258
Squaw Valley (Calif.), 170

St. Ignatius (San Francisco), 82
St. Mary's Chinese Girls Drum Corps, 225
Stadtman, Verne A., 442n.42
Standard Oil, 226
Stanislaus State College ("Turkey Tech"),
    136–37
Starr, Kevin, 3
State Compensation Insurance Fund, 26
State Water Project/bonds campaign, 209,
    213–16, 217–18, 219–23, 225–28, 251,
    349, 424n.28
Stegner, Wallace, 114; *The Big Rock Candy
    Mountain*, 102
Steinbeck, John: *The Grapes of Wrath*, 350
Stephens, June, 100
Stevenson, Adlai: and EGB, 69, 80–81, 251;
    losses by, 184; presidential bid (1956),
    83–84, 94, 297; presidential bid
    (1960), 182, 195, 198, 200, 203
Stevenson Clubs, 72–73, 127, 195
Stiern, Walt, 152
Stone, Irving, 71
Strong, Edward, 292–93, 302, 307
student protests (Berkeley, 1964), 296–313;
    arrests of students, 3, 293, 299, 307–8,
    310–12; Board of Regents capitulation
    following, 309–10, 443n.62; and
    changes in student body, 296; faculty
    involvement in, 308–9; Free Speech
    Movement, 301–2, 308, 309, 311, 315,
    443n.62; growth of issues, 298; influ-
    ence of, 2, 293, 310, 362, 363, 454n.81;
    passive resistance in, 292, 299, 308;
    police brought in, 305–7, 310–11,
    442n.45; police brutality in, 240; po-
    lice car captured by sit-down,
    299–301, 304; public reaction to,
    312–13; release of students from jail,
    308; Savio's role, 299, 301–3, 309,
    443n.62; Sproul Hall occupation, 292,
    302–4, 305, 307; Strong's role, 292–93,
    302, 307; university crackdown on
    student activism, 297–98, 440n.13;
    Weinberg's role, 298–301
suburban sprawl, 382
Sutter Club (Sacramento), 127
Swig, Ben, 92, 361, 367

Taft, Robert, 88–89
taxes: beer, 121, 130; capital gains, 121; evils
    of, 382–83; gasoline, 130, 410n.62;
    highway, 410nn.62–63; income,
    120–21, 125–26, 128, 132, 133, 134; in-
    heritance, 121; oil/natural gas, 121,
    131–32; tobacco, 121, 128, 130, 133
Teamsters, 351–52
Teeters, Negley, 157
Tehachapi Mountains, 209
Tejon Ranch, 226
television, 81, 107, 121–22, 357, 382. *See also
    under* Brown, Edmund G., POLITICAL
    CAREER
Thompson, John, 316
Thoreau, Henry David, 302, 441n.36
Tilles, Michael, 379
Time, 101, 141, 201
Tito, Josip Broz, 269, 270
tobacco taxes, 121, 128, 130, 133
Tobriner, Matt, 25, 73, 353, 415n.18
Tower of Jewels (San Francisco), 11
Treuhaft, Robert, 307–8
Trombley, Bill, 356
Truman, Harry: EGB's support of, 46, 47,
    55–59, 65, 69–70, 399n.49; liberalism
    of, 80; on Richard Nixon, 239; popu-
    larity of, 51, 65; presidential election
    of, 361
Truman Library (Missouri), 92
Tuck, Dick, 171, 242
"Turkey Tech" (Stanislaus State College),
    136–37

UC Berkeley (University of California,
    Berkeley): aerospace research at, 141;
    agricultural research at, 141; bound-
    aries of, 297; budget for, 142–43, 149,
    294, 412n.25, 439n.4; Fuck Rally at,
    316–17; growth/reach of, 135–36,
    140–41, 294; as knowledge factory,
    298; lobbying by, 150; as an open
    forum, 310; and Ph.D. controversy,
    143–44; reputation/stature of, 140;
    student politics restricted at, 296–97;
    student protests in, 2, 3; support for,
    139. *See also* student protests

UC Davis (University of California, Davis), 308–9
UC Irvine (University of California, Irvine), 136
UCLA (University of California, Los Angeles): budget for, 149, 294, 439n.4; growth of, 135, 294; lobbying by, 150; Pauley's donations to, 93; and Ph.D. controversy, 143–44
UC Merced (University of California, Merced), 457n.3
UC San Diego (University of California, San Diego), 136
UC Santa Barbara (University of California, Santa Barbara), 136
UC Santa Cruz (University of California, Santa Cruz), 136, 138–39
Udall, Stewart, 267
The Ugly American (Burdick), 102
Un-American Activities Committee (California), 127
unemployment insurance, 133, 251
unemployment rate, 237, 428n.25
unions: AFL-CIO, 216; collective bargaining by, 100; EGB's support by members, 363, 454n.81; farmworkers', 130–31, 350–51; regulation of, 130; Teamsters, 351–52; on water-project bond issue, 216
United World Federalists, 343
universities: admissions standards of, 147, 148–49; vs. colleges, 136–38, 141–49; elitism of, 148–49; growth of, 135–37, 143, 153, 251, 383
University of Alabama, 264
University of California: growth of, 135–39, 294, 383, 457n.3; Master Plan for, 138–39, 147–53, 293–94, 296. See also individual campuses
University of California, Los Angeles. See UCLA
University of Mississippi, 262
University of Strathclyde (Scotland), 310
University Society of Individualists, 298
Unruh, Jesse: background of, 278–79; and California delegation of 1960, 202; at Democratic National Convention

(1964), 286, 287; EGB seeks help from, 360; EGB's feud with, 278–81, 283–84, 287, 315–16, 342, 347–48; gubernatorial aspirations of, 347–48, 450n.21; on interest rates, 132–34; and Kennedy administration, 279; personality of, 279; popularity/status of, 268–69, 338, 348, 369, 450n.22; and Rumford Act, 265; on social programs/civil rights, 279; and State Water Project, 215; on student protests, 309; as Ways and Means chair, 125, 279
Urban League, 315
U.S. Bureau of Reclamation, 207
U.S. News and World Report, 338
U.S. Supreme Court, 69, 168

Venice (Italy), 269
Veterans Administration, 260
Vietnam War, 345–46, 348, 369
Vinson, Fred, 76
Voting Rights Act (1965), 334

Wallace, George, 264, 267
Wallace, Henry, 45–47, 56, 62–63, 399n.49
Warren, Earl: Chessman denied clemency by, 163; crime commission formed by, 60 (see also Commission on Organized Crime); and EGB, 68, 364; executions commuted by, 257; hunting by, 224; Kenny's challenge of, 47–48; and William Knowland, 88; on migration to California, 66, 400n.1; political maneuvering by, 59–60; popularity of, 75, 76; Jimmy Roosevelt's challenge of, 62; and Shattuck, 63–65; on Supreme Court, 59, 76, 90; on water project, 216, 224
Warschaw, Carmen, 282
Washington, D.C., racial discrimination in, 265
water, 205–28; for big landowners, 207–8, 226; Central Valley Project/160-acre limit, 206–8, 209, 212, 225; for Central Valley/South Coast farms and cities, 99, 204, 206; Colorado River,

205, 221; constitutional amendment for water project, 212; counties of origin of, 212, 424n.15; dams/canals for, generally, 210, 211–12, 227, 426n.67; Delta, 209, 211, 214, 218, 227; and Department of Water Resources, 209–10, 218; and environmental movement, 227; Feather River dam, 206, 208–9, 211, 217–19, 220, 223, 225, 227–28; Los Angeles's supply of, 205; and Metropolitan Water District, 215, 220–22, 223, 226; northerners vs. southerners on, 211–12, 213, 214–15, 217; Owens River tapped, 205; San Francisco's supply of, 205, 206; shortages/rationing of, 213; for small farmers, 207–8; State Water Project/bonds campaign, 209, 213–16, 217–18, 219–23, 225–28, 251, 349, 424n.28

Watts, Julia A., 319

Watts riots (Los Angeles, 1965), 2, 3, 319–40; Anderson's role, 324–28, 331, 338–39; Army involvement, 330–31; casualties of/property damage from, 329–30, 333, 448n.71; causes of, 334–37; Champion's role, 314, 327–28, 330–31, 339, 447n.54; curfew imposed, 331–32, 333, 339, 449n.91; EGB's role, 328–33, 335–36, 338–39; and Marquette Frye's drunk-driving arrest, 321–22; Martin Luther King's role, 335, 336; legacy of, 337–38, 340, 363, 454n.81; and Los Angeles County Human Relations Commission, 323; Lynch's role, 327–28; McCone Commission's investigation/recommendations, 336–37; National Guard involvement, 314, 325, 326–32, 333–34, 339; Parker's role, 318, 326, 327, 332, 335, 336, 337, 449n.91; police involvement/brutality, 314, 321–24, 325–27, 329–30, 333, 337; settlement/growth/neglect of Watts, 319–20; violence of, 322–24, 325–27, 329–30, 333, 335, 448n.71; whites' vs. blacks' reactions to, 334, 335–36; Yorty's role, 326, 332, 335, 337, 338, 347

Ways and Means Committee (California), 131, 279

wealth, 134, 410n.75

Wein, Eddie, 162, 165, 166–67, 376–77

Weinberg, Jack, 298–301

Welch, Robert, 234–35

West Coast invasion fears, 31–32

"What's Wrong with the Democratic Party in California?" (Asilomar), 72–73

Wheeler, Burton, 29

White, Lee, 330

White, Thomas P., 174

white backlash, 356–57, 362

whites vs. minorities, income of, 259–60

whorehouses, 42, 122

Williamson, Ray, 19, 20

Wilson, Harold, 268

Wilson, James Q., 401n.21

Wilson, Woodrow, 71

Winter Olympics (Squaw Valley, Calif.), 170

working-class cities, 363, 454n.83

World Congress of the American Hellenic Educational Progressive Association, 314

World War I, 12, 13

World War II, 31–34, 52, 208

Wrigley Field (Chicago), 29

Wyman, Gene, 341, 369

Wyman, Jane, 343

Wyntoon (near Mount Shasta), 236–37

Yale University, 140

Yorty, Sam: background of, 346; as congressman, 347; EGB seeks help from, 360–61; EGB's feud with, 78, 347; gubernatorial bid (1966), 355, 452n.47; Kuchel's defeat of, 80; as mayor of Los Angeles, 347; personality of, 346–47; popularity of, 338; as reactionary, 78; and Watts riots, 326, 332, 335, 337, 338, 347

Yosemite, 15

Young Socialist Alliance, 298

"Youth, Don't Be a Chump" (EGB), 43

Yuba County, 223

Ziffren, Paul, 194, 196

Indexer:	Carol Roberts
Compositor:	Binghamton Valley Composition
Text:	11.25/13.5 Adobe Garamond
Display:	Knockout HTF No. 46 Flyweight
Printer and binder:	Friesens Corporation